WESTERN LANDS AND THE AMERICAN REVOLUTION

THE UNIVERSITY OF VIRGINIA
INSTITUTE FOR RESEARCH IN THE
SOCIAL SCIENCES

JOHN LLOYD NEWCOMB, B.A., C.E., D.Sc., LL.D.
President of the University

WILSON GEE, M.A., PH.D., D.Sc.
Director of the Institute

Western Lands
and
The American Revolution

BY

THOMAS PERKINS ABERNETHY

NEW YORK

RUSSELL & RUSSELL · INC

1959

The Library of Congress has cataloged this book
as follows:

Abernethy, Thomas Perkins, 1890–
    Western lands and the American revolution. New York,
Russell & Russell, 1959.

    413 p. illus. 23 cm. (University of Virginia Institute for Re-
search in the Social Sciences. Institute monograph no. 25)

    1. Land tenure—U. S.—Hist. 2. U. S.—Public lands. 3. U. S.—
Hist.—Revolution—Causes. 4. Mississippi Valley—Hist.—To 1803.
I. Title.

E210.A15 1959   973.311   59–62504 ‡

Library of Congress

To

IDA ROBERTSON ABERNETHY

COLLABORATOR

PREFACE

IN his work, *The Mississippi Valley in British Politics,* Professor
Clarence W. Alvord dealt with the problem of the American West
during the colonial period, treating it from the point of view of the
imperial administration. Various studies dealing with the American side
of the question have been made, all of which deal with special areas or
phases of the subject. The object of this volume is to bring together in
a single narrative an account of the American West from the time when
its exploitation was begun by English colonists to the end of the Confederation period. The term "West" as used herein includes the country
lying between the Appalachian divide and the Mississippi River. The
area situated north of the Ohio is not discussed beyond the time when
it passed under the control of Congress in 1784. To trace the development of the legislation and the land companies which shaped its destinies
would be to retell a story that has often been told, and one which should
be carried beyond the limits of the Confederation period if its significance
is to be made clear.

With the exception of Professor Alvord's treatment of the British
phase of the subject, most of the writings on the West have dealt primarily with the problem of frontier development rather than with the political aspects of the matter. Since the main object of this study is to treat
of the political problem no attempt has been made to deal with all phases
of the question of Western lands, but only those which had some demon-
strable political effect. To this end it has been necessary to pay some
attention to the policy of the Continental Congress and to that of several
of the colonies and States in dealing with the West. Since Virginia lay
claim to so much of the country involved her activities are of paramount
interest, and this side of the problem has, in the past, been peculiarly
neglected. Historians have commonly manifested a leaning toward the
side of her opponents, taking the attitude that because her claims were
large, they were consequently unjust. In doing this, they have often
neglected the legal phases of the question. The author hopes that he has
succeeded in adhering strictly to the legal and political points involved,
but the matter is so complicated and controversial that he cannot hope
to have escaped all error.

Men generally appear at their worst when in pursuit of material gain.

vii

The land question was closely bound up with the commercial interests of the period; it affected the policies of Congress and of the various States, and even diplomacy came within the scope of the land speculator. Most of the leading characters of the Revolutionary era were concerned in one way or another. Some were quite willing that the Appalachians should form the western boundary of the new Union; others were ready to thwart the formation of the Union in the interest of their Western lands; and still others engineered the separatist movements in the West in an effort to protect their land claims. The very integrity of the young Republic depended on the contest of the speculators. Consequently, a study of land speculation does not present an altogether flattering picture of the "Fathers" of the Revolutionary period. It has been undertaken, not with a desire to cast aspersions, but in the belief that actions speak louder than words and that public professions should be checked against private activities. These activities, as far as they concerned land speculation, were usually kept as private as possible, and for that reason it is a difficult task to follow them. There are many gaps in the documents which bear silent testimony to the discretion of the speculators.

The author has no intention of condemning speculators merely as such. Speculation is a fairly normal phase of man's economic existence. It matters not that men speculated in lands, but it does matter that men in high place should have used their official position to fasten their claim on the one great asset the nation possessed. Some resorted to more overt forms of peculation. The record speaks for itself, and it is interesting to note how few of the regular officers of the line were concerned in profiteering schemes and how many of those who were connected with the service of supply, chiefly merchants and traders by occupation, were guilty of exploiting the public.

This study owes its existence to the Institute for Research in the Social Sciences of the University of Virginia and to its director, Professor Wilson Gee, under whose auspices it was undertaken. The Institute financed the extensive travel which was necessary in the collection of manuscript material and, through liberal grants during two summers, enabled the writer to give undivided attention to the study. To Professor Gee, for whole-hearted and understanding cooperation at every stage of the work, I am deeply grateful. I am indebted also to Mrs. Adele S. Hall, of his secretarial staff, for painstaking care in the preparation of the manuscript. The Richmond Alumni Association, by the establishment of a research professorship, was instrumental in affording the author opportunity to devote his time largely to the writing of the book.

The manuscript has had the advantage of a critical reading by Judge

Samuel M. Wilson, of Lexington, Kentucky, and Dr. Louise Phelps Kellogg, of the Wisconsin Historical Society. I am beholden to them both for many valuable suggestions. I wish to acknowledge my indebtedness also to Mr. William S. Mason, of Evanston, Illinois, whose generosity placed at my disposal his magnificent collection of Frankliniana and other manuscripts; and to Mr. William Marshall Bullitt, of Louisville, Kentucky, who graciously permitted me to use his family papers. The following have been particularly helpful in making available to me the manuscript collections under their charge: Dr. Louise Phelps Kellogg and Miss Alice Smith, of the Wisconsin Historical Society; Dr. T. P. Martin, of the Library of Congress; Mr. Morgan Robinson, of the Archives Department of the Virginia State Library; Mrs. Nell M. Nugent, of the Virginia Land Office; Mr. Robert A. Lancaster, of the Virginia Historical Society; Miss Mary Townsend, of the Pennsylvania Historical Society; Miss Ludie Kinkead, of the Filson Club; Miss Susan S. Towles, of the Henderson (Ky.) Library; Professor A. R. Newsome, formerly of the North Carolina Historical Commission; Miss Josie Cerf, of the Louisiana Historical Museum; Mr. John Wyllie, Curator of Virginiana, University of Virginia Library, and officials of the British Museum and the Public Record Office. To these and to all others who have helped to smooth the maze of involved research, I offer here an expression of deep appreciation. Throughout the research and the preparation of the manuscript, I have had the assistance of Ida Robertson Abernethy, my wife.

THOMAS PERKINS ABERNETHY

The University of Virginia

ABBREVIATIONS USED IN THE NOTES

A.E., E.U.—Affaires Étrangères, Correspondance Politique, États-Unis

Add. MSS.—Additional Manuscripts, British Museum

A.H.R.—American Historical Review

Am. Arch.—American Archives

A.P.S.—American Philosophical Society, Philadelphia

A.S.P.—American State Papers

A.W.I.—American and West Indies, Public Record Office, Colonial Office papers

Br. Mus.—British Museum

C.O.—Colonial Office papers, Public Record Office, London

C.V.S.P.—Calendar of Virginia State Papers

Dip. Cor.—The Revolutionary Diplomatic Correspondence of the United States, Francis Wharton, editor

G.D.A.—Georgia Department of Archives, Atlanta

H.S.P.—Historical Society of Pennsylvania

L. of C.—Library of Congress

M.V.H.R.—Mississippi Valley Historical Review

N.C.H.C.—North Carolina Historical Commission

N.C.S.R.—North Carolina State Records

N.Y.P.L.—New York Public Library

Pa. Arch.—Pennsylvania Archives, Samuel Hazard, editor

P.C.—Privy Council papers

P.E.I.K.—Petitions of the Early Inhabitants of Kentucky to the Assembly of Virginia, J. R. Robertson, editor

P.R.O.—Public Record Office, London

U. of C.—University of Chicago

Va. Arch.—Virginia State Archives

W. and L.U.—Washington and Lee University.

CONTENTS

		PAGE
PREFACE		vii
LIST OF ABBREVIATIONS USED IN NOTES		xi

CHAPTER

I	VIRGINIA LOOKS BEYOND THE MOUNTAINS	1
II	FRANKLIN AND HIS FRIENDS CONSIDER THE WEST	14
III	VANDALIA	40
IV	VIRGINIA'S INDIAN BOUNDARY	59
V	EXTENSION OF THE VIRGINIA FRONTIER, 1769–1773	79
VI	THE VIRGINIA-PENNSYLVANIA BOUNDARY DISPUTE	91
VII	STRUGGLE WITH THE SHAWNEE FOR KENTUCKY	98
VIII	THE ILLINOIS AND WABASH LAND COMPANIES	116
IX	VIRGINIA AND THE TRANSYLVANIA COMPANY	123
X	WEST AUGUSTA AND INDIANA	136
XI	RADICALS AND CONSERVATIVES IN VIRGINIA	149
XII	INDEPENDENCE AND VIRGINIA'S WESTERN LAND PROBLEM	162
XIII	THE LAND QUESTION AND THE CONTINENTAL CONGRESS, 1776	169
XIV	WATCHFUL WAITING, 1777	180
XV	THE CONQUEST OF THE ILLINOIS	193
XVI	CONGRESSIONAL POLITICS, 1778	205
XVII	VIRGINIA'S WESTERN LAND POLICY, 1778–1779	217
XVIII	CONGRESS AND THE WEST, 1779	230
XIX	VIRGINIA AND THE WEST, 1780–1781	242
XX	VIRGINIA AND THE WEST, 1782–1783	258
XXI	THE TREATY OF 1783 AND THE WEST	274
XXII	THE MOVEMENT FOR NEW WESTERN STATES, 1784–1785	288

xiv   CONTENTS

CHAPTER   PAGE
XXIII THE WEST IN DISTRESS, 1786 311

XXIV   A YEAR OF CONFUSION, 1787. 325

 XXV   SPANISH AND BRITISH INTRIGUE IN THE WEST, 1788–
       1789 338

XXVI   RETROSPECT 362

BIBLIOGRAPHY 370

INDEX 393

PUBLICATIONS OF THE INSTITUTE FOR RESEARCH IN THE SOCIAL
       SCIENCES 411

LIST OF MAPS

MAP   PAGE

1 John Henry's Map of Virginia, 1770 . . . . . *facing* 2

2 Indian Boundary Line Proposed by the Board of Trade,
   1768 . . . . *facing* 34

3 Vandalia as Originally Plotted on Evans' Map . . . 39

4 John Stuart's Map of Vandalia and the Cherokee Boundary Line, 1772 . . . . *facing* 54

5 Western Virginia, 1780 65

6 John Filson's Map of Kentucky, 1784 . . . . . *facing* 124

7 Arthur Campbell's Proposed State of Franklin, 1784 . . 292

CHAPTER I

VIRGINIA LOOKS BEYOND THE MOUNTAINS

JUST as Virginia was the first transatlantic experiment of the Mother Country, so was the Old Dominion the first colony to venture across the Appalachians. Almost a century and a quarter elapsed between England's transatlantic and Virginia's transmontane advance. While they hugged the coast for decade after decade, the colonists were ever aware of the exciting possibilities of the unknown and fearful hinterland: furs and precious stones; mines and lush acres; and, most important of all, that intriguing *ignis fatuus,* a short route to the wealth of the Indies. In 1626 Governor Yeardley wrote to the Privy Council that "discoveries by land . . . are of great hope both for the riches of the mountains and the probabilities of finding the passage to the South Sea. . . ." In 1642 the House of Burgesses passed an act for the encouragement of Western exploration. Ten years later a second act was passed giving first choice of land to the explorer, but prohibiting him from excluding others. Following the calamitous Indian uprising of 1644 the defenseless state of the colony was remedied by the erection of a chain of inland forts at the fall line of the rivers. These strongholds gave a new fillip to Western explorations. They furnished the most satisfactory base for such operations, and they bred a new race of men. Here an individualistic, hardy generation grew to maturity—our first backwoodsmen, facing with greater intrepidity the evils of the ancient forests in whose shadow they had been reared.

In 1650 a little company led by Edward Bland and Captain Abraham Wood filed out from one of these outposts, located on the site where Petersburg was to rise, and traveled southwestward for sixty-five miles, discovering "New Brittaine, a pleasant Country, of temperate Ayre, and fertile Soyle." Wood was for many years in command at Fort Henry whence they started on the journey and was an important factor in Western explorations at this period, sending out several expeditions. There is evidence tending to show that he himself reached one of the westward flowing rivers as early as 1654.

From the time of Sir William Berkeley's arrival in Virginia in 1642 he took an active interest in exploring the West. He encouraged Captain Wood in his Western enterprises, and year after year he himself planned

1

"to goe along . . . to find out the East India sea . . ." and whatever silver mines and riches the wilderness might disgorge. He never got round to it, but in 1669 he backed the expedition of John Lederer, a German physician of fertile imagination. Lederer started from the Falls of the Pamunkey, traveling up the river, and then northwestward through the Piedmont region. He reached the summit of the Blue Ridge from whence next morning he "had a beautiful prospect of the Atlantick-Ocean washing the Virginian-shore." He was of opinion "that the Indian Ocean does stretch an arm or bay from California as far as the Apalatean Mountains. . . ."

In 1671 there set out, under Captain Abraham Wood's auspices, Thomas Batts, Robert Fallam, and Thomas Wood for the purpose of "finding out the ebbing and flowing of the Waters on the other side of the Mountains in order to the discovery of the South Sea." They crossed the Appalachians and reached New River. In their wanderings they found various initials carved on the smooth beech trees, showing that other unsung adventurers had been before them. Leaving Wood dead in the wilderness, Batts and Fallam returned to their frontier outpost, happy in the belief that from the mountain tops they had seen "sayles" on the South Sea.

In 1673 James Needham, accompanied by a servant of Abraham Wood named Gabriel Arthur, was dispatched from Fort Henry and ultimately crossed the Carolina Blue Ridge. On a subsequent expedition Needham perished at the hands of Indians, but soon others were to follow the trail he had blazed.[1]

Long before the end of the century, however, the Virginians found that the Powhatan had been right—there was no salt sea beyond the great mountains; there was no short route to India. But there was an unending vista of virgin lands to be had for the taking. Writing in 1705, Robert Beverley, the historian of Virginia, described his compatriots as people "not minding anything but to be masters of great tracts of land—lords of vast territory." The era of prodigal land grants began a few years after Governor Alexander Spotswood in 1716 led his convivial Knights of the Golden Horseshoe on their theatrical pilgrimage to the peaks of the Blue Ridge.

The sporadic expeditions of Lederer and Fallam and Needham had been waves which receded but they showed that the tide was inevitably coming in. A little more than a century later Harriet Martineau saw it in full surge:

[1] For the journals of these early expeditions see C. W. Alvord and Lee Bidgood, *The First Explorations of the Trans-Allegheny Region by the Virginians, 1650–1674* (Cleveland, 1912) *passim.*

The possession of land is the aim of all action, generally speaking, and the cure for all social evils, among men in the United States. If a man is disappointed in politics or love, he goes and buys land. If he disgraces himself, he betakes himself to a lot in the west. If the demand for any article of manufacture slackens, the operatives drop into the unsettled lands. If a citizen's neighbours rise above him in the towns, he betakes himself where he can be monarch of all he surveys. An artisan works, that he may die on land of his own. He is frugal, that he may enable his son to be a landowner. . . .

A member of Congress . . . told me that . . . any man would be pronounced 'imbecile' who, having enough for his moderate wants, should prefer the enjoyment of his patrimony, his family relations, and intercourse with the society in which he was brought up, to wandering away in pursuit of more land . . . ; that there was no character of permanence in anything;—all was fluctuation, except the passion for land, which, under the name of enterprise, or patriotism, or something else that was creditable, would last till his countrymen had pushed their out-posts to the Pacific.[2]

Early in the eighteenth century, Soame Jenyns, one of the British Lords Commissioners for Trade and Plantations who attempted to recoup his own fortune in American lands, wrote in *The Modern Fine Gentleman*, "On Parchment wings his acres take their flight." "Westward the course of empire takes its way," was penned by George Berkeley, Bishop of Cloyne, at about the same time. Here is cause and effect. When his estate dwindled away a man could turn to the New World where he might have one, for little more than the asking, a hundred times as large. The demand for land grew; the frontier steadily receded. It was to be only a matter of time now from the pirogue to the clipper ship, from the packhorse to the covered wagon.

When the transmontane advance started Virginia's domain, according to her claim under the charter of 1609, was bounded on the south by a line represented by the present southern boundary of Kentucky, on the west by the "South Sea," and on the north by the Great Lakes. While the tidewater population was gradually spreading westward to the eastern slopes of the Blue Ridge another stream was flowing down the Shenandoah Valley from Pennsylvania, and by 1736 it had reached the neighborhood where Staunton developed. Here William Beverley, son of the historian, acquired a grant of more than one hundred thousand acres in that year. Benjamin Borden, a New Jersey trader who had ingratiated himself with Governor Gooch, secured an immense grant in the same vicinity. Farther up the Valley, near the present Winchester, Yost Heyt, a German from Pennsylvania who came to be known as Jost Hite, was peopling his huge tract, patented in 1730, with industrious German settlers. The great

[2] Harriet Martineau, *Society in America* (New York, 1837) I, 292, 331–332.

exodus from the German Palatinate and from Ulster began about this time and aided the colonization of the Valley. Immigrant ships were met with enticing advertisements of this El Dorado in Virginia, and during the decade several important Irish and Scotch-Irish families settled west of the Blue Ridge.

James Patton, from Donegal, was the head of one of these. He had formerly been a sea captain and had crossed the ocean many times, his vessel crowded with redemptioners for Virginia, some of whom were bound for Beverley's estate. It was inevitable that Patton himself should get the contagion for a fling at fortune in the New World. In 1736 he, with his brother-in-law John Preston, formerly a ship's carpenter, settled together on Beverley's grant. Preston's son William and his sons-in-law Robert Breckinridge and John Brown were destined to be leaders in the West, as was also Patton's son-in-law John Buchanan.[3]

Probably the earliest settler in this neighborhood was John Lewis, an Ulsterman who under great provocation had killed his landlord and fled to America. In 1732 he settled in what was soon to be "Beverley Manor" and surveyed the town of Staunton for Beverley in 1748. There came with him to America three young sons: Andrew—whom some Virginians thought should have been given command of the Revolutionary Army instead of Washington—Thomas and William. These together with Charles, born in Virginia and who was to die at Point Pleasant, became important figures on the frontier.[4] A third family of equal importance was that of John Campbell who, like Lewis, was an early Scotch-Irish settler in the neighborhood. His descendants were numerous and distinguished, but the most famous in the early period were General William Campbell of King's Mountain fame and Colonel Arthur Campbell of separatist tendencies.[5]

When Augusta County, including most of Virginia west of the Blue Ridge, was organized in 1745 Patton became its first high sheriff and Thomas Lewis its first surveyor.[6] In the same year the governor and council of Virginia granted Patton and others a tract of one hundred twenty thousand acres to be located at the southern end of the great

[3] Lewis Preston Summers, *History of Southwest Virginia* (Richmond, 1903) p. 43; Joseph A. Waddell, *Annals of Augusta County, Virginia* (Staunton, 1902) pp. 30, 57–58; R. A. Brock, ed., "The Official Records of Robert Dinwiddie, Lieutenant-Governor of the Colony of Virginia, 1751–1758," *Collections of the Virginia Historical Society,* new series, II–III (Richmond, 1883–1884) I, 8n.

[4] Archibald Henderson, *Dr. Thomas Walker and the Loyal Company of Virginia,* reprinted from the *Proceedings of the American Antiquarian Society* (Worcester, 1931) p. 14; Summers, *op. cit.,* p. 41; Waddell, *op. cit.,* pp. 24, 64; John Haywood, *The Civil and Political History of the State of Tennessee* (Nashville, 1915) pp. 45–46, 48–49, 88.

[5] *Virginia Magazine of History and Biography,* VII, 126–127; Waddell, *op. cit.,* pp. 147–150.

[6] Summers, *op. cit.,* p. 42.

Valley of Virginia.[7] It looked as though the old sailor's dream of wealth was about to be realized, and in 1748 a party was organized to explore the princely domain. In addition to Patton himself, its more important members were his son-in-law, John Buchanan; Charles Campbell, son to John; and Dr. Thomas Walker, a land magnate from Albemarle County who soon took up a large acreage where Abingdon now stands. He called this place Wolf Hills.[8] Daniel Smith, whose later land speculations were to carry him far, was the young school teacher in this wilderness settlement. Thomas Lewis and John Buchanan, his deputy, had been surveying in the neighborhood as early as 1746, and in 1750 they laid off a tract for Edmund Pendleton which was supposed to lie within Virginia, but which was actually in North Carolina and is now in Tennessee.[9]

Thus by the middle of the eighteenth century the southern end of the Valley was being exploited, and at about this time the settlement of Draper's Meadows was established, the first in Virginia to lie on the "western waters." On Fry's and Jefferson's map of 1751 Stalnaker's settlement on the Holston was given as the extreme Western outpost. While population was thus flowing southward down the Valley, a strenuous effort was being made to push the Virginia frontier northwestward to the Ohio River. In 1747 Thomas Lee, president of the Virginia Council of State, organized the Ohio Company, the object of which was trade with the Indians and land speculation. In 1744 Lee had acted as one of the Virginia commissioners at the Indian treaty at Lancaster, in Pennsylvania, then one of the last outposts of the frontier, and it was probably this experience which first interested him in Western lands. His technical adviser in the business was Thomas Cresap, a seasoned Maryland trader who lived high up on the Potomac and whose one hundred and six years of existence seem to have been one long adventure. In 1748 the petition of the company for a grant of two hundred thousand acres near the Forks of the Ohio was approved by the King and Council, and in July, 1749, the governor and council of Virginia made the grant. It was conditioned, however, on the building of a fort near the Forks and the settlement of a hundred families upon the land within seven years.[10]

[7] *Virginia Magazine of History and Biography,* V, 175–180, a list of early Virginia grants; Judge Lyman Chalkley, "Before the Gates of the Wilderness Road," *ibid.,* XXX, 183–204.

[8] William M. Darlington, ed., *Christopher Gist's Journals* (Cleveland, 1893) pp. 23–25; Henderson, *op. cit.,* p. 12.

[9] Summers, *op. cit.,* pp. 44–45.

[10] Herbert T. Leyland, "The Ohio Company," *Quarterly Publication of the Historical and Philosophical Society of Ohio,* XVI, 5–20; Samuel M. Wilson, "The Ohio Company of Virginia" (pamphlet, Lexington, Ky., 1926); Kate Mason Rowland, "The Ohio Company," *William and Mary Quarterly Historical Magazine,* I, 197–203; Corra Bacon-Foster, *Early Chapters in the Development of the Potomac Route*

The company proceeded with its major plan of opening a route from the Potomac to the Ohio and commencing trade with the Western Indians. In 1749 goods for this purpose were ordered from John Hanbury, a merchant of London who had been admitted to the company and who was its spokesman before the Board of Trade. The following year a storehouse with loopholes was erected at Will's Creek, opposite the present site of Cumberland, Maryland, to receive the supplies. In 1751 Cresap was directed to blaze a trail from this point to Redstone Creek, a tributary of the Monongahela, which he did with the aid of the Indian, Nemacolin. Christopher Gist, another adventurous Marylander and a friend of Cresap, was employed to explore the lands on both sides of the Ohio as low down as the Falls.[11] In 1750 he set out on his first excursion and on the way westward called at the Indian trading post at Logstown, eighteen miles below the Forks of the Ohio. Here he met George Croghan [pronounced "Crawn"], "the fat old trader" who had settled at Carlisle shortly after his arrival from Dublin in 1741 and who had since then shifted the place of his residence with the shifting of the frontier. Now he had trading houses scattered throughout the upper Ohio region from which he dispensed vermilion, brass kettles, ammunition, knives, looking-glasses, strouds, matchcoating, wampum, and rum. Although he was illiterate and in the beginning without backing, there went out from his trading houses something more far-reaching than Indian goods: intrigue and pretentious schemes for vast wealth and empire in which he involved many prominent figures of his day. At this time he was acting as unofficial Indian agent for the governor of Pennsylvania.[12] On Gist's arrival at Logstown he found also William Trent, Croghan's business partner and brother-in-law. The batteaux on the rivers, the packhorse trains on the wilderness trails, the endless bartering with Indians, negotiations with factors in the East, the spying out and surveying of choice acres, all required trusted employees. Trent was one of a/group of numerous kinsmen whom Croghan gathered about him to serve his interest, and

to the West (Washington, 1912) pp. 3–16; Jared Sparks, ed., The Writings of George Washington (New York, 1847) II, 478–483; Executive Journal of the Council of Virginia, July 12, 1749, British transcripts, Library of Congress, Public Record Office, Colonial Office, series 5, 1348.

[11] A. B. Hulbert, Historic Highways of America, III, Washington's Road (Cleveland, 1903) pp. 95–96; Louis K. Koontz, The Virginia Frontier, 1754–1763 (Baltimore, 1925) pp. 115, 136; Darlington, Gist, pp. 31–32, 88–89; James Veech, The Monongahela of Old (Pittsburgh, 1910) p. 26; Sparks, Washington, II, 479–480; John C. Fitzpatrick, ed., The Writings of George Washington (Washington, 1931) I, 19–20n.

[12] Albert T. Volwiler, George Croghan and the Westward Movement (Cleveland, 1926) pp. 25, 41; Darlington, op. cit., pp. 32, 249; Samuel Hazard, ed., Pennsylvania Archives, Colonial Records (Philadelphia, 1852–1856) V, 461; Neville B. Craig, ed., The Olden Time (Cincinnati, 1876) II, 182.

together they were a menace to all rival traders in the West. After Gist's visit Croghan and Trent were to play an important part in the history of the Ohio Company and of Virginia.

Having thus launched upon a bold program of development, the Ohio Company ran into difficulties from the first day of its existence. It had secured its charter by the grace of the Duke of Bedford and the British Ministry, not by that of the Virginia council. John Robinson of King and Queen County was the most powerful member of the ruling clique. He had long been interested in Western lands, having secured a grant of 100,000 acres on Greenbrier River in 1745. He combined in his person the offices of speaker of the House of Burgesses and treasurer of the colony, and for a quarter of a century was, under the governor, the dominant influence in the government of Virginia.[13] And this influence was not used in favor of the Ohio Company. In fact, as soon as it was known in Virginia that the company had secured the approval of the King and Council, certain members of the local council bestirred themselves to organize a still more extensive scheme. A grant of eight hundred thousand acres to lie along the southern edge of the Virginia frontier was made to a group of speculators known as the Loyal Company. The most prominent of these were John Lewis, Dr. Thomas Walker, Peter Jefferson, father of Thomas, Col. Joshua Fry—an Oxford graduate who had settled in the Piedmont region near Jefferson and who had in 1742 proposed to the burgesses to make an exact survey of the colony—Thomas Meriwether, John Harvie, Francis Thornton, and Edmund Pendleton. Of these men, Lewis represented the Shenandoah Valley interest, Pendleton was a protégé of the Robinson family, and most of the others constituted an Albemarle County coterie. Four years were allowed them to make the surveys and pay the fees. No colonization was required, and speculation was the only object of the organization.[14] This grant would seem to have been separated from that of the Ohio Company by a sufficient distance to prevent conflicts, but in neither case were definite boundaries fixed and competing claims might easily occur. In 1750 the Loyal Company sent Dr. Thomas Walker, who had already penetrated the wilderness with Patton, to explore its lands and to make surveys,[15] but the College of William and Mary, whose duty it was to certify all public surveyors, re-

[13] T. P. Abernethy, "John Robinson," *Dictionary of American Biography* (New York, 1935) XVI, 46.
[14] Executive Journal of the Council of Virginia, July 12, 1749, P.R.O., C.O., series 5, 1423 (photostatic copy in library of Virginia Historical Society). The Loyal Company grant was made by the council on the same day that it confirmed the royal grant to the Ohio Company.
[15] William C. Pendleton, *History of Tazewell County and Southwest Virginia* (Richmond, 1920) pp. 224–229; Henderson, *Walker,* pp. 16–17.

fused to qualify Christopher Gist, the appointee of the Ohio Company. This group then retaliated by taking out caveats against the surveys of the Loyal Company, thus interrupting its work.[16] Closely allied with the Loyal Company in all its struggles was the Greenbrier Company, organized by Speaker Robinson and Thomas Nelson in 1751.[17] The rivalry for Western domain had started in earnest in Virginia.

Such a situation called for prompt action. Robert Dinwiddie became lieutenant-governor of Virginia in 1751. The Ohio Company without loss of time proceeded to bolster its influence by taking the new executive into the organization, and throughout his administration he continued to be its strongest champion. Governor Arthur Dobbs, of North Carolina, was also a member, as were George Fairfax, Lawrence and Augustine Washington, Robert Carter, John Tayloe, Francis Thornton, and several other prominent Virginians. Thomas Lee, however, died while developments were still in the early stages, as did Lawrence Washington who had succeeded him as president of the company. Some of the original members, including Thomas Nelson, Francis Thornton, and George Fairfax, withdrew in 1749; new members were presently added, and in 1751 the company was reorganized. Soon, therefore, John Mercer and his sons George and Hugh, George Mason, Richard Henry Lee—son of the original president—and George Washington were the most conspicuous members of the group. All these were neighbors in the Northern Neck and at Fredericksburg; and the rival interests of this Ohio Company group on the one hand and of the Albemarle-Valley membership in the Loyal and Greenbrier Companies on the other created a cleavage which may be traced down the years in Virginia politics.

Nothing daunted by adversity, the Ohio Company proceeded with its plans. In 1752 Governor Dinwiddie in its behalf called a conference with the Six Nations and Western Indians at Logstown. The company was represented by Christopher Gist, whereas spokesmen for the colony were James Patton, Joshua Fry, and Lunsford Lomax. Among witnesses were Trent, Croghan, Gist, and Patton's nephew William Preston. Here the Indians surrendered their claim to lands south of the Ohio River, verifying a similar agreement made with the Six Nations at the treaty of Lancaster in 1744. They also agreed that the company might make settlements upon its lands and build a fort.[18] In 1753 a storehouse was erected at

[16] Summers, *op. cit.*, p. 51; Pendleton, *op. cit.*, pp. 224–229.

[17] James Hall, *Sketches of History, Life, and Manners in the West* (Philadelphia, 1835) I, 237–238; *Va. Magazine of History and Biography*, V, 175–180.

[18] Brock, *Official Records of Robert Dinwiddie*, I, 7–10, 17–19; Darlington, *Gist*, pp. 220–227; Richard Channing Moore Page, *Genealogy of the Page Family in Virginia* (New York, 1893) p. 205; Executive Journal of the Council of Virginia, Nov. 2, 1752, P.R.O., C.O., series 5, 1429 (photostatic copy in library U. of Va.); petition of

Redstone Creek, and a commission as surveyor was secured for Christopher Gist, who now established himself with eleven other families in the neighborhood and began making surveys for the company.

During the previous year the company had petitioned the Crown for a general extension of its grant, asking that half a million acres be given them and that, in order to avoid conflicts, their boundaries be fixed at the Ohio River, the Appalachian watershed, and the Great Kanawha River. The King and Council granted the request, but the next year the Virginia council made large grants to a group of its own members and their friends which might easily conflict with the Ohio Company claims.[19] In 1752 the House of Burgesses passed an act granting a ten-year exemption from taxation to settlers upon the Western waters.[20] But when, in 1754, the home government directed that one thousand acres, free of quit-rents for ten years, be donated to Western settlers, the land companies had reason to fear a new form of competition.[21]

The immediate response of the French to the establishment of the Ohio Company had been the departure of the Céleron expedition from Montreal in June, 1749, for the Ohio region. Now that the French were threatening British domination in this area the colonial governors were instructed by England to use force if necessary to protect their frontiers. In the autumn of 1753 Governor Dinwiddie sent the youthful George Washington—who had volunteered for the service after the failure of the original appointees, William Russell and William Trent, to undertake it— to notify the French that they were trespassing on British soil: in other words, on land of the Ohio Company, of which both the governor and the young messenger were members. William Trent left his Indian trade and intrigue long enough to view the site for a fort. The next year he was commissioned captain and ordered to begin work on a fortification at the Forks of the Ohio,[22] for which the Ohio Company had purchased twenty swivel guns. At the same time the governor offered two hundred thousand acres of Western land to officers and men who would volunteer for service in the regiment he was organizing for duty in this area, to

the Ohio Company to General Assembly of Virginia, Nov. 20, 1778, Va. Archives, petitions.

[19] Executive Journal of the Council of Virginia, June 15, 1753, P.R.O., C.O., series 5 (photostatic copy in library of U. of Va.) ; Darlington, *Gist,* pp. 226–229.

[20] Hayes Baker-Crothers, *Virginia and the French and Indian War* (Chicago, 1928) p. 31; William Waller Hening, ed., *The Statutes-at-Large, being a Collection of all the Laws of Virginia* (Richmond, 1819) VI, 258.

[21] Clarence W. Alvord, *The Mississippi Valley in British Politics* (Cleveland, 1917) I, 89.

[22] Deposition of Edward Ward, June 13, 1765, Ohio Company MSS., Historical Society of Pennsylvania; *Pa. Arch., Colonial Records,* V, 660; Veech, *Monongahela of Old,* pp. 79, iii; Executive Journal, Virginia Council, June 14, Oct. 27, Oct. 31, 1753, P.R.O., C.O., series 5 (photostatic copy in library of U. of Va.).

protect His Majesty's soil which happened to be also the soil of the Ohio Company. Colonel Joshua Fry was put in command of this force, and George Washington was designated second in command.[23] The governor of Pennsylvania protested that the Forks of the Ohio lay within his jurisdiction, and Dinwiddie agreed that the quit-rents should go to Penn if the lands were found to lie within his boundaries. The Quaker assembly of Pennsylvania, however, refused to back the governor and denied that its jurisdiction extended to the Ohio, thus making it logical for that body to refuse military aid for the coming conflict.[24] Meanwhile the Pennsylvanians, who had hitherto largely monopolized Indian trade in that region, stirred up the savages against the Virginians. In this state of affairs the French struck before the British were ready; took the fort which Trent had not completed, renaming it Duquesne for the governor of New France; and at the Great Meadows defeated Washington, who, with Joshua Fry dead on the march, had succeeded to the command and had fortified this position near Redstone. This was the beginning of the French and Indian War.[25]

The outbreak of hostilities put a stop to the activities of land companies. The British flag did not fly in the country west of the Alleghenies until General John Forbes captured Fort Duquesne in 1758. Thus, one plan of the Ohio Company was at last carried out, but Forbes did not march to his victory by way of the old road from Will's Creek which the company had marked at great expense and which Braddock of the Coldstream Guards, "the poor, prodigal ex-governor of Gibraltar," had found so disastrous. The Ohio Company suffered another reverse in the same year when Governor Dinwiddie was replaced by Francis Fauquier. Dinwiddie's membership in the land company and his sponsorship of the War were inseparably connected in the minds of the Virginians, and his policies had not been popular.[26] During Fauquier's ten years as governor he did nothing to advance the interests of the Ohio Company, but on several

[23] Louis K. Koontz, "Washington on the Frontier," *Virginia Magazine of History and Biography*, XXXVI, 305–327; Will H. Lowdermilk, *History of Cumberland, Maryland* (Washington, 1878) pp. 46–54; Darlington, *Gist*, pp. 236–237; President Nelson to Board of Trade, Oct. 18, 1770, inclosing copy of Dinwiddie's proclamation of 1754, British transcripts, L. of C., P.R.O., C.O., series 5, 1348; deposition of Major Ward, Draper MSS., ICC137, Wisconsin Historical Society; Brock, *Dinwiddie*, I, 56–57.

[24] W. Neil Franklin, "Pennsylvania-Virginia Rivalry for the Indian Trade of the Ohio Valley," *Mississippi Valley Historical Review*, XX, 463–480; Boyd Crumrine, *History of Washington County, Pennsylvania* (Philadelphia, 1882) pp. 158ff., 165; *Pa. Arch.*, V, 422–423, VI, 27; Volwiler, *Croghan*, p. 85; Brock, *Dinwiddie*, I, 23n.

[25] *Pa. Arch.*, VI, 28–29; John C. Fitzpatrick, *George Washington Himself* (Indianapolis, 1933) pp. 64–69; Charles H. Ambler, *George Washington and the West* (Chapel Hill, 1936) pp. 30–109.

[26] Alvord, *op. cit.*, I, 88.

occasions showed a preference for the rival Loyal Company and the men who were associated in it. Unlike his predecessor, he appears not to have been personally interested in Western lands. Having lost his entire patrimony at cards in one night's play, no doubt speculation of all kinds was distasteful to him.

These were not propitious years for any Western land enterprises. In 1758 Pennsylvania made a treaty with the Delaware Indians and agreed that no new settlements should be made on their lands. In 1760, Colonel Henry Bouquet, a Swiss officer in British service and now in command at Fort Pitt, wrote to Fauquier that, though Virginia was not a party to this pact, she would doubtless be expected to abide by its terms. Bouquet had expressed his willingness to become a member of the Ohio Company, and a share of its stock, equal to twenty-five thousand acres, was offered him. Having been won over to the Pennsylvania interest, he now made a virtue of declining it and in 1761 issued a proclamation on authority of the home government prohibiting settlements west of the Appalachian divide.[27] Virginia had issued patents for lands in the southern end of the Valley, notably those falling within James Patton's large grant, which lay west of this line. Governor Fauquier now asked Bouquet what were his intentions in regard to such lands. Bouquet referred the question to General Jeffrey Amherst, in command of the British forces in America, who interpreted the proclamation as intended merely to prevent encroachment upon lands belonging to the Indians.[28] When peace came in 1763 and the famous proclamation of that year was issued, definite royal authority was given to Colonel Bouquet's policy. There were valid titles in Virginia to lands lying west of the proclamation line, and these titles were never revoked nor could they have been invalidated without due process of law. Indeed, in 1766 the auditor-general of the colonies, Robert Cholmondeley, became much exercised because claimants refused to pay quit-rents on them.[29] It was later argued by interested parties that this proclamation line established a new western boundary for Virginia, but it was never argued that it did the same for Pennsylvania. It did, however, establish a new policy according to which the Indian claim to lands west of the line was recognized as valid—except in the case of lands previously patented as above mentioned—and

[27] *Ibid.,* I, 121, 126–127; Darlington, *Gist,* pp. 194–195; John Hughes to Commissioners of the Stamp Office, Nov. 2, 1765, *A Collection of Interesting Authentic Papers,* printed for John Almon (London, 1777) p. 53.

[28] Douglas Brymner, *Report on Canadian Archives, 1889* (Ottawa, 1890) pp. 72–79.

[29] Thatcher notes from British archives, Council minutes, June 5, 1766, L. of C., P.R.O., C.O., 323, 324, *ibid.,* P.R.O., C.O., 391, 73; Board of Trade MSS., Plantations General, 1766–1768, XXVI, 15–18, Historical Society of Pennsylvania transcripts.

extinguishable only by treaty made under royal authority.[30] Before this time grants had often been made with no regard for the Indian claims.

As soon as hostilities ceased the land companies resumed aggressive activities. The Loyal Company petitioned the Virginia government for a renewal of its grant, but this was refused because to accede would have meant a violation of the proclamation of 1763.[31] But by 1766 the company was urging all who had quitted their claims during the War to return to them on pain of forfeiture. Though there was no legal ground for this action, the company was assured the support of William and Thomas Nelson of the council and apparently of that of the governor also.[32]

The Ohio Company was as active as its rival, but less fortunate. In 1761 it attempted to re-open negotiations with the home government, and in 1763 George Mercer was dispatched to London as its agent. Here he eloped with a young noblewoman, was imprisoned for debt, and for six years sought the ear of the Ministry in behalf of his patrons. Never during that time did he receive the slightest encouragement in the business of the land company. The Board of Trade referred his petition back to the governor of Virginia for advice, and the Ohio Company rightly looked upon that action as a negative answer.[33]

After eighteen years of effort these rival companies were left without an acre of land which was legally theirs. In both cases their grants were made with certain conditions attached, and both had failed to meet the terms. They maintained, and with justice, that it was the War which had prevented the maturation of their plans, but the proclamation of 1763 had forestalled any possibility of further legal development for the time being, and future prospects looked doubtful. Then, in 1766, a new disturbing element entered the picture. Certain settlers upon the Western waters, who, of course, had no legal right to be there, represented to the Virginia assembly that their settlements were being molested by the land companies who lay claim to their farms. The House of Burgesses took the matter under consideration and drafted an address to the home

[30] Gage to Halifax, Jan. 7, 1764, C. E. Carter, ed., *The Correspondence of General Thomas Gage with the Secretaries of State* (New Haven, 1931) I, 9–11.
[31] Copy of attest by John Blair, n.d., British transcripts, L. of C., P.R.O., C.O., series 5, 1349, f. 23.
[32] Henderson, *Walker*, pp. 26–27, 68; *Journal of the Virginia House of Delegates, 1777–1780*, p. 88.
[33] Brock, *Dinwiddie*, I, 17–18; Kate Mason Rowland, *The Life of George Mason* (New York, 1892) I, 78, 131–132; Board of Trade to Committee on Plantation Affairs, June 26, 1767, British transcripts, L. of C., P.R.O., C.O., series 5, 1368, f. 324; *Ibid.*, P.R.O., C.O., series 5, 1331, ff. 411, 413; *ibid.*, P.R.O., C.O., series 5, 1332ff., 301, 307; Board of Trade minutes, Jan. 3, 1770, Thatcher notes, L. of C., C.O., 391, 71; George Mercer to Ohio Company, Nov. 21, 1767, *William and Mary Quarterly Historical Magazine*, I, 200–204.

government asking that settlement of the Western lands be permitted.[34]

The enormous grants of the early years were justifiable under the theory that the best way to settle the frontier was by means of importation of redemptioners by capitalistic speculators. If the frontier was to be settled by immigrants who came on their own responsibility then the large grants were not only unnecessary they were impolitic. None, in fact, had been made in Virginia since 1754,[35] and the future belonged to the many, though the struggle was to be a harder one than could have been imagined, and in its varied story lies the provenience of our early democracy.

[34] British transcripts, L. of C., P.R.O., C.O., series 5, 1333, f. 405ff.; a petition of sundry inhabitants of Augusta County, Nov. 7, 1766, *Journals of the House of Burgesses of Virginia, 1766–1769,* p. 37.

[35] Copy of attest by John Blair, n.d., British transcripts, L. of C., P.R.O., C.O., series 5, 1349, f. 23.

CHAPTER II

FRANKLIN AND HIS FRIENDS CONSIDER THE WEST

WHEN, in 1754, Virginia through the operations of the Ohio Company became involved in the French and Indian War, she called upon seven of her sister colonies for aid. Only North Carolina heeded the request. Being pacifically inclined, the Quaker assembly of Pennsylvania declared that the Forks of the Ohio lay outside the chartered limits of the province and hence declined to render assistance. The Penn family and its representative, Governor Hamilton, naturally took a different view of the matter, but were powerless to raise funds without consent of the Quaker majority in the assembly. Benjamin Franklin usually cooperated in political matters with the Quakers, but in this affair took the side of the governor and proved himself a masterly ally.[1]

Upon the outbreak of hostilities the home government authorized the colonies north of the Potomac to send delegates to Albany to negotiate with the Six Nations of Indians in order to prevent their aiding the French. Franklin was one of the Pennsylvania delegates at this Albany congress and here, without authority for so doing and entirely upon his own initiative, he presented his famous plan of colonial union. It was his idea that this plan for inter-colonial government should be submitted to the British Parliament for enactment, and the individual colonies, including those to the South which were not represented at Albany, were expected to acquiesce without question in this curtailment of their authority and territory. The fact that Franklin could devise such a plan showed how little he was able to anticipate events which were soon to crowd upon him. Fortunately for him, the issue between Parliament and the colonies was not joined in this connection. Not only the colonial governments but the British Board of Trade disapproved the scheme, and it was dropped without ever being submitted to Parliament.[2]

It might seem strange that so practical a man as Franklin would have shot so wide of the mark in this matter, but this is explained by reference

[1] W. Neil Franklin, "Pennsylvania-Virginia Rivalry for the Indian Trade of the Ohio Valley," *Mississippi Valley Historical Review*, XX, 463–480.
[2] John Bigelow, ed., *The Works of Benjamin Franklin* (New York, 1904) III, 12–14, 21–25, 35–39.

to certain circumstances surrounding the incident. Virginia had started a war for the back country, and the Northern colonies were standing aloof. In case of a successful issue Virginia might be expected to reap the lion's share of the reward, for she had a charter claim to most of the territory in dispute and it looked as though she might fortify this claim through conquest. The Quaker majority in the Pennsylvania assembly would be able, and seemed certain, to keep its government from doing anything effective in the emergency. But a central colonial government would take the matter out of the hands of Virginia. In fact, this was obviously one of the main objects which Franklin had in mind, for his instrument contained a statement that the boundaries of those colonies having extensive Western claims could be curtailed, and a provision that the right to purchase land from the Indians and to provide governments for the same should be restricted to the new central government which he proposed to create.

When two years had passed and nothing had been done toward putting the Albany plan into operation Franklin came forward with another proposition. It was a less ambitious scheme, but the chief objective remained the same. The proposal was for the creation of two new colonies north of the Ohio River, in territory claimed by Virginia but held by the French.[3] This plan was presented in England by Thomas Pownall, brother to John Pownall, the secretary to the Lords of Trade and Plantations, through whose influence he had been appointed lieutenant-governor of New Jersey in 1755. Pownall had been associated with Franklin at Albany. Another representative at the Albany congress had been a young member of the New York council, William Johnson, who was to leave an enduring mark on the West. Pownall became his and Franklin's staunch ally in all their land speculations. Nothing came of Franklin's proposals at the time but some years later Pownall played an important part in the revival of this scheme.[4]

Meanwhile the French and Indian War was in progress. After the defeat of Braddock the Pennsylvanians were shaken out of their lethargy, and Franklin was able to get the assembly to provide men and money for the defense of the frontier.[5] The fur trade was an important consideration in Philadelphia and Lancaster, and it was in this connection that the struggle came home to the Quakers. At this time the Indian depart-

[3] *Ibid.*, III, 148–157; William Vincent Byars, ed., *B. and M. Gratz* (Jefferson City, Mo., 1916) pp. 335ff.
[4] James Sullivan and A. C. Flick, eds., *The Papers of Sir William Johnson* (Albany, 1921–1933) I, 853, 994, II, 559–560; W. V. Byars, "The First American Movement West," MS. collection, H.S.P., p. 4; J. Almon, ed., *The Remembrancer* (London, 1776) pp. 131–133.
[5] Bigelow, *Franklin*, III, 93ff.

ment was subordinate to the military, and General Braddock, in 1755, put Colonel William Johnson in charge of relations with the Six Nations, and the following year he was made a baronet and Superintendent of Indian Affairs for the Northern Department. Johnson was an Irish gentleman by birth, the nephew of Sir Peter Warren, commander of the fleet that had captured Louisbourg in 1745. Through Sir Peter's marriage with Miss De Lancey of New York, he acquired a vast tract of land in the Mohawk Valley and turned to his young nephew as the man to develop this estate. Thus, Johnson came out to America early in life and took up his residence in the wilderness. Here he built a fine stockaded mansion where he lived in feudal magnificence. His household included a personal physician, a dwarf as a jester, a secretary, a tailor, a butler, and a large retinue of other servants. After the death of his wife he took to his bed and board Molly, the sixteen-year-old sister of the Mohawk chief, Joseph Brant, who bore him eight children and was usually spoken of as "the Indian Lady Johnson." Johnson had sent Chief Brant, when nineteen years old, to the mission school which grew into Dartmouth College, and the young savage acquired many of the vices and virtues of the whites, proving ever thereafter an indispensable intermediary between Johnson and the Indians. Johnson learned to speak the Mohawk language and often wore the native dress. He flattered the gullible chiefs and acquired great influence over them; the Indians swarmed over his house and grounds like bees, and he bore with them with patience. He once ordered from England several suits of clothes, richly laced. One of the chiefs was present when they arrived and admired them inordinately. In a few days he returned and informed the superintendent that he dreamed he had presented him with one of the suits, which Sir William did. Later Sir William dreamed in turn that the chief gave him a very valuable tract of land on the Mohawk, which the chief did, saying "Now, Sir William, I will never dream with you again, you dream too hard for me." Johnson appointed as his deputy agent George Croghan, who was doubtless aided in his delicate mission by the fact that his daughter by a Mohawk woman had married Chief Brant. His connection with the Ohio Company and his career as an Indian trader in western Pennsylvania have been mentioned.[6]

Because of Croghan's official position, he was now no longer ostensibly in business, but in 1760 Trent, his partner, became connected with a powerful group of Jewish merchants of Lancaster, headed by Joseph Simon, Levy Andrew Levy, and David Franks. The last-named was a member of the important Philadelphia house of Plumstead and Franks,

[6] *Papers of Sir William Johnson,* I, 539–540; III, 269–275.

and his brother Moses was a well-known London merchant. With this group became associated Bernard and Michael Gratz, natives of Langerdorf in Germany, who had formerly been in business in London. Bernard came to Philadelphia in 1754 and served an apprenticeship in the business of David Franks until 1758. In that year he wrote to his brother Michael to come over from London and take his place as he was adventuring into business on his own account. On learning of this, the elder brother Hayim Grätzer, wrote from Silesia:

. . . You write that you are again going across the sea,—to Philadelphia. From appearances you wish perhaps to become an English nabob. . . . Dont dare on any account to leave London without first informing me how much you have profitted and how much you are worth. . . . If you are able to bring home at least a thousand dollars in cash, then come to me. With the help of God, I will take care that you make a good match and have a living also. . . . I am surprised that our brother Bernard has changed his nature so much and has no intention of coming hither. . . . My desire is, if he will take my advice, to come home with you. If you [both] have it in mind to become rich men, you can become so here. . . .[7]

But the enterprising young Jews did not return to Silesia. Their destiny lay in America, and here they did indeed become "nabobs." They were soon leading members of the Lancaster firm. Michael married Miriam, daughter to Joseph Simon. He made business connections in New York and in 1765 formed a partnership with the Miranda Brothers of Curaçao, who traded extensively to the West Indies and the American colonies. Meanwhile Bernard was making connections in Virginia and engaging in the coastwise trade between New Orleans and Quebec.

In addition to his connection with Trent and this group of Jewish merchants, George Croghan became allied during the years of the War with another and equally important coterie. A certain John Campbell, who had become an intimate in his home, soon made a name for himself as a trader in association with the Franks-Gratz group. Thomas Hutchins was a young man from New Jersey who started out as a trader under Croghan's wing and finally became an engineer and army officer whose later career is of considerable interest. And lastly, Alexander

---

[7] Sulzberger MSS., American Jewish Historical Society, Philadelphia (published in Byars, *Gratz*, pp. 37–38) ; Volwiler, *George Croghan and the Westward Movement*, pp. 150–151. Trent was the son of William Trent, one-time Chief-Justice of the New Jersey Supreme Court. He was born in Lancaster in 1715 ; enaged in the Indian trade, learned the Indian languages and acquired much influence among them. He and William Franklin were life-long friends. He had lost an eye and was often referred to as the "One-Eyed Major." Washington had a poor opinion of him; concerning Trent's behavior at the surrender of the Ohio Company's fort, he wrote: ". . . Capt. Trent's behavior has been very tardy, and has convinced the world of what they before suspected, his great timidity." Washington to Gov. Dinwiddie, June 12, 1754, Fitzpatrick, *Washington's Correspondence*, I, 76–84.

McKee, said to have been a half-breed, became his associate in the Indian agency and was a close friend for many years.[8]

Through his connections with Sir William Johnson and the merchants and traders mentioned above Croghan exercised an influence in Western affairs which was certainly equal to that of any man of his day. To his extensive family connection the great West was a treasure chest. Beside William Trent, his brother-in-law, there were Edward Ward, his half-brother; Dr. John Connolly, his nephew; his cousins, Thomas Smallman, William Powell, and Daniel Clark—who came from Ireland to be his clerk; Lieutenant Augustine Prevost, son of the general of that name and Croghan's son-in-law; and William Croghan, his nephew, who married the sister of George Rogers Clark. Sir William Johnson depended greatly upon the old trader's knowledge of the Indians and appointed him as his representative to negotiate a treaty between Pennsylvania and the Delawares at Easton in 1757.

Here a peculiar situation developed. Four years previously a group of Connecticut speculators had organized themselves as the Susquehannah [sic] Company and purchased from the Six Nations a large tract of land in the Susquehanna Valley of Pennsylvania. Connecticut claimed this land by virtue of her sea-to-sea charter, and the assembly of that colony gave its sanction to the undertaking. The Penn family, proprietors of Pennsylvania, of course opposed the claim, but the Quaker faction in Philadelphia, led by Joseph Galloway and Benjamin Franklin and in control of the assembly of the province, was at odds with the Penns. This Quaker group now formed a "Friendly Association" which collected more than four thousand pounds in order to increase its influence among the Indians by means of presents.

At the treaty of Easton the Delawares were represented by Chief Teedyuscung, the Penn interest chiefly by Governor William Denny and Richard Peters, and the Quaker influence by several members of the assembly. This last group now contrived that Teedyuscung should demand a secretary of his own choosing and that Charles Thomson, a Quaker school teacher of Philadelphia and protégé of Benjamin Franklin, should serve in that capacity. The proprietary agents resisted this demand, but finally gave way. Thomson now insisted that the Proprietors produce all the documents representing their purchase of lands from the Delawares. This led to much argument, and later Croghan presented the Pennsylvania authorities with a paper setting forth the contention of the Indians that some of their Susquehanna lands had been claimed

[8] Volwiler, *George Croghan and the Westward Movement*, 143–144; Charles A. Hanna, *The Wilderness Trail* (New York, 1911) II, 5, 83; Thomas Hutchins MSS., H.S.P.

illegally by the Penns. This document, though transmitted by Croghan, was in the hand of Charles Thomson. Yet Croghan signed it when required to do so. The truth was that the Quakers, through the instrumentality of Isaac Norris, had brought pressure to bear on Croghan and thought that they had him in their interest, but his conduct at the treaty was not satisfactory to them. It seems highly probable that the Quakers were acting here in collaboration with the Susquehannah Company of Connecticut in trying to undermine the claim of the Penns to lands which the company was attempting to settle. The fact that Benjamin Franklin, a leader of the Quaker faction, was active in behalf of the Susquehannah Company and that he personally presented to the British Ministry a demand for investigation of the charges of the Delawares against the Penns, lends weight to this view. Croghan and Sir William Johnson, however, from this time forward opposed the Connecticut claim.[9]

The recapture by the British of the fort at the Forks of the Ohio was the climax of the military developments in 1758. General Forbes, sent from England to accomplish the task, landed in Philadelphia and at once developed connections with the merchants of that city.[10] The colonies were called on for assistance, and Virginia came forward with the most liberal aid, raising twenty-five hundred men and appropriating thirty-two thousand pounds for frontier defense. On the other hand, Franklin found it so difficult to induce the Proprietary and Quaker parties to cooperate in Pennsylvania that no aid was forthcoming from that quarter until eight days before the expedition was to march.[11] George Washington, commanding the Virginia detachment sent to join Forbes, strongly urged that the march be made over the old Ohio Company's road, or Braddock's Road, as it had come to be called. Philadelphia interests, however, persuaded Forbes to cut a new path over the mountains through Pennsylvania. This was a shorter route, but one much more difficult to accomplish. Its selection did, in fact, so delay the expedition that it was on the point of failure, and Virginia was on the point of withdrawing

---

[9] Julian P. Boyd, ed., *The Susquehannah Company Papers* (Wilkes-Barre, Pa., 1930) II, x–xvi, 37, 253, 261, 265; W. M. Smith, ed., *Franklin and Galloway—Some Unpublished Letters* (Worcester, 1925) pp. 26–28n; *Papers of Sir William Johnson*, I, 493–495, II, 438–440, III, 822–823, VI, 335–336; Franklin MSS., I, 50, XLIV, 40, XLVII, pt. 2, 9; American Philosophical Society; *Pa. Arch.*, VII, 656–657, 671–672, 677–678, 680–683, 686–687, 690–691, 698; Lewis R. Harley, *Life of Charles Thomson* (Philadelphia, 1900) pp. 45–47; Journals of the Board of Trade, XLV, 254, 290–292, H.S.P. transcripts; Benjamin to Deborah Franklin, April 12, 1759, in I. M. Hays, ed., *Calendar of the Papers of Benjamin Franklin in the Library of the American Philosophical Society* (Philadelphia, 1908) III, 448.

[10] *Papers of Sir William Johnson*, II, 890–892.

[11] Hayes Baker-Crothers, *Virginia and the French and Indian War*, pp. 128–139.

her support when Forbes made a last-minute dash which proved successful. Fort Duquesne was now renamed Fort Pitt, and when a village grew up about the place the name Pittsburgh came to be generally used. The British flag was again flying on the Western waters, but this time the Ohio Company did not form a part of the picture. Pennsylvania merchants were soon plying their trade in the area, and Governor Fauquier of Virginia took no active interest in the situation.

It was not until February 10, 1763, that peace was declared, and immediately thereafter the Indians rose up and smote the traders who had penetrated their fastnesses. Pontiac's War followed the French and Indian War, and it was two years before the British were able to occupy the territory they had conquered in the West. But the land speculators were busy even if the traders were not. The French had given up all claim to lands east of the Mississippi, and thus a vast new field was opened to those who sought broad acres. It was at this time that the Ohio Company, though altogether lacking in official support even in Virginia, sent George Mercer to London to plead its claims. Practically the same group of Virginians, with George Washington and the Lee family among its influential members, organized the Mississippi Company and petitioned for a huge tract of land to include the junction of the Ohio and Mississippi Rivers. Benjamin Franklin interested himself in the old claim of one Daniel Coxe, and various similar schemes were set on foot for exploiting the new country, but the gods did not smile at this time upon the speculating proponents of the far-flung frontier.[12]

Their dreams were cut short by promulgation of the royal proclamation of 1763. On May 5, 1763, shortly after the Treaty of Paris had ended the Seven Years' War and secured Canada to England, Lord Egremont, Secretary of State, wrote to Lord Shelburne, President of the Board of Trade, as follows:

The country called Canada is of such vast extent that for the greater convenience of governing its inhabitants, there seems to be a necessity of dividing it into two provinces and establishing in each a distinct government. It might also be necessary to fix upon some line for a western boundary to our ancient provinces beyond which our people at present should not be permitted to settle, hence as their numbers increased, they would emigrate to Nova Scotia or the provinces on the Southern Quarter [the Floridas]— where they would be useful to their Mother Country instead of planting themselves in the Heart of America, out of reach of Government where from the great difficulty of procuring European commodities, they would

12 Alvord, *The Mississippi Valley in British Politics,* I, 95; Franklin MSS., I, 77, 83, L. pt. 2, 28, A.P.S.; Thatcher notes from British documents, L. of C., box 1, quoting P.R.O., C.O., series 5, 978, f. 149.

be compelled to commerce and manufactures to the infinite prejudice of Britain. . . .[13]

For this and various other weighty reasons, the Ministry adopted the plan of limiting settlement, and in October the proclamation was issued. This not only prohibited settlement beyond the Appalachian watershed, but provided that land purchases from the Indians could henceforth be made only through the instrumentality of imperial agents or provincial proprietors. In this connection it should be noted that the British government had never recognized the sovereignty of the natives over any soil whatever on the ground that the Indians were nomads of whom few maintained permanent occupation of any definite area and who had no established form of government. However, Sir William Johnson wrote to the Lords of Trade in 1764:

> That it is a difficult matter to discover the true owner of any lands among the Indians is a gross error, which must arise from ignorance of the matter or from a cause which does not require explanation.
> Each nation is perfectly well acquainted with its exact original bounds; the same is again divided into due proportions for each tribe and afterwards subdivided into shares to each family, with all which they are most particularly acquainted. Neither do they ever infringe upon one another or invade their neighbour's hunting grounds.[14]

It was customary to purchase the putative title of the natives before taking possession of their lands merely for the sake of peace with the red men. The governors and proprietors of the several colonies exercised the right of granting unappropriated lands, and up to this time it was they who had been in the habit of negotiating with the Indians for cessions.[15] Private purchases such as that made by Croghan in 1749 and a large one made by Sir William Johnson in New York in 1760 had often been arranged, but since the natives did not possess an absolute or unassailable title, they could hardly have invested the purchaser with one. Despite the famous Camden-Yorke opinion, which, in its origin, had no reference or relation to North America, there were never any legal grounds to sustain the validity of a private purchase of lands from the Indians in America.

Since the line designated by the proclamation of 1763 was adopted merely because of the ease with which it could be delineated and since it left within the Indian country some lands which had been legally

[13] Egremont to Shelburne, May 5, 1763, *ibid.*, box 4, quoting P.R.O., C.O., 323, 16.
[14] Stephen L. Mershon, *English Crown Grants* (New York, 1918) p. 91.
[15] *Papers of Sir William Johnson*, I, 528–530, IV, 817–819; B. A. Hinsdale, "The Western Land Policy of the British Government from 1763–1775," *Ohio Archæological and Historical Quarterly*, I, 207–229.

patented in Virginia, it was naturally looked upon as only a temporary expedient. In 1764 the Ministry promulgated a supplementary body of instructions regarding Indian affairs in America. Sir William Johnson was largely responsible for suggesting the details. The enforcement of these regulations would have involved considerable expense, and a tax on the trade with the natives was proposed as a means of defraying it. Consequently, a Parliamentary enactment would have been necessary before the plan could be completely carried out. On account of political complications this was never accomplished, but both John Stuart and Sir William Johnson, Indian agents for the Southern and Northern departments respectively, were instructed to carry them out as far as was practicable. These regulations stated that a new Indian boundary line was to be negotiated as soon as possible, forbade Indian agents or their deputies to engage in private business, and made illegal all trade with the Indians in certain articles such as rum and rifled guns. The governors of the several provinces were to license traders, and these were to confine their activities to designated posts on the frontier.[16] The currency value of peltry was rigidly fixed, the trade equivalents in Indian goods being set by Sir William Johnson.[17]

A number of traders had lost goods by Indian depredations in 1754 and 1763. Croghan and Trent figured conspicuously among them. At the end of the War they and their associates at once made claim for restitution by the British government.[18] A meeting of the despoiled traders was held at the Indian Queen tavern in Philadelphia, and Croghan was dispatched to London to present their demands, as well as to negotiate some private business for Sir William Johnson. His journey was financed by a group of capitalists which came to be known as the Burlington Company because it had its headquarters in Burlington, New Jersey. William Franklin, governor of New Jersey, was the active head of this group. He was the illegitimate son of Benjamin Franklin, who "found a home under the parental roof when one year old." He had accompanied his father to England in 1756 to study law and won the friendship of the Earl of Bute, through whose influence he was in 1762 appointed governor of "Nova Cæsarea or New Jersey in America." This appointment

---

[16] Helen L. Shaw, *British Administration of the Southern Indians* (Lancaster, 1931) pp. 27ff.; Volwiler, *Croghan,* pp. 171ff.; Board of Trade MSS., Plantations General, XVIII, 272, H.S.P.; Louise Phelps Kellogg, *The British Régime in Wisconsin and the Northwest* (Madison, 1935) pp. 28–32.

[17] *Sir William Johnson Papers,* IV, 48–91.

[18] General Bouquet wrote to Benjamin Franklin, Aug. 27, 1764, ". . . I have the mortification to inform you *privately* that Bradstreet has granted peace to the Delawares & Shawnees without insisting on the least satisfaction for their murders & insults. . . ." Franklin MSS., I, 96, A.P.S.

John Penn termed a "shameful affair," saying that it had been put through in so private a manner that not a tittle of it escaped until it was seen in the public prints; that it was an insult to the people of New Jersey; and that he was so astonished and enraged that he could scarcely contain himself at the thought of it.[19] It is worth noting here that Benjamin Franklin was also dispatched to London in 1764 by the Quaker majority in the Pennsylvania assembly to work for the revocation of the Penn proprietorship. In this movement, as in many others, his closest associate was Joseph Galloway.[20]

Croghan now made ready to take his departure. He wrote Colonel Bouquet that it was necessary for him to go and solicit restitution for his losses in the Indian country or "Resk loosing every Thing I have depending in England and content myself at ye tail of a plow some where on ye frontier." He carried letters of introduction from the firm of Baynton, Wharton and Morgan to the great English merchants, Richard Neave and Son and David Barclay and Sons of London. Sailing from Philadelphia in December, 1763, he reached London after experiencing shipwreck on the coast of France early in 1764.[21] Croghan, fresh from his family of half-breeds in his wilderness home, from intercourse with his savage neighbors and calculating traders, was shocked by the pride and poverty of European civilization in France and London and by the corruption prevalent in the British government!

He was received "very politely" by Lord Hillsborough and had an early conference with Thomas Pownall who advised that the time was not ripe to present the memorial because of reports, principally by General Amherst, of injustice done the Indians. General Amherst, Croghan reported to Sir William Johnson, "is no body heer Nor has he been askt a question with Respect to ye affairs of amerrica Sence he Came over which a gentleman might nott ask his footman." In his report to Sir William he was pessimistic: ". . . What measures they will take ye Lord

---

[19] John Penn to Stirling, Sept. 3, 1762, W. A. Duer, *The Life of William Alexander, Earl of Stirling, with Selections from his Correspondence* (New York, 1847) 69–70; Frederick W. Ricord and William Nelson, eds., *Archives of the State of New Jersey*, Series 1 (Newark, 1886) IX, 368. Honor and ease evidently agreed with the new governor. The following year he wrote to his friend, William Strahan, in London: ". . . Please tell Mr. Myers (if it is possible that he has not yet finished the miniatures) that Mrs. Franklin would be glad to have them made a little fatter, as I have encreased considerably in Flesh since I left London." Wm. Franklin to Wm. Strahan, Dec. 18, 1763, *Pennsylvania Magazine of History*, XII, 381.

[20] Volwiler, *Croghan*, pp. 167–170, 200; Byars, *Gratz*, pp. 71ff.; *Papers of Sir William Johnson*, IV, 204, 264–266, 631–632; Baynton, Wharton and Morgan to David Barclay and Sons, Dec. 26, 1763, Baynton, Wharton and Morgan letter book, Pa. State Archives.

[21] Sidney George Fisher, *Pennsylvania, Colony and Commonwealth* (Philadelphia, 1897) pp. 255–267.

knows butt." After cooling his heels for three months he despaired altogether and wrote to his superior that he saw little probability of getting any restitution:

. . . there has been Nothing Don Sence I Came to London by the Grate ones butt Squbeling & fighting See who will keep in power the publick Intrest is Neglected to Serve privet-Intrest & I blive itt is hard to Say wh. party is ye honistist was I to Spake My Mind I wold Say they are all R — g — e — s — aLicke I am Nott Sorry I Came hear as it will Larn Me to be Contented on a Litle farm in amerrica if I Can gett one when I go back Butt I ashure yr. honour I am Sick of London & harttily Tierᵈ of ye pride & pompe of the Slaves in power hear which are to be pitied tho they Dont Deserve itt [22]

Croghan not only failed to secure any compensation for the traders, but made no progress toward getting a confirmation of the large grant of land made to Sir William in New York by the Six Nations.[23] He did not find Thomas Pownall "so willing to push itt as I Could wish tho he is very polite & Conlesant Butt ye more I am Acquainted with those peple ye Less I find them Sinceer." He discussed the possibility of the creation of new Western colonies with Thomas Pownall and his brother John. At the instigation of Lord Halifax, Croghan went so far as to suggest the idea to the Board of Trade. The plan was practically identical with that which Franklin had proposed in 1756, and its revival at this time was due to him and to the Pownalls.[24] It is significant that Croghan was instructed by Sir William to seek a grant of land south of the Ohio to satisfy the claims of the Ohio Company of Virginia and of the soldiers who were promised grants by Dinwiddie's proclamation of 1754. This and other evidence shows that Sir William and Virginia were on good terms.[25]

When Croghan returned to Philadelphia the latter part of 1764 he was at once exposed to the influence of the firm of Baynton, Wharton and Morgan. This was one of the most powerful commercial houses of the city and, along with the Franks, had lost heavily in the Indian depredations. Samuel Wharton now suggested to George Morgan that he invite Croghan to visit him at his home. Out of this contact there grew

[22] Geo. Croghan to Sir Wm. Johnson, April 14, 1764, *Papers of Sir William Johnson,* IV, 399.
[23] Thatcher notes, box 1, P.R.O., C.O., series 5, 1276, f. 691; *Papers of Sir William Johnson,* IV, 462–465, 567, 614–616.
[24] C. E. Carter, *Great Britain and the Illinois Country* (Washington, 1910) p. 111; Alvord, *The Mississippi Valley in British Politics,* I, 214; *Papers of Sir William Johnson,* IV, 339–341, 362–363, 419–422; Board of Trade MSS., *loc. cit.,* XIX, 305–310.
[25] Executive Journal of the Council of Virginia, Oct. 20, 1767, P.R.O., C.O., series 5, 1435 (photostatic copy in the library of U. of Va.); Justin Winsor, *The Westward Movement* (Boston, 1897) pp. 8–9.

a plan for the development of Western trade and Western empire. Morgan himself did not favor the plan, but Wharton did, and Croghan was highly in favor of it. British troops had not yet been able to occupy the Illinois country, and trade with the natives was not allowed, even at Fort Pitt. Sir William Johnson, however, was sending Croghan to negotiate with the natives for peace and had some hope of securing from them the cession of the Illinois region. A large supply of Indian goods would be necessary for this transaction, and Croghan planned to do some private trading on the side. He, Robert Field, the firm of Baynton, Wharton and Morgan, and their agent at Lancaster, Robert Callender, each took a fourth interest in the venture.[26] Callender had long been active on the frontier, having in 1755 recruited at the request of Washington some "likely Fellows who know the woods." Colonel Bouquet, in command at Fort Pitt, gave his consent to the mercantile adventure, and word was sent to the Indians in the neighborhood of the Fort to assemble for purposes of negotiation and trade. Plans were made for transporting a large supply of goods to that point, some for account of the government, some on private account.

Unfortunately for the traders, the inhabitants who lived along the route from Lancaster to Fort Pitt discovered that an illegal trade was being opened, and they did not intend to see their enemies supplied with the sinews of war. Collecting in armed bands they attacked the supply trains and destroyed several thousand pounds' worth of merchandise. Thomas Wharton, the Quaker, wrote in great agitation of the affair to Benjamin Franklin in London, saying that his brother Samuel had gone to Sir William Johnson's to inform him of it; that the head of one of the casks fell out whereby "they [the inhabitants] discovered that scalping knives or as some called them, pruning knives were sent up." He had, he wrote, satisfied himself that they were merely cutting knives such as the Indians used to carve their victuals. Nevertheless, both civil and military authorities found themselves unable to deal with the situation, and the offenders were acquitted by sympathetic juries when brought to trial.[27]

Sir William Johnson and General Gage were apprised of the situation and the Commander-in-Chief undertook to discover the facts. But this proved to be a difficult matter. The instructions of 1764 had prohibited Indian agents from engaging in trade, and consequently Croghan

[26] *Papers of Sir William Johnson,* IV, 623–626; Franklin MSS., I, 113, LVIII, 32, A.P.S.
[27] *Ibid.,* I, 131, 138, LII, 47–48; Max Savelle, *George Morgan, Colony Builder* (New York, 1932) pp. 18–24; Hanna, *Wilderness Trail,* II, 32; Volwiler, *Croghan,* p. 177.

denied that he was personally concerned in the venture. Wharton also told a crooked tale, and Gage became disgusted with the entire situation, stating it was owing "to Mr. Croghan's troubling his Head more about Trade than the business he is employed in, . . . that he thought to take advantage of his Employment to be first at the market & to make his business an affair of trade instead of carrying on the Service." [28] Despite this bad start, Croghan's negotiations with the Indians proved eminently successful, and through his efforts troops were enabled to occupy the Illinois country without a further struggle. Peace was then declared and trade with the natives was reopened in 1765 by official proclamation.[29]

In 1766 Baynton, Wharton and Morgan were ready to engage in earnest in Western traffic. In September of that year the partners wrote John Irwin, their Pittsburgh agent, that they were sending up a large number of wagons and 600 packhorses in order to load all boats, which they wished to leave not later than November, one to be built with "a small booby House in order that Mr. Wharton may be entirely sheltered from the weather." Two large flotillas finally were ready to sail from Fort Pitt, Fort Chartres in the Illinois being their destination. But Mr. Wharton was not in the small booby house. There went in his stead George Morgan, the youngest member of the firm, then twenty-three. He had left his fifteen-year-old bride, daughter to his partner John Baynton, much against his inclination. As a lad of thirteen he had been apprenticed under his father's will to the mercantile house of Baynton and Wharton and in 1763 had been made a partner to bolster the fortunes of that failing firm, the reorganization of which was completed with the aid of Richard Neave and Son of London.

Morgan was very comfortable in his specially constructed boat, its furnishings being a gun, pistol, sword, spy glass, speaking trumpet, tea chest, compass, pen and ink, and a chest of drawers which served as a desk at which he wrote the voluminous letters he sent back by Indian runner to his bride.

George Croghan was going out to the Illinois on a special mission to the Indians, and was in reality in command of Morgan's flotilla, although that over-confident young merchant declared he would look on himself "as perfectly safe without as with him, & my Journey would be ten times

[28] *Papers of Sir William Johnson,* IV, 704–707, 710–711, 712–714, 717–718, 729–730, 731–732, 735–736, 737–738, 770, 798–800; Samuel Wharton to John Baynton and George Morgan, April 2, 1765, Dreer MSS., members of Old Congress, H.S.P. In this letter Wharton reveals himself quite clearly.

[29] Croghan to Franklin, Dec. 12, 1765, P.R.O., C.O., series 5, 66; William Franklin to Benjamin Franklin, Dec. 17, 1765, *New Jersey Archives,* IX, 521–524; *Papers of Sir William Johnson,* IV, 787–788, 886–889.

more agreeable to myself, . . ." He added, "But above all Mr. Croghan is the most enterprising man, He can appear highly pleased when most chagrined and show the greatest indifference when most pleased." With the Illinois "adventurers" went also Thomas Hutchins and John Finley.[30] Finley apparently had traded in Kentucky under Croghan's auspices as early as 1753 and was at Fort Pitt in 1760. He hunted in Kentucky as the boats passed down the river.[31]

The old Quaker, John Baynton, thought Morgan "not only ought to have the prayers of our Congregation, but of every well wisher to North America, as the peace of it is intimately concerned in his undertaking." He thought a liberal trade with the Indians was necessary for peace with them, stating "The Supplys that we shall send to them by our several Divisions will far exceed any they ever had introduced to them— and can be afforded infinitely cheaper to them, than what they formerly received from the French, who usually sold their goods to them [many of the Articles were shockingly sophisticated] at 1000 Pct proffit. If our Compy disposes of their effects at 200 Pct I may sit down very easy the remainder of my Days as to Money Matters." [32]

The "Illinois adventurers" carried on their affairs under the most favorable auspices. General Gage instructed Colonel Wilkins, commanding in the Illinois, to favor their firm, and Samuel Wharton contracted to allow Wilkins five per cent on sales in return for his carrying out these instructions. Wilkins granted the firm thirty thousand acres of land between Kaskaskia and Prairie du Rocher because the firm "trading in this country have greatly contributed to his Majesty's service." He later accepted one fifth of the grants for himself.[33] James Rumsey, inventor of the steamboat, appeared in the Illinois in 1766 with a cargo of slaves from Jamaica for the firm. Here there was always a great demand for this human commodity. Early the following year the senior member of the company wrote him, "The inexpressible fatigues that you have undergone with the Negroes & your prudent management of them will do you honor as long as the facts can be remembered. And the whole of

[30] C. W. Alvord and C. E. Carter, *The New Régime, 1765–1767, Collections of the Illinois State Historical Library,* Vol. XI, British series, Vol. II (Springfield, 1916) 383–384; Hanna, *Wilderness Trail,* II, 38.

[31] *Pennsylvania Magazine of History and Biography,* II, 303–304; Lucien Beckner, "John Findley," *Filson Club Quarterly,* I, 118–119; W. H. Perrin, J. H. Battle, G. C. Kniffin, *Kentucky, a History of the State* (Louisville, 1888) p. 109; Hanna, *Wilderness Trail,* II, 2.

[32] John Baynton to Mary Morgan, July 11, 1766, in Alvord and Carter, *New Régime,* pp. 336–337.

[33] T. C. and M. J. Pease, *George Rogers Clark and the Revolution in Illinois* (Springfield, 1929) p. 15; Lt. Col. John Wilkins to Samuel Wharton, May 28, 1768, George Morgan MSS., Illinois Historical Survey, Urbana, Ill.

your conduct respecting them from the time you bought them at Jamaica to your landing them at Kaskaskia, has so endeared you to me that it will be my ambition to promote your interest. . . ." He advised Rumsey to remain at the Illinois at least a year, as a civil government was expected to be established there and "something great in the Company's affairs will very probably arise, that may enable them to serve you, as they could wish—effectively." [34]

The company's hunters were busy in the forest supplying meat and perhaps some of the furs which were shipped down the river to New Orleans and from there re-shipped to Philadelphia. Several of them were in the Kentucky country before Daniel Boone; one of these, Simon Girty, was "particularly attached" to Morgan. [35]

Despite all their efforts, Baynton, Wharton and Morgan's venture in Western trade did not turn out successfully. The French habitants of the Illinois country and those who had moved across the Mississippi to the Spanish side still got a large share of the fur trade, the Indians preferring the ingratiating manners of the French despite their higher prices, and they sent their pelts to New Orleans, whence they were supplied with British goods by the British merchants of Mobile and Pensacola. [36] Morgan charged the government double prices for his goods, but quarreled with Croghan, who had become secretly interested in the business, and involved himself and his associates in various difficulties. The great rival firm of Gratz and Simon was beginning active trade in the region, and as a result of these and other troubles, Baynton, Wharton and Morgan went into the hands of receivers in 1767. [37]

When the high hopes of Croghan and his associates for wealth from Western trade began to wane they turned their attention more and more to recouping their losses through land-jobbing and promoting new colonies. When Croghan returned in 1766 from his second journey into the Northwest, he called on Sir William Johnson at Johnson Hall, his palatial wilderness home. There they discussed a scheme for purchasing lands from the French habitants of the Illinois. He then journeyed to Philadelphia, from which place he wrote Sir William on March 30:

[34] John Baynton to James Rumsey, March 1, 1767, Ohio Company MSS., H.S.P.
[35] A. S. Withers, Chronicles of Border Warfare (Cincinnati, 1920) pp. 112–114; Samuel G. Drake, Indian Captivities (New York, 1872) pt. 2, pp. 178–264.
[36] Croghan to Sir William Johnson, Jan. 16, 1767, MSS. Collection, Illinois State Historical Library; C. H. Ambler, A History of West Virginia (New York, 1933) pp. 98–100.
[37] Franklin MSS., I, 145, XLVIII, 129, A.P.S.; C. W. Alvord and C. E. Carter, Trade and Politics, 1767–1769, Collections of the Illinois State Historical Library, Vol. XVI, British series, Vol. III (Springfield, 1921) 84–87; Alvord and Carter, New Régime, pp. 473–476; Savelle, Morgan, pp. 36–41; Volwiler, Croghan, p. 191; Franklin MSS., I, 94, A.P.S.; Byars, Gratz, p. 120; Savelle, Morgan, pp. 36–41.

Soon after My Return hear from your Honours I Wrote you about the Scheme of purchesing what Ever grants the French was posesed of in the Illineois Cuntry and Informd your honour that Governor Franklin with some other Gentlemen hear had formd the Same Scheme and offerd Me to be Concernd with them and your honour. Sence wh I heve Agreed with them in behalf of yr honour & Myself

By Leters from England there is the Greatest Reson to blive that a government will Soon Take place there, if So a thing of this Kind Must be Very Valuable provided we succeed, . . . itt is preposed that its nott to appear till ye Success of our plan is known that your honour & Governor Franklin is Concernd as itts thought you Can be of more Service by Nott being thought Concernd . . .

itt is Likewise preposed to aply for a Grant of 120000 acerrs of Lands to the Crown in that Cuntry and to Take into this Grant two or three Gentlemen of fortune & Influence In England, and Governor franklan and those other Gentlemen Desier to know whome your honour wold Chouse there to be Concernd & thet you wold Write to them if you Should nott Name the Whole you wold Chouse they Designe to Leve the Nomination of such as you Dont to Dr franklin who they prepose to send the pre-poseals to. . . .

Inclosd is the preposeals Drawn up by Governer franklin for yr honours per-ruseal and Such amendments or alterations as you May Judge Nesesery and when you perruse them & Make any alterations you will please to Inclose them to Governor franklin and write him what you think Nesesary on the ocation

When a fair Copey will be Sent you Signd by all those Gentlemen with a Memororial Requesting your honour's aperobation of thire preposial wh will give you an opertunity of Giveing your Sentiments to the ministry on the Subject wh will be of Infinet service to the Company & then the preposials will be Sent home to Doctor franklen to present his Majesty & Council for thire Confermation.

the Sooner your honour Considers this plan & Writes to Governor franklin the Beter as one half of England is Now Land Mad & Every body there has thire Eys fixt on this Cuntry, . . .[38]

A company was accordingly organized, including, beside Croghan and Sir William, the two Franklins, Joseph Galloway, John Hughes, John Baynton, George Morgan, and three Whartons. They proposed to ask for a grant of 1,200,000 acres lying between the Illinois and Mississippi Rivers, but the bounds of the colony were to extend as far east as the Wabash and as far north as the Wisconsin. Sir William Johnson was to be groomed for the governorship and Benjamin Franklin was to pro-mote the scheme in London.[39] Sir William Johnson wrote to Governor

[38] George Croghan to Sir William Johnson, March 30, 1766, *Johnson Papers*, V, 128–130.
[39] Franklin MSS., L, pt. 1, 47, A.P.S.; Alvord and Carter, *New Régime*, pp. 196–197, 203–204, 205–206, 214, 220; Calendar of Sir William Johnson MSS., *Proceedings of the American Antiquarian Society*, new series, XVIII, 367–384; Temple Bodley, *History of Kentucky before the Louisiana Purchase* (Chicago, 1928) I, 53–59; Vol-wiler, *Croghan*, pp. 261–265; MS. articles of agreement, March 29, 1766, box 9,

Franklin in high approval of the scheme, adding "I am of Opinion it would answer better that I recommended it in Gen¹ Terms, as an Affair I had heard was in Agitation, . . ." [40] Accordingly, he wrote the Chief Secretary of State, Henry S. Conway, enclosing the scheme "at the request of several Gentlemen of fortune & character," emphasizing the benefits which would accrue to England and the provinces from such a new colony, but saying nothing of those which would accrue to himself. [41] Sir Henry Moore, governor of New York, was taken into the company, and William Franklin wrote to his father in London that he thought it of little avail to buy lands in the Illinois unless a colony were established there and he had accordingly drawn up proposals for that purpose. He added that if his father favored the proposition he could add to the company himself and such men in England as would be most likely to promote the undertaking. Benjamin Franklin replied that he liked the prospect of the new colony and would do his utmost to promote it in England; he deplored the fact that he was not permitted to nominate additional members to the company, since, according to his reckoning "there would be near 63,000,000 acres,—enough to content a large number of reasonable people." He stated he had reason to hope for Shelburne's good opinion of the proposal, but that Hillsborough was "terribly afraid of dispeopling Ireland." [42]

The Philadelphia Philosopher carried out his functions with remarkable success. In 1767 he succeeded in bringing over to the cause Lord Shelburne, Secretary of State for the Southern Department, under whose jurisdiction the colonies fell, and Shelburne converted the Council to the plan. The proposal was next submitted to the Board of Trade, three distinct Western colonies being suggested, but the Board, with Lord Hillsborough as president, did not approve. As affairs of the American department became more important and complicated, the office of Secretary of State for the Colonies was created in 1768. With Hillsborough's appointment to this new position, the Illinois Company saw the death of its dream of a Western empire in America. [43]

H.S.P.; *The Centennial History of Illinois*, I, C. W. Alvord, *The Illinois Country, 1673–1818* (Chicago, 1922) 287–290; Bigelow, *Franklin*, IV, 137–139.

[40] Sir William Johnson to William Franklin, June 20, 1766, in Alvord and Carter, *New Régime*, pp. 318–319; Kellogg, *British Régime*, pp. 117–119.

[41] Sir William Johnson to Henry S. Conway, July 10, 1766, P.R.O., C.O., series 5, 67.

[42] Benjamin to Wm. Franklin, Sept. 12, 1766, Bigelow, *Franklin*, IV, 417–419.

[43] William Franklin to Benjamin Franklin, Dec. 17, 1765, *New Jersey Archives*, IX, 521–524; Benjamin Franklin to Sir William Johnson, Sept. 12, 1766, Gratz MSS., H.S.P.; Thomas Wharton to Benjamin Franklin, Nov. 11, 1766, Franklin MSS., H.S.P.; Carter, *Great Britain and the Illinois Country*, pp. 115–144; Alvord and Carter, *New Régime*, pp. 233, 337–338, 370; Alvord and Carter, *Trade and Politics*, pp. xv, 1–3, 12–21; Alvord, *Mississippi Valley in British Politics*, I, 347.

But Franklin and his friends had more than one string to their bow, and they were by no means downhearted because of this reverse. Another and even more promising plan had been taking shape for some years, and it began to assume definite form just as the sun of the Illinois Company was setting. The Ministerial plan of 1764 had provided for a new Indian boundary, and in 1765 Sir William Johnson had arranged with the Six Nations to draw a line down the Ohio River to the mouth of the Tennessee and thence up that river to its source. This would open up to speculation a fine new territory and provide an opportunity for the indemnification of the traders who had suffered by Indian depredations · in 1763. Croghan had failed in 1764 to secure in England a monetary compensation for them, and now turned to the possibility of securing a grant of land. On December 12, 1765, he sent Benjamin Franklin a copy of a journal he had kept on his tour into the Indian country, and wrote him as follows:

. . . In my public and private conferences with the Shawnese, Delawares, and Wyandotts, and the Several other tribes, who had robbed and murdered our Traders, I very frequently represented to them, their unparalleled breach of public faith, & that it, almost, compeled us to think them, unworthy of the least degree, of future confidence.

They as often expressed their sinsibility & Sorrow for it, and say'd, they were *not only very willing but anxious, to make a reparation* to the representatives of the unhappy Sufferers. Yet constantly urged, that they had no ways of doing it, except by *a Surrender of a part of their Country,* which they would *most chearfully* do, and especially of that part which lies on this side of the River Ohio (on the back part of Virginia) as it was now of no use to them, for Hunting Ground. . . .

In my return to New York, I called at Sir William Johnson's, where I was informed by him that when he settled the preliminaries of peace last Spring with the Deputys of the above Tribes,—he had also described to them, their faithless conduct towards the poor traders, and insisted, as one of the preliminary conditions of a pacification, that they should make a restitution—to which they as fully and chearfully consented as they had before, done to me—But alledged, at the same time, that they had no other manner of doing it, except by requesting the representatives of the Murdered Traders, to accept from them, *a part of their Country,* on this side of the River Ohio. . . .[44]

William Trent and John Hughes busied themselves in buying up the claims of the actual traders and transferring them to a group which now organized itself as the "Suffering Traders," consisting of Sir William Johnson, Benjamin Franklin, Governor William Franklin, John Baynton, Samuel Wharton, George Morgan, Charles Wharton, Joseph

[44] Geo. Croghan to Benj. Franklin, Dec. 12, 1765, British transcripts, L. of C., P.R.O., C.O., series 5, 66.

Galloway, and Robert Callender.[45] This was almost the same personnel as that of the Illinois Company. The firm of Baynton, Wharton and Morgan, frantically trying to stave off bankruptcy at this time, was particularly interested in the retribution scheme. The partners wrote to Benjamin Franklin in the summer of 1766:

. . . Sir William Johnson has been & is very desirous, to do us an essential Piece of Service, in respect to Indian Losses & Therefore When He was directed, to treat with the Six Nations, about a *Boundary*, He took that opportunity, of requiring Them to grant a Part of the Country, with that *Boundary* by way of Retribution for their Robbery—which They agreed to;—That is, when the Treaty is to be held, for the ascertaining & paying for the Land, *within it*,—They will acquaint Sir William, That they will not receive any Pay from the Crown, for such a particular part of the Land, within the Boundary (which we shall take care to be limited, by natural & imoveable Bounds)—As They give it, to the *Indian Traders*, as a Restitution for the Goods, They stole from Them.

You will please therefore, Good Sir, to observe That the Order to Sir William, for purchasing the *Boundary*, is the Basis, On which, We can Only Obtain the Indian Grant; for Unless, that is ordered to be purchased, —The Indians cannot give us the Land. . . .[46]

In accordance with these suggestions, Joseph Galloway, Sir William Johnson, and the Franklins, father and son, urged upon the Ministry the necessity of confirming the boundary, pleading that failure to do so would mean an Indian war.

With their creditors becoming more importunate, the "Illinois adventurers" were desperate, and Samuel Wharton wrote to William Franklin requesting that he urge his father to drop the Illinois affair rather than miss succeeding in the restitution grant, "for be assured, the Latter would be an immediate very great Thing & is of infinitely more consequence, to you & us, than the former. I have so lately, had an Opportunity of discovering the Inclination of Our frontier People, to settle On the Ohio, That I am persuaded—We could soon convert a very considerable part of the Indian Grant, into Money." [47] Wharton then wrote to Dr. Franklin that unless the boundary were confirmed, as fixed by Sir William Johnson in 1765, an Indian war would "infallibly happen

[45] MS. deed of declaration, May 24, 1766, George Morgan MSS., Illinois Historical Survey, Urbana, Ill.; Croghan to Franklin, Feb. 25, 1766, P.R.O., C.O., series 5, 66; A. Mitchell to S. Wharton, March 1, 1766, Ohio Company MSS., H.S.P.; *Collections of the Massachusetts Historical Society*, fourth series, X, pt. 2 (Boston, 1871) 604–608; Alvord and Carter, *New Régime*, pp. 207–209, 364–366; Byars, *Gratz*, pp. 340–353; *Papers of Sir William Johnson*, V, 16–17.

[46] Baynton, Wharton and Morgan to Benj. Franklin, Aug. 28, 1766, Franklin MSS., I, Miscellaneous, L. of C.

[47] Samuel Wharton to Wm. Franklin, [Not dated, but obviously written in 1767], Franklin MSS., XLVIII, 147, A.P.S.

this Winter or next spring." [48] Basing his arguments largely upon the inevitability of an Indian war, Dr. Franklin now initiated a strenuous campaign for confirming the boundary, thereby making the "Suffering Traders'" grant possible, and Shelburne was finally stirred to action. The earlier letters of Sir William on the subject had been misplaced, but they were sought and found, and just before turning over the colonial administration to Hillsborough, Shelburne, on January 5, 1768, issued orders for the demarcation of a new Indian boundary for the middle colonies.[49] It looked as though the "suffering traders" were to be put out of their suffering at last.

Sir William accordingly proceeded to assemble the Indians at Fort Stanwix the following September to negotiate for the new boundary. Twenty large batteaux laden with presents were conveyed to that place, and large quantities of food ordered, Sir William saying that on such occasions the Indians ate twice as much as Americans; they also constantly demanded of the white men rum, "which God has taught you how to make."

Not long after Hillsborough took over colonial affairs Sir William Johnson discovered that their ideas were not in harmony. According to Hillsborough's direction, the Indian boundary line was to run from Owego on the Susquehanna, near the southern boundary of New York, to the Ohio above Fort Pitt, and thence down that river to the mouth of the Great Kanawha, where it was to meet the line to be arranged by John Stuart with the Cherokee.[50] Not satisfied with this, Johnson got permission to extend the line northward on the New York frontier, but the Indians required considerable cash and cajolery before it was arranged. This increase of available lands in New York enabled Sir William, the Whartons, Trent, Croghan, and William Franklin and his "Burlington Company" to get large grants for themselves on the head-

[48] *Trade and Politics*, pp. 71–74.

[49] Bigelow, *Franklin*, IV, 330–334, 422–424; Volwiler, *Croghan*, pp. 221–222; Alvord, *Mississippi Valley in British Politics*, I, 354; Alvord and Carter, *Trade and Politics*, pp. 102, 118–120; Board of Trade MSS., XXVI, 483–484, XXVII, 1–10, H.S.P.; Croghan to Franklin, Oct. 2. 1767, Franklin MSS., I, 97, A.P.S.; C. E. Carter, ed., *The Correspondence of General Thomas Gage with the Secretaries of State, 1763–1775* (New Haven, 1931–1933) II, 53–54; *Papers of Sir William Johnson*, V, 855, VI, 22–23, 32, 66, 127–130; Board of Trade to Shelburne, Dec. 23, 1767, P.R.O., C.O., series 5, 68. Shelburne had apparently advised that the line go farther down the Ohio than the Great Kanawha, but the Board of Trade said it should stop there as the Cherokee occupied the country below, despite the claim of the Six Nations. C. W. Alvord, "The British Ministry and the Treaty of Fort Stanwix," *Proceedings of the State Historical Society of Wisconsin*, 1908, pp. 165–183.

[50] Hillsborough to Gage, Johnson, etc., Jan. 30, 1768, P.R.O., C.O., series 5, 69; William Franklin to Sir William Johnson, May 23, 1768, Gratz MSS., H.S.P., *Papers of Sir William Johnson*, VI, 146–148, 407–408; Bigelow, *Franklin*, IV, 424; Carter, *Gage*, II, 63.

waters of the Delaware and Susquehanna, including the huge tract which
the Six Nations had granted to Johnson some years earlier. Sir Henry
Moore, governor of New York and member of the Illinois Company, had
no part in the negotiation of the treaty, but he gave full support to all
these plans.[51]

Virginia's interest in the Treaty of Fort Stanwix was even keener
than that of New York. She also stood a chance to get considerable
extension of available territory, and she planned to make the most of
it. Early in 1768 Governor Fauquier had been succeeded, *pro tempore,*
by John Blair, president of the council. Blair appointed Colonel Andrew
Lewis and Dr. Thomas Walker to represent Virginia at Fort Stanwix.
But Johnson was so slow in assembling the Indians that Lewis was unable to await him, and consequently Walker alone spoke for Virginia
at the conference.[52]

It has been stated that Sir William's agreement of 1765 with the Six
Nations provided that the line should run to the mouth of the Tennessee
River and up that stream to its source. The Board of Trade specifically
rejected this plan and required that the line terminate at the Great
Kanawha, where the Cherokee boundary was to join it. When Lewis and
Walker heard of this governmental action, they denied the right of the
Cherokee to the land in question and urged Sir William to disregard his
instructions. He accordingly averred that the Six Nations insisted upon
the surrender of their claims south of the Ohio as far down as the Tennessee. Twice before, at the treaties of Lancaster and Logstown in 1744
and 1752 respectively, the Six Nations had given up all claim to this
land, and they were ready to do so again. They undertook to speak for
their dependents, the Delawares and Shawnee also, but these nations
rather than the Iroquois were immediately concerned in the region, and
were not ready to acquiesce in its surrender. The Cherokee, in spite of
Sir William's testimony to the contrary, had no intention of surrendering
lands at the behest of the Iroquois. But Sir William, the Six Nations,
and Virginia were in full accord, and conflicting Indian claims were
brushed aside.[53]

[51] Ruth L. Higgins, *Expansion in New York* (Columbus, Ohio, 1931) pp. 93–94;
Volwiler, *Croghan,* pp. 249–250; *Papers of Sir William Johnson,* V, 631–632; William
Franklin to Thomas Wharton, March 6, 1770, MS. collection, H.S.P.; Peters MSS.,
VI, 89, H.S.P.
[52] *Proceedings of the American Antiquarian Society,* new series, XVIII, 391;
Papers of Sir William Johnson, VI, 297–298, 316–317.
[53] William Franklin to Benjamin Franklin, Dec. 17, 1765, P.R.O., C.O., series 5, 66;
Board of Trade to the King, March 7, 1768, P.R.O., C.O., series 5, 69; Sir William
Johnson to Hillsborough, Nov. 18, 1768, *ibid.;* Samuel Wharton's journal of Indian
congress at Johnson Hall, April 29–May 22, 1765, Continental Congress MSS., Indian affairs, L. of C., no. 56, p. 83; S. Wharton to T. Wharton, June 23, 1768, Whar-

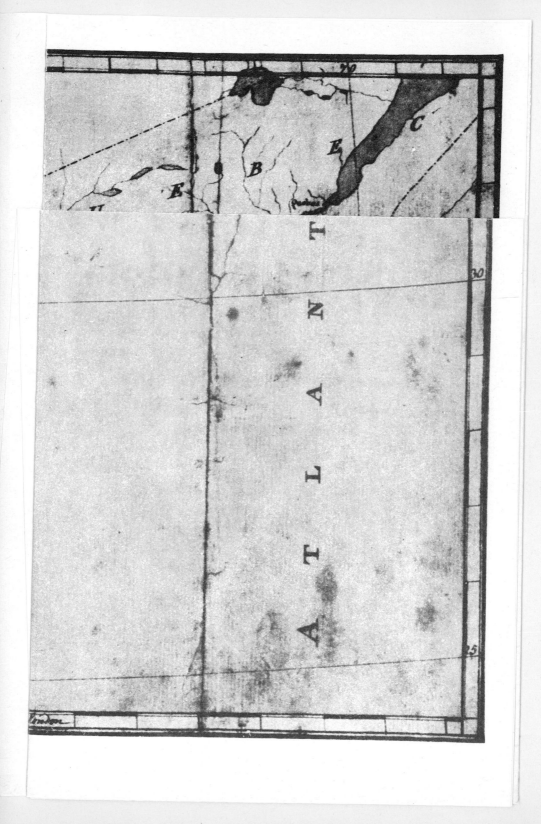

colony directly interested in the treaty. The proposed line would open up much new land in that province, and Governor Penn and Sir William worked in harmony to accomplish it. Richard Peters and James Tilghman of the council were the official representatives of Pennsylvania. The proprietors paid in cash for the lands they got and seemed quite satisfied with the bargain. Fort Pitt and the surrounding country were opened to settlement, but the treaty did not decide whether the territory belonged to Virginia or Pennsylvania. All inter-colonial boundary disputes were left unsettled.[55]

When Baynton, Wharton and Morgan had failed some months earlier the business was put into the hands of trustees appointed by the creditors. At this juncture Joseph Galloway had written to William Franklin:

> . . . Our Friend S. W. apprehends, and I think with good Reason, that Some Pains will be taken to Send him to the Illinois (some of the Company must be there), to transact their Affairs. The Impropriety of which will, I am certain, strike you on the first Mention of it, You will know of how much Importance Mr. W's Presence and Attention will be in obtaining a Retribution for the Indian Losses; and that no other Person for many Reasons can he [sic] negotiate that Matter with Sir W. J. & Mr C(roghan) but himself. Indeed, it appears to Mr. James & myself that this important Affair must drop, shoud it be determined that he sh^d go to the Indian Country. Mr. Wh. thinks that a Letter from you to Mr. James Signifying the Necessity of Mr. Whartons Staying to transact this Affair with Sir W, to be shewn to the Creditors, will have the Wished for Effect.
> Since I wrote the above, from Some Things I have heard, I do think it absolutely necessary that you should come down, by which means alone Mr. Wharton's Journey to the Illinois can be prevented, and thereby our great Object obtained. . . .[56]

Young George Morgan was sent back to the Illinois to look after the company's affairs there, and Samuel Wharton, after spending several weeks in the Indian villages in company with William Trent, was now in attendance at the negotiations for a treaty at Fort Stanwix, where, according to Morgan, he "had a fine field for the exercise of his Invention, Prudence & Retorick."

New Jersey had no Western lands and her governor had no official business at the treaty, but William Franklin was there also, as was William Trent. Their business, of course, concerned the grant to the "despoiled traders." The fact that the traders' losses were suffered in 1763 at the hands of the Northwestern tribes under Pontiac, with the Six

[55] *Pennsylvania Archives, Colonial Records,* IX, 492–495; *Papers of Sir William Johnson,* VI, 107–111, 168–170, 200–201.
[56] Joseph Galloway to Wm. Franklin, Sept. 6, 1767, Franklin MSS., XLVIII, 134, A.P.S.

Nations only slightly involved, was of no consequence to the Superintendent of Indian Affairs. The Iroquois made restitution by granting to the Wharton-Trent group a tract of land bounded by the Ohio River on the west, the Allegheny Mountains on the east, and the Little Kanawha on the south. The grant was made to the King in trust for "the only use, benefit and behoof of the despoiled traders," the object being to leave the government no choice in the matter. This came to be known as the Indiana grant and the grantees as the Indiana Company.[57]

There was yet another interest in which Sir William Johnson was concerned. George Croghan individually claimed 200,000 acres in the neighborhood of Fort Pitt by cession from the natives in 1749. The Indians obligingly made a request that if his lands should fall within the Pennsylvania boundary, which seemed likely, that he might be compensated out of the ceded lands which should fall within the King's territory; that is, in Virginia.

Sir William had been instructed to consult all the governors concerned in the making of the treaty, and he had cooperated with those of New York, Pennsylvania, and Virginia. Connecticut lay claim to some of the Western lands involved, and the fact that she was not consulted amounted to an official slight of her claim. A group of speculators, headed by Phineas Lyman, had revived a scheme originated by Samuel Hazard in 1755 to make a settlement on these lands. Lyman was in London lobbying for his claim. He had lost all patience waiting on the Ministry and was threatening to take his settlers out without leave.[58] Franklin took an interest in the scheme, but Sir William did nothing for the Connecticut group. In fact, two missionaries from Connecticut, apparently representing the interest of the Susquehannah Company, came to Fort Stanwix to connive with the Indians against the treaty.[59]

But Sir William had laid the ground work perfectly, and all went through as he had planned. At this time there was no question of the ownership of the Western lands lying south of the Ohio River. They were acknowledged in all official communications as belonging to Virginia, and now that colony got an extensive, if dubious, surrender of the native claim. But Sir William was a good trader and got something in return.

---

[57] *Papers of Sir William Johnson,* VI, 394–395; deposition of Samuel Wharton, Dec. 11, 1782, Cont. Cong. MSS., 77; *New Jersey Archives,* X, 55–56; Bodley, *Kentucky,* p. 64; Alvord, *Mississippi Valley in British Politics,* I, 187.

[58] Benjamin to William Franklin, June 13, 1767, Bigelow, *Franklin,* IV, 420.

[59] Franklin MSS., L, pt. 2, 28, LVIII, 114, A.P.S.; *Susquehannah Company Papers,* III, ix–xi; memorial of Phineas Lyman to the King in Council, 1767, P.R.O., C.O., series 6, 67; Darlington, *Christopher Gist's Journals,* pp. 261–266; George H. Alden, *New Governments West of the Alleghenies before 1780* (Madison, Wis., 1897) p. 7; *Papers of Sir William Johnson,* VI, 472–473, 513–514.

The Indiana grant overlay land that had long been claimed by the Ohio Company of Virginia, and now Virginia gave her aid to the competing Indiana Company. It is not without significance that Dr. Thomas Walker, who signed the treaty in the name of Virginia, was the agent of the Loyal Company, ancient rival of the Ohio Company group. In appointing him, President Blair was only pursuing the policy of Governor Fauquier in regard to these rival companies. Though he made no complaint at the time, later on when severely criticized in Virginia for his action in signing the treaty of Fort Stanwix, Walker said that he was not admitted to the private conferences there and that he signed the treaty only as a witness. The first of these statements was true; the latter was not. He was the fully accredited agent of Virginia at the treaty and signed the articles as such.[60] Virginia thereby consented to the Indiana Company claim in exchange for the surrender by the natives of all their remaining claims south of the Ohio River.

[60] J. P. Kennedy, ed., *Journals of the House of Burgesses of Virginia, 1766–1769,* pp. xxvi–xxxviii; Alvord, *Mississippi Valley in British Politics,* II, 69–71; Archibald Henderson, *Dr. Thomas Walker and the Loyal Company of Virginia,* pp. 30, 73–74; proceedings of the treaty of Fort Stanwix, Oct. 24–Nov. 5, 1768, P.R.O., C.O., series 5, 69. On Sept. 30, William Trent wrote from Fort Stanwix to John Baynton: "I am sorry to find that you as well as the rest of our friends have been so much alarmed. I really think if you had attended to a letter Mr. Wharton wrote you about the Virga Commisn. you would have been convinced that we are fully acquainted with every circumstance of the affair which has given you so much uneasiness and been the cause of this express. Pray make yourself easie and rest assured if there is any faith in a man of as good a character as Sir Wm. Johnson's that every thing will be settled to our entire satisfaction before we leave this place. As to Dr. Coxe he cannot hurt us." Ohio Company papers, H.S.P. See also Hillsborough to Sir William Johnson, Oct. 12, 1768, P.R.O., C.O., series 5, 69; Alvord and Carter, *Trade and Politics,* pp. 540–541. George Mason said that the entire transaction "wore the face of mystery and knavery." Ambler, *West Virginia,* pp. 100–103.

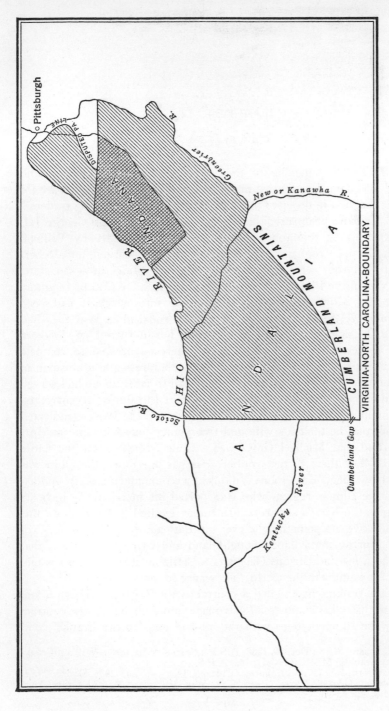

MAP 3. VANDALIA AS ORIGINALLY PLOTTED ON EVANS' MAP

Shaded area represents original plan of the Walpole Company for a proprietary colony, December 27, 1769. Unshaded area represents the revised plan of May 6, 1773 for the colony of Vandalia, the proprietary area remaining unchanged.

CHAPTER III

VANDALIA

WITH the opening of the year 1769 Samuel Wharton and William Trent were making final preparations to depart for London in order to plead the cause of the "suffering traders," alias the "Indiana Company," before the ministers of King George III. Their expenses on this journey were to be paid jointly by William Franklin, George Croghan, John Baynton, George Morgan, and Robert Callender; but they were leaving their financial affairs in a sad state. Morgan was in the Illinois country trying to rescue the firm of Baynton, Wharton and Morgan from the receivership into which it had been thrown in 1767.[1] Since the end of the French and Indian War they had been the only English traders in the Illinois, but in July, 1768, William Murray, representing the Franks-Gratz interests, arrived to compete with them. Murray was a man of considerable address and a kinsman of Lord Dunmore. He knew the problems he had to face, for he had served as captain of the British forces stationed at Fort Pitt during recent years. That he intended to make a considerable sojourn in the West is indicated by the fact that he took his wife and two young sons with him to Fort Chartres and that Michael Gratz was seeking "Masters for the Little Ones" to follow them to the frontier. His passage down the Ohio was facilitated by Lieut.-Col. John Wilkins, the commandant of troops assigned to the Illinois region, who transported his merchandise in boats belonging to the King's service, and Murray exulted to Gratz that "this affair will save us something clever in Batteaumen's Wages & Provisions." Murray immediately bought land and wrote his partners that if they had a few industrious Germans to settle on it, the Illinois would be the finest country in the world, "allowance for ague excepted." [2]

Although Wilkins had signed a contract with Baynton, Wharton and Morgan to throw his commercial patronage into their hands, the contract to supply the Illinois troops with rations had gone to the Franks' com-

[1] Ohio Company MSS., Dec. 30, 1768, H.S.P.; Samuel Wharton to William Franklin (1769?) Franklin MSS., XLVIII, 147, A.P.S.
[2] C. W. Alvord, *The Illinois Country* (Chicago, 1922) pp. 283–285; Alvord, *Trade and Politics*, pp. 342–349; Byars, *Gratz*, p. 87; Wm. Murray to B. & M. Gratz, April 24, 1769, *ibid.*, pp. 93–94.

pany despite Wharton's attempt to bribe Lachlan Macleane, Lord Shelburne's secretary, to use his influence for them. Morgan was notified of this at about the time of Murray's arrival, and life at once took on a very somber complexion for him. He presently quarreled with Wilkins over the five per cent commission which the latter was to receive, and one of his principal aides, James Rumsey the slave-trader, went over to his rivals, becoming secretary to Murray. Matters went from bad to worse; Wilkins finally put Morgan under arrest, causing him to decamp from the Western country in March, 1771, and return to Philadelphia, leaving his affairs in the hands of John Finley. By 1772 the house of Baynton, Wharton and Morgan had practically ceased to exist.[3]

As a result of all these misfortunes, Morgan, who had never wished to engage in Western trade, became greatly irritated with Samuel Wharton, whose entire attention was now taken up in London with the Indiana and other land speculating ventures. "The worst wish I pray may happen to this Generous gratefull, Polite Partner of ours," Morgan wrote to Baynton, "is Abundant Success in all his honest undertakings."[4] This reminds one of George Croghan's frequent complaints against "Land Jobbers." Wharton, with the ocean between them, refused to reply to letters from his partners, and they thought, not without reason, that he was trying to exclude them from the new land company. Baynton wrote him early in 1770, stating that, as he deemed himself a principal in the affairs of their firm, he was not fond of applying to others regarding the negotiations and instructed Wharton to report to him on the progress of their affairs.[5] Still the absent partner did not respond, and Morgan, with creditors becoming more importunate, wrote in great exasperation:

. . . As some Letters mentioned your having had an offer of this New Government I would wish you Joy on the Occasion did I not think You and I stood full as great a Chance of being Govern-ed elsewhere—for several Suits have been lately commenced against us. . . . For my own part I continue of the same Disposition as when I wrote to you last on this Subject Viz. That we must & shall make over to our Creditors or to Trustees for their Use, all our Proportions of the Western Lands—And further, That each & every of our Relations whose Names you have made Use of for Shares in the 72 Proprietorships shall & must do the same. This our already too much injured Creditors have an Undoubted Right to insist upon

[3] *Ibid.*, pp. 115–117, 120, 340–353; Savelle, *George Morgan*, pp. 36, 49, 71–72; memorandum of a conversation between Col. Wilkins and George Morgan, Dec. 23, 1770, George Morgan MSS., Ill. Hist. Survey, Urbana, Ill.; Morgan, advertisement of his intended departure, Kaskaskia, Dec. 20, 1770, *ibid.*; certificate of Col. Wilkins, March 16, 1771, *ibid.*; Morgan to Wilkins and Wilkins to Morgan, March 23, 1771, *ibid.*

[4] John Hughes to Thomas Wharton, June 7, 1769, Wharton MSS., H.S.P.; Savelle, *Morgan*, pp. 80, 82.

[5] John Baynton to Samuel Wharton, Jan. 3, 1770, Baynton's private letter book, Pa. State Archives.

& which Mr. Baynton & myself shall joyfully agree to; for you well know that neither Ours or any of your Relations have been anyways instrumental or assisting (further than we were justly entitled to demand from them) in this Business. This is so reasonable & just that I shall not Suffer myself to doubt your & your Relations ready Acquiescence therein nor need you be uneasy or fearfull that Mr. Baynton's or my Brothers etc. will hesitate to comply with this just Proposal—More particularly as they must at any rate assign to us their Shares—Their names being only borrow'd upon the Occasion in order that we might have the greater number of Shares. . . . I am very fearfull that you will be much longer delay'd in your Business than is generally imagined by your Relations, etc.—for I look upon your Demands on Pennsylvania as very unreasonable. I mean your Proposal to prevent Mr. Penn's just Claim to five Degrees of Longitude taking Place . . . for you, your Brothers & Colonel Croghan to talk of having Fort Pitt left out of Pennsylvania 20, 30 or 40 Miles is in my Opinion highly preposterous. . . . Yet I must confess that although I am convinced Mr. Penn is entitled not only to take Fort Pitt in but also to comprehend 4/5ths of what we call the Traders Grant, I say notwithstanding this, I wish my Judgement to be erroneous. . . .[6]

Morgan had more and more reason as time went on to fear that his partner in London was not working for the benefit of their creditors.

During the same years Croghan's affairs also became hopelessly involved. In connection with the Burlington Company, he had taken a leading part in the purchase of the 100,000 acres in New York known as the "Otsego tract." His interest in this, as well as certain other holdings, was heavily mortgaged to Richard Peters, Senior, and to the Burlington Company. Both creditors were anxious to get their hands upon the property, and a judgment was finally rendered against Croghan in 1772. The Gratz brothers, who also had an interest in his affairs, liquidated the estate for him and apparently tried to save what they could. But little was left, and a large part of his Western holdings finally passed into the hands of Bernard and Michael Gratz.[7]

[6] George Morgan to S. Wharton, Feb. 1, 1773, Baynton, Wharton and Morgan letter book, Pa. State Archives.

[7] Extracts of letters, Wm. Franklin to Croghan and *vice versa,* 1772–1773, Society collection, H.S.P.; Trent to Wharton, Nov. 16, 1770, *ibid.;* William Franklin to Trent, Jan. 14, 1771, *New Jersey Archives,* X, 227–228; also *ibid.,* X, 111–113; Wm. Franklin to Richard Peters, April 30, 1770, Peters MSS., VI, 108, H.S.P.; Croghan to Peters, Sept. 7, 1769, *ibid.,* VI, 86; same to same, Jan. 2, 1772, *ibid.,* VII, 97; memorandum, May 14, 1788, Ohio Company MSS., H.S.P.; Croghan to B. & M. Gratz, July 4, 1772, *ibid.;* Croghan to Trent, Jan. 18, 1769, Lamberton Scotch-Irish MSS., I, 86, H.S.P.; Burlington Company to Thomas Wharton, May 22, 1772, Wharton MSS., H.S.P.; Gratz–Croghan MSS., April 22, July 7, 1772, H.S.P.; Wm. Franklin to M. Gratz, Sept. 28, 1772, Etting MSS., Governors, I, 52, H.S.P.; state of Croghan's indebtedness, Oct. 26, 1772, Gratz MSS., Ridgway Library, Philadelphia; Byars, *Gratz,* pp. 112–113, 123, 131–132, 134–135; *Papers of Sir William Johnson,* VII, 487, 650–654; Volwiler, *Croghan,* 214–215; F. W. Halsey, ed., *A Tour of Four Great Rivers—being the Journal of Richard Smith* (New York, 1906) pp. xv, 36–37.

Croghan was thus not able to pay his share of the expenses of Wharton and Trent during their prolonged sojourn in London. Sir William Franklin, apparently with good reason, refused to pay his assessment; he bemoaned his difficulties in the "cursed Otsego business" and stated that he had more than one reason to regret having gone to the treaty at Fort Stanwix.[8] Trent was so impoverished that he hardly contributed at all to the support of his wife and five children during these years, Thomas Wharton, brother to Samuel, finding it necessary to come to their relief. Samuel's expenses were paid to the amount of ten thousand pounds from the funds of the insolvent firm of Baynton, Wharton and Morgan.[9]

Thus Trent and Wharton were indeed in desperate circumstances when they repaired to London in January, 1769, but they put their trust in the Indiana Company which was expected to deliver them from all their adversities. This, however, proved to be a forlorn hope. On their arrival they discovered that Lord Hillsborough had set himself against their project. The treaty of Fort Stanwix had irritated him no little, not only because Sir William Johnson had broken his instructions in carrying the line down the Ohio beyond the mouth of the Great Kanawha but because the grant of lands to the King had been made upon condition that the grants to Croghan and to the "suffering traders" should be ratified, although the government had never been consulted in regard to them nor the deeds submitted. Furthermore, it was charged that Hillsborough detected misinformation about the country concerned in Wharton's statements that thirty thousand people were settled on it, that hemp of good texture grew wild there and could be loaded on ships and sent safely down the Ohio to the Gulf of Mexico, and that naval stores could be sent as cheaply from thence as from New York or Philadelphia. The Secretary for the Colonies and the Board of Trade determined to reject the Croghan and Indiana grants and so notified Sir William Johnson. Sir William, in a lame attempt to explain his action in negotiating for an Indian boundary in territory outside his jurisdiction, had informed the home government that the red men would not accept any other boundary, that they insisted on making the larger cession

---

[8] Wm. Franklin to Wm. Trent, Jan. 14, 1771, *New Jersey Archives,* series 1, X, 227–228.

[9] Indenture dated Feb. 28, 1769, Lamberton Scotch-Irish MSS., I, 94, H.S.P.; Edmd. Milne to Trent, Oct. 7, 1769, Ohio Company MSS., H.S.P.; Croghan to Trent, Nov. 30, 1769, Gratz-Croghan MSS., H.S.P.; Wharton to Wm. Franklin, July 21, 1771, Franklin MSS., III, 70, A.P.S.; Thomas Wharton to Wm. Franklin, Oct. 12, 1771, *ibid.,* III, 70b; W. to B. Franklin, July 29, 1773, *ibid.,* III, 159; George Morgan to S. Wharton, June 11, 1774, Baynton, Wharton and Morgan letter book, Pa. State Archives; *Papers of Sir William Johnson,* VII, 477–478; Sarah Trent to Thomas Wharton, Sept. 9, 1771, Wharton MSS., H.S.P.; Wm. Franklin to Thos. Wharton, April 27, 1772, MS. collection, H.S.P.

rather than the one for which he had been instructed to negotiate. Hillsborough now instructed him, perhaps not without a touch of sarcasm, that the lands below the mouth of the Great Kanawha should be retroceded to the natives if it could be done without giving them offense.[10]

But in this action Hillsborough moved too precipitately. He had taken it without first consulting the Privy Council, and that body was jealous of its rights. It did, in fact, over-rule Hillsborough as far as the grant to the Crown was concerned, and Johnson was then notified to accept the whole grant as far as the Tennessee River in case the Six Nations would be offended by the raising of any question as to their claim to the territory. This, of course, meant that Sir William's arrangements in this respect would be carried through. But Hillsborough had his way about the Croghan and Indiana grants, and they were laid aside for future consideration. This amounted to rejection.[11]

Thus the hopes of Wharton and Trent were dashed to the ground, and not even Benjamin Franklin, who had been in London since 1764 as agent for several of the colonies and as postmaster-general of America, could aid them. On the contrary, according to William Strahan, member of Parliament and King's printer, Franklin "could not stir in this business as he is not only on bad terms with Lord Hillsborough, but with the *Ministry in general*. Besides, his temper has grown so very reserved, which adds greatly to his *natural inactivity*, that there is no getting him to take part in *anything*." [12] But Wharton was a smooth person, and there were few in England so great that they could not be interested by accounts, enthusiastically colored by his imagination, of the great fortunes to be amassed in American lands. Through various connections he was enabled to rescue his affairs temporarily from total wreck. For his purposes the most important personages were Franklin's old friend, Thomas Pownall, and the great London banker and member of Parliament, Thomas Walpole, son of Horatio Lord Walpole and cousin to Horace of epistolary fame.

Wharton met this kindred spirit on June 14, 1769, and had a long conversation with him. Walpole told Wharton that he had supped the

[10] Report of the Board of Trade, April 25, 1769, P.R.O., C.O., series 5, 70; *Papers of Sir William Johnson,* VI, 652–653; Morgan to S. Wharton, Oct. 14, 1772, Baynton, Wharton and Morgan letter book, Pa. State Archives.

[11] Hillsborough to Johnson, Jan. 4, 1769, P.R.O., C.O., series 5, p. 70; same to same, May 13, 1769, Dec. 9, 1769, *ibid.; Papers of Sir William Johnson,* VII, 118–120, 495, 496; Geo. Morgan to S. Wharton, Oct. 14, 1772, Baynton Wharton and Morgan letter book, Pa. State Archives.

[12] Wm. Strahan to Wm. Franklin, Apr. 3, 1771, Franklin MSS., XLVIII, 139, A.P.S.

night before with Camden, the Lord Chancellor, and Camden had confided that the Ministry was entirely out of sympathy with Hillsborough in his policy on the Fort Stanwix treaty and that it had over-ruled his first decision on it.[13] Hope was not dead after all, and an idea began to take shape. Walpole was keenly interested in American lands, and he had funds at his disposal as well as a certain amount of political influence. By July 24th a company had been organized. Its personnel was selected with shrewd care. Beside Walpole and Pownall, some of its important English members were Lord Hertford, who filled the office of lord chamberlain; Lord Camden, still in the Ministry; Richard Jackson, known as "Omniscient Jackson," counsellor to the Board of Trade and former secretary to George Grenville; Grenville himself; Lord Gower and Lord Rochford, members of the Privy Council; Lachlan Macleane, member of Parliament; John Robinson, an under-secretary of the treasury; Grey Cooper, joint secretary of the treasury; Earl Temple, Thomas Bradshaw, a tool of the Duke of Grafton, soon to be succeeded as principal minister by Lord North; Thomas Pitt; Anthony Todd, British Postmaster-General; William Strahan, King's printer and member of Parliament; Sir George Colebrook, director of the East India Company; John Sargent; Richard and Robert Walpole; and other men of affairs. Being thus bulwarked by shareholders of high place and great fortune in England and by men of influence in America such as Sir William Johnson, the Whartons, Franklins, Croghan, Trent, Galloway, the Franks, and others, the prospects of the company were bright indeed. Its plan was to purchase 2,400,000 acres of the lands ceded by the Indians at the treaty of Fort Stanwix for ten thousand four hundred sixty pounds, which was the sum later set by the government to be paid for the grant. The "suffering traders" were incorporated in the new company, Trent being their agent, and their claims were to be made good.[14]

When this proposal was heard by the Board of Trade on December 20th Hillsborough was surprisingly amiable and amenable. He proposed that the petitioners ask for a larger grant—one large enough for the creation of a new Western colony. He further suggested that they should

[13] (Trent) to Croghan, June 11, 1769, Ohio Company MSS., H.S.P.; *Papers of Sir William Johnson,* VII, 16–17.
[14] Petition of Benjamin Franklin and Samuel Wharton to Congress, Feb. 25, 1780, Cont. Cong. MSS., 77 (printed in Bigelow, *Franklin,* XII, 341–367); petition of the Walpole Company to the King, July 24, 1769, P.R.O., T. I, 470 (referred to Board of Trade, Nov. 20, 1769, P.R.O., C.O., series 5, 1332, f. 283); Samuel Wharton, *Facts and Observations* (London, 1775) appendix 2, pp. 136ff.; Sparks, *Washington,* II, 483–485; *Papers of Sir William Johnson,* VI, 568–569, VII, 590–592; Alvord, *Mississippi Valley,* II, 102; Fitzpatrick, *Writings of Washington,* III, 49n.

go to the Lords of the Treasury to discuss the financial aspects of the matter, since it was a purchase that they contemplated.[15]

It did not take Walpole and his associates long to act upon these suggestions. On December 27th a meeting was held in the Crown and Anchor Tavern and the Grand Ohio Company was organized. The members now proposed to ask for a tract of land to be bounded on the west by a line to run from the point on the Ohio opposite the mouth of the Scioto River southward to the Cumberland Gap, thence following the Cumberland Mountains to the point where the Greenbrier River flows into the Kanawha, thence to the source of the Greenbrier, and then along the Allegheny, or "Endless," Mountains to the western boundaries of Maryland and Pennsylvania. The fact that the western boundary of Pennsylvania was in dispute was beside the point. This was estimated to embrace about twenty million acres, and it included certain tracts on the Greenbrier which had been patented by the government of Virginia. It was to be a proprietary government, with the company paying expenses of the civil establishment until it should become self-supporting. After twenty years quit-rents were to be paid to the Crown on such lands as had been settled at that time.[16]

Hillsborough later confessed that he had encouraged Walpole and Wharton to ask for so much in the hope that, their request being so unreasonable, they would not get it. He evidently thought that the Treasury would consider the compensation inadequate for such an immense grant, and the colony of Virginia was expected to oppose the lopping off of so large a part of her Western domain. But on January 4, 1770, the Lords of the Treasury assented to the terms proposed by the Grand Ohio Company. The various shareholders connected with that august body had done their work well.[17]

Life was taking on a rosier hue for Wharton and Trent, but their troubles were not yet over—not by any means. Immediately upon hearing of their agreement with the Treasury, Edward Montagu, agent for Virginia, notified the committee of correspondence of that colony and entered a caveat against the new company, asking that nothing further be done in the matter until his constituents could be heard from. Strangely

[15] Wharton, *Facts and Observations*, pp. 2ff.; Journal of the Board of Trade, Dec. 20, 1769, LXXVII, 298–300, H.S.P. transcripts.

[16] Extract from the minutes of the meeting of Dec. 27, 1769, Ohio Company MSS., H.S.P. Camden, Thomas Pitt, and such high personages seem to have worked only behind the scenes. They were not present at this meeting, but Thomas Pownall and Walpole were. Franklin acted as chairman.

[17] P.R.O., C.O., series 5, 1332, f. 315; P.R.O., T.I., 476; Journal of the Board of Trade, Jan. 17, 1770, LXXVIII, 14, H.S.P.; John Pownall to Grey Cooper, Jan. 19, 1770, P.R.O., C.O., series 5, 1369.

enough, though this letter was duly received in Virginia, no protest was forthcoming. Fauquier had died two years previously. On August 13, 1768, Horace Walpole wrote to his friend, Horace Mann, of the unrest in America, stating: "Virginia, though not the most mutinous, contains the best heads and the principal *boutesfeux*. It was thought necessary that the governor should reside there. At the same time, Lord Botetourt, a court favorite, Groom of the Bedchamber to George III, yet ruined in fortune, was thought of by his friend Lord Hillsborough." [18] Botetourt took office late in 1768, and, though he and Virginia failed to live up to his friend Hillsborough's expectations in this matter, there were several private interests ready to make trouble for Walpole and his company.

Arthur Lee, in London at the time, soon heard of the new land company and wrote to his brother Richard Henry that the Ministry, which set everything to sale, was going to make a grant of *their* lands to a company of adventurers "headed by the mercenary & infamous Ld Hertford." Lee, in behalf of the Mississippi Company organized by the Lees, Washington, and their friends in 1763, immediately presented to the Ministry a petition asking that the lands in question be not granted to the Grand Ohio Company until his company could be apprised of the terms on which they would be granted. The Mississippi Company was now asking for two million five hundred thousand acres to lie between the Alleghenies and the Ohio and between the thirty-eighth and forty-second parallels.[19] This would have overlapped the lands for which Walpole and Wharton were petitioning, and it likewise conflicted with the claims of the old Ohio Company of Virginia, to which the Lees and Washingtons also belonged. This company was still pressing its claim in London through the agency of George Mercer, who represented also the bounty claims of Washington's soldiers under the proclamation of Governor

---

[18] Montagu to Virginia Committee of Correspondence, Jan. 18, 1770, *Virginia Magazine of History and Biography,* XII, 159–161; Walpole to Mann, Aug. 13, 1768, Peter Cunningham, ed., *Letters of Horace Walpole* (London, 1866) V, 120; T. Falconer wrote to Charles Grey, Aug. 2, 1768: "What will Ld Botetourt do at Virginia? I fear he wants the necessary knowledge and takes the government to restore his disordered finances. What[ever] comes of this nomination, I am glad Sir Jeffrey A(mherst) is removed. His excuse was beneath a soldier . . . and no man of honour would have insisted on non-residence when his country was at stake." *Historical Manuscripts Commission, Fourteenth Report,* Appendix, Part IX, p. 303; John Pownall to Grey Cooper, Feb. 15, 1770, P.R.O., C.O., series 5, 1369; P.R.O., C.O., series 5, 1332, f. 323

[19] Arthur to R. H. Lee, Feb. 15, 1770, Lee MSS., U. of Va. library; *The American Historical Review,* XVI, 312–317; Alvord and Carter, *New Régime,* pp. 516–518, 570–572; *Trade and Politics,* pp. 144–146, 543; Continental Congress MSS., 77, ff. 210–214; Arthur Lee to R. H. Lee, Dec. 23, 1768, Lee MSS., U. of Va. library; Journal of the Board of Trade, May 9, 1769, LXXVII, 43–44; *ibid.,* Jan. 24, 1770, LXXVIII, 15–16; Board of Trade papers, Plantations General, XXX, 127ff.; R. H. Lee, *Life of Arthur Lee* (Boston, 1829) I, 197, 198, 205.

Dinwiddie of 1754.[20] General Phineas Lyman was still in London petitioning for Western lands for his "Military Adventurers"; the Penns were demanding all papers in connection with the Grand Ohio Company, fearing their interests were involved; and the "suffering traders" of 1754 were making trouble.[21]

When Sir William Johnson had obtained the Indiana grant at Fort Stanwix only the traders who had lost goods in 1763 were included. Trent, acting for the Wharton group, had bought up a large part of the claims of those who had suffered in that year, as well as of those who had lost goods in 1754. Some, however, had not sold out to him. Now, the sufferers of 1754 who had not benefited under the Indiana grant and who charged that Sir William and his friends had acted clandestinely were agitating for a part of this tract or for a separate allotment of land. Moses Franks of London was at one time authorized to act for them, and they employed other counsel at different times; but Wharton and Trent were able to quiet their agitation by taking several of the Franks group into the Indiana Company.[22]

George Mercer was also bought off. According to his agreement the Ohio Company of Virginia was absorbed by the Grand Ohio Company. Two shares, out of the total of seventy-two into which the new enterprise was divided, were granted to the Virginia company, and Mercer individually was to have one share. He was also given to understand that he might become governor of the new province. His bargain was repudiated by the Virginia Ohio Company as soon as it was made known to it and the matter was laid before the Virginia council which decided that no action on its part was necessary. But it does not appear that the Grand Ohio Company was ever notified of the repudiation, for the Virginia company and Mercer appear to have been included as members of the new company until its sun had set behind the clouds of revolution.[23]

Washington's regiment of 1754 was also provided for, the 200,000

[20] Journal of the Board of Trade, Jan. 3, 1770, LXXVIII, 3; John Pownall to Grey Cooper, Jan. 29, 1770, P.R.O., C.O., series 5, 1369.
[21] Journal of the Board of Trade, May 4, 1769, LXXVII, 59–60; Memorial of Proprietors of Pennsylvania, Feb. 15, 1770, ibid., LXXXVIII, 38; Board of Trade MSS., Plantations General, H.S.P. transcripts, March 2, 1769, XXX, 21; P.R.O., C.O., series 5, 1369, f. 18; P.R.O., P.C. 1, 59, May 11, 1769.
[22] Arthur Lee to R. H. Lee, July 12, 1770, Lee MSS., U. of Va. library; memorial of the "sufferers of 1754," May 12, 1770, Ohio Company MSS., H.S.P.; Trent to Moses Franks, Jan. 1, 1773, ibid.; Trent to one of the traders, Dec. 1, 1768, ibid.; petition of the "sufferers of 1754," Jan. 4, 1767, ibid.; powers of attorney, Jan. 17, 1769, ibid.; power of attorney, Trent to Wharton, Feb. 20, 1769, ibid.; P.R.O., P.C. 1, 59, June 9, 1769; Savelle, Morgan, p. 79; Papers of Sir William Johnson, VI, 578–582.
[23] Darlington, Gist, p. 244; P.R.O., C.O., series 5, 1332, f. 383; Geo. Mercer to Thos. Wharton, Jan. 6, 1773, Wharton MSS., H.S.P.; Executive Journal of the Council of Virginia, July 27, 1772, P.R.O., C.O., series 5, 1440.

acres pledged by Governor Dinwiddie being promised to them in one survey out of the lands of the Walpole Company. Washington was shrewd enough to enter his personal allotment in the very neighborhood, near the confluence of the Great Kanawha and Ohio Rivers, where the Walpole Company planned to locate the seat of government for their new colony. All prior rights, whether legal or equitable, to lands in the new province were to be preserved. Thus practically all conflicting interests were taken care of. The Ministry paid no attention to the petitions of Arthur Lee or Phineas Lyman, and Virginia had not been heard from. It looked as though, with powerful politicians on its side, the Walpole Company would have clear sailing. Accordingly on May 8th, it presented its second petition to the Board of Trade.

The question was now again up to Hillsborough. He had failed to get the support of the Treasury or of Virginia, and most of the ministers were against him. In fact, nearly all of them were members of the Walpole Company which was now more British than American.[24] With such a personnel Arthur Lee had good reason to state that nothing could defeat their scheme except a heavier purse. But in December, 1769, Virginia had sent Hillsborough a proposal for buying up all the lands claimed by the Cherokee within the colony, and a report showing that previous to 1754 several companies had been formed among members of the local council for the purpose of speculating in Western lands. About the middle of May, 1770, Hillsborough called this matter to Walpole's attention, and copies of the papers were delivered to him. When, on July 18, Walpole presented his case before the Board of Trade he cast aspersions on these Virginia companies and Hillsborough seized the opportunity for delay. He demanded time to consult Botetourt concerning Virginia's activities and interests, and, meanwhile, the Virginia governor was ordered to make no grants of Western lands pending further instructions. But Botetourt died before he had opportunity to answer this communication from his friend and patron, and it fell to President Nelson of the Virginia council, who succeeded him temporarily, to reply. He was able to explain that Virginia had made no large grants since 1754, and that all those except that to the Loyal Company and that to Colonel James Patton had lapsed because of failure to carry out the conditions. He hoped that all legal and equitable claims would be made good, but stated that "we do not presume to say to whom our gracious sovereign

[24] John Blackburn to Johnson, Sept. 2, 1772, *Papers of Sir William Johnson*, VIII, 588–589. Here it is stated that the company consisted of "many noble lords and all the secretaries in office." Camden's name, for instance, does not appear on any of the earlier lists of members of the company, yet he was almost certainly a member from the first. If so, he was not the only silent partner in the enterprise.

shall grant his vacant lands nor do I set myself as an opponent to Mr. Walpole and his associates." [25]

This communication was dispatched by Nelson on October 18, and it reached London before the end of the year, but Hillsborough did not permit the Walpole associates to have any information concerning it until February 28, 1771, though they had heard some time before that the letter had been received. On March 5, the Walpole Company presented the Lords of Trade and Plantations with its answer to President Nelson's letter. But Hillsborough was obdurate and as long as he remained at the head of colonial administration it was obvious that nothing further could be accomplished toward the establishment of the new colony.

It was not until April, 1772, that Hillsborough brought himself and the Board of Trade to report on the second Walpole petition. As was to have been expected, the answer was unfavorable. The facts that Virginia had adverse claims and that new inland colonies would not promote trade but would draw off population from the empire were stressed.[26] Now at last the Walpole affair began to move rapidly to a crisis. Either Hillsborough had to be silenced or the company had to give up the fight. It was an embarrassing dilemma for the administration and a tense moment for the land speculators. Wharton composed a long answer to Hillsborough's report, and on July 1 the Committee of Council for Plantation Affairs was ready to go on record as in opposition to the Board of Trade. This was an extraordinary state of affairs. Lord North, now Prime Minister, was much disturbed. He did not want Hillsborough to resign, but Lord Gower, a shareholder in the Walpole Company and still a member of the Privy Council, would not yield, and North found it impossible to find any solution that would satisfy both sides, despite the conciliatory attitude of Lord Suffolk. Consequently, on August 1, Hillsborough gave up his offices, and five days later the deposed colonial secretary was made an English earl.[27] Benjamin Franklin wrote jubilantly of the resignation to his son:

[25] Journal of the Board of Trade, Dec. 6, 1769, LXXVII, 229; *ibid.*, July 18, 1770, LXXVIII, 162–163; a letter [Pownall] to Walpole, July 9, 1770, P.R.O., C.O., series 5, 1333, f. 385ff.; Walpole to Hillsborough, July 16, 1770, P.R.O., C.O., series 5, 1332, f. 403; President Nelson to Hillsborough, Oct. 18, 1770, P.R.O., C.O., series 5, 1348: "The Case with Respect to Virginia," n.d., n.s., Ohio Company MSS., H.S.P.

[26] Bigelow, *Franklin*, V, 408–432, VI, 3–49; P.R.O., C.O., series 5, 1333, f. 365ff., March 5, 1771; Thatcher notes, box 3, April 15, 1772, P.R.O., C.O., series 391, 79, f. 74.

[27] Suffolk to the King, July 21, 1772, Sir John Fortescue, ed., *The Correspondence of King George the Third from 1760–1783* (London, 1927–1928) II, 369–370; The King replied to Suffolk: ". . . After your departure into the Country, Lord North wrote to Lord Gower to desire the report on the Ohio business might be postponed,

At length we have got rid of Lord Hillsborough. . . . You will hear it said among you, I suppose, that the interest of the Ohio planters has ousted him; but the truth is, what I wrote you long since, that all his brother ministers disliked him extremely, and wished for a fair occasion of tripping up his heels; so, seeing that he made a point of defeating our scheme, they made another of supporting it on purpose to mortify him, which they knew his pride could not bear. . . . The King's dislike made the others more firmly united in the resolution of disgracing Hillsborough, by setting at naught his famous report.[28]

However, the version of that astute observer, Horace Walpole, differed from this. He wrote in his journal: "On the 7th Lord Hillsborough resigned, and on the 12th was created an English earl to indemnify him. As he had a large estate in Ireland and was extremely desirous of being viceroy of that country, it was believed that half his discontent was feigned in order to obtain an earl's coronet which raised him to a rank proper for that dignity."

Though Walpole did not think highly of him and historians have usually tended to take the same view, Hillsborough was apparently sincere in his belief that Westward expansion was not to the advantage of the Empire; he was consistent in the maintenance of his views; and it does not appear that there were any selfish motives back of his official acts. This is more than can be said for most of those who opposed him. The opinion of his King was that he "always puts things off to the last minute,

---

to which he received an answer that consented to it if the Cabinet but particularly You and Lord Rochford came into it; but the latter was certainly cold, the debating at Cabinet whether a report directed by the Privy Council should remain dormant was a new idea; Your Brother Secretary who though possessed of many amiable qualities is not very prudent on receiving your letter (wherein you thought this unnecessary but chose Lord North as he had got into the puzzle should extricate himself out of it) writes to the President that the two Secretaries were averse to the proposal, upon which Gower directs him to report it directly, that he has communicated to L^d. Hillsborough who means to resign in a few days, but by the letter Lord Rochford sent me yesterday I find Lord North takes the thing much to heart and has certainly been actuated upon by Lord Hillsborough, whose natural suspicion is greatly encreased by the whole of this transaction and if care is not taken may be productive of some personal unpleasant thing between Rochford and him, by this short state of the affair You must see Lord North's natural good nature and love of indecision, added to too much precipitation in Lord Rochford, and suspicion in Lord Hillsborough, with want of confidence in all the parties have brought this to the present strange situation which is rather difficult to be unravelled. . . . You must not forget that in trying to keep Lord Hillsborough care must be taken of the danger of offending Lord Gower. . . ." The King to Suffolk, July 22d, 1772, Fortescue, *Correspondence of King George the Third*, II, 370. This will give some insight into the intricacies of the question, politically, in England. It should be remembered that Lord Gower was a member of the Vandalia Company. John Doran, ed., *Last Journals of Horace Walpole* (New York, 1910) I, 125–128; Darlington, *Gist*, 241ff.

[28] Benj. Franklin to Wm. Franklin, Aug. 17, 1772, *New Jersey Archives*, series 1, X, 377–378n.

and though an amiable man, the least a man of business I ever knew." [29]
He was by no means an unobservant spectator of what was passing in
the colonies, and he was not as completely hoodwinked by the fine-spun
reports of Sir William Johnson as that official believed.

Hillsborough was succeeded at the Board of Trade by William Legge,
Earl of Dartmouth, whose widowed mother had married the Earl of Guil-
ford, Lord North's father. The new Colonial Secretary and the Prime
Minister, had, therefore, been reared as brothers and were very close.
The King spoke of his "great and known piety," and it was of Dart-
mouth the poet Cowper wrote,

> We boast some rich ones whom the Gospel sways,
> And one who wears a coronet, and prays.

Dartmouth was himself interested in American lands, having obtained
a large grant in 1770; and three years later Joseph Reed, of Pennsylvania, whose career was yet to be made, wrote offering his services in the
purchase of lands from the Indians. [30] Dartmouth proved to be entirely
satisfactory from the Walpole point of view, and on August 11 the Board
of Trade issued a report in favor of the new colony. On August 14 the
King and Council gave their approval, and the matter seemed to be settled. The colony was to be called "Pittsylvania" in honor of the great
Premier so cordially hated by George the Third. Somewhat prematurely
the Wharton family in Philadelphia had rejoiced greatly over hearing
the news that "His Excellency Samuel Wharton, Esq[re], Governor and
Commander in Chief of the Province of Charlotta on the Ohio" had kissed
His Majesty's hand on being appointed governor of "Charlottina" or
"Charlotta."

As success seemed assured, the Whartons became more ambitious:
Thomas, Senior, tried first to buy out Robert Callender; next he sent one
of his sons to Sir William Franklin—to that gentleman's great resentment—to demand of him whether he would sell his share in the company. Franklin instructed his son, Sir William, since he would now have
a large landed property, to make his will and secure it to Temple, his
illegitimate son. [31] But George Morgan had less cause to rejoice. He had

---

[29] Horace Walpole to Horace Mann, July 29, 1772, *Last Journals of Horace Walpole,* I, 227–228; Peter Cunningham, ed., *The Letters of Horace Walpole,* V, 401;
Fortescue, *Correspondence of King George the Third,* V, 418.

[30] Manuscripts of the Earl of Dartmouth, *Historical Manuscripts Commission,
Eleventh Report,* Appendix, Part V (London, 1887), p. 337; report on memorial of
Earl of Dartmouth and others praying for a grant of land, P.R.O., C.O. 391, 71.

[31] Geo. Morgan to Samuel Wharton, Oct. 14, 1771, MS. Letter Book of Prominent
Men West of Alleghenies, 1769–1771, Pa. State Archives. (While thus titled, the
book contains letters of George Morgan only) ; Wm. to Benj. Franklin, Jan. 5, 1773,

asked Wharton again and again to state that the firm, not Wharton alone, was interested in all his negotiations at Fort Stanwix and in London, but Wharton ignored his letters. When he learned of the grant Morgan wrote:

> . . . Your elder Brother has modestly given it out that 'John Baynton will be concerned a small share in the Grant to the 72 Proprietors, but as to Geo. Morgan he has no right to expect it'—You & Your Brother cannot put Mr'. Baynton off with a single Share or even 10 shares provided you & all your Fathers Family & Your own all together enjoy *one single share* more than I ALONE DO. You have had your day of Festivity & Galantry in England Whilst I have been exposed at the Illinois. It is over! . . . I will esteem you more than I have for many years past if upon landing you will appoint a time & place for me to give you satisfaction for these remarks.[32]

Morgan was soon left to carry on the firm's tangled affairs alone, the old Quaker, John Baynton, dying about this time. His death Morgan attributed to the ill-usage of their partner, Wharton, from whom he had not heard direct in nearly four years.[33]

Since the situation in America had changed somewhat since 1769, the boundary of the new colony was now modified in several respects. It was to run from the point on the Ohio opposite the mouth of the Scioto River to Cumberland Gap, but instead of following the Cumberland Mountains from that point, the line followed the Virginia-North Carolina boundary to the Alleghenies, and up these mountains to the western boundaries of Maryland and Pennsylvania. Thus some well-established settlements in southwest Virginia were cut off from the colony and added to "Pittsylvania." Meanwhile, Virginia had established a new boundary in 1770 between her lands and those reserved to the Cherokee. Since this line ran eastward of the western limit of the new colony, settlements were forbidden in the area lying between the two lines. But while the boundaries of the new colony were altered, the boundaries of the lands granted to the Walpole Company as proprietors remained as before; that is, the line ran from Cumberland Gap along the Cumberland Mountains and did not include the settlements of southwest Virginia. This is a point which will be shown later to have had considerable

Franklin MSS., III, 135, A.P.S.; Benj. to Wm. Franklin, August 3, 1773, Bigelow, *Franklin,* VI, 189–190.

[32] Geo. Morgan to S. Wharton, Nov. 2, 1772, Baynton, Wharton and Morgan letter book, Pa. State Archives.

[33] Geo. Morgan to Geo. Croghan, Aug. 1, 1773, Baynton, Wharton and Morgan letter book, Pa. State Archives. In this letter, Morgan demanded that Croghan write him if he did not think himself liable "for your one-fourth the Loss in our joint Adventure to the Illinois, by your leading us into which, you Sir, was the cause of *our Ruin. . . .*"

significance. The Indian agents, Sir William Johnson and John Stuart, were instructed to notify the natives of these arrangements.[34]

The next step was the drafting of a charter for the infant colony and making provision for putting the new plan into operation. The Board of Trade was directed to report on these matters. On May 6 this body came forward with a surprising proposition. On February 25, 1773, John Stuart [35] had dispatched to the home government a map purporting to show the line agreed on between the Cherokee and Virginia. This line, as surveyed by John Donelson in 1771, varied from that agreed on·at the treaty of Lochaber in 1770, running down the Kentucky River instead of to the mouth of the Kanawha, thus adding a large area to that which was supposed to have been ceded by the Indians. This change seems not to have been fully appreciated by the Ministry until Stuart's map arrived, nor had it ever been approved. Dartmouth, however, was delighted with the arrangement and now proposed that the new colony include all these newly acquired lands as far as the Kentucky River. The proprietary grant was to remain as before. And, in a facetious vein or unconscious irony, it was further proposed that the new colony should be re-christened "Vandalia," in honor of Queen Charlotte, "as her Majesty is descended from the Vandals." Sir William Johnson was usually spoken of as the prospective governor, but neither he, nor George Mercer, nor Samuel Wharton were being considered for the office. Dartmouth planned to give the place to his cousin Major William Legge, at a salary of one thousand pounds.[36]

This was the high-water mark in the history of the group which came to be known as the Vandalia Company, though the name Vandalia was really to be applied only to the colony, the company being officially known as the Grand Ohio Company but often called simply the Walpole Company. The project seemed to have passed all the important hurdles; with the approval of the Lords of Trade and Plantations and of the Privy

[34] Ohio Company MSS., Aug. 14, 1772, H.S.P.; P.R.O., C.O., series 5, 1333, f. 485ff.

[35] While Sir William Johnson had been busy with his land schemes in the Northern Department John Stuart had not been idle in the Southern. He was a native of Scotland who came to America in 1748 and served as captain in the Provincial troops raised by South Carolina in 1757. He accumulated a vast landed property and over 200 slaves, only a very small part of which was obtained before he became Indian Superintendent. Shaw, *British Administration of the Southern Indians,* p. 18.

[36] Dartmouth to Stuart, May 5, 1773, P.R.O., C.O., series 5, 74; Stuart to Dartmouth, Jan. 4, 1773, *ibid.;* same to same, Feb. 25, 1773, *ibid.;* C.O., series 5, 1369, f. 326; C.O., series 5, 232, f. 347ff.; Bigelow, *Franklin,* V, 344–345; E. B. O'Callaghan, ed., *Documents Relative to the Colonial History of the State of New York* (Albany, 1857) VIII, 311; Dartmouth to Legge, March 17, 1773, *Manuscripts of the Earl of Dartmouth, Historical Manuscripts Commission, Eleventh Report,* Appendix, Part V, p. 335; Journal of the Board of Trade, LXXXI, 76–77; report of the Board of Trade, May 6, 1773, Ohio Company MSS., H.S.P. Also in C.O., series 5, 1369, f. 326ff.

Council, what could stand in the way of its fulfillment? Yet something did stand in its way and ultimately defeated its accomplishment.

It is impossible to say definitely what that something was. General Thomas Gage returned to England in the summer of 1773. In his American command it had been necessary for him to work in harmony with Sir William Johnson and his friends, but Gage often bristled at Johnson's methods of exploiting his official position, and he had never taken any part in the Vandalia scheme while Johnson was secretly included in it. That his influence told heavily against the project on his return to England was stated on good authority, and there is little reason to doubt that there was truth in the statement. There is evidence to the effect that the Earl of Suffolk, Secretary for the Southern Department and thought by some to have the chief voice in the Privy Council touching American affairs, changed his mind on the subject at this time. Of less significance for the moment, but highly interesting, is the fact that Shelburne and his friends, though favorable to Franklin's earlier Illinois project, gave no aid or comfort to the Vandalia scheme, though Wharton was careful to seek them out.[37] Dartmouth had received reports, too, that the people of New York, Connecticut, and Massachusetts thought Sir William Johnson "has attended more to his own private interests than to the good of the State." Even before this time Chief Justice Frederick Smyth of New Jersey had reported to the home government that he had sounded opinion of people in general in New York and New Jersey and that opposition to the new colony was highly applauded by everybody except Sir William Franklin.[38] This coincided with a report Lord Dunmore made to Hillsborough when the former was governor of New York. There was of course a strong current of opposition at all times from interested quarters in Virginia—which will be discussed later—although efforts to appease it were made not only by providing for conflicting claims, but by propaganda in various public prints stressing the great benefit which would accrue to that colony because the proprietors of Vandalia would contribute largely to the opening of the James and Potomac Rivers.[39]

[37] Gage had written to Hillsborough, July 22, 1769, "It is apprehended, those Grants, and some others, have been obtained by unwarrantable Practices and private Intrigues with the Indians, as well before, as at the time of the Treaty [of Fort Stanwix]; by which Means it is confidently said, People have acquired large Tracts of Country; Some of Whom, by Virtue of Grants so obtained, begin to claim the Property of other People acquired by legal Methods, so as to have occasioned lately an Outcry in this Place." Carter, *Correspondence of General Gage*, I, 231–232. Also, *ibid.*, II, 615–616; *Papers of Sir William Johnson*, VI, 627–628, VII, 65–67, 1123–1124, VIII, 112–113; Joseph Wharton to Thomas Wharton, Oct. 10, 1773, Wharton MSS., H.S.P.; Alvord, *Mississippi Valley*, I, 349, II, 97–98.
[38] Smyth to Hillsborough, Oct. 5, 1772, *New Jersey Archives,* series 1, X, 379–382.
[39] *Pennsylvania Gazette,* June 4, 1773, Draper MSS. 13J147.

John Murray, Earl of Dunmore, was now governor of Virginia; he had a greedy interest in land but no interest in the new proprietary government. He had come to America to better his fortune and planned to settle his family in this country. Virginia's great Western domain beckoned to him irresistibly. Doubtless his influence told in England where he was powerfully connected, his daughter presently marrying the Duke of Sussex, son of George the Third. There was evidently much dissatisfaction in England over the entire business of Vandalia, since it was at this time that the advisability of creating an office of inspector-general of the sales and grants of lands in America was urged upon Dartmouth.[40]

On July 3, 1773, Alexander Wedderburn, the solicitor-general, and Edward Thurlow, the attorney-general, were directed by the Board of Trade to draw up the papers for making the grant to the Vandalia Company. On July 13 these officials presented a report making some objections to the proposed charter. These were discussed and apparently removed, for on October 28 the same officials were directed to proceed with the draft. However, this was not done. On December 25 George Croghan in America heard rumors that the Vandalia cause was lost, and George Morgan wrote to upbraid his lobbying partner in London, lamenting:

. . . that my Plan was not Pursued, viz. to take immediate Possession of the Lands ceded to us by the Indians & dispose of them at a moderate Price, suppose 5£ per 100 Acres. By this means all our Debts would have been paid many years ago. . . . But your Plan . . . to strike some great Stroke in England to make a grand Fortune has put mine out of our Power in a great Degree, for our having waited & Sollicited a Confirmation of the Indian Grant so many years is a full Acknowledgement that our Title without it would not be good. . . .

Wharton, who had been so calculating in selecting the personnel of his organization for their influence and their purse, would certainly have omitted the Philadelphia Philosopher could he have looked forward to December 25th of that year. On this day Benjamin Franklin found it necessary to admit that he had been responsible for the publication of the famous Hutchinson letters, and on January 29, 1774, he was summoned before the Privy Council and bitterly denounced by Wedderburn, the solicitor-general. Three weeks before, Thomas Wharton had written to his brother in London that he did "most ardently wish thou may be in possession of the Grant before the arrival of the full accounts respecting the conduct of the Americans touching the tea, as I fear it

---

[40] *Manuscripts of the Earl of Dartmouth, Historical Manuscripts Commission, Fourteenth Report,* Appendix, Part X (London, 1895) p. 53.

will strengthen our enemies to oppose the confirmation thereof." [41] Indeed, how could the Ministry, without appearing to water the seeds of treason itself, grant a great proprietary government in the heart of its already restless American dominion to this arch enemy, his son and associates? Since the early days of the venture Franklin had never seemed entirely optimistic about its success, and it is certain that his affiliation with the revolutionary movement in America hurt his political influence in England even before the affair of the Hutchinson letters broke it down completely. As early as 1771 William Strahan had written to Franklin's son warning him to be as circumspect as possible if he did not wish to jeopardize the grant, as it was thought in England that he entertained the same political opinions as his father and was actuated by the same motives with regard to Britain and America.[42]

Here the history of Vandalia really ends. Wharton struggled on manfully until the outbreak of the Revolution, and in the spring of 1775 the draft of the grant was actually completed, but laid aside pending settlement of the dispute with the colonies. In the meantime the two emissaries were having difficulties of a more personal nature. William Trent's wife, who had not heard from him in a year, and who avowed she was starving, made provision for her children and planned to embark for London to see for herself what he was about. George Morgan, who had discovered that Samuel Wharton had taken a deed in fee simple to himself for a seventh part of the Indian grant to the "sufferers in 1763," which had been originally taken in Croghan's name for the firm of Baynton, Wharton and Morgan, was threatening to come to London and demand an accounting for this and other wrongs. Wharton was thoroughly frightened, and his brother "took the most effectual steps to discover if he [Morgan] really had Intentions of going over," adding "if he should know thy fears on his going home, it might stimulate him & his abbetors to pursue the measure; if anything occurs which points that way, I shall do everything in my power to set it aside." But Morgan did not go to England. His fortune was sunk in the disastrous venture in Western trade; he accused Samuel Wharton of saddling Baynton, Wharton and Morgan with debts made by the firm before he was taken into it; his house had paid ten thousand pounds for the expenses of the lobbying

---

[41] Alvord, *Mississippi Valley*, II, 157–163, 247–248; Hanna, *Wilderness Trail*, II, 69–70; Rochford to Dartmouth, Sept. 7, 1773, *Manuscripts of the Earl of Dartmouth, Historical Manuscripts Commission, Fourteenth Report*, Appendix, Part X, pp. 172–173; Geo. Morgan to S. Wharton, June 11, 1773, Baynton, Wharton and Morgan letter book, Pa. State Archives; Thos. to Samuel Wharton, Jan. 7, 1774, Wharton letter book, H.S.P.

[42] Wm. Strahan to Wm. Franklin, Apr. 3, 1771, Franklin MSS. XLVIII, 139, A.P.S.

partner who now was endeavoring to leave him out of the land deal. He was in dire straits, and at the end of the year Thomas Wharton reported to Samuel that Morgan "is removed to the North end of Third Street where he proposed to take in some children to board & try to get into some grocery business." [43]

Still Samuel Wharton tarried in London. He had done most of the actual work of promotion, and took most of the credit to himself—to such an extent, in fact, that William Franklin was disgusted with what looked to him like an attempt to discredit his father. Wharton kept himself clear of revolutionary entanglements and was spoken of in England as "of thoroughly British principles." However, no friction appears to have developed between Wharton and Franklin in England.[44] In fact, they were able to cooperate for years afterward and under very changed conditions. A part of their later work was to bring the ghost of Vandalia before the Revolutionary Continental Congress.

[43] Thos. Wharton to Samuel Wharton, May 17, 1774, Wharton letter book, H.S.P.; same to same, May 3, 1774, *ibid.;* same to same, Dec. 6, 1774, *ibid.;* Geo. Morgan to Samuel Wharton, Dec. 1, 1773, Baynton, Wharton and Morgan letter book, Pa. State Arch.

[44] Wm. Franklin to Strahan, June 18, 1771, Franklin MSS., XLVIII, 139, A.P.S.; William to Benjamin Franklin, Jan. 5, 1773, *ibid.*, III, 135; also *ibid.*, III, 145, 149; Bigelow, *Franklin*, V, 320–322.

CHAPTER IV

VIRGINIA'S INDIAN BOUNDARY

WHEN Sir William Johnson agreed with the Six Nations that they would surrender their claim to all territory lying south of the Ohio River as far down as the Tennessee and that traders who lost goods in 1763 would be compensated by a grant of land, his negotiations concerned territory not in his own department but in that of John Stuart, the Southern superintendent. It is certain that neither Sir William nor any of the group with which he was associated had any organized designs on the area lying below the Little Kanawha. Why then did he make this plan so early and go to so much trouble to carry it through at Fort Stanwix in 1768? Here is a mystery the documents do not solve, and one is left to formulate the best theory which appears to fit the facts. Sir William knew that the lands which the "suffering traders" coveted were admitted to lie within Virginia, and that the old Ohio Company was still pressing its claim to this same area. He would, therefore, very naturally have expected trouble from that quarter over the traders' grant. But he knew also that Virginia was keenly anxious to extend her western boundary against the Indians, and a new cession from the Six Nations would be of some assistance toward that end. The fact that Dr. Thomas Walker, the accredited agent of Virginia for that purpose, gave his unqualified sanction at Fort Stanwix to this arrangement certainly tends to substantiate the view that a bargain had been made in advance. Indeed, while the treaty was in progress of negotiation, Thomas Wharton in Philadelphia heard something that caused him to become alarmed over possible opposition from Virginia. Croghan wrote him that if he had read his brother Samuel's last letter, he would have known that there was nothing to fear from that quarter.[1]

Dr. Walker had served as commissary for Virginia troops during the French and Indian War. In that capacity he had visited Philadelphia and become acquainted with Benjamin Franklin and some of the important merchants. His home in Virginia was near that of Peter Jefferson. After the death of Jefferson he acted as guardian for the fatherless, red-headed, freckle-faced lad, Thomas Jefferson. Walker had powerful connections

[1] Also Johnson to Hillsborough, June 26, 1769, P.R.O., C.O., series 5, 70.

among the political leaders of Tidewater and among the magnates of the Valley. No other Virginian could rival him in these matters, and from the end of the French and Indian War to the end of the Revolution he effectually dominated the land speculating interests in the Old Dominion. He was the active head of the Loyal Company; that company—and it only—always got whatever it wanted so long as it was within the power of the government of Virginia. The struggle of this colony to establish a new Indian boundary cannot be understood without some knowledge of the influence and ideas of this shrewd physician.[2]

The whole question of the Indian boundary goes back to the proclamation of 1763. The line established by that decree was a purely temporary one, and in 1764 plans were formulated under the influence of Lord Shelburne for fixing a new one all along the western frontier of the colonies. John Stuart, in the Southern Department, began negotiations with the natives for this purpose in 1765, just as Sir William Johnson did in the Northern Department, but the business moved more rapidly with him than it did with Sir William. Before the end of 1766, Stuart had drawn a new line back of the Georgia and Carolina settlements and was ready to accomplish the same work for Virginia. Why Shelburne allowed Sir William to wait so impatiently for the completion of his plans for the boundary, while Stuart was allowed to go ahead so quickly requires some explanation. All the Northern colonies had restricted, if not definite, western boundaries, whereas the western limits of those south of Maryland were indeterminate. Shelburne's plan, as explained in Chapter II, was to create definite western limits for the Southern colonies.[3]

The boundary line from North Carolina had been arranged as far as Chiswell's Mine on the upper waters of the New or Kanawha River in the Valley of Virginia. Stuart planned to complete the work during 1766 by arranging with the Cherokee for the continuation of the line back of Virginia. He wrote several letters to Governor Fauquier urging that this be done, but received no reply to his communications.[4] This silence on the part of the governor of Virginia is puzzling. He was in ill health, and for this reason he may have neglected the matter. But the frontier question was a live one at just this time and the governor was not by any means indifferent to it. In 1765 settlers beyond the proclamation line of 1763 had refused to pay quit-rents because the proclamation seemed to deny

[2] Archibald Henderson, *Dr. Thomas Walker and the Loyal Company of Virginia* (Worcester, Mass., 1931) *passim;* T. P. Abernethy, Sketch of Thomas Walker, *Dictionary of American Biography.*

[3] George Mercer to the Ohio Company, Nov. 21, 1767, *William and Mary Quarterly Historical Magazine,* I, 200–204; Shelburne to Gage, Nov. 14, 1767, *Correspondence of General Thomas Gage,* II, 53–54.

[4] Stuart to Shelburne, April 1, 1767, P.R.O., C.O., series 5, 68.

their right to settle where they were. But the auditor-general of North America did not believe that earlier grants could be revoked in this way.[5] In 1766 the Loyal Company advised those who claimed lands under its grant to return to their settlements on threat of being dispossessed. Though the company had no legal title to the lands it claimed, it appears that it was encouraged in this stand by certain people high in authority in Virginia.[6] The settlers petitioned the House of Burgesses against the pretensions of the Loyal Company, and that body sent a petition to the home government urging that settlements beyond the mountains be permitted, but saying nothing of the claims of the Loyal Company.[7] It was certainly to the interest of the company that Virginia's western boundary should not be fixed as John Stuart would have fixed it, and it is most likely that Fauquier was silent for this reason.

In the spring of 1767 Shelburne instructed Stuart to establish Virginia's western boundary but Fauquier wrote to Stuart that he knew nothing of the proclamation of 1763 nor of any subsequent orders for completing the line.[8] Finally on November 14 of that year Shelburne wrote to Fauquier requiring that the work be completed and directing that the line run from Chiswell's Mine on the Kanawha to "that point from whence the Northern Provinces set out." This was interpreted to mean the southwest corner of Pennsylvania, but this point had not yet been determined.[9]

While these questions were in agitation the following very significant letter was written by Patrick Henry to Captain William Fleming and delivered to Dr. Thomas Walker:

Agreeable to my promise I have conversed with Mr. Walker on the subject of your going out to reconnoitre the lands lying on the Mississippi near its Junction with the Ohio. He is pleased to say that you are very agreeable to him & that he shall be satisfied to rely on your prudence & veracity in viewing that country & in fixing on some such spot as would be proper for the first company of adventurers to begin the execution of the Scheme I hinted to you. I must refer you to that Gentleman for the explanation of many particulars relative to the affair which are not yet

[5] R. Cholmondeley, Auditor-General of North America, to the Board of Trade, April 17, 1766, Board of Trade MSS., Plantations General, XXVI, 15–18.
[6] *Journal of the House of Delegates, 1777–1780*, p. 88; Henderson, *Walker*, 28.
[7] P.R.O., C.O., series 5, 1333, 405ff.; *Journal of the Board of Trade*, July 11, Nov. 6, 14, LXXIV, 260, 390.
[8] Executive Journal of the Virginia Council, Sept. 8, 1767, P.R.O., C.O., series 5, 1435; Stuart to Shelburne, July 28, 1767, P.R.O., C.O., series 5, 68; Fauquier to Stuart, Sept. 17, 1767, P.R.O., C.O., series 5, 69; Hillsborough to Stuart, May 12, 1768, *ibid.;* Fauquier to Stuart, May 6, 1767, C.O., series 5, 70; Stuart to Fauquier, July 21, 1767, *ibid.*, Stuart to Fauquier, April 11, 1767, C.O., series 5, p. 68.
[9] *Papers of Sir William Johnson*, V, 793; Executive Journal of the Virginia Council, March 10, 1768, P.R.O., C.O., series 5, 1435.

bro[t] to any fixed point, I mean that the outlines of the Scheme are only plan'd as yet. However before any great or Effectual headway can be made in it I think some knowledge of the country is obviously necessary. Pardon me if I recommend to you a diary. Even the trees, herbs grass stones hills etc. I think ou[gh]t to be described. The reason I wish you to be so particular is that a succinct account of your Journal may be printed in order to invite our countrymen to become settlers. The Task is arduous, to View that vast forest, describe the face of the Country & such of the rivers Creeks etc. as present themselves to view is a work of much Trouble, hazard & fatigue & will in my Judgement intitle you to the favourable notice of every gentleman engaged in the Scheme. I think you'll not have Time from (—) [sic] to finish the Jaunt. I wish it was convenient for you to begin sooner. Whenever you go I wish you a safe Journey & that Success which those who labor for prosperity deserve. . . . I have mentioned your going out to other sundry gentlemen & every body is fond of it.[10]

Unless Henry, Walker, and Fleming knew something of Sir William Johnson's plans, it is hard to see why they imagined that Virginia could expect to grant titles to lands so far west as the junction of the Ohio and Mississippi Rivers. Two years later, with much better prospects of success, an affiliated group was apparently working on a similar scheme.[11] When the lands in central Kentucky were finally opened to survey it was they who directed the work, with Henry and his connections primarily involved in the undertaking.

When the next move was made in the boundary controversy the situation had changed materially. Sir William Johnson's Philadelphia coterie had brought pressure to bear upon Shelburne through Dr. Franklin. It wished to persuade him to carry out the plans of 1765 and extend the line down the Ohio River to the mouth of the Tennessee. Shelburne took the advice of the Board of Trade, which reported on December 23, 1767, that the claim of the Six Nations to lands below the Great Kanawha was not tenable, and that Sir William should extend the line only as far as this point. Stuart was to extend the line back of Virginia to meet here, and orders were given to both superintendents to this effect.[12] The House of Burgesses was again petitioning that settlements beyond the mountains should be allowed, and the Board of Trade answered that it must await the drawing of this new boundary.[13]

Sir William was not to be defeated without a struggle. Before any fur-

---

[10] Henry to Fleming, June 10, 1767, Draper MSS., 15ZZ3.
[11] Thomas Lewis to William Preston, Draper MSS., 2QQ112.
[12] Board of Trade to Shelburne, Dec. 23, 1767, P.R.O., C.O., series 5, 68; Stuart to Shelburne, May 7, 1768, P.R.O., C.O., series 5, 69.
[13] Hillsborough to Board of Trade, May 17, 1768, P.R.O., C.O., series 5, 1332; Journal of the Board of Trade, May 17, 31, June 7, 1768, LXXIV, 110, 113, 118; Board of Trade to Hillsborough, June 10, 1768, C.O., series 5, 1346.

ther steps could be taken, however, the personnel involved in the matter had been changed in two cases. Shelburne had been succeeded by Hillsborough as Secretary in charge of colonial affairs; Fauquier had died and John Blair, president of the Virginia council, had taken his place until a new governor should be appointed. A triangular correspondence now took place between Johnson, Blair, and Stuart. The Northern superintendent indicated to the Southern that he would not permit the claim of the Six Nations to extend down the Ohio farther than the Great Kanawha River and apparently suggested to Stuart that he should purchase from the Cherokee their claim to the lands from that point to the Tennessee River. Stuart then wrote to Hillsborough that it would be easy for him to secure a surrender of Indian territory as far down as the Kentucky River and offered to do so if it were desired.[14]

The readiness of the Cherokee to sell is as easy to understand as is that of the Six Nations. Stuart stated that they claimed the lands south of the Great Kanawha, which amounted to saying that they did not claim anything north or east of that river. Their nearest villages were in what is now southeastern Tennessee. Naturally any pretensions that they could set up to lands as far away as the Kentucky River were very vague and insubstantial. Hillsborough, however, decided against the additional cession and was content to have the line run from Chiswell's Mine down the Great Kanawha to the Ohio. It appeared that Sir William was not to have his way.[15]

It was now necessary for Stuart, Johnson, and Blair to cooperate in making plans for holding conferences with the Cherokee and Six Nations in order to agree with them on the line. During this correspondence, Blair showed himself to be quite ignorant on the subject of Indian affairs, but ready to expedite the business. He complained that grantees of lands beyond the mountains refused to pay quit-rents because their lands had been left in the Indian country. He now appointed Dr. Thomas Walker and Andrew Lewis, the most important of the grantees, as the Virginia commissioners for fixing the boundary.[16] This fact speaks eloquently of the influence wielded by these two men and the land companies they represented.

[14] Blair succeeded Fauquier, March 4, 1768, *Papers of Sir William Johnson*, VI, 224–226; Blair to Stuart, June 18, 1768, C.O., series 5, 70. Sir William had given Blair to understand that the Board of Trade had decided the line should run to the Tennessee. Stuart to Hillsborough, July 14, Aug. 16, 1768, C.O., series 5, 69.
[15] Hillsborough to Stuart, Sept. 15, 1768, C.O., series 5, 69; Stuart to Hillsborough, Feb. 12, 1769, C.O., series 5, 70.
[16] Executive Journal of the Council of Virginia, June 15, 1768, C.O., series 5, 1435; Blair to Stuart, Aug. 3, 1768, C.O., series 5, 70; Blair to Hillsborough, Sept. 27, 1768, P.R.O., C.O., 5, 1346; *Papers of Sir William Johnson*, VI, 143–144.

Since the conference with the Six Nations was supposed to be held before that with the Cherokee, Walker and Lewis were sent off to join Sir William Johnson, though the place where he was to meet the Indians had not been designated to them. It turned out that the treaty at Fort Stanwix was slow in getting under way, and it was decided that Lewis should leave Walker with Sir William and make his way southward to join Stuart for the Cherokee treaty, which Stuart had arranged to hold at Chiswell's Mine on October 25. Traveling at a rapid pace, Lewis reached Chiswell's Mine, only to be informed by a letter from Governor Botetourt, who had succeeded Blair, that the negotiations had been postponed.[17] But this was not exactly what had happened. In good faith Blair had collected goods for presents to the Indians and provisions for the conference. But Stuart, setting out from Charleston in September, had traveled into the Indian country and met the Cherokee at Hard Labor on October 14, eleven days before the time on which he had agreed with Blair. Here he negotiated a treaty whereby the natives consented to a boundary line that would run from Chiswell's Mine directly to the mouth of the Great Kanawha. According to previous plans the line was expected to follow the river, but Stuart's arrangement gave Virginia appreciably more territory than the river boundary. It had been Stuart's original plan that the Virginia commissioners should meet the Cherokee at the Mine on November 10 to begin the survey of the boundary, but, since the cross-country line would require considerably more surveying than the line originally intended, the Indians urged a delay, and April 10, 1769, was agreed on as the time to begin the work. It was this delay, rather than a delay of the negotiations, of which Stuart notified Botetourt, and Botetourt notified Lewis.[18]

The Indian superintendents had been instructed to cooperate with the interested governors in making all these arrangements. Why Stuart felt himself authorized to steal a march on Blair and establish Virginia's Indian boundary without the cooperation of a Virginia representative—though one had been appointed for that purpose and was doing everything possible to carry out his mission—does not appear, nor is it clear why he changed the line so as to give Virginia more territory. He evidently was afraid that Virginia might throw some obstacle in the way of his negotiation and wished to get it done before that could happen. At the same time

[17] Executive Journal of the Council of Virginia, June 30, Nov. 1, 1768, C.O., series 5, 1435; Botetourt to Andrew Lewis and Israel Christian, Nov. 6, 1768, C.O., series 5, 1347.
[18] Journal of Stuart's proceedings from Sept. 28, 1768, C.O., series 5, 70; Stuart to Blair, Oct. 17, 1768, C.O., series 5, 1347; Executive Journal of the Council of Virginia, Oct. 19, Nov. 5, 1768, C.O., series 5, 1435; Lewis to Botetourt, Nov. 14, 1768, C.O., series 5, 1332; William Christian to Botetourt, same date, ibid.; Stuart to Hillsborough, Dec. 28, 1768, C.O., series 5, 70.

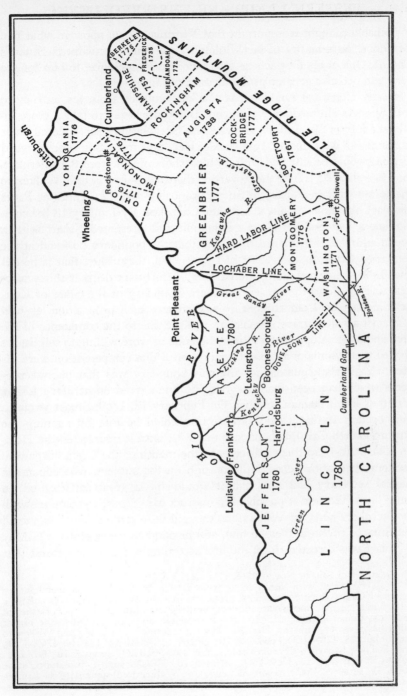

MAP 5. WESTERN VIRGINIA, 1780

he probably thought it important that Virginia should approve what had been done. As a matter of fact, Botetourt made no complaint of Stuart's conduct. One of his first acts as governor was to apologize to him for the delay and promise greater promptness in the future.[19]

Shortly afterward Dr. Thomas Walker returned from his journey to Fort Stanwix; immediately Governor Botetourt began to take a more intelligent interest in Indian affairs. The Six Nations surrendered their claims as far west as the Tennessee River, and from this time forward Virginia would be satisfied with nothing short of this from the Cherokee. On December 20, 1768, the governor dispatched Lewis and Walker to Charleston with an address to Stuart proposing that the Tennessee River boundary should be arranged with the Cherokee. By January 18 the commissioners had reached their destination and presented Stuart with a formal address. But instead of asking that the boundary be fixed at the Tennessee River, as Botetourt had instructed, they asked that it be extended due westward along the parallel of thirty-six degrees thirty minutes, that is, along the present southern boundary of the State of Kentucky. Stuart held out stubbornly against any such proposition, as well as against an alternative proposal to run the line to the confluence of the Ohio and Mississippi Rivers. Since the Indians were willing to sell Stuart advised them to make a modest concession if due compensation were offered. Virginia's argument for the new boundary was that many settlements which had been made beyond the line agreed on at Hard Labor were thus left in Indian country. On February 12, 1769, Stuart wrote to Hillsborough stating that this objection could be met by running the Virginia-North Carolina boundary due west until it intersected the Holston River and from thence directly to the mouth of the Great Kanawha. Botetourt had approached Hillsborough on the subject, whereupon the colonial secretary had said that it would "be a great satisfaction" to him if he should find it possible "to instruct Mr. Stuart to complete with the Cherokees what Sir William has thought fit to settle at Fort Stanwix." But Stuart's proposal pleased him, and he adopted it gratefully. On May 13 Stuart was directed to fix the line accordingly.[20] It is significant that

[19] Botetourt to Stuart, Nov. 6, 1768, C.O., series 5, 70.

[20] Walker carried with him a letter from David Ross, a Virginia merchant, to Alexander Cameron, Stuart's deputy, proposing that Sir William Johnson's policy be imitated in securing some private grants from the Indians and having them ratified at the treaty. Cameron notified Stuart of the proposal, and Stuart notified the higher authorities. Ross to Cameron, Dec. 20, 1768, C.O., series 5, 71; Lewis and Walker to Stuart, Jan. 18, 1769, C.O., series 5, 70; Stuart to Botetourt, Jan. 19, 1769, C.O., series 5, 1347; Stuart to Cherokee chiefs, Jan. 19, 1769, C.O., series 5, 70; Hillsborough to Stuart, May 13, 1769, C.O., series 5, 70; Hillsborough to Botetourt, same date, C.O., series 5, 1347; Report of Lewis and Walker to Botetourt, Feb. 2, 1769, *ibid.;* Stuart to Hillsborough, Feb. 12, 1769, C.O., series 5, 70; Hillsborough to Bote-

this was the day on which he notified Sir William Johnson, against his own judgment, to ratify the Tennessee River boundary as fixed with the Six Nations at Fort Stanwix. However, it was stipulated that no settlement was to be permitted west of the Cherokee boundary as marked on the Virginia frontier.

Hillsborough was playing an astute game—one which was certainly lacking in directness. Being forced by the Privy Council to make a concession to the Wharton-Walpole associates, he at the same moment made an agreement with Virginia which would apparently deprive them of much of the land for which they were contending. As late as May 14, 1772, they were uninformed of his decision regarding the Virginia boundary. On the other hand, with the probable exception of Dr. Walker and a few speculators, no one in Virginia yet appeared to know anything of the plans of the Philadelphia magnates.[21]

Though the concession was much less than he had asked, Botetourt was prepared to make the most of it. A part of the proposal was that Virginia should pay for the additional lands which she was to acquire from the Cherokee. This would demand an appropriation, which required the consent of the House of Burgesses. Accordingly, on August 14 Botetourt issued a call for that body to meet on November 7. The burgesses on convening expressed their dissatisfaction with the line proposed by Stuart and Hillsborough and asked that the southern boundary of the province be extended due west to the Ohio River. Though well-informed men knew better, the governor apparently thought that a due west line would actually intersect the Ohio. He, therefore, wrote Hillsborough that he was "extremely anxious for the success of everything that has been desired by the present Assembly." While making their representation to the home government the burgesses agreed that if no better line could be obtained than the one proposed by Stuart the requisite twenty-five hundred pounds should be forthcoming. They furthermore protested against the monopoly of Western lands, directing that a full report be made to them of all orders of council for granting lands beyond the Alleghenies.[22]

tourt, March 1, 1769, C.O., series 5, 1347; Botetourt to Hillsborough, with inclosures, Dec. 24, 1768, *ibid.;* Botetourt to Stuart, Dec. 20, 1768, C.O., series 5, 70.

[21] As late as Jan. 6, 1772, so important a person as Governor William Franklin was uninformed as to developments in Virginia. Franklin MSS., III, 84, 126, 129, A.P.S.; C.O., series 5, 1333 f.; 431; Journal of the Board of Trade, May 15, 1772, LXXX, 92; Hillsborough to Johnson, May 13, 1769, *Documents Relative to the Colonial History of the State of New York,* VIII, 165–166.

[22] Botetourt to Hillsborough, Sept. 23, 1769, C.O., series 5, 1347; *Virginia Magazine of History and Biography,* XII, 227 ff.; address of House of Burgesses to Botetourt, Jan. 20, 1770, C.O., series 5, 71; *Journals of House of Burgesses, 1766–1769,* pp. 318–319, 334–336; Botetourt to Hillsborough, Jan. (?), 1770, C.O., series 5, 1348.

This report was presently made and a copy of it sent to the home government. It showed that between 1745 and 1754 many enormous grants had been made and that most, if not all, of the members of the Virginia council had figured in them, including John Blair, the Nelsons, the Pages, and many others. No large grants had been made since 1754, however, and nearly all the early ones had lapsed because of failure of the grantees to carry out the conditions.[23] It was this report which was used by Walpole to discredit Virginia in his second appeal to the Board of Trade.

So far the House of Burgesses appeared to be on the side of the settlers as opposed to the great land companies. Their memorials spoke such language, but their statutes belied it, for Thomas Walker and his friends were busy with propaganda. Since many settlers were causing litigation by entering caveats against the land companies it was enacted that any one entering a caveat must stand the costs in case he lost his suit, and he was required to post security to guarantee such payment. It was enacted also that any one questioning a survey and demanding a new one should also post security to pay the costs in case he lost. Thus, the cards were stacked against the settler by the very body which was pretending to speak in his defense. That was politics in the modern manner.[24]

It might be assumed from what has been stated up to this point that Dr. Thomas Walker and his associates were the only people in Virginia who were interested in Western lands at this time. The truth is that, next to Walker, George Washington was the most important figure in this aspect of Virginia affairs. As early as 1767 he was informed of Sir William Johnson's plans for the Indian boundary in Pennsylvania and planned to buy lands in the area that would fall to the lot of Pennsylvania when the line should be drawn. This was accomplished in 1769 and William Crawford, Washington's agent in that neighborhood, proceeded to make the purchases as planned.[25] Lands lying in the Pittsburgh neighborhood, but beyond the acknowledged limits of Pennsylvania, afforded Washington a knotty problem. Pennsylvania's western boundary was left undetermined when the Indian boundary was fixed at Fort Stanwix and that province and Virginia contested a considerable area. The old Ohio Company still had its claims in the region and George Croghan

[23] C.O., series 5, 1333, 133ff., printed in *Virginia Magazine of History and Biography*, V, 175–180.
[24] Hening, *Statutes*, VIII, 386–388; Thos. Walker to Wm. Preston, Jan. 24, 1770, Draper MSS., 2QQ116.
[25] C. W. Butterfield, *The Washington–Crawford Letters* (Cincinnati, 1877) pp. 1–5, 10–12, 13, 16–17; Washington to John Armstrong, Sept. 21, 1767, Fitzpatrick, *Writings of George Washington*, II, 471–473.

claimed two hundred thousand acres by his Indian grant of 1749, to say nothing of the designs of the "suffering traders." In the fall of 1767 Washington wrote to Crawford:

The other matter, . . . which I proposed in my last to join you in attempting to secure some of the most valuable Lands in the King's part which I think may be accomplished after a while notwithstanding the Proclamation that restrains it at present and prohibits the settling of Them at all for I can never look upon that Proclamation in any other light (but this I say between ourselves) than as a temporary expedient to quiet the Minds of the Indians and must fall of course in a few years especially when those Indians are consenting to our Occupying the Lands. Any person therefore who neglects the present oppertunity of hunting out good Lands and in some measure marking and distinguishing them for their own (in order to keep others from settling them) will never regain it, if therefore you will be at the trouble of seeking out the Lands I will take upon me the part of securing them as soon as there is a possibility of doing it. . . . By this time it may be easy for you to discover, that my Plan is to secure a good deal of Land. . . .[26]

He informed Crawford that he might be censured for his opinion of the King's proclamation if it were known and advised him to carry on his operations "snugly under pretence of hunting other Game . . . and leave the rest to time and my own Assiduity to Accomplish." Crawford had known Washington since their school days; he had been with the Virginia troops under Braddock in 1755 and with Forbes in 1758. On these expeditions he had won Washington's confidence. He was to meet an appalling death by being burnt at the stake by Indians, but now his "assiduity" matched that of his chief and he spied out and marked thousands of choice acres. After the Fort Stanwix treaty Croghan, who extended his boundary to take in any good land he saw, began selling off his claims as rapidly as possible, despite the fact that the confirmation of them which the Six Nations attempted to make to him by that treaty was rejected by the British government.[27] Washington, through Crawford, consulted Croghan regarding a purchase of fifteen thousand acres and also considered buying his interest in the Walpole Company, but finding that Croghan's claim was too nebulous, he finally decided against the move. However, Washington did acquire, by grants, some of these lands claimed by Croghan, and he had to resort to litigation at a later date to enforce his rights.[28]

[26] Washington to Wm. Crawford, Sept. 21, 1767, *ibid.*, II, 468–470.
[27] Volwiler, *Croghan,* pp. 291–293; *Washington–Crawford Letters,* pp. 5–10.
[28] Croghan said that Washington actually purchased of him. Croghan to Gratz, Feb. 20, 1771, Gratz MSS., H.S.P. But a little later Crawford reported unfavorably on the advisability of such a purchase. Crawford to Washington, April 20, Aug. 2,

These were minor speculations, however, compared to the main one in which Washington was concerned at this time. It will be recalled that in 1754 Governor Dinwiddie promised two hundred thousand acres of land to the regiment which Washington commanded in the Great Meadows campaign. The proclamation of 1763 prevented the fulfillment of this promise for the time being, but the drawing of a new Indian boundary seemed to open the door of hope. This was somewhat dimmed when, on December 8, 1769, Dr. Thomas Walker informed Washington that the lands near Fort Pitt were reserved to the "suffering traders" under the treaty of Fort Stanwix. Finally, on December 15, 1769, the Virginia council promised that Washington and his regiment might take up the grant in not more than twenty surveys. This occurred after the House of Burgesses had voted money to establish the new boundary. The home government had given its assent to the proceeding, and it was natural to assume that the new territory would be thrown open to settlement. And, finally, Wharton and his friends had not yet even thought of organizing a new Western colony. In other words, the council had every reason to believe that it was within its rights in making this agreement with Washington, and having made the agreement under so much color of authority, it is doubtful whether any subsequent orders, even from the home government, could have legally annulled it.[29]

During the spring of 1770 Governor Botetourt received his first news of the formation of the Walpole Company. He sent a message to Washington asking his opinion. On April 15 Washington replied with a round condemnation of the scheme. By it, he said, Virginia would lose four fifths of the land for the purchase of which she had recently appropriated £2,500.[30] That autumn he journeyed down the Ohio from Fort Pitt in company with William Crawford and several others and made his surveys of land lying between the Little and Great Kanawha Rivers, thus avoiding conflict with claims of the "suffering traders," but placing the surveys within the bounds of the Walpole Company's territory. On his return home he received a letter from George Mercer informing him that the Walpole organization agreed to allow the claims of his regiment out of their grant, the whole to be laid off in one survey of two hundred thou-

1771, *Washington–Crawford Letters*, pp. 18–19, 20–21. Crawford to James Tilghman, Aug. 9, 1771, *ibid.*, pp. 22–23; Washington to Croghan, Nov. 24, 1770, Fitzpatrick, *Writings of Washington*, III, 29–30; Croghan to Washington, Aug. 18, 1771, S. M. Hamilton, ed., *Letters to Washington* (Boston, 1901) IV, 78–79; A. B. Hulbert, ed., *Washington and the West* (New York, 1905) pp. 146–148.

[29] Executive Journal of the Council of Virginia, Dec. 15, 1769, C.O., series 5, 1440; Washington to Botetourt, Dec. 8, 1769, Fitzpatrick, *op. cit.*, II, 528–532.

[30] Washington to Botetourt, April 15, 1770, Sparks, *Washington*, II, 355ff.

sand acres. When Washington answered this letter he made no reference to the proposition.[31]

On June 12, 1770, Hillsborough wrote to Botetourt, sending a copy of the Vandalia petition and promising that Virginia's rights would be considered. But Virginia did not wait for any official authorization. Two days after this letter was written the House of Burgesses decided to accept the Indian boundary which Stuart had proposed the year before. The twenty-five hundred pounds was made immediately available and Botetourt, with the advice of the council, sent word to Stuart that he should proceed at once with the negotiation.[32] This was accomplished on October 18, 1770, at the treaty of Lochaber, South Carolina. Here the line was agreed on as Stuart had previously proposed except that the Cherokee refused to give up the Long Island in the Holston River. For this reason it was agreed that the boundary should run a due west course to a point six miles east of this island, thence north to the Holston, and thence direct to the mouth of the Great Kanawha. The Indians offered to let the line run a more westerly course after it left the Holston in order to compensate for the concession regarding the Long Island, but Stuart did not feel himself authorized to accept any more territory and rejected the offer. However, he suggested that the home government might be appealed to on the subject. By appointment of the governor and council, Colonel John Donelson of Pittsylvania County made his bow to history at this conference as official representative of Virginia. It was he who later led a band of immigrants to the wilds of Tennessee and helped to establish Nashville, and whose daughter married Andrew Jackson. He was a burgess and an outstanding figure on the frontier, having taken up lands in Pittsylvania as early as 1744. He owned the first iron works, known as the Bloomery, in his section. He now made a favorable impression on Stuart, who had apparently harbored prejudice against Virginia up to this time. Donelson was presently to use his newly acquired influence to good advantage.[33]

On October 15, before this work was finished, the very popular Governor Botetourt died and was succeeded *pro tempore* by President Wil-

[31] Craig, *Olden Time*, I, 416ff., for journal of the expedition. Fitzpatrick, III, 66–67; Hamilton, *Letters to Washington*, IV, 39–40.

[32] *Journals of the House of Burgesses, 1770–1772*, p. xiii.

[33] Stuart had approached the Indians on the subject of the new boundary as early as April 10th of the same year. Minutes of congress held at Congaree, S. C., C.O., series 5, 71; Stuart to Hillsborough, Nov. 28, 1770, C.O., series 5, 72; Executive Journal of the Council of Virginia, June 18, 1770, July 13, 1771, C.O., series 5, 1440; Stuart to Botetourt, Oct. 25, 1770, C.O., series 5, 1345; Botetourt to Stuart, June 21, Aug. 9, 1770, C.O., series 5, 1348; *Virginia Magazine of History and Biography*, XII, 352–364; *ibid.*, IX, 360–364, for text of treaty.

liam Nelson of the council. By this time Virginia had received four official notices of the organization of the Grand Ohio Company. The first two were sent by Montagu on January 18 and February 16, 1770. They were acknowledged on July 5 in a surprisingly perfunctory manner by the committee of correspondence. On June 12 Hillsborough wrote to Botetourt about the matter. On July 20 the Board of Trade again addressed Botetourt and asked various questions suggested by Walpole's representations. On the last day of July the governor of Virginia was ordered to make no more grants of Western lands pending further notice.[34]

When Nelson came into office he found this last communication to Botetourt unanswered and one of his first duties was to act upon it. On October 18, the day of the treaty of Lochaber, he wrote home the first official letter on the subject of Vandalia. This dispatch, so disappointing to Hillsborough, can hardly be called a protest. Nelson admitted the right of the King to grant his lands to whom he pleased, but hoped that all legal and equitable claims to lands in the area of the new colony would be protected. Among those which should be so protected, he mentioned the claims of Washington's regiment, the claim of the old Ohio Company of Virginia, and those of Colonel James Patton and of the Loyal Company.[35] But long before this, on May 8 of the same year, the Walpole Company had arranged to satisfy the demands of Washington's troops by allowing them the promised two hundred thousand acres in *one* survey, and Mercer had arranged his merger of the Virginia Ohio Company with the Walpole Company. No attempt was here made to satisfy the Patton claim or the Loyal Company, but their claims lay principally in southwest Virginia, and by following the line of the Cumberland Mountains the boundary of the new colony would avoid encroaching too much upon their special preserve. The fact that this line was so arranged from the beginning is a further indication that there must have been some cooperation between the Loyal Company interests in Virginia and the Wharton interests in Philadelphia. An even stronger indication is the fact that the Loyal Company group did not once raise its voice in protest against the cutting off of Virginia's Western territory.

It is generally assumed that Virginia bitterly resented this threatened loss of her transmontane region. But Nelson's letter is the nearest thing to a protest emanating from Virginia, with the exception of Washington's strong dissent which Botetourt enclosed in one of his communi-

[34] *Virginia Magazine of History and Biography,* XII, 159–161, 164–165; Board of Trade to Botetourt, July 20, 1770, C.O., series 5, 1369; Hillsborough to Botetourt, June 12, July 31, C.O., series 5, 1348; Nelson to Hillsborough, Oct. 15, 1770, *ibid.*
[35] Nelson to Hillsborough, Oct. 18, 1770, C.O., series 5, 1348.

cations. It is true that Botetourt collaborated with Hillsborough to secure a new Indian boundary for Virginia that was expected to cramp the Vandalia project, but he did not directly challenge the project for a new colony. Walker and the Loyal Company, who had more than once swayed legislation, surely had enough influence to have secured some kind of protest if they had wanted it. The fact that it was not forthcoming is very good evidence that they did not desire it.[36]

On the surface it would seem queer that Virginia should have devoted such strenuous efforts in order to get a more extended western boundary and at the same time paid so little attention to a movement that would have taken from her an enormous stretch of territory. But a little reflection makes the situation entirely clear. Most of the Tidewater magnates of Virginia, members of the council and their friends, had already discovered that they were not in position to speculate successfully in Western lands. Western connections were necessary for this purpose, and only Dr. Walker, Washington, Patrick Henry, William Byrd III, and a few others had such connections. The council was willing enough to accommodate such speculators, despite the general Eastern conviction that the frontier was a terrible place inhabited by terrible people whose main business in life was stirring up Indian wars for which Easterners had to pay. Thus, the problem was mainly a question of what a few powerful speculators wanted, and such men did not look far into the future. An immediate opening of lands for exploitation was their object, and they had found that the Lochaber line was the best they could get from Hillsborough and Stuart. If the new colony should be established and its eastern boundary become the western boundary of Virginia, that would open more land in southwest Virginia than would the Holston-Kanawha line. Walker seemed to be satisfied with the situation.

On December 11, 1770, the Earl of Dunmore was transferred from the governorship of New York to that of Virginia. Goldsbrow Banyar, judge of probate of New York, wrote Sir William Johnson, "you cannot conceive how reluctantly he [Dunmore] leaves this Province." One reason for the Scottish nobleman's reluctance was that he had enormous holdings of land in western New York which he was planning to settle with immigrants from his own country, and his removal at this time interfered with the scheme.[37] It was October 12, 1771, before he reported

[36] On May 27, 1771, Walker wrote to Preston that there had been "some alarming accounts of an enormous grant on our Frontiers," but though he had been in Williamsburg for some time and in close touch with the provincial administration, he had taken no steps to protest against the plan. Draper MSS., 2QQ125–126. Walker to Preston, Jan. 24, 1770, ibid., 116.

[37] Goldsbrow Banyar to Sir Wm. Johnson, July 18, 1771, Papers of Sir William Johnson, VIII, 192–195.

at his new post of duty. Before leaving his old government he had expressed decided disapproval of the Vandalia Company, and his arrival in Virginia was no good omen for that enterprise.

Washington immediately besought the new governor to issue patents on his surveys, but imperial instructions forbade it and nothing was accomplished at the moment. Colonel Thomas Cresap had returned from England with such alarming news regarding establishment of a new colony by the Walpole Company that Washington wrote to Mercer in the fall of 1771 to know how cheaply a share in that enterprise might be bought. If Washington was disturbed by the activities of the Walpole associates, so were they thoroughly alarmed by his plans. Dr. John Connolly, in fact, tried to persuade him to transfer his efforts to the Natchez region and so remove himself from their sphere of influence. But the Virginia colonel got the upper hand. On November 4, 1772, he petitioned Dunmore and the council to issue patents on the surveys which he and Crawford had made for the regiment; two days later this request was granted to the extent of one hundred twenty-two thousand two hundred ninety-three acres. On December 15 the patents were actually made out.[38] Why Dunmore changed his mind and decided to violate his instructions does not appear. This measure has often been looked upon as quite irregular. It is true that orders had been issued to prohibit the granting of Western lands in Virginia, but the order in council of 1769 under which Dunmore acted was made before these prohibitory instructions were issued. It is at least arguable that Dunmore was within his rights in this matter. There can scarcely be any doubt that substantial justice was on his side.[39]

During the spring of 1771 John Donelson surveyed the Indian boundary which had been agreed on at Lochaber. He was accompanied by Alexander Cameron, deputy Indian agent under John Stuart, and several of the Cherokee chiefs. When they arrived at a river which Donelson called the Louisa the chiefs, according to Donelson, suggested that they break off there and let the line run down the river. This would save a great deal of work and give Virginia more land. Donelson readily agreed, and the line was so arranged. But the question later arose as to which river was the Louisa. It had originally been named by Dr. Thomas

---

[38] Hamilton, *Letters to Washington*, IV, 152–156; Fitzpatrick, III, 72; *Washington–Crawford Letters*, pp. 23–26; George Morgan to Thomas Wharton, May 6, 1772, Wharton MSS., H.S.P.; Executive Journal of the Council of Virginia, Nov. 4 and 6, 1772, C.O., series 5, 1440; Virginia Land Office records, Patents, XLI, 66, 77, 80, 94–100.

[39] Dunmore to Hillsborough, Nov. 12, 1770, *Documents Relative to Colonial History of New York*, VIII, 252–253; Hillsborough to Nelson, Dec. 11, 1770, C.O., series 5, 1348.

Walker on his exploring expedition of 1750. He gave the name to the west fork of the Big Sandy, and Professor Alvord has decided that this was the river which Donelson designated.[40] So it would have been if Donelson had been going in the right direction and had followed the first tributary of the Ohio which he crossed. The maps commonly used at this time, Mitchell's and Evans', show the Louisa as a branch of the Great Kanawha. To have taken this river as the line would have given Virginia much less territory than the treaty line would have given her. According to these maps the Kentucky River is the only one which lay in the path of the surveyors, though actually they had to turn from their course and cross the Cumberland Mountains in order to reach it. The fact is that Cameron in his report (the map with which he accompanied this document has never been found) spoke of the surveying party leaving off at "Cedar River," a small stream and a tributary of the Kentucky. Despite Professor Alvord's reasoning, there are various other indications, including an affidavit by Donelson, that it was the Kentucky River to which he referred. Dunmore sent a map of the survey with his report to Hillsborough, but it also has been lost. Stuart excused himself from sending a map with his report—a rather suspicious circumstance—but he did later prepare one which showed the Kentucky River as the one down which the boundary line ran.[41] This he sent to the Cherokee with a map of Vandalia when he notified them late in 1772 of the intended establishment of the new province. His orders instructed him to forbid settlement between the Lochaber line and the western boundary of Vandalia. He told the Indians that settlement would not be permitted between the western boundary of Vandalia and the Kentucky, not the Kanawha. Thus he turned the whole affair to the advantage of the Vandalia proprietors. It was at least two months later before he sent a map of the new line to the home government.

The question arises as to why Stuart, after having taken the initiative in the fight to restrict Virginia's western boundary, should so suddenly have changed his mind and consented to extend it. There are two circumstances which may help to explain it. He and Donelson had become good friends, and Donelson represented the expansionist interests in Virginia. But perhaps the more important consideration is that at this time it was generally expected that the Vandalia project would succeed. If it did this extension of territory would probably be added to the new

[40] J. S. Johnston, ed., *First Explorations of Kentucky* (Louisville, 1898) pp. 63, 67; Henderson, *Walker*, p. 69; Executive Journal of the Council of Virginia, April 17, 1771, C.O., series 5, 1440; Dunmore to Hillsborough, March (?), 1772, C.O., series 5, 1350.

[41] James Hall, *Sketches of History, Life, and Manners in the West* (Philadelphia, 1835) I, 248; Stuart to Hillsborough, Sept. 24, 1771, C.O., series 5, 72; for Stuart's map, see plate iv, *ante*.

colony, not to Virginia. Stuart had usually made it his first business to carry out instructions from home, and it is likely that he knew the way the wind was blowing there in spite of Hillsborough.[42]

In March, 1772, Dunmore sent Donelson's report and a map of the new line to Hillsborough. On June 6 Hillsborough answered. He did not complain of the change which had been made, but said the matter was under advisement. He also reiterated the instruction not to grant lands beyond the line of the proclamation of 1763. About a week before this date he had made his last report against the Vandalia Company, stressing Virginia's prior rights. On July 1 the Committee of Council for Plantation Affairs took issue with him, favoring Vandalia, but stipulating that no settlements should be made beyond the Kanawha. One month later Hillsborough resigned, and on August 14 the King and Council gave their official approval to the establishment of "Pittsylvania." The stipulation that no settlements should be made beyond the Lochaber line was retained, but the eastern boundary of the colony was to be advanced from the line of the Cumberlands to that of the Alleghenies. The new territory, however, was not to be added to the grant to the Walpole Company as proprietors, their boundary stopping at the Cumberland Mountains as before. This change is interesting. With Hillsborough out and Dartmouth in, the Vandalia group was taking a stronger stand. This new boundary would cut off many long-established Virginia settlements. Moreover, these settlements lay in the special preserve of the Loyal Company. Yet no complaint was heard from Dr. Walker or from Dunmore. The Virginia governor did protest, however, because he was not allowed to grant lands west of the mountains. Since this territory would not be included in the proprietary grant to the Walpole Company, Walker evidently believed that the claims which he represented would be undisturbed, and he apparently thought that his land-speculating future would be as bright under the ægis of Vandalia as under that of Virginia.[43]

It was not until February 23, 1773, that Stuart transmitted his map of the new line to London. It seems that the significance of the changed boundary was not clear to the home government until this was received. The map certainly clarified it, and on May 6 the Board of Trade made its report, bestowing the name of Vandalia on the new colony and proposing that its western boundary be extended to the Kentucky. The boundaries of the proprietary grant remained as before.

[42] Stuart to Oukonnestotah (no date, but late in 1772), Cont. Cong. MSS., I, 71, II, 193, L. of C.; Dartmouth to Stuart, Sept. 2, 1772, C.O., series 5, 73.
[43] Hillsborough to Dunmore, June 6, 1772, C.O., series 5, 1350; Dunmore to Hillsborough, Nov. 16, 1772, C.O., series 5, 1351.

Thus, while Virginia fought stubbornly for a more extended western boundary against the Cherokee, the Vandalia project had grown to full flower without her having made any definite protest. Only one conclusion is possible: that the great majority of Virginians, including most of the leaders with the exception of Washington and other members of the Ohio Company, were indifferent in the matter of Western lands. The one other group that was seriously concerned, the Loyal Company and its allies, was sufficiently powerful to have made trouble. Its interests were paramount in the boundary controversy, and its agent, Dr. Walker, was an active propagandist in its behalf. The fact that he did not interfere indicates that he did not wish to do so. The explanation is that the opening of available lands was the principal object of the Loyal Company, and the Vandalia government could be as useful in that connection as could that of Virginia, perhaps even more so.[44] In December, 1772, the *soi-disant* "Lord" Stirling of New Jersey visited Williamsburg and talked with Speaker Randolph. He wrote to Governor William Franklin that he was "told here that there will be no room for contention between this colony and the new colony; they say that the grantees of the new colony have consented that all the *regular* grants under this province shall be confirmed," meaning such as had been officially entered, though not surveyed. Another indication of cooperation between Lord Botetourt, the Loyal Company, and the Vandalia interests is the fact that, while such great concern was manifest by the Botetourt administration over the settlers of southwest Virginia, those who had settled under the leadership of Cresap and others in the neighborhood of Redstone, the old stamping ground of the Ohio Company of Virginia, were given to understand that they could expect no countenance from the Old Dominion.[45]

That the Nelson administration had a kindly feeling for the Loyal Company is shown by an incident of May 5, 1772. On that day a communication was presented to the council by Dr. Thomas Walker, lieutenant of Botetourt County, representing that settlers from other colonies were coming in and, taking advantage of the proclamation of 1763, seating themselves upon lands which had previously been granted to others, that is, to him and his associates in the Loyal Company. The council

[44] Stuart gave Walker and Lewis credit for the lion's share of the interest in and agitation of the boundary question. Stuart to Hillsborough, Jan. 20, 1770, C.O., series 5, 71. Walpole gave them credit for having directed Botetourt's boundary policy. Memorial to the Board of Trade, March 5, 1771, C.O., series 5, 1333; minutes of Virginia Council, Aug. 17, 1770, C.O., series 5, 72; Stirling to Wm. Franklin, Dec. 5, 1772, Franklin MSS., XLVIII, 143, A.P.S.

[45] Adam Stephen to Botetourt, July 29, 1769, and minutes of council upon the same, Aug. 8, 1769, C.O., series 5, 1347.

ordered that the sheriff, with the assistance of all officers and citizens, remove the offenders.[46] If the claims of the Loyal Company were to be thus upheld no one could settle any Western land in Virginia without the liability of being forced to purchase from it, for no bounds had been specified for its enormous grant and it might locate its tracts wherever it chose in the great transmontane region.

[46] Executive Journal of the Council of Virginia, May 5, 1772, C.O., series 5, 1440.

CHAPTER V

EXTENSION OF THE VIRGINIA FRONTIER, 1769–1773

DURING the French and Indian War the settlement at Draper's Meadows, then the outpost of civilization in the Valley of Virginia, was wiped out by an Indian massacre. Colonel James Patton, the old sea captain who had weathered many voyages bringing over redemptioners to Hobbs Hole and carrying back furs and tobacco, who had spent more than twenty hazardous years on the frontier, now paid the penalty for his hardihood, being slain along with several others. With one exception no other important settlement was made in this area until some time after these hostilities had ceased. This exception was Chiswell's Mine. Colonel John Chiswell of Williamsburg, proprietor of the famous Raleigh Tavern, was son-in-law to Colonel William Randolph and father-in-law of Speaker John Robinson. In 1766 he killed a man in a tavern brawl and committed suicide. Ten years before he had discovered the lead mine on the upper waters of the New or Kanawha River, which came to bear his name. It was put into operation almost immediately under the management of Colonel William Byrd, Chiswell, and Robinson. Byrd built a fort near the place in 1758. The interests of the operators extended at times to land speculation in addition to mining, and Edmund Pendleton, Robinson's protégé, came to take part in this phase of Western development.[1]

It was not until the year 1770 approached that any other establishments of consequence were made in the neighborhood. At about this time John and Arthur Campbell moved from their home near Staunton and settled on a tract of land at Wolf Hills on the Holston River, where Abingdon now stands. This had been purchased from the Patton estate in 1765, and it did not concern them that it lay west of the proclamation line of 1763. At about the same time other settlers, including several friends of the Campbells from the Staunton neighborhood, established homes in the vicinity. Captain William Russell was the son of a prominent lawyer who had studied in the Temple; he was one of the Knights of the Golden

---

[1] Edmund Pendleton to William Preston, Feb. 6, 1768, Draper MSS., 2QQ103–104; *Va. Mag. Hist. and Biog.*, IX, 85–88, XVII, 318–319; Samuel M. Wilson, "West Fincastle—Now Kentucky," *Filson Club History Quarterly*, Apr., 1935, pp. 75–80.

Horseshoe and a great landholder of Orange County. The younger Russell was educated at the College of William and Mary and in 1770 established himself at "Castlewoods" in the valley of the Clinch, west of Holston and near the North Carolina boundary. He was presently to marry the widow of General Campbell, who was a sister of Patrick Henry. William Christian, another prominent pioneer who settled in the neighborhood in 1770, had studied law under Henry and married his sister Anne. Christian's father, Israel, was a successful merchant of Staunton and at one time a burgess from his county. His daughter married Dr. William Fleming of the same community. Fleming had studied medicine at the University of Edinburgh and had served as surgeon in the British navy. In 1755 he came to Virginia where he was soon attached to Washington's regiment as a lieutenant. Perhaps the most important of all these pioneers of southwestern Virginia was William Preston, son of the emigrant John, who left the Staunton neighborhood in 1773 and established his home at the old Draper's Meadows site, renaming it "Smithfield." Evan Shelby, who settled on the Holston in 1771, was a newcomer. When a lad of about fifteen, he came from Wales with his father and settled eventually near Hagerstown. Before 1763 he was engaged in extensive fur trade at Fort Pitt, Michillimaccinac, and Green Bay. His mercantile enterprises brought him at times into relation with the firm of Baynton, Wharton and Morgan. As one of the "suffering traders," he was a member of the Indiana Company, and the losses he sustained were a leading cause of his removal from Maryland to Virginia. He had been in Braddock's campaign and served under Forbes in 1758.[2]

This practically completes the list of early leaders of southwestern Virginia. Almost all other inhabitants of the region who attained any prominence, such as the Todds, the Browns, Breckinridges, Roanes, Wallaces, the McDowells, the Triggs and Bullitts, were connected with these by family ties. Most of them were of Scotch-Irish stock, and, contrary to the popular conception that those who pushed the frontier westward were uncouth, uneducated but picturesque figures such as Daniel Boone, most of them were men of position and good education. Through Byrd, Patrick Henry, and Pendleton they had important Eastern connections, and their influence in Virginia politics was of first-rate im-

---

[2] Anne Christian to Anne Fleming, Dec. 3, 1770, Fleming MSS., Washington and Lee University library; Shelby to Wm. Campbell, Nov. 9, 1772, Campbell–Preston MSS., L. of C.; Edmund Moran to Evan Shelby, April 7, 1764, June 20, 1765, etc., Durrett misc. MSS., University of Chicago library; Waddell, *Annals of Augusta County*, p. 181; Hale, *Trans-Allegheny Pioneers*, p. 100; *Va. Mag. Hist., and Biog.*, VII, 126–127.

portance. Leadership on this frontier was at least as restricted as it was in the older communities. The men who held the offices also fastened their claim on the land.

By 1769 the Holston area was rapidly filling up with men of the less conspicuous sort. Some of them passed the Virginia boundary and established on the Watauga River the first transmontane settlements in North Carolina.[3] Among them were hunters and explorers constantly seeking new frontiers to conquer. Beyond the Holston flowed the Clinch, and Powell's Valley lay just a little to the westward. The famous gap in the Cumberland Mountains was not far away—the gateway to Kentucky, the path to empire. Explorers could have wished no fairer field.

It had been nearly twenty years since Dr. Thomas Walker and Christopher Gist ventured into the dark and bloody ground that was Kentucky. The French and Indian War had intervened to discourage further activities of this kind, but now fine herds of big game and virgin lands were beckoning again.

Hunters were in the neighborhood of Cumberland Gap in 1761, and by 1764 Daniel Boone and others had penetrated into the Kentucky country. In 1766 James Smith of western Pennsylvania, who led the "Black Boys" in the destruction of Croghan's goods in 1765, penetrated even farther into the hinterland. He had been in captivity among the Indians for twenty-four years, and it is probable that in company with the migratory red men he had already been over this territory many times. Having heard of Sir William Johnson's plan to purchase from the Six Nations all of the Kentucky country as far down as the Tennessee River, Smith set out in 1766 with several companions, passed through the Holston country to the Cumberland Gap, and explored the region beyond. During the same year, while the goods of Baynton, Wharton and Morgan were being transported to the Illinois country down the Ohio River, several of the hunters attached to the convoy explored the Kentucky shore of the river. Among them was John Finley, who continued to work for Morgan in the Illinois and in whose hands Morgan left his affairs when he quitted that region in 1769. Finley was still there in October, 1771, making it obvious that this could not have been the man of the same name, living in western Virginia, who accompanied Dr. Walker on his expedition in 1748 and who in 1767 passed through Kentucky to the Ohio River.[4]

[3] T. P. Abernethy, *From Frontier to Plantation in Tennessee* (Chapel Hill, 1932) pp. 1–18.

[4] Draper is responsible for confusing the two Finleys (or Findlays according to Draper), Hanna, *Wilderness Trail*, II, 212–215. Filson, an almost contemporary writer, says in his *Kentucky* that Finley lived in North Carolina, p. 8; and John Brad-

The year 1767 saw various other explorers in Kentucky. Daniel Boone again visited the eastern fringe of that country in this year. Samuel Harrod, brother to James, and George Michael Holsteiner, otherwise known as Michael Stoner, reached the site of Nashville the same season.[5]

Many unrecorded explorations must have been made in this and the following year, but it was 1769 before these activities came to be impressive. Daniel Boone's famous expedition in company with John Finley is the best known, but it is hardly the most picturesque. In the same year Hancock Taylor from Orange County, Virginia, uncle of President Zachary Taylor, led a group of explorers and hunters into Kentucky. He and several others launched a boat on the Ohio and sailed down to New Orleans, returning home overland. This was also the year in which James Knox and his famous band of "Long Hunters" began their expeditions into Kentucky, which were continued during 1770 and 1771. Knox was a native of Ireland who had come to America at the age of fourteen. He was to give a good account of himself at the head of one of Morgan's companies of riflemen at Saratoga. The "Long Hunter," with otter or beaver cap, heavy buckskin moccasins and leggins, long hunting shirt of soft leather, hatchet stuck in his belt, his hunting knife in a sheath attached to the strap of his shot-pouch, his long black rifle in the crook of his arm, was a rugged figure, fittingly dressed for the wilderness in the regalia he had adopted from the Indian. He set out with several packhorses, carrying provisions to last only two days from the settlement, for afterward the wilderness yielded abundance. Knox's hunters went through Cumberland Gap to the Barrens of Kentucky. Here immense herds of buffalo, elk, and other game roamed. Their trails could be easily followed by their well-beaten paths to the salt licks. The hunters erected a rude "skin-house," and when it was filled with as much peltry as their packhorses could carry they began the trek back to the settlements. Among Knox's companions were Anthony and Isaac Bledsoe, Casper Mansker, a German who was born while his parents were crossing the Atlantic to America, and several others who came to be well-known in the early annals of Tennessee and Kentucky. Most, if not all, of them lived at this time in the Holston country. Ten of the "Long Hunters" built two boats and two trapping canoes, loaded them with their peltry and floated down the Cumberland River. They came to a trading post of the French *voyageurs* called French

---

ford, in his "Notes on Kentucky," *Kentucky Gazette*, Sept. 1, 1826, says the same thing. See also, Hall, *Sketches of the West*, I, 240; and Hale, *Trans-Allegheny Pioneers*, p. 267; Baynton, Wharton and Morgan to John Finley, Oct. 8, 1771, Baynton, Wharton, and Morgan letter book, Pa. State Archives.

[5] W. R. Jillson, *Tales of the Dark and Bloody Ground* (Louisville, 1930) pp. 21–25; *Register of the Kentucky State Historical Society*, XXX, 224.

Lick, now Nashville, and here discovered such great herds of buffalo that they were afraid to disembark for fear of being trampled to death. A salt-lick nearby was deserted, but on the ground bleached bones and skulls were so thickly strewn that the hunters could walk several hundred yards without touching earth. The French hunters had slaughtered entire herds for their tongues and tallow.[6]

Although these intrepid woodsmen made extended sojourns in Kentucky on their hunting expeditions, no efforts were made to establish settlements there during these years, and a significant attempt to push the frontier of southwestern Virginia almost to Cumberland Gap in 1769 failed signally. It will be recalled that at this time the colony of Virginia was, largely under the influence of the Loyal Company, struggling desperately to extend its Indian boundary in order to include as much of this country as possible in the area open to settlement. This explains why it was that Dr. Walker, in 1769, made an agreement with several parties of adventurers that if they would settle Powell's Valley, just east of the Gap, each man would be given one thousand acres of land, the first comers to have first choice. Joseph Martin of Albemarle County led a band of twenty-one settlers, reached the Valley first, and preempted the choicest land. However, Indians molested his camp and he and his companions decided to abandon the enterprise. The result was that no settlements were made in Powell's Valley at this time, but Martin later came to be Patrick Henry's land agent and an important figure in the development of the early Southwest.[7]

Despite this misadventure, population was moving so fast into southwestern Virginia that in November, 1769, an act was passed to divide Augusta County, which had heretofore included nearly all of Virginia west of the mountains. The southwestern section was now erected into the county and parish of Botetourt. The expansion continuing, Botetourt was divided in February, 1772, and that part which lay west of the New or Kanawha River became the county of Fincastle. Though Dunmore had had orders to create no new Western counties, he excused himself to the home government for assenting to this act and it was allowed to stand. William Christian was made high sheriff of the Fincastle jurisdiction, and William Preston became commander of the militia and county surveyor. John Floyd, Daniel Smith, the young teacher from Wolf Hills, William Russell, Robert Preston, son of William, Robert Doak, and

[6] Brent Altsheler, "The Long Hunters and James Knox their Leader," *Filson Club Historical Quarterly*, V, 169–185. William Miller was the longest surviving Long Hunter, dying in 1841.

[7] William Martin to L. C. Draper, Sept. 6, 1842, Draper MSS., 3XX7; Walker to Martin, Sept. 23, 1771, *ibid.*, 1XX1; Abernethy, *op. cit.*, p. 6.

James Douglas were appointed deputy surveyors. Preston was thus the central figure in the land situation when the settlement of the Kentucky country began.[8]

Attempts in this direction had been long delayed by the proclamation of 1763, by the difficulty of establishing the new Indian boundary, and by the hostility of the natives, but the treaty of Lochaber with the Cherokee had been made in 1770 and Donelson had surveyed his line in 1771. If the home government ratified this arrangement Virginia could expect to occupy lands as far west as the Kentucky River. But the Vandalia Company had fair prospects of getting this new territory. Because of these complications Dunmore was first instructed on February 7, 1771, not to issue grants for more than one thousand acres, and then, on June 6, 1772, he was ordered not to grant any land west of the old line of 1763.[9]

In the face of these instructions the governor pursued a peculiar policy. The royal proclamation of 1763, while closing the frontier beyond the mountains to promiscuous settlement, promised grants of land to soldiers who had served in the French and Indian War. Whether this applied to those who had served under the authority of the different colonies as well as to those who had served in the royal army was uncertain, but both groups were pressing their claims. Colonel William Byrd III had commanded a Virginia regiment in the War, and, on September 2, 1772, he advised the soldiers who had served under him to make surveys of the lands they claimed. He knew that the governor could not patent these tracts to them at once, but thought their prior rights would be respected whenever it became possible to issue patents. On October 30 following Captain Thomas Bullitt, who had served under Washington in the late War, advertised in the Virginia and Pennsylvania gazettes that he was going out to Kentucky the following spring to survey lands claimed under the proclamation of 1763, and that those wishing to have their claims surveyed should meet him on the Ohio River in the spring. He had secured an appointment as surveyor of lands on the Ohio from the College of William and Mary, and the boldness of his proposal would have led any one to suspect that Lord Dunmore had given his approval to the plan.[10]

In response to this invitation some of the officers in the Fredericksburg

[8] Dunmore to Dartmouth, May 25, 1773, P.R.O., C.O., series 5, 1351; Pendleton, *Tazewell County*, p. 258.

[9] C. H. Laub, "British Regulation of Crown Lands," *William and Mary Quarterly Historical Magazine*, X, 52–55.

[10] Lord Stirling to Wm. Franklin, Dec. 5, 1772, Franklin MSS., XLVIII, 143, A.P.S.

neighborhood, Dr. Hugh Mercer among them, met to make plans for securing their surveys. Not taking a fancy to Bullitt, they commissioned Hancock Taylor to go with him and attend to their interests. Not only Mercer but Washington and others who came in contact with Bullitt entertained some dislike of him.[11] Before he set out down the Ohio in the spring he entered into a correspondence with George Morgan, lately of the Illinois country and now in desperate financial straits, to seek to establish a monopoly of salt springs and lead mines that might be located in the country Bullitt was to explore. Under date of March 6, 1773, Bullitt wrote Morgan:

On considering your proposals of joyning a company of you in Phila. as you have very able men amongst you, and the prosecuting the scheme of salt & lead works must be of advantage to the country have resolved to come into a scheme of that sort—but must beg leave that the whole affair is not left on me to chuse and survey for two reasons—the first, I may be senshured to undertake such a thing if I take all the land you may buy, it may be said I am making deep strokes of monopoly in the West—when men are engaging in weighty affairs its but right they should be their own judges. I will endeavor to procure for us the half of the Bigg Bone salt spring and any other that may be found and the lead mine—I shall without doubt be about fort Pitt the 20th April and shall be glad to see one of you.[12]

When spring came Bullitt assembled his military adventurers at the mouth of the Great Kanawha. He was aided by James Douglas and Hancock Taylor, the experienced woodsmen who were later deputy surveyors of Fincastle County. James Harrod and Isaac Hite also accompanied him. He was to have been met at the Scioto by William Thompson, with James Finley, James Smith, whose odyssey through the Gap into the wilds of Kentucky had brought him reputation as explorer and woodsman, and about sixty others who represented the interests of the veterans of Pennsylvania, but Thompson arrived after Bullitt had passed down the Ohio. His supply train was attacked with the loss of several men and all the packhorses. He nevertheless made a number of surveys and decided to try to get a commission from the College of William and Mary on his own account. In this effort he succeeded during the next year, but Colonel Preston, the surveyor of Fincastle, refused to validate surveys not made under his authority and Thompson's claims

[11] In writing of Bullitt, Washington stated: "Bullitt is no favorite of mine, and therefore I shall say nothing more of him, than that his own opinion of himself always kept pace with what others are pleased to think of him—if anything, rather ran ahead of it." Washington to John A. Washington, March 31, 1776, *American Archives*, series 4, V, 561–562.

[12] Thos. Bullitt to Geo. Morgan, March 6, 1773, autograph collection of Simon Gratz, H.S.P.; Hugh Mercer to Joseph Shippen, June 9, 1773, Irvine MSS., XVI, 66, H.S.P.

were later rejected on this ground.[13] Another party of prospectors came overland from Preston's place in Fincastle and joined Bullitt near the Kentucky River. This party was headed by James McAfee, an Irishman from County Armagh who had settled in Augusta County, and included his brothers George and Robert. They made surveys on the Kentucky and Salt Rivers with the expectation that Bullitt would authenticate their work. It appears that this expectation was warranted, for Bullitt and his men worked in harmony with the McAfees. The fact that they set out from Preston's estate indicates that they had his backing. It is noteworthy that the McAfees surveyed not only soldiers' plats, but tracts of four hundred acres which were intended for settlement rights under the old colonial system.[14]

While the McAfees awaited on the Ohio Bullitt made an excursion into the Wabash country to have a conference with the Shawnee Indians. They had never given their assent to the treaty of Fort Stanwix and continued to declare that they would oppose the occupation of the country south of the Ohio which the Six Nations had ceded. At this time Guy Johnson, son-in-law of Sir William, wrote to General Haldimand—who, like Bouquet, was a Swiss officer in British service and had just replaced Gage as commander of military forces in North America—that the eagerness with which the people in the more Southern provinces were pushing to the Ohio could not but prove alarming to the Indians. He stated that settlements were projected far beyond the prescribed limits, and that evil consequences could be prevented only by restraining the eager pioneers. The object of Bullitt's visit to the Shawnee was to get their consent to his surveying operations and to the settlement which was expected to follow. He came upon them at their town of Chillicothe unexpectedly, and their attitude at first was hostile. Speeches were exchanged, and friendship appeared to have been established under the influence of Richard Butler, the Pittsburgh trader, who was making a sojourn at Chillicothe and who interpreted the speeches, giving the answer of the Shawnee to Bullitt in written form, signed by himself. In return for permission to survey and settle in Kentucky Bullitt agreed that the Shawnee should be allowed to hunt south of the river and that they should be paid for their

[13] Dunmore to Thompson, April 2, 1774, Irvine MSS., XVI, 69, H.S.P.; *ibid.*, pp. 70, 72; Patrick Work to James Burd, July 18, 1773, *ibid.*, p. 67; Hugh Mercer to Dr. John Morgan, Sept. 8, 1773, *ibid.*, p. 68; Hamilton, *Letters to Washington*, IV, 248–250, 290–293; Draper MSS., 8CC10–12; *American State Papers, Public Lands*, I, 583–584.

[14] Neander M. Woods, *The Woods-McAfee Memorial* (Louisville, 1905) p. 169ff.; Journals of James and Robert McAfee, *ibid.*, 428–440; James McAfee's Journal, 1773, Draper MSS., 4CC1–12; Butler, *Kentucky*, pp. 20–22. Alvord erroneously states that Harrodsburg was founded in 1773. *Mississippi Valley in British Politics*, II, 187.

claims to the soil which the Six Nations had denied at Fort Stanwix. They were told also that the great men from Virginia were coming among them for this purpose. No sooner was Bullitt gone than the Indians sent messengers to Pittsburgh to notify Alexander McKee, who had succeeded Croghan there as deputy Indian agent, of what had happened. McKee gave them an evasive answer which neither condemned nor approved what the Virginians were doing. He did mention, however, that the King was to establish a new government south of the Ohio.[15]

While Bullitt was thus progressing down the Ohio in the summer of 1773 Dunmore visited Pittsburgh. Trouble had broken out between the settlers in that neighborhood on account of the boundary dispute between Virginia and Pennsylvania, so the governor wished to view the situation first hand. He wished perhaps to view the land also, since, on his return from the West, he petitioned the King for a grant of one hundred thousand acres "in the back part of Virginia free of quit rents." [16] Washington was to have gone with him, but circumstances prevented. Though he could not be there in person, the master of Mount Vernon advised Dunmore to consult William Crawford and George Croghan. On June 29, Croghan's nephew, Dr. John Connolly, wrote to Washington asking his aid in securing from Dunmore a grant for two thousand acres under the proclamation of 1763. He had already arranged with Bullitt to make a location at the Falls of the Ohio for him. It is not certain that Washington took a hand in it, but Bullitt surveyed that choice tract and Dunmore granted to Connolly the site on which the city of Louisville was to rise. At the same time an adjoining tract was granted to one Charles Warnsdorf and presently transferred to Connolly and John Campbell jointly. Other tracts contiguous to these were surveyed at the same time for Edward Ward, Croghan's half-brother, and others closely associated with the old trader.[17]

These were choice tracts of land and Dunmore was baiting his hook for no small fry. This was the beginning of the alliance between the governor of Virginia and the Croghan faction in the struggle against the governor of Pennsylvania for control of Pittsburgh and its environs.

It is hard to see how Dunmore thought he had a right to grant the

[15] McKee to Haldimand, June 20, 1773, Add. MSS., 21670, Br. Mus.; *Papers of Sir William Johnson,* VIII, 834–835, 888–891; C.O., series 5, 74, 345; Jillson, *Tales of the Dark and Bloody Ground,* pp. 34–58; Guy Johnson to Haldimand, Aug. 26, 1773, *Papers of Sir William Johnson,* VIII, 875–876.

[16] Petition of Earl Dunmore, British transcripts, L. of C., C.O., series 5, 1334, f. 195.

[17] Virginia Land Office, Patents, book 42, pp. 505–507, Dec. 16, 1773 (copy of the Connolly patent, dated Oct. 7, 1773, is in the Durrett misc. MSS., University of Chicago library); Sparks, *Writings of Washington,* II, 373–374; Hamilton, *Letters to Washington,* IV, 208–216, 253–254.

lands in question. They lay below the Kentucky River and, therefore, beyond the limits established by Donelson with the Cherokee Nation. The only claim that Virginia could set up to the right to occupy this area was under the treaty of Fort Stanwix. In fact, Virginia was always prepared to make the most of this treaty. Connolly's warrant was granted on the basis of service as a surgeon's mate in the French and Indian War, and hence under the proclamation of 1763. In April Dunmore had been ordered by the home government, along with other colonial governors, to grant no more lands for the time being except under this proclamation. But he knew that this did not give him a free hand regarding Western lands even in the case of military claimants.[18]

Washington, hearing of Bullitt's activities, purchased two officers' warrants and sent word to him to survey ten thousand acres on his account. At the same time he wrote to the governor asking if grants under the proclamation were to be made. One day, on his return home from the Annapolis races, Washington found a letter from Dunmore which stated that he did not consider himself at present authorized to make them. As for Bullitt, he said he knew nothing of his surveys and had sent a messenger to order him in. It seems that the latter part of the statement was true, for both Connolly and Dunmore became dissatisfied with Bullitt, and in the following October the governor and council of Virginia proposed to the College of William and Mary to revoke his surveyor's commission on the ground that he was causing trouble with the Indians and it was accordingly revoked. His promises to the Shawnee may possibly explain this action, or he may have shown too much interest in salt springs and lead mines. Dunmore, at the very time petitioning for his own huge grant, would scarcely have been complacent over seeing these alienated to Bullitt and his Philadelphia group which sought to monopolize them.[19]

Washington was not the only seeker after lands to whom the governor's policy was enigmatical in the spring of 1773. On April 30, Dr. Thomas Walker wrote to William Preston that Arthur Campbell had assured him nothing had been done relative to surveying on the Western waters.[20] Certain it is that Dunmore had not yet committed himself to granting any patents under the proclamation of 1763, despite his grant to Connolly and Campbell, though he appears to have held out to Bullitt and others hope that it might be done.

[18] Board of Trade papers, Plantations General, XXIX, 365–367.
[19] Executive Journal of the Council of Virginia, Oct. 14, 1773, C.O., series 5, 1440; Sparks, *Writings of Washington,* II, 375–380; *Washington-Crawford Letters,* pp. 33, 34–36; Fitzpatrick, *Writings of Washington,* III, 155–156.
[20] Draper MSS., 2QQ145.

By the fall of 1773 the prospects of the Vandalia project were known in America to be on the decline. It must have been this fact that prompted the governor of Virginia to come forward with a bold and definite Western policy. Not until October 11 did he notify the council of instructions on granting land which had been issued the previous April. He had at that time protested against the application of the new instructions to warrants already issued. The Virginia council now decided grants should continue to be made on such warrants, and a little later the home government coincided in this interpretation.[21] This ruling might have been stretched to cover even the case of the Loyal Company, and it is not unlikely that some such purpose was in view.

It was on the same day, October 11, that Dunmore took his first decisive step in the boundary dispute with Pennsylvania. The alliance with Croghan which he had made in this connection would have been impossible had Croghan not been doubtful of the success of Vandalia. And one other factor may help to explain Dunmore's audacity. His secretary, Captain E. Foy, was sending Lord Dartmouth detailed information "to aid his Lordship in choice of locations" of Western lands.[22] Dartmouth's interest in American lands will be recalled; he and his sons had already taken up thousands of acres.

Finally, on November 4, 1773, the governor and council of Virginia granted to George Washington and his associates several additional tracts of Western lands as part of the 200,000 acres promised him and his regiment under Dinwiddie's proclamation of 1754. At the same time the council agreed to issue him warrants under the proclamation of 1763, this action solving the mystery of Bullitt's surveying expedition. Two days later it was reported to the council that, in anticipation of this decision, certain combinations had been formed to take premature advantage of it; Dr. Thomas Walker, John Byrd and John May were appointed to examine the books of the surveyors of Augusta, Botetourt and Fincastle Counties. This was a case of appointing the cats to guard the mice.[23]

Following logically upon these developments the climax in the whole drama of land speculation was reached on December 16. Western settlers, who had a preemption right to fifty acres and an equal amount for each

[21] Dunmore to Dartmouth, July 4, 1773, and Dartmouth to Dunmore, Oct. 27, 1773, C.O., series 5, 1351; Executive Journal of the Council of Virginia, Oct. 11 and 19, 1773, C.O., series 5, 1440.

[22] E. Foy to Dartmouth, Sept. 22, 1773, *British Historical Manuscripts Commission, Fourteenth Report,* Appendix, part X, Vol. ii, 173–174.

[23] Executive Journal of the Council of Virginia, Nov. 4 and 6, 1773, C.O., series 5, 1440; Virginia Land Office, Patents, book 42, pp. 492, 496, 500, 503. A copy of the deed to John Fry and others for 21,941 acres, dated Dec. 1, 1773, is in the Illinois State Historical Library.

three acres cleared, complained that surveys for the soldiers were interfering with their claims. The governor and council took the matter under
consideration and issued an order declaring that soldiers might make
their surveys wherever they wished so long as they did not interfere with
actual settlements or with legal surveys previously made. As to the
settlers, they might purchase their lands either from the soldiers who had
warrants, or from the Loyal or Greenbrier Land Companies.[24] This was
the only official act, either colonial or imperial, which gave tacit recognition to the claims of the Loyal Company after the issuance of the proclamation of 1763. The company had failed to carry out the terms of its
charter which had subsequently become defunct. In this indirect way
Dunmore and his council now managed to grant it a certain recognition.
Furthermore, it is obvious from this decision that any settler who had
occupied lands in the western part of Virginia could be pounced upon by
agents of the Loyal Company and forced to pay its price of three pounds
per hundred acres for the lands to which he had a right of preemption.
Prior to 1756, one hundred fifty-six thousand one hundred sixty-four
acres had been surveyed for the company. Between this time and the
outbreak of the Revolution, forty-five thousand three hundred forty
additional acres were surveyed.[25] It is hardly necessary to add that the
old Ohio Company of Virginia was not included with the Loyal Company
in the favor of the governor and council.

[24] Executive Journal of the Council of Virginia, Dec. 15 and 16, 1773, C.O., series 5,
1440.
[25] Walker to Preston, Dec. 15, 1773, Draper MSS., 2QQ157.

CHAPTER VI

VIRGINIA-PENNSYLVANIA BOUNDARY DISPUTE

IN 1767 Mason and Dixon's line was completed between Maryland and Pennsylvania. In fact, it was continued somewhat beyond the western extremity of Maryland, but not to the western end of Pennsylvania. After the limits of Maryland were passed, the line separated Pennsylvania from Virginia, but Virginia had no part in the running of it. When the proprietors of Pennsylvania in 1768 agreed on an Indian boundary within their province and purchased from the Six Nations the lands that the natives surrendered east of this line, no attempt was made to establish the western boundary between Pennsylvania and Virginia. It was clear enough that the southern limit of the Quaker colony should extend five degrees westward from the Delaware River, and Virginia was never inclined to question seriously the proposition that Mason and Dixon's line should be extended due west to the full extent of five degrees. But the western end of this line had not been determined. No one knew just where it would fall, or whether Pennsylvania's western boundary, which would spring from that point, should run due north or follow the meanders of the Delaware at that distance.[1] The crux of the argument was whether Pittsburgh, the trade-center and strategic focus for that whole region, would fall to one colony or the other. There was good reason for doubt on this subject, and both sides at times admitted this to be the case. It will be recalled that during the French and Indian War the governor of Pennsylvania laid claim to the Fort Pitt area as within his province, but the assembly of the colony denied this and, on that ground, at first refused to aid in its protection.

Despite all this uncertainty as to their jurisdiction, the proprietors of Pennsylvania awaited only the demarcation of the Fort Stanwix boundary line in 1769 before surveying and selling lands in the region. Further-

---

[1] Boyd Crumrine, "The Boundary Controversy between Pennsylvania and Virginia, 1748–1785," *Annals of the Carnegie Museum*, I, 505–524; James Veech, *The Monongahela of Old* (Pittsburgh, 1910) pp. 89–96, 238–239; T. J. Chapman, *Old Pittsburgh Days* (Pittsburgh, 1900) pp. 101–105; Craig, *The Olden Time*, I, 433ff.; Executive Journal of the Council of Virginia, Feb. 20, 1770, C.O., series 5, 1440; Croghan to Wharton, June 21, 1769, *Pa. Mag. Hist. and Biog.*, XV, 430–431; John Penn to Dunmore, March 31, 1774, *Pa. Arch.*, X, 161.

more, in 1771 their government established the county of Bedford and included the Pittsburgh country within its indefinite bounds. Archibald Lochry was made treasurer of the new jurisdiction and William Thompson represented it in the assembly. Among its justices were George Wilson, Dorsey Pentecost—a Virginian who dwelt on a large estate called "Greenway" in the forks of the Youghiogheny—and William Croghan, a nephew of Colonel George Croghan who later married Lucy, sister to George Rogers Clark.[2] At this measure the Vandalia proprietors took alarm, as did George Croghan, both for them and for himself. If all this country should fall to Pennsylvania, the Walpole Company, the "suffering traders," and Croghan personally would lose large tracts for which they were contending. When Wharton and his London associates heard of Penn's pretensions they discussed the matter and decided to take it up with their friends in the government.[3]

But it was not only the Croghan and Walpole groups which objected to Pennsylvania jurisdiction. The Cresap settlement at Redstone had been making trouble for its Pennsylvania neighbors since 1766, and here was new cause for agitation in which the Cresaps took a leading part.[4]

The chief partisan of the Penns in the disputed area at this time was Arthur St. Clair (pronounced "Sinkler"; the pioneers named Sinkler Bottom in his honor) a kinsman of General Gage, through whose influence he obtained, at the age of twenty-three, a commission as ensign in the 60th Royal American Regiment. He came from his native Scotland in time to take part in the engagement on the Plains of Abraham. Resigning from the service, he had settled in Boston, from whence he removed to western Pennsylvania where he owned huge tracts of land in the Ligonier Valley. Here he was the trusted agent and friend of the Penns, and between the Cresaps and Colonel Croghan he had his hands full. He strongly suspected the Vandalia partisans in Philadelphia of adding fuel to the fire. The Virginia contingent, which constituted the majority of the population in the disputed area, appealed to Governor Dunmore. Dr. John Connolly took a leading part in the movement and presented a petition with nearly six hundred signatures asking that Virginia take the territory under her jurisdiction. The governor was not

[2] Boyd Crumrine, *History of Washington County, Pennsylvania* (Philadelphia, 1882) pp. 147–149; Samuel Wharton to T(homas) W(harton) and J(oseph) G(alloway), April 9, 1773, Franklin MSS. III, 145, A.P.S.; memorandum for Geo. Morgan, March 6, 1772, Baynton, Wharton and Morgan letter book, Pa. State Archives.

[3] William Henry Smith, ed., *The St. Clair Papers,* (Cincinnati, 1882) I, 262–264, 267–268.

[4] *Ibid.,* I, 257–259, 260–262, 264; *Papers of Sir William Johnson,* VII, 96–97; Botetourt to Hillsborough, Sept. 30, 1769, C.O., series 5, 1348; Crumrine, *Washington County,* p. 168.

uninterested in the situation, though his immediate predecessors had paid no attention to the aggressive policy of the Penns.[5]

Toward the end of 1771 Croghan resigned his deputy Indian agency to Alexander McKee in order to devote his entire time to trade and his landed interests. He and his kinsman Thomas Smallman were closely associated in the Indian trade, as were McKee and Alexander Ross, a Scotsman who had acquired much land in the Pittsburgh neighborhood and who had been commissary for the garrison at Fort Pitt. The Pittsburgh partnership of Joseph Simon and John Campbell was still flourishing, with Simon keeping headquarters at Lancaster and Campbell taking care of the Pittsburgh end of the business. Both these partnerships had various traders who went into the Indian country to collect pelts, and both were financed largely by the Gratz brothers of Philadelphia. This Jewish family had supplanted Baynton, Wharton and Morgan in the Western trade and now practically controlled that part of it which centered around Pittsburgh.[6]

In an attempt to forestall the proprietary claims, Croghan had some of his Indian grants laid off and began selling tracts to Bernard Gratz and others. His surveys were first made by William Thompson, but Thompson's work proving unsatisfactory, John Campbell was employed. Campbell's work likewise not coming up to expectations, he was replaced by Robert Lettis Hooper, who in turn was supplanted by Dorsey Pentecost. Eventually Croghan dispensed with Pentecost and called on his half-brother Edward Ward to do the work. Ward's final surveys took in far more territory than had been included previously, and encroached on purchases which Washington and Crawford had made from the Penns. Croghan settled a number of people on these tracts, and Washington had much difficulty in ridding himself of them.[7]

In October, 1772, the garrison at Fort Pitt was abolished and the buildings of the fort were sold to Alexander Ross and William Thompson.[8] In February, 1773, Westmoreland County was organized by Pennsylvania. It included all the province lying west of the mountains.

[5] *Ibid.*, pp. 166–167; *St. Clair Papers*, I, 265–267, 284–285; Craig, *The Olden Time*, I, 475; Dunmore to Dartmouth, March 18, 1774, C.O., series 5, 1352; *Am. Arch.*, series 4, I, 275.

[6] Carter, *Correspondence of General Thomas Gage*, I, 314–315; Byars, *B. and M. Gratz*, pp. 15, 128–129, 133; Croghan to B. Gratz, May 11, 1773, Draper MSS., 7J136.

[7] Indenture, Geo. Croghan to Edward Hand, Dec. 29, 1770, H.S.P.; *Papers of Sir William Johnson*, VII, 1132–1133; William Crawford to James Tilghman, Aug. 9, 1771, *Washington-Crawford Letters*, pp. 22–23; Crawford to Washington, Dec. 29, 1773, *ibid.*, pp. 37–39; Hanna, *Wilderness Trail*, II, 68; Crumrine, *Washington County*, p. 167n; Byars, *B. & M. Gratz*, pp. 141–142.

[8] *Proceedings of the Convention . . . of Virginia, Dec., 1775* (Richmond, 1816) Jan. 6, 1776, pp. 87–88; Croghan to Capt. Marcus Prevost, June 27, 1773, Add. MSS., 21, 730, Br. Mus.; *St. Clair Papers*, I, 599; Chapman, *Old Pittsburgh Days*, p. 101.

The seat of justice was fixed at Hanna's Town, about thirty miles east of Pittsburgh. William Crawford was made presiding judge of the court, and Arthur St. Clair, Alexander McKee, William Lochry, and Alexander Ross were numbered among the justices.[9] This development gave a new impetus to the boundary dispute. During the following summer Dunmore visited Pittsburgh and promised the before-mentioned tracts of land at the Falls of the Ohio to Connolly, Campbell, and Ward.[10] His alliance with the Croghan faction, which these grants indicated, was a perfectly natural one. They were both interested in limiting the claims of Pennsylvania, and it was logical that they should work together. But some of the consequences of this alignment proved to be almost fantastic.

On October 11, 1773, the governor and council of Virginia, in answer to a petition from settlers near Fort Pitt complaining of the creation of Westmoreland County by Pennsylvania, established the District of West Augusta and appointed Croghan, Connolly, Ward, Thomas Smallman, Pentecost, and John Gibson as additional justices. From time to time the court of Augusta was to be adjourned from Staunton to Pittsburgh and these new justices were to serve as the court at the latter place.[11] This was a technical way of getting around the prohibition against establishing new counties, which had been ignored in 1772 in the case of Fincastle. As to the new justices, they were all kinsmen or friends of Colonel George Croghan. Connolly was in Williamsburg at about the time the action was taken, and he and Washington appear to have collaborated in urging the governor to pursue this course. Here was a powerful weapon to be used against the Penns; from this time on the tension between the two parties tightened. Dunmore paid for this alliance by agreeing to validate Croghan's Indian grants which the home government had refused to recognize. And it was rumored that the firm of Simon and Campbell was to have special trading privileges under the new régime.[12] However, Croghan had not altogether given up hope for Vandalia, though doubt was increasing. During the fall of 1773 while he was making these terms with Dunmore he was also corresponding

[9] Col. Wm. Byrd to (?), Sept. 12, 1772, Draper MSS., 4ZZ56; Hassler, *Old Westmoreland*, pp. 5–9; Crumrine, *Washington County*, p. 149.

[10] Hall, *Trans-Allegheny Pioneers*, p. 202.

[11] Executive Journal of the Council of Virginia, C.O., series 5, 1440; *Virginia Gazette*, Sept. 8, 1774.

[12] W. Neil Franklin, "Pennsylvania-Virginia Rivalry for the Indian Trade in the Ohio Valley," *Mississippi Valley Historical Review*, XX, 478–479; Hamilton, *Letters to Washington*, IV, 289–290, 310–312; Croghan to B. Gratz, Sept. 24, 1774, Gratz-Croghan MSS., I, 38, H.S.P.; Volwiler, *Croghan*, pp. 301–302; Byars, *B. and M. Gratz*, pp. 340-353.

with Wharton and trying to explain to the Indians why the governor of the new province did not arrive.[13]

Connolly had gone to Williamsburg to secure the grant of land at the Falls which Dunmore had promised him. Before the end of the year he was back in Pittsburgh and on January 1, 1774, in the capacity of a Virginia captain he signed a proclamation summoning the militia of the Pittsburgh area to assemble on the 25th of that month. He planned also that the newly appointed justices for Augusta County should hold court in Pittsburgh on the 20th. Croghan and his supporters were widely suspected of complicity in these measures, but, while they were interested in undermining Governor Penn's jurisdiction, they did not wish to assist Dunmore openly as long as there was a chance that Vandalia colony might be established and their land claims made good without the assistance of Virginia. Consequently, the justices neither refused nor exercised their commissions and the court did not meet on the 20th.[14]

But "the haughty and imperious" Connolly was not inclined to mince matters. He was going ahead with his plans to assemble the militia when he was arrested and confined to jail by Arthur St. Clair, now clerk of the court of Westmoreland. When the 25th arrived the militiamen, mostly of Croghan's following, assembled at Pittsburgh, and finding their commander in the calaboose they marched to the fort and decapitated a keg of rum. Here an address demanding their allegiance to the Pennsylvania authority was read to them by St. Clair and a group of justices of Westmoreland County. Of Croghan's immediate friends, only Alexander McKee, the deputy Indian agent for the district, adhered to the Pennsylvania faction. No serious clashes occurring, the militiamen presently dispersed to their homes, but Dorsey Pentecost, one of Connolly's lieutenants, went down to the Redstone settlements to organize the Virginia adherents in that neighborhood.[15]

Connolly remained in jail only a few days and then secured his release on condition that he was to answer for his conduct before the court of Westmoreland County. Upon his enlargement, he made his way to Staunton, the seat of justice for Augusta County, Virginia, and qualified

[13] Croghan to T. Wharton, Nov. 11, Dec. 23, 1772, May 11, Oct. 15, Dec. 9, 1773, *Pa. Mag. Hist. and Biog.*, XV, 431–437; T. Wharton to Croghan, Dec. 25, 1773, Wharton letter book, H.S.P.; T. Wharton to Thos. Walpole, Dec. 27, 1773, *ibid.*

[14] C. M. Burton, *John Connolly, a Tory of the Revolution* (Worcester, Mass, 1909), pp. 3–14; T. Wharton to Croghan, March 17 and 21, 1774, Wharton letter book, H.S.P.; *St. Clair Papers*, I, 271–272; *Papers of Sir William Johnson*, VIII, 1062–1066.

[15] Hamilton, *Letters to Washington*, IV, 318–321; *St. Clair Papers*, I, 279-283, 284; Craig, *The Olden Time*, I, 472–476; Crumrine, *Washington County*, p. 170; Executive Journal of the Council of Virginia, Feb. 28, 1774, C.O., series 5, 1440; *Virginia Gazette*, March 3, 1774.

to act under his commission as a magistrate in that jurisdiction. Returning to Pittsburgh, he assembled a military force, took possession of the
old Fort Pitt, evacuated by the regular troops in 1772, and renamed it
Fort Dunmore.

Meanwhile Governor Penn had entered into correspondence with the
governor of Virginia. Penn demanded that Dunmore evacuate Pittsburgh
pending a settlement of the boundary controversy, and Dunmore demanded that Penn dismiss St. Clair because of his arrest of Connolly.
The council of Virginia upheld the governor; a military force to support
Connolly was authorized and a proclamation issued to that effect.[16]

Early in April Connolly prepared to keep his appointment with the
court of Westmoreland. Collecting between a hundred and fifty and two
hundred men, he appeared before that body and demanded an audience.
Not knowing what else to do, the court granted the parley. Thereupon
the captain read a manifesto in which he denied their jurisdiction over
his person. But, he said, in order to avoid undue friction, he would not
interfere with their proceedings in such cases as might be brought before
them.[17]

The president of the Westmoreland court at this time was Colonel
William Crawford, Washington's faithful land agent. He at once wrote
a letter to Governor Penn describing the indignities heaped upon his
court by Connolly. The document was transmitted by Colonel George
Wilson, another native of Virginia who was active on the Pennsylvania
side of the controversy. A little later Crawford took a military commission under Connolly in order to repel an Indian attack, and for this act
was dismissed from his Pennsylvania office as justice of the peace. Yet
Crawford's sympathy for the Penn interest in the boundary dispute was
undoubtedly sincere, and it is significant, for his interest and that of
George Washington were the same. They were having trouble with
Croghan because he claimed lands which they had bought from the
Penns, and Dunmore was supporting Croghan's claim.[18] Even Connolly
could not face with equanimity the possibility of a wholesale validation
of Croghan's enormous land claims in the Pittsburgh area, and friction
presently arose between the Captain and his uncle on this score. But,

[16] Executive Journal of the Council of Virginia, Feb. 28, April 10, 1774, C.O., series
5, 1440; proclamation by Dunmore, April 25, 1774, Ohio Company MSS., H.S.P.;
St. Clair Papers, I, 287–291; Crumrine, Washington County, 170–172.
[17] Croghan to David Sample, April 4, 1774, Pa. Arch., series 1, IV, 483–484; Craig,
The Olden Time, I, 478–480, 482.
[18] Ibid., I, 464–468; Crumrine, Washington County, p. 173; St. Clair Papers, I, 291–
294, 352; Virginia Archives, petitions, Sept. 22, 1774; Washington-Crawford Letters,
pp. 42–46; Hamilton, Letters to Washington, IV, 378–379.

for the time being, these two Irish Pennsylvanians were working together for Dunmore and Virginia.[19]

When Connolly returned to Pittsburgh from Hanna's Town, where the court of Westmoreland was held, he immediately proceeded to arrest three of the justices who happened to live within his reach—Æneas Mackay, Andrew McFarlane, and Devereaux Smith. He packed them off to Staunton to be incarcerated, but they appealed to Dunmore and he released them. Not only that, but he reproved Connolly for the rashness of his act, warning him not to do as the Pennsylvanians did.[20] Governor Penn, nevertheless, took alarm and sent two commissioners to Williamsburg to treat with Dunmore about the boundary. They proposed an appeal to the Crown to fix the line, to which Dunmore was willing to agree, but he was not willing that Virginia should bear any part of the expense. They proposed also that Dunmore evacuate all territory east of the Monongahela pending the fixing of a permanent boundary, but this would have meant the surrender of Pittsburgh, and to that the governor of Virginia would not consent. Penn would make no terms without this condition; consequently, the negotiations broke down on the point. While Dunmore's attitude has appeared unreasonable to most writers on the subject, yet to have given up Pittsburgh would have been a complete surrender on his part.[21]

By the beginning of May, 1774, the boundary controversy seemed thus to have reached an impasse. And by this time the first blows had been struck in the struggle that came to be known as "Dunmore's War." In order to elucidate the events of this conflict it is necessary at this point to turn back to the beginning of the year and to recall the attempts that were being made to plant the first white settlements in Kentucky.

[19] Volwiler, *Croghan,* p. 301; *St. Clair Papers,* I, 313–314.

[20] Dunmore to Connolly, April 25, 1774, C.O., series 5, 1352; Executive Journal of the Council of Virginia, April 25, 1774, C.O., series 5, 1440; Devereaux Smith to Gov. Penn, June 12, 1774, *Am. Arch.,* series 4, I, 467.

[21] Crumrine, *Washington County,* pp. 175–176; Dunmore to Dartmouth, June 4, 1774, C.O., series 5, 1350; *Pa. Arch.,* X, 182–183; *Virginia Gazette,* Sept. 8, 1774.

CHAPTER VII

STRUGGLE WITH THE SHAWNEE FOR
KENTUCKY

IN September, 1773, a party of more than thirty adventurers from the Yadkin, reinforced in Powell's Valley by recruits from the Holston settlements, set out for the Kentucky country lying beyond Cumberland Gap. Their object was to seek fertile tracts of land where they might make their homes. They had not proceeded far when Indians surprised them and killed several of their number, including sons of Daniel Boone and William Russell. The whole party then retreated, and no further attempts were made to explore Kentucky during that year. Boone accompanied Russell to his home in the Clinch River valley and remained in the neighborhood until June of the following year. But before that date another and more formidable movement into Kentucky had begun.[1]

Several antagonistic factors were involved in this attempt to plant the first settlements in the remote wilderness of Kentucky, and it is only by tracing their interplay that this fascinating phase of our history can be understood. The government of Virginia, as represented by Lord Dunmore with his council and the House of Burgesses, was the most important of these factors, for nothing of a legal nature could be done without its sanction. Yet relatively little attention has been paid to governmental activities, while the adventures of the pioneers, to which time has lent the color of romance, have been dwelt upon in great detail.

The Indians, particularly the Shawnee who determined that Kentucky should not be settled by the whites, doubtless come next in importance. The murder of young Boone and Russell was supposed at the time to have been committed by the Cherokee, but it was later discovered that a roving band of Shawnee were the perpetrators. This tribe lived north of the Ohio in the valley of the Scioto, but they often hunted in Kentucky and they did not intend to have their supply of game disturbed. While the Six Nations had sold and ceded all the land on the south

---

[1] Arthur Campbell to Dunmore, Dec. 14, 1773, Add. MSS., 21672, Br. Mus. In his report of the murders, Campbell does not mention Boone. *Washington-Crawford Letters,* p. 68; Filson, *Kentucke,* p. 57.

side of the Ohio to the whites, the Shawnee, though vassals of the Six Nations, resented this disregard of what they conceived to be their rights and in 1769 formed a confederacy of Western tribes to oppose any movement of the whites into the country which they claimed. From time to time intruders were murdered, and it was abundantly clear, even before 1774, that Kentucky could not be settled without an Indian war.[2]

Another interested party was the group of Pennsylvania traders who lived about Pittsburgh and at whose head was the redoubtable George Croghan, loved by the red man but distrusted by many of those who knew him best. Of a visit made by Croghan into Virginia at this time, Levy Andrew Levy wrote to Michael Gratz, his financial backer, "he is such an artful person I make no doubt he will take some persons in in Virginia."[3] Croghan and his fellow traders carried on a traffic with the Delawares and Shawnee, and any frontier disturbance was sure to hurt their business. They therefore dreaded Indian wars, particularly as the natives often made the traders who happened to be among them the first victims of their fury. Furthermore, Croghan and several of his associates were interested in the Vandalia scheme and, therefore, did not wish to see the Virginians occupy any of the country which their organization was striving so hard to acquire.

On the Virginia side it was not Dunmore, really, who took the lead in the movement to settle Kentucky. The governor was indeed the ally, and to some extent the victim, of several groups of land-hungry Virginians. Only two of these groups were of any real importance during 1774, and hence only they will be considered at this time. Colonel George Washington as a leading proponent of the land claims of the veterans of the French and Indian War has been mentioned; and Colonel William Preston, who held nearly all the high offices, including that of surveyor, of the frontier county of Fincastle, which comprised all the Kentucky country, also has been discussed.

Among Preston's friends and associates in Fincastle Colonel William Christian is a familiar figure. Arthur Campbell and the entire Campbell connection were associates and friends of Preston. This frontier

[2] Affidavit of Thomas Sharp, Feb. 20, 1774, C.O., series 5, 75, f. 335; Dunmore to Stuart, April 5, 1774, *ibid.*, f. 339; John Stuart to Dartmouth, Dec. 15, 1774, C.O., series 5, 76; Johnson to Hillsborough, April 4, 1772, C.O., series 5, 73; Hillsborough to Johnson, July 1, 1772, A.W.I., Plantations General, 276; *Papers of Sir William Johnson,* VII, 107–108, 140–141, 182–185, 314–315, 315–317, 332, 650–654, VIII, 647–649; *Docs. Rel. Col. Hist. N. Y.,* VIII, 222–223; Carter, *Correspondence of General Thomas Gage,* I, 253–255; Shaw, *British Administration of the Southern Indians,* pp. 85–86.

[3] Byars, *B. & M. Gratz,* pp. 145–146; Hamilton, *Letters to Washington,* V, 8–9; St. Clair to Penn, June 8, 1774, *Am. Arch.,* series 4, I, 465; Craig, *The Olden Time,* II, 12–13.

magnate was also associated with Dr. Thomas Walker of the Loyal Company and was connected with Edmund Pendleton, administrator of the estate of Speaker Robinson, and with Colonel William Byrd III in the operation of Chiswell's lead mine, at which place Dunmore fixed the seat of justice of Fincastle County.[4]

Thus the speculators of Virginia's southwestern frontier had influence in Williamsburg, for Colonel Byrd was a power in official circles and Patrick Henry kept himself well informed as to Dunmore's interest in lands. It is clear, at any rate, that the governor cooperated heartily with both groups of land speculators throughout the earlier part of the year 1774. But his hands were tied to a considerable extent by orders from England.

According to the instructions of April 7, 1773, no lands were to be granted except to officers and soldiers of the French and Indian War, who had been promised tracts under the proclamation of 1763. Though it was not entirely clear that colonial troops were included in the benefits of this proclamation, Dunmore had taken a stand in favor of their claims by his action in council on the previous December 16, and had made up his mind to pursue the line of policy then initiated. Accordingly, on January 27, 1774, Preston issued notice that all those interested in taking up lands under the proclamation should meet his deputy surveyors at the mouth of the Great Kanawha on the 14th of April following.[5]

On February 2 the British Government adopted an entirely new set of instructions for the granting of lands in America. Tracts were to be surveyed in advance, and plots of one hundred to one thousand acres sold at auction to the highest bidder. At the same time the quit-rents were increased. There immediately followed a chorus of protests from colonial governors that lands could not be sold on these terms, that the incomes of the governors would be reduced by the loss of fees from this source. Shortly thereafter the home authorities made a concession by ruling that in cases where the initial steps toward taking up lands had been made before the issuance of the new regulations, grants should be made under the old system. Claims under the proclamation of 1763 had been exempted from the operation of the new instructions, but on April 6 Dunmore was given positive orders from Dartmouth not to make any grants under the proclamation pending further instructions on that head. For the time being he kept all these orders quite to him-

---

[4] Preston to Byrd, May 14, 1774, Draper MSS., 3QQ24; Preston to Pendleton, May 14, 1774, *ibid.*, 3QQ25; Pendleton to Preston, June 4, 1774, *ibid.*, 3QQ36.
[5] Hugh Mercer to Preston, Jan. 8, 1774, Draper MSS., 3QQ1; *Washington-Crawford Letters*, pp. 47–48; *Maryland Gazette*, March 10, 1774.

self, and the Virginia council went on record as favoring the claims of colonial troops, while Dartmouth expressed his doubts regarding them.[6] The manner in which the governor of Virginia flew directly in the face of his superiors at Westminster and proceeded with his Kentucky policy has been to historians a source of amazement and a cause for censure. His audacity is indeed remarkable, but the circumstances prompting it have not been adequately presented. Dunmore was fully aware that Dartmouth and a number of his associates high in the British Ministry were personally interested in the Vandalia Company. He knew also that the Kentucky River, under his own direction and with the consent of the home government, had been established as the boundary between Virginia and the Cherokee, the colony paying the expenses of the negotiations with the Indians. The lands, therefore, as far south and west as the Kentucky were definitely under the complete jurisdiction of the government of Virginia. The Vandalia project, in favor of which Dartmouth issued his prohibition against the claimants under the proclamation of 1763, had as yet no legal standing whatever. Dunmore could have been dismissed for disobeying instructions, but it is very doubtful whether grants made by him in face of those instructions could have been legally overthrown. The claims under the proclamation had been excepted from the operation of the general instructions of February 2; whereas Dartmouth, apparently on his own responsibility, issued the prohibitory orders of April 6 to Dunmore.[7] It is by no means clear that the Secretary had a right to set aside the general instructions of the Board of Trade and Privy Council by issuing these special instructions.

The hostility between Virginia and the Vandalia Company has usually been taken for granted. However, it has been pointed out in earlier chapters that the Vandalia group had powerful friends in Virginia and that the Old Dominion was remarkably passive in its attitude toward the company up until this time. But now, on April 2, 1774, a petition from the three frontier counties of Augusta, Botetourt, and Fincastle protested against the encroachment of the Vandalia claim upon lands which had been taken up under Virginia enactments. This petition

[6] Yet Thomas Lewis did hear something about the prohibitory order. Lewis to Preston, June 8, 1774, Draper MSS., 3QQ38. St. George L. Sioussat, "The Breakdown of the Royal Management of Lands in the Southern Provinces, 1773–1775," *Agricultural History*, III, 68–71; C. H. Laub, "British Regulation of Crown Lands in the West, Last Phase, 1773–1775," *William and Mary Quarterly Historical Magazine*, X (new series), 52–55; Board of Trade MSS., Oct. 28, 1773, XXXI, 1ff., H.S.P.; Orders in Council, Feb. 2, 1774, C.O., series 5, 29; Dartmouth to Dunmore, April 6, 1774, C.O., series 5, 1352; Executive Journal of the Council of Virginia, April 20, 1774, C.O., series 5, 1440.

[7] Dunmore to Dartmouth, June 9, 1774, C.O., series 5, 1350.

was presented by the governor to the assembly and forwarded to the home government. It had the approval of Dunmore, and there can be no doubt that it had the backing of that group of Western speculators which operated under the leadership of Dr. Thomas Walker and William Preston.[8]

When spring came and travelling through the back country became practicable, the new movement to Kentucky got under way. On April 7, John Floyd, a deputy surveyor of Fincastle, set out from Preston's house for Kentucky. Two other deputies, James Douglas and Hancock Taylor, went with him. Both these had accompanied Bullitt the previous year, but at that time they were not deputy surveyors under Preston. Beside the surveyors, there were Isaac Hite, grandson of the old German pioneer, Thomas Hanson, Alexander Spotswood Dandridge, grandson of Governor Spotswood, James Knox, and a number of chain carriers and others. They found their way down the Kanawha River to its mouth, meeting several parties of white men on the journey and learning from them that Indian hostilities had already occurred in the neighborhood. The Shawnee apparently under the influence of Croghan's partisans, let it be understood that they intended to kill the Long Knives, as they called the Virginians, and rob the Pennsylvanians whom they might find in the country.

On reaching the mouth of the Kentucky, Floyd's party made camp and waited several days for a group which Colonel William Russell, on instructions from Preston, was sending out to locate the line John Donelson had surveyed in 1771. They were not certain whether it followed the Kentucky or Cumberland River, and Floyd understood that the explorers were to meet him at the mouth of the former stream in case the line ran that way. But no one came to them and they proceeded down the Ohio to the Falls.[9]

Here they resurveyed the plots which Bullitt had marked out for Connolly and Campbell the previous year. This was not merely a matter of form, though Dunmore had already granted patents on these tracts. Preston had signed Bullitt's original surveys when urged to do so by the governor, but this had raised a storm of protest, he said, and he accordingly refused to authenticate any other surveys made by surveyors not properly deputized by him. Since Dr. Thomas Walker con-

[8] Dunmore to Dartmouth, April 2, 1774, C.O., series 5, 1352. A copy of the petition and correspondence concerned therewith, under date of June 9, is to be found in P.R.O., P.C. 1, 60 (Colonial B, 10).

[9] Deposition of John Floyd, Oct. 28, 1776, *C.V.S.P.*, I, 309–311; Thwaites and Kellogg, eds., *Dunmore's War*, pp. 4–6; Hanson's journal, *ibid.*, pp. 110ff.; original in Draper MSS., 24CC1–40.

sulted with Preston and Thomas Lewis in the matter one is led to suspect that it was he who registered the objection to Bullitt's surveys. Certainly Preston and Walker meant to keep Kentucky in their own hands.[10]

Bullitt's backers were sufficiently influential to secure from the governor and council, on May 3, 1774, a recommendation to Preston that his surveys of 1773 be validated, but Preston ignored the request. The consequence was that, except for the Connolly and Campbell tracts at the Falls, Bullitt's surveys were either resurveyed or completely disregarded by Floyd and his men. Several of the choice salt-lick tracts, which Bullitt had hoped to secure for himself, were resurveyed by Floyd's party for William Christian.[11]

The surveys made by Floyd, Taylor, and Douglas were in tracts of one, two, and three thousand acres and were executed under authority of the proclamation of 1763. Some of them were for actual veterans of the last war, but many were for men who had bought the rights of such veterans. Whether coming under the one category or the other, most of the beneficiaries were of the Preston-Walker group of speculators, including Patrick Henry, William Byrd III, John May, William Fleming, Andrew Lewis, Arthur Campbell, William Christian and their friends. One of the first surveys, however, was executed for Colonel George Washington.[12]

The exploring party which failed to meet Floyd at the mouth of the Kentucky actually performed the task assigned to it and traced Donelson's survey to the Kentucky River. But instead of following that stream to its mouth where Floyd awaited, it retraced its steps and reported the result of its work to Preston.[13] It was now understood that Virginia had no right to grant lands beyond or below the Kentucky except such as it acquired by cession of the Six Nations at Fort Stanwix. And there were positive orders from England not to occupy this

[10] *C.V.S.P.*, I, 307–319; Hamilton, *Letters to Washington,* IV, 345–347; Walker to Lewis, March 1, 1774, Draper MSS., 3QQ10; Thomas Lewis to Preston, March 15, 1774, *ibid.*, 3QQ13; Henderson, *Walker,* pp. 72–73.

[11] Bullitt to Fleming, March 12, 1774, Fleming MSS., W. and L. U. library; Bullitt to Preston, May 4, 1774, Draper MSS., 3QQ22; Executive Journal of the Council, of Virginia, May 3, 1774, C.O., series 5, 1440.

[12] Philip Fall Taylor, "Calendar of Warrants for Land in Kentucky Granted for Service in the French and Indian War," *Kentucky Society of Colonial Wars* (Frankfort, 1917) pp. 64ff.; "Leestown," address by Judge S. M. Wilson, *Register of the Kentucky State Historical Society,* XXIX, 385; list of surveys, 1774, Breckinridge MSS., L. of C.; Floyd to Preston, April 26, 1774, *Dunmore's War,* p. 7; Dandridge to Preston, May 15, 1774, Draper MSS., 3QQ26.

[13] Russell to Preston, May 7, 1774, *Dunmore's War,* pp. 19–22; Preston to Samuel McDowell, May 27, 1774, *ibid.*, pp. 25–26; Russell to Preston, May 7, 1774, Hamilton, *Letters to Washington,* V., 2.

territory. Hence, no one could have expected that Floyd's surveys at the Falls would lead to any actual grants in the near future. The object in such cases always was to get a claim marked out with the hope that this would give a prior right when it finally became possible to secure grants in the region.

While Floyd and his party, the official Virginia surveyors, were carrying on their work in Kentucky, several other groups of speculators were in the same country carrying on the same work in a quasi-official capacity. Colonel, later General, William Thompson, who had visited Kentucky in 1773 in the interest of the Pennsylvania claimants under the proclamation of 1763, returned in 1774. In the meantime he had organized his clients and had gone to Williamsburg and secured a commission as deputy surveyor from the College of William and Mary. He now made a number of surveys on the north fork of the Licking and the next year returned to the Virginia capital to get his work ratified, but Preston's stand had blocked the path of any one who surveyed in Kentucky without his approval, even though holding a commission from the College, and Thompson came off empty-handed.[14]

But a greater man than Thompson was in the field. Colonel George Washington had enough influence in Williamsburg to secure a commission from the College for his land agent, William Crawford. Not only this, but he was able to bring enough pressure to bear upon Thomas Lewis, surveyor of Augusta County, to have Crawford made a deputy surveyor for that jurisdiction. Lewis complied grudgingly, but both he and Preston refused to approve the surveys which had previously been made for Washington by Crawford in the expectation that it would fall to the Vandalia government to validate them.[15] Yet Washington had as much influence with Dunmore as did Preston, and he and Crawford could now proceed with their plans without hindrance. Their immediate scheme was to settle a colony of German redemptioners on the Kanawha tract which Dunmore had already granted to the master of Mount Vernon under the proclamation of 1754. Crawford collected the laborers and supplies at his home on the Monongahela and was preparing to send them down the river when a temporary stop was put to his plans by the outbreak of Indian disturbances.[16]

[14] A.S.P., XVI, Public Lands, I, 583.
[15] Washington to Preston, Feb. 28, 1774, letter in possession of Mrs. John Preston, Seven Mile Ford, Va.; Thomas Lewis to Preston, March 15, 1774, Draper MSS., 3QQ13; Washington to Thomas Lewis, Feb. 17, 1774, Fitzpatrick, Writings of George Washington, III, 182–184; Hamilton Letters to Washington, IV, 331-332.
[16] During the previous year Washington had tried to lease some of these lands. Draper MSS., 13J179; Hamilton, Letters to Washington, IV., 251–252; Washington-

Both Crawford and Thompson had standing as surveyors, but an equally famous man made his way to Kentucky in the spring of 1774 without legal backing of any kind. This was James Harrod of the Monongahela country who, despite the handicap of being unable to read or write, was becoming a power in the West. Leaving his home on Ten Mile Creek in May, he returned to the spot which he had visited in 1773 and, with a party of forty-one men, began laying the foundations of Harrodsburg on Salt River.[17] This place was southwest of the Kentucky, and hence it certainly was not open to occupation, nor did Harrod have any claims under the proclamation of 1763. The tracts which he surveyed were of four hundred acres, known as settlement rights, with a thousand acres additional, known as preemption rights. He was pinning his hope to the old statutes of 1752 and 1754 for encouraging settlers on the waters of the Mississippi. He knew that it might be some years before he could get legal grants, but whenever the country should be opened he expected to be on the ground with the first claim. And he knew that Dunmore was doing all he could to hasten the day. Speculation in those times was real speculation.

Still another group of prospectors should be considered. While Floyd was making his way to the mouth of the Kentucky an obscure young man by the name of George Rogers Clark was at the mouth of the Little Kanawha with a party of eighty or ninety men, which included Michael Cresap, son of Thomas and leading spirit in the Redstone settlement, and Isaac Zane, founder of Wheeling. In the fall of 1772 Clark, a native of Albemarle County, Virginia, had settled at Fish Creek on the Ohio and had been clearing a farm and carrying on surveying operations in the neighborhood.[18] Now his party was supplied with all necessary provisions and planned to descend the Ohio and cooperate with Floyd in taking up lands under the proclamation of 1763. But an untoward train of events occurred to interrupt their proceedings.

Hearing that a band of Indians had attacked a small party of whites a few miles below their camp, the men on the Little Kanawha held a council to decide what to do. They were determined not to turn back,

Crawford Letters, 46–50; 85–92; Roy B. Cook, *Washington's Western Lands,* p. 38.
[17] Gen'l Robert B. McAfee to Benjamin Hardin, n.d., Durrett MSS., University of Chicago; Withers, 190–191. A list of the members of the party is given in Draper MSS., 14J128.
[18] John B. Ray to Jonathan Clark, Nov. 22, 1772, Draper MSS., IL8; George R. Clark to Jonathan Clark, Jan. 7, 1773, *ibid.,* IL9; James A. James, ed., *George Rogers Clark Papers* (Springfield, 1926) p. 2.

and their first impulse was to attack an Indian village at the mouth of the Scioto. Electing Michael Cresap their leader, they took his advice and refrained from attacking at once, but fell back up the Ohio to Wheeling to await developments.[19] From this point they got in touch with Captain John Connolly at Pittsburgh. Connolly sent couriers to the Shawnee to know their intentions and received replies indicating that they intended to take to the war-path. On April 21 he sent a message to Cresap to this effect, and on the 26th following, Cresap communicated the information to his men.[20]

The next day a boat came down the river containing two traders and two Indians, who were in the employ of Richard Butler of Pittsburgh. The Indians were fired on and killed, and it seems certain that Cresap's party was responsible. The following day his men attacked a small party of Shawnee, killing one of them, and on the 30th Chief Logan's family was murdered in a most atrocious manner by one Greathouse and his party at Baker's Bottom. Some Delawares and a few Cherokee were involved in this bush-whacking warfare, but the Shawnee were the principal objects of attack on the part of the Virginians.[21]

An Indian war was now almost inevitable. Dunmore and Connolly are commonly given credit for having fomented it to further their own ends, but it is hard to see how this could have been the case. Surveyors would certainly not have been sent into Kentucky and then the Indians turned loose on them. War was resolved upon only when it became clear that the Shawnee did not intend to permit the peaceable settlement of the country, and Connolly seems to have acted with reasonable restraint. Though Cresap discouraged attacks on several occasions and though he was not guilty of the murder of Logan's family, yet he led several forays and may be said to have taken the lead in fomenting hostilities, but he did it only after he had received word from Connolly that peace could not be expected. What Cresap and his men really wanted was to settle Kentucky, not to engage in an Indian war which would postpone settlement.[22]

Connolly at once communicated with Dunmore; and the governor, on April 28, authorized him to call out the militia and to take all pos-

[19] George R. Clark's letter, June 17, 1798, Draper MSS., 27CC45–46.
[20] Letters from Redstone, Oct., 1774, *Am. Arch.*, series 4, I, 1015–1016.
[21] Withers, p. 134ff.; Doddridge, p. 229; Hall, *Sketches of the West*, I, 196ff.; affidavit of John Gibson, *Writings of Thomas Jefferson* (Mem. ed.) II, 308–310; Ebenezer Zane to John Brown, Feb. 3, 1800, *ibid.*, II, 310–311; deposition of James Chambers, *ibid.*, 313–315; *Pennsylvania Gazette*, May 25, 1774, Draper MSS., 14J56; Devereux Smith to Dr. Smith, June 10, 1774, *Am. Arch.*, series 4, I, 467–471.
[22] Virgil A. Lewis, *History of the Battle of Point Pleasant* (Charleston, W. Va., 1909) pp. 15–16.

sible measures for the protection of the inhabitants. Nevertheless, the country west of the Monongahela was almost completely evacuated as soon as hostilities began. In order to check this panic-stricken movement of the frontier people Connolly sent a hundred militiamen down to Wheeling, and under the management of Colonels William Crawford, Angus McDonald, and Dorsey Pentecost they commenced the construction of Fort Fincastle at that place.[23]

Dunmore called on the House of Burgesses for help, but that body authorized him to go no further than to use the militia under existing statutes. Almost immediately afterward it was dissolved by the governor for having voted, in Puritanical fashion, for a day of fasting and prayer on the occasion of the passage of the Boston Port Bill.[24] The elderly but irate Landon Carter wrote that the governor and council "wants 1200 men to fight the Pennsylvanians. I'd rather save them for Boston a great deal." Richard Henry Lee wrote to his brother William, "Our assembly meets in February next, when it is expected much dislike will be taken at the Indian measures of Lord Dunmore on our frontier this summer. We hear that more than £100,000 will not defray expence. . . ." Tidewater Virginians in general had little interest in Indian wars. They knew the cost to them would much outweigh any immediate benefits. Even in the West there was a feeling among the people that they were being called on to fight the Indians for the benefit of a few speculators. It is noteworthy also that the passage of the momentous Quebec Act in April, 1774, produced so little excitement in Virginia, although, in extending the Canadian boundary to the Ohio, it deprived Virginia of millions of acres which she had hitherto claimed.[25]

All that Dunmore could do for the moment, therefore, was to instruct the commanders of the western counties to raise sufficient militia to enable Colonel Andrew Lewis to build and man a fort at the mouth of the Great Kanawha. Connolly did all in his power to put Fort Dun-

---

[23] *Papers of Sir William Johnson*, VIII, 1152–1153; Hamilton, *Letters to Washington*, V, 3–7; *Dunmore's War*, pp. 37–38, 101–102; Pentecost to Wm. Harrod, July 20, 1774, Draper MSS., 4NN9; *Am. Arch.*, series 4, I, 454; Crumrine, *Washington County*, pp. 65–74; *Virginia Gazette*, June 9, 23, 1774.

[24] *Journals of the House of Burgesses, 1773–1776*, May 12, 1774, pp. 92–93; notice posted by Dunmore, June 10, 1774, C.O., series 5, 1353; Justin Winsor, "Virginia and the Quebec Bill," *American Historical Review*, I, 436–443.

[25] R. H. Lee to Wm. Lee, Dec. 15, 1774, misc. MSS., library of W. H. Mason, Evanston, Ill. (now in Yale library); Edmund Randolph, "Essay on the Revolutionary History of Virginia," *Virginia Magazine of History and Biography*, XLIII, 211–213; deposition of Adam Wallace, *ibid.*, XIII, 45–46; *William and Mary Quarterly Historical Magazine*, XIV, 183. The author has not been able to find any complaint against the territorial phase of the Quebec Act. Its religious provisions were criticized in the *Virginia Gazette*, Sept. 1, 15, 29, Oct. 6, 1774. See C. H. Metzger, *The Quebec Act* (New York, 1936) pp. 68, 84, 90.

more, at Pittsburgh, in readiness, and this chain of forts was to furnish the nucleus for a defensive war against the Shawnee.[26]

Meanwhile the Pennsylvania traders who had headquarters at Pittsburgh were much excited over the situation. Their agents who happened to be in the Shawnee towns when hostilities broke out were in grave danger. They might lose their lives, and their employers their profits. But anxiety was relieved when three Shawnee chiefs conducted the traders safely to Croghan's house. Here, however, the chiefs were fired upon by some of Connolly's men, and immediately afterward Connolly posted notice forbidding all trade with hostile Indians. Croghan now wrote to Governor Penn that Connolly was trying to destroy the trade of the community and proposed that the Pennsylvania merchants should evacuate Pittsburgh and establish a trading post at Kittanning.[27] At the same time Croghan cooperated with Connolly, Campbell, and McKee to keep the Delawares peaceable, in which effort they succeeded. Simultaneously Sir William Johnson was holding a conference with the Six Nations at Johnson Hall; they also were kept out of the fight, but death overtook Sir William before the conference was ended.[28]

It appears from this that Croghan's position was peculiar in the circumstances. Two conflicting interests were involved, trade and land speculation, and he was affected by both. On one hand, he was cooperating with Penn, St. Clair, and the Pennsylvania merchants to keep the Indian trade open; and on the other, he was still in touch with Dunmore, Campbell, and his nephew Connolly. John Campbell, though a Pennsylvanian trader of the Gratz group, cooperated with Connolly because of their joint interests in land, and possibly in trade also.[29]

The Virginians did not intend to permit the Indian trade to go on while hostilities were in progress, for the sinews of war, in the form of arms and ammunition, were furnished the savages through that channel.

[26] Apparently the first plan was for Lewis to build a fort at the mouth of the Kentucky, Dunmore to A. Lewis, July 12, 1774, Draper MSS., 46J7. Dunmore to Preston, July 3, 1774, ibid., 3QQ53; Randolph C. Downes, "Dunmore's War, an Interpretation," in M.V.H.R., XXI, 325–326; John Campbell to M. Gratz, May 30, 1774, misc. MSS., I, 152, H. S. P.; Virginia Gazette, July 14, 1774; St. Clair Papers, I, 322–323.

[27] Ibid., I, 312–313, 316, 325–327, 340–343; Pa. Arch., series 1, IV, 521; Am. Arch., series 4, I, 429, 473–475, 483; Wm. Wilson to Gratz Brothers, May 31, 1774, Byars, B. & M. Gratz, p. 144; Craig, Olden Time, I, 499–500.

[28] McKee's journal, May 1 to June 9, 1774, Am. Arch., series 4, I, 475–483; Sir Wm. Johnson to Gov. Franklin, June 27, 1774, Add. MSS., 29237, Br. Mus.; Pa. Arch., series 1, IV, 531–533; St. Clair Papers, I, 327–331; Croghan to Thomas Wharton, Aug. 10 and 12, 1774, Pa. Mag. Hist. and Biog., XV, 437–439.

[29] Executive Journal of the Council of Virginia, May 26, 1774, C.O., series 5, 1440; St. Clair to Penn, May 29, 1774, Am. Arch., series 4, I, 463; Croghan to St. Clair, June 4, 1774, ibid., I, 465–466; Byars, B. & M. Gratz, pp. 142–143; St. Clair Papers, I, 303–304.

The Pennsylvanians were equally determined that the trade should not be interrupted. In the usual American fashion, historians have put a righteous face upon the cause of the merchants. In this case their glory lay in their friendship for the natives and their pacifism. On the other hand, they were often charged with buying goods the natives had stolen from the whites, and it was suspected that they had a hand in encouraging the Shawnee to repel or kill the Virginians who were attempting to settle Kentucky.[30]

Thus, in the Pittsburgh area the war developed into a struggle between Pennsylvania merchants and Virginia land speculators, quite as much as a war between the whites and the Indians. And the boundary controversy between Virginia and Pennsylvania, being at its height, came in to complicate matters further. Both sides had, of course, appealed to the home government. Dartmouth wrote to Dunmore that the difference could not be settled by the British authorities on their responsibility alone, but that commissioners from the two provinces involved would have to be appointed and their expenses provided for and that he did not suppose Virginia would be interested in doing this until she knew definitely whether or not the Vandalia Company would control the lands west and south of the Pennsylvania line when established. For the time being Dartmouth gave his approval to Dunmore's control of Pittsburgh, and the Virginia council fixed upon Turtle Creek as the eastern limit of her *de facto* jurisdiction in that neighborhood.[31]

Meanwhile the surveyors who were operating in Kentucky were in great danger. Christian, Preston, and Arthur Campbell were much concerned about the safety of Floyd and his men, but it was William Russell who acted in their behalf. Daniel Boone, a ranger of considerable experience but not yet known to fame, had been living in Russell's Clinch River neighborhood ever since the repulse of his Kentucky expedition of the previous year. Russell now engaged him and Michael Stoner, another experienced woodsman, to go to the Falls of the Ohio to warn Floyd and the other surveyors that the Indians were on the war-path. They set out on June 26 and were gone for the space of sixty-two days. We know that they visited Harrod who was busily laying the foundations of his Salt-River settlement, but there is no record of

[30] Connolly to Washington, June 7, 1774, Hamilton, *Letters to Washington,* V, 8–9; Adam Stephen to R. H. Lee, Aug. 27, 1774, *Am. Arch.,* series 4, I, 739–740; *ibid.,* I, 872–876.

[31] Executive Journal of the Council of Virginia, May 28, 1774, C.O., series 5, 1440; Dartmouth to Dunmore, June 1, 1774, C.O., series 5, 1352; same to same, Aug. 3, 1774, *ibid.*

their having made direct contact with Floyd's party. If they reached the Falls of the Ohio, Floyd had returned to the region of the Kentucky River before they got there. Hanson, who kept a journal of Floyd's expedition, makes no mention of Boone. If Boone, according to his claim, as phrased by Filson, conducted the surveyors back to the settlements it was not the surveyors whom he went especially to warn.[32]

What actually happened was this: a party of ten prospectors, including James Knox, who were in the neighborhood of Harrod's cabins, were attacked on July 8 by the Indians, and two of them were killed. On July 10 the survivors warned Harrod and his party of thirty-five, who at once quitted the country. On the 8th, Floyd's party, which was surveying on the Kentucky River, divided into two groups with the agreement that they were to meet at Harrod's. One of these parties, including James Douglas and Isaac Hite, reached the rendezvous on July 22. It evidently discovered what had happened and immediately left, some of its members going back to the settlements and some going down the river to New Orleans. When Floyd's party reached the spot two days later it found two fires burning and a note on a tree telling of the circumstances under which the camp had been evacuated. Floyd and his men also retreated to the settlements, but Hancock Taylor did not accompany them. He was killed· by the Indians as he traveled homeward. Thus the end of the year 1774 found Kentucky with many new land claims established by the surveyors, but not a single white man had yet made his home permanently in the vast region.[33]

While the surveyors were still in Kentucky, Dunmore, on July 5, signed a large number of land grants. Most of them were for small tracts in the eastern part of Virginia. The usual payment of ten shillings per hundred acres was made, and the governor was acting quite within his instructions in case the initial steps had been taken by the grantees before the orders of February 2, 1774, were issued. But a few of the grants of this date were made under authority of the proclamation of 1763. None of them involved Kentucky lands, but two tracts were in the much-disputed area about Pittsburgh. One of these lay on Chartiers' Creek, land which George Croghan had long claimed, and it was issued to Colonel George Washington. Dartmouth now wrote Dunmore, ap-

[32] R. S. Cotterill, "Kentucky in 1774," Filson Club, *Historical Quarterly*, I, 25–34; Christian to Preston, June 22, 1774, Draper MSS., 3QQ42; Russell to Preston, June 26, 1774, *ibid.*, 3QQ46; *Dunmore's War*, pp. 49–51, 52–55.

[33] Hanson's journal, *Dunmore's War*, pp. 130–133; *Kentucky Society of Colonial Wars*, p. 65; Preston to Printer of the *Virginia Gazette*, Aug. 13, 1774, *Virginia Gazette*, Sept. 8, 1774, also in *Am. Arch.*, series 4, I, 707–708; report of Sept. 14, 1774, *ibid.*, I, 787; *Virginia Gazette*, Sept. 15, 1774.

parently at the instance of Samuel Wharton, a pointed letter again forbidding the granting of Western lands.[34]

On July 24, the day Floyd arrived at Harrod's deserted camp, Dunmore gave up his defensive policy against the Shawnee and directed Andrew Lewis to march his forces to Point Pleasant, at the mouth of the Great Kanawha. He was to build a fort there and await the arrival of the governor with another body of men who were to come down the Ohio from Pittsburgh.[35] In order to direct operations from thence, the governor proceeded in person to that point, issued a proclamation asserting the jurisdiction of Virginia, and was soon in conference with the local leaders. Croghan consulted him and gave it out that the governor had promised to validate his land claims in the neighborhood, though it is not certain that Dunmore knew just how extensive these were. Croghan still had hopes, however, that the Vandalia colony might be established and that he might hold his lands under that jurisdiction.[36]

But if Croghan was still hopeful and Dartmouth was still persistent in regard to Vandalia, Joseph Galloway and Governor William Franklin were losing confidence, and Sir William Johnson, shortly before his death, was writing to Dunmore in behalf of Joseph Chew who sought a grant from Virginia. Samuel Wharton and Walpole presented another Vandalia petition to the government during this period. But Benjamin Franklin had lost office and influence and had given up his holdings in the company with the understanding that he was to be reinstated in case the situation should ever take on a brighter face. At this time he wrote to his friend, the Bishop of St. Asaph, that he would as soon see the emigrants people Nova Scotia, where he owned land, as to move to Ohio, for he had declined his share in the Ohio purchase.[37]

Croghan made himself useful to Dunmore in bringing the Indian chiefs to confer with him, and in this manner friendly relations with

[34] Virginia Land Office, Patents, book 42, pp. 516, 520, et passim; Dartmouth to Dunmore, July 6, 1774, C.O., series 5, 1352; Thomas to Samuel Wharton, July 5, 1774, Pa. Mag. Hist. and Biog., XXXIII, 433.

[35] Dunmore to Lewis, July 24, 1774, Dunmore's War, pp. 97–98; Virginia Gazette, Oct. 13, 1774.

[36] Dunmore to Dartmouth, Aug. 14, 1774, C.O., series 5, 1352; "extract of a letter from a gentleman at Redstone," Aug. 18, 1774, Am. Arch., series 4, I, 722–724; Craig, Olden Time, I, 506; Croghan to B. Gratz, Sept. 24, 1774, Gratz-Croghan MSS., I, 38, H.S.P.

[37] Thomas Wharton to Walpole, May 2, 1774, Pa. Mag. Hist. and Biog., XXXIII, 330–332; T. to S. Wharton, May 5, 1774, Wharton letter book, H.S.P.; T. Wharton to Walpole, Aug. 2, 1774, ibid.; Wm. Franklin to Sir Wm. Johnson, May 25, 1774, Add. MSS., 29237, Br. Mus.; Galloway to Richard Jackson, Aug. 10, 1774, Historical Manuscripts Commission, Fourteenth Report, Appendix, Part X, p. 242; Benj. Franklin to the Bishop of St. Asaph, March 15, 1774, Franklin-St. Asaph MSS., library of W. H. Mason, Evanston, Illinois.

the Delawares were maintained, Chief White Eyes being particularly helpful. Largely through this channel contact was made with the Shawnee, and Croghan was hopeful that peace might be established with them also. It was agreed that White Eyes and a few other Delawares were to visit their towns and bring their chiefs to consult with Dunmore at the mouth of the Little Kanawha. On September 14 the Virginia Executive issued an order, in pursuance of royal instructions, proclaiming his jurisdiction over the country west of Laurel Hill, and on the 17th he marched with about twelve hundred men for the Indian country.[38]

When Colonel Lewis reached Point Pleasant, he found in a hollow tree a message from the governor.[39] It was an order to march on and join forces with Dunmore at the mouth of the Little Kanawha. But Lewis had to await arrival of supplies and was still at Point Pleasant when day began to break on October 10. Two members of the force who had gone out early for the purpose of hunting were fired on by Indians who had crossed the Ohio on rafts during the night. A general engagement followed which has come to be known as the Battle of Point Pleasant. The contest was severe and the issue doubtful until a flank movement led by Captains George Matthews and John Stuart and Lieutenant Isaac Shelby caused Cornstalk, the Shawnee chief, to believe that reinforcements had arrived, and the Indians retired. Young Lieutenant Shelby was the son of the Welsh pioneer, Evan Shelby, who also was in the battle in command of the Fincastle troops and who near the close of the fray directed the action at the front. Colonel Andrew Lewis had lost his brother, Major Charles Lewis, and Colonel William Fleming had been seriously wounded. The casualties were heavy on both sides, for it was the greatest pitched battle fought with the natives between the French and Indian War and the outbreak of the Revolution.[40]

Meanwhile Dunmore had received word by Chief White Eyes that the Shawnee refused to make peace; he at once broke camp and marched toward their villages on the Scioto, sending word to Lewis to meet him on the march. Reaching these towns, he found them deserted and soon learned that the native denizens had engaged Colonel Andrew Lewis at Point Pleasant. They were now ready to sue for peace and

---

[38] Dunmore to Dartmouth, Sept. 16, 1774, C.O., series 5, 1353; *St. Clair Papers*, I, 331–335; *Dunmore's War*, pp. x–xi; Valentine Crawford to Washington, Oct. 1, 1774, *Washington-Crawford Letters*, pp. 97–100; *Virginia Gazette*, Nov. 17, 1774.

[39] *Dunmore's War*, p. 285 and note.

[40] Some accounts say they were to meet at the mouth of Hockhocking. Col. John Stuart, "Memoir of Indian Wars," *Collections of the Virginia Historical and Philosophical Society*, I, 37–66; J. F. D. Smyth, *A Tour in the United States of America* (London, 1784) II, 158–173; Virgil A. Lewis, *History of the Battle of Point Pleasant* p. 48.

Dunmore readily accepted their proposition; the treaty of Camp Charlotte was accordingly drawn up. The Shawnee agreed to return all prisoners, to refrain from hunting on the south side of the Ohio, and they gave hostages for their good conduct. A young Englishman saw these hostages in Winchester, on their way to Williamsburg, and described them as follows:

They are tall, manly, well-shaped men, of a Copper colour with black hair, quick piercing eyes, and good features. They have rings of silver in their nose and bobs to them which hang over their upper lip. Their ears are cut from the tips two thirds of the way round and the piece extended with brass wire till it touches their shoulders, in this part they hang a thin silver plate, wrought in flourishes about three inches diameter, with plates of silver round their arms and in the hair, which is all cut off except a long lock on the top of the head. They are in white men's dress, except breeches which they refuse to wear, instead of which they have a girdle round them with a piece of cloth drawn through their legs and turned over the girdle, and appears like a short apron before and behind. All the hair is pulled from their eye-brows and eyelashes and their faces painted in different parts with Vermilion. They walk remarkably straight and cut a grotesque appearance in this mixed dress.[41]

At Camp Charlotte, Dunmore arranged for another conference to be held at Pittsburgh the following year to arrive at a more formal agreement.[42]

Thus ended Dunmore's War. The home government and the Virginia House of Burgesses opposed the governor's policy, and Lewis's army was disgusted that it was not allowed to pursue its advantage to a more convincing conclusion. It was clear from the first that Dunmore wished nothing more than that the Shawnee cease interfering in the settlement of Kentucky.[43]

Numerous charges have been made to the effect that Dunmore's activities in this whole struggle were thoroughly aggressive and purely selfish. It should already be apparent that his policy was by no means excessively aggressive so far as the Indians were concerned. As for his selfish aims, it is certainly true that he was ambitious to acquire lands. He was interested in one important land company, and on June 20 the

---

[41] *Journal of Nicholas Cresswell*, p. 49.

[42] Chief Logan's famous speech [see *Jefferson's Notes on the State of Virginia* (Baltimore, 1800) appendix no. 4] is supposed to have been delivered to John Gibson, interpreter at this treaty. John J. Jacob, in his *Life of the Late Captain Michael Cresap* (Cincinnati, 1866) pp. 94–95, says that Logan was not present on the occasion, and that Gibson, whose Indian wife was Logan's sister, composed the speech. Yet Draper came to the conclusion that Logan actually delivered it. Dunmore to Dartmouth, Dec. 24, 1774, C.O., series 5, 1353; T. to S. Wharton, Oct. 25, 1774, Wharton letter book, H.S.P.; *Dunmore's War*, p. 303; *Washington-Crawford Letters*, pp. 54–57.

[43] Dartmouth to Dunmore, Nov. 2, 1774, C.O., series 5, 1352.

Board of Trade had rejected his petition for a grant of one hundred thousand acres to himself individually.[44] Patrick Henry, in Philadelphia to attend the Continental Congress, grew very chatty on the subject over Thomas Wharton's breakfast table. An account of this conversation regarding Dunmore's activities was immediately relayed by Wharton to Thomas Walpole in London:

. . . As I am on the subject of Vandalia, I cannot help but give you a detail of a very singular annecdote I was yesterday favored with by Mr. Henry, one of the Delegates from Virginia, attending the Congress. He is a man of the highest character, an Eminent Lawyer, & man of greatest activities. He called at my House to Breakfast with me, & we soon entered into conversation respecting the new Colony; as he was very desirous of knowing the general tenor of the constitution, I gave it to him, to which he said that on these General & Catholic principles, there cannot be the least doubt but that it would Settle at a most rapid rate. I told him certainly would had not their governor (Lord Dunmore) taken up arms against the Indians, which created a war between them & us & consequently drove the inhabitants from the New Colony, who were making very great improvements. He replied, Lord Dunmore is your greatest friend, what he is doing will forever hereafter secure the peace of your Colony by driving the Indians to an amazing distance from you. I opposed this by such arguments as occurred & put some leading questions to discover if possible the real intentions of Dunmore for prosecuting this unjust war and was happy enough to succeed. He replied that he was well acquainted with the Secret Springs of this affair & knew it would ultimately tend in the greatest happiness of the proprietors of Vandalia. I then begged him to explain himself, as we were really ignorant thereof, on which he said that he was at Williamburg with Ld Dunmore when Doct Connolly first came there, that Connolly is a chatty, Sensible man, & informed Dunmore of the Extream richness of the Land which lay on both sides of the Ohio; that the prohibitive orders which had just been sent him relative to the Land on the hither side (or Vandalia) had caused him to turn his thoughts to the opposite shore, and that as his Lordship was determined to settle his family in America, he was really pursuing this war in order to obtain by purchase or treaty from the Natives a tract of Territory on that Side; he then told me he was convinced from every authority that the law knew that a purchase from the natives was as full & ample a title as could be obtained; that they had Ld Camden & Mr. Yorke's opinions on that head, which opinion with some others Ld Dunmore had consulted, had, with the knowledge Connolly had given him of the quality of the Country & his determined resolution to Settle his family on this continent, were the real motives or springs to the present expedition. This gentleman than asked me if I knew where he could buy some Indian goods, I told him where but said it is not possible you mean to enter the Indian Trade at this period. He laughingly said the Wish World is my Hobby horse, from whence I

[44] Board of Trade to Committee of Council for Plantation Affairs, June 20, 1774, C.O., series 5, 1369, f. 363; Journal of the Board of Trade, Feb. 4, 1774, LXXXII, 14, H.S.P.; *St. Clair Papers*, I, 296–302.

concluded he has some prospect of making a purchase of the Natives, but where I know not. It seems he has a Survey on the Ohio just below the Scioto, he also said that he with two other lawyers had been consulted on the right the Crown had to make our Grant, as it was within the limits of Virginia. Their reply was that the Crown had an undoubted right to grant the territory of Vandalia & that We sh^d have no opposition, he believed, from Virginia. . . .[45]

Patrick Henry's version was only partly correct. Certainly it was not customary for royal governors personally to lead the militia against savages who were threatening frontiersmen on the rim of civilization. It is probable that Dunmore seized this opportunity to judge for himself of the desirability of the land to the westward. He certainly must have hoped to profit in some way from his policy, but Henry was apparently wrong in thinking that the lands north of the Ohio were his immediate objective. The settlement of central Kentucky was obviously his chief concern. The treaty at Fort Charlotte proves that he had no immediate intention of opening up the lands north of the Ohio. On the other hand, it was alleged at the time, and apparently with much reason, that he was Connolly's secret partner in speculations in Kentucky lands. Needless to say, his activities did not give much satisfaction to the Pennsylvanians, and he was little more successful in winning supporters in Virginia. His historical reputation has suffered from this fact.

[45] Thos. Wharton to Thos. Walpole, Sept. 23, 1774, Wharton letter book, H.S.P. Wharton already had information of the Camden-Yorke opinion, and he probably knew how Dunmore had been apprised of it. See following chapter.

CHAPTER VIII

THE ILLINOIS AND WABASH LAND COMPANIES

IT is difficult to follow the tracks of land speculators, so eager were many of them to pass on to posterity or to unsuspecting investors the property which they had acquired without leaving too much evidence as to the means by which they acquired it. In this manner they paid a delicate and undeserved compliment to the economic conscience of the American people. But "for ways that were dark and for tricks that were vain," the Illinois and Wabash Companies were peculiar. The little that is known of them leaves much to be desired, but even that little makes a stranger story than has yet been told in regard to their operations.

In 1757 Charles Pratt, then the English attorney-general and later to become the Earl of Camden, in conjunction with Charles Yorke, solicitor-general and son of Lord Chancellor Hardwicke, issued a legal opinion to the Crown in which they stated that "In respect to such places, as have been or shall be acquired by treaty or grant from the Grand Mogul or any of the Indian princes or governments, your Majesties letters patents are not necessary, the property of the soil vesting in the grantees by the Indian grants." [1] On April 1, 1772, William Trent made a copy of this opinion, leaving out the words "the Grand Mogul," thereby making it appear that the opinion might be applied to "Indian princes" in America. Trent was not the man to have dug up this opinion for himself, and by 1772 Yorke was dead. Camden, however, was now a leading member of the Vandalia Company and in that connection had had considerable business with Trent. It must have been Camden who suggested to Trent the copying of the opinion which he and his colleague had handed down in 1757 in regard to India. [2]

With the opinion there went a letter to George Croghan signed by

---

[1] C. W. Alvord, ed., *Illinois-Ouabache Land Company Manuscripts* (Chicago, 1915) p. 11; T. C. and M. J. Pease, *George Rogers Clark and the Revolution in Illinois, 1763–1787* (Springfield, 1929) pp. 23–25; Alvord, *Mississippi Valley in British Politics,* II, 200.

[2] Alvord, *The Illinois Country, 1673–1818* (Chicago, 1922) pp. 300–302; Alvord, *The Illinois-Ouabache Manuscripts,* pp. 1–19.

Thomas Walpole, Samuel Wharton, Lord C[amden], Lord G[ower?] and by two others, instructing Croghan to use it as the basis for purchasing a large tract of land lying north of the Ohio River, heretofore inviolate Indian territory. It is significant that Benjamin Franklin was left out of the deal, and it was not until January, 1775, that Samuel Wharton explained the inwardness of its workings to his brother Thomas.[3] Even with the aid of the specious Camden-Yorke opinion, such a purchase was not a simple matter. Goods had to be provided to pay the natives for their land, and secrecy had to be maintained, for this was a game at which only a few hands could play. Consequently, a rather complicated scheme was devised. William Trent, who had tarried in London with Samuel Wharton lobbying for the Vandalia Company, was to return to America with a cargo of Indian goods which was to be landed on the Potomac River, rather than in Philadelphia, and forwarded at the proper time to Croghan for treaty-making purposes.[4]

In addition, letters were written to Croghan telling him that the governor of Vandalia and his suite could be expected at Pittsburgh during the following summer. All was to be got in readiness and the impression was to be created that the shipment of goods was intended to be used for a present to the Indians on that occasion. Thus, the real motive of the shipment could be masked. Whether any one thought that the governor of Vandalia, apparently in the person of Samuel Wharton, and his suite would really arrive cannot be stated with certainty. Croghan at least did not fail to make it appear that he expected them.

Eventually the Camden-Yorke opinion and the accompanying letters reached Thomas Wharton in Philadelphia and he, manifesting an inexplicable degree of confidence in human nature, entrusted them to William Murray to deliver to Croghan.[5] It was during the previous year that the firm of Baynton, Wharton and Morgan had finally withdrawn from Western trade. At this time Murray was the principal Western agent of David Franks and Company, whose members included James Rumsey and Alexander Ross in addition to Murray, Franks, and the Gratz brothers. They were old rivals of the Wharton combination. Croghan, of course, now carried on his trade through the Franks-Gratz group, but he was still in correspondence with the Whartons in regard to Vandalia and related land speculations. The sanctity of the post was little regarded in those days, and it is fairly evident

[3] Thomas to Samuel Wharton, Nov. 30, 1773, Wharton letter book, H.S.P.; S. to (T) Wharton, Jan. 31, 1775, Wharton MSS., H.S.P.
[4] Volwiler, *Croghan,* pp. 297–298.
[5] Croghan to Bernard Gratz, May 11, 1773, Draper MSS., 7J136–138.

that Thomas Wharton read these letters before committing them to Murray. One cannot escape the conclusion that Murray read them and copied the Camden-Yorke opinion as soon as he got his hands on them. The reason for this conclusion is that before leaving Philadelphia he engaged the Franks-Gratz connection in a combination and secured goods from them with which to make a purchase of land from the Indians. It appears that he planned to use the opinion as his authority for such purchase as soon as he should reach the Illinois country whither he was bound.[6] When he arrived at Pittsburgh on May 10, 1773, he turned the letters over to Croghan and tarried for a few days in the company of this genial trader. Writing back to Gratz to inform him of his progress, he mentioned that John Campbell, William Thompson, and Robert Callender had been added to the land company and that Croghan had told him he had been informed of the Camden-Yorke opinion when he was in England in 1764. Evidently Croghan could not keep his counsel, for George Morgan happened to be in the neighborhood and he too got wind of the opinion as well as of Croghan's intended purchase of land on the strength of it.[7]

Since his retirement from the Illinois country, Morgan had apparently not been profitably engaged. Making his headquarters in Philadelphia, he carried on a bitter correspondence with Samuel Wharton, whom he blamed—and with some justice—for all his woes. Morgan had been left out of the Vandalia Company, although Wharton had used enough of the funds of the bankrupt house of Baynton, Wharton and Morgan while lobbying for the land company in London to have bought thousands of acres for the firm. Vandalia's other agent in London stood little higher in Morgan's esteem. "With regard to that contemptible wretch Trent," he opined, "he is not worth a Kick." [8]

After a few days Murray began his journey from Pittsburgh into the Illinois country. He arrived there on June 11 and on July 5 he purchased from the Illinois Indians two large tracts of land, one at the junction of the Illinois and Mississippi Rivers, the other at the confluence of the Ohio and Mississippi. Thus did the Illinois Company get its feet on the ground.[9]

In the meantime Croghan was not idle. In the autumn he assembled

[6] Byars, *Gratz,* p. 120.
[7] Murray to B. and M. Gratz, May 15, 1773, Ohio Company MSS., H.S.P.; T. to S. Wharton, Nov. 30, 1773, Wharton letter book, H.S.P.
[8] *Papers of Sir William Johnson,* VIII, 1024; George Morgan to Samuel Wharton, June 11, 1773, Baynton, Wharton and Morgan letter book, Pennsylvania State Archives.
[9] A copy of the deed, dated July 20, 1773, is in the Fleming MSS., W. and L. U. library. Byars, *Gratz,* pp. 136–137.

some of the chiefs of the Six Nations as he had been instructed to do, but no governor appeared nor had the goods for presents arrived. Yet Indians could not be sent home empty-handed without serious embarrassment, and Croghan was equal to the emergency. He got together a supply of goods, probably on credit from local merchants, and made a deal with the natives for one and a half million acres of virgin lands north of the Ohio.[10]

The wily trader now wrote to Thomas Wharton urging that three thousand pounds be supplied to defray expenses of the Indian conference, and Wharton appealed to Joseph Galloway to help raise the money from the Vandalia associates. Galloway went to William Franklin, and they agreed there was something suspicious about the affair, and they were certain that the report about the expected arrival of the governor of Vandalia was false. Benjamin Franklin was consulted, and he assured them the report was without foundation. Finally the Wharton family raised one hundred and sixty pounds in Philadelphia and sent it to Croghan. This, of course, was quite inadequate and Croghan repaid them by keeping his own counsel about his land purchase. He later gave it out that he had paid six thousand dollars for it, but it is hard to conjecture how he could have raised that sum—if, indeed, he did raise it.[11]

The Gratz-Franks merchants had scooped the Whartons on this occasion, and not one of the latter connection, not even Croghan, was admitted to a share in Murray's venture. But Disraeli was not to be born for a quarter of a century yet, and in the meanwhile Jewish influence was not overly powerful at Westminster. Even though armed with the Camden-Yorke opinion, land speculators needed friends with political influence, and in this matter the Quaker Whartons had all the best of it. But the Gratzes were not lacking in shrewdness; they applied their wits on the occasion to very good effect. In short, they decided to take the governor of Virginia, Lord Dunmore, into their counsel. Here was a man with some power and much resourcefulness and with no love for the Vandalia Company or any of its works. Accordingly, on April 19, 1774, the Illinois Company addressed a petition to that personage, recognizing the authority of Virginia north of the Ohio and asking Lord Dunmore to intercede for it with the home government.[12] This Dunmore straightway did and was as promptly told by Dartmouth

---

[10] Croghan to Trent, July 15, 1775, Ohio Company MSS., II, 6, H.S.P.

[11] T. Wharton to Croghan, Aug. 28, 1774, Wharton letter book, H.S.P.; T. Wharton to T. Walpole, Sept. 3, 1774, Pa. Mag. History and Biog., XXXIII, 443; Joseph Galloway to Wm. Franklin, Nov. 25, 1773, Franklin MSS., XLVIII, 144, A.P.S.

[12] Petition of David Franks, John Murray and John Campbell to Dunmore, Apr. 19, 1774, C.O., series 5, 1352, f. 151.

that His Majesty's Government would have none of it. Gage and Sir William Johnson were equally positive in their opposition to the Illinois Company; Captain Lord, commanding in the Illinois country and who had opposed Murray's purchase from the first, was instructed to make a public disavowal of it.[13]

Finally, on July 25, 1774, word was received that Trent's cargo of Indian goods had arrived at Georgetown, Maryland. It was consigned to Thomas Wharton, and he was to have it delivered to Croghan whenever the time was ripe for the Indian purchase. But Dunmore's War was now brewing and the Virginians would not look with complacency upon the delivery of powder to the natives. Consequently, the business had to be postponed. As soon as the war was over, winter was at hand, and in the spring the powder was taken and paid for by the county committee which was preparing for the struggle with Great Britain.[14]

Shortly after this, Croghan had a letter from Trent wishing to know what had been done about the land deal. Thus reminded of the matter and knowing that the Wharton connection had little chance of raising sufficient funds for the purpose, Croghan got nine hundred pounds from some Virginians—presumably Dr. Thomas Walker and his associates— and on July 10, 1775, purchased six million acres from the Six Nations. The tract lay just across the Ohio from Pittsburgh, and twelve thousand dollars was supposed to be the purchase price. Five days later Croghan answered Trent's letter. He did remember, he wrote, that over three years ago—it was actually two years—Wharton had written him to investigate the possibilities of such a purchase, and he had heard nothing more of it since. He had supposed the matter had been dropped, but he had made on his own account a small purchase of one and a half million acres for six thousand dollars. He was now on his way to the Warm Springs of Virginia to meet the gentlemen from whom he had borrowed the money, and unless he could repay what he owed, he must surrender to them two thirds of the original purchase. But if Trent would come

[13] Johnson to Haldimand, March 31, 1774, Add. MSS., 21670, Br. Mus.; Haldimand to Johnson, Sept. 15, 1773, *ibid.; Papers of Sir William Johnson*, VIII, 844–845, 885– 886, 898–899, 905–906, 931–932, 1104–1105, 1118–1119, 1140–1146; Arthur C. Boggess, "The Settlement of Illinois," *Chicago Historical Society's Collection*, (Chicago, 1908) V, 10–11; Dunmore to Dartmouth, May 16, 1774, C.O., series 5, 1352; Dartmouth to Dunmore, July 6, 1774, *ibid.*, same to same, Sept. 8, 1774, *ibid.;* Dunmore to Dartmouth, Dec. 24, 1774, Force Transcripts, L. of C.

[14] T. Wharton to Croghan, July 25, 1774, Wharton letter book, H.S.P.; T. Wharton to Thomas Richardson, Aug. 20, 1774, *ibid.;* T. Wharton to Croghan, Sept. 30, 1774, *ibid.;* T. Wharton to Richardson, Jan. 17, 1775, *ibid.;* T. to S. Wharton, June 28, 1775, *ibid.;* Richardson to Trent, Jan. 18, 1776, Ohio Company MSS., II, 18, H.S.P.; Croghan to T. Wharton, Aug. 10, 1774, *Pa. Mag. Hist. and Biog.*, XV, 43.

to the Springs and bring four thousand dollars in cash, he and his partners might have the two thirds interest.[15]

Croghan knew he was safe in making this proposition because Trent
was not likely to be able to raise the ready money. Nothing more was
heard from him on this head. Just what happened at the Warm Springs
cannot be stated, but four days before Croghan was to have met the
"Virginia gentlemen" there Dr. Thomas Walker and his son John were
given leave to be absent from their seats in the Virginia convention for
the remainder of the session. Dr. John Connolly and his commercial associates, John Campbell and Joseph Simon, with three Indian chiefs,
also had business at the Warm Springs at the same time. Since Connolly's
itinerary carried him from the Warm Springs to Williamsburg for a
conference with Lord Dunmore, one is led to suspect that the governor
of Virginia may have been concerned in these transactions. Two years
later Croghan and Trent visited the Warm Springs and sold one forty
eighth part of the six-million-acre grant to Dr. Thomas Walker and a
group of his Albemarle neighbors for five thousand dollars. These scattered facts are all that we have in regard to these purchases of Croghan,
but they are sufficient to show that a large number of important speculators must have been concerned in the scheme.[16]

It is probable that Patrick Henry was also interested. On August 7,
1775, Wharton wrote from London to his brother Thomas in Philadelphia. He and Dr. Edward Bancroft were busying themselves with the
details of the new land purchase, and they desired Thomas to be equally
active with members of the Continental Congress. He trusted that the
purchase had been accomplished by this time, and it was imperative that
the Continental Congress pass a resolution validating purchases made
from the natives. In order to assist the passage of such a resolution, he
proposed that half shares in the company be given to eight useful members of Congress—this, he stated, in addition to the share already set
aside for Patrick Henry. Thomas Wharton, it will be recalled, had met
Henry on September 23 of the previous year while he was in Philadelphia in attendance on the first Congress. At that time Henry informed

[15] Croghan to Trent, July 15, 1775, Ohio Company MSS., II, 6, H.S.P.; Volwiler,
Croghan, pp. 296–297.

[16] Trent to Todd, Aug. 1, 1777, C.O., series 5, 134, no. 15; Connolly to George
Rootes, Aug. 1, 1775, *Va. Mag. Hist. and Biog.*, XIV, 78–79; R.C.M. Page, *Genealogy
of the Page Family of Virginia* (New York, 1893) pp. 206–209; Waddell, *Augusta
County*, p. 89; John Connolly, "A Narrative of the Transactions, Imprisonment, and
Sufferings of John Connolly," p. 322, *Pa. Mag. Hist. and Biog.*, XII, 310–324. Copy of
the original cession to Croghan by the Six Nations, and of Croghan's deed to Walker
and associates furnished the author by Mr. H. W. Walsh of Charlottesville, Va.

Wharton that Dunmore was fighting the Shawnee in order to get land north of the Ohio under the terms of the Illinois grant. Henry was mistaken in some of his statements, but he had become aware that Dunmore was made acquainted with the Camden-Yorke opinion when the Illinois Company presented their petition to him.[17]

If Dunmore was not friendly toward the Vandalia Company, Patrick Henry was—so much so that he obliged that body with a written legal opinion that its claim upon Virginia's western territory was good, and in Congress he favored Franklin's proposed Articles of Confederation which would have given control of the Western lands to that body.[18]

As late as March 19, 1776, Samuel Wharton was still busy in London with the affairs of the new speculation. On that date he wrote to Trent indicating that Virginia was a party to the scheme and that Henry was already engaged in it. The letter, partly in cipher, was intercepted by the British authorities.[19] His ally in all these operations was Dr. Edward Bancroft, a native of Massachusetts, who had studied medicine in England and was now resident in London. Some years before he had gone out to Borneo and managed the plantation of his friend Paul Wentworth, and while there had made important experiments in dyes. He had something of a reputation as a naturalist and chemist, and these interests formed a close bond between him and Benjamin Franklin.

It is not to be supposed that the Gratz group was idle while Wharton and Bancroft were lobbying for Vandalia. For some time Murray had been busy reorganizing his company, and on October 18, 1775, he engineered the purchase of two additional tracts of land north of the Ohio from Piankeshaw Indians of the Vincennes area. This was done in the name of the new "Wabash" company, with Governors Dunmore of Virginia and Thomas Johnson of Maryland heading its list of members, which included Charles Carroll and a strong group of Baltimore merchants. Evidently they thought the British government was going to have a hard time enforcing its will in America. And evidently the Wharton group as well as the Gratz group decided that it was well to make friends in Virginia. The Revolutionary struggle was to be considerably affected by all these events.[20]

[17] The Gratz group was also cultivating Henry. M. to B. Gratz, May 30, 1775, Gratz MSS., Ridgway Library, Philadelphia. Hall, *Sketches of the West*, pp. 248–249; T. Wharton to T. Walpole, Sept. 23, 1774, Wharton letter book, H.S.P.; S. to T. Wharton, Aug. 7, 1775, Wharton MSS., H.S.P.
[18] W. W. Henry, *Patrick Henry* (New York, 1891) I, 303–304; Alvord, *Mississippi Valley in British Politics*, II, 201 n. 368.
[19] S. Wharton to Trent, March 19, 1776, C.O., series 5, 40.
[20] Murray to B. Gratz, May 16, 1774, Ohio Company MSS., I, 108, H.S.P.

CHAPTER IX

VIRGINIA AND THE TRANSYLVANIA COMPANY

WHEN Virginia's Indian boundary was established in 1771 by the marking of Donelson's line from the Holston to the mouth of the Kentucky, much desirable land lying in Clinch and Powell's Valleys, just east of Cumberland Gap, was left in the Indian country. At the time when settlers were moving across the Virginia line into the Watauga Valley, others were occupying the valley of the Clinch. Prominent among them were William Russell, son of the Knight of the Golden Horseshoe from Orange, and Daniel Smith, the erstwhile school-teacher from Wolf Hills. In 1772 the Watauga people leased their lands from the Cherokee and established a committee to administer affairs pending a more permanent arrangement. The Clinch settlers continued to consider their territory as being in Virginia and to take an active part in the government of Fincastle County.[1]

Naturally this situation could not exist indefinitely. In the spring of 1774 a group of speculators, including three members of the governor's council—William Byrd, John Page and Ralph Wormeley, along with Patrick Henry and his brother-in-law William Christian—determined to make an effort to buy from the Cherokee the lands in question. They sent William Kennedy to consult the natives, and he returned with a favorable reply. On April 5 Governor Dunmore wrote to John Stuart, the Indian agent, instructing him to take measures to defeat the designs of a group of men who were trying to buy lands from the Cherokee. It seems highly probable that it was the Byrd group which he had in mind, particularly in view of the fact that nothing more was ever heard of their scheme. It was not until April 19 that William Murray wrote the petition which notified Dunmore of the Camden-Yorke opinion; consequently, Byrd and his associates may have proceeded without a knowledge of it.[2]

The next plan to buy these lands from the Cherokee came out of North Carolina. The organizers of the movement were Judge Richard

---

[1] T. P. Abernethy, *From Frontier to Plantation in Tennessee,* map p. 5, p. 9.

[2] Deposition of William Christian, June 3, 1777, *C.V.S.P.,* I, 288–289; deposition of Patrick Henry, June 4, 1777, *ibid.,* 289–290; Dunmore to Stuart, April 5, 1774, C.O., series 5, 1353.

Henderson of Hillsborough; and his law partner, John Williams; Thomas and Nathaniel Hart, planters and merchants of the same vicinity; and their friends John Luttrell and William Johnston, nephew to Samuel Johnston of North Carolina. Most of these men were originally from Virginia, and they still had connections in that colony, particularly in the nearby county of Pittsylvania, where Colonel John Donelson was the official surveyor and where Harry and James Innes were leading attorneys.[3]

On August 27, 1774, this North Carolina group organized a land speculating combine which it called Richard Henderson and Company. In November Henderson and Nathaniel Hart went into the Cherokee country and made an agreement with the chiefs of that nation to buy from them all the land lying south of the Ohio and between the mouth of the Great Kanawha and Tennessee Rivers. Chief Little Carpenter returned with them to help select the goods which were to be given in payment. Before winter closed in the goods were purchased and transported to Sycamore Shoals on the Watauga, where the formal treaty was to be made.[4]

On January 6, 1775, the Henderson Company was reorganized, its name changed to the "Transylvania Company," and a few additional members taken in, among them being James Hogg, a kinsman of Sir Walter Scott who had only the year before come to America. Plans were now made for establishing a new colony in the West. The intention of the partners was to pay quit-rents if the King would recognize their title; otherwise, they would declare their independence of him. In any event they meant to establish their own government and administer their own laws. They had heard that Dunmore had a copy of the Camden-Yorke opinion, but apparently they had not yet seen it. However, a copy of Trent's draft of this famous document is preserved among the papers of Judge Henderson. Just when he obtained it can never be known.[5]

Major Arthur Campbell of Fincastle, whom a contemporary characterized as "very able, mean-spirited and jealous," accompanied Hender-

[3] J. F. D. Smyth, *A Tour in the United States of America* (London, 1784) I, 124–128; Draper MSS., ICC2, 27; *Journal of the Department of History of the Presbyterian Church of the United States of America*, XIV, 313–314; Hart MSS., Presbyterian Historical Society, Philadelphia; Archibald Henderson, "The Transylvania Company and the Founding of Henderson, Kentucky" (pamphlet, n.d., n.p.), p. 5; MS. account book of Harry Innes, no. 4, Kentucky Historical Society; William S. Lester, *The Transylvania Colony* (Spencer, Indiana, 1935) pp. 17–28.

[4] Archibald Henderson, *Richard Henderson and the Occupation of Kentucky, 1775, M.V.H.R.,* I, 341–363.

[5] Deed book "D," pp. 272ff., Court of Appeals of Kentucky, Frankfort, Ky.; Preston to Dunmore, Jan. 23, 1775, C.O., series 5, 1353; Kellogg, *British Régime*, p. 127n.

son on at least a part of his journey into the Indian country. The Patrick Henry group considered joining in the venture but later decided against the move on political grounds. Colonel William Preston heard of the plans of the Transylvania Company from Campbell and wrote to Dunmore on January 23, denouncing the scheme. On February 7, Dunmore relayed the information to Dartmouth.[6]

In March, 1775, Henderson and certain of his associates met twelve or thirteen hundred Cherokee at the Sycamore Shoals and on the 17th of that month the Transylvania Company formally traded goods for the lands between the Kentucky and the waters of the Cumberland which were claimed by the Cherokee. At the same time the Watauga settlers purchased the lands on which they were living. But the Transylvania partners did not get all that was included in Henderson's original plan. They accepted the Kentucky rather than the Kanawha as the northern and eastern limit of their purchase, and the Cumberland watershed rather than the Tennessee River on the south and west, thus leaving to Virginia the purchase that Donelson had made when he surveyed the boundary line. The money promised the Indians by Donelson had never been paid, and they were apparently ready to sell all that Henderson and his co-partners cared to buy, but the Judge had friends in Virginia and he doubtless wished to avoid antagonizing certain interests in the Old Dominion.[7]

Even before the treaty was concluded, Daniel Boone, now living in Virginia on the Clinch but who originally hailed from western North Carolina and was well-known to Henderson and the Harts, set out with an advance party of twenty men to clear a trail through Cumberland Gap to the blue grass region of Kentucky. As soon as possible Henderson, Nathaniel Hart, and John Luttrell of the company, followed with a party of about thirty. When they got to Powell's Valley, they halted to give Boone time to finish the trail and bridle-path for their pack-animals. Here, during the previous January, Joseph Martin had established a settlement. It will be recalled that back in 1769, under the influence of the Loyal Company, he had attempted to make a settlement here but the Indians had shown a hostile front, causing him to abandon the attempt. Martin had been appointed by the Cherokee, along with John Farrar, to

[6] Deposition of Arthur Campbell, Oct. 21, 1778, *C.V.S.P.*, I, 303–304; Campbell to Preston, Nov. 21, 1774, Draper MSS., 3QQ134; *ibid.*, 1CC160–161; Stuart to Dartmouth, Jan. 3, 1775, C.O., series 5, 76; Cameron to Stuart, Dec. 17, 1774, *ibid.*; Dunmore to Dartmouth, Feb. 7, 1775, C.O., series 5, 1353.

[7] Cameron to Stuart, Feb. 23, March 2, 1775, C.O., series 5, 76; *Journals of the House of Burgesses, 1770–1772*, p. xxxiv; *Bureau of American Ethnology, Fifth Annual Report* (1883–1884) plate 8; Hamilton, *Letters to Washington*, V, 152–153.

represent them in the conveyance of the lands to the Transylvania partnership, and he was now working as a protégé of the Henderson organization.[8]

William Calk, of Prince William County, Virginia—who left us an interesting diary with an originality in spelling that fascinates—with a small party of adventurers joined Henderson and the rest at Martin's Station. They finally got word from Boone that he had blazed the way as far as Otter Creek on the Kentucky, the neighborhood in which they wished to settle, and was having trouble with the Indians. Consequently, on April 8, Henderson and his party hurried forward. When they reached the camp which Boone had established on the west bank of the Kentucky they were welcomed by a volley from the rifles of the pioneers of Boonesborough.[9]

But Boonesborough was not the first settlement established in Kentucky. The earliest recorded party to reach Kentucky in the spring of 1775 was that of the McAfee brothers from Virginia. Preceding the Henderson party through the Gap, they reached the Boiling Spring on Salt River on March 11, just one day after Boone started for Kentucky. Here they had made surveys two years previously. They were busy making improvements when, on March 15, James Harrod and his party of forty-two men from the Monongahela country passed them and halted a few miles beyond at a group of cabins from which the Indians had driven them the year before. A few days later the McAfees set out on a return trip to Virginia, leaving two men to take care of their improvements. On the way they met the Henderson party coming out, and Henderson persuaded George, Robert, and William to return with him and assist in the establishment of Boonesborough. James and Samuel refused to join him and rode on toward Virginia over the Wilderness Trail—a pathway destined to become the slender road to an empire so great that it would have staggered the imagination of even the ambitious Henderson. Thus, Harrodsburg was founded about two weeks before Boone reached Kentucky and was the first permanent settlement made in that country.[10]

Surveyors, prospectors, and settlers swarmed into the new region during the spring of 1775. Hancock Lee and his party, who were com-

---

[8] *Va. Mag. of Hist. and Biog.*, VII, 9; *Register of the Kentucky State Historical Society*, XXIII, 143; Henderson to Martin, June 12, 1775, Draper MSS., 1CC215; Floyd to Preston, April 15, 21, 1775, *ibid.*, 17CC165, 167; Henderson to Martin, July 20, 1775, *ibid.*, 1CC216–217.

[9] "Journal of William Calk," in *M.V.H.R.*, VII, 365–377.

[10] Neander M. Woods, *The Woods-McAfee Memorial* (Louisville, 1905) p. 176; Genl. Robert B. McAfee to Benjamin Hardin, n.d., Durrett collection, University of Chicago; A. G. Bradley ed., *The Journal of Nicholas Cresswell* (New York, 1928) pp. 78–79; Thwaites and Kellogg, *Dunmore's War*, p. 207n.

missioned to make an enormous survey for the old Ohio Company of
Virginia, now beginning to show new signs of life, established Leestown
about a mile below the site of Frankfort, founded by James Wilkinson
in 1786. Numerous parties from Pennsylvania were scattered through
the area east of the Kentucky. One of these groups, led by Robert Patterson and John McClelland of that province, established McClelland's
Station which became in later years the village of Georgetown. These
were the only important developments of the year on the eastern side
of the Kentucky, but a few smaller stations, including Hinkston's and
Martin's, were also established. The surveys made by such parties were
mostly four-hundred-acre plots which were expected to be patented later
as settlement rights. To mark a few trees and construct a rude cabin
on such a plot or to clear and plant a small corn-patch was supposed to
give one the right to consider himself, legally, a superior claimant to the
designated tract.[11]

There were two other interesting parties in Kentucky during this
spring. One of these made dug-out canoes at Washington's bottom on
the Monongahela where a backwoodsman named Simpson was building
a grist mill for the future father of his country. A leader of this party
was Nicholas Cresswell, a young English gentleman who had acquired
some interest in William Murray's Illinois Company and who was also
in search of virgin lands in Kentucky. The other was James Nourse, who
in 1769 had come with his wife, nine children and a great array of goods,
from Hertfordshire, England, to seek his fortune in the New World and
had established a home near the present location of Charleston, West
Virginia. After stopping at Fort Pitt and dining with the trader John
Campbell they floated on down the Ohio to Grave Creek. Here they
halted to view the large Indian mound which was responsible for the
lugubrious name of the stream. It was near this spot that the young
George Rogers Clark had made his first experiment as a settler in the
winter of 1772–1773, and in this vicinity Clark joined the Englishmen,
who found him an "intelligent man," and came down the Ohio and as-
cended the Kentucky River with them. On reaching the vicinity of the
Elkhorn Clark quitted his English friends to join the party of Hancock
and Willis Lee.[12]

George Mason, for the old Ohio Company, had employed this latter

---

[11] Withers, *Chronicles of Border Warfare,* pp. 97n., 196; S. M. Wilson, *The First
Land Court of Kentucky* (Lexington, 1923) p. 18; Z. F. Smith, *History of Kentucky*
(Louisville, 1886) p. 54.

[12] *Journal of Nicholas Cresswell,* pp. 51–52, 67–68; M. C. N. Lyle, *James Nourse
and his Descendants* (Lexington, 1897) pp. 10–15; diary of James Nourse, Durrett
MSS., U. of C. library; *Va. Mag. of Hist. and Biog.,* VIII, 199–202.

group to survey the two hundred thousand acres which that organization had been trying to acquire ever since 1748. In 1773 the Ohio Company had secured from the College of William and Mary a surveyor's commission for William Crawford. The next year Hancock Lee was made his official assistant, and George Rogers Clark was employed as one of his deputies. None of them had authority from Preston to work in Fincastle County, though John Tayloe appealed to Preston for such a concession. Nevertheless the two hundred thousand acres (actually embracing close to eight hundred thousand acres) were laid out in one survey, partly on the north fork of Elkhorn but mainly on the waters of Licking, and the settlement of Leestown, as previously stated, was established nearby on the Kentucky. Mason was a persistent man.[13]

On March 14, three days before the treaty of Sycamore Shoals was signed, Dunmore wrote to Dartmouth that he had issued a proclamation against Henderson and his confederates, and sent surveyors to Kentucky. On the 21st, four days after the treaty, he actually issued his proclamation. This document, in addition to condemning Henderson "and other disorderly persons, his associates," made public for the first time the instructions which the governor had received more than a year previously in regard to the disposal of the public domain. The new policy called for the survey of bodies of land in tracts of from one hundred to one thousand acres. These were to be sold at public auction to the highest bidder, who should thereafter pay a quit-rent of half-penny an acre. This more than doubled the customary quit-rent and the prospect was that the original purchase price would be much greater than the ten shillings per hundred acres which had theretofore been charged.[14]

Though these instructions had not before been made public, the president of the council and some other influential men knew of their existence. Thomas Lewis had, in fact, written to Preston on June 19, 1775, that he knew of them and also that Dunmore had been ordered to suspend their operation and to make no more grants to provincial soldiers. Now, Preston suggested to the governor that he use the instructions as a wedge against Henderson, and Dunmore took the advice. Preston was

[13] Draper MSS., 16J50; John Tayloe to Preston, Jan. 28, 1775, *ibid.*, 4QQ5; Wilson, *The Ohio Company,* pp. 29–39; James A. James, *George Rogers Clark Papers* (Springfield, 1912) p. 9; petition of the Ohio Company to General Assembly of Virginia, Nov. 20, 1778, Va. Arch., petitions.

[14] *Am. Arch.,* series 4, II, 174; Dunmore to Dartmouth, March 14, 1775, C.O., series 5, 1353; C. H. Laub, "British Regulation of Crown Lands in the West, the Last Phase," *William and Mary Quarterly Historical Magazine,* new series, X, 52–55; St. George L. Sioussat, "The Breakdown of the Royal Management of Lands in the Southern Provinces, 1773–1775," *Agricultural History,* III, 92–97.

accordingly directed to send surveyors into Kentucky to mark off certain tracts where the new system might be given a trial. It was very doubtful whether lands could be sold under the new regulations, and Preston professed to have had trouble in finding surveyors who were willing to take chances on getting any fees for their work. But John Floyd and other "assistant" or deputy surveyors, were dispatched to Kentucky with orders to confine themselves to the lands east of the Kentucky River and to take care not to encroach upon the claims of the Walpole Company. In addition to making these surveys under the new instructions, Floyd and his fellow deputies also had authority to mark some plats for the military claimants under the proclamation of 1763.[15]

Floyd set out for the wilderness with Alexander Spotswood Dandridge, John Todd and others, and we find them presently south of the Kentucky River and in the act of establishing St. Asaph's Station in conjunction with Benjamin Logan. Logan was a settler of the Holston region who had started for Kentucky with Henderson. On reaching Rockcastle River the two had parted, and Logan, veering somewhat toward a point southwestward of Boonesborough, collaborated in the establishment of St. Asaph's, which was often known as Logan's Fort.[16]

On March 27, the Virginia convention condemned the new land policy which Dunmore had so tardily announced, and appointed committees to inquire "whether His Majesty may, of right, advance the terms of granting land in this colony." This was taking the same tone which Jefferson had taken in his "Summary View" of the previous year. Here the eminent domain of the Crown was denied, and it was argued that the land ultimately belonged to the people or to their local governments. Thus, two diametrically opposite principles of government were brought into conflict over the land question, and John Locke was at the bottom of it.[17]

Colonel William Christian wrote to Harrod in Kentucky to discourage the surveying of land under the new instructions and Captain William Russell, now in command of Fort Blair at Point Pleasant, used his in-

[15] As late as Sept. 8, 1774, Dunmore had been forbidden to make any surveys beyond the Kanawha, Dartmouth to Dunmore, C.O., series 5, 1352; *Papers of Sir William Johnson*, VIII, 1074; Preston to Dunmore, March 10, 1775, Draper MSS., 4QQ7; Dunmore to Preston, March 21, 1775, *ibid.*, 4QQ9; Lewis to Preston, June 19, 1775, *ibid.*, 4QQ20.

[16] *Register of the Kentucky State Historical Society*, XIV, 20–22; Bradford, "Notes on Kentucky," *Kentucky Gazette*, Sept. 15, 1826; R. S. Cotterill, *History of Pioneer Kentucky* (Cincinnati, 1917) p. 91; Humphrey Marshall, *The History of Kentucky* (Frankfort, 1824) I, 29; John Floyd to Preston, May 30, 1775, Draper MSS., 17CC180–181.

[17] *Proceedings of the Convention*, March 27, 1775, p. 8; *Am. Arch.*, series 4, II, 172.

fluence to the same end, notifying Preston of his action. For these or other reasons, Floyd presented himself at Boonesborough on May 3 and inquired of Judge Henderson as to his terms of granting land. Henderson professed to be no little surprised and a bit suspicious, but he struck a bargain with the Virginian and proposed to let each of the principal men of Floyd's party have a thousand acres on the terms offered to the first settlers: that is, at twenty shillings per hundred acres. Presently Floyd was made entry-taker for the Transylvania Company. Harrod and his associates at Harrodsburg and at the Boiling Spring had already ostensibly joined forces with Henderson, so that now he had no opposition in the land which he and his co-proprietors claimed west and south of the Kentucky except that Thomas Bullitt reappeared at the Falls of the Ohio with unknown designs.[18]

It was a propitious time for the establishment of a government. The proprietors made no secret of their aims, writing of themselves as the "true and absolute Proprietors of the Colony of Transylvania." Acting in the capacity of governor and council, Henderson and his associates called for an election of members from the different stations to meet as a House of Delegates. From St. Asaph's, Floyd, Todd, Dandridge and Samuel Wood were chosen; from the Boiling Spring, James Harrod, Nathan Hammond, Isaac Hite, and Azariah Davis were the delegates; from Harrodsburg, Thomas Slaughter, John Lythe, James Douglas, and Valentine Harmon were elected; and from Boonesborough, Daniel Boone and his brother Squire, William Cocke, Samuel Henderson, William Moore, and Richard Calloway made up the delegation. On May 23 the body assembled and listened to a speech from Henderson in which he urged the necessity of establishing courts and a militia system. The House at once proceeded to work on this suggestion. In June the proprietors appointed justices of the peace for the different settlements.[19]

One immediately begins to wonder what Henderson's plans could have been as to the relation of Transylvania to Virginia, to the Continental Congress, and to the British Crown. The answer to this question came when, in September, James Hogg was dispatched to Philadelphia with a petition from the Transylvania Company to the Congress. Here it was stated that the new colony did not wish to throw off allegiance to His Britannic Majesty, but did wish to be admitted to membership in Con-

---

[18] Wm. Madison to Preston, July (?), 1775, Draper MSS., 4QQ30; Henderson's journal, ibid., 1CC209; Russell to Preston, June 12, 1775, ibid., 4QQ19; Henderson to the Proprietors, June 12, 1775, George W. Ranck, *Boonesborough* (Louisville, 1901) pp. 189–190.

[19] Jefferson MSS., June 5, 1775, II, 54, L. of C.; Draper MSS., 1CC202–206; Virginia Archives, petitions, June 5, 1775, printed in *Va. Mag. Hist. and Biog.*, XIX, 265–266; *ibid.*, XVIII, 379–380.

gress on an equal footing with the other colonies, Mr. Hogg serving as its delegate.[20]

Messrs. Hewes and Hooper, two of the delegates from North Carolina, accompanied Hogg to Philadelphia and introduced him to the two Adamses. These gentlemen professed to be interested in his proposition, but suggested that he talk with the delegates from Virginia, "since Transylvania lay within the bounds of that colony." Hogg accordingly had a conference with Jefferson and Wythe and found that they, though favoring the establishment of a liberal government in the back country which should extend to the Mississippi on both sides of the Ohio to the charter limits, would not consent to its being done without the sanction of the Virginia convention. Richard Henry Lee apparently concurred in this opinion. Seeing that he was not likely to overcome this opposition, Hogg decided not to present his petition. But he had made some friends among the Northern delegates, and some member of the Illinois Company furnished him with a copy of the Camden-Yorke opinion. Silas Deane of Connecticut appeared to be especially interested in Transylvania. He held out hopes that he might bless the new colony with a migration of his constituents if the government were sufficiently liberal and the land sufficiently cheap. We shall find that Deane did not easily forget his early interest in Western lands.[21]

While the movement to Kentucky was at its height in March, 1775, Virginia's second convention was in session. It would have been strange indeed, in view of conditions, if the question of Western lands had not been speedily brought before this body. It has already been mentioned that resolutions were passed condemning the new regulations for the sale of public lands. This came two days after Dunmore had been thanked by that body for his successful Indian war of the previous year. Yet Henderson's activities are not mentioned in the journal of the convention. We know, however, from other sources that this subject was discussed; that Arthur Campbell, Patrick Henry, and others defended Henderson; and the fact that the convention did not assert Virginia's claim to the lands which Henderson was settling was looked upon as a distinct triumph by the Transylvania Company—so much so that the organization wrote a letter to Henry thanking him for his assistance.[22]

Henderson's position was, indeed, rather strong. While the governor

---

[20] *Am. Arch.,* series 4, IV, 546; Ranck, *Boonesborough,* pp. 212ff.

[21] Deane to Henry, Jan. 2, 1775, Stan V. Henkels, *The Patrick Henry Papers and Relics* (catalogue, Philadelphia, 1910) ; C. F. Adams, *The Works of John Adams* (Boston, 1850) II, 430; *Am. Arch.,* series 4, IV, 543–546.

[22] Richard Henderson and Company to Patrick Henry, April 26, 1775, Ranck, *Boonesborough,* pp. 194–195; Thomas Lewis to Preston, June 19, 1775, Draper MSS., 4QQ20.

of North Carolina, as well as Dunmore, had issued a proclamation condemning the activities of the Transylvania Company, in North Carolina it had the support of such powerful men as Joseph Hewes, William Hooper, Willie and Allan Jones, Thomas Burke, and others. In Virginia Patrick Henry was a tower of strength, and he evidently had the majority in the convention with him. The reason for this is that independence was not anticipated in Virginia at this time, and the outlook, so far as Western lands were concerned, left a choice only between Henderson's project and Dunmore's lately announced instructions. The great majority of people in eastern Virginia were not interested in the West. It was a liability rather than an asset. It bred expensive Indian wars and drained off population. Jefferson and the Lees were developing an imperialistic attitude which even Washington did not share. But they were exceptional men. To the average land speculator of the stamp of Henry, Preston and Walker the price of land and the prospect of future development made all the difference. If Henderson offered better terms than Virginia, Virginia speculators were ready to support him. George Rogers Clark and John Floyd actually took up lands under Henderson, and Arthur Campbell, who aspired to be surveyor to the company, and many other Virginians were supporting him.[23]

But a split had developed in the ranks of the Virginia speculators. Preston had to think of his official position as surveyor of Fincastle County. The idea of sending Floyd to Kentucky to try out the new instructions as a weapon against Henderson originally came from him, and he could not afford to break with the governor. As soon as it was known in Fincastle that he was responsible for this scheme Christian called a meeting of the county committee which drew up a memorial to the convention protesting against the making of any surveys under Dunmore's instructions. Thomas Lewis, surveyor of Augusta County and still a member of the Loyal Company, did what he could to put Preston's case in a favorable light before the convention, and since Christian and practically all the Western leaders were his friends the surveyor of Fincastle escaped without personal censure, but his policy was condemned. The convention ordered that there should be no surveys under the instructions.[24]

[23] Campbell–Preston MSS., Dec. 27, 1775, L. of C.; deposition of James Douglas Oct. 28, 1778, C.V.S.P., I, 307–309; Edna Kenton, Simon Kenton (Garden City, N. Y., 1930) pp. 64–65; James, Clark Papers, pp. 9–10; William Christian to Preston, Aug., 1775, Draper MSS., 4QQ32; John Williams to Joseph Martin, Dec. 3, 1775, ibid., 1CC218–219.

[24] Proceedings of the Convention, July 18, Aug. 11, 15, 1775, pp. 4, 14, 16–17; Christian to Preston, July 25, 1775, Hart MSS., Presbyterian Historical Society, Philadelphia; Lewis to Preston, Aug. 19, 1775, Draper MSS., 4QQ29; Preston to

The friends of the Loyal Company were doubtless willing enough to acquiesce in the decision, but they were also hostile toward Henderson. Among the Western leaders, only the Lewises actually belonged to the company, but Preston was closely associated with it. How many others may have been drawn within its sphere of influence cannot be stated, but those who supported Henderson could not have been deeply involved. George Mason and George Washington of the Ohio Company were no less hostile to the Henderson group than were the members of the Loyal Company.[25]

This division in interest among a group of Western leaders who had long worked together and who were bound by ties of blood and friendship did not prove really serious at the moment, but it was to have some long-range results. For the time being Preston was willing enough to bow to the will of the convention. In fact, Floyd had anticipated this train of events and had made no surveys under the governor's new instructions. On the contrary, as has been seen, he temporarily joined forces with Henderson, but not, it would seem, without reservations.

One other incident occurred during the spring of 1775 which throws considerable light on the political situation as it affected the question of public lands in Virginia. The surveys which Willis and Hancock Lee were making for the Ohio Company in Kentucky under authority of William Crawford afforded the Loyal Company much concern. Crawford not only had a commission as surveyor from the College of William and Mary, but was a deputy under Thomas Lewis, surveyor of Augusta, and a considerable number of his surveys had already been patented to Washington. It looked as though the Ohio Company was finally about to solve its problem. Its claim was certainly as good as that of the Loyal Company, and all that it needed in order to put itself on an equal footing was an accredited surveyor. But the Loyal Company meant to brook no rival. Preston took the matter up with John May, clerk of Botetourt and a man of considerable influence in Williamsburg. Together they concocted a letter to an attorney of that capital, the object of which was to bring about an investigation of the legality of Crawford's appointment as surveyor. If they could have succeeded in carrying their point most of Washington's lands, including those granted him under the proclamation of 1754, would have been lost to him. He got word of this threatened

Christian, n.d. (1775) ibid., 4QQ32; William Russell to Daniel Smith, ibid., 16J12; Christian to Preston, July 12, 1775, ibid., 4QQ25; Preston to the Virginia Convention, n.d. (1775) Virginia Archives, petitions; Committee of Fincastle to the Convention, July 18, 1775, ibid., printed in Va. Mag. Hist. and Biog., XV, 16.

[25] Filson Club, History Quarterly, VI, 223–226; Hamilton, Letters to Washington, V, 133–135; Fitzpatrick, Writings of George Washington, III, 278–280.

calamity and wrote to Dunmore for the facts. The governor replied that the legality of Crawford's appointment was being questioned and in case the decision went against him, all his surveys would be held invalid and the grants made upon them would hence be void. Washington must have spent some uneasy hours as a result of this letter. But the threatened catastrophe did not occur. On September 25 he wrote Crawford requesting when he went down the river that he would endeavor to get a license from Bullitt to survey his ten thousand acres so that he could proceed to patent it. Washington added, ". . . though I know I gave him mortal offense by interesting myself in procuring commission for you, yet I believe he will comply." It is probable that the Colonel induced the Ohio Company, of which he was still a member, to take a less dangerous course, and Willis Lee was selected to survey its claim. The Loyal Company was apparently satisfied that it could deal with this situation, for Lee had no authority to work under any county surveyor.[26]

The contemplated action against Crawford was dropped since the only object had been to prevent his working for the Ohio Company. But John Camm, commissary to the Bishop of London and hence head of the established Church in Virginia, president of the College of William and Mary and clerk of the governor's council, wrote to William Preston and complained on behalf of the College of the action of surveyors of Fincastle, Botetourt and Augusta in the case of Colonel Crawford. The College had, all along, shown itself to be favorable to Washington and the Ohio Company by commissioning surveyors of their nomination.[27]

The attitude of the governor's council was crucial in administrative matters, and a poll of its members and their landed interests would be significant in this connection. There were, at this time, ten members of that body, including Camm, who apparently had no personal interest in land speculating ventures. The same seems to have been true in the case of Robert Burwell. Of the remaining eight, Thomas Nelson and Richard Corbin belonged to the Loyal Company; Philip Ludwell Lee, John Tayloe and Robert Carter were members of the Ohio Company, while William Byrd, Ralph Wormeley and John Page had been associated with Patrick Henry in his unsuccessful plan to buy lands from the Cherokee in the spring of 1774.[28]

[26] Washington to Crawford, Sept. 25, 1775, *ibid.*, III, 152–153; *ibid.*, III, 280–281; Hamilton, *Letters to Washington*, V, 158; Preston to Camm, May 1, 1775, Draper MSS., 4QQ13; Roy B. Cook, *Washington's Western Lands* (Strasburg, Va., 1930) pp. 37–39.

[27] Camm to Preston, March 10, 1775, Draper MSS., 4QQ10; *Dictionary of American Biography*, III, 440–441.

[28] List of members of the Loyal Land Company, April 24, 1775, in Campbell–Preston MSS., L. of C.

Since the Ohio Company had more members on the council than did the Loyal, it is not easy to see why the latter group always had the inside track with colonial authorities. It appears that Carter, and possibly Lee as well as Colonel Washington, had lost hope for the Ohio Company, leaving George Mason to assume practically the whole burden of fighting its battles. It is likely that Henry's friend, Colonel Byrd, was inclined to support the interests of the Loyal Company. Moreover, Henry had real influence, and his relations with Preston were very close in regard to land matters, despite the Henderson affair. And finally, there are many indications that Dr. Thomas Walker was a powerful man in Williamsburg as well as in Albemarle.[29]

[29] Rowland, *Mason,* I, 214–215.

CHAPTER X

WEST AUGUSTA AND INDIANA

O N December 6, 1774, Governor Dunmore issued commissions
for the organization of a court at Pittsburgh for the District of
West Augusta. The justices, as members of the Augusta County
court, had been appointed earlier in the year, but most of them had never
qualified under their commissions, though Connolly had been adminis-
tering a military régime for some time. It was planned that the court
should assemble, by adjournment from Staunton, the chief county seat,
on December 20, but it did not actually get down to business until February 21, 1775. On that day George Croghan assumed office as presiding justice of a panel which included John Campbell, John Connolly,
John Gibson, Thomas Smallman, Dorsey Pentecost, David Shepherd, and
William Crawford.[1] Most of the justices were Croghan's friends and kinsmen, though a few could not be placed in that category. This was manifest
when, on September 23, Croghan registered his Indian deed of 1768 for
two hundred thousand acres. Gibson made formal protest, Pentecost absented himself, and while Crawford kept his seat, he had every reason
to oppose Croghan's claim and probably did so. Dr. Thomas Walker and
his son John were present to witness the deed.[2]

At about the time of the first assembling of the court the Virginia
partisans in the District of West Augusta selected John Harvie, recently
of Albemarle County, and John Neville, late of Winchester, land speculators both, to represent them in the Virginia convention. Though there
was no previous authority for this action and apparently no machinery
for a regular election, the delegates were duly seated by the convention
when it assembled on March 20. Thus, the only practical respects in
which the District of West Augusta differed from a separate county were
that its court could meet only by adjournment from Staunton, that it

[1] Boyd Crumrine, ed., Minute Book of the Virginia Court . . . for the District
of West Augusta, *Annals of the Carnegie Museum*, I, 525–568; Crumrine, *Washington County*, p. 178; Lyman Chalkley, ed., *Chronicles of the Scotch-Irish Settlement
in Virginia; Extracts from the Original Court Records of Augusta County, 1745–
1800* (Rosslyn, Va., 1912) I, 177, 183.
[2] Minute Book of Court of West Augusta, *loc. cit.*, pp. 553–554.

had only a deputy sheriff, and that a single clerk, in the person of John Madison, Junior, served both at Staunton and at Pittsburgh.[3]

While this organization was being carried through, the Pennsylvania court for the county of Westmoreland was meeting at nearby Hanna's Town, and the changed situation did not improve relations. On February 7 a group of Connolly's men had broken open the jail at Hanna's Town and made prisoners of two Pennsylvania adherents. Pennsylvania officials were not permitted to exercise their functions in the neighborhood of Pittsburgh, and, of course, it was difficult for either side to establish any systematic enforcement of the law.[4]

The need of discipline was particularly urgent in such a frontier community as Pittsburgh. The low moral tone of the neighborhood is graphically described in the journal of Nicholas Cresswell, and the records of the court of West Augusta give proof of the lawlessness of the community.[5] Such unseemly diversions as street fights and tavern brawls over concubines were interrupted by the exigencies of serious business. The battle of Lexington was fought on April 19, and on May 16 a committee of safety was organized for the District of West Augusta. Its panel was practically identical with that of the court, Croghan presiding over both bodies. An announcement of principles was issued by the committee; its sentiments were in line with those being expressed throughout the colonies. Loyalty to the King was declared, but British encroachments upon American liberties would be resisted by force of arms.[6] Though pronounced differences of opinion were later to develop in this group, they did not come to the surface during 1775. Connolly appeared to inspire general confidence, and, even after it was reported that Dunmore had removed the powder from Williamsburg and threatened to encourage the Indians to attack the border settlements, a large number of Virginia partisans in West Augusta, including William and Valentine Crawford and most of the leaders, expressed their disbelief in the report and their continued confidence in the governor. This was looked upon by Connolly and Dunmore as a declaration of Tory principles on the part of the signers, but it is clear that some of them were not Tories.[7]

The Pennsylvania partisans were in substantial agreement with the

[3] *Proceedings of the Convention . . . of Virginia*, March 21, 1775, p. 4.

[4] T. to S. Wharton, Feb. 28, 1775, Wharton letter book, H.S.P.; *Am. Arch.*, series 4, I, 1272, II, 683–684; Craig, *Olden Time*, I, 444, 512.

[5] Aeneas Mackey to James Wilson, Oct. 31, 1775, Gratz MSS., H.S.P.; Nicholas Cresswell, *Journal, . . .* pp. 98–99.

[6] Craig, *History of Pittsburgh*, p. 114; Volwiler, *Croghan*, p. 325; Crumrine, *Washington County*, pp. 74–76.

[7] Address of the inhabitants of transmontane Augusta County to Dunmore, Sept. 24, 1775, C.O., series 5, 1353; Hanna, *Wilderness Trail*, II, 79; C. W. Butterfield, *History of the Girtys* (Cincinnati, 1890) p. 32.

Virginians in their attitude toward British encroachments. The West-morelanders organized a committee of safety at Hanna's Town on May 17, the day following that on which West Augusta organized her committee. The political sentiments which they expressed were not different from those emanating from Pittsburgh, but St. Clair did not seem at all happy about the situation, writing that he feared success almost as much as failure in this enterprise.[8]

Yet among the Virginians at Pittsburgh there was not quite so much unanimity as appeared on the surface. At the end of his Shawnee campaign of the fall of 1774, Dunmore, it will be recalled, made peace with the natives at Camp Charlotte. Hostages were given by the Indians, and a definitive peace was to be concluded the following spring. But during the spring of 1775 Dunmore was too busy at Williamsburg to pay much attention to Pittsburgh, and the Shawnee were clamoring for the return of their hostages and the promised treaty, which always meant drinks and trinkets. Connolly felt that it was obligatory upon him to do something about the situation and, accordingly, in May sent word to the Shawnee to meet him at Pittsburgh for negotiations.[9]

On June 1, 1775, Congress received a communication from the committee of West Augusta stating that they feared Dunmore's designs in connection with the Indians and asking that Virginia and Pennsylvania send commissioners to treat with the red men. The petition was referred to the delegates from those colonies, and Richard Bland referred it to the Virginia House of Burgesses which was then meeting for the last time, Dunmore already having fled the colony. On June 24, the day of its final adjournment, this body appointed Colonel George Washington, Dr. Thomas Walker, Colonel Adam Stephen, James Wood, Colonel Andrew Lewis, and John Walker as a commission to meet the Western Indians at Pittsburgh. On July 12, Congress created three Indian departments to be responsible for all relations with the natives, and as commissioners of the Middle Department it selected Patrick Henry, Benjamin Franklin, and James Wilson.[10]

Meanwhile Connolly proceeded with his own plans for a treaty with the Shawnee. The Mingoes and Delawares were assembled at Pittsburgh

[8] St. Clair to Shippen, May 18, 1775, *Am. Arch.*, series 4, II, 633–634; E. W. Hassler, *Old Westmoreland* (Pittsburgh, 1900) pp. 13–17. At this time death removed from the scene one of the staunchest Virginia partisans who had long been active on the frontier. Michael Cresap led a company of riflemen from Maryland to join Washington at Boston and died in New York while on his way home.

[9] Hamilton, *Letters to Washington*, V, 101–102; *St. Clair Papers*, I, 354–355.

[10] *Journals of the House of Burgesses, 1773–1776*, pp. 230, 246, 277, 282; *Am. Arch.*, series 4, II, 1240; *Journals of the Continental Congress*, II, 174–177, 183, 251; Lewis, *Battle of Point Pleasant*, pp. 62–69; Thwaites and Kellogg, eds., *The Revolution on the Upper Ohio* (Madison, 1908) pp. XI–XII; Savelle, *Morgan*, p. 133.

but the Shawnee did not come. On June 21, the day before the negotiations were to begin, the Pennsylvania partisans seized Connolly and carried him off a prisoner. A group of Connolly's friends from Croghan's neighborhood made reprisal by seizing three of the Westmoreland magistrates who had taken part in Connolly's capture. The committee of West Augusta at once demanded release; since this was the stronger party the demand was complied with. Connolly then returned to Pittsburgh, and the treaty was completed, the terms being the same as those arranged the previous year by Dunmore. This document was laid before the Virginia convention on July 21, and on the 25th it was approved with thanks.[11]

When Connolly wrote his own account of these transactions he stated that he completely deceived the revolutionary party, that while publicly making a treaty which satisfied Virginia, he carried on secret negotiations with the natives the object of which was to align them with the Loyalist cause.[12]

Whether the Pennsylvanians had arrested him because they suspected his motives and wished to deprive him of opportunity to influence the Shawnee or whether this was merely another move in the ever-present boundary dispute cannot be stated. Connolly seemed to think that the Pennsylvanians arrested him because they were Whigs and that the West Augusta authorities supported him because they were his friends. Certainly the West Augusta committee as a whole was still loyal to Dunmore and willing to support his agent. As it turned out later, some members of that committee took the Loyalist side, some became good Whigs, and some played a double game. But independence was not yet expected, and for the present they were all giving their support to the cause of Congress and of the colonies in asserting American rights as against "ministerial" oppression. A war for independence and a war for American rights within the Empire were two very different things. As for Connolly, despite the apparent unanimity existing between him and the committee of West Augusta, some of that body evidently did not trust him implicitly or they would not have appealed to Congress in the matter of the treaty with the Shawnee.

It is natural that at this time the question of the military occupation of Fort Pitt, alias Fort Dunmore, should have arisen. Whatever may have

[11] Proceedings of the Convention . . . of Virginia, July 21, 25, pp. 5, 6; Va. Mag. Hist. and Biog., XIV, 54–79; St. Clair Papers, I, 356–357; Washington–Crawford Letters, pp. 101–103.

[12] Copy of a talk sent from the Shawnee, Mingoes, etc., to Dunmore, July 6, 1775, C.O., series 5, 1353; Am. Arch., series 4, III, 76–78, 717–718, IV, 100–111; St. Clair Papers, I, 358, 361.

been the attitude of the committee of West Augusta, neither Congress nor Virginia could have thought of permitting its continued control by an agent of the fugitive governor of Virginia. Edmund Pendleton stated at a later date that the matter was debated in Congress in 1775, that Maryland objected to having Congress held liable for such frontier defense, and that Virginia and Pennsylvania consequently raised two hundred men each for that service.[13] The accuracy of this statement appears doubtful. Actually the Westmoreland committee passed resolutions providing for the occupation of the fort by the Pennsylvania militia of that county, but on August 7 the Virginia convention ordered Captain John Neville to march from Winchester with his company and occupy the fort. This he accomplished on September 11. Meanwhile the Virginia and Pennsylvania delegates in Congress had urged those of their respective constituents who were parties to the boundary controversy to pursue a policy of peace until the difficult question could be settled. Dunmore had received instructions from Dartmouth to establish the meridian of the Monongahela as a temporary boundary line, but that bellicose governor was now out of the picture, and Neville promised not to interfere in the controversy, though outbreaks continued to occur between the partisans at Pittsburgh.[14]

As soon as Connolly had completed his negotiations with the Indians he set out with three of their chiefs for Williamsburg. He was accompanied also by the two Pittsburgh business partners, Joseph Simon and John Campbell, with whom his relations were close. They went by way of Winchester, and from there made a detour to the Warm Springs for business reasons. What that business may have been has been explained in Chapter VIII. The committee at the Warm Springs was suspicious of Connolly and gave him considerable trouble, but his treaty had received the approval of the convention, and Peyton and John Randolph as well as Pendleton desired to see him and the chiefs at Richmond. He was accordingly allowed to proceed on his journey, but instead of appearing in Richmond, he joined Lord Dunmore on board the *Fowey* and made plans to return to Pittsburgh to organize an Indian campaign against the colonies.[15] As he was making his way toward his former headquarters for

[13] Pendleton to Madison, Sept. 25, 1780, *Journals of the Continental Congress*, V, 505.

[14] Petition of Alexander Ross, Va. Archives, petitions, 1775; Neville, *Olden Time*, I, 445; Journals of the Board of Trade, May 22, 1775, LXXXIII, 68–69; Dartmouth to Dunmore, May 30, 1775, C.O., series 5, 1353; Wm. Thompson to Jas. Wilson, June 20, 1775, Gratz MSS., H.S.P.; John Irvine to B. Gratz, June 20, 1775, Ohio Company MSS., H.S.P.

[15] Robert Campbell to B. Gratz, July 6, 1775, Gratz–Croghan MSS., H.S.P.; *Pa. Mag. Hist. and Biog.*, XII, 310–324.

this purpose, he, together with the Scot, J. F. D. Smyth, was captured on November 23 by the revolutionists at Frederick, Maryland, and committed to prison. He was thus removed from the scene for the time being, but we shall meet him again.[16]

On September 12, the day after the arrival of Captain John Neville with his Virginia troops at Fort Pitt, the commissioners from Virginia and the Congress assembled under the shadow of the fort for their negotiations with the natives. Henry and Franklin had declined to act for Congress and Dr. Thomas Walker of Virginia and Lewis Morris of New York had been chosen to serve in their places. The natives had not yet arrived nor had Dr. Walker; the other two Congressional commissioners improved their time by making strenuous protests against the presence of Neville's Virginia troops, but they were unable to do anything about it. Before mid-October, both Walker and the Indians having arrived, they got down to the business of treaty-making. Since Walker was a member of both the Congressional and the Virginia commissions he was selected to preside over the joint meetings, and Arthur St. Clair served as secretary. James Wood, an Oxford graduate who came out to America early in life and founded Winchester, had made a long and hazardous journey through the Indian country of the Northwest to invite the natives to Pittsburgh. He had found that the British authorities at Detroit had been busy stirring up the red men to oppose the colonies, and several times his life was in danger. He explained that the colonies desired only the neutrality of the natives in the conflict with the mother country. The Americans would not cross the Ohio River to attack them if they would agree not to molest the settlements south of that stream. This was the policy adopted by Congress, and these were the terms agreed upon at Pittsburgh.[17]

As to the wisdom of this course, much of a controversial nature might be said. Only a small group of Delawares were positively sympathetic with the Americans. The Six Nations, with the Shawnee and the rest of the Northwestern Indians, were much under British influence, and from the first the imperial authorities did not hesitate to incite the natives to active warfare, at times even paying for scalps. Washington early opposed the Congressional idea of Indian neutrality, but George

[16] *Am. Arch.*, series 4, III, 1047–1048, 1660–1662, IV, 615–618; J. F. D. Smyth, *A Tour in the United States*, pp. 191ff.; Alexander to Duncan Cameron, Nov. 11, 1775, papers of the Continental Congress, 51, Vol. I; Sparks, *Writings of Washington*, III, 211–212.

[17] James A. James, "Indian Diplomacy and the Opening of the Revolution in the West," Wisconsin Historical Society, *Proceedings*, 1909, pp. 127–133; Thwaites and Kellogg, eds., *Revolution on the Upper Ohio*, pp. 25ff.; *Journals of the Continental Congress*, II, 251; *St. Clair Papers*, I, 14–15; Albach, *Annals of the West*, p. 244.

Morgan, who in 1776 succeeded Richard Butler as Congressional Indian agent at Pittsburgh, was persistent, if not consistent, in maintaining the policy which Congress itself maintained far beyond its usefulness.[18]

There can be no question that this policy was highly advantageous to the mercantile interests. As long as it was maintained, Morgan and his friends could carry on their trade in the Illinois country. The new Indian agent had established connections with Richard Winston—an original member of Vandalia—and Daniel Kennedy in the Illinois, and they carried on a traffic in flour down the Mississippi to New Orleans, where Daniel Clark and Oliver Pollock acted as agents in this business. Robert Morris, the great merchant of Philadelphia, was also interested in it, having a monopoly of the trade with the Spanish governor at New Orleans.[19]

It seems likely also that those who were interested in the Illinois and Wabash Land Companies as well as those who were connected with Croghan in his six-million-acre grant north of the Ohio, favored the policy of Indian neutrality. But the bearing of this question will be discussed in another connection. Certain it is that the Kentucky settlements were left open to Indian attack with little chance that Congress would assist them. Virginia, however, in 1775 maintained not only the garrison in Fort Pitt but one in Fort Fincastle—soon to be known as Fort Henry—at Wheeling and another in Fort Blair at Point Pleasant. The intrepid Captain William Russell was in command of the latter post.[20]

While the struggle between the Virginia and Pennsylvania factions was going on at Pittsburgh and while Indian treaties were being arranged and negotiated, still a third matter came up for debate and agitation in that turbulent little community of Indian traders and adventurers. It is hardly necessary to say that this was another phase of the land question.

It should be recalled that William Trent returned from London in the spring of 1775 after long and fruitless lobbying in which he assisted Benjamin Franklin and Samuel Wharton on behalf of the Vandalia Company. Franklin also returned to America, leaving Wharton and his friend Dr. Edward Bancroft, with the aid of Thomas Walpole and other English associates, to carry on as best they might. Trent was made American agent for the company and armed with instructions drawn up by Wharton which gave minute directions as to the manner of handling various phases of their speculations.[21]

The outbreak of the war had put an end to any immediate hope that

[18] Savelle, *Morgan,* p. 131; Volwiler, *Croghan,* p. 324; Perkins, *Annals of the West,* p. 148.
[19] Daniel Clark to George Morgan, Feb. 13, 1775, George Morgan MSS., L. of C.
[20] Dunmore to Dartmouth, Sept. 24, 1775, C.O., series 5, 1353.
[21] Agreement signed April 11, 1775, Etting (large) misc. MSS., f. 59, H.S.P.

the Vandalia charter would be signed, though Walpole assured Franklin that this would be done as soon as the rupture with the colonies could be healed. Meanwhile, he advised Franklin and Trent to arrange to have the Vandalia lands seized and leased in behalf of the company, but the operation was to be accomplished with great secrecy because news of it in England would have a bad effect. The senior Franklin corresponded with his son William about the project, and the latter argued against it on the ground that it would be altogether too risky, since secrecy could scarcely be maintained. It is interesting to find the two Franklins thus cooperating in private matters after they had publicly parted ways in the political field. One of Vandalia's leading spirits was soon to be exiled by the new State of Pennsylvania and his estates confiscated. This was Thomas Wharton, Senior, who wrote to his son Samuel in London that he hoped "something would happen to prevent the independence so much desired by some but dreaded by others." [22]

Whatever Walpole's plan may have been, no great confidence was placed in it by his American associates, and during 1775 Wharton and Bancroft busied themselves in London with a simpler and less ambitious scheme. Knowing that success for Vandalia was temporarily out of the question, since that depended upon the action of the British government, they raised the ghost of Indiana to play the leading rôle in their little drama.

The claim of the suffering traders of 1763 had been incorporated with and swallowed up by Vandalia ever since 1769, but now it was to be put upon its own feet again. Trent and Wharton and several of the Franks clan were members of both companies, but Morgan and Croghan, Callender, Gibson and John Campbell, along with several others who had long been connected with the Pittsburgh trade, were concerned only in the Indiana grant. This grant, it will be recalled, was made at the treaty of Fort Stanwix in 1768, but when the home government ratified that treaty, it refused to give its assent to the Indiana claim or to the grant which the Six Nations made to George Croghan at the same time. The deed from the Indians was, therefore, the only ground upon which the Indiana Company could base its claim, and their hopes consequently depended upon the recognition in America of the principles of the Camden-Yorke opinion.

In order to fortify their case, Wharton, with the aid of Dr. Bancroft, wrote a pamplet entitled *View of the Title to Indiana,* which he published

[22] T. to S. Wharton, Sept. 8, 1775, *Historical Manuscripts Commission, Fourteenth Report,* p. 1376; T. Wharton to Croghan, April 27, 1775, Wharton letter book, H.S.P.; Wm. to Benjamin Franklin, Aug. 14, 1775, Franklin MSS., IV, 66, A.P.S.

in London in 1775 and republished in Philadelphia in 1776. Not wishing
to rely solely on the Camden-Yorke opinion, the two pamphleteers secured
similar opinions from two eminent London jurists, Sergeant Glynn and
Henry Dagge, the latter a member of the Vandalia Company. While in
Philadelphia Benjamin Franklin, James Wilson, and Patrick Henry gave
their views to the same effect. Wilson received monetary compensation
for this service, but Henry, though usually inclined to be avaricious, declined such obvious recompense. William Grayson, who was soon to become a member of Congress from Virginia, was taken into the company.
At a later date Edmund Pendleton, chairman of the Virginia convention,
gave the weight of his legal opinion in favor of the Indiana claim. It is
clear that a campaign was on foot to bring Congress around to these
views.[23]

In addition to this line of activity, it was necessary to reorganize the
old Indiana Company. Trent was to take the leading part in this phase
of the business, but his first move was an appeal to George Morgan to
consult Governor William Franklin, a member of the company. Accordingly, on August 8 Morgan wrote to the younger Franklin explaining
Trent's plan for reorganization.

Virginia was fast occupying the land, and something had to be done
quickly. Seeing that an Indian cession, even in the eyes of Camden and
Yorke, was supposed to give only title to the soil and not the right to
govern it and seeing also that the Indiana claim was bounded on the north
and west by the Ohio River, on the east by the Pennsylvania and Maryland lines, and on the south by the Little Kanawha—an area in which
Virginia's jurisdiction had never been questioned—there seemed to be
no choice but to recognize the jurisdiction of the Old Dominion. This
Trent proposed to do. His intention in this respect was made perfectly
clear to Morgan, and by Morgan it was explained to William Franklin.[24]

Going ahead with his plans, Trent called a meeting of the Indiana
Company to assemble at Pittsburgh on September 21, 1775. Morgan and
the members of the company who lived in the neighborhood attended, but
none of the Whartons or Franks were there. The nine who were present
wrote to Samuel Wharton for the original deed and agreed to open a
land office with Morgan in charge. Actual settlers were to be allowed to

[23] Copy of 1776 edition of *View of the Title to Indiana* in rare book room, L. of C.;
S. Wharton to Franklin, April 17, 1775, *Pa. Mag. Hist. and Biog.*, XXVII, 151–152;
Bancroft to Franklin, Aug. 7, 1775, *ibid.*, pp. 161–162; S. Wharton to James Wilson,
n.d., Wilson MSS., III, 71, H.S.P.; memorandum book of William Trent, March 10,
1782, Ohio Company MSS., H.S.P.
[24] Trent to Morgan, July 10, 1775, Morgan MSS., Ill. Hist. Survey, Urbana,
Ill.; Morgan to Wm. Franklin, Aug. 8, 1775, Franklin MSS., IV, 62, A.P.S.; Morgan
to Trent, n.d. (1775) Ohio Company MSS., H.S.P.

purchase their tracts from the proprietors, and an advertisement to that effect was prepared. But a number of these settlers either had Virginia warrants for their claims or were tenants of men who had them; William Crawford was at the time busy making new surveys for Virginians. One of the absentee proprietors was the former Colonel, now General, George Washington, to whom Dunmore had just made, on July 5, 1775, a grant of nearly three thousand acres, known as the Mount Pleasant tract, on Chartiers Creek, land long claimed by Croghan. This was three weeks after John Adams arose in Congress and nominated the Virginia Colonel —the only member habitually to appear in uniform—to command the Revolutionary army. The modest Colonel immediately darted out of the room, and Adams noted, not without malice, that the face of the chairman, John Hancock, who aspired to the command himself, bore a look of "mortification and resentment." [25]

While Washington was struggling with his motley army certain difficulties arose which threw the plans of the land speculators at Pittsburgh into confusion. The original grant had been made to the company by the Indians to pay for certain losses suffered by a group of traders in 1763. Most of these traders had made their claims over to the company, and most of them were to receive thirty per cent of the face value of their claims in case the grant went through. But it seems that some of them had got better terms than others, and now the latter were inclined to repudiate their original agreement and demand fifty per cent instead of thirty. It appears that Trent promised to meet their terms. After two days the meeting was adjourned to assemble later at Carlisle.[26]

It was not long after this Pittsburgh meeting that Trent got a letter from Thomas Wharton criticizing him pointedly for his actions. He maintained that the Philadelphia group had not been consulted as to the place of the next meeting or as to the plan of reorganization. So disgusted was Trent at this that he did not appear at the Carlisle meeting, and it finally took the genius of Benjamin Franklin to bring the warring factions together again.[27]

It has generally been assumed that the difference arose because of Trent's plan to recognize the jurisdiction of Virginia. As a matter of fact, no other plan had been thought of, for it would have been difficult indeed to find any theory on which Virginia's jurisdiction could have been denied.

[25] T. to S. Wharton, March 30, 1775, Wharton letter book, H.S.P.; *Washington-Crawford Letters*, p. 73; Byars, *Gratz*, pp. 350–353; Craig, *Olden Time*, I, 516; Crumrine, *Washington County*, p. 189n.

[26] Minutes of the Indiana Company meeting, Sept. 21–22, 1775, Ohio Company MSS., II, 9, H.S.P.; Darlington, *Gist*, pp. 245–247.

[27] T. Wharton to Trent, Nov. 8, 1775, Wharton letter book, H.S.P.; Levy Andrew Levy to Trent, Nov. 15, 1775, Ohio Company MSS., H.S.P.

The real difficulty arose over two points of a strictly business nature. Thomas Wharton objected to Trent's having given in to the demand of the original "sufferers," and his brother Samuel refused to give up some stock which he held under suspicious circumstances.

When the firm of Baynton, Wharton and Morgan had gone into bankruptcy some years before, the Indiana stock which the partners held had been assigned to the trustees along with the other assets of the company. Robert Morris was one of these trustees and took the leading part on their behalf in the dispute which now arose. Beside this company stock, Samuel Wharton held seven shares in the Indiana grant which had been assigned to him by another person, and which Trent said was supposed to have been turned over by him to the company. But Wharton insisted on holding this stock as his individual property and refused to surrender it to the trustees.[28]

Finally that venerable philosopher, Benjamin Franklin, stepped in to smooth out these difficulties in his own inimitable way. Though the Doctor was not a member of the company, he now acted as proxy for his son, the governor. It then turned out that Samuel Wharton had to surrender his stock, and the original "sufferers" got their fifty per cent, much against the wishes of Franklin and Morgan. Then, by an arrangement of January 19, 1776, the entire stock of the company was transferred to Richard Bache, Franklin's son-in-law; Owen Jones, Junior; and Isaac Wharton, brother to Samuel and Thomas. They were to act for a year as trustees for the company.[29]

On March 20 a meeting of the company was held at the Indian Queen Tavern in Philadelphia, with Dr. Franklin in the chair. It was arranged to open the land office with George Morgan as principal agent and to sell four hundred acres each to actual settlers at fifty dollars per hundred acres, free of quit-rent. Robert Lettis Hooper, a friend of William Franklin and some time surveyor to George Croghan, was made surveyor-general. Joseph Galloway became president of the company. This arrangement had one very pleasing aspect for the organization. Over eight thousand pounds had been borrowed in 1768 by Croghan, Trent and Samuel Wharton from one Alexander Lourie for use in purchase of the

---

[28] T. to S. Wharton, Nov. 30, 1775, Wharton letter book, H.S.P.; Morgan to S. Wharton, Dec. 1, 1773 (1775?), Baynton, Wharton and Morgan letter book, Pa. State Library; indenture, April 9, 1776, Morgan MSS., Ill. Hist. Survey, Urbana, Ill.; Savelle, *Morgan*, p. 74.

[29] T. to S. Wharton, Feb. 25, 1776, Wharton letter book, H.S.P.; Byars, *Gratz*, p. 353; indenture of Jan. 19, 1776, Indiana Company Papers, Wharton MSS., H.S.P.; Trent to Wm. Buchanan, Feb. 6, 1776, Ohio Company MSS., II, 18, H.S.P. By this last letter it appears that Croghan had sold more lands than he was entitled to under the company. This was not an unusual procedure with Croghan.

Indiana lands. It was to be repaid four years after the ratification of the
grant by the home government. Now, since governmental ratification was
not a part of the plan, the loan would never have to be repaid. It is interesting to see how Whigs and Tories could thus bury the political hatchet
and cooperate so heartily in the pastime of land speculation.[30]

On April 15 Morgan published an advertisement to the effect that the
Indiana Company would soon open an office at Pittsburgh for the sale of
its lands. On the 17th the company's deed was registered with the court
of West Augusta County, thus tacitly recognizing Virginia's jurisdiction.[31]

Immediately on seeing Morgan's advertisement, the Virginia delegation in Congress, consisting of R. H. Lee, Wythe, Harrison, and Braxton,
waited on Thomas Wharton. They desired to know Morgan's authority
for selling the land in question. They also wished to know whether
Wharton had ever heard that Virginia had bought the same land from
the Six Nations at the treaty of Lancaster in 1752 or whether he knew
that Virginia had passed an act in 1754 which forbade the private purchase
of lands from the natives. They warned the Indiana claimants not to
proceed without laying their case before the Virginia convention.[32]

These questions put Wharton in a dilemma. He had never heard of
either the treaty or the statute, and he realized that they threatened to cut
the ground from under his feet. In his perplexity he was inclined to throw
upon Trent the whole blame for having overlooked the Lancaster treaty.
Hurriedly he consulted Galloway, and together they framed some an-
swers, but they were not very convincing even to their authors. A second
line of defense offered definitely more hope. Wharton had another conference with some of the Virginia delegates, and at least one of them appeared to be sympathetic. Wharton's advisers had at first thought of
appealing to the Virginia convention, but to do so would be to give
definite recognition to the jurisdiction of that colony and bring her law
of 1754 into baneful operation. Instead Wharton now appealed to Morgan to try to forestall the registration of the Indiana deed at Pittsburgh.
But the change of mind came too late, for this had already been accomplished. Now it was decided that the Virginia delegates should bring the
matter before their convention, and this was a safer course, for the company would not thereby be committed.[33]

---

[30] Byars, *Gratz*, p. 24.
[31] Virgil A. Lewis, "The Original Indiana Territory" (pamphlet in L. of C., 1895)
pp. 11–12; Draper MSS., IZZ2.
[32] T. Wharton to Trent, April 17, 1776, Wharton letter book, H.S.P.; Volwiler,
Croghan, pp. 298–300.
[33] Crumrine, ed., Minute book of the Virginia Court . . . for the District of West
Augusta, *loc. cit.*, I, 562–563; action of debt, Alexander Lourie vs. William Trent,
March, 1776, Ohio Company MSS., H.S.P.; T. Wharton to Morgan, April 22, 1776,

Of the four Virginia delegates, Lee and Wythe were inclined to assert Virginia's jurisdiction over the Western lands, and neither of them would have been likely to make common cause with Wharton. But both Benjamin Harrison and Carter Braxton had important business connections with Robert Morris and other Philadelphia merchants. It was probably one of them who held out hope for Indiana.

Yet such hope as may have been held out proved illusory for the time being. On June 24, 1776, the Virginia convention condemned all private purchases of land from the Indians unless the legislature of the colony should give its approval and declared that actual settlers should have the right of preemption. On June 29 was adopted the constitution of the new State which defined Virginia's boundaries as including the Indiana claim and a far greater extent of Western territory. It is worthy of note that this was the first sweeping assertion by Virginia of her right to jurisdiction over all the land remaining within the boundaries fixed by the charter of 1609. Until Jefferson propounded a contrary theory in 1774 it was admitted that the King might change the boundaries when he chose, and as the Indians occupied much of the country the question of actual ownership of the soil would have been largely academic at an earlier date.[34]

Only one course now remained for Indiana. In July of the previous year Benjamin Franklin had submitted to Congress his plan for union. That plan proposed to put the back country under jurisdiction of Congress and to give that body authority to determine boundaries of the States and the right to create new ones. Now, two weeks after Virginia's assertion of her claim to Western territory, John Dickinson prepared the first draft of the Articles of Confederation, and in it incorporated Franklin's proposals. This was the door of hope not only for the Indiana claimants but for Vandalia as well.

Wharton letter book, H.S.P.; T. Wharton to John Hough, April 22, 1776, *ibid.*, T. Wharton to Joseph Simon, April 26, 1776, *ibid.*; T. Wharton to Morgan, May 14, 1776, *ibid.*; Byars, *Gratz*, pp. 154–155.

[34] *Proceedings of the Convention of . . . Virginia,* June 24, 1775, p. 63; Constitution of 1776, final section, given in Poore's *Federal and State Constitutions* (Washington, 1878) II, 1912.

CHAPTER XI

RADICALS AND CONSERVATIVES IN VIRGINIA

HAVING arrived at the fateful year during which the American colonies declared their independence from Great Britain and set up establishments of their own, it is well to turn aside from the discussion of Western land problems and consider the political situation which existed in Virginia in 1776. This is necessary because of the part played by political faction in the settlement of important questions arising at this critical time in connection with the extensive Western land claims of the Old Dominion.

The terms "radical" and "conservative" are commonly used to describe the two groups into which Virginia's leaders were divided during the Revolutionary epoch, and there is good contemporary authority for classifying Patrick Henry, Richard Henry Lee, and Thomas Jefferson as the captains of the former and such men as Edmund Pendleton, Robert Carter Nicholas, Benjamin Harrison of Berkeley, and Archibald Cary as the most important of the latter group. Their respective stands on the question of resistance to England is apparently the test by which their affiliation has usually been determined. But this classification, though probably as good as any other that could be made, is not entirely satisfactory as a key to Revolutionary-Virginia politics. In fact, Jefferson himself, who gives such a classification, says that the difference between the factions was one of method rather than of principle. Both radicals and conservatives favored resistance, the distinction being that the radicals were a bit more precipitate in their methods. And this difference in method has received more attention than it really deserves.[1]

There can be no question that the points of view which underlay the factional divisions in Virginia can be traced back to a period well before the struggle over the Stamp Act. From the political standpoint three of the most powerful families in Virginia, if not the three most powerful, during this period were the Lees, the Randolphs, and the Robinsons. Thomas Lee had served as president of the council, and John Robinson was treasurer of the colony and speaker of the House of Burgesses from 1738 until 1766. Peyton, John, and Edmund Randolph suc-

[1] Diary of Landon Carter, *W. & M. Quarterly*, XIV, 183ff.

ceeded each other as attorney-general of the colony and State during a period of many years. The Robinsons and Randolphs were related by marriage and were closely associated in politics, but the Lees, while not lacking family connections throughout Tidewater, formed a rival group. This rivalry went back at least to the time when the competing Loyal and Ohio land companies were organized in 1748.[2] It was revived when the Stamp Act came up for consideration.

It was not the radicals but the conservatives who first introduced resolutions condemning the proposed Stamp Act. These were passed by the House of Burgesses on December 18, 1764, and Landon Carter, related to both the Lees and the Randolphs and a thorough-going conservative, claimed credit for having initiated the movement.[3] When the assembly met on May 1, 1765, the definitive Stamp Act had been passed, but nothing was done about it until the session was nearly over and most of the members had gone home. Then, on May 29, Patrick Henry, a new member who lacked connections with the ruling families, but whose simple geniality, whose volatile emotions and ready tongue gave him a command over men, arose in his place to present a series of resolutions which he had drafted. They were seven in number and in strong language condemned the attempt of Parliament to tax Virginia. The first five were passed by the rump of the House which remained in session, but the fifth got by with a majority of only one vote. The next day the House reversed its action on the fifth resolution and Peyton Randolph tried to find a precedent for expunging it from the journal, but it was not expunged. The remaining two were never presented, but they were published in the Newport *Mercury* on June 24. Richard Henry Lee supported Patrick Henry in this movement, and its real significance lies in the effect which it had upon the careers of these two men who had so little else in common.[4]

At a later date Edmund Randolph wrote that up to this time the political control of the colony had been in the hands of a well-entrenched group of Tidewater planters. Under the leadership of the Randolphs and the Robinsons it had kept the situation well in hand for a number of years, but there were many men in the House, particularly the younger ones and those from the upper counties, who were not connected with the ruling families. Lacking a leader they had heretofore exercised little

[2] See Chap. I.
[3] Diary of Landon Carter, *loc. cit.*, XV, 173ff.
[4] Edmund Randolph says that the resolutions of 1765 were understood to have been written by John Fleming of Cumberland County, but Henry claimed to have written them himself, though the only known copy is not in his hand. Randolph, "MS. History of Virginia," p. 107; Stan V. Henkels, *The Patrick Henry Papers* (Phila., 1910) pp. 36–38; *Journals of House of Burgesses, 1761–1765*, pp. liv–lxxi; Fauquier to Board of Trade, June 5, 1765, C.O., series 5, 1331, f. 69.

influence, but Henry now emerged as their chief, and with their support this ambitious but ungrammatical young lawyer became a power in the land. One of his contemporaries said of him about this time that he was "very stern and steady in his country's cause and at the same time such a fool that I verily believe it w'd puzzle even a king to buy him off." [5] His new ally, Richard Henry Lee, though belonging to a family of distinction and political ambition, had not fared well since 1748. While Thomas Ludwell Lee became a member of the council, his brother Richard Henry, the most able of the clan, had failed of preferment. In alliance with Henry he now had a chance to change the situation, and this he meant to do. [6]

The year 1765 was a momentous one in his career, for, in addition to the Stamp Act, another political situation arose to furnish him with excellent material for agitation. During the French and Indian War Virginia had emitted some paper currency, certain issues of which were redeemable in 1765. But laws were passed for the earlier redemption of the notes. John Robinson, as treasurer, was in charge of this business, and in 1760 and 1761 the burgesses passed resolutions requiring the burning of the redeemed notes as fast as they came in, and appointing a committee to see that the burning was actually accomplished. Robinson's friends thought that this action on the part of the House showed a lack of confidence in his administration, and there were those who attributed to Richard Henry Lee the motive force behind the movement. When 1765 arrived and one of the issues became due some of the notes were presented to the treasury for redemption. Robinson's reports showed a substantial balance on hand, but it developed that there was an actual shortage of specie with which to take up the notes. Suspicion was naturally aroused, and Lee and Patrick Henry secured the passage of an act providing for an investigation. [7]

But the committee appointed to make the inquiry brought in a report that the treasury was in sound condition. It appears that the members of the committee were in the habit of taking the treasurer's word for the condition of his books—for were they not all gentlemen? [8] Unfortunately for Robinson, he died the next year, and Governor Fauquier appointed Robert Carter Nicholas to take his place pending an election by the House

[5] Roger Atkinson to Samuel Pleasants, 1774, *Va. Mag. of Hist. and Biog.*, XVI, p. 356.

[6] Edmund Randolph, "MS. History of Virginia," pp. 104–105.

[7] The journals do not show that R. H. Lee attended the session of 1765, though he was a member. Yet the journals always omitted many matters and there is considerable evidence to connect him with this move for investigation. Hening, VII, 353, 466, 468–469; David Boyd to R. H. Lee, Nov. 17, 1766, Lee MSS., U. of Va. library.

[8] *Journals of House of Burgesses, 1761–1765*, May 24, 1763, p. 177, May 29, 1765, pp. 356–357.

of Burgesses. Nicholas at once started an investigation on his own account, and it was presently discovered that the late treasurer's accounts were short by a neat one hundred and two thousand pounds, though all the paper currency was accounted for.[9]

Just before this crisis arose, Governor Fauquier had received instructions from home to separate the offices of speaker and treasurer. The House of Burgesses elected both officials, but the governor had to approve the latter. After adjournment of the House in 1765 Fauquier had written home to say that in case Robinson were again elected speaker he thought he should be allowed to continue in the office of treasurer because of his valuable services, but in case some other speaker should be elected, that would afford an opportunity to separate the offices. When Robinson died Fauquier supported Peyton Randolph, the attorney-general and a close friend of Robinson, for the speakership; George Wythe—who with the Randolphs and Pendleton had stoutly opposed Henry's Stamp Act resolutions—was suggested as his successor in the post of attorney-general. Nicholas was put forward for the treasury by his friends, and the governor gave him the *pro tempore* appointment. The House elected Peyton Randolph as its speaker in 1765, but John Randolph—quite unpopular since the Stamp-Act controversy—was made attorney-general instead of Wythe. The burgesses then fell in with the governor's idea on the question of the treasurer and elected Nicholas.[10]

It was not without opposition that Peyton Randolph had been elected to the speakership. Richard Henry Lee coveted that honorable post, and his friends were legion. Richard Bland also wanted it, but he wrote to Lee that he hoped they could work together for the creation of a commission to handle the treasury. It is ordinarily assumed that Lee was largely responsible for the movement to separate the speakership from the treasury, but it is now clear that this move was planned by the home government entirely independently of Lee's known interest in the matter. It is also clear that Lee, while hostile to the Randolphs and Robinsons, had cordial relations with several important men who were of that faction, including Bland and Nicholas. The division was therefore primarily a personal matter.[11]

When Robinson died Edmund Pendleton—a protégé of the family—Peter Randolph, and Peter Lyons were the executors of his will. They

[9] *Journals of House of Burgesses*, 1766–1769, pp. xi–xxiii; *Virginia Gazette*, June 27, Sept. 5, 1766.

[10] Fauquier to Board of Trade, June 5, 1765, May 11, May 22, Nov. 10, 1766, C.O., series 5, 1331, ff. 69, 203, 207, 345; Nicholas to Lee, May 23, 1766, Lee MSS., U. of Va. library; *Virginia Gazette*, May 16, 23, 1766.

[11] Bland to Lee, May 22, 1766, Lee MSS., U. of Va. library; *Virginia Gazette*, Aug. 1, 1766.

undertook to pay off the indebtedness to the colony as rapidly as possible, but this was no simple matter. It appeared that Robinson had made large loans of public funds to personal friends, and the obvious method of procedure would have been to bring action against those who were indebted to the Robinson estate. It was believed, however, that many of the most important men in the colony were among those who had been indulged by Robinson at public expense, and there was no desire to expose them. Such action as was taken was carried on in a quiet manner, and, though the treasury never recovered all its losses, a large part of the defalcation was made good by the executors. Among the various persons who were involved with Robinson, it is possible to name only Archibald Cary, William Byrd, and Colonel John Chiswell as three who definitely were.[12]

It is impossible to identify many of the partisans of the opposing sides in these disputes because no votes were recorded in the House of Burgesses, but one bit of information is especially helpful toward this end. As the treasury crisis of 1765 approached, it was proposed in the House that the colony establish a loan office, borrowing money in England for that purpose. In this manner Robinson's debtors might have transferred their loans to the public office and thus have relieved the treasurer of personal responsibility. The loan office bill was passed by the House on May 24, 1765, and Peyton Randolph, his son-in-law Benjamin Harrison, Edmund Pendleton, Archibald Cary, Robert Burwell, Carter Braxton, and Dr. William Fleming were appointed managers on the part of the House to confer with the council. That body defeated the measure.[13]

Two points of significance may be inferred from these facts. First, the managers may be assumed to have supported the loan office bill and, therefore, may be looked upon as Robinson partisans. Such an assumption is supported in several cases by other information, and it tends to clarify the whole situation. Furthermore, it is evident from the action of the council that that body was not necessarily in close affiliation with the Robinson-Randolph group which dominated the House of Burgesses.

A few other happenings of this period throw additional light upon the political situation. At about the time of Robinson's death, his father-in-law, Colonel John Chiswell, it will be recalled, killed a man in a tavern brawl. It appears from the evidence taken at the time that the victim was drunk and unarmed, whereas Chiswell was under the influence of nothing but his passions. A preliminary hearing was held and Chiswell was com-

[12] George Wythe, ed., *Decisions of Cases in Virginia by the High Court of Chancery* (Richmond, 1852) pp. 127–132; *Virginia Gazette,* June 13, Aug. 15, 1766.
[13] *Journals of House of Burgesses, 1766–1769,* p. xviii.

mitted to the sheriff for imprisonment pending trial, but he was taken from the custody of the sheriff and bailed by three judges of the general court. These three were William Byrd, Pressley Thornton, and John Blair, president of the council. George Wythe gave his opinion that the judges were within their rights in admitting Chiswell to bail, and Peyton Randolph, the attorney-general, absented himself from the county during the hearing, but a bitter controversy arose over this action. It was stoutly maintained by several writers in the *Virginia Gazette* that the three judges went quite beyond their jurisdiction and, because of a personal interest, interfered with the course of justice.[14]

Still one more dispute arose at the same time to trouble the waters of local politics. Under the Stamp Act George Mercer had been appointed agent for Virginia, but when he arrived in Williamsburg, a "mob" of merchants and planters forced him to resign. Richard Henry Lee also sought the appointment, but he was now charged with joining in a celebration at Fredericksburg whereat Mercer was burned in effigy. Several articles on this subject appeared in the *Gazette,* but the Mercers resented outside interference and George's father, John, and his brother, James, took up the cudgels against Lee. Fauquier charged him with fomenting trouble in the Northern Neck in order to gain the speaker's chair.[15]

These incidents of 1765 and 1766 make it clear that Virginia politics did not run in a placid stream, and personal animosities were generated as a result. Lee and Patrick Henry stood out against the entrenched interests and leadership of the ruling families. They were powerful in the House of Burgesses and out of doors, but they were challenging a mighty clique, and that was dangerous business. Though friendly relations were maintained between many men who were in different political camps, the Lees seem to have imbibed a permanent antipathy for Carter Braxton and Benjamin Harrison. Some of the reasons for this will be brought out later. It does not speak well for the consistency of Richard Henry Lee that he was seeking the office of agent under the Stamp Act at the time he was joining with Patrick Henry in denunciation of that measure.

It was 1774 before another really serious crisis arose in Virginia. The passage of the Boston Port Bill prompted the House of Burgesses to set aside, in good Puritan fashion, a day of fasting and prayer. The governor repaid this act of devotion by dissolving the House, but the members met at

---

[14] *Virginia Gazette,* July 4, 11, 18, 25, Aug. 1, 1766.
[15] Fauquier to Board of Trade, Oct. 2, Nov. 3, 1765, April 7, 1766, C.O., series 5, 1331, ff. 123, 137, 189; *Virginia Gazette,* July 18, 25, Sept. 26, Nov. 3, 1766.

the Raleigh Tavern and, with Peyton Randolph in the chair, proposed a Continental Congress, adopted a non-importation association, and called a colonial convention to meet the following August. During the next year three similar conventions assembled. The first one, which met in March under Henry's strenuous leadership, passed by a majority of one vote resolutions for arming the colony. The next month Governor Dunmore brought down a storm upon his head by removing a store of powder from the arsenal in Williamsburg. At Fredericksburg and in Hanover, under the leadership of Henry, military forces assembled to descend upon the colonial capitol, but conservative leaders succeeded in preventing an armed clash.[16]

Henry and some of the radical leaders were urging the colony to armed resistance, while the conservatives were striving for conciliation, but even here there was no difference in fundamental principles. The conservatives had no more intention than did the radicals of submitting to taxation without representation or to other acts of the British government which were considered arbitrary. And not even the inflammable Patrick Henry had yet advocated independence in Virginia. It was again merely a question of method, with Henry and his allies trying to make political capital out of the situation.

On June 1 the House of Burgesses met for what proved to be its last regular session. On the 8th the governor fled the colony and took refuge on board H.M.S. *Fowey* which lay in York River. On June 24 the burgesses, just before adjourning, declared their loyalty to the Crown. In July the second convention of the year assembled and established a committee of safety, made up largely of conservative men with Pendleton at their head, to conduct the administration of the colony. During August Dunmore began to make forays upon the coast of the province and was planning, with the approval of the British government, to enlist the Negroes and Indians in his service. Thus actual war began in Virginia, the governor striking the first blow. The committee of safety then began to take measures for defense. In spite of all Henry's efforts, it was not he who brought on the crisis. Dunmore did that for him.[17]

When the fateful year of 1776 dawned upon the New World it could not yet be said that any political leader in Virginia had come out openly

[16] The association was generally opposed by the merchants, who said that debts had to be paid to English creditors. William Lee said that Pendleton, Nicholas, Charles Carter, Thomas Nelson, and Carrington also opposed it. William to R. H. Lee, Sept. 10, 1774, *Letters of William Lee*, I, 87–100; list of signers of the association, Aug. 1–6, 1774, C.O., series 5, 1352; Dunmore to Dartmouth, May 15, 1775, C.O., series 5, 1353.

[17] H. J. Eckenrode, *The Revolution in Virginia* (Boston, 1916) pp. 32–57; Dartmouth to Dunmore, July 12, 1775, C.O., series 5, 1353; *Am. Arch.*, series 4, II, 1240.

for independence. In fact, it cannot be stated positively that any of the leaders desired it. In March Joseph Reed of Philadelphia had written to George Washington: "It is said that the Virginians are so alarmed at the idea of independence that they have sent Mr. Braxton on purpose to turn the vote of that Colony, if any question on that subject should come before Congress." [18] George Mason later said that he decided for independence only when the last petition of Congress was rejected by Great Britain. On October 15, 1775, Pendleton had written to Richard Henry Lee to say that he had not been unprepared for the disagreeable intelligence of the small hope of accommodation. But, though the hope was small, most Virginians still ardently desired it. The following April Pendleton wrote that he thought independence inevitable after a few months; and then exclaimed: "Oh Britain how has[sic] thou suffered thy renowned arms to be degraded, by employing them in the cause of Tyranny and Oppression, when Virtue and liberty was the Shield and Spear wch made them Formidable!" On the same day Lee wrote to Henry that independence was necessary because European help was indispensable. On May 20 Henry wrote to John Adams that a French alliance was to him everything.[19]

Thus within a few months the situation began to change perceptibly. By February leading men were beginning to believe that acceptable concessions were not to be expected from the home government and that there was no alternative but separation. In this change of sentiment the conservatives were quite as forward as the radicals, so that by April there were only a few of them who still held out against crossing the Rubicon. Nicholas, Braxton, and Landon Carter were the most outspoken of these, but even they were only asking for delay. It is true that four members of the council—William Byrd, Richard Corbin, Ralph Wormeley, and John Camm—opposed independence altogether, and they were supported by John Randolph and a few others. Yet their influence was inconsiderable among the planters of the Tidewater or elsewhere in Virginia.[20]

When the last colonial convention met in May, 1776, Peyton Randolph was dead, and Pendleton was chosen to preside. In his opening speech he

[18] Reed to Washington, March 15, 1776, Reed, *Life and Correspondence of Joseph Reed*, I, 171–174.
[19] George Mason to George Mercer, Oct. 2, 1778, *Va. Historical Register*, II, 28–31; Pendleton to Lee, Oct. 15, 1775, *Am. Arch.*, series 4, III, 1067–1068; same to same, April 20, 1776, Lee MSS., U. of Va. library; Reed, *Life of Joseph Reed*, I, 171–174; Landon Carter's diary, March 28, 1776, *loc. cit.*, XVI, 257; R. H. Lee to Henry, Henkels, *op. cit.*, pp. 47–48; Henry to John Adams, May 20, 1776, C. F. Adams, *Life and Works of John Adams* (Boston, 1851) IV, 201–202.
[20] Dunmore to Dartmouth, June 25, 1775, C.O., series 5, 1353.

told the members that the questions of independence and a form of government were two of the principal subjects to be considered. And now at last the radicals and conservatives began to manifest some real differences in their political views. The Lees and their friends wished to have Congress declare the colonies independent and that body was then to establish a uniform plan of colonial government. On the other hand, the conservatives favored an immediate declaration of independence by Virginia, and she was then to draw up her own plan of government. In other words, the radicals were the Federalists, the conservatives the State-rights group.[21]

The reasons for this alignment are not far to seek. The Lees had a long-standing friendship with the two Adamses of Massachusetts, and in Congress the New England vote had been a tower of strength to them when confronted by the relatively conservative members from the middle colonies. John Adams had furnished the radical leaders with a plan of government which was supposed to be quite liberal, and the Lees and their following apparently wished Virginia to imitate the democracy of New England. As for the conservatives, they were extremely jealous of their local independence and leadership. They also had their plans for government. Their main object was to safeguard their position of leadership under the new order, and Carter Braxton drew up a proposed constitution which was far more illiberal than was the régime of the late colonial period.

No great internal political revolution had taken place as a result of the unsettled times, and, though there were new faces, the old leaders still had the ascendancy in the May convention of 1776. But on the question of independence the radicals won a victory. On May 15 the convention instructed its delegates in Congress to work for a declaration of independence by that body, and Pendleton drafted the resolutions to that effect. On the question of the frame of government the conservatives had their way, and a committee was appointed to draw up a declaration of rights and a constitution. Archibald Cary was placed at the head of this committee, but George Mason was its guiding spirit, for it was his draft which served as the ground-work for both the bill of rights and the constitution.

Mason's position in the convention requires a little explanation. In the Northern Neck he was a neighbor of the Lees, and with them he was associated in the business of the old Ohio Company. He is usually classified as a radical, and it is true that he normally cooperated in political meas-

21 Robert Leroy Hilldrup, "The Virginia Convention of 1776," (MS. dissertation in U. of Va. library) p. 156.

ures with the Lees and Henry, the latter of whom he considered "the first man upon the continent." But the bill of rights and the constitution which he so largely produced were distinctly conservative. That is to say, the suffrage was not extended, the Church was not disestablished, nor was the dominant position of the Tidewater aristocracy challenged. His phrase in the bill of rights that "all men are by nature equally free and independent" meant that men were equal only in respect to freedom, and a mental reservation was made as to the slaves. Nearly all the Virginia leaders at the time opposed slavery as an institution, but none favored extending equal political rights to Negroes. Mason gave voice also to Lockian principles of government and to certain political rights which had been well-established in England. There was certainly nothing radical in this.[22]

But what was Henry doing while these crucial questions were being discussed, and what of the Lees? Richard Henry Lee and Jefferson were absent in Congress, but Henry was in the convention, and so was Philip Ludwell Lee. Together they succeeded in striking from the declaration of rights a provision against bills of attainder, the conservatives standing more squarely for inalienable rights than the radicals. Philip Ludwell Lee does seem to have stood for certain liberal principles, but Henry expressed himself as satisfied with the constitution which was produced, and the truth appears to be that he formed a tacit alliance with the conservatives in order to be elected the first governor under the new régime. Richard Henry Lee supported Thomas Nelson, Senior, for that office, while Edmund Randolph supported Henry, who won by sixty votes to forty-five.[23]

It is clear that the radicals had no definite program for a liberal form of government. The John Adams plan which they had praised so highly cannot be said to have furnished such a model. Its only definite provisions were as to the machinery of government, and it put all faith in annual elections and an all-powerful lower house of assembly. Both governor and council were to be elected by this body. Though giving lip service to liberal principles, nothing definite was said as to the suffrage or apportionment of representation or the established Church, and these were the crucial questions.[24]

It was Thomas Jefferson who furnished the only constructive ideas

[22] James P. Holcomb, *Sketches of the Political Issues and Controversies of the Revolution* (Richmond, 1856) p. 114; Mason to Martin Cockburn, May 26, 1774, *Va. Historical Register,* III, 27–28.

[23] Hilldrup, *op. cit.,* pp. 202–205; R. H. Lee to Pendleton (?) May 12, 1776, Ballagh, I, 190–192.

[24] Adams, *Works of John Adams,* IV, 193–200.

along this line. The plan of government which he drew up and presented
to the convention, when it was too late for it to have much effect, had
several noteworthy features. It provided against future purchase of land
from the Indians except on behalf of and by authority of the assembly,
and enabled that body to establish future governments in the West. This
feature of his plan was actually added to the constitution, whereas the bill
of rights had said that no government separate from Virginia ought to be
established within her limits. These two provisions meant very different
things. Jefferson also advocated a freehold suffrage, but provided that
fifty acres of land should be granted to every "person of full age" who
did not own so much, and that "no other person shall be capable of taking
an appropriation." The plan also advocated apportionment of representation in accord with population, provided for disestablishment of the
Church, and said that no person thereafter coming into the State should
be held in slavery. These were strikingly liberal innovations, and Jefferson thus stands out as the first real progressive of the period in Virginia.[25]

Whereas the independence resolution of May 15 was not, in form,
a separate declaration of independence by Virginia, it was generally so
considered, and when it was adopted the British flag was pulled down in
Williamsburg. The constitution, which was adopted on June 29, included
a declaration of independence which was conclusive for Virginia individually, and it would be hard to deny that the Old Dominion became a free
State a week before the united colonies declared their independence in
Congress.

During the progress of the convention one incident came up which,
while not of major importance, throws a flood of light upon the political
situation in Virginia. Among the seven delegates who had been sent to
Congress in 1775 were Carter Braxton and Benjamin Harrison. They
belonged to wealthy and powerful families, and they were probably the
only dominant figures in Virginia who were extensively engaged in commerce. Both Harrison and Braxton had close business relations with
Robert Morris of Philadelphia, and they had no idea of failing to take
advantage of the eclipse of the Scottish merchants who had heretofore
so largely controlled the tobacco trade. Furthermore, Morris was now
the financial agent of the Congress, and Harrison's son, Benjamin, was
paymaster of the forces in Virginia.[26] The younger Harrison and Morris
took this occasion to agree on a scheme whereby each was to charge a

[25] P. L. Ford, ed., *The Writings of Thomas Jefferson* (New York, 1893) II,
25–26.
[26] Carter Braxton to Wm. Armistead, Sept. 17, 1776, *Tyler's Quarterly*, I, 92–93;
ibid., II, 171–173; Thomas Adams to John M. Jordan and Co., Oct. 23, 1770, *Va. Mag.
Hist. and Biog.*, XXIII, 57–59.

premium of two per cent on any bills which he drew on the other in connection with the public business. Great objection was made in Virginia
against paying the two per cent. The matter was taken up in the convention, and Harrison was called before that body and asked for an explanation. Afterward he wrote to Morris and said that he had satisfied his
inquisitors but that the relation between them should be kept a profound
secret for the present or else he would have trouble. He thought they
might later hit upon some scheme for carrying out their ideas, but for
the present the paymaster's account would have to be handled in some
other way.[27]

While this affair was being agitated a new election of delegates to
Congress occurred in the convention, and Harrison and Braxton were
dropped from the list. The younger Harrison indicated that his father was
simply being made to pay for the commercial affairs of the family. Charges
had been made against Braxton by the Lees, and Henry opposed him.
When the storm died down and Jefferson resigned from Congress, Harrison was elected in October to take his place, but Braxton remained at
home.[28]

Throughout the Revolution there were two opposing camps among the
leaders in Virginia. Braxton and Harrison were among the dominant
figures on one side, and the Lees stood in the front ranks of the other.
It was still true that personal antagonism did not extend much beyond
these central points, but Henry and Pendleton had their differences, while
Mason was no friend to either Braxton or Cary. These factions should
not be looked upon as political parties with a definite cleavage between
them, nor is it possible to trace any definite cleavage between the eastern
and western parts of Virginia. Washington can hardly be said to have
belonged to either faction, for he had friendly relations with both Harrison
and the Lees, and there were many men who changed sides as the issues
changed.

In connection with this political discussion it will be interesting to
consider briefly the mooted question as to why Virginia deserted her
allegiance to the British Crown with so much conviction and promptness.
The situation regarding planter debts to British merchants and the question of Western lands have usually been brought forward by modern
writers as the principal forces back of the desire for independence. It

[27] Harrison to Willing, Morris and Co., April 4, May 17, May 26, June 7, June 15,
accounts of July 28–Aug. 10, 1776, Robert Morris MSS., L. of C.
[28] Harrison to Robert Morris, June 29, 1776, *ibid.*; Willing and Morris to William
Bingham, July 24, 1776, *ibid.*; E(dmund?) R(andolph?) to Jefferson, June 23, 1776,
Jefferson MSS., L. of C.; *Journal of the Virginia House of Delegates,* Oct. 10, 1776,
p. 6.

should be clear, however, from this study that the resentment against the Vandalia project was much less widespread than has usually been supposed. This also appears to have been the case in regard to the Quebec Act. Very few Virginians had any interest in the lands north of the Ohio River before the Revolution; the complaints made against the act were based upon religious and political rather than economic grounds. As to planter debts, members of the conservative Tidewater gentry owed most of them, and they, in the majority of cases, went over to the cause of independence only as a last resort. Though some of them were certainly glad to use the disturbances of 1774 and 1775 in order to get a respite from their creditors, they surely would have sought independence at the first opportunity if final escape from their creditors had been their primary object. Furthermore, many of them really had a high sense of honor in such matters.[29]

What the planters actually wanted was a restoration of the situation as it had been prior to 1763. They would have insisted that Western lands be left open to settlement, that no further taxes be imposed on them by Parliament, and that no American bishop be appointed to deprive the vestries of the patronage of their parishes. They desired the non-interference of Parliament in their local government and the continuance of all their ancient privileges. Granted these, they would gladly have avoided the democratic dangers which a revolution held over their heads.[30]

[29] Thomas Adams to T. Hall, Nov. (?), 1774, *Va. Mag. Hist. and Biog.*, XXIII, 178–179.

[30] Richard Bland to Thomas Adams, Aug. 1, 1771, *Va. Mag. Hist. and Biog.*, VI, 127–134; Diary of Landon Carter, *loc. cit.*, XVIII, 37–44.

CHAPTER XII

INDEPENDENCE AND VIRGINIA'S WESTERN
LAND PROBLEM

NO group of people in America was more deeply affected by the declaration of independence than were the land speculators. All their plans were changed by that political event. Even the anticipation of it caused them grave concern, for successful speculation was never more dependent upon a shrewd prognostication of events than in this case. As soon, therefore, as independence became a probability, the dealers in Western land schemes began to shape their courses accordingly. Both in Kentucky and in the Pittsburgh area there was much uneasiness as to the attitude which might be assumed by the government of Virginia.

Until the latter part of 1775 the Transylvania Company had had smooth sailing in Kentucky. Most of the Virginians who had come out to that country were working in apparent harmony with it, for Dunmore certainly had no authority to open to settlement any land which lay beyond the Kentucky River to the west and south, and his orders actually forbade the opening of any beyond the Alleghenies. The only hope was in Henderson and the specious Camden-Yorke opinion. But now the situation began to change. The Transylvania proprietors were marking out for themselves large tracts near the Falls of the Ohio, where Douglas, Hite, and Floyd had previously made surveys for a number of influential Virginians. It is not surprising, therefore, that Isaac Hite, now living at Harrodsburg, should begin to show signs of opposition to Henderson and his associates.

In December, 1775, we find him, along with the Harrods, McAfees, and other settlers of Harrodsburg, sending a protest to the Transylvania Company complaining that it had raised the price of its lands. The act complained of was quite in accord with the plans of the company, for only the first settlers were to be allowed to purchase at the original price, and no one had previously complained of the arrangement. The representatives of the company thought that the surveys at the Falls lay behind the protest, and they agreed to limit the grants which should be made in that neighborhood to one thousand acres, and this to be allowed to settlers only. But the trouble continued, the Harrodsburg men refusing to take up any lands under the company. John Williams, agent for Transylvania, called off the meeting of a second assembly which he had planned for the spring.[1]

It is noteworthy that John Floyd continued to act as surveyor for the Transylvania Company during the year 1776, and spoke of the Harrodsburg men as "banditti." John Todd, a friend of Preston who was in Kentucky at the time, took no part in the affair, but, on the contrary, was dickering with Henderson about some of William Fleming's claims at the Falls. On April 2, Willis Lee was killed in this neighborhood while acting in conjunction with a party led to that place by Henderson himself. Joseph Martin, at his settlement in Powell's Valley, also showed no signs of breaking with Henderson. These men were closer to those occupying the seats of the mighty in Virginia than were Harrod and Hite, and their attitude is significant on that account. Dr. Thomas Walker wrote to Joseph Martin about this time, indicating his willingness to take up lands under the Transylvania Company and instructed Martin to inquire of Henderson concerning his terms. In fact, the first tangible evidence of a change of sentiment on the part of any of the leading figures of the Preston group is to be found in a letter of October 23, 1776, from Christian to Henry, and even here there is nothing more than a hint of the change.[2]

The movement against the Transylvania Company, therefore, seems to have had its origin in the stockaded fort at Harrodsburg. Its leaders must have thought that there was a fair prospect that independence would be declared, for there would have been slim chance indeed of their getting any immediate grants from the royal government had it remained in power. That this sentiment should have developed in the West before it did in the East is not altogether surprising. Neither Henry nor any other Eastern leader had yet declared for independence when Hite made his first protest. By this time some of them certainly realized the possibility of it, but they were not staking their land claims upon it. Hence, they were not yet ready to break with Henderson entirely.

On the other hand, the Harrodsburg men meant business. On May 18, 1776, three days after the Virginia convention passed its independence resolution, that body was presented with a petition from the frontier

[1] C.V.S.P., I, 274–275; Ranck, Boonesborough, pp. 232–239; Williams to Joseph Martin, March 3, 1776, Draper MSS., 16J54; Lester, The Transylvania Colony, Chap. VIII.

[2] John Todd to Wm. Fleming, May 3, 1776, Fleming MSS., W. and L. U. library; Dorsey Pentecost to Committee of Safety, May 15, 1776, Va. Mag. Hist. and Biog., XVI, 41–42; Floyd to Martin, May 19, 1776, Draper MSS., 1XX10; Christian to Henry, Oct. 23, 1776, Henry, Henry, III, 128.

outpost at Harrodsburg making charges against the Transylvania Company. It presently received from John Craig another which stated that the Transylvanians were undertaking to establish a separate government. On May 20 there was read in the convention the advertisement published by George Morgan wherein he proposed to sell Virginia lands in the name of the Indiana Company. During June a petition was presented from Fincastle complaining that the agents of the land companies were trying to collect large sums from settlers. Thus the question of Western land claims, in several of its phases, was placed before the convention which already had its hands full.[3]

One could not accuse Judge Henderson of being neglectful of his interests. He and most of his company were in Williamsburg while these events were taking place; on June 15 they presented the convention with a counter-petition. In this they made the erroneous statement that they had not tried to establish a new government, but they made it quite clear that they denied Virginia's claim to the soil in question. On June 24 the convention answered this by passing a resolution declaring that purchases of lands from Indians would not be considered valid unless approved by the legislature. The act also provided that actual settlers should have preemption of the land upon which they were established. Henderson's next move was to issue a proclamation warning squatters off his domain. Then, on July 4, the convention created a committee, made up largely of interested parties, to take evidence against the companies which claimed Virginia land by virtue of Indian deed. This was cold comfort for the Transylvania and Indiana Companies, yet it left their cases open. After hearing the evidence which the committee was to collect, the legislature was still free to approve their claims. And both companies had powerful friends in Virginia.[4]

Meanwhile, the anti-Transylvania movement in Kentucky was gaining momentum. The Harrodsburg leaders had decided to take matters into their own hands and sent out a call for an assembly of the people to gather at that place on June 8. The meeting took place as scheduled and remained in session until the 15th. Captain John Gabriel Jones was selected to preside over the assembly. He was the nephew of Gabriel Jones, said to have been Jefferson's first law partner, the first attorney to practice in the Valley of Virginia and the father-in-law of John Harvie, of Albemarle, who later became head of Virginia's land office. A committee, similar to the county committees which had been organized elsewhere,

---

[3] *Proceedings of the Convention of Virginia,* May, 1776, pp. 18–19, 20, 39–40.
[4] *Ibid.,* pp. 51–53, 63, 83–84; minutes of the Convention, June 15, 1776, Jefferson MSS., L. of C.; *Am. Arch.,* series 4, VI, 1573–1576; *C.V.S.P.,* I, 271–272.

was chosen and a petition was addressed to the convention requesting that West Fincastle be organized as a separate county. The organization of a separate government for West Augusta was cited as a precedent in case the royal instructions against establishment of new counties should stand in the way. Furthermore, two delegates were elected to carry this petition to Richmond and to present themselves to the convention as the representatives of West Fincastle. The presiding officer, Jones, and Captain George Rogers Clark were selected for this mission.[5]

Clark had been in Kentucky the previous year, but he did not reach Harrodsburg on this occasion until after his election as a delegate. Taking this into consideration, along with the fact that he was only twenty-four years of age and not a resident of Kentucky, his selection is not a little surprising. Some one must have fixed it for him, and it is not unlikely that Jones was that man. Clark's family was living in Caroline County at this time, and they had business connections with Thomas Marshall, father of the future Chief Justice, and with the Bullitts, the Hites, and the Madisons. These facts and his Western experiences of the past few years are sufficient to show that Clark was not an altogether unknown young man at the time. Despite his own claim to that effect, he had not been among the leaders of the anti-Transylvania movement at Harrodsburg, and it must have been Jones's influence, rather than his own, which put him forward on the occasion.[6]

Jones and Clark did not present their petition to the convention of 1776. That body adjourned on July 5th, before they reached Richmond. On the way down Jones made a detour to the Holston country, and Clark held a conference with Patrick Henry, who had just been elected governor of Virginia. This is the first known contact between these two men, and its importance can hardly be over-estimated. From this time until the end of the Revolution they worked continuously together, and Clark, whose account of their transactions is the one usually followed, represents himself as the leader and Henry as the collaborator in all that they did. Clark's account doubtless is colored with the inflated egoism of the very young, for, while there is no way of knowing in detail what actually passed between them, considering the relative age, experience,

[5] James R. Robertson, ed., *Petitions of the Early Inhabitants of Kentucky to the General Assembly of Virginia, 1769–1792* (Louisville, 1914) pp. 36–39; *Va. Mag. of Hist. and Biog.,* XVI, 157–160; there are originals of these petitions in the Virginia Archives, petitions, and in the Draper MSS., 14J148–152 is a petition signed at Harrodsburg, June 15, 1776, by Abraham Hite, clerk.

[6] Clark apparently entered land with the Transylvania Company as late as April 9, 1776. John Williams to John Floyd, Draper MSS., 16DD6; G. R. Clark to Jonathan Clark, Feb. 26, 1776, *ibid.,* 1L23; Jonathan Clark to John Clark, Jr., June 13, 1776, *ibid.,* 1L30; John Clark, Jr. to "Brother," Aug. 12, 1776, *ibid.,* 1L31.

and political sagacity of the two, it is not likely that the young stripling from the frontier played the leading part in shaping their ideas, and that the versatile new governor of Virginia merely fell in with them. Henry, as well as young Clark, knew the West. Had he not for years and years pinned his hope for a fortune on the boundless free lands beyond the mountains?

By the time Clark reached Richmond the government under the new constitution was in operation, but the House of Delegates had not yet convened. He appealed to the Council of State for a supply of powder for Kentucky, but this body was dominated by conservative men and it was not until after he had threatened that Kentucky would seek friends elsewhere if not aided by Virginia, that he prevailed on them to furnish transportation for the powder which they had granted.[7]

When the House of Delegates assembled Jones had already arrived in Richmond. What his business in the Holston country may have been, we have no way of knowing. On October 8 Jones and Clark presented to the House of Delegates the petition of West Fincastle. They were not allowed to take seats as representatives of the district, and they soon found that there was strong opposition to the creation of a new county in the Kentucky country. Richard Henderson was on hand to oppose the move, and he was aided by Arthur Campbell, lieutenant of Fincastle. These leaders found many sympathizers in the ranks of Virginia's conservative politicians, but Jefferson and Mason sided with Kentucky. It was not until December 7, 1776, that the battle was won by the West. Fincastle County, whose name was connected with the now odious rule of Lord Dunmore, was abolished and three new counties were set up in its stead. Kentucky was one of these. John Todd became the first presiding justice, with Logan and Floyd members of the court. While this was a blow to the Henderson régime, it had no bearing upon the claim to the soil of Transylvania. That question was left for settlement at a later date.[8]

Turning now to the Pittsburgh area, we find the boundary controversy still raging. The delegates of Virginia and Pennsylvania in the Continental Congress had urged moderation on the settlers, but this had not quieted them. During 1776 the Virginia convention made two propositions to Pennsylvania for settling the dispute, but these did not go far enough to satisfy the Quaker State, and no serious attention was paid

---

[7] James, *Clark Papers, 1771–1781*, pp. 208–213.
[8] *Journal of the House of Delegates*, Oct. 8, 11, 19, 1776, pp. 4, 8–9, 19; *ibid.*, Dec. 7, 1776, p. 87; Hening, IX, 257; Va. Archives, petitions, Oct. 19, 1776.

to them in that quarter. On the other hand, Pennsylvania, which had remained on the defensive during the Dunmore régime, now assumed the offensive in the quarrel. Officials were appointed to exercise jurisdiction in areas which, up to that time, had been under Virginia control. Thomas Scott was one of these, and he presently found an opportunity to arrest and incarcerate Dorsey Pentecost, the Virginia lieutenant of the District of West Augusta.[9]

The majority of the Virginia leaders as well as the people in the area concerned were evidently wishing for a peaceful settlement of this annoying controversy, for, after all, it was of small weight in comparison to the war which the colonies were waging in common. And it was a small matter when lumped with Virginia's whole problem of Western lands. These larger problems now engrossed the attention of the Old Dominion.[10]

Not long before Dunmore abdicated his government he gave orders for the evacuation of the Western forts which had been established during his campaign against the Shawnee in 1774. At Fort Blair on the Kanawha the evacuation was carried out, and the revolutionary government of Virginia took the first opportunity to authorize garrisons both here and at the old Fort Fincastle, now Fort Henry, at Wheeling—this in addition to the forces it was maintaining at Redstone and Pittsburgh. Thus Virginia established a line of frontier defense while Congress was working for a truce with the Indians. But Virginia cooperated with the Congressional policy so far as to pass, on May 21, an ordinance which prohibited settlements north of the Ohio River.[11]

On November 6 Virginia divided the old District of West Augusta into the three new counties of Yohogania, Monongalia, and Ohio. The seat of government for West Augusta had already been transferred from Pittsburgh to Catfish Camp. The evacuation of Pittsburgh indicated the weakness of the Virginia party at this time. Croghan, impoverished and under suspicion of Loyalism, no longer took an active part in public affairs, but some of his confederates were still busy in the administration of Yohogania, the panel of justices for this county being much the same as that which had acted for West Augusta. The creation of these new counties was in line with the policy which Clark and the Virginia radicals

[9] Dorsey Pentecost to Committee of Safety, June 2, 4, 1776, *Va. Mag. of Hist. and Biog.*, XVI, 48–49, 50-51; Pentecost to Henry, Nov. 5, 1776, *ibid.*, XVII, 161–163; *Am. Arch.*, series 4, VI, 1576; Papers of Continental Congress, Va. State Papers, I, 71.

[10] Va. Archives, petitions, June 29, 1776.

[11] *Am. Arch.*, series 4, VI, 1532; *Va. Mag. Hist. and Biog.*, XVIII, 33; Pendleton, *Tazewell County*, p. 356; Withers, 216.

had been able to put through for strengthening the political interest of the West. On this issue there was a clearer division between the two factions than on any other that had yet arisen. But as far as the Pittsburgh area was concerned the creation of new counties appears as an attempt to bolster a losing cause.[12]

[12] *Journal of the House of Delegates,* Nov. 6, 1776, p. 43; Hening, IX, 262.

CHAPTER XIII

THE LAND QUESTION AND THE CONTINENTAL CONGRESS, 1776

DURING 1776 the Continental Congress continued to be divided between the two major factions which had taken shape during the earlier sessions. From the geographical point of view it can be said that New England and the South were combined against the middle colonies. From the economic angle it is an almost equally good generalization to state that the agrarian interests of the former group predominated over the commercial interests of the latter. But, of course, both interests were represented in all the colonies, and the geographical alignment was therefore not clearcut.

As to Virginia, Carter Braxton and Benjamin Harrison represented the commercial interest in Congress, but the Lees, with the support of Jefferson and Wythe, were able to maintain a majority against them. John Hancock likewise typified the commercial element of New England, though the two Adamses were able to carry, not only Massachusetts, but a majority of the New England delegates along with them.

Whether the coalition between the Lees and the Adamses was based on their long-standing personal friendship or upon a similarity of interests, it is true that in combination they were generally able to dominate the deliberations of Congress and to carry their program against the majority of the delegates from the middle colonies.

At the head of this opposition group stood Robert Morris and Benjamin Franklin of Pennsylvania. Franklin's poltical career had been a strange one, and nothing in it was stranger than his cooperation with Morris in Congressional matters. In 1764 he had stood with the Quakers in opposition to the Proprietary party in Pennsylvania and had been sent to England by the Galloway-Wharton group to work for the revocation of the Penn charter. While the Quakers, who had a majority in the assembly, were inclined to submit to the Stamp Act, the merchants and lawyers of the Morris, Willing, and Dickinson faction came out with the Proprietary party, the Presbyterians and Anglicans against it. They were able in this way to make capital against the anti-Proprietary party, and enlisted the Scotch-Irish and some of the Germans in their cause.

The tide was too strong, and presently Franklin came out against the Stamp Act.

Opposition to the British acts of 1774 was led by the same group of merchants and lawyers in Pennsylvania, and now Franklin was clearly on its side. But when the question of independence came up Morris, Willing, and Dickinson stood with Galloway, the Whartons, and a majority of the Quakers in opposing it, but Franklin was one of its strongest proponents. He was also in opposition to Morris and the merchants when he favored the democratic constitution which the radical party of Presbyterians and proletariat promulgated for Pennsylvania in 1776. Yet in Congress he joined Morris and his group in opposition to the Adams-Lee faction.[1]

It thus appears that in the struggles leading up to the Revolution the mercantile group of Pennsylvania occupied practically the same ground which was occupied in Virginia by Harrison and Braxton, while Franklin ran almost the identical course which was run by Patrick Henry in the Old Dominion. Political expediency appears to have been the watchword of both.

New Jersey and Delaware were under the political influence of Pennsylvania, and Maryland was also a commercial colony with many interests in common. These four governments, therefore, usually stood together with Robert Morris as their mentor, though by no means their only powerful personage.

It was the Lees and the Adamses who pushed through the program of independence and the appointment of Washington to the command of the army, the former encountering strong opposition from the middle colonies. The Adams-Lee coalition dominated also the discussions of the crucial question of public lands.[2]

A determined effort was made by Franklin, Dickinson, and their

---

[1] C. H. Lincoln, *The Revolutionary Movement in Pennsylvania* (Philadelphia, 1901) pp. 172ff.; W. Roy Smith, "Sectionalism in Pennsylvania during the Revolution," *Political Science Quarterly*, XXIV, 208–235; Samuel B. Harding, "Party Struggles over the First Pennsylvania Constitution," American Historical Association, *Annual Report*, 1894, pp. 371–402; James P. Holcombe, "Sketches of the Political Issues and Controversies of the Revolution" (pamphlet in the Library of Congress, 1856) p. 38; Sydney George Fisher, *Pennsylvania: Colony and Commonwealth* (Philadelphia, 1907) pp. 255–267, 297–298, 319–235, 335–336; Samuel Wharton to William Franklin, Sept. 29, 1765, Franklin MSS., I, 159, A.P.S.; Thomas Wharton to Benjamin Franklin, Aug. 14, 1765, *ibid.*, I, 156; John Hughes to Commissioners of Stamp Office, Oct. 12, 1765, J. Almon, *Collection of Interesting Authentic Papers*, p. 47; *New Jersey Archives*, V, 575–586; W. B. Reed, *Life and Correspondence of Joseph Reed* (Philadelphia, 1847) I, 65ff., 151–154; Alexander Graydon, *Memoirs of his own Time*, (J. S. Littell, ed., Philadelphia, 1846) pp. 118–122.

[2] C. F. Adams, *Works of John Adams*, III, 31–32; J. B. Sanders, *Evolution of Executive Departments of the Continental Congress* (Chapel Hill, 1935) pp. 41–42.

friends to secure for Congress under the Articles of Confederation the right to fix boundaries of the States claiming Western lands and to make all purchases of territory from the Indians. This was opposed by the Virginia delegates, and with the aid of North Carolina, Georgia, and New England they were able to defeat the project, with the result, however, that the Articles were not adopted until the following year.[3]

Even from the first Maryland took the lead in the fight against Virginia's extensive Western claims, and the conflict extended to various questions not immediately connected with the Articles of Confederation. On September 16 Congress proposed to give a bounty of land to Continental troops who enlisted for the duration of the War. The lands were to be purchased with funds from the general treasury, and Maryland at once objected. The fight was led on her part by Thomas Johnson and Samuel Chase, both members of the Wabash Land Company.[4]

If one were to judge by the records of Congress he would have to assume that the great land companies were remarkably quiet during 1776, for not a single petition from any of them is mentioned in the journals. It is true that their promoters were a bit bewildered by the changing political scene, and that Congress did not, for the moment, hold out much hope for them except in the fight Maryland and her sister States of the center were making to limit the extent of those States which claimed their borders reached to the Mississippi. If this were accomplished the land companies would have a vast field open to their operations, for not a word to the prejudice of their claims was said by the proponents of the Maryland cause. Since Franklin, Morris, James Wilson, George Ross, and others from Pennsylvania, as well as Johnson, Chase, Carroll, and Robert Morris's brother-in-law William Paca, of Maryland, were members of these companies, this circumstance is easily understood.[5]

Virginia's claim was the principal object of attack during the discussions of this year. New York had not yet thought up the fine-spun claim which she later advanced and surrendered with such fine dramatic effect. Massachusetts was not pushing her case, and Connecticut was devoting her energies to her dispute with Pennsylvania over the Wyoming Valley. North Carolina and Georgia were certainly influenced by their ambitions,

[3] *Journals of the Continental Congress,* July 21, 1775, II, 198; *ibid.,* Aug. 20, 1776, V, 679–680; E. S. Corwin, *French Policy and the American Alliance of 1778* (Princeton, 1916) p. 219; Walter H. Mohr, *Federal Indian Relations, 1774–1788,* pp. 176–177.

[4] *Am. Arch.,* series 5, III, 53, 120, 134, 508, 660–661, 787–788, 827; *Journals of the Continental Congress,* Nov. 23, 1776, VI, 978; Kathryn Sullivan, *Maryland and France* (Philadelphia, 1936) pp. 18–23.

[5] Thomas Wharton to Levy A. Levy, July 28, 1776, Wharton letter book, H.S.P.; Thomas Wharton to ———— (?), Sept. 18, 1776, *ibid.;* E. S. Delaplaine, *Life of Thomas Johnson* (New York, 1927) pp. 140ff.

but it appears that New England in her alliance with Virginia was expecting her compensation otherwise than in Western lands.

The struggle, then, was not one between the large States and the small ones, between those having Western claims and those possessing none. It was rather a contest between certain States claiming Western lands for themselves, on one side, and those claiming it in the interest of certain land companies on the other, the middle group of States being controlled largely by members of the great land companies.[6]

While the Adams-Lee faction was victorious in most of the important struggles, the Franklin-Morris group got the upper hand in one phase of Congressional activity which was of utmost significance. On November 29, 1775, the Committee of Secret Correspondence was organized, with Franklin, Robert Morris, Harrison, Thomas Johnson, Dickinson, and Jay as its members. The duties of this body were both diplomatic and commercial. It was to make contacts with foreign governments and, with the aid of the Secret Commercial Committee, secure supplies from abroad. On March 3, 1776, it dispatched Silas Deane to France where he was to act as commercial and diplomatic agent for the committee and as private commercial agent for Robert Morris. Shortly Morris's brother Thomas and John Ross were dispatched to assist Deane in commercial matters of both private and public character. William Bingham was similarly sent to Martinique whence goods from the Continent were to be transshipped, and when the French government made him a loan of sixty thousand livres for his operations, he was able to amass a large private fortune. These agents were instructed to get in touch with Messrs. S. and J. H. Delap of Bordeaux, Messrs. Clifford and Teysett of Amsterdam, and with other commercial houses in the principal ports of the Continent. Morris also had business relations with the leading merchants in the colonies, including Harrison and Braxton in Virginia, Hooper and Hewes in North Carolina, and others.[7]

Since most of the foreign commerce of the colonies had been carried on by British and Scottish merchants before the War the door was left wide open for American enterprise when hostilities began. It was Morris who took advantage of that opportunity, and his private agents served

---

[6] See for a different interpretation, James C. Welling, *The Land Politics of the United States* (New York, 1888) pp. 6ff.

[7] Minutes of the French legation in the United States (L. of C. photostat from William S. Mason's library, Evanston, Ill.) Vol. 1, book 6, list of members of Congress, 1788; Wharton, *Diplomatic Correspondence of the Revolution*, I, 559–560, II, 78–80; J. B. Sanders, *op. cit.*, pp. 38–39; *Am. Arch.*, series 4, VI, 783; Willing and Morris to Samuel Beall, March 6, 1776, Morris MSS., L. of C.; Deane to Morris, May 2, 1776, *ibid.*; Deane to Morris, June 23, 1776, *ibid.*; Willing and Morris to Bingham, Sept. 14, 1776, *ibid.*; same to same, Oct. 20, 1776, *ibid.*; same to same, Dec. 3, 1776, *ibid.*

also as the agents of the Congress in commercial matters. This mingling of private and public business was subject to great abuse, and there is no question that Morris abused it. Not only was he able to charge Congress his own prices for the goods which he furnished the government, but it happened more than once that when his ships were lost and his private property destroyed, Congress assumed the risk and paid the bill. Furthermore, when the American cause began to look somewhat unpromising in the fall of 1776 Morris wrote to Bingham that if things got any worse, "it might not be a desirable thing to bring property hither." The idea that Morris financed the Revolution out of his own pocket is purely mythological. The truth is that the Revolution financed Robert Morris.[8] Brissot de Warville thought that it was "scarcely to be credited that amidst the disaster of America, Mr. Morris, the inhabitant of a town just emancipated from the English, should possess a fortune of eight millions." It is, however, the Frenchman added, "in the most critical times that great fortunes are acquired . . . commerce bears everywhere the same character . . . it is a citizen of the universe, it excludes alike the virtues and the prejudices that stand in the way of its interest." [9]

These remarks may seem to be aside from the main subject under discussion, but Morris was a land speculator as well as a merchant and politician, and each one of these interests had a bearing upon the other. The connection is indicated by the fact that Deane had scarcely reached France before he began to write home about plans to organize a great European-American land company to exploit the country north of the Ohio. Furthermore, the factional strife in Congress centered largely around the operations of the Committee of Secret Correspondence, and we shall have cause, from time to time, to revert to the subject.[10]

While Franklin was much concerned in the operations of this committee, it is not to be supposed that he forgot his interest in the land companies. His attitude in the matter of the Articles of Confederation is evidence to that effect. Though Vandalia presented no petition to Congress during 1776, the situation in the Pittsburgh area showed that the child was not dead, nor yet altogether unconscious.

The factional strife in that stormy neighborhood—always acute—was now, if anything, more complicated than ever. In the days of Lord Dun-

[8] Willing and Morris to Bingham, Sept. 27, 1776, *ibid.;* Deane to Morris, Dec. 4, 1776, misc. MSS., William S. Mason library; Sumner, *Morris,* I, 308.
[9] Brissot de Warville, *New Travels in the United States, 1788,* (London, 1794) p. 387.
[10] Wharton, *Diplomatic Correspondence of the Revolution,* II, 153–157; *Am. Arch.,* series 5, III, 1019–1022.

more, Croghan's following had cooperated with the Virginia governor against St. Clair and the party which adhered to the Pennsylvania proprietors. Now Dunmore was gone and Croghan was no longer taking an active part in the politics of West Augusta, though he was still nominally chairman of the county committee. Among his followers, Alexander Ross and Alexander McKee were both detected in correspondence with the enemy. Ross was arrested in Maryland but liberated by Congress and soon made his way from Pittsburgh to the Natchez country on the lower Mississippi. Here we shall hear of him again. McKee was carrying on his correspondence in line of duty as deputy Indian agent under the British régime. Richard Butler, Indian agent under Congress, turned his letters over to the county authorities, and McKee was put upon parole, but allowed to go about his personal business with the natives. Smallman seems to have taken over Croghan's functions on the county committee, and Edward Ward was still active in this connection. John Campbell and John Gibson were also officials of the county, and they were working in cooperation with the Virginia faction, whereas the remainder of Croghan's old following presumably remained true to the Vandalia-Indiana interests.[11]

The Virginia party was now headed by Captain John Neville who commanded the Virginia troops, which constituted the only military force in the neighborhood. His principal supporters, like William Crawford and Dorsey Pentecost, were connected with the military organization of the county. Then there was St. Clair's old Pennsylvania following, which had represented the Proprietary interest in opposition both to Vandalia and to Virginia. It remained faithful to Pennsylvania under the new régime, and kept its hold on the organization of Westmoreland County. The boundary dispute with Virginia still went on, but both Pennsylvania and Virginia factions were strongly Whig in principle, while the loyalty of the Croghan following, and even that of Croghan himself, was under some suspicion.

The situation was further complicated when Congress created an Indian commission for the Middle Department and established its headquarters at Pittsburgh. Dr. Thomas Walker and John Harvie, both of Albemarle County, Virginia, and Jasper Yeates and John Montgomery, of Pennsylvania, both friends of James Wilson, now constituted that

---

[11] Minutes of Indian commissioners, Aug. 29, 1776, Yeates papers, H.S.P.; certificate of A. McKee, May 9, 1776, Dreer MSS., French Refugees, Colonial and Indian Affairs, H.S.P., *Am. Arch.*, series 4, V, 815–819; *ibid.*, series 5, I, 1607; *Journals of the Continental Congress*, IV, 317, V, 652; Continental Congress papers, 69, I, f. 119; Mrs. Dunbar Rowland, *Life, Letters and Papers of William Dunbar* (Jackson, Miss., 1930) pp. 38, 50, 51.

commission; on April 10, Congress, without any obviously good reason, deposed Richard Butler as Indian agent for the district and appointed George Morgan in his stead. Morgan had not prospered since the disruption of his commercial partnership with Baynton and Wharton, but he had taken a leading part in the recent reorganization of the Indiana Company; and now he was to act at Pittsburgh as agent both for that body and for Congress. The minions of the Franklin-Morris group in Congress had a positive genius for combining public and private business, and Morgan was no exception to the rule.[12]

At the beginning of the War, Congress had adopted a policy of encouraging the Western Indians to maintain a status of neutrality. While carrying on offensive operations against Quebec this neutral policy was adhered to on the Pittsburgh front during the first half of 1776. As far as the Delawares, Shawnee, and Iroquois were concerned it was reasonably successful, these tribes agreeing to a neutrality policy at a conference held at Fort Pitt on July 6. It appears that Sir John Johnson, son and successor of Sir William, did nothing to upset the arrangement. But the Wyandottes and more Western tribes were under the influence of the British administration at Detroit, and that government did not hesitate to make active use of them from the first.[13]

Thus when Morgan was dispatched to Pittsburgh neutrality was still the policy of his government, but most of the Pennsylvania and Virginia leaders in the region were of a different opinion. In 1775 St. Clair had urged an expedition against Detroit, and the leaders about Pittsburgh, including George Rogers Clark, David Rogers, William Harrod, and Hancock Lee prepared to carry out the plan. Despite the advocacy of the expedition by James Wilson and Lewis Morris, Congress refused to give its assent and the propitious moment was allowed to pass.[14]

For some time Washington had been urging that the Indians should be enlisted in the American cause. On May 21, 1776, the convention of Virginia commissioned John Gibson to solicit the aid of the friendly tribes, but Morgan tried to forestall him. On May 25 Congress passed a resolution to the effect that it was "highly expedient to engage the Indians in the service of the United Colonies," and a proposition for an expedition against Detroit was taken under advisement. This was just six weeks after Morgan's appointment, but it had no effect on his policy. He con-

[12] Wilson to Yeates, July 10, 1776, Gratz MSS., H.S.P.
[13] Joseph Chew to (Dartmouth?) Jan. 7, 1776, Add. MSS., 29237, Br. Mus.; *Am. Arch.*, series 5, I, 36–37, III, 599–600; Hildreth, *Pioneer History*, p. 109.
[14] Alexander Blain to Matthew Elliott, Feb. 7, 1776, Add. MSS., 21845, Br. Mus.; Wm. Thompson, to Jas. Wilson, Apr. 15, 1776, Gratz MSS., H.S.P.; *St. Clair Papers*, I, 14–15; Draper MSS., 16J3–4; *Am. Arch.*, series 4, III, 717; see also Alvord, *The Illinois Country*, 315; Burnett, I, 193.

tinued to insist on neutrality, and Congress failed to come to any decision about the campaign against Detroit during this year, in spite of Washington's apparent desire for such a measure.[15]

By this time Morgan was immersed in several activities which had no bearing on his work for the Continental Congress. He already had connections with the two traders, Richard Winston and Daniel Kennedy, at Kaskaskia who were carrying on a traffic with New Orleans in flour and other goods. Robert Morris was their backer in Philadelphia, and Oliver Pollock was their agent in New Orleans. Morgan kept in touch with them and also had relations with other traders, notably Matthew Elliott and David Duncan who operated from Pittsburgh. Trading in the Indian country was always dangerous business in time of war, but this trade was of more than merely commercial importance. It enabled Morgan, through the contacts of his agents with the Indians, to get information of the situation of affairs at Niagara and Detroit and even to carry on a correspondence with those British posts.[16]

Interesting as these activities were, they take on a real significance only when considered in connection with other developments which unfolded themselves shortly after Morgan reached Pittsburgh. One was an attempt to establish a new government in the area. During June, 1776, plans were made for calling a convention of the people to draw up a constitution and to apply to Congress for admission as a fourteenth colony, and a memorial to Congress was drafted. When some opposition to this plan developed, anonymous advertisements were published setting forth that the conflicting interests of Virginia and Pennsylvania and the land claims of Croghan and the Indiana and Vandalia Companies made some decisive action necessary. The people were asked to meet at the polls during August and express their opinions as to whether it were best to appeal directly to Congress to intervene or to frame a local government to deal independently with the situation. In case they decided to pursue the latter course they were to elect a constitutional convention according to the original plan. The boundaries of the new State on the west were to be the same as those formerly planned for the Vandalia colony, but it was to include also the Pennsylvania lands lying west of the Fort Stanwix line. The claims of the Walpole Company were stated in the most favorable terms.[17] The only name mentioned in connection

[15] Savelle, *Morgan*, p. 138; *Am. Arch.*, series 4, VI, 1532, 1677; *Journals of the Continental Congress*, IV, 394, 396, V, 452.

[16] Elliott to Morgan, Oct. 17, 1776, Add. MSS., 21845, Br. Mus.; Wm. Wilson to Elliott, Nov. 19, 1776, *ibid.*; Hanna, *Wilderness Trail*, II, 81; Alvord, *Kaskaskia Records*, p. 2.

[17] Copies of the memorial and the advertisement are preserved in the Yeates MSS., H.S.P.; see also Crumrine, *Washington County*, pp. 185–188; F. J. Turner, "Western

with this scheme was that of David Rogers, an old associate of the Cresap family, who now represented West Augusta in the Virginia House of Delegates and who was to perish at the hands of Indians while bringing powder from New Orleans. His connection indicates that some Virginians must have been concerned in the scheme, although Neville was assisted by John Campbell and John Gibson, along with the majority of the committee of West Augusta, in putting it down, and Edmund Pendleton, in retiring from the presidency of the Virginia committee of safety when the new State government was organized in July, stated that the Croghan, Indiana, and Vandalia interests were back of the project. However, Croghan's following apparently opposed the plan and pinned its hope on the old alliance with Virginia which had been established during the Dunmore régime. The fact that Charles Simms, a Virginian and intimate friend of Neville, at this time bought some of Croghan's claims further indicates that this was the case. Moreover, those Pennsylvanians, like St. Clair, who were not connected with the land companies, must have objected to the proposed truncation of the State. The circumstances would point to George Morgan and the Vandalia interests centering about Franklin and the Whartons as having been the prime movers in the business. It is probable that Jasper Yeates assisted them. Shortly after Franklin returned from England, Walpole and Sargent had written of a scheme which had been developed for seizing and leasing the Vandalia country during the period of hostilities, after which, as they were assured on the best authority, their grant would be ratified in England. Great secrecy was to be maintained in carrying out this plan, and William Franklin thought it was risky business. It is not unlikely that there was some connection between that plan and this attempt to establish a fourteenth State by the name of Westsylvania. At least they had the same object in view.[18]

The only practical result of the Westsylvania movement was Virginia's division in November of the old West Augusta jurisdiction. This was apparently an attempt to strengthen her political organization in the face of danger. The seat of local government, it will be recalled, had recently

State-Making in the Revolutionary Era," *The Significance of Sections in American History* (New York, 1932) pp. 103–106.

[18] Pendleton to Virginia delegates in Congress, July 15, 1776, Jefferson MSS., L. of C.; Thwaites and Kellogg, *Revolution on the Upper Ohio*, p. 232; William to Benjamin Franklin, Aug. 14, 1775, *Pa. Mag. of Hist. and Biog.*, XXVII, 163–164; Neville to President of Virginia Committee of Safety, June 13, 1776, *Va. Mag. of Hist. and Biog.*, XVI, 53–54; *Journal of the House of Delegates*, Oct. 24, 1776, p. 26; power of attorney, Aug. 26, 1775, Charles Simms MSS., L. of C.; a copy of the petition of the Committee of West Augusta to the Virginia House of Delegates condemning the Westsylvania scheme is in the Yeates MSS., H.S.P.; and also in the Draper MSS., 4NN32.

been shifted from Pittsburgh to a place called Catfish Camp or Augusta Town, and now the county court of Yohogania was established there. The present town of Washington, Pennsylvania, occupies the spot and preserves the records of these early Virginia courts.[19]

Whether or not George Morgan was the principal organizer of the Westsylvania movement, he was concerned at the same time in a still more extensive and elusive scheme which had to do with Western lands. During November Dr. Walker received reliable information that plans were being made at Niagara and Detroit to send attacking forces against Pittsburgh. He communicated this intelligence to the other commissioners, and they warned Dorsey Pentecost, the county lieutenant of Yohogania, who at once notified the Continental Congress and Governor Henry of Virginia. The commissioners authorized the strengthening of posts along the upper Ohio, and Pentecost proceeded to collect a militia force which he considered adequate for defense.[20]

Morgan now wrote to Pentecost, branded his information as incorrect, and rebuked him for spreading rumors of an attack. Pentecost replied by giving the source of his information and stating that he had notified Congress of his acts. After this Morgan ceased to report to the commissioners at Pittsburgh, but dealt directly with Congress. Why that body permitted him to pursue a policy differing from its own cannot be stated. The question of a campaign against Detroit did not develop to the point of a practical issue, and Morgan doubtless kept most of his business privy to himself and his associates.[21]

There must have been some ulterior motive behind his insistence upon keeping the Indian nations neutral during the War. Of course his trading interests were concerned, but there are many indications that something more than trade was involved. The most interesting evidence in this connection is furnished by a letter which he wrote on June 10 to Henry Hamilton, the British lieutenant-governor and commandant at Detroit. It was forwarded secretly by an intermediary who was to deliver it to Hamilton and inform him that no attack was to be made against his

[19] Minute book of the Virginia Court held for Yohogania County, Boyd Crumrine ed., *Annals of the Carnegie Museum* (1904–1905), II, 71–429; Hening, *Statutes*, IX, 262.

[20] *Va. Mag. of Hist. and Biog.*, XVII, 260–261; Thwaites and Kellogg, *Revolution on the Upper Ohio*, pp. 190–191, 195–196, 199, 218–220; Pentecost (?) to Henry, Aug. 31, 1776, Yeates MSS., H.S.P.; Pentecost to the Commissioners, Sept. 6, 1776, *ibid.*; Henry to the Commissioners, Sept. 23, 1776, *ibid.*; Alvord, *The Illinois Country*, p. 313; *Am. Arch.*, series 5, II, 511–513; Henry to Pentecost, Dec. 13, 1776, *Official Letters of the Governors of the State of Virginia* (H. R. McIlwaine, ed., Richmond, 1926——) I, 76–77.

[21] Savelle, *Morgan*, p. 141; Morgan to Pentecost, Nov. 17, 1776, Dreer MSS., French Refugees, Colonial and Indian Affairs, H.S.P.; Pentecost to Morgan, Nov. 19, 1776, *ibid.*

post unless he made the first move. Morgan's object was to establish a correspondence and to induce Hamilton to join him in a neutrality program, but it is difficult to see how he could have presumed to state positively that no attack would be made against Detroit when Congress was actually contemplating one. How a copy of this letter came to be preserved in the papers of Jasper Yeates, one of the commissioners, is also a mystery. It is clear, however, that Hamilton would have nothing to do with Morgan.[22]

Another letter which throws further light on the situation was written by Morgan on July 6 to Winston and Kennedy at Kaskaskia. Morgan was trying to get horses and supplies from Kaskaskia and informed the two traders that he would hold an Indian treaty at Pittsburgh in the fall and that it would be much to their interest for one of them to be present. He cautioned them to keep his business very secret and inquired if they could have supplies for about two companies of men at Kaskaskia on December 25.[23]

Was Morgan trying to neutralize Congress and the Indians and the post at Detroit and planning to seize the Illinois country by means of a private expedition conducted in the dead of winter? Without the co-operation of his friends of the Franklin group in Congress and of Hamilton at Detroit such a plan could hardly have succeeded for long, but with millions of acres of land as a bait he could probably have organized his own régime in the Illinois before he could have been dislodged—a plan somewhat similar to the Westsylvania scheme—and then secured recognition by Congress of a new State in the Illinois. And if Congress would not listen he and his associates were not without friends on the other side. It is not known, of course, just what his plan was, but the letters to Hamilton and to Winston and Kennedy indicate that some such secret scheme existed. His Indian policy certainly requires an explanation, and his later career shows clearly that he was eminently capable of such plotting.

[22] Morgan to Hamilton, dated May 31, but actually written June 10, 1776, Dreer MSS., Soldiers of the American Revolution, H.S.P.; Hildreth, *Pioneer History*, pp. 98–108.

[23] Morgan to Winston and Kennedy, July 6, 1776, Add. MSS., 21845, f. 498, Br. Mus.; also in Alvord, *Kaskaskia Records*, p. 1.

CHAPTER XIV

WATCHFUL WAITING, 1777

D
URING 1777 the partisan struggle in Congress was becoming more acute. Its ramifications included many issues in addition to that of Western lands, and because of the interrelation of various questions it seems desirable to touch upon at least two of them in order to clarify the general situation.

When in 1770 Dennys de Berdt—father-in-law of Joseph Reed of Pennsylvania and long agent for Massachusetts—died in London, Benjamin Franklin had been appointed by that province to succeed him. Upon being deposed as postmaster-general in 1774 Franklin made ready to return to America after an absence of ten years and suggested to Massachusetts authorities that he resign their agency into the hands of his deputy, Arthur Lee, "a young man of parts and ability." Lee was the youngest of six sons of Thomas Lee, organizer of the Ohio Company, and had been living in London for some time where he was an intimate of Lord Shelburne. His brother William was also resident in the British Capital where he looked after the tobacco interests of his Virginia family and friends; in 1775 he and another American, Stephen Sayre, his business partner, were elected Aldermen of the City of London—two "foreigners" chosen by the "City men" to show their contempt for the existing government.

When the Committee of Secret Correspondence was formed in Congress it appointed Arthur Lee as its agent in London. He was to sound European opinion and was instructed to act in "impenetrable secrecy."

Ever since losing Canada to England in 1763 France had kept an observer in the British colonies, watching with satisfaction the growing discontent in America and biding her time. Now, in the present crisis, she also dispatched an observer to London in the person of Pierre-Augustin Caron, watchmaker, musician, playwright, adventurer, who, as an aid to his social climbing, had assumed the noble name of Beaumarchais. He was no stranger to London, having recently been involved in a profitable blackmail scheme with Théveneau de Morande, an expatriate Frenchman resident in that city, whose former mistress had been du Barry. The author of *Figaro* was not only an unscrupulous blackmailer, but had been suspected of murder under strongly incriminating circumstances.

The home of John Wilkes, the radical lord mayor, was open to any who opposed the government, and here Beaumarchais and Arthur Lee met. Beaumarchais had one passion in life—to rise in the world and to amass a fortune to support the position to which he aspired. He had already had a fling at trade under the tutelage of one of the shrewdest business men in France and had at that time become interested in the colonies of France and Spain to which he traded. Having failed in that venture and in his plan to marry a West Indian sugar heiress, it now behooved him to acquire a fortune in some other manner. Arthur Lee opened to him new possibilities: vast stretches of virgin lands, great cargoes of tobacco, an incredibly profitable trade which the colonies heretofore had been forced to carry on with England only.[1]

The British secretary for foreign affairs, Lord Rochford, was also a friend of Beaumarchais, appreciating his gifts as a writer and musician. From him the Frenchman learned that England would never grant the demands of her rebellious colonies; from Arthur Lee he learned that the colonies would never yield. Anglo-American affairs were at an impasse. The hour of revenge for which France had long waited was at hand, and, incidentally, the opportunity for which Beaumarchais yearned. He reported faithfully to the Comte de Vergennes, French minister of foreign affairs, and soon he was able to inform Arthur Lee that on June 10, 1776, his government had made a gift of a million livres for the aid of the revolutionary colonists. The management of this fund was turned over to Beaumarchais, who, to mask its real source, carried on trading operations under the fictitious name of *Roderigue Hortalez et Cie.*[2]

The situation now demanded that America send a more formidable mission to France, and, in December, 1776, Benjamin Franklin was dispatched to Paris to join Silas Deane. Early in 1774 Franklin had written to his son, Sir William—who, like all the other royal governors except Jonathan Trumbull of Connecticut, had adhered to the British cause —that so far as public affairs were concerned ". . . my intention is to decline all interest in them, and every active part, except where it can serve a friend . . . ; for being now about entering my 69th year & having lived so great a part of my life to the public, it seems but fair that I should be allowed to live the small remainder to myself and to my

[1] Paul Frischauer, *Beaumarchais* (New York, 1935) *passim.*
[2] T. P. Abernethy, "Commercial Activities of Silas Deane in France," *American Historical Review,* XXXIX, 477–485; J. Almon, *The Remembrancer,* 1777, p. 96.

friends." [3] On being appointed to France, whatever his motive he accepted, saying "I am old and good for nothing, but as drapers say of their fag ends of cloth, you may have me for what you please." The course he had run in the last few tumultuous years had been more vacillating than that of most American leaders who, at first opposing independence, had as a result of events come over whole-heartedly to the cause. Before leaving England, Franklin had in 1774 assured the Earl of Chatham, who trustingly sought his cooperation to heal the breach, that he had never heard "from any person, drunk or sober, in any part of the Continent, the least expression of a wish for separation." At that very time, in November, 1774, Josiah Quincy wrote from England to his Boston friends: "Dr. Franklin is an American in heart and soul; you may trust him; his ideas are not contracted within the narrow limits of exemption from taxes, but are extended upon the broad scale of total emancipation.—He is explicit and bold upon the Subject." [4] Notwithstanding this statement, a year later the Philadelphia Philosopher was writing to John Hughes: ". . . a firm Loyalty to the Crown and faithful adherence to the Government of this Nation, which it is the Safety as well as Honour of the Colonies to be connected with, will always be the wisest course for you and I to take, whatever may be the madness of the Populace or their blind leaders, who can only bring themselves and Country into Trouble, and draw on greater Burthens by Acts of rebellious Tendency." [5] Now, he was in Paris as representative of these "blind leaders" and here, where he already had considerable reputation, he created something of a sensation. The Comte de Segur, brother-in-law to Lafayette, was very much intrigued by the sight of "an old man whose grey hair is visible under a marten-skin cap, walking about amongst the powdered heads of Paris." French aristocrats aped the style of this American rebel's trousers, untroubled by any visions of the *sans-culottes* of another revolution.

Arthur Lee, who two years previously had worked so amicably with Franklin in the cause of American interests, now came over from London to complete the American mission. Franklin and Deane were immediately taken under the protecting wing of M. Donatien le Rey de Chaumont, a kinsman of the Comte de Maurepas, French principal minister. Chaumont, a prosperous merchant of Blois, was now a government contractor and a member of the Farmers-General. He made his

---

[3] Benjamin to William Franklin, Jan. 5, 1774, Bigelow, *Works*, VI, 267–268.
[4] Philip Henry Stanhope, Lord Mahon, *History of England from the Peace of Utrecht to the Treaty of Versailles, 1713–1783*, (Boston, 1853) VI, 23–24.
[5] Benjamin Franklin to John Hughes, Sydney George Fisher, *Pennsylvania: Colony and Commonwealth* (Philadelphia, 1907) pp. 313–314.

home upon an elaborate estate at Passy, where Maurepas was a frequent visitor. Franklin and Deane were lodged upon this estate, and here they made their headquarters as long as Deane remained in France, but Lee did not join their congenial circle. Franklin occupied Chaumont's house for nine years and placed on it the first lightning rod ever put up in France. The Frenchman refused to accept any rent, but said that Congress, if it saw fit, could compensate him with a grant of land.

Between Deane and Lee there soon arose a quarrel. There was some jealousy between them because of the fact that the former laid claim to all credit for securing supplies which the French Ministry was furnishing Congress through the instrumentality of Beaumarchais and for which Lee had arranged before Deane arrived in France. He soon discovered that Congress was being asked to pay for them, whereas he had understood that a free gift was intended. Fuel was added to the fire when Lee found that Deane was devoting most of his time to private speculations. With Chaumont as his backer and through the connivance of the French Ministry, he was fitting out privateers and selling prizes in French ports. In combination with Chaumont, Robert Morris, and Thomas Walpole, he organized an international trading company and carried on a far-flung commerce with America. Jonathan Williams, nephew to Franklin, had, in the absence of Lee and without authority from Congress, been made commercial agent to the American commission; this young man of twenty-two years was now established at Nantes as the principal agent of Deane's trading company. By authority of the Comte de Sartine, French minister of marine, Chaumont was put in charge of the privateering business in which the American agents were permitted by the French Ministry to engage clandestinely up to the time when France entered the War. This gave his company unrivaled opportunity, for operations had to be carried on secretly and no prizes could be sold except upon terms dictated by Chaumont. As purchasing agents for Congress, he and Williams bought the captured goods which, as prize agents, they sold to their own associates. According to Franklin's own testimony, they sometimes made as much as eight thousand per cent on their transactions. Charles Willing was located in the Barbadoes to attend to the transshipment of goods from that point; Bingham and other agents also were active in the West Indies, while Oliver Pollock still acted for Morris at New Orleans. Soon John Ross was sent over from Philadelphia to look after the commercial affairs of Morris in Paris.

Thomas Morris, half-brother to Robert, and William Lee, brother to Arthur, had been appointed by Congress to manage commercial affairs in Europe, but the Franklin-Deane coterie prevented William Lee from acting under his commission, and it was this situation which precipitated the open break between the Lees and their colleagues.

Robert Morris thus held the keys to America's foreign trade, and through his agents he was able to exert a powerful influence upon the foreign policy of Congress. On March 28, 1777, Patrick Henry wrote to Richard Henry Lee, "Mr. Morris has speculated very largely in such articles as the army wants. The Public Agent complains he is anticipated. I hope this practice will be effectually stopped or fatal consequences must ensue." That Washington, too, had strong feelings on the subject of profiteering is shown by a letter which he wrote the following year to Joseph Reed. In it he said:

It gives me very sincere pleasure to find that there is likely to be a coalition of Whigs in your state . . . , and that the Assembly of it are so well disposed to second your endeavours in bringing those murderers of our cause—the monopolizers, forestallers, and engrossers to condign punishment. It is much to be lamented that each state, long ere this, has not hunted them down as the pests of society, and the greatest enemies we have to the happiness of America.

He and the Lees constantly complained of the tendency of the mercantile interests to make capital out of the calamities of their country. About the same time Washington wrote to General Andrew Lewis:

Want of virtie . . . is infinitely more to be dreaded, than the whole force of Great Britain, assisted as they are by Hessian, Indian, and Negro allies; for certain I am, that, unless extortion, forestalling, and other practices, which have crept in and become exceedingly prevalent and injurious to the common cause, can meet with proper checks, we must inevitably sink under such a load of accumulated oppression. To make and extort money in every shape that can be devised, and at the same time to decry its value, seems to have become a mere business and an epidemical disease, calling for the interposition of every good man and body of men.[6]

On May 26 Mann Page wrote from Philadelphia that he understood an entire change in the Virginia delegation was expected and urged that no man who was engaged in trade should be sent to Congress. This was necessary, he said, because Congress had to make returns to Europe for

[6] Morris to Bingham, Feb. 15, 1777, Morris MSS., L. of C.; Deane to Morris, April 11, 1777, *ibid.*; Morris to Bingham, April 25, 1777, *ibid.*; Henry to Lee, March 28, 1777, Henkels, *Patrick Henry Papers*, p. 39; Mann Page to (John Page?) May 26, 1777, *William and Mary Quarterly* (n.s.) VII, 215–216; Secret Committee to Pollock, June 12, 1777, Continental Congress papers, Pollock MSS., f. 50; Washington to Reed, Dec. 12, 1778, Wm. B. Reed, *Life and Correspondence of Joseph Reed* (Philadelphia, 1847) II, 41–42, also pp. 223–228; Washington to Lewis, Dec. 12, 1778, Sparks, *Writings of George Washington,* VI, 91.

supplies furnished them and delegates could use inside information and make large profits, letting the public pay for any losses which they might sustain.

Such "inside information" in France, Arthur Lee soon discovered, was also a source of profit to Deane. Having free access to Franklin's papers, he was in possession of secret information from the French Court as well as from Congress, and he made use of this to speculate clandestinely in British stocks. He used Dr. Edward Bancroft as his secretary and courier, and Samuel Wharton, still tarrying in England, and Thomas Walpole as his London agents for this purpose, with Walpole apparently putting up the money. Bancroft was now a double spy in the pay of both America and England, but George III—who was by no means the stupid man American tradition has made him—took his reports with a grain of salt, saying it should ever be borne in mind that he was a stock-jobber. Vergennes evidently was equally distrustful of certain of the American agents. In 1780 he wrote, "In truth Congress has sorry agents. I believe they are more concerned with their private speculations than with the interest of their principals."

These debasing activities of America's first foreign mission did not come prominently before Congress until the following year, but one other of Deane's enterprises gave rise to a bitter struggle during 1777. At the instance of Beaumarchais, Deane made agreements with various officers who desired positions of high command in the American army. Among these was the Baron von Steuben, a veteran of the school of Frederick II, who could not teach or drill or even swear at Washington's army without the aid of an interpreter, and the redheaded, awkward, adolescent millionaire, the Marquis de LaFayette, who was fired with zeal to fight for the oppressed Americans. Among them, too, were the Colonels Mottin de la Balme and Thomas Conway, Knight of the Order of St. Louis. Of the former we shall hear more anon. The latter was an Irishman who had served for thirty years in the French army as an officer in the Irish brigades. He had the great advantage of a fluent command of both the English and the French tongue and was not handicapped by any marked degree of modesty. Arriving in Boston he presented himself to Washington, who referred him to Congress. That body at once made him a Brigadier-General and presently proposed to appoint him Adjutant-General of the army with the rank of Major-General. This caused a furor among Washington's officers, several of whom threatened to resign. Washington protested in strong terms against the measure, but it was carried in spite of him. At the same time Congress reorganized the Board of War and put Washington's rival, General Horatio Gates, godson of Horace Walpole, at the head of it.[7]

These measures formed the basis of the so-called "Conway Cabal," and they are supposed to have been the work of an anti-Washington clique in Congress. They certainly constituted an affront to the Commander-in-Chief at a time when his fortunes had reached their nadir at Valley Forge and when Gates was riding the crest of a wave of popularity following the victory at Saratoga. The usual impression is that the Adams-Lee faction in Congress was responsible for their enactment, and the evidence for this view seems impressive at first glance.

On several occasions Lee and the Adamses were named as the principal conspirators, and they did not rush into print with denials, but certain facts make this charge appear in a very doubtful light. Lee corresponded with Washington about the Conway appointment throughout the time when it was being carried through, assuring Washington that he would support his views. Samuel Adams said that John Hancock and Robert Morris—the latter admitting that he had interested himself in getting a commission for Conway—were responsible for linking his name with the conspiracy. Henry Laurens was the most outspoken opponent of the cabal, and he was a firm adherent of the Adams-Lee group. Patrick Henry, governor of Virginia and a strong supporter of Lee at this time, was also a staunch supporter of Washington. Thomas Mifflin and Dr. Benjamin Rush of Pennsylvania, leading conspirators, belonged to the opposition group in Congress, as did most of the members of the Board of War. Laurens pointed in the same direction when he said that the cabal was directed by a group in Congress whose influence centered in the Board of War and the Board of Treasury. Though James Lovell and John Adams apparently supported Gates, they were not fond of Deane's military protégés, and Lovell wrote to Washington to complain of them. There is, therefore, much reason to believe that the "conspiracy" was fathered by the Morris adherents, but that they tried in devious ways to throw the odium of it upon their opponents, It is a remarkable fact that on April 1, 1777, before Conway arrived in America, Patrick Henry wrote to Richard Henry Lee, "You are again traduced by a certain set . . . who say that you are engaged in a scheme to discard Genl. Washington. I know you too well to suppose you attempt anything not evidently calculated to serve the cause of Whigism." A little later Lee wrote

---

[7] *Journals of the Continental Congress,* VII, 347, 349, IX, 762, 958, 971–972, 1023, 1026; W. Heath to Washington, April 26, 1777, Washington MSS., L. of C.; Washington to Congress, May 9, 1777, *ibid.;* R. H. Lee to Washington, Oct. 20, 1777, *ibid.;* Sparks, *Writings of George Washington,* V, 97–100; Sparks, *Letters to Washington,* II, 10–12, 44–48; Sullivan, *Maryland and France,* p. 128.

to Henry that he entertained ". . . a strong belief that a change is wished, in order to remove obstruction feared from me, and to prepare the way for the execution of private plans, in which the public will not be gainer." He said the New England and Virginia men were strongly united against Great Britain, but that Virginia had many enemies in the central States. On June 4, 1777, James Milligan wrote from Lancaster to General Hand: "We have nothing to fear but from villians among ourselves, & this tide of avarice and avidity which overflows the country like a Torrent, but more especially in this accursed state where they seem anxious for nothing but sordid wealth, such blood sucking vipers have my hearty curses."

Certainly the evidence against Lee and Samuel Adams is to be found only in the statements of their opponents, notably in that of Conway himself whose connection with Deane would not have endeared him to the Lees.[8]

Lee's and Milligan's statements have certain significant implications when it is recalled that on the line-up in Congress depended not only various incredibly profitable trade enterprises, but the cause of Vandalia and other land schemes. Congress now, not the British government, was to be the arbiter, and if men with a tender feeling toward the land companies should be kept in high places, there was an excellent chance to salvage those schemes.

The factional differences which lay behind the Deane and Conway conflicts influenced practically every problem that Congress touched,—lands, trade, and military questions including that of frontier defense.

At Pittsburgh partisan strife tended to subside at this time, and efforts were being made to settle the boundary controversy. John Campbell now became lieutenant of the new county of Yohogania, Zackwell Morgan of Monongalia, and David Rogers of Ohio. George Morgan was still using his influence in favor of the policy of Indian neutrality which Congress had previously given up. Hostilities committed by the Mingoes of Pluggy's Town caused Congress and Virginia to collaborate on a punitive expedition in the spring of 1777, but Morgan used his influence to have the plan abandoned.[9] Shortly afterward Congress, for the first time,

---

[8] *Ibid.;* I, 408–414; John Fiske, "The French Alliance and the Conway Cabal," *Atlantic Monthly,* LXIV, 220–239; James Milligan to Genl. Hand, June 4, 1777, Draper MSS., Indian Wars, I; Burnett, *Letters of Members of the Continental Congress,* II, 386, 570, 583, III, viii, 63–64, 263; Sparks, *op. cit.,* V, 493, 499; Fitzpatrick, *George Washington Himself,* pp. 333ff.; Morris to Bingham, Feb. 16, 1777, Morris MSS., L. of C.; Henry to Lee, April 1, 1777, Henkels, *Patrick Henry Papers,* p. 41; Lee to Henry, May 26, 1777, W. W. Henry, *Patrick Henry,* III, 73–74.

[9] Henry to David Shepherd, April 12, 1777, Draper MSS., 1SS51–52; John Page to Morgan and Neville, April 15, 1777, *ibid.,* 1SS53–54; H. R. McIlwaine, ed., *Official*

took charge of the military situation in that neighborhood, and General Edward Hand, a former officer in the British forces stationed at Fort Pitt and related by marriage to Jasper Yeates, was sent to Pittsburgh to take command. He arrived on June 1, but the Virginia militia made up the greater part of the available force, and it took orders only from the governor of Virginia. However, Governor Patrick Henry showed every inclination to cooperate with the Continental commander.[10]

During the summer George Morgan, John Campbell, Alexander McKee, Simon Girty and several of their friends were accused of treasonable practices. These charges grew out of an Indian attack on Fort Henry at Wheeling. The natives were aided by Tories, who were known to be numerous in the neighborhood, and suspicion fell upon Morgan and his friends. It was Colonel Zackwell Morgan who made the complaint, and soon counter-complaints were made against him for having drowned a Tory. The county court of Monongalia prepared to send Colonel Morgan to Richmond for trial, and the militia threatened to go on strike in protest. George Morgan and his associates were put under arrest by General Hand, and Congress appointed a committee to investigate their case. No sufficient evidence was found to convict them, and hence they were released.[11]

The British were doing all in their power to stir up the natives against the Americans, and numerous hostilities were committed. During the late summer plans were made for a punitive expedition, but nothing was accomplished in this direction. Thus Morgan was completely successful in maintaining his policy of inaction throughout the year. He, along with John Neville, went so far as to suggest to Governor Henry that the Virginia settlements in Kentucky should be abandoned. His ultimate object is hard to fathom.[12]

Letters of the Governors of Virginia, I, 104, 120–121; Thwaites and Kellogg, *The Revolution on the Upper Ohio,* pp. 236–238, 247–250; Henry, *Henry,* III, 46–47.

[10] Henry to Hand, July 3, 1777, Draper MSS., 15ZZ7; Abraham Hite to Hand, July 3, 1777, *ibid.,* 1U61; Henry to William Fleming, Sept. 7, 1777, *ibid.,* 15ZZ11; Thwaites and Kellogg, *Frontier Defense,* pp. 74–76; *ibid.,* 5–7; W. H. Mohr, *Federal Indian Relations,* pp. 50–51.

[11] John Campbell to Commissioners of Congress, Nov. 19, 1777, Dreer MSS., French Refugees, etc., H.S.P.; John Proctor to same, Dec. 1, 1777, *ibid.;* Morgan to same, Nov. 11, 1777, Dreer MSS., Soldiers of the Revolution, III, H.S.P.; Gibson to Hand, Sept. 4, 1777, Thwaites and Kellogg, *Frontier Defense,* p. 73; *ibid.,* pp. 128, 142, 184–187; James Chew to Hand, Oct. 23, 1777, Draper MSS., 1U124; Burnett, *op. cit.,* II, 533; *Journal of the House of Delegates,* Dec. 10, 1777, p. 72; Savelle, *Morgan,* pp. 154–155; Darlington, *Fort Pitt,* p. 225; *Journals of the Continental Congress,* IX, 831, 942–945; W. H. Siebert, *Loyalists of Pennsylvania,* p. 9.

[12] Morgan and Neville to Henry, April 1, 1777, Draper MSS., 1NN3; Hand to William Fleming, Aug. 12, 1777, Thwaites and Kellogg, *Frontier Defense,* pp. 42–43; article for the *Federal Gazette,* in Morgan's hand (1777 ?), Morgan MSS., Ill. Hist. Survey, Urbana, Ill.

The attitude of Virginia on frontier questions is easier to understand. Committees of her assembly were busy investigating the claims of the Henderson and Indiana companies whose pretensions were at times discussed on the floor of that body, but no decision was reached in either case during the year. The influence of Dr. Thomas Walker and the Loyal Company was being used against Henderson, but he still had friends in Virginia, and strenuous efforts were made to get Samuel Johnston and Willie Jones, leaders of the conservative and radical parties respectively in North Carolina, to appear at Richmond in his behalf.[13]

George Croghan and Michael Gratz came to Virginia to plead their private claims, as well as those of the Indiana Company. On June 3 a petition was presented to the assembly in behalf of the company, but no definite action was taken. There is every reason to believe, however, that the prospects of this group were far from hopeless. There was a fairly clear division between the local parties on the subject. Liberals of the Jefferson and Lee stamp had no proclivities for the Indiana Company, but among the conservatives the situation was different.[14]

In his 1776 plan of government for Virginia, Carter Braxton had recognized the validity of the Fort Stanwix treaty and of the Indiana grant which formed an original part of that instrument. Braxton had had cordial relations with Thomas Walker while in attendance on Congress during 1776, and his attitude probably grew out of that connection. Edmund Pendleton had had legal dealings with the Whartons, and he also favored Indiana. So did James Mercer and apparently Archibald Cary. It was during 1777 that Dr. Walker and a group of his friends bought a share in Croghan's six-million-acre purchase west of the Ohio, and his friend John Harvie undertook to have the Indiana title recorded in Virginia for Morgan. On August 19 Croghan's deed was recorded in Staunton, and when that speculator left Virginia Patrick Henry dispatched letters by him. Thus it appears that a large part of the leadership of the Virginia conservatives, Dr. Walker and presumably the Loyal Company which he represented, and Patrick Henry as well as James Wood, Charles Simms, James Innes and other Virginians at Pittsburgh, had some connection with the Indiana group. The fact that neither the Indiana nor Vandalia Company presented petitions to Congress during this year indicates that the latter was in abeyance and the former pinning its faith on Virginia. But the liberals of the Lee-Adams group kept

---

[13] *Journals of the House of Delegates,* June 7, 26, 1777, pp. 65, 97–98; *ibid.,* Nov. 24, 1777, p. 41; Jones to Johnson, Oct. 9, 1777, misc. MSS., Hayes papers, N.C.H.C.; Henderson, *Walker,* pp. 74–77.

[14] *Journal of the House of Delegates,* June 3, 1777, p. 55; Byars, *Gratz,* p. 165; *Tyler's Quarterly,* I, 145; Draper MSS., ICC140–146.

the upper hand both in Congress and in Virginia, and the land companies made no progress at this time.[15]

Whatever Patrick Henry's attitude toward the Indiana Company may have been at this period, his main interest centered in Kentucky. His principal objective for the time being was the negotiation of a treaty with the Cherokee whereby their boundary line might be pushed far enough west to clear Cumberland Gap and thus secure the route to the blue grass country. His plans for this move were delayed by a Cherokee war during the summer in which both Virginia and North Carolina were involved, but the treaty which ended it brought the fulfillment of Henry's designs. The Indian boundary was extended westward from the Holston River to a high peak just beyond the great Gap. At the same time a trading post was established on the Long Island of the Holston, and Joseph ·Martin, once agent for Dr. Walker and later connected with Henderson with whom he was still in correspondence, was made Indian agent for both Virginia and North Carolina with his headquarters on the Island.[16]

At this time a significant development was taking place in the neighboring southwestern counties of Virginia. In 1773 the council had issued an order that frontier settlers should have the preemption of the lands on which they were settled, but they were to pay three pounds per hundred acres to the land companies or else hold under the soldiers who had claims under the proclamation of 1763. The Loyal and Greenbrier Companies had surveyed many of these settlers' claims, but they had never been able to make titles nor had there been any land office open for that purpose since Lord Dunmore left Virginia. Plans were now being made to establish one, and frontier settlers began to dread the payments which they must make to the land companies, whose claims, as a matter of fact, were very tenuous indeed.

Petitions protesting against their demands were circulated in the counties where the land company claims were most numerous. A protest was also made against the existing method of appointing county surveyors, for the land companies had usually seen to it that their friends occupied these positions in the Western counties. The popular election of sur-

---

[15] Henry to Hand, July 27, 1777, Draper MSS., 18J26; T. Wharton to Braxton, Aug. 26, 1777, Wharton MSS., H.S.P.; T. Wharton to Levy A. Levy, July 28, 1776, Wharton letter book, H.S.P.; C.V.S.P., I, 277–282, 297; Volwiler, Croghan, p. 310; Byars, Gratz, pp. 358–360; R.C.M. Page, Page Family of Virginia, 206–207.
[16] Journal of the House of Delegates, Dec. 5, 1777, p. 57; Henderson to Martin, April 13, 1777, Draper MSS., ICC226; Henry to Martin, Nov. 3, 1777, ibid., 1XX29; Henry to Oconostotah, Nov. 15, 1777, Continental Congress papers, 71, II, 209; ibid., 71, II, 208, 213, 221–222; Henry, Henry, I, 464; McIlwaine, Letters of the Governors of Virginia, I, 94–95; Mohr, Federal Indian Relations, pp. 54–55.

veyors was now proposed, but the right of the College of William and Mary, or some other educational foundation, to pass on qualifications and receive perquisites was not questioned. Several such petitions were presented to the assembly at the same time, and a number of prominent names were signed to them. Those of David and Arthur Campbell, William Cocke, David Craig, Gilbert Christian, and several members of county courts were among the signatories. Evidently these petitions were inspired by a group of leaders who were taking a stand in opposition to the land companies.[17]

Though the question was now under discussion, no general land act was passed at this time. However, quit-rents were abolished except in the Northern Neck, and settlers on the Western waters were confirmed in their preemption right to four hundred acres of land. This had been promised them during the previous year, but taxes were now levied upon their holdings as though they had actual titles. Yet all previous claims were to remain unaffected by this legislation, and the land companies could still claim all tracts which they had surveyed. Many settlers in southwest Virginia were affected by this situation.[18]

Within a few years Arthur Campbell was to lead a movement for the secession of southwest Virginia from the State, and David Campbell, William Cocke, David Craig, Gilbert Christian—the same men who had signed the protest regarding the land situation—were to be connected with the State of Franklin movement in 1784. Arthur Campbell's scheme was closely allied with the State of Franklin, and the seed of his future opposition to the government of Virginia is to be seen in these petitions which championed the rights of the settlers against the land companies. For the present he tried to avoid giving testimony that would reveal Henry's former interest in the Henderson company. His own connection with that group may explain his whole attitude on the land question.[19]

During this year Kentucky was faring badly. On account of Indian hostilities, all the settlements except Harrodsburg and Boonesborough were abandoned, and only about forty families inhabited these two. Governor Henry sent two hundred men under Colonel John Bowman to aid in their defense, yet this was an insufficient force. In spite of the lean times, the county government which had been established by law the previous year was put into operation. The court included John Bowman, Richard Calloway, John Todd, John Floyd, and Benjamin Logan. John

[17] *Journal of the House of Delegates*, May 21, 24, 1777, pp. 23, 31; *ibid.*, Nov. 6, Nov. 8, pp. 13, 14, 15, 18. See in Virginia Archives, petitions.
[18] Hening, *Statutes*, IX, 355ff.
[19] *Journal of the House of Delegates*, Nov. 25, 1777, p. 43.

Bowman became county lieutenant, Anthony Bledsoe lieutenant-colonel and George May, surveyor. The defenders at Boonesborough were put under command of Boone and Calloway, and George Rogers Clark, with rank of major, commanded at Harrodsburg. During the next year this young man was to achieve considerable reputation for himself.[20]

[20] *Journals of the House of Delegates,* June 21, 1777, p. 87; *ibid.,* Dec. 1, 1777, p. 50; Draper MSS., 8CC2–3; petition of Feb. 27, 1777, *ibid.,* 4CC29–30; Marshall, *Kentucky,* I, 47; Cotterill, *History of Pioneer Kentucky,* p. 120; Bradford's "Notes on Kentucky," *Kentucky Gazette,* Sept. 15, 1826.

CHAPTER XV

THE CONQUEST OF THE ILLINOIS

I N order to penetrate the springs of George Rogers Clark's movement against Kaskaskia in 1778 it is necessary to turn back two years
and consider the commercial situation which existed in that French
village in 1776. William Murray had for several years been the agent
there for the Franks brothers. Early in this year he went down to New
Orleans to attend to business which came to that frontier metropolis from
the Illinois country. His brother Daniel was left in charge of the business at Kaskaskia. Richard Winston and Daniel Kennedy were there
receiving orders from George Morgan and Robert Morris and sending
peltry and flour down to New Orleans, where Oliver Pollock, in collaboration with the Spanish governor, had a monopoly of the flour trade.
Daniel Clark, a nephew of George Croghan, had originally gone to New
Orleans to attend to the commercial interests of his uncle, and he was
long to remain an important merchant there. Another American merchant
doing business in Kaskaskia was Thomas Bentley, a close friend to
Colonel John Rogers of the Pittsburgh area. Thus was maintained an
avenue of trade from Philadelphia through Pittsburgh and Kaskaskia to
New Orleans, and it was kept open during the War despite the fact that
the Illinois villages were in British hands and their merchants found it
necessary to accept British sovereignty.

With direct trade to England cut off at the beginning of the conflict,
the insurgent colonials experienced much difficulty in securing an adequate supply of the munitions of war, especially powder. Large supplies
of this precious article were stored in the royal magazines at New
Orleans, and the British fleet could not block the way to that city. The
merchants named above and their associates were practically the only
people in the colonies who understood the trade to New Orleans. Certainly no one in Williamsburg knew anything about it.

How Williamsburg came to be involved is an interesting question. Of
course Virginia claimed jurisdiction over the Illinois country, and certain land companies had made purchases from the Indians in that region.
The principal of these were the Illinois and Wabash Companies organized by William Murray. His brother Daniel as well as John Campbell,

county lieutenant of Yohogania, were members, and Winston and Kennedy had witnessed the original purchase from the natives. Croghan had also made large purchases in the region, but his property had passed largely into the hands of the Gratz brothers, with whom Murray was connected. The defunct firm of Baynton, Wharton and Morgan likewise had claims in the area which had been sold to Richard Winston. These companies had made no plans to set up independent governments in the Illinois, but were prepared to accept the jurisdiction of Virginia if she would recognize their claims to the soil.[1]

The French *habitants* of the Illinois country, though living under British rule, were inclined to favor the American cause, and most of the Indians of that neighborhood could be managed with the aid of the French villagers and American merchants. If powder could be got from New Orleans and if Virginia would furnish the troops the country might easily be conquered, and both Virginia and the land companies would profit thereby. Who was responsible for such a scheme can perhaps never be known, but that such a scheme was laid during 1776 is proved by the facts now to be narrated.

In May of this year Colonel George Gibson, of the Continental line, set out from Pennsylvania on a momentous journey to Williamsburg. He was brother to Colonel John Gibson, who was an old associate of Croghan in the Indian trade, a member of the Virginia faction in the Pittsburgh area since the days of Lord Dunmore and now commander of one of the Virginia regiments on that frontier. Colonel John was also a member of the Indiana Company. In other words, he was thoroughly versed in all matters relating to trade and politics in western Pennsylvania, and his connections were with the Croghan-Morgan group in that neighborhood. That his brother was selected for the journey to Williamsburg is not surprising. That he did not go entirely on his own initiative is clear, for many diverse elements were involved in his mission.

On reaching the Virginia capital Gibson consulted with General Charles Lee and the committee of safety, of which Edmund Pendleton was president. From Lee and the committee he secured letters addressed to Oliver Pollock of New Orleans.[2]

[1] Savelle, *Morgan,* p. 73; Alvord, *Cahokia Records,* p. xxxiii; H. W. Beckwith, ed., Letters from Canadian Archives, *Collections of the Illinois State Historical Library* (Springfield, 1903) I, 295–298; Crumrine, "Minute book of Yohogania County," *Annals of the Carnegie Museum,* II, 118–119; Thwaites and Kellogg, *Frontier Defense,* p. 292; Alvord, *The County of Illinois,* introduction; petition of William Murray to governor of Virginia, Jan. 11, 1786, Va. Arch., petitions.

[2] James A. James, "Oliver Pollock, Financier of the Revolution in the West," *Mississippi Valley Historical Review,* XVI, 67–80; James A. James, "Oliver Pollock and the Winning of the Illinois Country," Illinois Historical Society, *Transactions,* 1934, pp. 33–59.

Returning at once to Pittsburgh, Gibson set out with Lieutenant William Linn and fifteen men on the long river voyage down to New Orleans. His object was to secure powder from the Spanish arsenals. During August he reached his destination, and Pollock arranged with the governor, Luis de Unzaga, for twelve thousand pounds of powder for which eighteen hundred and fifty dollars was paid by Virginia. Thus the Pennsylvania-New Orleans trading interests and the governor of Louisiana cooperated with Virginia to secure the powder from the Spanish arsenals.

The British had control of Natchez and other settlements on the Mississippi above New Orleans, and Spain was ostensibly a neutral nation. Pressure was brought to bear upon Unzaga, and for the sake of appearances he had to arrest Gibson and detain him as a prisoner. The governor secretly did all he could for Pollock and the American cause, and on September 22 Linn started back up the river with his precious cargo. A Spanish convoy and a Spanish flag were necessary in order to get past the British posts, but this was accomplished in safety and by the middle of the winter the boats had reached the Arkansas River, above the British zone.[3]

Meanwhile Unzaga had been succeeded at New Orleans by Don Bernardo de Gálvez, and Patrick Henry had become governor of Virginia under her new constitution. About January 1, 1777, Henry wrote to Dorsey Pentecost to send out an expedition to locate Linn's cargo, supposedly in the neighborhood of the Spanish post at St. Louis. Captain William Harrod was dispatched on this mission, but no word being received from him, Henry wrote to John Campbell, the Yohogania County lieutenant, to send another expedition in search of Linn; Morgan and John Neville consulted about the matter and wrote to Henry that they did not know where St. Louis was located. It was at the same time that they suggested the Kentucky settlements be abandoned in order to avoid trouble with the Indians.[4]

Linn, however, had been able to manage very well. Early in the spring he arrived at the mouth of the Ohio, and there was met by Thomas Bentley from Kaskaskia, who furnished him with necessary supplies. To Bentley, Linn delivered a letter from William Murray at New Orleans. He had one also from Murray to his brother Daniel at Kaskaskia. They contained information that spies were to be sent to the Illinois in the interest of the American cause, and the Kaskaskia merchants were di-

[3] *Journal of the Virginia House of Delegates*, June 28, 1777, p. 110; John W. Caughey, *Bernardo de Gálvez in Louisiana* (Berkeley, 1934) p. 86.
[4] Morgan and Neville to Henry, April 1, 1777, Draper MSS., 1NN3; Pentecost to Harrod, Jan. 28, 1777, *ibid.*, 4NN46.

rected to receive any party of Americans which might arrive.[5] On April 20 Major George Rogers Clark, commanding officer at Harrodsburg, sent Benjamin Linn, Samuel Moore, and two other woodsmen as spies to Kaskaskia. At about the same time he dispatched Harrod on an unknown mission to Pittsburgh. On May 2 Linn reached Wheeling with his cargo of powder.[6]

That George Morgan was interested in these proceedings is shown by a letter which he wrote on April 22 to Governor Gálvez proposing that Spain and America join forces against the British in the conquest of Mobile, Pensacola, Niagara, and Detroit. This is most surprising, for Morgan had discouraged every previous attempt to organize expeditions into the Illinois country. On July 19 Congress passed a resolution authorizing Morgan to go to New Orleans to enlist the cooperation of Gálvez in an attack on Mobile and Pensacola. This campaign had been planned by Morgan and Arnold, and the American troops were to be led by General Hand. On October 18 Patrick Henry corresponded with Gálvez about such a plan.[7]

Henry Laurens, president of Congress, defeated the scheme for the Pensacola campaign,[8] but on November 21 the Committee of Commerce, headed by Robert Morris and, it will be recalled, made up largely of his friends, on its own initiative and without the sanction of Congress as a whole, dispatched James Willing down the Mississippi. Willing was brother to Morris's business partner, Thomas Willing, and a commission as naval captain was conferred upon him for the purpose of this enterprise. He was ordered to call on General Hand at Pittsburgh for boats and supplies; his instructions were to capture British property on the river, to clear the stream for the passage of American commerce, and to get powder and supplies in New Orleans to be sent up the Mississippi. On January 10, 1778, he set off in the *Rattletrap* from Pittsburgh with a party of about thirty men.[9]

[5] Bentley was imprisoned by the British for this act. Deposition of Thomas Bentley, Aug. 1, 1777, Add. MSS., 21, 845, Br. Mu.; proclamation by Hamilton, Aug. 15, 1777, *ibid.;* Hamilton to Haldimand, April 25, 1778, *ibid.,* 21, 782; Alvord, *Illinois-Ouabache Land Company Manuscripts,* p. 20; Alvord, *The Illinois Country,* pp. 320–321; Alvord, *Kaskaskia Records,* pp. xix–xx.

[6] Bradford, "Notes on Kentucky," *Kentucky Gazette,* Sept. 15, 1826; Robertson, *Petitions of the Early Inhabitants of Kentucky,* pp. 57–59; Cotterill, *History of Pioneer Kentucky,* p. 122.

[7] *Papeles de Cuba,* L. of C. transcripts, *legajo* 1281, f. 113; Paul C. Phillips, *The West in the Diplomacy of the American Revolution* (Urbana, 1913) p. 67; Savelle, *Morgan,* pp. 175ff.; *Journals of Congress,* VIII, 566–567.

[8] David Duncan Wallace, *The Life of Henry Laurens* (New York, 1915) p. 242.

[9] Commercial Committee to Edward Hand, Nov. 21, 1777, Burnett, II, 565; John Caughey, "Willing's expedition Down the Mississippi," *Louisiana Historical Quarterly,* XV, 5–36; J. F. H. Claiborne, *Mississippi as a Province, Territory and State*

Arthur Lee in London was bidding for Spanish support at the same time he was trying to enlist France in America's cause, and he had, on June 27, 1776, secured from the Spanish government a secret gift of one million livres for the Continental Congress. In July, 1777, two thousand barrels of powder and other supplies, presumably a part of this gift, were deposited by Spain in New Orleans for the use of the Americans.

In October George Gibson, having been released, returned with the remainder of the powder which he had secured from Pollock and delivered letters from New Orleans to Congress. It is probable that he gave information of the new supplies received from Spain and that this was the principal motive for sending Willing down the river, but it is significant that Willing acted only for the Committee of Commerce and not for Congress as a whole. His expedition, therefore, had merely a semi-official status.

On November 20, the day before the dispatch of Willing, Congress provided for the sending of a commission to Pittsburgh to investigate the feasibility of an attack on Detroit. It was also to investigate the charges against Morgan for complicity in disloyal acts, but at the same time Morgan, still Indian agent, was made deputy commissary-general for the department including Pittsburgh.

On June 22 Clark's spies returned from Kaskaskia with favorable reports on conditions in that vicinity. Clark was soon on his way to Williamsburg, and on December 10 he unfolded to the governor his plan for the conquest of the Illinois. On the same day the House of Delegates, in committee of the whole, passed a resolution "that it is the opinion of this committee that the Governor be empowered, with the advice of Council, to order such part of the militia of this commonwealth as may be most convenient, and as they judge necessary . . . to act with any troops on an expedition that may be undertaken against any of our western enemies." [10]

On January 2, 1778, Henry informed the council that he "had had some conversation with several gentlemen who were well acquainted with the western frontiers of Virginia and the situation at Kaskasky." The council advised him to send an expedition against Kaskaskia under command of Lieutenant-Colonel Clark, twelve hundred pounds being appropriated for that purpose. The same day Governor Henry gave Clark

(Jackson, Miss., 1880) I, 116–122; James, *Clark,* pp. 104–108; Thwaites and Kellogg, *Frontier Defense,* pp. 198–199; Francis Lewis to Robert Morris, Feb. 21, 1778, Stan V. Henkels, pub., *The Private Correspondence of Robert Morris* (Philadelphia, 1917) p. 32.

[10] *Journal of the Virginia House of Delegates,* Dec. 10, 1777, p. 72; Mann Butler, *History of the Commonwealth of Kentucky* (Louisville, 1834) p. 46.

his secret instructions. He was to apply to General Hand at Pittsburgh
for boats and ammunition, to take Kaskaskia, and to prepare for the
establishment of a fort at the mouth of the Ohio. For necessary funds
he was to draw on Oliver Pollock at New Orleans. The purpose of the
expedition was to be kept as secret as possible. In a letter of the same
date the governor called on General Hand to furnish boats for several
companies of militia. On the following day Henry consulted Jefferson,
Mason, and Wythe—none of them members of the council—who agreed
to combine their influence to secure grants of land for the troops who
should be used in this campaign. It was on this day that Clark said he
was taken into partnership by Governor Henry in locating a body of
land.[11]

A few points are of interest in connection with these plans. The idea
of the campaign is generally supposed to have originated with Clark, but
the Spanish agent Miralles thought that Bentley and Henry were the
prime movers, and Bentley's close relations with John and David Rogers
give strength to this view. Clark's sending of the spies so exactly coincided with Murray's suggestion that it is hard to escape the conclusion
that he was working in cooperation with the Kaskaskia merchants,
especially since one of them, Benjamin Linn, was related to the William
Linn who went with Gibson to New Orleans. And how would Henry,
except through this channel, have known that Pollock was prepared to
cooperate? The continued cooperation between Clark and the traders
throughout the proceedings in the Illinois country makes this conclusion
still more convincing.[12]

Though designed to be carried on in a secret manner, the campaign
was entirely official as far as Virginia was concerned. The House of
Delegates approved it in general terms; the governor and council sanctioned it specifically. The strange part of it is that General Hand was
called upon to furnish the sinews of war. Hand held his command under
Congress, and Congress had no part whatsoever in this campaign. That
body did not even have any knowledge of it in advance, nor did Hand
for that matter. But Henry did not seem to doubt his compliance. In
this he was correct, for the General showed every inclination to comply
on his own authority, but since he was not pressed for time, he consulted
General Horatio Gates of the Board of War in regard to the project.

---

[11] Queries by and instructions from Governor Henry, n.d., Fleming MSS., W. and
L. U. library; James, *Clark Papers*, p. 27; McIlwaine, *Official Letters of the Governors of the State of Virginia*, I, 222–224; Henry, *Henry*, I, 592–593; Thwaites and
Kellogg, *Frontier Defense*, pp. 196–197.
[12] Alvord, "Virginia and the West, an Interpretation," *Mississippi Valley Historical Review*, III, 31–32.

Clark got his boats and then drew on George Morgan for commissary supplies. He was able to raise few recruits in the Pittsburgh area, nor was he able to get many in Kentucky.[13]

A few days after arranging for this campaign Henry dispatched another expedition into the West. On January 15 Colonel David Rogers, late lieutenant of Ohio County, was sent to Pittsburgh with authority from the Board of War to call on General Hand to furnish him with boats for an excursion down to New Orleans. He carried a letter from Henry to Governor Gálvez saying that he came to get the supplies which Gálvez had stated in a letter to Congress were lodged at New Orleans for the use of Virginia. Henry also told Gálvez that he planned to build a fort at the mouth of the Ohio for the protection of commerce on the Mississippi and asked the Spanish governor if he did not think the annexation of West Florida to the United States would have a good effect in curtailing British trade in that quarter. Henry also requested a loan, to be repaid in goods. Gálvez transmitted this letter to the Court of Spain and held out hope that every request would be complied with.[14]

It thus happened that three expeditions set off from Pittsburgh early in 1778. Willing and Rogers went to New Orleans, Clark to the Illinois. The first was sent by a committee of Congress, the other two by Virginia. Their purposes all blended into one scheme of conquering the country north of the Ohio, opening the navigation of the Mississippi, and keeping it open by means of a fort at the mouth of the Ohio. Gálvez showed every inclination to cooperate with the Americans, even to the extent of a joint campaign against Mobile and Pensacola. Though Congress did not sanction such a campaign and though that body as a whole had not even authorized that of Willing, it is clear that the Morris group was sympathetic with these measures, while Laurens opposed them, and apparently his friends of the Adams-Lee faction were able to keep Congress from entering into the schemes of Henry, Morgan, and Gálvez.

It is obvious that the Illinois land-company interests, through the Kaskaskia merchants and apparently through General Hand who had bought thousands of acres from Croghan and was otherwise connected with them, were cooperating with Henry in the conquest of the Northwest. Clark was also assisted by de Leyba, the Spanish governor at St. Louis, and

[13] Savelle, *Morgan*, p. 179; Cotterill, *History of Pioneer Kentucky*, pp. 127–128; Thwaites and Kellogg, *Frontier Defense*, pp. 202–203, 227, 271–272; Kellogg, *Frontier Advance on the Upper Ohio* (Madison, 1916) pp. 49–51, 122.

[14] Henry to Gálvez, Jan. 14, 1778, Douglas Brymner, *Report on Canadian Archives*, 1888, pp. 105ff.; Pickering to Rogers, May 25, 1778, *ibid.*, p. 110; Rogers to Henry, Oct. 4, 1778, Add. MSS., 21, 844, Br. Mus.; Thwaites and Kellogg, *Revolution on the Upper Ohio*, p. 232; Thwaites and Kellogg, *Frontier Defense*, pp. 199, 278–279; Kellogg, *Frontier Advance*, p. 91.

his agent, M. Francis Vigo.[15] Since Morgan had opposed all former plans for such a conquest but gave his support to this one he must have had great confidence in the prospect that Virginia would validate the land purchases made by the companies in that area. In 1775 Patrick Henry had signed a statement to the effect that he considered these purchases from the natives as conveying a valid title to lands. It is natural that he would, two years later, have been credited with holding the same opinion, but it is hard to escape the conviction—for which there is no documentary evidence, however—that the Pennsylvania speculators must have had some rather definite commitments made to them by the Virginia leaders of the Henry and Pendleton groups. Except for Henry, their connections were all with the mercantile and conservative factions in Virginia, led by Pendleton and Harrison, the progressives of the Jefferson and Lee following having no dealings with them.

Thus the mercantile-conservatives in Virginia seem to have been in alliance with the mercantile-conservatives of the Morris faction in Congress favoring an expansionist policy in the West. On the other hand, the Lee-Adams liberals in Virginia and in Congress appear to have had little interest in expansion at this time. It is important, of course, that the cause of expansion was inextricably identified with the cause of certain land companies during 1778.

After much delay the commission provided by Congress assembled at Pittsburgh. It consisted of Sampson Matthews of Virginia and George Clymer of Pennsylvania. One of its first important acts was to clear George Morgan of the charges of disloyalty which had been lodged against him. The next day Morgan's friends and associates, Alexander McKee, Matthew Elliott, and Simon Girty, escaped from Pittsburgh and joined the British. Though they did not show themselves capable of consistent patriotism, they did show great consideration for their friend Morgan by delaying their departure until he was cleared.[16]

On April 27 the commissioners advised Congress to undertake a campaign against Detroit and to appoint negotiators to make a new treaty with the Indians. In May General Lachlan McIntosh was appointed to succeed Hand in the command at Pittsburgh, and on June 1 Timothy Pickering of the Board of War expressed a desire to consult with him and Morgan about the proposed Detroit campaign. On the eleventh of

[15] Thwaites and Kellogg, *Frontier Defense*, pp. 200–201; de Leyba to Clark, July 8, 1778, *American Historical Review*, XLI, 94; de Leyba to Gálvez Aug. 6, 1778, *ibid.*, p. 99; Willing to Clark, Aug. 22, 1778, James, *Clark Papers*, p. 66; Bruno Roselli, *Vigo* (Boston, 1933) p. 82ff.

[16] Matthews to President of Congress, Feb. 13, 1778, Cont. Cong. MSS., LVI, 89; Thomas Wharton to Laurens, May 2, 1778, *ibid.*, 69, I, 497; *Pa. Arch.*, series 1, VI, 386–387; Thwaites and Kellogg, *Frontier Defense*, pp. 249–251.

this month Congress gave its sanction to this expedition. Thus Continental plans for the taking of Detroit had been definitely laid when Clark captured Kaskaskia without a struggle on the night of July 4–5, 1778. On July 7 the council of Virginia passed resolutions disapproving of the proposed Congressional campaign, and the next day Governor Henry gave notice to that effect. On July 25 Congress abandoned the idea, but authorized McIntosh to lead an expedition against the hostile Indian tribes. This officer did not reach Pittsburgh until August, and shortly thereafter Morgan departed for the East. Though Morgan had approved the Detroit expedition, he had no liking for McIntosh, who was not a land speculator; neither he nor Virginia gave any support to the Indian expedition which that officer now undertook.[17]

On September 17 Andrew and Thomas Lewis, the commissioners appointed for the purpose under the authority of Congress, concluded a new treaty with the Delawares. Morgan's old policy of neutrality was now definitely broken, and the natives agreed to take up the hatchet in the American cause and permit the passage of an army through their country to attack Detroit. Furthermore, they criticized Morgan's conduct as Indian agent and asked that Colonel John Gibson be appointed in his stead. No cession of lands was requested, and the establishment of an Indian State with representatives in Congress was held out as a hope for the future. It is not surprising that Morgan presently criticized this treaty in strong terms, saying that a sufficient grant of land could have been got from the Delawares to satisfy the demands of the Continental soldiers. Shortly thereafter he resigned as Indian agent for the Middle Department.[18]

The conquest of the Illinois was apparently not known in Virginia until the beginning of October. On the twentieth of November, it was reported in Williamsburg that "Major Rogers Clark, the Conqueror of the Illinois, has marched against D'Etroit, which from want of provisions and defense, it will doubtless be reduced to obedience to the United States." Henry notified the Virginia delegates in Congress of Clark's

[17] David I. Bushnell, Jr., "The Virginia Frontier in History," *Va. Mag. of Hist. and Biog.,* XXIII, 256–268; Savelle, *Morgan,* p. 179; Kellogg, *Frontier Advance,* pp. 26–27, 104, 112–113; *William and Mary Quarterly Historical Magazine,* V (n.s.) 163; Morgan to Hand, May 16, 1778, Draper MSS., 2U18; Henry to County Lieutenant of Botetourt, Nov. 20, 1778, *ibid.,* 2U50; Christian to Henry, Nov. 22, 1778, *ibid.,* 2U51; Pickering to Morgan, June 1, 1778, Morgan MSS., L. of C.; *Journals of the Continental Congress,* XI, 588–590, 720; Henry to Laurens, July 18, 1778, Cont. Cong. MSS., 71, I, 165.

[18] Bushnell, *op. cit., Va. Mag. of Hist. and Biog.,* XXXIV, 44–45; Mohr, *Federal Indian Relations,* pp. 72–73; Savelle, *Morgan,* pp. 256–262; Kellogg, *Frontier Advance,* pp. 127–128; Draper MSS., 1H10; Hildreth, *Pioneer History,* p. 133; *Treaties between the United States of America and the several Indian Tribes* (Washington, 1837) pp. 1–4.

victory in the Illinois and organized a county government for the whole region north of the Ohio. John Todd, a close friend of Clark who had been with him on the Kaskaskia expedition, was made county lieutenant and given authority to appoint his subordinates. He named Richard Winston, the trader and land speculator, as sheriff. The governor was authorized to send a force of five hundred men for the protection of the country, but otherwise the inhabitants were to be interfered with as little as possible by the new régime. They were to elect their customary officials, pay them in the usual way, and enforce the customary law. This government was of a purely temporary nature, for the act was to expire at the end of the year. By subsequent acts it was continued until 1781.[19]

Knowledge of Clark's exploit apparently reached Pennsylvania before November 3, for on that date the Illinois and Wabash Land Companies held a joint meeting and planned to unite their interests. They drafted a memorial which was presented to the Virginia House of Delegates on December 26. In it they asked no favors, but stated their intention to take possession of the lands which they had bought from the Indians in 1773 and 1775. M. Gérard, who was in Philadelphia at the time, stated that plans were being made by members of Congress to settle the country by means of companies already formed and that they expected to have twenty thousand settlers on the land within four years.[20]

In view of these facts and of the fact that the idea of the conquest of the Illinois by Virginia appears to have originated with Thomas Bentley at Kaskaskia and William Murray in New Orleans and in view of the close cooperation between Clark and the Illinois merchants who were friends and associates of Murray, it seems clear that it was the collaboration of the interests supporting the land companies and the Henry administration in Virginia which made the result possible.

That Gálvez had given such generous aid and that he was also willing to cooperate with the rebels in an attack on West Florida is equally significant. As early as February 10, 1778, Arthur Lee understood that Spain desired possession of Pensacola, but the treaty of alliance with France left the United States free to conquer any of the existing or former possessions of Great Britain in America. In March the Count Floridablanca, Spanish Secretary of State, expressed himself as satisfied

[19] For Todd, see Chicago Historical Society, *Collections,* IV, 285–288; Carl Evans Boyd, "The County of Illinois," *American Historical Review,* IV, 623–635; Hening, IX, 552; Henry to Virginia delegates in Congress, Nov. 14, 1778, Cont. Cong. MSS., 71, I, 189.
[20] Gérard to Vergennes, Nov. 10, 1778, *Affaires Étrangères, États-Unis,* L. of C. transcripts, V, 68; James A. James, "Oliver Pollock and the Free Navigation of the Mississippi River," *Mississippi Valley Historical Review,* XIX, 334; Alvord, *The Illinois Country,* pp. 340–342; *Pennsylvania Packet,* Dec. 12, 1778.

with the Mississippi River as a boundary between Spain and the revolt-
ing colonies, and as late as June 1, the question was still an open one
at the Courts of France and Spain. Gálvez was ready to help the American forces clear the navigation of the Mississippi of British obstruction,
and he did not raise any question as to who should control West Florida
in case it should be conquered. The plan to accomplish this object, so
zealously fostered by Henry and Morgan in their correspondence with
the Spanish governor, was finally quashed by Congress on October 31,
1778. The Board of War, reporting on letters from Willing, Pollock, and
Gálvez, pronounced the proposed joint expedition to be beyond the means
of Congress to support.[21]

This marks the end of complete harmony between Spanish and American officials in dealing with the Western problem. The turn in affairs
came with the arrival of Don Juan de Miralles, Spanish agent and unofficial observer in America. This gentleman had landed at Charleston in
January and had discussed with Governor Henry of Virginia the proposed joint expedition against Florida. In July he proceeded to Philadelphia and in October entered into collaboration with the French minister, Gérard. Gérard wrote to Vergennes that he had not seen Miralles'
instructions, but could discover them from his conversation. They insisted on an exclusion of America from the navigation of the Mississippi,
on Spanish control of West Florida, and support of British jurisdiction
in Canada and the Northwest. America was to be aided in order to distress Britain, but she was not to be allowed to become too powerful.
Vergennes thought that Canada, Nova Scotia and the Newfoundland
fisheries should be left to Britain, that Spain should have the disposition
of Florida, but that Congress would demand navigation of the Mississippi, and Gérard should avoid difficulties on this head if possible.[22]

The French minister in Philadelphia seemed more ready to cater to
Spanish ambitions as represented by Miralles than was his master, Vergennes. On October 20 he reported a conversation with Robert Morris
and some of his Congressional friends in which Morris expressed the

[21] Miralles to Gálvez, June 6, 1778, *papeles de Cuba,* L. of C. transcripts, *legajo*
1281, part I, p. 50; Lee, *Arthur Lee,* II, 34–35, 55; Craig, *History of Pittsburgh,* pp.
128–129; S. F. Bemis, *Pinckney's Treaty* (Baltimore, 1926) pp. 21–22; *Journals of
the Continental Congress,* XII, 1083; Clymer to President of Congress, March 7, 1778,
Cont. Cong. MSS., LVI, 93; Laurens to Clymer, March 27, 1778, Burnett, III, 144;
Phillips, *The West in the Diplomacy of the Revolution,* pp. 65–66, 95; McKee to
Haldimand, Sept. 6, 1778, Add. MSS., 21, 876, Br. Mus.; Caughey, *Gálvez,* pp. 88, 90;
Bemis, *Diplomacy of the American Revolution,* 60, 94–95.

[22] Gérard's instruction, March 29, 1778, *Affaires Étrangères États-Unis,* III, f. 159–
164; Gérard to Vergennes, July 25, 1778, *ibid.,* IV, 41; Vergennes to Gérard, Oct. 26,
1778, *ibid.,* V, 43; Paul C. Phillips, "American Opinion Regarding the West, 1778–
1783," M.V.H.A., *Proceedings,* VII, 290–300; Phillips, *The West in the Diplomacy
of the Revolution,* pp. 103–104.

opinion that Congress should surrender the navigation of the Mississippi and the Southwestern territory to Spain. He said that the strength of the Confederacy lay in the North and that the North should be kept in the ascendancy by curtailing the territory on the Southwest.

Furthermore, the territory north of the Ohio River could be kept in political and commercial league with the East only if the navigation of the Mississippi were given up and that region forced to trade to the East. John Jay stated that "our empire is already too great to be well governed," and he, Gouverneur Morris, and the entire Robert Morris bloc in Congress gave general support to these principles, and Gérard became their active champion.[23]

This, of course, meant the end of the alliance between this group and the Henry administration in Virginia, but at least one of the Virginia Congressmen sympathized with Morris's ideas. With the Illinois already conquered, Virginia's aid was no longer essential; the situation in the Old Dominion was not looking altogether propitious for the land companies; and the Morris group was gaining strength in Congress. During the remainder of the War there was to be a bitter fight between the supporters of Virginia's claims on one side and the Congressional advocates of a restricted western boundary, led by Morris and Gérard, on the other.

[23] Gérard to Vergennes, Oct. 20, 1778, *Affaires Étrangères, États-Unis,* V, 33; James, "Pollock and the Navigation of the Mississippi," *loc. cit.,* p. 335; Bemis, *Pinckney's Treaty,* pp. 22–24; Phillips, *The West in the Diplomacy of the Revolution,* pp. 108–115; Wharton, *Diplomatic Correspondence,* I, 362.

CHAPTER XVI

CONGRESSIONAL POLITICS, 1778

IT has been seen to what extent, during the early years of the Revolution while the insurgent colonies were fighting with no great success for what they deemed to be their rights, attempts were usually made to sidestep factional differences for the sake of the common cause and how in 1777 friction in Congress was aroused as a result of the Conway cabal. The year 1778 brought with it a crisis that forced partisan strife in Congress into the foreground, and during the remainder of the War two antagonistic groups struggled openly for control of that body.

The natural line of cleavage was between the Northern and the Southern colonies, and this for two main reasons. The major part of the Western lands was claimed by the Southern group, and many issues grew out of this fact. Then again, the land-owning Anglican aristocracy of the South possessed a different standard of values from that of the small-farmer and mercantile society of the North. On many issues this sectional division came to the fore, notably in connection with sumptuary and sabbatical legislation brought forward by the Northern Puritanical element in Congress.[1] But it has been shown how the purely sectional division was cut across and largely submerged by the alliance between the Virginia Lees and the Massachusetts Adamses in Congress. A personal element was involved in this coalition, but it represented primarily an alliance of the predominantly agricultural forces as opposed to the commercial. The fact that the opposition was led by the great merchant, Robert Morris, and that its policies usually involved mercantile interests was the central fact in the situation.[2]

Strangely enough, the events which brought to a crisis this hostility between merchant and farmer occurred in Paris. At the beginning of 1778 Franklin, Deane, and Lee still represented the cause of America in

---

[1] Gérard to Vergennes, Aug. 24, 1778, *Correspondence Politique, Affaires Étrangères, États-Unis,* L. of C. transcripts, IV, 98 : same to same, Oct. 4, 1778, *ibid.,* V, 8.

[2] De Francy wrote, "Robert Morris in his time has had much influence, but since it appeared that he occupied himself only with his own affairs in appearing to occupy himself with those of the public, the confidence which was reposed in him infinitely diminished." John Bigelow, ed., *Beaumarchais the Merchant: Letters of Théveneau de Francy, 1777–1780* (New York, 1870) pp. 12–13. See also Worthington C. Ford, ed., *Letters of William Lee* (Brooklyn, 1891) III, 947.

that Capital. Deane had just been recalled on account of his improvident contracts with French officers for service in the American army, but he had not yet received notice of that fact. Lee was increasingly at odds with his colleagues but striving to maintain an appearance of unity; not even his brother Richard Henry had heard anything of the differences that were developing.

Franklin, Deane, and Bancroft were still domiciled with Chaumont at Passy, and their politician-merchant host was in close touch with the Comte de Vergennes, French foreign minister. Conrad Alexandre Gérard de Rayneval, Vergennes' chief clerk, served along with Chaumont as an intermediary between the French Court and the American agents, and Maurepas and Sartine were closely associated with the foreign minister in his American enterprises.[3]

On January 8, after the victory at Saratoga gave some assurance of the Revolution's success, the French Ministry notified the American agents that the King was prepared to enter into treaties of amity and commerce with the rebel colonies. The creator of *Figaro* drafted the manifesto whereby the King acknowledged the independence of the United States. Immediately Deane authorized Bancroft to hie himself to London and use the advance knowledge of this event for speculating purposes. Bancroft had been sent on a similar errand when news of Burgoyne's defeat had been received the preceding autumn. Walpole had usually put up the money for their joint speculations, but on February 17 Deane sent Wharton nineteen thousand five hundred and ten livres from the funds of the commission. A British secret service agent, learning of the remittance, gave it out that Wharton was "a creature of and supported by Dr. Franklin." While Deane and Bancroft made such use of the information they gathered from official sources under Franklin's nose, they were both engaged in selling the same information to agents of the British government.[4]

[3] Gérard to Vergennes, Dec. 4, 1778, *A.E., E.U.,* V, 97; Vergennes to Franklin, March 18, 1779, *ibid.,* VII, 160; Jonathan Williams to Vergennes, Oct. 6, 1778, *ibid.,* V, 26; Chaumont to Vergennes, Oct. 10, 1778, *ibid.,* V, 39; same to same, Oct. 28, 1778, *ibid.,* V, 116; same to same, Nov. (?) 1778, *ibid.,* V, 215; Comte de Lauraguais to Maurepas, March 3, 1778, Stevens facsimiles, no. 802; Bigelow, *Works of Benjamin Franklin,* VII, 338; Winslow C. Watson, ed., *Men and Times of the Revolution, or Memoirs of Elkanah Watson* (New York, 1856) p. 87; *Life and Correspondence of John Paul Jones—from original Letters and Manuscripts in the Possession of Miss Janette Taylor* (editor not given, New York, 1830) pp. 133–134.

[4] Franklin himself was in direct correspondence with Walpole at this time. William Strahan, the King's printer, to whom Franklin had written the famous letter announcing that "You and I were long friends, but you are now my enemy and I am yours," sent him and Deane a Stilton cheese on Feb. 13, 1778. Strahan to W. T. Franklin, Franklin MSS., XLIV, 21, A.P.S.; Walpole to Franklin, Dec. 23, 1777, *ibid.,* VII, 177. See also Temple Franklin to Bancroft, n.d., *ibid.,* CVII, 153; Bancroft to W. T.

On the same day that the Franco-American treaty was announced to Franklin and Deane another spy whom they had taken into their camp as secretary returned from a journey to London. This person, John Thornton, made the mistake of letting it be known that he had discovered in London that the Ministry knew of Bancroft's speculating journeys and that they understood he was sent by the three American commissioners in Paris. Shortly afterward Franklin suggested to Lee that he use Thornton as his secretary. The offer was accepted and Lee sent Thornton to London to act as a spy in the American cause. Lee, of course, did not know that Thornton was a British spy, nor did Franklin suspect either him or Bancroft or Deane. But Franklin did know of the speculation that was going on, and he could hardly have helped knowing that secret official information was being used for that purpose by Bancroft, since he had had, and continued to have, access to all private papers in possession of the American commission.[5] In fact, when Arthur Lee heard accidently of Bancroft's trips across the Channel he expostulated with Franklin saying that such journeys were astonishing if Bancroft held any office of trust under the commission. If he did not hold such office, the Virginian continued, it was even more surprising that he had access to papers of the commission and even had the key to them, which he himself, a joint commissioner, had respectfully asked for in vain.[6]

Instead of doing anything to stop this leakage at the point where he knew it was taking place Franklin now joined Deane in a successful attempt to discredit Lee in the eyes of the French Ministry. On reaching London Thornton got in contact with Samuel Wharton and his brother Joseph, and these two Quakers sent word to Paris that secret information was being divulged through Thornton. This statement was true enough, but all parties concerned knew that Bancroft and the Whartons

Franklin, n.d., *ibid.*, CVIII, 64; Bancroft to B. Franklin, n.d., *ibid.*, LXX, 22; Wharton to (B. Franklin, 1778), *ibid.*, XLI, 99; same to same, March 3, 1778, *ibid.*, VIII, 147; Hutton to Franklin, April 19, 1778, *ibid.*, IX, 60; Wharton to Deane, May 19, 1778, *ibid.*, XLVII, pt. 2, 114; Wharton to Bancroft, May 22, 1778, *ibid.*, XLVII, 116, 117; Wentworth to Eden, sketches of Americans, 1778, Stevens facsimiles, no. 487, Wentworth to Eden, Jan. 10, 1778, *ibid.*, no. 335; Wentworth to Eden, March 27, 1778, *ibid.*, no. 342; E. D. Ingraham, ed., *Papers Relating to the Case of Silas Deane*, (Phila., 1855) pp. 63–65, 110; Lee, *Arthur Lee*, II, 45, 103; Lord North to the King, Jan. 30, 1778, Fortescue, *Correspondence of King George the Third*, IV, 29–30; the King to North, Feb. 3, 1778, *ibid.*, IV, 34; also *ibid.*, IV, 45–46, 50–51; Wharton to Deane, Feb. 21, 1778, Add. MSS., 24, 321, Br. Mus.; same to same, March 13, 1778, *ibid.*; Digges to A. Lee, Aug. 30, 1778, Arthur Lee MSS., Harvard U. library; Horace Walpole, *Letters*, VII, 31n.

[5] Thornton to the Commissioners, Jan. 3, 1778, Arthur Lee MSS., Harvard U. library; Thornton's depositions, April 4, 13, 1778, Lee MSS., U. of Va. library; Lee, *Arthur Lee*, I, 374–375, II, 47–48; Franklin to Bancroft, April 16, 1778, Bigelow, *Works of Benjamin Franklin*, VII, 290–291.

[6] Lee, *Arthur Lee*, I, 366–367.

were merchants of secret information, that they depended on it for their "dabbling in the Alley." On receipt of this tip regarding Thornton, Deane, and Franklin insinuated to Vergennes that Lee—for whom Thornton had been acting as secretary since his recommendation for that post by Franklin—could not be trusted with official secrets. Furthermore, a letter, apparently forged by Thornton, which was supposed to have been written by Lee to Lord Shelburne expressing some regret over the necessity of the French alliance, was transmitted to Vergennes. A copy of this document is preserved in the Franklin papers. Lee had already been practically excluded from all important business of the commission, but this manipulation now put a better official face upon the situation, and presently Congress was notified through Vergennes and his minister at Philadelphia that Lee was not trusted by the French Ministry. Thus was Franklin's object accomplished.[7]

While Deane and Franklin had many irons in the fire, one of their most important concerns still centered about the commercial establishment at Nantes headed by Franklin's nephew, Jonathan Williams, a youthful profiteer who had formerly been employed in a London confectionery. He had been provided with a commodious storehouse for his operations, and Deane, with Franklin's approval, furnished him with ample funds from the exchequer of the American commission, for which no accounting was required. After Lee had been beseeching for more businesslike procedure Franklin wrote to his nephew that he need be under no concern that his orders came from Deane only; "you would be justified," he added, "if you had no orders at all."[8]

Now that France was openly at war with England privateering was engaging an increasingly large number of adventurers. Among these was the Scotchman, John Paul, who in 1773 had gone to Virginia to take charge of his deceased brother's estate on the Rappahannock and had assumed the name Jones. He was fitted out with a fleet of five privateers, and his prizes were sold through the agency of Chaumont. On several occasions Jones protested indignantly at the terms forced on him, but he had no choice in the matter for the booty could not be sold except on terms dictated by Chaumont. William Carmichael, also tainted with trea-

[7] Bancroft to Franklin, Sept. 14, 1778, Arthur Lee MSS., Harvard U. library; M. Livingston to A. Lee, July 15, 1778, ibid.; Thornton to A. Lee, May 5, 7, 16, 22, 1778, ibid.; same to same, May 30, 1778, ibid.; Lee, Arthur Lee, II, 50, 70–71; Wharton, Diplomatic Correspondence, I, 639, 659–661; E. S. Corwin, French Policy and the American Alliance of 1778 (Princeton, 1916) pp. 166–167n.; Thornton to W(?), May 13, 1778, Franklin MSS., XLVII, 112, A.P.S.; Fortescue, Correspondence of George the Third, IV, 133–135.
[8] Benjamin Franklin to Jonathan Williams, Dec. 22, 1777, Lee MSS., U. of Va. library; Ingraham, Papers Relating to Silas Deane, pp. 39–42, 141–149, 173.

son, who had acted as Deane's secretary and was in position to know, later testified before Congress that some of the public funds of the American commissioners were used to outfit privateers to cruise in the Mediterranean! On one occasion Franklin wrote to Jones that the French government was preparing to provide him with a super-privateer. Thus were public and private concerns combined, and the principals were careful to keep no intelligible records of the transactions. Later, when Congress was trying to bring some order out of the chaos of expenditures, Franklin wrote to Chaumont: "If we agree and make a settlement so that the state of our accounts may appear clear to my constituents, I shall make no difficulty of advancing the sum you require." [9]

Washington's army at this time was all but perishing for want of the supplies which were delayed by operations of the spies and traitors at Franklin's headquarters. That venerable philosopher, however, deep in his meditations, sent no word to commanders of privateers except an order to watch out for Captain Cook, then expected to be on his return from the South Seas, and to give him every aid as a friend to mankind. This reminds one of Gibbon, the historian, sitting silently in Parliament day after day, musing on the decline and fall of the Roman Empire while an imperial domain was slipping from Britain.

Deane had become the collaborator and partner of Beaumarchais in the management of the fund which the French Ministry had turned over to the playwright for the use of America. While it had been intended, for diplomatic reasons, to give only the appearance of a commercial transaction to the shipment of supplies for the rebel army, Beaumarchais and Deane undertook to make it in truth a commercial affair. They demanded that Congress make full payment for all goods sent, in spite of the fact that that body had no voice as to what should be sent and received no accurate account of shipments made. It is clear that the King of France really intended to make a gift of the million livres, and Beaumarchais acted as if the gift were made to him personally. Much special pleading has been done in his behalf, but it is clear enough that he and Deane made shipments on their private accounts, with no effort to keep them separate from the public account, claiming payment for all on the same basis. Franklin disliked Beaumarchais, and the American commission in

[9] Taylor, *Life and Correspondence of John Paul Jones*, pp. 109–110, 113–114, 136–137, 156–161, 164, 204–205, 258; Almon, *Remembrancer, 1778*, p. 373; Chaumont to Vergennes, Jan. 5, 1778, Stevens facsimiles, no. 771; Lee to Franklin, Jan. 10, 1778, A. Lee MSS., Harvard U. library; John Ross to B. Franklin, March 7, 1778, Franklin MSS., VIII, 157, A.P.S.; Wharton to Chaumont, March 23, 1778, *ibid.*, VIII, 186; Ford, *Letters of William Lee*, II, 406–408, 418–424; W. G. Sumner, *Financier and Finances of the American Revolution*, I, 183–184; Franklin to Chaumont, May 2, 1784, Franklin MSS., LIV, 125, no. 7, A.P.S.

Paris officially denied that the Frenchman had a right to claim payment for all the supplies, but Deane, having a private interest in the matter, supported all claims of the playwright.[10]

On September 26 of the preceding year Beaumarchais had sent an agent to America in the person of Théveneau de Francy, his confidential clerk and nephew of his former partner in blackmail, Théveneau de Morande, to collect his claims from Congress. He was still in America, and on July 31, 1778, he wrote to his patron:

> . . . You will have difficulty in believing that the Committee on Commerce would never consent that the returns destined for you should be consigned to you directly. Mr. Robert Morris was one of those who opposed it most, & as he is the only merchant in Congress who has ever conducted large commercial operations, his opinion is law. He wishes these returns to be consigned to one of their commercial agents in France who should sell the cargoes as fast as they arrive and remit to you the proceeds— He thus finds means of employing people with whom he is always *de moitie*. *Il fait ses affaires de toutes celles de la republique.* As he is a very great influence and has a very great credit, and as, in the beginning of the Revolution especially, no one could render greater service to America than he, through his connections in the four quarters of the globe, he has done whatever he pleased. All the money destined to make purchases abroad has been confided to him. Consequently, he has sent agents into all parts of Virginia & in general everywhere whence they could export anything, to make purchases of tobacco & other products. The vessels which are loaded with this merchandise usually belong to Mr. Morris, & he freights them for account of Congress. He always takes care to insure the tenth or twelfth part of the cargo belonging to him, and the vessel is thus sent by his agent in Virginia, consigned to his agent in France, and as this Virginia agent is not required to render any account of his shipment, they have ample time to ascertain whether the vessel has arrived or has been taken. In the first case, it belongs to Mr. Morris; in the second, it belongs to Congress. . . . It was the fear of seeing all this business go out of his or his agents' hands that prevented his consenting that the returns be consigned directly to you. . . .[11]

As has been seen, Morris was not the only one who "worked for himself in working for the republic." While his associates were largely taken up with immediate profits to be made from the supplies which the Americans, fighting for their lives, so desperately needed they did not forget their erstwhile land interests. As long as he remained in Paris Deane was constantly trying to induce Congress to take possession of the Western land for payment of military bounties and for purposes of speculation in Europe. He concocted a lottery scheme to dispose of twenty millions of

[10] Lee, *Arthur Lee*, I, 306–308, 373–374.

[11] de Francy to Beaumarchais, July 31, 1778, *Letters of Théveneau de Francy*, p. 10. When de Francy heard that Adams had been elected to replace Deane he wrote to Beaumarchais that he should get his accounts in shape. *Ibid.*, pp. 5–6.

acres to be laid out on the Ohio and Mississippi Rivers and had a company ready—organized from among his European associates—which was prepared to take advantage of the opportunity as soon as Congress should assent. He wrote Congress that this plan was approved by the Court of France. When the Secret Committee reported that it was not clear that Congress possessed any Western lands in its own right Deane's chagrin was equal to his economic disappointment. Chaumont individually soon possessed one share of stock in Vandalia, and "Chaumont & Company" held another. After the Revolution his son came to America to look after the landed property. In truth, there was much talk of Vandalia among the partners as they gathered around Chaumont's hospitable dinner-table. That gentleman announced his intention to remove to the "Paradise on Earth" into which the American wilds were expected to be transformed, and Silas Deane gave it out that he and his family also would make their home in Vandalia. Richard Neave, Junior, of the London mercantile firm which some years before had saved the tottering house of Baynton and Wharton, in order to make certain of the share which had come into his possession, repaired to France and before Benjamin Franklin took the oath of allegiance to the United States. Dr. Bancroft, too, had acquired a share in Vandalia during this period, and in a petition of that organization to Congress three years later he was described as a loyal American citizen! By the end of the next year we shall see that various Frenchmen, including Ferdinand Grand, banker to the American commission (though Deane's original instructions had directed him to another) ; Gérard, the chief clerk of Vergennes ; and John Holker had been added to the personnel of the Illinois and Wabash Companies, while Deane and Morris were leading spirits in them.[12]

Holker was a protégé of Chaumont and an associate of Deane. He was the son of an English Jacobite who had migrated to France and amassed a large fortune as a result of commercial operations. On December 27, 1777, he left France for America in company with Simeon Deane, brother to Silas, fortified with a letter of recommendation from Franklin to John Hancock. On March 4, 1778, Silas Deane received notice of his recall, and on April 1 he and Gérard, who was now to act as French minister to the United States, set out to submit their cause to the Continental Congress. Holker also was to have an official status, for he was made consul-general of France and agent-general of the Royal Marine in America. In addition, he was to act as the commercial agent for Chau-

---

[12] Ingraham, *Papers Relating to Silas Deane,* pp. 44–46; list of members of Illinois and Ouabache (*sic*) companies, Jefferson MSS., L. of C. ; *ibid.,* list of proprietors of Vandalia ; petition of Vandalia Company, Lee MSS., Harvard U. library.

mont. John Adams, able, honest and stubborn, was elected by Congress
to replace Deane in France, and he arrived in that country at about the
time of his predecessor's departure. But Deane's place in Franklin's
household was really taken by Dr. Bancroft, to whom Franklin turned
over Deane's correspondence. Early the next year Samuel Wharton
quitted London and joined this agreeable household at Passy.[13]

The return of Silas Deane and the advent of de Francy, Holker, and
Gérard precipitated a political crisis in Congress. During May, 1778,
Richard Henry Lee began receiving complaints from his brother Arthur
about the situation at Passy. Arthur soon began laying his complaints
also before the Committee for Foreign Affairs, of which his brother was
a member.[14]

Before Deane set out on his return Lee urged that the public accounts
be settled, since Deane had possession of all the vouchers. Franklin ignored the request, although Deane had had ample time to comply with
it. According to de Francy, he had not only refrained from preparing his
own but had persuaded Beaumarchais ·not to prepare his accounts so
that their business relations with the French officers whom they had
sent to America might not be revealed to Deane's colleagues. At about
the same time the three commissioners, under promptings from Franklin,
adopted a resolution advising Congress that there was a mixture of public and private property involved in the Beaumarchais accounts and that
they could best be settled at Passy. Whatever the reason for it, Congress
got no accounts.[15]

With this handicap to face, Deane realized he would have need of
friends in Congress and prepared for that emergency with considerable
foresight. Beaumarchais was instrumental in securing a letter from Vergennes speaking of Deane's work in glowing terms. The King presented
him a likeness of His Most Christian Majesty, and Franklin added a
letter of tribute. Deane wrote that he had "not taken a single step but
by the advice of Doctor Franklin," and he counted heavily on the support
of this great name. The lack of accounts might be forgiven in the face
of such testimony. Furthermore, Gérard had instructions from Vergennes

[13] Franklin to Hancock, Dec. 4, 1777, Franklin MSS., Misc., II, U. of Pa. library;
Ingraham, *Papers Relating to Silas Deane*, pp. 44–46; Sumner, *op. cit.*, II, 163; *A.E.,
E.U.*, VII, 55–59; Holker to Chaumont, May 13, 1778, John Holker MSS., I, L. of C.;
Franklin to A. Lee, May 17, 1778, Bigelow, VII, 301; Sullivan, *Maryland and France*,
p. 46.
[14] Lee, *Arthur Lee*, II, 34–35, 127–128, 134; Ballagh, *Letters of Richard Henry Lee*,
I, 465.
[15] Lee to Franklin, April 2, 1778, Bigelow, VIII, 277–279; de Francy to Beaumarchais, May 14, 1778, Bigelow, *Letters of de Francy*, pp. 8–9; Lee, *Arthur Lee*, II, 37.

to champion the cause of Deane in Congress, but this was to be done in a quiet manner in order not to attract too much attention.[16]

Deane and his coterie soon found many things in America beside politics to engage their attention. The States, of course, still needed supplies and Europe needed tobacco, and the trade could be transacted on one side of the Atlantic as well as the other. Privateering was a lucrative enterprise, but the demand was not satisfied on either side, and large profits awaited the successful speculator. Robert Morris continued to be the general in command on the economic front, and Deane's relations with him, it will be recalled, had been close ever since he first went to France as agent of the Secret Committee of Congress and of Willing, Morris and Company. Deane's brother Simeon now took the active lead in commercial matters; in collaboration with John Holker he proceeded to build up, with the backing of Morris, an elaborate trading system. Holker remained for the greater part of the time in Pennsylania, keeping up contacts with Morris and Congress on one side and with Chaumont on the other, while Simeon Deane betook himself to Virginia and established connections with a number of important merchants of that State for the purpose of purchasing tobacco for shipment to Europe. He formed a partnership with the brothers Richard and Thomas Adams and wrote to Temple Franklin, illegitimate son of Sir William who was now acting as secretary to his grandfather in Paris, that they employed a clerk for the French language and begged to be recommended to such as might inquire. He also had relations with Norton, Beall and Company; Pleasants, Shore and Company; and other Virginia merchants. His most important personal contacts were with Benjamin Harrison of Brandon and Governor Patrick Henry. Henry's connection is surprising, for the governor was openly acting as a political ally of Richard Henry Lee and the anti-Deane group in Congress, but de Francy pictures Henry as privately opposing the Lees at this time, and the governor certainly befriended Deane.[17]

---

[16] Vergennes to Gérard, April 22, 1778, *A.E., E.U.,* III, 97; Wharton, *Diplomatic Correspondence,* I, 542; W. M. Van der Weyde, *The Life and Works of Thomas Paine* (New Rochelle, 1925) I, 58–59; *Magazine of American History,* III, 631–635.

[17] Simeon Deane to Temple Franklin, Oct. 2, 1778, Franklin MSS., LVIII, 67, A.P.S.; Simeon to Silas Deane, pub. Aug. 26, 1778, Ingraham, *Papers Relating to Silas Deane,* pp. 124–126; Simeon Deane to Holker, Oct. 13, 1778, Holker MSS., L. of C.; Morris to Holker, Oct. 19, 1778, *ibid.;* same to same, Oct. 27, 1778, *ibid.;* same to same, Nov. 3, 1778, *ibid.;* John Holker's observations on Mr. Morris's statements, 1778, *ibid.;* Simeon Deane to Holker, May 16, 1778, *ibid.;* same to same, May 30, 1778, *ibid.;* Holker to Chaumont, June 19, 1778, *ibid.;* Simeon Deane to Holker, June 20, 1778, *ibid.;* Benjamin Harrison to Holker, Aug. 20, 1778, *ibid.;* Holker to Chaumont, Aug. 25, 1778, *ibid.;* Wharton *et. al. vs.* Morris *et. al.,* A. J. Dallas, *Reports of Cases*

With these commercial activities in progress the Deane question was taken up for investigation by Congress. On July 18, Gérard reported that he found no appreciable opposition to Silas Deane in that body, but twice during August the former commissioner was questioned by a committee. His case did not present itself in a favorable light, and for the time being the matter was dropped. Deane now began vociferously to demand a hearing; finally, on December 1 he was instructed to appear again before Congress. His case was taken up and on December 5 he was notified to re-appear. On the same day he published in the *Pennsylvania Packet* a diatribe against Arthur Lee. This was too much for Henry Laurens, president of Congress, who insisted that Deane should not now be permitted a personal appearance but should be required to present his case in writing. On this stand Laurens was defeated by one vote. Deane was permitted his hearing, and Laurens resigned the presidency to be succeeded by John Jay.[18]

Thomas Paine, the famous author of *Common Sense,* was serving as secretary to the Committee for Foreign Affairs, and in this capacity he had become familiar with the correspondence which had been carried on by that body and the American commissioners in Paris. Paine had formerly been employed to use his powerful pen in defense of the title of the Vandalia Company and to deride Virgina's extensive claims to Western land, but Deane's close association with Franklin and other promoters of that company did not prevent Paine from becoming indignant at his effrontery. On December 15 he published in the *Packet* an answer to the article by Deane. Among other things, he struck at Beaumarchais' claims and made some reference to the gift which the French government had made to the colonies.[19]

Gérard now rose up and, having failed in an effort to bribe Paine, demanded that Congress discipline him. France, though at this time openly at war with England, could not, according to Gérard, admit that she had aided the rebels before joining the conflict, and Congress thought

. . . in the Courts of Pennsylvania (Philadelphia, 1790) pp. 125–126; Simeon Deane to Thomas Adams, June 22, 1778, Va. Historical Society MSS., File 1; Holker to Chaumont, July 13, 1778, Holker MSS., William S. Mason library; de Francy to Thomas Adams, July 15, 1778, Va. Historical Society MSS., File 1; Lee, *Arthur Lee,* II, 152–153.

[18] Gérard to Vergennes, July 18, 1778, *A.E., E.U.,* IV, 27; same to same, Aug. 16, 1778, *ibid.,* IV, 85; same to same, Oct. 4, 1778, *ibid.,* V, 8. A similar address by Deane was published in Almon's *Remembrancer* under date of Nov., 1778, pp. 185–190. Ingraham, *Papers Relating to Silas Deane,* pp. 84, 128–129; *Pennsylvania Packet,* Dec. 5, 1778; *Journals of the Continental Congress,* XII, 1181, 1192, 1200, 1202; *Pa. Mag. Hist. and Biog.,* XIII, 232–236.

[19] Conway, *Life of Thomas Paine,* (New York, 1892) I, 125–137, 438n.; *Pennsylvania Packet,* Dec. 15, 1778, Jan. 16, 19, 1779; William M. Van der Weyde, *Life and Works of Thomas Paine,* I, 61.

it necessary to meet the demand of the minister of her ally. Paine's writings were accordingly condemned, and Congress, much to its confusion later, put itself on record as denying that any gift had been made by the French government. Paine resigned his secretaryship, and Deane was able to gloat over his victory. Certainly it looked as though Congress would have to pay for that which it had admitted was not a gift. Gérard had proved a powerful friend and his influence with Congress, on account of gratitude for French aid, was indeed great.[20]

But the victory of Deane's friends and the commercial faction in Congress was not as complete as they could have wished. From its first organization Morris and his adherents had controlled the important Committee of Commerce; but on December 14 Henry Laurens took revenge for his recent defeat by presenting a letter which he had received from Richard Henry Lee, who was not present in Congress at this time. The letter revealed that a commercial agent of Carter Braxton had been guilty of improper conduct in connection with some purchases of tobacco in Virginia. Braxton was acting for Robert Morris and the affair cast a very unfavorable light upon the activities of the Commercial Committee. Accordingly, this committee was abolished and a new one of a different complexion appointed. All the papers of the old Committee of Commerce and of the Secret Committee were to be turned over to the new one, which might call to account any person found to be involved. Morris's enemies could now contemplate the pleasure of investigating the affairs of this great financier.[21] The Adamses, the Lees, and Laurens were still able to hold their own in Congress against the forces of Morris, Hancock, and such Virginians as John Banister, John Harvie, Carter Braxton, and Benjamin Harrison—all business associates of Robert Morris.[22]

A little thought will readily show what bearing this factional strife had upon the question of Western lands. Soon petitions from the land companies were to rain upon Congress, and the question of the cession of Western claims was to come before that body. The cleavage which took place on trade issues held when the land question was in the fore. Indeed,

[20] Conway, *Paine,* I, 125; Lee, *Arthur Lee,* I, 301–302.

[21] Braxton to Jonathan Hudson, Nov. 27, 1777, Sprague MSS., II, 452, H.S.P.; Morris to John Bradford, April 4, 1777, Morris MSS., N.Y.P.L.; *Journals of the Continental Congress,* Jan. 6, 1779, XIII, 30; also *ibid.,* XII, 1216–1217; Ballagh, *Letters of Richard Henry Lee,* II, 71–72.

[22] *Collections of the New York Historical Society, 1878, Revolutionary Papers,* "Letters to Robert Morris," I, pp. 407–412, 431, 436–437; Braxton to (?), June 19, 1777, Gratz MSS., H.S.P.; Harrison to Theodorick Bland, Sept. 8, 1777, *Tyler's Quarterly,* XII, 132–133; Deane to Harrison, Sept. 17, 1777, Stevens facsimiles, no. 194; Morris to John Brown, Feb. 1, 1778, Morris MSS., N.Y.P.L.; Brown to Morris, Feb. 13, 1778, *ibid.;* Bigelow, *Letters of de Francy,* p. 12n.; Morris to Holker, Oct. 8, 1778, Holker MSS., L. of C.

it is almost impossible to separate the two interests, so closely were they intertwined, for usually the merchants and the speculators were identical. To those of commercial bent the West was not a great public resource to be used for the benefit of the people, but a commodity to be used in trade. Robert Morris, for instance, who led the mercantile cohorts in Congress, possessed one and a half million acres in Virginia alone, and some years later he disposed, in one sale, of four million acres to the Holland Land Company. When Samuel Wharton, another great Philadelphia merchant, left London to join Franklin in Paris he had spent ten fruitless years and every shilling he could raise, as resident agent of the Indiana Company and of Vandalia in the British Capital. Thomas Walpole, member of Parliament and one of the partners in the concern organized by Morris and Deane for trading with the enemy, was likewise one of the chief promoters and largest shareholders of Vandalia. Chaumont, Bancroft, Joseph Wharton, and lesser figures of Franklin's coterie were also members of that enterprise. Thus Franklin's organization in Europe was made up largely of his Vandalia associates, and Lee's hostility to them may well have grown out of his old hostility to that company. Doubtless he remembered all too keenly how Vandalia had thwarted the ambitions of the Mississippi Company for which he had acted as agent back in colonial days and how it had effaced the Ohio Company, founded by his father long years before Vandalia was ever thought of. This is not admitting, however, that Arthur Lee's attitude can be accounted for solely on such a basis. It is admitting only that this rivalry probably accelerated his zeal and lent enthusiasm to his task of exposing the peculiar activities of his fellow commissioners.

It appears that Franklin and his friends, while not entirely abandoning hope for Vandalia, were becoming increasingly interested in the lands north of the Ohio River. We shall presently see this interest ripen into something of real consequence. For the present, young George Rogers Clark seemed to have the situation in that area well in hand. His capture of Kaskaskia was publicly announced in Philadelphia on December 12.[23]

[23] Wentworth to Suffolk, Sept. 24, 1777, Add. MSS., 34, 413, Br. Mus.; Wentworth to Eden, Jan. 1, 1778, Stevens facsimiles, no. 327; same to same, Jan. 7, 1778, *ibid.,* no. 489; Lee, *Arthur Lee,* II, 129–130, *Pennsylvania Packet,* Dec. 12, 1778.

CHAPTER XVII

VIRGINIA'S WESTERN LAND POLICY, 1778–1779

DURING 1778 the political situation in Virginia remained much as it had been since the beginning of the War, but the land question now emerged as a definite issue in party strife. The liberal element was led by the same small group which had largely dominated Virginia politics since 1776. Richard Henry Lee, Patrick Henry, Thomas Jefferson, George Mason, and George Wythe made up the inner circle, but such men as John Taylor, John Tyler, Senior, and the young James Madison were valuable allies. Neither Mason nor Wythe had been "forward" on the question of resistance to Britain, and both Jefferson and Henry on occasion spoke with scorn of the rank and file of Western pioneers, but this was the party of expansion and progress. Lawyers and planters, its members were inclined to look upon government with a somewhat visionary eye, and their interest in the West was not due to any feeling of kinship with frontiersmen or to the fact that they were leaders in land speculation, but to a tinge of imperialism. It is true that Jefferson had inherited his father's share in the Loyal Company, and that Mason and Lee were active in the councils of the old Ohio Company and were still trying to salvage something from this investment, but their public policy does not appear to have been affected more than incidentally by this interest.

Patrick Henry stands in a class by himself. Ostensibly he was cooperating whole-heartedly with the liberal group, but he had private connections with their conservative rivals. Being governor of the State, he did not have to show his hand in the assembly and his stand on the land question is difficult if not impossible to fathom.[1]

The conservatives were still led by Benjamin Harrison, Carter Braxton, Archibald Cary, and Edmund Pendleton. Substantial planters of the Tidewater section, a few of them were lawyers, but a large number were merchants as well as planters. It is worthy of particular note that not one of the liberal group had large mercantile interests, whereas many of the conservatives did. They were "practical" men, in the accepted modern

---

[1] George Mason to George Mercer, Oct. 2, 1778, *Va. Historical Register*, II, 28–31; Ballagh, *Letters of Richard Henry Lee*, I, 106; Henry, *Henry*, III, 144–148.

American sense of that word. They took an interest in public affairs; but, in the old colonial as well as modern American fashion, they hoped to steer the ship of state into channels that would prove profitable to themselves. This situation had an important bearing upon the issues that confronted Virginia at this time in connection with the land question.[2]

Since the end of the colonial régime no land office had been opened and no lands had been granted in Virginia. Yet settlers were daily filtering in and establishing themselves upon soil to which it was impossible at the time to obtain title. The claims of the great land companies were so extensive and, in the case of the Virginia companies, so vague as to boundaries, that any settler was in danger of eviction whenever the companies might find it possible to push their pretensions. Realizing their position, the "squatters" began to agitate at an early date, and they brought enough pressure to bear upon the convention to secure the passage of a resolution on May 14, 1776, which promised preemption rights to actual settlers whenever the lands upon which they were established should be put on the market. The colonial period had known no such situation and no such legislation. In October, 1777, four hundred acres was fixed as the amount which such settlers could claim, and they were taxed upon this holding even though they did not yet have a legal title. This acreage satisfied the "squatters," for the lowly frontiersmen always considered it discreditable for one man to amass more land than he could actually settle and cultivate.[3]

By the beginning of 1778 the leaders of the liberal faction were prepared to establish a land office. There were several reasons for this. The currency was beginning to depreciate, and they wanted to obtain from the sale of lands funds with which to restore the credit of the State. They wished also to undermine the claims of non-Virginian speculators who were trying to get possession of lands which Virginia claimed for herself. And they desired to avoid further confusion by settling all outstanding claims to Western lands.

In view of these considerations Jefferson and Mason collaborated in the preparation of a land office bill. They apparently hoped to have it passed during January, 1778, but in this they were disappointed. The conservatives opposed their plan and were able to prevent its enactment. The Harrison-Pendleton faction had several reasons for this action. To

[2] Braxton to Capt. Conyngham, Dec. 16, 1779, Arthur Lee papers, Harvard U. library.
[3] Wm. Thompson vs. James Boydstone, Nov. 13, 1773, Summers, *Annals of Southwest Virginia*, pp. 166–167; *Proceedings of the Convention of Virginia*, June 24, 1776, p. 63; John Todd to Preston, May 17, June 22, 1776, Draper MSS., 4QQ41, 52; Wilson, *First Kentucky Land Court*, p. 27; Hening, *Statutes*, IX, 349, 355–356; Marshall, *Kentucky*, I, 45.

sell Western lands would draw off population from the East and depreciate the value of Eastern property. It would also draw off soldiers from the army, and Washington and other officers opposed the plan on that account. Furthermore, the conservatives supported the cause of the Indiana Company and did not wish to see its claim undermined, whereas that was one of the chief aims of the liberals.[4]

Although they did not succeed in their main objective, the proponents of a land office secured the passage of legislation looking toward the later accomplishment of their purpose. In order to prevent a constant increase in the number of outstanding land claims, it was resolved, on January 24, 1778, that no entry or survey made after that date and before the opening of a land office should be valid. It was further declared that persons thereafter settling on the Western waters should have the preemption of not over four hundred acres at the price to be fixed for the sale of public lands. At the same time the papers relating to the claims of the Henderson and Indiana companies were turned over to Jefferson and Mason for study. Bills to confiscate British property and British debts were also passed at the time, this, too, being a part of the liberal program.[5]

Yet the liberals were not able to get more than a moiety of their wishes put into effect. The May session of the 1778 assembly elected Harrison as speaker, and Henry retained the governorship. Thomas Adams, John Harvie, John Banister, F. L. Lee, Meriwether Smith, R. H. Lee, and Cyrus Griffin were elected to Congress in that order of preference. Adams, Harvie, and Banister all had mercantile ambitions, and they, like Henry, were either at the time involved in the transactions of Morris, Deane, de Francy, Holker, and their associates or were soon to become involved. The fact that they received much larger votes than did the two Lees is significant of the political trend at this period. The conservatives were giving the liberals a hard battle and were generally getting the best of it, at least temporarily.[6]

When the fall session of the 1778 assembly convened the land question at once became an issue of major importance. The land companies had

[4] Rowland, *Mason*, I, 291–292; Wm. Russell to Wm. Fleming, Oct. 7, 1778, Draper MSS., 2U47; Mason to Jefferson, April 3, 1779, Jefferson MSS., L. of C.; Jefferson to Fleming, June 8, 1779, *Official Letters of the Governors of Virginia*, II, 4n.
[5] *Journal of the House of Delegates*, Jan. 13, 23, 24, 1778, pp. 113, 132, 136; Randall, *Jefferson*, I, 215; Rowland, *Mason*, I, 289.
[6] Silas Deane to Thomas Adams, June 25, 1779, *Va. Mag. of Hist. and Biog.*, VI, 32; Richard to Thomas Adams, June 1, 1778, *ibid.*, V, 293–297; same to same, July 4, 1778, *ibid.*, V, 294–296; same to same, July 20, 1778, *ibid.*, XXII, 395; Silas Deane to Benjamin Harrison, Sept. 17, 1777, Stevens facsimiles, II, no. 194; Carter Braxton to Todd and Swan, April 23, 1762, Society collection, H.S.P.; David Stewart to Robert Morris, Jan. 20, 1778, Robert Morris MSS., L. of C.; Joseph Jones to George Washington, Jan. 22, 1778, *Letters of Joseph Jones*, pp. 5–7; *Journal of the House of Delegates*, May 29, 1778, p. 26.

been instructed to present their claims at this time, and they were not loath to comply. Thomas Walker presented a petition in behalf of the Loyal Company, and Archibald Cary, speaker of the Senate, made a report recommending that all actual surveys made by that company be carried into grants. These amounted to slightly more than two hundred thousand acres out of the eight hundred thousand to which they had originally had pretensions.[7]

Henderson's company was prepared to accept a compromise. The North Carolina judge now admitted the validity of the purchase made from the Six Nations at Fort Stanwix by which Virginia secured a claim upon the lands lying south of the Ohio River. Henderson's purchase from the Cherokee overlapped this territory, and he declared his willingness to accept a grant of only a part of his company's original claim, and that subject to Virginia's jurisdiction. Accordingly two hundred thousand acres on Green River in Kentucky were granted to him.[8] This tract was not surveyed until 1796, and it is probable that the Henderson interests still hoped, until that time, for the validation of purchases of lands from the Indians.

The Ohio Company submitted a petition and the Indiana Company was apparently quite certain of success.[9] A meeting was called and plans made to employ John Harvie, one of the Virginia delegates in Congress, to act as their attorney and to take out caveats against any trespassers on the lands which they claimed. No agent was sent to lay their claims before the House of Delegates, but Edmund Randolph ably represented their cause in that body. Pendleton and other prominent conservatives favored their claim, and it did look as though their chance of success was considerable.[10] Nor were the conservatives without good reason for their

[7] *Journal of the House of Delegates,* Oct. 27, 29, 1778, pp. 28, 35, Nov. 5, 11, 26, pp. 43, 53–54, 87–88; Thomas Walker to William Preston, Oct. 28, 1778, Draper MSS., 4QQ183; James Nourse to his wife, Nov. 5, 1778, *Va. Mag. Hist. and Biog.,* VIII, 199–202.

[8] Henry seems to have been on friendly terms with Henderson at this time. Henry to Fleming, May 5, 1778, Draper MSS., 4QQ167. *Journal of the House of Delegates,* Oct. 26, 28, 29, 1778, pp. 28, 31, 36, Nov. 4, 23, pp. 42, 79, Dec. 8, p. 105; Rowland, *Mason,* I, 305; Henderson to John Williams, (?) 1778, Misc. MSS., N.C.H.C.; deed of Col. William Dry to Charles Drayton, Feb. 24, 1778, Alves MSS., Henderson, Ky.; *C.V.S.P.,* I, 305–307, 309–311; Wm. Blount to Sec. of War, Nov. 8, 1792, *Territorial Papers of the United States, Territory South of the Ohio River,* IV, 211.

[9] *Journal of the House of Delegates,* Nov. 20, 1778, p. 74; Byars, *Gratz,* pp. 360–362; Rowland, *Mason,* I, 301; Memorial of the Ohio Company, Nov. 20, 1778, Va. Arch., petitions.

[10] Address to the Virginia assembly, by a "Native," presumably Edmund Randolph, June, 1776, *Am. Arch.,* series 4, VI, 754; Trent to B. Gratz, Sept. 24, 1778, Ridgway Library MSS., Philadelphia; Morgan to Trent, Sept. 27, 1778, Ohio Company MSS., H.S.P.; same to same, Dec. 1, 1778, *ibid.;* Trent to B. Gratz, Dec. 14, 1778, Gratz

stand. Many of them, it will be recalled, had legal or commercial relations with the Philadelphia merchants, notably Morris, the Whartons, and the Gratz brothers, who were, in one way or another, interested in the Indiana and Vandalia claims. Furthermore, Virginia had acquired her most defensible title to Kentucky at the treaty of Fort Stanwix, and the Indiana grant was a part of that treaty. It is true that the British administration had refused to ratify the grant to the "suffering traders" when it accepted the treaty, but through the agency of Dr. Thomas Walker, Virginia had made a tacit bargain which involved acquiescence in the Indiana claim in order to secure the large cession of Kentucky lands, and those who had participated in that bargain should have stood by it regardless of the attitude of the home government. It was the conservatives who had supported Walker all along, and it was logical that he and they should support Indiana now. The liberals had no such connections or obligations.[11]

Despite all this the assembly passed a resolution disallowing every unauthorized private purchase of lands from the Indians. This was not propitious for the cause of the Indiana proprietors, but it was not yet considered by any means hopeless.[12]

The anxiety of the soldiers over the prospect of having a land office opened and the public domain sold off while the men were in the field and unable to attend to their private interests has been mentioned. Their fears were duly brought to the attention of the assembly, and a resolution was passed providing for a grant of two hundred acres to each enlisted soldier, and a large district in Kentucky was set aside for their claims.[13]

One other major factor was involved in the Virginia land question at this time—the interest of the humble settler. All the land companies threatened his simple abode in the forest. He could do little against them

MSS., H.S.P.; Byars, *Gratz*, p. 172; *Journal of the House of Delegates*, Dec. 10, 1778, p. 108.

[11] Lord Stirling to Wm. Franklin, Dec. 5, 1772, Franklin MSS., XLVIII, 143, A.P.S.; deposition of Thomas Walker, *C.V.S.P.*, I, 197–198; Tench Tilghman to Robert Morris, Feb. 24, 1777, Letters to Robert Morris, *Collections of the New York Historical Society*, 1878, p. 421; Joseph Simon to Patrick Rice, July 20, 1778, Ridgway Library MSS., Philadelphia; draft of a memorial, apparently by Trent (1779?) Ohio Company MSS., H.S.P.; Thomas to Joseph Wharton, May 6, 1775, Wharton letter book, H.S.P.; Thomas Wharton to Edmund Pendleton, Oct. 10, 1778, *ibid.*; Volwiler, *Croghan*, p. 310; Byars, *Gratz*, pp. 18–19, 21, 177, 183–185.

[12] *Journal of the House of Delegates*, Nov. 4, 1778, p. 42.

[13] James Wood to Washington, Nov. 12, 1778, Sparks, *Letters to Washington*, II, 229–232; *Journal of the House of Delegates*, Dec. 19, 1778, p. 126; Wm. Russell to Wm. Fleming, July 25, 1779, Draper MSS., 2U65; Abraham to David Shepherd, Aug. 20, 1779, *ibid.*, 1SS167–169; Jefferson to Washington, Dec. 10, 1779, *Writings of Thomas Jefferson* (Mem. ed.), IV, 81.

without leadership, and leadership is rare among such people. Fortunately for them, there were a few of the more important men who were interested in their cause, and by this means their case was laid before the legislature. Petitions inveighing against the land companies and their extensive claims came in from all parts of the West, and copies or originals of most of them are to be found in the papers of Arthur Campbell thereby giving a clue to the identity of their foremost champion.[14]

The activities of this man are very strange. He was closely affiliated with the powerful Valley group which was led by Preston, Christian, Fleming, William Russell, Stephen Trigg, and others of the Scotch-Irish strain. Preston was agent under Walker for the Loyal Company and most of the group were supporters of that combination. Christian was, and Russell was to become, brother-in-law to Patrick Henry. Christian was brother-in-law also to Fleming, Trigg, and Caleb Wallace. Thus the interests of the Loyal Company and of Governor Henry were combined in this closely-related group of western Virginians. But Arthur Campbell, though he held lands under the Loyal Company and was still on good terms with several of this group, had already given evidence of hostility to that organization. He was to give much more evidence of it in future, and his method was to stir up the simple settlers against its claims. It has been alleged that his stand was due to personal pique, but it seems more probable that it was due to political ambition.[15]

With the advent of 1779 the stage was set for the climax of Virginia's drama of the public lands. The political situation changed in favor of the liberals, due doubtless to the scandals of the previous year which had connected the names of certain leading conservatives with unsavory commercial transactions and caused reverberations on the floor of Congress. As a result the liberals were able largely to put their program of land legislation into effect. Jefferson was chosen over Thomas Nelson and John Page to succeed Henry as governor. Henry was elected to Congress along with Edmund Randolph, Gabriel Jones, James Mercer, William Fitzhugh, Meriwether Smith, and Cyrus Griffin, but he declined the

[14] The memorial and remonstrance of Kentucky (1779?), Campbell-Preston MSS., II, 151, L. of C.; similar memorials from Washington and Montgomery Counties in *ibid.*; Walker to Preston, March 23, 1778, Draper MSS., 4QQ164; same to same, May 29, 1778, *ibid.*, 4QQ172; same to same, July 9, 1778, *ibid.*, 4QQ179; Va. Arch., petitions, May 23, Oct. 24, 1778; *Journal of the House of Delegates,* May 23, Oct. 27, 29, 1778, pp. 1, 28, 35.

[15] *C.V.S.P.*, I, 303–304, 315; Stephen Trigg to Preston, May 16, 1778, Draper MSS., 4QQ169; Walker to Preston, Oct. 23, 1778, *ibid.*, 4QQ183; same to same, Dec. 16, 1778, *ibid.*, 4QQ184; Andrew Lewis to Preston, Aug. 4, 1779, *ibid.*, 5QQ5; Walker to Preston, Aug. 14, 1779, *ibid.*, 5QQ6; Christian to Preston, Oct. 22, 1779, *ibid.*, 5QQ11; *Official Letters of the Governors of Virginia,* I, 306; Preston to Fleming, July 31, 1779, Fleming MSS., W. and L. U. library; William H. Whitsitt, *Life and Times of Judge Caleb Wallace* (Louisville, 1888) pp. 82, 87–88.

honor and retired to the fastness of his Leatherwood estate in Henry County.[16]

There was no apparent break in Western policy, however, for Jefferson was prepared to carry on the major enterprises undertaken by Henry. Plans had been made for Clark to errect a fort at the mouth of the Ohio, and this was actually accomplished during the fall of 1779 under Jefferson's direction, the post being christened Fort Jefferson. The main object was to control the trade of the Mississippi at that point, and commerce with New Orleans was expected to be stimulated by the move. Another of Henry's projects had been a campaign against the Chickamauga Indians who obstructed the navigation of the Tennessee River where it cuts through the Cumberland Mountains. Evan Shelby, who had lately removed to the Holston country, was to command the expedition, and here again Henry was thinking of trade with the Spanish at New Orleans. But the British held Natchez, and until that place could be taken the West would not be entirely open to American trade. For this reason Henry had appealed to Congress to organize an expedition against that post, but he received no reply.[17]

It was realized in Virginia that one State, singlehanded, could not control the entire West. Up to this time, Henry had had the cooperation of certain Pennsylvania interests, but this could no longer be expected if the Indiana claims were denied, and it was beginning to look as though the liberals would be able to defeat them. But the liberals, led by Richard Henry Lee, had their own program of cooperation. Realizing that the Articles of Confederation—by which Congress was given no jurisdiction over Virginia's Western claims except indirectly in the case of boundary disputes—were not likely to be adopted without some compromise on the question of lands, Lee had proposed to Henry on November 5, 1778, that Virginia surrender her claim to the territory north of the Ohio River. Accordingly, on December 17 of the same year the assembly proposed to Congress that Virginia would join with the other landed States in surrendering sufficient Western territory for bounties to the soldiers of the landless States, provided that these landless States would accede to the Articles of Confederation. But this was not enough to satisfy

[16] William Christian to "dear Brother" (William Fleming?) July 11, 1779, Campbell-Preston MSS., L. of C.; *Journal of the House of Delegates,* June 1, 18, 1779, pp. 29, 55.

[17] Governor Henry to Governor Caswell, Jan. 8, 1779, misc. MSS., N.C.H.C.; Henry to Fleming, Feb. 13, 1779, Draper MSS., 2U60; John Floyd to (Preston) Nov. 26, 1779, *ibid.,* 17CC186–187; Wm. to Anne Fleming, Dec. 15, 1779, Fleming MSS., W. and L. U. library; Henry to Washington, March 13, 1779, Sparks, *Letters to Washington,* II, 260–262; Clark to Jefferson, Sept. 23, 1779, Add. MSS., 21, 844, Br. Mus.; Jefferson to Gálvez, Nov. 8, 1779, *Va. Mag. Hist. and Biog.,* VI, 284–288; Henderson, *Walker,* p. 6.

Maryland and the other objectors, and nothing immediately came of it.[18]

Finally, on June 22, 1779, Mason succeeded in having his land office bill passed by the assembly. Connected with it was another bill, a twin measure, for settling all outstanding claims for unpatented lands before surveys on treasury warrants under the new legislation should commence. The terms of this act are decidedly complicated, but the main features are not difficult to understand. Before the closing of the colonial land offices, as well as since that time, preliminary steps had been taken toward the acquisition of numerous tracts of land, but for various reasons patents had not been granted in many cases. It was these unperfected and often conflicting claims that now had to be determined, and they were of numerous different types. In cases where actual surveys had been made by accredited county surveyors or their deputies before the passage of the act of January 24, 1778, the problem was simple. Such claims were validated, and thus the Loyal Company got its two hundred thousand acres, pending, however, formal adjudication before the court of appeals. Entries made on the Western waters before the proclamation of 1763 and involving not over four hundred acres were validated even though no official survey had been made. This was meritorious consideration for those intrepid settlers who had formed the vanguard of pioneers on the frontier. The officers and soldiers who claimed under Dinwiddie's proclamation of 1754 had already secured patents from Dunmore for most of their lands, but there were some left over, and these were validated even though the surveyor who ran the lines had authority only of the College of William and Mary and lacked an appointment under a county surveyor. The Ohio Company stood in the same situation regarding its surveyors, but it failed to get the same exception made in its case. The conservatives strongly opposed its pretensions and Mason was unable to carry the point. Thus when its case came before the court of appeals the fact that Preston, Thomas Lewis, and the other surveyors of the Western counties had long been under the influence of the Loyal Company and had refused to permit the accrediting of an Ohio Company surveyor resulted in the total loss of its claims. It is rather ironical that Mason thus failed to profit by his own bill.

All actual settlers before January 1, 1778, were granted four hundred

[18] On August 10, 1778, R. H. Lee wrote to Jefferson, "I heartily wish that the wisdom of our country (Virginia) may be early next session employed to regulate our finance, restore public credit, determine about our back lands, and if possible, get rid of our public commerce." Jefferson MSS., L. of C.; R. H. Lee to Henry, Nov. 15, 1778, Burnett, *Letters of Members of the Continental Congress,* III, 495; resolves of the Virginia House of Delegates, Dec. 17, 1778, Cont. Cong. MSS., 71, I; Thomas Nelson to Washington, Nov. 28, 1779, Sparks, *Letters to Washington,* II, 362; Henry, *Henry,* III, 166.

acres at a nominal price, and they were given the preemption of an additional thousand acres at the regular price of forty pounds the hundred acres. Settlers who moved in after that date but before the passage of the act were to have the preemption of four hundred acres at the regular price. No provision was made for future settlers, and therein lay one fatal weakness of the bill.

The western counties of Virginia were divided into four districts and a commission was to be appointed by the governor to hear and determine all claims set up under this act. Its decisions were to be final even in cases where settlers had had their tracts surveyed by the land companies and were to make their purchases from them.

After all such previous claims were settled the remaining lands were to be put on the market and sold at forty pounds the hundred acres, no limitation being placed on the amount that might be purchased by one man. It was estimated that this price was about equivalent in the depreciated currency of the time to the old colonial price of ten shillings the hundred, taking into account the fact that the former quit-rent of two shillings the hundred was abolished and titles were granted in fee simple. Lands still in possession of the Indians, the military reservation, the Transylvania tract, and all lands north of the Ohio River were reserved from sale. John Harvie, a friend and neighbor of Jefferson in Albemarle, was put in charge of the land office.[19]

Having had so little success during the previous year, the Pennsylvania speculators were more active during 1779. The Indiana claim was brought again before the assembly while the land office bill was under consideration. George Croghan and Bernard Gratz were on hand to push its case and Dr. Thomas Walker testified in its behalf, but to no avail. By a very narrow margin its petition was finally defeated. Faced with this reverse, it now prepared for the first time to lay its case before Congress, and on November 11 it presented a memorial to that body in which it took the new departure of denying the right of Virginia to the soil. The Vandalia Company, taking a new lease on life, also presented its first memorial to Congress at about the same time. Virginia at once protested against this action and a memorial on the subject, drawn by Munford, Mason, and Henry, was sent to Congress. From now on that

[19] Jefferson said that one of the principal objects of the act was to abolish the large unsurveyed claims on the Western waters. Jefferson's notes on the case between himself and John Harvie, U. of Va. photostats from Jefferson MSS., Massachusetts Historical Society; Jefferson to Gérard de Reyneval, March 20, 1801, *Writings of Thomas Jefferson* (Mem. ed.) X, 225–227; Henderson, *Walker,* pp. 39–40; Perrin, *Kentucky,* pp. 221–224; Wilson, *First Kentucky Land Court,* p. 10; C. H. Laub, "Revolutionary Virginia and the Crown Lands," *William and Mary Quarterly Historical Magazine,* XI, 307; Hening, *Statutes,* X, 35–50, 50–65.

body was to be the arena of the major conflict between Virginia and these two companies, along with the Illinois-Wabash combination.[20]

Yet the fight in Virginia was not altogether abandoned. When the assembly convened in the autumn, George Morgan was on hand to present another memorial in behalf of Indiana, and Bernard Gratz was present to press the claims of George Croghan to his old grant of two hundred thousand acres from the Six Nations. They made excuses for the Indiana appeal to Congress and urged the obligations under which they conceived that Virginia lay in the matter of their claims. But the only action which resulted was the adoption by the assembly of a protest, the work of George Mason, to Congress. By this instrument Virginia denied that Congress had any jurisdiction over the Western lands. It was maintained that all State boundaries rested upon colonial charters and that no authority had been given Congress to change them. In case the articles were ratified, however, that body might use its good offices to arbitrate in boundary disputes. Virginia was united in support of this theory, for to grant the Indiana or any other claim to certain lands was one thing, but to admit the jurisdiction of Congress in the matter was quite another. It is hard to see how any valid legal arguments could have been brought against the Virginia contention, but many feeble theories have been concocted for that purpose. For the time being Congress did not make so bold as to assert its jurisdiction.[21]

In the case of another question growing out of Croghan's claim the stand taken by Virginia legislators was of an altogether different complexion. Charles Simms, along with John Harvie and John Neville, was one of those Virginians who had cooperated with Croghan's partisans in the Pittsburgh area during the early days of the War. Simms, who was now serving as an officer in Washington's army, appealed to his commander for leave to go to Virginia to look after his landed interests. Washington denied this request; Simms thereupon appealed to Congress and secured a reversal of the General's decision. He then repaired to Williamsburg and laid his case before the assembly. Simms explained that he had purchased a tract of nearly three thousand acres which was originally a part of Croghan's claim. He alleged that he had not been able to improve his holding because of his service in the army, and on this score the

[20] Petition of George Croghan, June 5, 9, 1779, Va. Arch., petitions; *Journal of the House of Delegates*, June 8, 9, 18, 1779, pp. 39–40, 44, 56, Dec. 10, p. 84; George Mason to R. H. Lee, June 19, 1779, Lee MSS., U. of Va. library; *Official Letters of the Governors of Virginia*, II, 66; Rowland, *Mason*, I, 34; Hening, *Statutes*, X, 557–559; Wm. Croghan to B. Gratz, Aug. 22, 1779, Croghan-Gratz MSS., H.S.P.

[21] Petition of Bernard Gratz, Nov. 10, 1779, Va. Arch., petitions; Trent to Edmund Randolph, Nov. 9, 1779, Ohio Company MSS., H.S.P.; Byars, *Gratz*, p. 188.

assembly made him the grant. Thus a patent was issued upon a claim which had already been invalidated by that body![22]

The stand of Patrick Henry on the question of the Indiana claim is a mystery. The liberals certainly thought that he was cooperating with them, and his approval of the land office bill is beyond question. But on November 10, 1778, Duncan Rose, a Virginia commissary official, wrote to Michael Gratz that the former governor would be a great aid to the cause of Croghan and Indiana if he were in Williamsburg, and Rose was in position to know. It will be remembered that in 1775 Henry had given a written legal opinion in support of the Indiana claim, and there is no record of his having changed his mind. The weight of evidence would seem to indicate that he had not changed it.[23]

The question of the Western lands could not be fully disposed of until the North Carolina boundary should be extended and the boundary dispute with Pennsylvania settled. This latter controversy had wearily dragged on through the years, but now in 1779 definite steps were taken to settle it. Virginia appointed commissioners to meet a similar delegation from Pennsylvania and reach an agreement on the question. They assembled in Baltimore on August 27, 1779, and agreed on the line which now separates the two States. Pennsylvania at once ratified the agreement, but Virginia delayed long enough to permit her commissioners under the land office act to adjudicate many titles in the disputed area. Pennsylvania looked upon this as an act of bad faith and protested, but on June 23, 1780, Virginia ratified the findings of the boundary commission on condition that Pennsylvania validate titles growing out of Virginia grants in the disputed area. On September 23 Pennsylvania acceded to this demand and the line was finally run in 1784–1785. Pennsylvania did not, however, entirely live up to her agreement in the matter of Virginia titles.[24]

During 1779 arrangements were also made for extending the North Carolina-Virginia boundary. Dr. Thomas Walker and his lieutenant Major Daniel Smith were appointed for that purpose on the part of Vir-

[22] Memorial of Charles Simms, Oct. 16, 1779, Va. Arch., petitions; *ibid.*, Nov. 19, 1778; *Journal of the House of Delegates,* Nov. 19, 1778, p. 72, Oct. 16, 1779, p. 11; Bacon-Foster, *Potomac Route to the West,* pp. 245–250; Hening, *Statutes,* X, 139–140; Byars, *Gratz,* pp. 184–185.

[23] Wm. to R. H. Lee, Oct. 30, 1779, Lee MSS., U. of Va. library; Duncan Rose to M. Gratz, Nov. 10, 1779, Byars, *Gratz,* pp. 188–189.

[24] *Journal of the House of Delegates,* Dec. 9, 12, 1778, pp. 106, 112, Nov. 8, 1779, p. 46; Virginia's proposals in the Pennsylvania boundary dispute, Cont. Cong. MSS., I, 71, L. of C.; Boyd Crumrine, "The Boundary Controversy between Pennsylvania and Virginia, 1748–1785," *Annals of the Carnegie Museum,* I, 505–524; Crumrine, *Washington County,* p. 190; Bacon-Foster, *Potomac Route to the West,* p. 251.

ginia, and Judge Richard Henderson, John Williams, and William Bailey Smith were to act for North Carolina. Henderson as well as Walker had a personal interest in the business, for he was busy preparing for the establishment of a setttlement at the French Lick on Cumberland River, where Nashville now stands.[25]

The commissioners had not proceeded far when they disagreed on the course of the line. The result was that Walker surveyed one line and Henderson another, thus originating a boundary dispute between the two States which was to vex them for many years. However, it was established that the French Lick lay in North Carolina and not in Virginia, as had been formerly supposed, and Henderson proceeded with his plans. Colonel William Byrd III and George Rogers Clark had purchased tracts of land at the French Lick, but both claims were now lost in favor of North Carolina.[26]

It remains to remark that the land office act of 1779 was a colossal mistake. In 1776 Jefferson had advocated the granting of tracts of fifty acres to each family lacking that amount. This would have been an improvement on the colonial head-right system, and it would have been a great aid to the growth of democracy in America. Any democracy, in order to be real, must have a sound economic basis, and diffusion of small land-holdings among the people is one of the most satisfactory means that has ever been devised to that end. There is an element of historical irony in the fact that Jefferson, the father of democracy, should have helped to draft the act by which democracy was defeated in Virginia at the moment when it might have had its birth. The result was that within a few years Robert Morris came to own one and a half million acres, and Alexander Walcott a million acres of Virginia's Western lands, and most of that remaining fell into the hands of other absentee speculators who paid, in depreciated currency, a price equivalent in some cases to about fifty cents the hundred acres. Thus the growth of the country was retarded, the resident population forced to protect the property of those who took no part in its defense, and the great public domain was exploited by a few individuals for their private gain.[27]

The settlers were quick to see the point and petitions remonstrating against this feature of the land act poured in upon the assembly during the fall of 1779. But the damage had been done and there was no chance

[25] Abernethy, *From Frontier to Plantation in Tennessee*, pp. 14–15, 29–30.
[26] Henry to Clark, Dec. 12, 1776, *Official Letters of the Governors of Virginia*, I, 340; James, *Clark Papers, 1771–1781*, p. 304.
[27] Nell M. Nugent, ed., *Cavaliers and Pioneers, Abstracts of Virginia Land Patents and Grants, 1623–1800* (Richmond, 1934) I, p. x.

to repair it. During the following years Virginia was to pay a heavy price for her folly.[28]

[28] Robertson, *Petitions of the Early Inhabitants of Kentucky*, pp. 45–47; James, *Clark*, pp. 182–183; *Journal of the House of Delegates*, Oct. 14, 1779, p. 8; Floyd to (Preston) Dec. 19, 1779, Draper MSS., 17CC121–124; petition of the inhabitants of Albemarle County, Oct. 14, 1779, Va. Arch., petitions; petition of Loudoun County, Oct. 18, 1779, *ibid.;* memorial of the inhabitants of Botetourt County, Nov. 22, 1779, *ibid.*

CHAPTER XVIII

CONGRESS AND THE WEST, 1779

ASERIES of events which occurred at the end of 1778, including Deane's publication of December 5 and Paine's altercation with Deane and Gérard and his final resignation from the secretaryship of the Committee for Foreign Affairs, made it clear that there would be much unsavory business in Congress during 1779. Our present interest in the events of that year centers around the questions of the Western boundary and the navigation of the Mississippi, but these matters were so inextricably involved in the factional strife then in progress that it is necessary to turn our attention first to that subject.

While Deane was waiting upon Congress for the settlement of his accounts Arthur Lee laid before that body his interpretation of the activities of the American commissioners in Paris both while Deane was there and after his departure. Franklin was still domiciled with Chaumont at Passy, and Dr. Bancroft and Samuel Wharton were in attendance upon him. Captain Thomas Hutchins of the British Army, the erstwhile surveyor for Vandalia, was in London carrying on his correspondence with Wharton and engaging, with Thomas Walpole, in speculation in British stocks on the basis of inside information received from Wharton.[1]

Franklin took no direct part in these transactions, but he had been warned that Bancroft was engaged in such speculations and he knew that information used for that purpose was very likely, if not certain, to be accessible to the British government also. Furthermore, it is extremely unlikely that Wharton and Hutchins could have carried on a correspondence through the necessary secret channels without Franklin knowing of it. These channels were open to Wharton only because Franklin controlled them. And if Franklin was not acquainted with the character of Bancroft, his long association with Wharton had made him thoroughly familiar with the dishonest methods of that merchant-speculator. Of the

---

[1] During this year Walpole sold his Vandalia stock to Bancroft. Ingraham, *Papers Relating to the Case of Silas Deane,* narrative of Arthur Lee, Feb. 10, 1779, pp. 151–182; Hutchins to Wharton, Feb. 27, Mar. 9, 1779, P.R.O., C.O., series 5, 38ff. 107–109; C.O., series 5, 7 entire; Wharton to John Almon, March 20, 1779, Add. MSS., 20, 733, Br. Mus.; Bigelow, *Franklin,* VIII, 46–57; Lovell to R. H. Lee, June 5, 1779, Lee MSS., U. of Va. library; V. I. Bertrand to Franklin, Sept. 14, 1779, Franklin MSS., XV, 167, A.P.S.

greedy profiteering that had been carried on by his nephew Jonathan Williams, Deane, Chaumont, and others there is documentary proof that he knew a great deal. Yet, on August 8, 1779, Franklin approved the accounts of John Ross because they had been inspected by Wharton and Bancroft, "men of integrity." On October 17 he wrote to Lovell that he still believed in Deane and had never intermeddled in the quarrels between him and Arthur Lee. If being a consistent partisan of Deane was not intermeddling, then his statement was correct.[2] But it cannot be forgotten that Franklin had taken part in Deane's scheme to throw upon Arthur Lee the blame for Bancroft's disclosures of secret information in London and to discredit the Virginian at the French Court by means of this and other imputations. On the other hand, John Adams wrote to Vergennes in defense of Lee. Of course the final object had been the removal of Lee from the scene of operations in France. This task was undertaken by the friends of Deane, Morris, and Gérard in Congress during the spring of 1779. The first move was the presentation of a statement by William Paca of Maryland—brother-in-law to Robert Morris— and Drayton of South Carolina, based upon information obtained from the French minister, that the French government was withholding communications from the American commissioners because Lee was not trusted. On May 3 a vote to recall him was taken, but the friends of the Lee-Adams group were able to prevent it by a tie vote of the States, though the majority of individual votes was cast against Lee. The desired object was, however, finally accomplished on June 10.[3]

Throughout the year Deane was actively engaged in commercial operations with Morris, Chaumont, Gérard, and John Holker. One of their operations had raised a storm of protest in Philadelphia where Morris's friends of the anti-constitutional or conservative party had lost control of the political situation, which was now in the hands of the constitutional

[2] Ingraham, *Papers of Silas Deane*, pp. 89–90; A. Lee to Franklin and Adams, Feb. 7, 1779, Franklin MSS., XIII, 86, A.P.S.; Franklin's certificate, Aug. 8, 1779, *ibid.*, LIV, 55; report of Committee on Foreign Affairs, March 24, 1779, Cont. Cong. MSS., 25 I, 83ff.; Ford, *Letters of William Lee*, II, 534n.; Franklin to Chaumont, May 19, 1779, Franklin MSS., Wm. S. Mason collection; Sumner, *Morris,* I, 219; Bigelow, *Franklin,* VIII, 147; report to James Milligan, Auditor-General, Jan. 5, 1781, A. Lee MSS., Harvard U. library.

[3] Richard Champion to A. Lee, July 25, 1779, Lee MSS., Harvard U. library; M. Livingston to John Paul Jones, March 13, 1779, *ibid.;* report of Paca and Drayton, April 30, 1779, *ibid.;* Ballagh, *Lee,* II, 58–59, 98–100, 108, 125–130; *Pennsylvania Packet,* Aug. 31, 1779; Wallace, *Henry Laurens,* pp. 307–310; Ford, *Letters of William Lee*, III, 19, 717; Archibald Cary to Jefferson, Aug. (?) 26, 1779, Jefferson MSS., L. of C.; Isham, *Deane Papers,* IV, 63–67, 73; George C. Wood, *Congressional Control of Foreign Relations during the American Revolution, 1774–1789* (Allentown, Pa., 1919) pp. 82–83; Wharton, *Diplomatic Correspondence,* III, 42–44; J. Almon, *The Remembrancer,* 1779, pp. 375ff.; *Journals of the Continental Congress,* XIII, 542, XIV, 714.

or radical party. The depreciation of the currency had caused much alarm because of the rapid rise in prices, and committees had been established throughout Pennsylvania to fix the maximum rates which could be charged for commodities. The Philadelphia committee had discovered that a boat-load of flour, which was supposed to belong to Silas Deane, had been sold to Morris, and that Morris had sold it to Holker for use of the French fleet. Congress had not been given a chance to purchase it, and there were suspicions that some of it was to be used for private trading and exported contrary to the provisions of the embargo. Gouverneur Morris, for the Congressional Committee of Commerce, stated these suspicions to Gérard, who denied them. The French minister also refused to appear before the Philadelphia committee to answer questions and appealed to Congress for protection. This was granted him, and the matter was hushed up. While the suspicions of the Philadelphia committee may have been without foundation in this case, the whole group involved in this deal made a habit of using public station for private ends, and there can be no wonder that they were looked upon with some degree of misgiving by disinterested persons who were acquainted with their transactions.[4]

Another ugly affair came to the attention of Congress in connection with the capture of a Portuguese ship by the American privateer *Phoenix*. The *Phoenix* was commanded by Captain Augustus Conyngham and owned jointly by Robert Morris, Carter Braxton, Dr. Thomas Walker, and Michael Gratz. This disregard of the neutral flag, however pleasing to France or Spain, could not be tolerated by Congress, and resolutions condemning Conyngham and Braxton were adopted by that body. It gave the Lees much pleasure to see their enemy thus humbled.[5]

Some knowledge of such dissensions will be of assistance in analyzing the votes which were cast in Congress during this year on questions of

[4] Richard Bache to Franklin, Oct. 22, 1778, Franklin MSS., XII, 68, A.P.S.; Abner Livingston to R. Morris, Jan. 23, 1777, Morris MSS., L. of C.; defense by Morris, Jan. 7, 1779, *ibid.*, published in *Pennsylvania Packet*, Jan. 9, 1779; Craig, *The Olden Time*, II, 322; Conway, *Paine*, I, 418; Mifflin to Morris, Jan. 26, 1779, *Collections of N. Y. Historical Society*, 1878, pp. 441–442; J. Dinant to Deane, Feb. 7, 1779, P.R.O., S.P., Dom. Geo. III, bundle 13, ff. 38–39; Wharton, *Diplomatic Correspondence*, III, 261–262; Gérard's memorial, July 26, 1779, Jefferson MSS., L. of C.; Meriwether Smith to Jefferson, June 25, 1779, *ibid.*; —(?) to Holker, Oct. 20, 1779, Holker MSS., Wm. S. Mason collection; Roche to Holker, June 2, 1779, *ibid.*; G. Morris to Holker, June 25, 1779, *ibid.*; Holker to Morris, June 28, 1779, *ibid.*; Paine to John Jay, April 23, 1779, Cont. Cong. MSS., 55, I, 363; Reed, *Reed*, II, 144; Ford, *Letters of William Lee*, II, 628–630; Burnett, IV, 227–229; Sumner, *Morris*, I, 229–230; *Pennsylvania Packet*, July 3, 20, 24, 1779.

[5] Randolph to Jefferson, Nov. 13, 1779, Cont. Cong. papers, 71 I.; R. Morris to James Searle, n.d., *Am. Arch.* series 5, III, 1373; Carter Braxton to M. Gratz, March 13, 1781, Etting collection, Signers, H.S.P.; Byars, *Gratz*, pp. 22, 204–205; *Pennsylvania Packet*, Oct. 28, 1779.

peace terms and Western boundaries, but it is necessary now to consider the military situation existing in the Western country at this time.

On February 24, George Rogers Clark took Vincennes and was soon busy making plans to lead an expedition against Detroit. But the credit of paper currency had finally been undermined in the West, and Oliver Pollock, de Leyba, and Clark's other financial backers could not stand up under the burden thus imposed upon them. De Leyba and Pollock were ruined because of the advances which they had made to the Virginia leader, and the problem of getting supplies in the Illinois became acute. Nevertheless, by June 28 Clark was preparing to march against Detroit. He was prevented from doing so not primarily because of lack of provisions but by the failure of recruits to arrive from Kentucky in sufficient numbers. Within a few weeks he found it necessary to forego the campaign and concentrate his attention on the establishment of the long-planned fort at the mouth of the Ohio. Meanwhile he maintained a post at the Falls of that river, but the Illinois country was practically evacuated by Virginia troops.[6]

In the Pittsburgh area a peculiar situation existed. McIntosh's abortive campaign of the previous year had failed, according to his own account, largely because of George Morgan's failure to furnish adequate supplies. Morgan had originally advocated the campaign, but after its failure he used all his influence to discredit the actions of the commander. McIntosh demanded an investigation, but Washington found it inconvenient to make one at the time.[7] Morgan also took much pains to discredit the treaty which had been made with the Delawares at Pittsburgh in the fall of 1778, sending agents into the Indian country to stir them up against it. Then he brought to his home a delegation of the Delawares—most of whom were now at war on the British side—and helped the Indians prepare an address to Congress. In this business he was assisted by Lewis Morris of New York, and by John Dodge and Daniel Sullivan, frontier adventurers of doubtful reputation. The document which they drafted laid claim to country as far west as the Wabash River—more than this na-

[6] Alvord, *The Illinois Country*, pp. 343–346; Bodley, *Clark*, pp. 136–138, 143; Clark to Henry, April 29, 1779, Cont. Cong. MSS., 71, I; John Rogers to Jonathan Clark, May 6, 1779, Draper MSS., 1L54; de Leyba to Gálvez, June 9, Oct. 18, 1779, *American Historical Review*, XLI, 109–110, 111–112; Wm. Crawford to Morgan, June 28, 1779, Morgan MSS., Ill. Hist. Survey, Urbana; Draper MSS., 46J49–51; James, *Clark*, pp. 170–171; Clark to Jefferson, Sept. 23, 1779, Add. MSS., 21, 844, Br. Mus.

[7] Washington to Brodhead, Feb. 15, 1779, Draper MSS., 1H24; Kellogg, *Frontier Advance*, pp. 252–253, 327–328; McIntosh to Washington, April 27, 1779, Sparks, *Letters to Washington*, II, 284–289; same to same, May 3, 1779, Washington MSS., CVII, 105, L. of C.; Alexander Hamilton to McIntosh,, May 14, 1779, Cont. Cong. papers, 152 VII, f349; same to Hamilton, May 14, 1779, *ibid.*, 152 VII, f365, charges against Morgan, May 16, 1779, *ibid.*, 152 VII, f353; Washington to Jay, May 16, 1779, *ibid.*, 152 VII, f345.

tion had previously claimed—and proposed to cede to Congress enough to enable it to make grants to the Continental troops. In addition, the Indians made Morgan a private offer of a choice tract of about eighteen square miles just across the Ohio from Pittsburgh. Morgan delivered himself of a pious speech and declined the offer, but the Indians were benevolently persistent and granted the land to Morgan's children. Congress did not see fit to do business with the Delaware delegation, and shortly afterward Morgan resigned his Indian agency. In this whole scheme there would seem to be an explanation of the policy of Indian neutrality which Morgan had pursued since the beginning of the War. The best way to get lands and to carry on trade on the frontier was to stay on good terms with the natives, not permitting the vicissitudes of war to interfere too much with the efforts to accumulate private fortunes.[8]

Colonel Daniel Brodhead succeeded McIntosh at Pittsburgh and in September, 1779, he was busy planning a move against Detroit. Morgan was on friendly terms with the new commander, who could not however, understand why Morgan now thought that five hundred men would be sufficient to take the British post whereas two years previously he had thought that eighteen hundred would be required, and the fortifications at Detroit had been strengthened in the meantime. But Brodhead found the organizing of an expedition about as hard as Clark had found it, and by the middle of October he had abandoned the enterprise.[9]

The question arises as to why Morgan was apparently so anxious to take Detroit at this time, whereas he had usually shown considerable dislike of expeditions into the Indian country. On November 3, 1778, at about the time when Clark's capture of Kaskaskia was known in Philadelphia, the Illinois and Wabash Companies held a joint meeting and planned to unite their interests and establish towns in the Illinois country. On March 26, 1779, they perfected their organization, and Silas Deane, Chaumont, Robert Morris, Gérard, the French minister, John Holker, and Grand, the Paris banker, were taken into the company.

[8] Savelle, *Morgan,* pp. 156–166; Kellogg, *Frontier Advance,* pp. 38–40, 193–194, 204, 217, 277, 313, 317–321, 345; Walter H. Mohr, *Federal Indian Relations,* pp. 77–79; Nathaniel Scudder to Morgan, Jan. 8, 1779, Morgan MSS., Ill. Hist. Survey, Urbana, Ill.; John Killbuck to John Montour, Jan. 18, 1779, Add. MSS., 21, 782, Br. Mus.; Heckwelder to John Gibson, Feb. 8, 1779, Washington MSS., L. of C.; Cont. Cong. MSS., 152 VII, 357; address of the Delawares to Morgan, May 12, 1779, Geo. Morgan MSS., Historical Society of Western Pennsylvania, Pittsburgh; Burnett, IV, 216; *Journals of the Continental Congress,* XV, 1154–1155.
[9] Brodhead to Washington, Nov. 10, 1779, Sparks, *Letters to Washington,* II, 349–352; Brodhead to Morgan, May 22, 1779, *Pa. Arch.,* series 1, XII, 116; same to same, Sept. 24, 1779, *ibid.,* pp. 159–160; Brodhead to David Shepherd, July 17, 1779, Draper MSS., 1SS165; Kellogg, *Frontier Retreat,* p. 16.

George Ross of Philadelphia became president of the combined companies, and Bernard Gratz was made secretary. William Murray, the original organizer of both companies, and John Campbell became agents for carrying on the active work of colonization. One cannot but be impressed with the political strength which this new organization brought to the company.[10]

Morgan was concerned with the Vandalia and Indiana Companies rather than with the Illinois and Wabash, but John Campbell, Robert Morris, the Gratz brothers and many others had a stake in both groups, and the paths which they trod in these days were never far apart. It is clear at any rate that the Philadelphia land speculating gentry had, through the Illinois and Wabash organization, an interest in the Illinois country and a considerable influence in Congress. When questions of Western boundaries and the navigation of the Mississippi River came up for discussion in that body, this situation had an important bearing.

From March until August, 1779, Congress was engaged in a debate over the terms of peace on which France should support America when the time came to make a settlement with Great Britain. Of major importance were the questions of the navigation of the Mississippi and the Western boundary of the States. The terms of the French alliance were not explicit on either point, and both Gérard and Vergennes were working with Spain to limit American ambitions in both directions. Gérard wrote to Vergennes advising that he encourage Spain to get possession of whatever posts she could in the Mississippi Valley. He informed Congress in no uncertain terms that its persistence in attempting to establish its power at Natchez, on the Ohio, and in the Illinois, would display an unfair spirit of conquest, that such acquisition was wholly foreign to the principles of the French-American alliance, and that his King would not prolong the War one day to help the Americans secure the possessions they coveted.[11]

Gérard had formed close connections with the leaders of the Morris faction in Congress, and, having won a signal triumph over Tom Paine, they were in strong position. The first vote on the question of the navigation of the Mississippi was taken on March 24, and Pennsylvania was the only State which cast a majority in favor of making an unqualified demand for that privilege. She was supported by both the Virginia Lees, but Laurens voted with all the other Southern members against it. This

[10] Alvord, *The Illinois Country*, p. 381; Byars, *Gratz*, p. 137; Alvord, *Cahokia Records*, p. lxx; Alvord, *Illinois-Ouabache Manuscripts*, pp. 18ff.

[11] Henri Doniol, *Histoire de la Participation de la France à l'Établissement des États-Unis d'Amérique* (Paris, 1890) IV, 72–75; Sullivan, *Maryland and France*, pp. 84–90.

can be explained only by the fact that a Spanish alliance was much desired at this time, and the South was willing to forego its interest for that object.[12]

The Lee-Adams faction was at this time the expansionist element in Congress and it generally stood firm in demanding the Mississippi boundary, navigation of the river to the sea, and unlimited fishing rights on the Newfoundland Banks. This amounted to a pooling of interests, and the fact that Massachusetts and Connecticut had land claims which overlapped those of Virginia seems to have served as a bond of union rather than as a cause of dissension at this time. It is possible that Richard Henry Lee's plan for the cession of the Northwest to Congress was the basis upon which this agreement rested.[13]

By August the hope of a Spanish alliance seems to have faded, and when another vote was taken the fifth of that month on the question of demanding the navigation of the Mississippi, the partisan situation in Congress was revealed. Massachusetts, New Jersey, Pennsylvania, Delaware, Virginia, North and South Carolina voted in favor of the proposition. Only New Hampshire, New York, and Maryland cast a majority vote against it.[14]

This alignment is significant for it shows a situation rather different from that which is usually pictured. The Adams faction was generally able to control the vote of Massachusetts and to rally a degree of strength in the other New England States, but it was rarely able to carry that whole section along with it. Morris and his friends had not only lost control of Pennsylvania, but of New Jersey and Delaware also. The radical party of Pennsylvania was especially strong in the western part of the State, and the merchants of Pittsburgh were keenly interested in the New Orleans trade. This explains the attitude of Pennsylvania on the navigation of the Mississippi. Maryland and New York were the mainstays of the Morris faction at the time, and, though it did not come out in this vote, they could now usually count on carrying Virginia and the Carolinas with them.

During 1779 Virginia was, at different times, represented in Congress by Richard Henry and Francis Lightfoot Lee, Edmund Randolph, Meriwether Smith, William Fleming, Cyrus Griffin, William Fitzhugh, and Thomas Nelson. None of these men serving along with the two Lees was friendly to the Lee connection, and they were almost uniformly able to carry the vote of the State against them. Of the North Carolina repre-

[12] Phillips, *The West in the Diplomacy of the American Revolution*, pp. 116–121, 123; *Journals of the Continental Congress*, XIII, 339–341, 369–370.
[13] John Page to A. Lee, Aug. 16, 1778, Lee, *Lee*, II, 327; Sumner, *Morris*, I, 218n.
[14] *Journals of the Continental Congress*, XIV, 926.

sentatives, Joseph Hewes was a business associate of Robert Morris, and the rest of the delegation voted almost invariably with him against the Adams-Lee interest. In South Carolina Henry Laurens was a staunch supporter of the Lees, but Drayton, a land speculator, was a partisan of the Morris group, and they usually tied the vote of their State. Langworthy of Georgia rarely voted, but when he did, he normally voted against the Lees. Thus the South was almost a unit against the party which best represented her interests. This alignment held good when personal questions involving the dispute between Deane and the Lees arose, but, of course, it broke down when the question of peace terms came up. Lovell and Holton of Massachusetts ordinarily carried their State for the expansionist program in the West, but the rest of New England did not follow them. The Lees and Laurens voted with New England on questions involving her interest, but they were alone in the South in such action. Thus majorities varied in accord with the nature of the question under consideration.

Having voted on July 12 to demand the fisheries and on August 5 to claim the right to navigate the Mississippi to the sea, on August 14 Congress reversed itself and adopted instructions to its peace commissioners which did not, in an unqualified manner, make either demand. But the Mississippi River boundary, at least from the forty-fifth to the thirty-first degree, was demanded. This retreat was obviously due to pressure brought to bear on Congress by Gérard. He and his friends professed to believe that the Adams-Lee group, which he styled the "anti-Gallican party," was prepared to break with France and treat directly with England for the navigation of the Mississippi. By August 12 it was known in Philadelphia that Gérard had been recalled by Vergennes, and it is presumable that he was able to make this fact appear as a mark of French disapproval of the stand taken by Congress on the peace terms. The fact that the reversal of policy came immediately after the announcement of his recall gives weight to this view, but whatever means were used, the language employed by Congress in its resolves makes it clear that French pressure was the cause of their action.[15]

It might seem strange that the question of the Western boundary caused so much less discussion than did that of the navigation of the

[15] S. F. Bemis, *The Diplomacy of the American Revolution* (New York, 1935) p. 101; Phillips, *The West in the Diplomacy of the American Revolution,* pp. 122–123, 134; J. B. Sanders, *Evolution of Executive Departments of the Continental Congress, 1774–1789* (Chapel Hill, 1935) p. 45; Nathanael Greene to Washington, April 26, 1779, Sparks, *Letters to Washington,* II, 279–281; William Fleming (?) to Jefferson, June 22, 1779, Jefferson MSS., L. of C.; R. H. Lee to Jefferson, Aug. 12, 1779, *ibid.; Journals of the Continental Congress,* XIII, 827–835, XIV, 920–922, 924, 956; Doniol, *op. cit.,* IV, 224.

Mississippi. This may be explained by the fact that the Morris group, and even the French agents, were share-holders in the Illinois-Wabash Land Company and desired the Mississippi River boundary on the Northwest for that reason. They would scarcely have had the hardihood to demand it in that quarter and depart from it to the southward, but to secure the boundary and give up the navigation would have strangled the Southwest while forcing the Northwest to trade toward the East. This was in accord with the previously-expressed ideas of Robert Morris, and it doubtless explains the action of his friends in Congress. Though Gérard talked a great deal about the plan to limit the Western boundary of the States, no such policy was actually pushed in Congress.[16]

When, on September 11, the Indiana and Vandalia land companies, after having consulted Benjamin Franklin, appealed to Congress through George Morgan and William Trent to substantiate their claims and deny the jurisdiction of Virginia, another issue of major importance came to the fore. William Grayson of Virginia had recently bought nine hundred shares in the Indiana claim, and these companies, combined with the Illinois-Wabash interest, now had a powerful contingent in Congress. The land-claiming States had much to fear.[17]

The Indiana and Vandalia petitions were referred to a committee, and when its report was made Congress passed resolutions requesting Virginia to revoke her land office act. On this question Griffin and Fitzhugh alone of the Virginia delegation voted, carrying the State against the proposal. Sharpe and Harnett of North Carolina carried their State on the same side of the question. The only other votes cast in opposition were those of Henry of Maryland and Gouverneur Morris. It is notable that while Morris and Jay of New York were staunch partisans of the Robert Morris faction on all questions relating to the Deane quarrel, neither of them manifested any concern over the interests of the land companies. New York, in fact, usually voted as a land-claiming State, but she was opposed to demanding free navigation of the Mississippi.[18]

During the whole of this year Maryland continued to agitate against

[16] Paul C. Phillips, "American Opinion Regarding the West, 1778–1783," the *M.V.H.A., Proceedings,* VII, 286–305; Phillips, *The West in the Diplomacy of the American Revolution,* pp. 124–127; Gérard to Vergennes, March 8, 10, 12, 18, 1779, *Affaires Étrangères, États-Unis,* VII, 135, 139, 143, 159; *Pennsylvania Packet,* July 20, 1779.

[17] Hope and Company to Franklin, Jan. 4, 1779, Franklin MSS., XIII, 9, A.P.S.; S. Wharton to Franklin, May 15, 1779, *ibid.,* XIV, 114; same to same, July 1, 1779, *ibid.,* CI, 114; indenture of May 1, 1779, Ohio Company MSS., H.S.P.; memorial of William Trent for Vandalia Company, Sept. 11, 1779, *ibid.;* petition of George Morgan for Indiana Company, same date, Cont. Cong. papers, 77, f. 234; Byars, *Gratz,* pp. 182–183; *Journals of the Continental Congress,* XV, 1063.

[18] *Ibid.,* Oct. 29, 30, 1779, XV, 1223–1224, 1229–1230; Burnett, IV, 513.

the adoption of the Articles of Confederation in their existing form and to demand that the Western lands should be surrendered to Congress for the common benefit. But, according to her proposal, this surrender for the common benefit was to be qualified by a statement that all grants and surveys made to or for individuals before the beginning of the War were to be made good. This would have taken care of the Illinois-Wabash claims, as well as of many others including the enormous grants made to George Croghan and his associates. There would indeed have been very little land left to be used for the common benefit. The fact that Governor Thomas Johnson, ex-governor William Paca, Samuel Chase, and Charles Carroll, with a number of other important Marylanders, were members of the Illinois-Wabash Company gives point to the stand taken by this State.[19]

Throughout most of the year the question of the settlement of Deane's accounts was pending before Congress. But, since he could make no accounting, he was not able to get the arbitrary settlement which he had expected. Finally, on August 6, Congress "discharged" him, the word "discharged" having been substituted in the resolution for the word "excused." Though Deane was anxious to be on his way, his friends apparently did not like the form of the action, and though all New England favored it, New York, Delaware, Maryland, Virginia (Smith, Fleming, and Randolph—the Lees not voting), North Carolina, and Drayton of South Carolina (Laurens not voting) opposed the resolution. This is a fair indication of the strength of Deane's friends in Congress.[20]

The erstwhile commissioner now made his way to Williamsburg where his brother Simeon was engaged with several important Virginia merchants in the tobacco business. He, Robert Morris, and James Wilson were in communication about trade and the affairs of the Illinois-Wabash Land Company, and it appears that they were planning still other adventures in land. Presently Deane sailed for France to renew, in an unofficial capacity, the contacts with Chaumont, Grand, and other French capitalists and merchants which had proved so profitable since the beginning of the War. We shall next hear of him in the pay of the British government.[21]

[19] Byars, *Gratz*, pp. 363–367, Rowland, *Mason*, I, 321; Burnett, IV, 507–518.
[20] Deane to Thomas Adams, June 25, 1779, *Va. Mag. of Hist. and Biog.*, VI, 32; Isham, *Deane Papers*, IV, 87–90; *Journals of the Continental Congress*, XIV, 930.
[21] Wallace, *Life of Henry Laurens*, p. 334; Sumner, *Morris*, I, 226–227, 271–272; Ford, *Letters of William Lee*, II, 594–602; Nathaniel Scudder to R. H. Lee, Nov. 16, 1779, Lee MSS., V, 169, Va. Historical Society; Deane to James Wilson, Nov. 29, 1779, James Wilson MSS., III, 7, H.S.P.; James Wilson to Holker, Dec. 15, 1779, Holker MSS., Wm. S. Mason collection; Deane to Morris, Dec. 29, 1779, Morris MSS., N. Y. P. L.

During the fall of this year an event occurred in the West which, while perhaps not of great importance, is sufficiently illuminating to deserve narration. In January, 1778, Governor Henry of Virginia had sent Captain George Gibson, brother to Colonel John Gibson, to New Orleans to emulate the achievement of David Rogers and bring back supplies from the Spanish governor. Gibson carried letters from Henry to Gálvez asking for a loan of money as well as for supplies. Oliver Pollock was still able and the governor was still willing to aid the American cause, and Gibson got several boat-loads of goods, which were sent back up the river. Finally, in August, 1779, the boats reached the Falls of the Ohio and late in September started on the last leg of the journey to Pittsburgh. John Campbell, lieutenant of Yohogania County, accompanied the flotilla, and Gibson carried letters from Clark and Colonel John Todd, now lieutenant of the Virginia county of Illinois, intended for Governor Jefferson. At the point where Cincinnati now stands the party was attacked by a band of Indians under Simon Girty and nearly all killed except Campbell, who was befriended by Girty and saved from the natives. He was turned over to the British authorities in Canada and all his papers seized. These included his title to the land which Dunmore had granted him and Connolly at the site where Louisville was even at the moment getting its first population in the persons of the settlers who gathered about Clark's headquarters there. Another of Campbell's documents was the instructions sent him by the united Illinois-Wabash Company in which he was authorized to act as its agent in the West. For some time Campbell was kept in confinement by the British, but finally he was exchanged and returned to the United States. In 1784 he settled in Louisville and renewed his activities as a land speculator and trader, but by 1788 we shall find him acting as secret agent of the British authorities in Canada. On that account his loyalty to the American cause must lie under some suspicion, as did that of a number of his old Pittsburgh associates.[22]

The Pittsburgh speculators continued to pursue Croghan's policy of cooperating with Virginia against Pennsylvania until the very end of 1779. This is brought out by the fact that on September 28 there was presented to the court of Yohogania for its approval a petition from the court of Monongalia County protesting against the recently-enacted

[22] Notice from *Maryland Journal*, Dec. 7, 1779, Draper MSS., 16J99ff.; Kellogg, *Frontier Advance*, pp. 49–51; Kellogg, *Frontier Retreat*, pp. 17–18, 93–94; *Richmond Times-Dispatch*, Feb. 24, 1935, quoting Richmond Hustings Court, order book, I, June 16, 1783; George Ross to John Campbell, March 25, 1779, Add. MSS., 21, 844, f. 123, Br. Mus.; John Todd to Governor of Virginia, Aug. 18, 1779, *ibid.*, 21, 844; published in *Michigan Pioneer Collections*, XIX, 456–458; *ibid.*, XIX, 376–377; papers taken from George Gibson, Brymner, *Canadian Archives*, 1888, pp. 896–899.

Virginia land office bill. The Yohogania court refused to sanction this protest, thereby expressing its approval of the Virginia legislation. Yohogania County included all the country which Virginia claimed in the Pittsburgh area and its court, sitting at Augusta Town, was still dominated by men of the Croghan school; that is, they hoped to get lands under Virginia laws more readily than they could be secured under Pennsylvania jurisdiction, and Croghan was still busy trying to establish old claims, using the court for that purpose. It is not likely that they had yet heard of the agreement which had just been reached by the Baltimore commission on the disputed boundary. This agreement was still to be ratified, and Virginia was yet to adjudicate many claims in the disputed area. Monongalia County lay largely outside that area, being in what is now West Virginia.[23]

[23] Boyd Crumrine, ed., Minute book of the Virginia Court held for Yohogania County, Sept. 28, 1779, *Annals of the Carnegie Museum,* II, 358ff.

CHAPTER XIX

VIRGINIA AND THE WEST, 1780–1781

BEFORE the year 1780 was far spent the vexed question of conflicting claims to Western lands raised its head once more in Congress, and soon it became evident that some progress was being made toward its settlement. On December 15, 1778, Maryland had adopted resolutions instructing her delegates in Congress to notify that body that she would never accede to the Articles of Confederation unless the States claiming Western lands should surrender them to the control of Congress. In 1775, however, she had helped to defeat a proposal that Congress provide for the defense of Pittsburgh, leaving Virginia and Pennsylvania to do so alone.[1]

On February 13 New York provided for the cession to Congress of the tract of Western lands which she claimed by virtue of her pretended jurisdiction over the Six Nations. This tract included all the Western parts of that vast and indefinite area to which the Six Nations had set up claims during the colonial period. Beside taking in the Shawnee and Delaware country north of the Ohio River, it extended over that tract south of the Ohio—in what is now Tennessee and Kentucky—which the Six Nations had ceded to the Crown at the treaty of Fort Stanwix and which the Cherokee also claimed. Thus it covered practically all of the Western country which Virginia claimed under her charter of 1609.[2]

As to New York's claim that she owned this territory because the Six Nations were subject to her jurisdiction, it is hard to see how any one could have taken it very seriously. It is true that the Iroquois had made a limited submission to New York during the colonial period, but it was admitted that this did not involve ownership of the soil, nor did it make the Six Nations a part of the colony of New York. During the later years of the colonial period these Indians were under the jurisdiction of Sir William Johnson, Indian agent for the Northern Department, and the governor of New York was consulted by him no more than were

---

[1] *Journals of the Continental Congress*, XIV, 619–622; Pendleton to James Madison, Sept. 25, 1780, Massachusetts Historical Society, *Proceedings*, series 2, XIX, 112–114; Craig, *The Olden Time*, I, 557 ff.

[2] Herbert B. Adams, *Maryland's Influence upon Land Cessions to the United States, Johns Hopkins University Studies in Historical and Political Science*, series 3, I, 32.

the governors of the other colonies within whose chartered limits any part of their country lay.

The idea of the cession by New York originated in the mind of General Schuyler when he heard that Congress was about to assume control of the Western lands on its own initiative and take from the Empire State more than she cared to part with. New York then decided to cede what she did not own in order to avoid a more difficult situation. Naturally the gesture was seized on by the anti-Virginia group in Congress with the object of undermining her charter claims.[3]

On June 26, 1780, the New York cession, the Maryland resolution, and the protest of Virginia against Congressional jurisdiction over Western lands, which had been presented to Congress on April 28, were submitted to a committee consisting of James Duane, John Henry, Joseph Jones, Roger Sherman, and Willie Jones. It is interesting that none of the land company petitions was placed before this committee.[4]

Four days after its appointment, one of the members of this committee, Joseph Jones of Virginia, wrote to Jefferson that Maryland would never confederate unless concessions were made and that Virginia ought to give up her claims to the country north of the Ohio. Shortly afterward John Walker, another member of the Virginia delegation, wrote a letter to the same effect. On September 12 Madison expressed himself similarly, and Washington and Richard Henry Lee favored such a move. In fact, Virginia had officially indicated her willingness to compromise as early as December of the previous year, and there seems to have been at that time little difference of opinion on the subject among her leaders. Pendleton, however, objected to bargaining with Maryland, especially on account of her connection with the land companies.[5]

On September 6 the Congressional committee reported on the subject submitted to them. The land-claiming States were pressed to cede a part of their territory to Congress. The committee congratulated New York on her action and urged Maryland to accede to the Articles.[6]

But Virginia wished to have a more definite basis on which to proceed. On July 27, Mason, replying to a letter from Joseph Jones on the subject, made several suggestions as to terms on which the cession should be made. Jones decided to attend the next meeting of the Virginia assembly in

[3] Ibid., pp. 30–32; Burnett, V, 20–22; Merrill Jensen, "The Cession of the Old Northwest," M.V.H.R., XXIII, 27–48.

[4] Journals of the Continental Congress, June 26, 1780, XVII, 559.

[5] H. B. Adams, op. cit., p. 29; Joseph Jones to Jefferson, June 30, 1780, Letters of Joseph Jones of Virginia, Worthington C. Ford, ed. (Washington, 1889) pp. 15–16; Jones to Washington, Oct. 2, 1780, ibid., pp. 32–34; John Walker to Jefferson, July 11, 1780, Jefferson MSS., L. of C.; Rives, Madison, I, 261–262.

[6] Journals of the Continental Congress, Sept. 6, 1780, XVII, 806–807.

order to work for the cause of cession, and Madison was to manage the business in Congress on behalf of his State. On October 10 a vote was taken on a series of resolutions prepared by Joseph Jones, on the terms on which cessions were to be made. It was agreed that new States with powers equal to those of the original thirteen should be created out of the Western territory which might come under the jurisdiction of Congress, and that the Confederation would reimburse individual States for expenses incurred in conquering and defending any country which might be ceded. But a provision that no purchases of lands from the Indians by private individuals or companies should be validated was stricken out. Madison voted against the resolutions in their emasculated form, but Walker and Bland voted in their favor. This showed which way the wind blew, but shortly afterward Madison wrote that he did not believe Congress meant to back the landjobbers, yet it was important that Virginia should annex to any cession she might make a proviso against the private purchases. Thus was the ground cleared for the struggle, and the lines of battle were already marked out.[7]

Evidently the land companies were worried about the situation. They had already presented several memorials and on November 16, some of their representatives proposed to the Virginia delegates that the question of their claims should be arbitrated under the jurisdiction of Congress. It is needless to say that this proposal was rejected by the Virginians.[8]

Finally, on January 2, 1781, the Virginia assembly passed resolutions providing for a cession of its claims to the country north of the Ohio River. At the same time it voted to instruct its delegates in Congress to vote for a relinquishment of the right to navigate the Mississippi in case a treaty could be made with Spain on that basis. This was the very last act of the session and it was passed on the day on which Benedict Arnold commenced his invasion of Virginia. The gloomy outlook envisaged by that event may have had some connection with the new stand taken on these two issues. Spain had long insisted on the exclusive use of the lower Mississippi, and the completion of the Confederation could be expected to have a favorable effect upon her attitude toward a treaty. Her aid was sorely needed.[9]

To her proposed cession Virginia annexed several conditions. The

[7] Rowland, *Mason*, I, 359–367; Burnett, V, pp. xxxix, 423–424, 454; Jones to Washington, Sept. 6, 1780, Sparks, *Letters to Washington*, III, 78–80; Jones to Madison, Oct. 2, 1780, *Letters of Joseph Jones*, pp. 34–35; Henry, *Henry*, II, 75ff.; *Journals of the Continental Congress*, XVIII, 915–916.

[8] Trent to Congress, Sept. 27, Oct. 13, 1780, Cont. Cong. MSS., 77, ff. 218, 230; Morgan to Congress, Nov. 30, 1780, *ibid.*, f. 206; Joseph Wharton to Trent, Oct. 13, 1780, Ohio Company MSS., H.S.P.

[9] *Journal of the House of Delegates*, Jan. 2, 1780, p. 81.

land between the Little Miami and Scioto Rivers was to be reserved
to her for payment of military bounties; the expenses of her Illinois campaign were to be met by Congress; the Confederation was to be completed
by the accession of Maryland; new States were to be erected out of the
ceded territory; Virginia's remaining claims were to be guaranteed by
Congress; and all private purchases of land from the Indians were to
be invalidated.[10]

On February 2, 1781, Maryland agreed to accede to the Articles. There
can hardly be a doubt that her previous attitude had been influenced by
the claims of the Illinois-Wabash Land Company, for, after reversing
herself in the matter of Congressional jurisdiction in the case of Pittsburgh, her proposals had been carefully worded so as to safeguard the
interests of the company. According to her stand ceded lands were to
be used for public purposes only after the private purchases had been
made good. But now, with Virginia's proviso denying their claims, Maryland gave way and came into the Confederation. La Luzerne, the French
minister, had brought pressure to bear, and this seems to have been
largely responsible for the change. Governor Thomas Johnson, a member
of the Illinois-Wabash Company, wrote that "We have sacrificed much
of our right according to our idea, to comply with the desire of other
states. May it have the wished-for effect on our friends the Spaniards
and our enemies." He and his Maryland associates deserve credit for
having put patriotism above private interest when the situation called
loudly for such action.[11]

They doubtless still hoped that Congress would force Virginia to back
down. This seems more likely in view of the flood of petitions which the
land companies now poured upon Congress. On the day after the action
of the Maryland assembly, the united Illinois-Wabash Company presented a new memorial to that body, and in March the "Passy" memorial,
drafted by Benjamin Franklin and Samuel Wharton, was presented on
behalf of the Vandalia Company. On May 21, Wharton, Trent, and
Bernard Gratz memorialized in favor of George Croghan's old claims,
and on July 20 Trent petitioned in behalf of the Indiana Company.[12]

Meanwhile, in October Connecticut had proposed to cede to Congress
her claims to Western soil, reserving to herself three and a half million

[10] *Ibid.*, p. 80.

[11] Thomas Johnson to James Duane, Feb. 3, 1781, *Publications of the Southern
History Association,* IX, 399–400; St. George L. Sioussat, "The Chevalier de la Lu-
zerne and the Ratification of the Articles of Confederation," *Pa. Mag. of Hist. and
Biog.,* LX, 391.

[12] Memorial of Franklin and Wharton, Feb. 26, 1780, Cont. Cong. MSS., 77, ff.
167–205; *ibid.,* 41, X, 87–89; *ibid.,* 77, f. 226; Alvord, *The Illinois Country,* p. 384;
Franklin to Richard Bache, Sept. 13, 1781, Franklin MSS., Misc., V, L. of C.

acres and jurisdiction over the area. This and the New York and Virginia cessions, along with the petitions of the land companies, were submitted to a committee. On June 27, 1781, this committee issued a report proposing to reject all three cessions and the fixing of a line by Congress beyond which it would not guarantee the claims of any of the States. This done, new States were to be erected in the territory west of the line.[13]

This was indeed strong medicine, for the newly adopted Articles did not give Congress the right to fix State boundaries on its own initiative. In fact, they specifically provided that Congress could deprive no State of any territory which it claimed, but that disputed boundary questions should be settled by a body of arbiters to be appointed through the cooperation of Congress and the States concerned.

It is easily discernible, therefore, why this report was not adopted, but a new committee was appointed and the whole question submitted to it for consideration. On October 16 Virginia protested against reception and consideration by Congress of the petitions of the land companies. Her cession, she claimed, had been made upon an understanding that questions of conflicting claims in the ceded area should not be entertained and the action of Congress was, therefore, a breach of faith. A vote was taken on the question, and all States north of Virginia opposed her stand, those to the South approved it. Nevertheless, during October the Illinois-Wabash and the Vandalia Companies favored Congress with new representations. Wharton and Trent, speaking for Vandalia, were so optimistic as to "hope that the wisdom and justice of Congress will be exercised toward" the British members of the company. Their hopes were further bolstered by the fact that Tom Paine had been employed to write a pamphlet, entitled "Public Good," in their behalf.[14]

Finally, on November 3, the second committee made its report. It recommended rejection of the proposals of Virginia and Connecticut, but acceptance of New York's which was said to include all the land which Virginia offered to cede. It further proposed that the claims of George Croghan and of the Indiana Company should be validated. This land, so far as it was not included in the boundaries of Pennsylvania, had always been admitted during the colonial period as belonging to Virginia, and thus the committee was proposing that Congress dispose of land lying within the undisputed bounds of one of the States. The committee also advised that the claim of the Vandalia Company was too extensive

---

[13] *Journals of the Continental Congress*, XX, 704.
[14] *Ibid.*, XXI, 1057–1058; Vandalia petition, Oct. 20, 1781, Jefferson MSS., L. of C.; refutation of *Public Good* pamphlet by Tom Paine, Oct. 28, 1781, Lee MSS., U. of Va. library.

to be validated, but recommended that its American members should be reimbursed in lands for the expense to which they had been put in prosecuting their claim. As to the united Illinois and Wabash companies, the committee ruled that their original purchases had not been sanctioned by constituted authority and that they should, therefore, be disallowed.[15]

Congress took no action on this report. For it to have undertaken to pass on claims of the land companies to territory over which the Articles gave it no jurisdiction would indeed have been going far. Some time was yet to elapse before the question of Western lands was to be settled. But the Articles of Confederation had been adopted, and at last the States could carry on their joint affairs under a loosely organized but regularly-constituted government.[16]

Meanwhile Virginia was having troubles in Kentucky as well as in Congress. On April 14, 1780, George Rogers Clark set out for the Iron Banks on the Mississippi, just below the mouth of the Ohio, where the construction of the long-planned Fort Jefferson was at last begun. Before the project had got well under way, Clark had to leave the work in charge of his subordinates in order to return to the Illinois country and defend that section against a British attack. While he was successfully defending Cahokia, Captain Bird and a party of Indians visited Kentucky and defeated the garrisons at Martin's and Ruddle's stations. In August Clark organized a punitive expedition against the Shawnee and defeated them at Piqua, but his operations were hampered by the fact that the Indians had been warned by the French villagers who were now under the influence of the French adventurer, Colonel Auguste Mottin de la Balme.[17]

This was he who had come to America early in 1777 in company with Colonel Conway, bringing recommendations from Benjamin Franklin and Silas Deane. Mottin de la Balme had served as captain in the French cavalry and had written authoritative works on that branch of the service. Congress conferred upon him a commission as lieutenant-colonel and made him inspector-general of cavalry. He had hoped to be given command of the entire cavalry establishment, but disappointed in that expectation, he resigned his commission before the end of the year. For a

---

[15] *Journals of the Continental Congress,* XXI, 1098; Cont. Cong. MSS., 30, f. 1, published in *Journals of the Continental Congress,* XXII, 223–232. A manuscript copy of this report is also in the Fleming papers, W. and L. U. library.

[16] Protest of the Virginia delegates, n.d., Cont. Cong. MSS., 30, f. 557.

[17] James, *Clark,* 206–213; A. C. Boggess, *The Settlement of the Illinois, Chicago Historical Society's Collection,* V, 34–35; J. A. James, "Significance of the Attack on St. Louis, 1780," M.V.H.A. *Proceedings,* II, 211; Bodley, *History of Kentucky,* I, 212; Jefferson to Joseph Martin, Jan. 24, 1780, Draper MSS., 46J57; Fleming's journal, April 6, 1780, *ibid.,* 2ZZ75/18; Jefferson to Clark, Jan. 29, 1780, Jefferson MSS., L. of C.

time he engaged in mercantile operations in Philadelphia, but on June 27, 1780, he set out for Pittsburgh and was soon establishing contacts with the neighboring Indians. In July he reached Vincennes and at once began stirring up the French against Clark and his men.[18]

Despite Clark's popularity and success, Virginia influence had been on the wane for some time in the Illinois. Virginia currency had so declined that it was now of little value, and the local merchants had lost heavily as a result of their advances to Clark. John Todd, the lieutenant of the Virginia county of Illinois, had left that country in November, 1779. On his departure, Richard Winston, George Morgan's former partner in trade and now sheriff of the county, was left in charge of affairs. Richard McCarty and John Dodge, another of Morgan's aides, were among the leaders of the American group. Thomas Bentley, also an associate of Morgan and a traitor to both sides, was engaged with Dodge in various operations of very questionable nature. They were, of course, not popular with the villagers.[19]

When Mottin de la Balme arrived, Dodge seems to have played into his hand, and he had little trouble in persuading the French that they had been mistreated by the Virginians and that the King of France was the one to whom they should look for deliverance. He reported his operations to Cesar Anne de la Luzerne, who had, in September, 1779, replaced Gérard as French minister at Philadelphia, and it is obvious that the two were working in concert. Furthermore, since Luzerne was maintaining the same connections in Congress which had been established by his predecessor and since Mottin de la Balme said that he had consulted certain members of that body, there can be little doubt that the Congressional group which opposed Virginia's claims to the Illinois country did not look with disfavor upon the operations of the Frenchman.[20]

This adventurer, having collected about a hundred Frenchmen and a few Indians, set out in October upon an expedition against Detroit. His little army did not display the American colors, but marched under the banner of the King of France. The feeling which his representations had aroused against Virginia had forced Clark to withdraw the last of his

[18] Benjamin Franklin to Charles Thomson, Jan. 20, 1777, Add. MSS., 21844, Br. Mus.; Stevens facsimiles, no. 176; Sparks, *Works of Benjamin Franklin,* VIII, 195–196; *Am. Arch.,* series 5, II, 1091–1092; Mottin de la Balme to Luzerne, June 27, 1780, Brymner, *Report on Canadian Archives,* 1888, pp. 865–866; *ibid.,* 1887, p. 228.

[19] *Cahokia Records,* pp. xcv–civ; Alvord, *The Illinois Country,* pp. 348–351; *Journal of the House of Delegates,* June 20, 1780, pp. 55–56; R. Matthews to Maj. De Peyster, Sept. 29, 1780, Add. MSS., 21982, Br. Mus.; Winston to Todd, Oct. 14, 1780, *C.V.S.P.,* I, 380–382.

[20] Alvord, *The Illinois Country,* pp. 350–351; Mottin de la Balme to Luzerne, Aug. 22, 1780, Add. MSS., 21844, Br. Mus.; inhabitants of Cahokia to Mottin de la Balme, Sept. 21, 1780, *ibid.;* McCarty to Clark, Oct. 14, 1780, *Cahokia Records,* pp. 618–621.

troops from the Illinois, and if Mottin de la Balme could take Detroit, his influence would be supreme throughout the region. There has been some speculation as to whether his object was to gain territory for France or for America. But it is clear that France had no territorial ambitions in the Illinois, and the Spanish at St. Louis were hostile to him. Obviously his only object was to gain the country for Congress and thereby undermine the claims of Virginia.[21]

But he did not succeed. Having waited for some time at one of the Miami villages for reinforcements which failed to arrive, he destroyed the village and began a retreat. The Indians, however, overtook him on his return march and, on November 5, cut his command to pieces, Mottin de la Balme losing his life in the struggle.[22]

As a result of the passage of the Virginia land act of 1779, hordes of Virginians had set their feet on the long trail which was to end only at the Pacific more than three quarters of a century later. Kentucky was flooded with immigrants during the early months of 1780. Wagons and boats were arriving at the Falls in large numbers. On the first of May George May opened the surveyor's office for Kentucky County in the neighborhood of Harrodsburg and the place swarmed with speculators. Before much business could be done, however, Clark took it upon himself to suspend operations in an attempt to turn the attention of those who had assembled from the acquisition of land to the defense of the Illinois.[23]

On account of the increased population the Virginia assembly at its May session of 1780 divided Kentucky into three new counties—Jefferson, Lincoln, and Fayette. John Todd was made colonel of Fayette, with Daniel Boone as his lieutenant-colonel, and Thomas Marshall was named county surveyor. Benjamin Logan was appointed colonel of Lincoln, Stephen Trigg being lieutenant-colonel and James Thompson surveyor. For Jefferson County, John Floyd was named colonel, William Pope lieutenant-colonel, and George May surveyor.[24]

Many of the new-comers to Kentucky were from Pennsylvania and other States than Virginia, and they found the situation in regard to the public lands anything but satisfactory. Much speculation was going on, the depreciation of Virginia paper to a rate of one thousand to one by

[21] *Cahokia Records,* pp. lxxxix-xciv; Brymner, *Report on Canadian Archives,* 1888, p. 882.

[22] De Peyster to Haldimand, Nov. 16, 1780, *ibid.,* 1887, p. 229; Haldimand to De Peyster, Jan. 6, 1781, *ibid.,* 1887, p. 230; Hamilton to De Peyster, Jan. 6, 1781, Add. MSS., 21783, Br. Mus.; De Peyster to Haldimand, Dec. 3, 1780, C.O., series 5, 42, f. 14.

[23] Bradford, "Notes on Kentucky," *Kentucky Gazette,* Oct. 13, 1826.

[24] Hening, *Statutes,* X, 315-317; Perkins, *Annals of the West,* pp. 234-235; Marshall, *History of Kentucky,* I, 119-121.

the end of 1781 making it a very profitable business. John Floyd was settled on Beargrass Creek near the Falls of the Ohio. He had recently had an exciting adventure when, as commander of a privateer, he had been captured and carried to England, from which place he made his way to Paris and borrowed money from Benjamin Franklin to enable him to return to America. Now he was in the wilderness looking after the Kentucky interests of William Preston and his connections. Among these were two young nephews of Preston who later were to play a large part in Kentucky affairs. One of them was John Brown, son of a Presbyterian clergyman of the same name, and now a student at the College of William and Mary. He was already corresponding with his uncle about Western land matters, and his interest was to increase with the years. William Breckinridge, another nephew, was on the Beargress with Floyd. We shall presently hear more of him and his family.[25] William Christian, William Fleming, Caleb Wallace, and Stephen Trigg were also very active in connection with Kentucky lands at this time. Trigg was already occupying an important position in the new country, and Caleb Wallace, a Presbyterian clergyman now living in the lower Valley, was planning to remove to the farther West. Christian himself was also considering such a possibility.[26]

Virginia land office treasury warrants were being bought up in large numbers, and many of them were sold in Philadelphia. When George May, the surveyor, opened his Kentucky office such warrants or certificates covering sixteen thousand acres were presented for entry, but the purchasers of State certificates under the Virginia land office act found that their investments were of doubtful value. Military warrants and settlement and preemption rights had precedence over the "treasury warrants," as they were called, and it was difficult to find good lands upon which they could be entered without conflicting with prior and better claims. Only with the aid of an experienced woodsman was there any chance of success.[27]

Most of the non-Virginian new-comers to Kentucky had put their faith

[25] Marshall, *History of Kentucky*, I, 124–125; Floyd to Preston, Sept. 5, 1780, Draper MSS., 17CC132–133; same to same, Dec. 8, 1780, *ibid.*, 17CC133–134; same to same, Jan. 19, 1780, *ibid.*, 17CC120–121; Russell to Preston, Feb. 26, 1780; *ibid.*, 5QQ19; John Brown, Jr. to Preston, Dec. 9, 1779, *ibid.*, 5QQ14; same to same, March 7, 1780, *ibid.*, 5QQ20; same to same, March 22, 1780, *ibid.*, 5QQ25; Floyd to Preston, May 31, 1780, *ibid.*, 17CC127–129; *ibid.*, 31CC1; William Breckinridge to Preston, June 1, 1780, *ibid.*, 5QQ31; James, *Clark Papers*, p. 384.
[26] Clark to Fleming, Jan. 19, 1780, Draper MSS., 46J53; Kellogg, *Frontier Retreat*, pp. 128–132, 137–138; Patrick Henry to Fleming, March 29, 1780, Fleming papers, W. and L. U. library; military surveys in Kentucky from Col. Preston's office, *ibid.*
[27] Floyd to Preston, May 5, 1780, Draper MSS., 17CC124–127; *Journal of the House of Delegates*, June 28, 1788, p. 150.

in these treasury warrants, and the outlook was most discouraging. Out of this situation there developed in the early months of 1780 a movement for the secession of Kentucky from Virginia and the creation of a new State in the region.

Matters were further complicated by another element of discontent. Clark had centered his attention on the Illinois country and on the posts at the Falls of the Ohio and at Fort Jefferson. The Kentucky settlers, a majority of whom lived in the neighborhood of the Kentucky River, felt that their cabin homes—whether singly or in clusters, commonly called "stations"—were not adequately protected from the savages. They desired that forts should be erected at the mouths of the Kentucky and Licking and more easterly streams flowing into the Ohio, and they made their needs known in Richmond. Orders were given Clark for the construction of the forts which the settlers desired, but no funds or manpower were provided and the object was not attained. Especially were the counties of Lincoln and Fayette irritated, since they were not in the least protected by the post at Louisville, and their colonels-commandant, Todd and Logan, began to take a critical attitude toward Clark.[28]

This situation added fuel to the fire of the secessionists; during 1780 several meetings were held and several petitions drawn up asking Congress to erect Kentucky into a new State under Continental authority. John Kinkead was one of the leaders and Todd appears to have taken some part in these activities. Other prominent Virginia settlers were concerned, but Clark said that the majority of those involved were of the non-Virginian element. He, indeed, was offered the leadership of the movement, but he refused it and with more than seventy others signed a petition to the Virginia assembly, begging its protection and virtually announcing that they would not submit to Congress.[29] Brodhead corresponded with Levin Powell, and John Dodge wrote George Morgan about conditions in the Western country. Morgan relayed information of the Kentucky secession movement to Congress for the bearing that it might have upon Virginia's Western ambitions. According to Luzerne, the news does seem to have had some effect, but Congress took no direct

---

[28] *Va. Mag. of Hist. and Biog.*, XXVII, 42–45; ——— (?) to Fleming, Oct. (?), 1780, Draper MSS., 46J58; *Journal of the House of Delegates*, Dec. 11, 1781, p. 35; Cotterill, *History of Pioneer Kentucky*, p. 202; Bodley, *Clark,* pp. 177–182; Bodley, *History of Kentucky*, I, 294–295.

[29] Frederick Jackson Turner, "Western State-Making in the Revolutionary Era," *A.H.R.*, I, 262; Bodley, *Kentucky,* I, 157–159, 279, 304–305; memorial of Illinois and Kentucky Counties to Congress, May 15, 1780, in Roosevelt, *Winning of the West* (New York, 1895) II, 398–399; the same, Aug. 24, 1780, Cont. Cong. MSS., 48; George Rogers to John Clark, Aug. 23, 1780, Draper MSS., 46J112; *ibid.*, 16CC40; *Kentucky Historical Register*, XL, 41–46.

action and the Kentucky secession movement gained no great momentum during 1780.[30]

All the while Clark had been contemplating another attempt to take Detroit. Governor Jefferson was in hearty accord with him on that subject, and in the early months of 1780 they began making plans. On February 10, Jefferson wrote to Washington and proposed that Virginia cooperate with Colonel Daniel Brodhead, commandant at Pittsburgh, in the intended expedition. At about the same time, Clark wrote to Brodhead offering to cooperate with him. Brodhead had been making plans of his own with the same object in view, but Washington was not able to supply troops for the purpose and it was decided that Brodhead could not, on that account, act alone. Cooperation between Continental and Virginia forces was the only practicable plan, and there were many difficulties in the way of such a consummation. It was thought that Brodhead would not serve under Clark nor Clark under Brodhead, but Washington and Jefferson were anxious to bring about some form of cooperation.[31]

No progress was made on these plans during the summer, but in the fall the question was again taken up. Washington was still unable to support Brodhead's plans, but Clark repaired to Richmond, and he and Jefferson worked out a scheme for a joint campaign. Virginia was to pay the costs of the expedition and furnish most of the troops, and Washington agreed that the artillery and a part of the garrison at Pittsburgh were to accompany the expedition, and this was sanctioned by Congress. In December Jefferson prepared instructions for Clark. He was to command the expedition and Washington sent orders to Brodhead to cooperate with him. Naturally this was a great disappointment to Brodhead, but both to Washington and to Clark he expressed his intention of complying with orders. Nevertheless, when Jefferson sent agents to Pittsburgh, in January, 1781, to purchase supplies for the expedition the Commandant protested on the ground that the garrison and settlers would suffer as a result.[32]

[30] Paul C. Phillips, "American Opinion Regarding the West, 1778–1783," loc. cit., p. 272n.; Kellogg, Frontier Retreat, pp. 22, 319; Morgan to Trent, Sept. 12, 1780, Draper MSS., 46J59; Levin Powell to Brodhead, Jan. 21, 1781, ibid., 1NN51–53; Morgan to John Dodge, Dec. 1, 1780, Kaskaskia Records, pp. 209–210.

[31] Washington to Brodhead, Jan. 4, 1780, Draper MSS., 1H122; Clark to Craig, March 23, 1781, ibid., 30J51–53; Jefferson to Washington, Feb. 10, 1780, Sparks, Letters to Washington, II, 394–395; Brodhead to Washington, March 18, 1780, ibid., II, 416–417; same to same, April 24, 1780, ibid., II, 437–439; Jefferson to Washington, Sept. 26, 1780, ibid., III, 98–101.

[32] Washington to Clark, April 25, 1781, Sparks, Writings of Washington, VIII, 25–26; Washington to Brodhead, Dec. 29, 1780, ibid., VII, 343–345; Jefferson to Washington, Dec. 13, 1780, Sparks, Letters to Washington, II, 175–178; Brodhead to

Clark set out for Pittsburgh on January 22, being raised to the rank of brigadier-general on the same day. On reaching his destination he found manifold difficulties confronting him. These were due in part to the old controversy over the Pennsylvania-Virginia boundary. The two States had agreed on a line, but it had not yet been surveyed. Pennsylvania had just divided the county of Westmoreland and created the new jurisdiction of Washington County in the long-disputed area. The Virginia counties of Ohio, Monongalia, and Yohogania covered much the same territory, but the State was no longer supporting their jurisdiction, and before the beginning of 1781 they seem to have ceased to function regularly, the Yohogania court holding its last session on August 28. Virginia had tried also to quiet the controversy over land titles by suspending in the disputed area the operations of the commissioners under the land office act of 1779.[33]

Yet the officers of the Virginia counties continued to exercise some of their functions during 1781, and it was to them that Clark appealed in his attempt to raise recruits in the Pittsburgh area. Dorsey Pentecost, acting as lieutenant of Yohogania, was his most active assistant, and his efforts caused considerable unrest among the settlers. Governor Joseph Reed and the council of Pennsylvania, having been appealed to by Clark, directed the officials of Washington and Westmoreland Counties to aid him. Archibald Lochry, lieutenant of Westmoreland, complied as best he could, but James Marshal, lieutenant of Washington County, refused to do so. Most of the old Pennsylvania party in the area, including Thomas Scott, sided with Marshal, whereas the old Croghan following took its traditional stand in favor of Virginia jurisdiction. Colonel John Gibson, now second in command of the garrison at Pittsburgh, was especially active in Clark's behalf. Furthermore, he, in partnership with the Gratz brothers, furnished Clark with a large quantity of supplies for the expedition.[34]

Washington, Feb. 25, 1781, *ibid.*, III, 243–244; Clark to Washington, May 26, 1781, *ibid.*, III, 323–325; Washington to Brodhead, Dec. 29, 1780, Craig, *The Olden Time*, II, 347; Brodhead to Jefferson, Jan. 17, 1781, *ibid.*, II, 380–381; also *ibid.*, II, 388; Crumrine, *Washington County*, pp. 94–95; Kellogg, *Frontier Retreat*, pp. 352–353; Mohr, *Federal Indian Relations*, p. 83; Cont. Cong. MSS., 60, f. 33.

[33] Crumrine, ed., "Minute book of the Virginia court held for Yohogania County," *loc. cit.*, II, 427–429; Crumrine, *Washington County*, p. 91; Jefferson to Joseph Reed, Feb. 9, 1780, Cont. Cong. MSS., 71; Jefferson to Pres. of Congress, Feb. 9, 1780, *Official Letters of the Governors of Virginia*, II, 97–100; Hening, *Statutes*, X, 237.

[34] Agreement between John Gibson and B. and M. Gratz, Sept. 25, 1780, Ohio Company papers, H.S.P.; Clark to Pres. Reed, March 23, 1781, Draper MSS., 1NN54–55; Pentecost to Reed, July 27, 1781, *ibid.*, 1NN60; also *ibid.*, 46J29; Reed to Clark, May 15, 1781, Crumrine, *Washington County*, pp. 195–196; James Marshal to Reed, *Pa. Arch.*, series 1, IX, 193–194; Pres. Reed and Council to Archibald Lochry, July 25, 1781, Add. MSS., 21845, Br. Mus.; *Journal of the House of Delegates*, June 11, 1781, p. 13; Byars, *Gratz*, pp. 23–24, 205.

Naturally most of the settlers were anxious to shun military duty, and they took advantage of the dual jurisdiction in order to avoid compliance with the authority of either State. And out of the general turmoil there arose another secession movement. It showed its head as early as April of 1780, and agitation continued intermittently throughout that and the succeeding year. The Pennsylvania emancipation act of 1780 may have been one of the contributing causes. Benjamin Johnson, deputy surveyor of Yohogania, was mentioned as one of the leaders, and he carried on a correspondence in that connection with Colonel David Shepherd, lieutenant of Ohio County. James Innes was sent to represent Yohogania in the House of Delegates in 1781, and he also is mentioned as one of the leaders among the separationists. Pentecost was likewise accused of vigorous activity in the cause.[35]

All these men were connected with the Virginia régime in the area, and the Pennsylvania partisans were not slow in accusing the partisans of the Old Dominion of being responsible for the plot. There are reasons for believing that they were correct in their charge. Lands were to be obtained more easily under Virginia than under Pennsylvania authority, and the Croghan group, animated largely by special claims, had long supported the cause of the former. There was now no chance that Virginia authority would be established in the Pittsburgh area, and the only way to avoid paying the Pennsylvania price for lands was to form a new State which would include the old disputed territory. The alignment of factions and the reason for their differences remained much the same as they had been in the time of Lord Dunmore and John Connolly.[36]

Finding it so difficult to raise volunteers, Clark finally resorted to impressment, and that naturally created a greater furor than ever. In the end his arduous efforts failed and early in August he set out down the Ohio from Wheeling with only about four hundred men. The artillery from Fort Pitt went with him, but Brodhead had refused to let Colonel Gibson take his regiment. He had used his influence in other ways to hamper Clark, and Washington presently relieved him of his command on account of his failure to carry out orders in this connection. Charges were brought against him of having used his post for his own personal ends, and, though he was not convicted by court-martial, he was evidently

[35] Turner, "Western State-Making in the Revolutionary Era," *loc. cit.*, 85; Sipe, *Fort Ligonier*, p. 498; Crumrine, *Washington County*, pp. 231–235; Gabriel to William Madison, April 10, 1780, Draper, MSS., 5ZZ73; B. Johnston to David Shepherd, Oct. 3, 1780, *ibid.*, 1SS231; Thos. Scott to Pres. Reed, Jan. 24, 1781, *Pa. Arch.*, series 1, VIII, 713–715; James Marshal to Pres. Reed, June 27, 1781, *ibid.*, IX, 233–234; *Journal of the House of Delegates*, Nov. 17, 1781, p. 41.

[36] Darlington, *Fort Pitt*, pp. 243–244; Crumrine, *Washington County*, p. 197; Byars, *Gratz*, pp. 370–371.

guilty of having carried on private trading in partnership with David Duncan while holding military command.[37]

When Clark set out from Wheeling the House of Delegates had, on June 21, already authorized the governor to countermand the expedition, but he apparently did not know of it. He hoped to find recruits from Kentucky when he reached the Falls of the Ohio, and to proceed with his plan. Colonel Lochry arrived at Wheeling with about a hundred men just after Clark left. He proceeded down the river to join his commander, but he was attacked by a body of Indians and he and nearly all his men perished. Clark himself narrowly escaped attack by the same force. On reaching Louisville—which town had been incorporated at the Falls by an act of June 23, 1780—he found that Fort Jefferson had been abandoned on June 8 for lack of supplies, and he was able to collect a force of no more than seven hundred thirty men. This was not adequate for his undertaking, and the expedition was abandoned.[38]

Clark at once set to work on the construction of a strong fort, christened Fort Nelson, at the Falls, and a number of the neighboring tribes of Indians made their submission on account of the threat of invasion, but the opportunity had passed and it was not to return. Arnold's invasion had led to the resignation of Governor Jefferson. He was succeeded for a time by General Thomas Nelson, but Nelson also resigned as soon as the military crisis was over, and on November 30, Benjamin Harrison was elected governor of Virginia. Harrison was not in favor of a forward Western policy and Clark was ordered to remain on the defensive. On account of certain criticisms, he offered to resign his military command but was persuaded to remain in the service. On December 14 the House of Delegates failed to renew the act, which expired by limitation, for the government of Illinois County, and the Northwest was thus left without a legal administration. Well might Clark have looked upon his work as having been done in vain.[39]

It remains to give in conclusion a brief account of a situation which developed in southwestern Virginia during the fall of 1781. Arthur Campbell, lieutenant of Washington County, had already given evidence of his

[37] Sipe, Fort Ligonier, pp. 523–524; Kellogg, Frontier Retreat, pp. 363–370, 397; Craig, The Olden Time, II, 393–395; Crumrine, Washington County, pp. 97–98; Clark to Pres. Reed, Aug. 4, 1781, Draper MSS., 46J67; Washington to Brodhead, Sept. 6, 1781, ibid., 1H155; Hassler, Old Westmoreland, p. 147; Gen. Irvine to Washington, Dec. 2, 1781, Sparks, Letters to Washington, III, 452–459.

[38] Journal of the House of Delegates, June 23, 1780, p. 60; Lochry to Clark, Aug. 8, 1781, Add. MSS., 21845, Br. Mus.; Floyd to Preston, Aug. 11, 1781, Draper MSS., 17CC138–139; Craig, The Olden Time, II, 533–534.

[39] Floyd to Preston, Jan. 1, 1782, Draper MSS., 17CC139–141; Journal of the House of Delegates, Nov. 30, 1781, p. 22; ibid., Dec. 14, 1781, p. 39; Bodley, Clark, pp. 213–216.

opposition to the claims of the Loyal Company which were confined principally to his section of the State. Without any legal claim except the
vague recognition which was expressed in the order of the Virginia
council handed down in 1773, the company had induced numerous settlers to have their lands surveyed by its agents under the direction of
Walker and Preston. The land act of 1779 had recognized the validity
of these surveys and had given final jurisdiction in the case to the court
of appeals. This meant that the settlers who had submitted to the surveys
would have to pay the higher price which the company demanded,
whereas they otherwise would have been entitled to grants by settlement
and preemption. Campbell held lands under the company and would
be adversely affected by this situation. So would a large number of
his neighbors.

The commission on land titles which was appointed for Washington
and Montgomery Counties under the act of 1779 consisted of Harry
Innes, and Nicholas and Joseph Cabell. On September 17, 1781, Innes
wrote to Campbell stating that the commission was concerned over the
advantage that the Loyal Company was taking of the settlers, and that
it would do the best it could to protect them. It was also discovered at
this time, through the activities of the commission, that John Buchanan,
who had made a number of surveys in southwestern Virginia for James
Patton under the authority of Thomas Lewis, surveyor for Augusta
County, had no commission to serve as deputy surveyor from the College
of William and Mary. This, according to the terms of the act of 1779,
should have invalidated all his work, which would have been a serious
blow to the Patton interests with which Walker, Preston, and Pendleton were connected.[40] The interested parties decided to keep the matter
as quiet as possible, and the commission seems not to have been able
to accomplish anything. The court, of course, validated the Loyal Company surveys, and Campbell and Innes were left to make the best of the
situation. But petitions from Washington County against the Loyal Company were presented to the House of Delegates on the 1st and 14th of
December, 1781. A copy of one of these memorials, together with a copy
of one from Montgomery County, is preserved in the Campbell papers.
Campbell thought that the assembly had not treated him justly in connection with an expedition which he had recently led against the Cherokee, and this may have added to his discontent. He seems also to have

[40] Henderson, *Walker*, pp. 83–85; Innes to Campbell, Sept. 17, 1781, Draper MSS.,
9DD29; Arthur Campbell to Col. Wm. Edmondson, Sept. 22, 1781, *ibid.*, 9DD30;
Pendleton to Preston, Nov. 1, 1781, *ibid.*, 5QQ99; *Journal of the House of Delegates*,
Nov. 21, 1781, p. 10.

had a grudge against Colonel William Russell, who was one of the Preston group of southwestern Virginia magnates.[41]

As a result of his Cherokee campaign Campbell was working at this time for the establishment of a military post at the mouth of the Holston River, near where Knoxville now stands, and he wrote to the president of Congress urging that Joseph Martin be made Indian agent for the Southern Department with headquarters at this place. It is possible that Martin's former connection with the Henderson company may have been in his mind. Be that as it may, it is significant that it was at this time that Campbell began planning for the secession of the five southwestern counties of Virginia and the two adjoining counties of North Carolina. We shall trace the development of this movement in the next chapter.[42]

[41] A. Campbell to Jefferson, June 20, 1781, Cont. Cong. MSS., 71 II, 141; *Journal of the House of Delegates*, Dec. 1, 14, 1781, pp. 24, 39.

[42] Summers, *History of Southwest Virginia*, p. 391 ff.; A. Campbell to Geo. Muter, Jan. 16, 1781, Cont. Cong. MSS., 71, II, 43; A. Campbell to Pres. of Congress, Sept. 28, 1781, *ibid.*, 78, VI, 55; *Journals of the Continental Congress*, XXI, 1088–1089.

CHAPTER XX

VIRGINIA AND THE WEST, 1782–1783

HAVING made his plans during 1781, Arthur Campbell proceeded during the two succeeding years to agitate for the creation of his new State. On February 19 he had a letter from William Christian in which the matter was discussed at length. The Congressional report of November, 1781, on Western land claims was the motive power for their plan. In that report it was proposed that Congress take over the country beyond the Allegheny watershed and create new States from the territory. Now, there was no precedent for such action, and the proponents of that policy in Congress certainly intended that the central authority should frame the government for the new States and take over the public lands for its own purposes. Campbell and Christian intended to forestall such a proceeding and lead the people in the organization of their own government, which was also to administer the public lands but turn the proceeds over to Congress. Thus would economic and political power be acquired by the local leaders. They proposed to hold an election in March, 1782, for delegates to a convention to meet the next month, consider the Congressional report, and decide what they would do in the circumstances. On April 20, 1782, Campbell received a letter from John Donelson, then in Kentucky, which shows that these two were collaborating in an effort to have the more distant settlements follow a course similar to that which was being pursued in southwestern Virginia.[1]

The connection of Christian with this movement is interesting. Being brother-in-law to Patrick Henry and closely associated with the Loyal Company interests, one would hardly expect to find him heading a secession movement. And his connection did not last long, for this communication is the only evidence which we have in his case. It is obvious from his letter that his principal desire was to forestall Congressional action when he thought it imminent, but when it became apparent that Congress was not likely to assume control of southwestern Virginia he was no

[1] Christian to Campbell, Feb. 19, 1782, Draper MSS., 9DD32; Donelson to Campbell, April 20, 1782, ibid., 9DD34; C.V.S.P., III, 414; Summers, Southwest Virginia, pp. 391–397.

longer willing to go along with Campbell. In May, 1783, the court of appeals finally validated the claims of the Loyal and Greenbrier Companies, and in one of Campbell's memorials the fees paid by the settlers to these companies were mentioned as a grievance. In this Campbell's interest apparently differed from that of Christian.[2]

On December 7 of the same year charges against Campbell were preferred in the House of Delegates because of his new-State proceedings. They were referred to a committee and nothing more was heard of them at this time. Neither did Governor Harrison take any action. Campbell was not disturbed in any of his offices, and Donelson was appointed by the governor to negotiate an important Indian treaty. In Kentucky Clark did not hesitate to accuse Harrison of favoring the secessionist party, and his charges can hardly be overlooked. The governor and the assembly were apparently willing for Congress to think that the people of the West were able to care for themselves in case that body should take a strong hand in their affairs.[3]

It is true that on January 8, 1783, Harrison wrote to Joseph Martin saying "When you were here last you mentioned to Mr. Hardy a letter you had received from Col. Arthur Campbell advising you to decline any further business with the Indians, and to let them break out on the Inhabitants with some reflections on the Executive for their inattention to you and to them." The governor said that this was too much to be borne and asked for a copy of Campbell's letter. He thought that Campbell should be called to account, but nothing was ever done by him in this direction.[4]

While the new-State movement was in progress Joseph Martin and his Virginia and Carolina associates found themselves much occupied by other land-speculating ventures. Martin was still acting as Indian agent for Virginia with headquarters at the Long Island in the Holston River, though this spot had now been found to lie within territory of North Carolina. Martin was also still closely associated with Patrick Henry and serving him in connection with Western land schemes. On October 15, 1782, Governor Harrison wrote to Martin that he had received a letter from Colonel John Donelson saying that the Creek and Chickasaw Indians wished to make peace with Virginia. The governor, having been authorized by the assembly to do so, proceeded to appoint Martin, Donel-

[2] Daniel Call, ed., *Reports of Cases . . . in the Court of Appeals of Virginia* (Richmond, 1833) IV, 21–32; Thomas Walker to Daniel Smith, May 20, 1783, Draper MSS., 1Q18; *Journal of the House of Delegates*, June 13, 1783, p. 53; *ibid.*, Nov. 25, 1783, pp. 32–33; Summers, *Southwest Virginia*, p. 396.

[3] *Journal of the House of Delegates*, Dec. 7, 1782, p. 58.

[4] Harrison to Martin, Jan. 8, 1783, *Official Letters of the Governors of Virginia*, III, 423–424.

son, and Isaac Shelby, who shortly afterward removed from the Holston country to Kentucky, to negotiate with the natives. They were warned, however, that in case any land cessions were made, nothing should be said to indicate that Virginia recognized the Indians as sovereigns of the soil claimed by the Old Dominion as lying within her boundaries.[5]

It is an interesting question as to whether Harrison was within his rights in thus undertaking a separate negotiation with the Indians. The Articles of Confederation stipulated that Congress should have entire control over those who were "not members of any of the States, provided that the legislative right of any State within its own limits be not infringed or violated." What Indians were members of the States might have proved a difficult question, but the phrase could have been construed as applying to Indians not living within the borders of any of the States. In that case Virginia would have had a right to make these treaties had the Indians concerned lived within her limits, but none of them actually did live within territory claimed by Virginia. Governor Harrison's treaties were to be made with Indians all of whom lived within the borders of North Carolina, and the place finally designated for the negotiation of the Chickasaw treaty, French Lick on the Cumberland— the Nashville settlement—was in that State. It was a queer situation, but North Carolina made no objections for reasons which will soon become apparent. It seems that Harrison actually considered the creation of a Southern confederation within the Confederation for the purpose of dealing with the Indians. This would have been clearly contrary to the provisions of the Articles. The governor of Virginia was certainly no strong supporter of the jurisdiction of Congress.[6]

Harrison had intended that the treaties should be made as speedily as possible, but Martin and Donelson were soon involved in a speculating scheme which delayed their official business. At this time William Blount was a leading, if not the leading, figure in North Carolina politics. He and Governor Richard Caswell cooperated in managing the affairs of that State, and both were inordinate land speculators.[7] On January 6, 1783, Blount wrote from Charleston to his brother John Gray Blount that he was attempting to form a company for the purchase of lands in

[5] Harrison to Martin, Oct. 15, 1782, *Official Letters of the Governors of Virginia,* III, 344; *Journal of the House of Delegates,* Dec. 11, 1782, p. 61; Harrison to Donelson, Martin, and Shelby, Jan. 11, 1783, Draper MSS., 1XX56; Martin to Benjamin Logan, Feb. 20, 1783, *ibid.,* 46J74.

[6] Campbell to Martin (1783), Draper MSS., 1XX66–67; Mohr, *Federal Indian Relations,* pp. 140–141.

[7] On Jan. 7, 1782, William Blount wrote to his brother John Gray Blount, "if it is possible . . . have it [land claim] condemned in Georgia either by Party, Bribery, or in any other way." John Gray Blount papers, N.C.H.C.

the "Great Bend" of the Tennessee—that is, the country lying north of the southernmost point on that river, where Decatur, Alabama, now stands. Both Georgia and South Carolina claimed jurisdiction over the region, and Blount was preparing to negotiate with both States and with the Indian claimants. On May 17 following he wrote to Donelson on the same business, and he and Martin were engaged to make the purchase from the Cherokee and attend to the surveying of the lands. Caswell, John Sevier—a Virginian from the Shenandoah Valley who had moved to the Holston country in 1773—Anthony Bledsoe, and Griffith Rutherford of North Carolina, Patrick Henry as well as Martin and Donelson of Virginia, Wade Hampton of South Carolina, and others were taken into the company.[8]

Finally, on August 21, William Blount wrote to his brother that Donelson had purchased the desired country from the Indians for one thousand pounds specie to be paid in goods, and plans were at once made for establishing a county government under the authority of Georgia and for making a settlement under the leadership of Sevier, Donelson, and Martin. It was not until 1784, however, that they could proceed with an attempt to carry these plans through.[9]

Meanwhile this group of speculators had other irons in the fire. In 1783 North Carolina passed an act which threw nearly all of her Western lands upon the market at ten pounds the hundred acres. This was equal to no more than five dollars in specie, and the speculators reaped a rich harvest during the seven months that elapsed before the act was repealed. The Western country soon swarmed with speculators. Caswell employed John Donelson and his son Stockley to locate tracts for a company which he formed to speculate in lands, and Joseph Martin was busy looking out for choice tracts for Henry. Arthur Campbell and John Adair were engaged in the same enterprise. Of course, there were many lesser speculators, and the claims thus established were finally made good even though the Indians had not yet relinquished their hold upon most of the country thus disposed of.[10]

[8] William to J. G. Blount, Jan. 6, 1783, *ibid.;* same to same, June 20, 1783, *ibid.;* Harrison to Martin, Jan. 6, 1783, Draper MSS., 1XX54; William Blount to Martin, Oct. 20, 1783, *ibid.,* 4XX17; Arthur P. Whitaker, *The Spanish-American Frontier, 1783–1795* (Boston, 1927) pp. 54–55; Abernethy, *From Frontier to Plantation in Tennessee,* pp. 64–66.
[9] William to J. G. Blount, Aug. 21, 1783, J. G. Blount papers, N.C.H.C.; Donelson to William Blount, Sept. 24, 1783, *ibid.*
[10] Martin and Christian jointly owned the land upon which Fort Patrick Henry stood near the Long Island of Holston. Document dated Aug. 10, 1783, William Marshall Bullitt MSS., Louisville, Ky.; Christian to Campbell, Sept. 6, 1783, Draper MSS., 9DD41; Abernethy, *From Frontier to Plantation in Tennessee,* pp. 49–54; Samuel Henderson to J. G. Blount, Aug. 12, 1782, J. G. Blount papers, N.C.H.C.;

At last, about the middle of November, 1783, Martin and Donelson completed their treaty with the Chickasaws at the French Lick. The natives expressed their friendship for the Americans, and never again did they make war upon them. It seems that Isaac Shelby, son of the Welsh pioneer Evan Shelby, refused to take part in the proceedings because he disapproved of the way in which his colleagues made use of their official position to engage in private speculations. Similar complaints were laid before Governor Harrison, and it was charged by Benjamin Logan that Martin and Donelson were probably being paid by Virginia while they were working for Blount and his associates. Harrison mildly expressed his disapproval of their conduct, not complaining of their purchase but only of the way in which his agents had neglected their official duty. In answering the governor's charges Donelson stated that the Muscle Shoals purchase was not made until after the treaty was concluded. This statement was contrary to fact.[11]

During 1782–1783 the separation movement in Kentucky progressed along lines similar to those which characterized the situation in southwest Virginia. This is made more evident by the cooperation between Arthur Campbell in the one region and John Donelson in the other. But the situation was more complicated in Kentucky. George Rogers Clark and other opponents of the movement always stressed the anti-Virginia sentiments of the immigrants from other States and gave them credit for furnishing the main support for the secessionist movement. Many of these, too, were men of small means, and they dreaded the thought of the lands being engrossed in large tracts by speculators while they were unable to secure titles to their little farms. The earlier settlers, the majority of whom were Virginians, had been given settlement and preemption rights under the land act of 1779. Even as late as 1781, needy settlers were allowed four hundred acres on credit, but those who came later had small chance to acquire farms. Naturally they were dissatisfied.[12]

Another grievance which affected Virginians and non-Virginians alike was that all legal business requiring a higher jurisdiction than that of a county court had to be taken to Richmond for transaction; there was no

(Blount?) to Donelson, May 17, 1783, *ibid.;* Thomas Polk to William Blount, July 5, 1783, *ibid.;* John Adair to Arthur Campbell, Dec. 10, 1783, Draper MSS., 9DD40; Henry, *Henry,* III, 243–244.

[11] Isaac Shelby to Martin, April 5, 1783, Draper MSS., 46J80; Harrison to Martin, Aug. 21, 1783, *ibid.,* 1XX63; same to same, Sept. 18, 1783, *ibid.,* 1XX64; *C.V.S.P.,* III, 522–523, 548; John Reid to Harrison, Feb. 23, 1784, Clark MSS., Va. Arch.; Donelson to Harrison, March 3, 1784, *ibid.*

[12] Hening, *Statutes,* X, 431–432; Walker Daniel to Fleming, April 14, 1783, Draper MSS., 46J78–79.

county-surveyor's office opened in Kentucky until November, 1782, except for the brief period in 1781 when George May opened his office in Jefferson County. Furthermore, taxes always bore heavily upon frontier settlements where currency was scarce.[13]

Perhaps more important than either of these elements, though much less numerous, were the great land speculators. During these years individual speculators were extremely active, and several powerful companies were formed for the purpose of dealing in Kentucky lands. The most interesting of these was organized by the Gratz brothers and Charles Willing in cooperation with Dorsey Pentecost. The Gratz brothers had become acquainted with Pentecost in connection with Clark's abortive campaign of 1781, and now that acquaintance was turned to practical account. The former were to purchase the land warrants and Pentecost was to attend to having them located. Thomas Marshall, surveyor of Fayette County, was in position to be useful and was taken into the company. He turned the Gratz warrants over to his son Charles, acting as deputy surveyor under his father, who was to locate them and get half the land as his compensation. Presently Robert Morris, James Wilson, and Levi Hollingsworth became connected with this group, and they had the cooperation of John Harvie who was in charge of the Virginia land office. Even Governor Harrison considered joining the Gratz brothers in their Kentucky speculations. Much could be accomplished by such a group as this, but they had many rivals at that time.[14]

Such speculators took up immense tracts, and they often found their surveys interfered with by soldiers' warrants and settlement and preemption claims, both of which, it will be recalled, had precedence over their "treasury warrants." They came to employ some of the most prominent men in Kentucky in their interest, and naturally it would have been a great advantage to them to have had the political destinies of the country in their own hands. There can be no doubt that Donelson and some of the leading Virginia settlers represented this interest. Opposed to them were the early immigrants who had their claims protected under Virginia law and certain cis-montane Virginians who had invested heavily in military warrants, especially those which had been surveyed under

[13] J. R. Robertson, ed., *Petitions of the Early Inhabitants of Kentucky*, pp. 62–66, 66–68; Marshall, *Kentucky*, I, 149–150; Smith, *Kentucky*, p. 225.

[14] Byars, *Gratz*, pp. 23–24, 26–27, 212, 214, 218, 221–222; Floyd to Preston, Oct. 19, 1782, Draper MSS., 17CC143–144; same to same, March 28, 1783, *ibid.*, 17CC144–149; James Wilson to William Bingham, May 27, 1783, Gratz MSS., H.S.P.; articles of agreement, Sept. 13, 1783, Innes MSS., XX, pt. 1, L. of C.; document, Dec. 25, 1783, *ibid.;* Jillson, *Kentucky Land Grants*, p. 7; MS. account book giving land claims of Robert Morris, most of which passed into his hands from this group of speculators, Va. Arch.

Preston's jurisdiction in the late colonial period. John Floyd had been their principal agent, and Patrick Henry, William Christian, the Lewises, and that entire group of Valley speculators had an interest in these early surveys. They had marked off the choicest tracts in the blue grass region, mostly east of the Kentucky River but also in the neighborhood of the Falls. These men would not easily consent to a change of jurisdiction in Kentucky. Thus it was largely a question of the interests of the early settlers as opposed to those of the new-comers and of early speculators as opposed to more recent adventurers.[15]

The old difficulty over the location of the frontier forts was still causing trouble. Clark and the Jefferson County authorities continued to favor a concentration at the Falls of the Ohio, while the Fayette and Lincoln people wanted posts farther upstream. Thomas Marshall admitted that such posts would really furnish little protection from the Indians, except as rallying points for expeditions into their country, and that he favored a fort at the mouth of the Limestone mainly for the purpose of facilitating immigration. On the other hand, the commissioners on the Western debt favored a post at the mouth of the Kentucky. It has already been pointed out that the secession movement was strongest in those counties which opposed Clark's Indian policy, and it is worth while to note that these were the counties in which most of the old military surveys were located.[16]

In spite of such opposition as Clark, Floyd, Walker Daniel, and their supporters could muster, Donelson called a meeting during the spring of 1782 and secured the adoption of a new-State resolution which was addressed to Congress in much the same tone as that which Campbell had sent from southwestern Virginia. An address was sent also to the Virginia assembly, and during the May session of that body a committee reported a resolution approving a future separation of Kentucky under the legal authority of the State, but not otherwise. Jefferson and most of the Virginia leaders took the same view. The petition to Congress was not presented until August 27, and no action was taken on it, but the Virginia delegates wrote to Harrison concerning it and he replied that he disapproved of the movement and of its backers in Philadelphia.[17]

[15] Henry to Christian, Sept. 19, 1782, William Marshall Bullitt collection, Louisville, Ky.; William Christian, power of attorney to Robert Daniel, Aug. 23, 1783, ibid.; Register of the Kentucky State Historical Society, XXV, 113.
[16] C.V.S.P., III, 301–302; Thomas Marshall to (?), Dec. 22, 1782, Draper MSS., 2U133; commissioners to Harrison, Dec. 23, 1782, ibid., 2U134; ibid., 46J75; Cotterill, Pioneer Kentucky, p. 183; Bodley, Clark, p. 191.
[17] Draper MSS., 5ZZ75, 46J78, 16CC40, 9DD34; Jefferson to Madison, March 24, 1782, Writings of Thomas Jefferson (Mem. ed.), IV, 190–191; Harrison to Virginia delegates, Sept. 20, 1782, Official Letters of the Governors of Virginia, III, 326;

Yet in Kentucky Clark complained bitterly that Harrison supported the secessionist party and thwarted his efforts to suppress it. There is much reason to think that he was justified in his opinion. It was Arthur Campbell who first reported that Clark was drinking heavily, and the governor credited and disseminated the rumor. Harrison found much to complain about also in connection with the settlement of Clark's accounts.[18]

By many in Kentucky the General was unjustly blamed for the defeat at the Blue Licks, in August, 1782, in which he had no part and in which Colonels John Todd and Stephen Trigg were killed. In carrying on his various campaigns, Clark had drawn heavily on Oliver Pollock, Daniel Clark, and other New Orleans merchants. John Todd and John Montgomery also had drawn on them, and now Daniel Clark was in Richmond and Pollock in Philadelphia seeking to settle their accounts. They maintained that all the drafts had been accepted on a specie basis whereas many of them had been drawn after specie ceased to circulate in Virginia.[19]

On June 21, 1781, the assembly had established a commission to investigate these Western accounts; Thomas Marshall, William Fleming, Samuel McDowell and Caleb Wallace had been appointed for that purpose. On February 17, 1783, they submitted their report, and from it and other evidence, it is clear that there was reason to doubt the accuracy of the accounts of the New Orleans merchants.[20]

In the first place, the merchants admitted that Western prices were very high, amounting to eight or nine hundred per cent advance on the original cost of the goods in Europe. The Virginia authorities insisted that they were so high as to indicate that the Virginia drafts had been accepted at a discount. Pollock and Daniel Clark denied this, and, though

C.V.S.P., III, 121–122; Papers of Charles Thomson, Collections of the New York Historical Society, 1878, pp. 145–150; Bodley, Kentucky, I, 299; Henry, Henry, II, 175; Bodley, Clark, p. 194.

[18] Harrison to Ky. Comrs., Oct. 16, Nov. 4, 1782, Draper MSS., 46J71–72; Harrison to Campbell, March 7, 1783, ibid., 9DD39; Jefferson to Clark, Nov. 26, 1782, James, Clark Papers, 1781–1783, pp. 155–156; ibid., pp. 159, 170–172, 178–180; C.V.S.P., III, 384–385; Bodley, Clark, pp. 223–225.

[19] Journal of the House of Delegates, Dec. 14, 25, 1781, pp. 38, 56; ibid., June 21, 1783, pp. 72–75; Morris to Harrison, Jan. 15, 1782, Robert Morris MSS., L. of C.; Morris to Daniel Clark, Jan. 14, 1782, ibid.; Harrison to the commissioners, Jan. 29, 1782, Draper MSS., 46J69; C.V.S.P., III, 323, 337, 433; report of Oliver Pollock to Congress, Sept. 18, 1782, Pollock papers, L. of C.; Simon Nathan to Pollock, Oct. 13, 1782, ibid.; Rowland, Mason, II, 62; Bodley, Clark, pp. 213–216; David Jameson to Harrison, Nov. 26, 1781, Tyler's Quarterly, IV, 417–418.

[20] Journal of the commissioners, James, Clark Papers, 1781–1783, pp. 90–412; Fleming to Preston, Dec. 20, 1781, Draper MSS., 5QQ102; McDowell to Fleming, March 24, 1782, ibid., 2U131; Thomas Marshall to Fleming, March 9, 1782, ibid., 2U130; commissioners to Harrison, Dec. 23, 1782, ibid., 2U134.

in the case of some merchants there is evidence to the contrary, George Rogers Clark supported Pollock's contention. Harrison and the Virginia assembly made many delays, but it seems that they were really trying to get at the truth of the matter, and some of the accounts were settled during this period. The weight of evidence appears to support the honesty of both George Rogers Clark and Pollock. Certain it is that both of them jeopardized their private credit for the sake of the government, which was very slow in doing them justice.[21]

Because of these and other difficulties Clark became more and more dissatisfied with his position. Yet in the fall of 1782 he took part in one last attempt to take Detroit. He was to advance from Kentucky into the Indian country while General William Irvine, with the backing of Washington, the Pennsylvania authorities and Congress, was to march from Pittsburgh. The two commanders made plans to synchronize their movements. Though their immediate object was a stroke against the natives, they hoped that, if successful in this, they might converge upon Detroit. Clark was able to advance as planned and won a victory over the Shawnee, but Shelburne had given orders to General Haldimand to put an end to Indian warfare, and on being informed of this Washington countermanded Irvine's expedition. Thus the Revolutionary War in the West came to an end. Clark continued to hold his command and to quarrel with Harrison until July 2, 1783, when the governor notified him of his release from the service of the State and thanked him profusely for the work that he had done.[22]

While military matters were causing dissension and the secession movement was in progress, the Virginia assembly was not altogether deaf to the pleas of her loyal citizens in Kentucky who submitted several petitions complaining of the legal disabilities under which they labored. In order to meet at least a part of these complaints a district court was provided for the three Kentucky counties during the May term of 1782. Harry Innes was presently appointed to act as presiding justice, and Caleb Wallace, John Floyd, and Samuel McDowell as associate justices. On March 3, 1783, the two last-named organized the court and appointed John May clerk and Walker Daniel district attorney. The clerk and the

[21] C.V.S.P., III, 25–29; James, Clark Papers, 1781–1783, pp. 32–34, 226; Harrison to Pollock, Nov. 7, 1783, Pollock MSS., L. of C.; Journal of the House of Delegates, Dec. 27, 1782, pp. 83–84; ibid., June 25, 1783, p. 83; ibid., Nov. 14, 19, 29, 1783, pp. 18, 23, 38; ibid., Dec. 1, 9, 20, 22, 1783, pp. 40–41, 56, 78, 81.

[22] Haldimand to Shelburne, July 17, 1782, P.R.O., C.O., series 5, 15; same to Townshend, ibid.; Clark to Irvine, Aug. 10, 1782, Irvine MSS., VI, 91, H.S.P.; Irvine to Clark, Sept. 9, 1782, ibid., VII, 19; deposition of William Bruce, Oct. 29, 1782, Add. MSS., 21783, f. 263, Br. Mus.; De Peyster to Haldimand, Jan. 7, 1783, ibid., f. 282; Haldimand to De Peyster, Feb. 19, 1783, ibid.; C.V.S.P., III, 452–454; Hassler, Old Westmoreland, pp. 182–188.

district attorney were delegated by the court to select a place for its meetings, and they chose the spot where Danville was soon located as the seat of justice.[23]

The year 1782 opened in the Pittsburgh area with one of the most shocking incidents of all our frontier history. Under the influence of the Moravian missionaries, David Zeisberger and John Heckwelder, the Delaware Indians of the Tuscarawas River had accepted Christianity. During the early years of the Revolution they had generally remained neutral, but maintained a friendly attitude toward the Americans. George Morgan had usually been able to make use of them in his trading operations, and while in their villages his agents got valuable information of British movements. But British traders also were often in the same villages, and they doubtless secured an equal amount of information. Toward the end of the War the Delawares showed signs of falling under the influence of the British, and on several occasions they were suspected of having committed atrocities in the neighborhood of Pittsburgh.

The excitement caused by these incidents was apparently stimulated by another factor. It was now known that when the boundary line between Virginia and Pennsylvania should be run, the lands in the Pittsburgh area which had long been claimed by George Croghan would fall within Pennsylvania, and Croghan, whatever Congress might do about his claim, would get none of them. Many settlers in the Chartiers Creek area claimed their lands under Croghan, and now they had no other prospect but to be dispossessed. There were not a few in these circumstances who urged that the settlers should cross the Ohio, attack the Indians, and settle on their lands. This cry was particularly strong among the Chartiers Creek settlers, and the Indian atrocities furnished a good excuse for executing such a plan.

James Marshal, commandant of Washington County, favored a retaliatory expedition, and Colonel David Williamson was authorized by him to carry it out. Marching with about three hundred men, he reached the Delaware village of Gnadenhutten on March 7. The Americans were received in a friendly manner by the natives and for three days they enjoyed the primitive hospitality of the Indians. Then on Sunday they gathered the villagers, about ninety in all, into their church, and while they were singing hymns, set upon them and massacred men, women and children, only one person escaping with his life.

When the victorious army returned to Pittsburgh it attacked a small

---

[23] Robertson, *Petitions of Early Inhabitants of Kentucky*, pp. 68–69; *C.V.S.P.*, III, 523; *Official Letters of the Governors of Virginia*, III, 368; Hening, *Statutes*, XI, 85; Marshall, *Kentucky*, I, 159; Butler, *Kentucky*, p. 141.

body of Indians who had been living on an island near the town and killed several of them. They wished to kill Colonel John Gibson and his squaw because he was supposed to be friendly to the natives, but General Irvine protected Gibson.[24]

Irvine wrote to his wife describing the massacre in all its brutality, but ended by saying that he did not know what was right in the matter and asking her not to talk of it. In other words, he knew that it was not safe to speak his mind. John Cannon and Dorsey Pentecost condemned it. Thus, as far as one can discover, the leaders of the Pennsylvania party in the region were responsible for the massacre, which was condemned by several leaders of the old Croghan-Virginia group. This was a reversal of rôles since the days of Dunmore and Connolly when the Virginia faction was bitterly condemned by the Pennsylvania adherents for their hostility toward the natives in the incidents leading up to Dunmore's War.[25]

The war party, not satisfied with the Gnadenhutten massacre, urged another campaign against the natives. Irvine used his influence to have William Crawford put in command of this expedition, and on May 25 he set out for the Wyandotte and Shawnee towns on the Sandusky. He had a force of about four hundred men with Colonel David Williamson as second in command. After a slow march he met the Indians in the neighborhood of the Sandusky towns. After getting the worst of the fight during that day and the next the American force retreated. Many were killed and some were cut off. Colonel Crawford was captured and slowly burned at the stake by the natives in their traditional manner. Simon Girty was a witness to this execution which is said to have been the last of its kind in this country.[26]

The political situation in western Pennsylvania was about as chaotic during 1782 as was the military. The new-State movement was being actively agitated by Pentecost, Benjamin Johnson, Thomas Smallman, and James Innes—all leaders of the Virginia-Croghan group. The adherents of this faction lived mostly in the region west of the Youghiogeny River, that is, in the area which had been claimed by Virginia and which was now recognized as a part of Pennsylvania.[27]

[24] James, Clark, pp. 263–264; Hassler, Old Westmoreland, pp. 156–160.

[25] Darlington, Fort Pitt, pp. 238–240; William Croghan to B. Gratz, April 20, 1782, Croghan–Gratz MSS., H.S.P.; Pentecost to Pres. Moore, May 8, 1782, Pa. Arch., series 1, IX, 540–541; Craig, The Olden Time, II, 536–537.

[26] Irvine to Washington, May 21, 1782, Sparks, Letters to Washington, III, 509–510; same to same, July 11, 1782, ibid., pp. 522–524; James, Clark, pp. 264–267; Kellogg, British Régime, pp. 182–183.

[27] Crumrine, Washington County, pp. 231–235; Irvine to Washington, April 20, 1782, Sparks, Letters to Washington, III, 501–504; Craig, The Olden Time, II, 536–537; Pa. Arch., series 1, IX, 572–573; Innes and Smallman to B. Gratz, Nov. 12,

The land claims of Croghan and the Indiana Company were partly responsible for the strength of the secession movement. Now that Pennsylvania's authority had been established Croghan would lose all his surveys and could hope only for compensation elsewhere, and the best of the Indiana lands would also fall within Pennsylvania. Since a committee of Congress had expressed itself favorably toward these claims there was at least some hope for remuneration. James Innes, having the situation of the settlers in mind, discussed the question with Edmund Randolph, who wrote to Governor Harrison suggesting that the Indiana tract be divided into two parts and half of it sold to the settlers at a low price, the proceeds being used to compensate the company. But the company was not overly optimistic since Virginia no longer had jurisdiction, and it was extremely doubtful whether it could, even with the backing of Congress, secure indemnification for its losses. At least General Irvine, a silent member of the company, held this view of the matter. On November 13, 1782, Samuel Wharton, who had returned from France the previous year, wrote from Philadelphia to Trent:

This hasty line is just to inform you and I desire you will write to Mr. Morgan—that the inhabitants westward of the Alleghany Mountains have by beat of drum declared themselves an independent state, by the name of *Transylvania*. It is said there are 5,000 men, good marksmen, who have associated themselves to defend their independence. Some of them have crossed the Ohio and are settling the Indian lands. This transaction, jointed with an important *late* one, will most probably bring western affairs to a quick issue. It is alleged that Mr. P-ti-co-t is at the bottom of this western Revolution. This is the substance of what Congress and the Council of Pennsylvania have received from Genl. Irvine. I submit to Mr. Morgan and you whether any measures should be taken by the company, or whether any person should, in their behalf, immediately proceed to Ft. Pitt and learn the true object in view.[28]

These Western activities looked ominous to the speculators, and Trent and the Gratz brothers, who were now concerned, bestirred themselves. Meetings of the company were held in Philadelphia and during April, 1783, Congress was again memorialized in behalf of both Indiana and the Vandalia organizations.[29]

1782, Ohio Company MSS., H.S.P.; Madison to Randolph, Nov. 19, 1782; Madison papers, L. of C.

[28] S(amuel) W(harton) to Trent, Nov. 13, 1782, Ohio Company MSS., H.S.P.

[29] Minutes of meeting of the Indiana Company, May 8, 1783, *ibid.;* Trent to Gratz, Dec. 6, 1782, *ibid.;* C.V.S.P., III, 133–135, 542; *Journal of the House of Delegates,* Nov. 16, 1783, p. 13; William Croghan to B. Gratz, Jan. 31, 1783, Gratz–Croghan MSS., H.S.P., pub. in Byars, *Gratz,* pp. 211–212; *ibid.,* p. 214; Trent to Irvine, April 9, 1783, Irvine MSS., VII, 110, H.S.P.; Irvine to Trent, April 23, 1783, Etting MSS., Generals of the Revolution, III, 69, H.S.P.; Cont. Cong. MSS., 77, f. 222; *Journals of the Continental Congress,* XXIV, 276, 322.

In the midst of the wrangle, death removed one of the principals. George Croghan—who could never resist pushing out his boundary to include any fine land he saw and of whom Crawford once wrote Washington that he "would not tell him where the Land Lys and I am Afraid to tell him till he Runs the Line for I think if he new of it he would run it in one [on] purpose to have the Seling of it to you,"—was in August, 1782, reduced to the ultimate six feet of earth. After so many years on the distant frontier, scheming for wealth and lands, he died possessed of scarcely more than the "litel farm" of which he had long before written to Sir William Johnson.

The political situation was further confused by suits which were brought in the courts of Washington and Westmoreland Counties against members of the Virginia party who had aided Clark in his efforts to raise troops in the neighborhood for his campaign of 1781. Clark's supporters—the men who acted as county officials under Virginia jurisdiction—were no longer protected by Virginia law, and were at the mercy of their opponents. This matter was brought to the attention of the Virginia assembly which refused to provide for the running of the boundary line unless Pennsylvania would agree to respect the previous acts of the Virginia counties formerly exercising jurisdiction in the disputed area, especially in regard to land titles. Pennsylvania met the terms, and during 1783 arrangements were made for the joint survey, which was finally accomplished the following year. Thus the long-drawn-out controversy was settled.[30]

Before that time the new-State movement had subsided. On December 3, 1782, Pennsylvania passed an act making it treason to advocate secession from the State, and the Reverend James Finley was sent to the Western country to investigate the situation. This seems to have put an end to the agitation, for little more was heard of it at this time.[31]

At the beginning of 1782 the question of the Virginia cession was still before Congress. The committee report of November 3 of the previous year had never been acted on, but on April 18 it was brought up for discussion. Arthur Lee then introduced a resolution providing that, before voting, every member should declare on oath whether or not he was directly or indirectly interested in any of the companies claiming lands in opposition to claims of those States which were offering to make cessions. His proposal was supported by the members from the Southern

---

[30] John Neville to Clark, April 14, 1782, Bodley, *Clark*, p. 173; *Journal of the House of Delegates*, June 15, 1783, p. 51; Thomas Hutchins, *et al.* to Rev. James Madison, *et al.*, Oct. 16, 1783, Hutchins MSS., H.S.P.; *Pa. Arch.*, series 1, X, 171.
[31] *Ibid.*, X, 40, 41, 168.

States, and further consideration of the committee report was dropped.[32]

The question was brought up again on May 1, when Theodorick Bland proposed a resolution to the same effect as that which Lee had introduced on the former occasion. The committee report was now spread on the journals for the first time, but further consideration was postponed, New York voting with the Southern delegates against postponement. The question was again introduced on May 6 and resulted in another postponement, only Virginia and South Carolina voting against it at this time.[33]

Virginia meanwhile was becoming thoroughly disgruntled at the way in which her proffered cession was treated by Congress, for she was convinced that it was the interests of the land companies which were preventing a settlement. Madison, one of the strongest proponents of the cession, wrote to Arthur Lee that he was ready to drop the whole business, and Patrick Henry and the Lees were showing signs of disaffection. The Virginia assembly appointed a committee, consisting of Jefferson, Mason, Randolph, Arthur Lee, and Thomas Walker, to draw up a statement vindicating the claim of the State to the Western territory. Randolph undertook the drafting of the report, but he made slow progress and the document was not submitted until the May session of 1784—too late to have any bearing on the settlement of the issue. He stressed especially the fact that the colonial governors of Virginia had made many grants of Western lands under British authority, though temporary restrictions were at times issued, and that their right to do this was not questioned before the Revolution. He pointed out also that the proclamation line of 1763 was not intended as a new Western boundary of the colonies. And, of course, the assumption that colonial charter boundaries were considered valid in the case of some of the States and not in the case of others would not bear scrutiny.[34]

On September 25, 1782, Congress again appealed to the States with Western lands to cede them without conditions, and on October 29 the

[32] *Journals of the Continental Congress*, XXII, 191–194; Sparks, *Writings of Washington*, VIII, 547–549; Craig, *The Olden Time*, I, 557ff.; J. C. Welling, *Land Politics of the United States*, pp. 20–24.

[33] *Journals of the Continental Congress*, XXII, 223–232, 234, 240–241; Madison to Arthur Lee, May (?), 1782, Arthur Lee MSS., Harvard U. library.

[34] George Mason to Randolph, Oct. 19, 1782, George Mason papers, L. of C.; *Journal of the House of Delegates*, Nov. 19, 1782, p. 24; *ibid.*, Nov. 26, 1783, p. 35; Turner, "Western State-Making," *A.H.R.*, I, 257; Rowland, *Mason*, II, 22, 65; Conway, *Randolph*, p. 47; Byars, *Gratz*, pp. 371–372; Fitzpatrick, *Writings of Washington*, II, 469n.; Henry, *Henry*, II, 219; Jefferson to Madison, June 17, 1783, *Writings of Jefferson* (Memorial ed.) IV, 443; Ford, *Letters of Joseph Jones*, pp. 90–91; Randolph to Arthur Lee, July 18, 1782, Arthur Lee MSS., Harvard U. library; same to same, Aug. 10, 1782, *ibid.*

New York cession was finally accepted. Another appeal was made to the States on April 18, 1783, but no progress at all was being made, and it was clear that there would have to be concessions by both sides before a settlement could be reached. Some members of Congress were for using a strong hand, but though the anti-Virginia group had a majority in that body and though they constantly argued that the right to the Western country had devolved upon Congress as a result of the War, yet no actual threat of forcible occupation was made. In the first place, the Articles of Confederation forbade it; in the second, if Congress were to determine the boundaries of Virginia, why might it not fix those of New York as well?—a question which the Vermont issue reduced to a very real basis.[35]

By June 4, 1783, Congress had decided to give ground. The matter of the Virginia cession was submitted to a new committee, which was directed to report without passing on the question of Virginia's title, and the land company claims were not brought forward in this connection. The New Jersey delegation, which now assumed the rôle of leading champion of the land companies, protested against this action but to no avail. On June 20 the committee reported, and New Jersey again protested. Finally, on September 13, the report was again taken up. It recommended acceptance of the Virginia cession minus the seventh and eighth reservations, which provided that Virginia's title to her remaining land be guaranteed by Congress and that all private land purchases from the natives in the ceded territory should be invalidated. By way of explanation it was stated that Congress had agreed not to go into the question of conflicting claims and that the provision that the land should be used for the common benefit of all the States should cover the proviso against private purchases from the Indians. The report was adopted, with Maryland and New Jersey dissenting.[36]

Joseph Jones thought that Virginia would agree to these terms, and he and Madison were indefatigable in promoting their cause in the State. Their efforts finally met with success; on December 22, 1783, the assembly agreed to the terms of Congress. The Indiana Company at this time induced New Jersey to appoint as its agent George Morgan, who was now living near Princeton, thus enabling him to present its case as one between the two States; but on March 1, 1784, Congress put its final seal upon the transaction.[37]

[35] Jones to Washington, Feb. 27, 1783, Ford, *Letters of Joseph Jones*, pp. 101–102.
[36] *Journals of the Continental Congress*, XXIV, 406–409, XXV, 554–564; Alvord, *The Illinois Country*, pp. 381 ff.
[37] Turner, "Western State-Making," *A.H.R.*, I, 254; Cont. Cong. MSS., 41, X, 99–103; Jones to Jefferson, Dec. 21, 1783, Ford, *Letters of Joseph Jones*, pp. 133–135;

It had been a long and bitter struggle, and neither side could claim to have won a complete victory. Virginia deserves well of the country for having defeated the schemes of the united Illinois and Wabash land companies, whose claims, in the first place, were based upon the shoddiest of foundations. Though she did not get an outright acknowledgment of her claims to the remaining territory, it can be said that a tacit recognition was implied, for if Congress considered Virginia's cession of the Northwest as worth anything, it had to admit that her claim to the unceded territory was also of value; and as to that area, there were no conflicting claims of jurisdiction with any of the States. Only the Indiana and Vandalia Companies disputed her title to the soil. Furthermore, when the final cession was made, a motion was introduced to add a proviso stating that acceptance of the cession should not be construed as implying the validity of Virginia's claim to the remaining territory, and this was voted down, with only Rhode Island, New Jersey, and Pennsylvania in favor. New Jersey alone voted against accepting the cession in its final form.[38]

same to same, Dec. 29, 1783, *ibid.*, pp. 135–138; also *ibid.*, pp. 132–133; *Journal of the House of Delegates*, Dec. 8, 1783, p. 53; *Journals of the Continental Congress*, XXVI, 89–90, 110–117; document dated Dec. 22, 1783, Arthur Lee MSS., Harvard U. library; Morgan's petition to Congress, March 1, 1784, Morgan MSS., Ill. Hist. Survey, Urbana, Ill.

[38] Mohr, *Federal Indian Relations*, p. 102ff.

CHAPTER XXI

THE TREATY OF 1783 AND THE WEST

DURING 1780 Franklin's situation at Passy underwent marked changes. Having been recalled by Congress, Arthur Lee prepared to return to America in the spring of that year, and Samuel Wharton and Thomas Hutchins planned to sail with him on the privateer frigate *Alliance*. Captain Hutchins had just been caught redhanded in his spying and speculating activities in London, and much of his correspondence with Wharton seized. After having been imprisoned for a time he was released and ordered by the British to join his regiment and sail for America, but gave it out that he had gone to Wales for his health. He hinted at a journey to Russia also, but actually he went to Paris and put himself under the protecting wing of Franklin. Bearing a letter of recommendation from the philosopher to Congress, he presently appeared before that body and was commissioned geographer of the United States and assigned to General Greene's army in the South.[1]

There was considerable difficulty over the sailing of the *Alliance* because Arthur Lee insisted that Congress had commissioned Captain Landais to command, while Franklin had put the ship under command of Captain John Paul Jones. Wharton finally was left behind, but made the crossing later in the year and was soon traitorously engaged in sending information to the British. During 1782 he and Arthur Lee faced each other again as members of Congress.[2]

As soon as Lee reached Philadelphia he submitted his accounts to Congress on October 17, 1780, and asked for a hearing, since he assumed that his recall implied censure of his conduct. He submitted also the be-

[1] Edward Williams to "Monsieur Chevalier," Feb. 22, 1780, Hutchins MSS., H.S.P.; same to Mons. P. Steptoe, March 13, 1780, *ibid.;* P. Drouillard to Hutchins, March 20, 1780, *ibid.;* Bigelow, *Works of Franklin,* VIII, 203–204; *Journals of the Continental Congress,* XIX, 187, XX, 475–476, 738.

[2] Arthur Lee to President of Congress, Aug. 13, 1781, Arthur Lee MSS., Harvard U. library; John Bondfield to Arthur Lee, April 15, 1780, *ibid.;* Lee, *Arthur Lee,* pp. 83, 272; Wharton to Franklin, May 15, 1780, Franklin MSS., XVIII, 86, A.P.S.; same to same, June 14, 1780, *ibid.,* XVIII, 141; same to same, Oct. 5, 1780, *ibid.,* XX, 13; Franklin to Coffyn, June 13, 1781, Franklin MSS., Misc. III, L. of C.; Cont. Cong. MSS., 193, ff. 73, 77, 89, 93, 97; Ford, *Letters of Joseph Jones,* pp. 68–70; Ford, *Letters of William Lee,* III, 800–801n., 851; Bigelow, *Works of Franklin,* VIII, 263–264; Isham, *Deane Papers,* I, 446–448; S(amuel) W(harton) to D. C(onway?), Jan. 25, 1781, P.R.O., C.O., series 5, 101, f. 529; *ibid.,* f. 533.

jeweled portrait of the King which had been presented to him on his departure from France. A vote was taken on committing this report, and only New York, New Jersey, and North Carolina opposed.[3]

On December 1, 1780, the committee reported that Lee should be allowed to keep the royal portrait and that no properly supported charges had been lodged against him. This was making very light of all that Deane had had to say regarding Lee, who was sufficiently encouraged to submit, on December 7, a letter criticizing Franklin's conduct of affairs in France, especially in its commercial phases. The committee to which this letter was submitted reported by Theodorick Bland, on January 2, 1781, that a day should be set aside to consider the recall of Franklin.[4]

On March 28 following the Board of War made a report on the supply business as conducted in France and gave a clean bill to Franklin and his aides, putting all the blame for the *Alliance* incident upon Lee. Having heard in France of the situation, Franklin tendered his resignation in April, but it was not accepted nor was the report of the committee which called for his removal ever acted upon. In fact, the spirit of Congress underwent a decided change during 1781, and Franklin's friends gained complete ascendancy.[5]

Franklin was now left alone in charge of the American mission at Passy, and there can be no doubt that he was much happier than he had been, even though he had to carry on much of the correspondence himself. His grandson Temple was still with him, acting in the capacity of secretary. Bancroft, too, was with him at times, but this enterprising person was often on his travels. It was unfortunate for Franklin that he now had to write many of his own letters, for this necessitated his putting his name to numerous documents which formerly would have been signed by Deane. It enables us, however, to know that the aged philosopher was fully concerned in the various commercial enterprises of which Deane had once had active charge.[6]

The arms furnished to Congress by France came directly out of the royal arsenals; the contracts for clothing were handled directly by Chaumont working in cooperation with Vergennes, the money for this purpose

[3] *Journals of the Continental Congress*, XVIII, 951–953.

[4] *Ibid.*, XVIII, 1114–1115; XIX, 13–14; Burnett, V, 425–426.

[5] *Journals of the Continental Congress*, XIX, 316; XXI, 900; Hale, *Franklin in France*, pp. 427–430, 450–451, 454.

[6] J. Holker to Franklin, April 16, 1780, Franklin MSS., XVIII, 47, A.P.S.; Bancroft to Franklin, Aug. 25, 1781, *ibid.*, XXII, 125; Holker to W. T. Franklin, Sept. 4, 1781, *ibid.*, CIII, 95; Bigelow, *Works of Franklin*, VIII, 344–345; John Shaffer(?) to Gérard, May 5, 1781, Franklin MSS., Misc., II, H.S.P.; John Shaffer to "Bernard," Aug. 10, 1781, *ibid.*; P. Thompson to Franklin, Aug. 24, 1781, *ibid.*; J. H. Shaffer to Franklin, Sept. 27, 1781, *ibid.*; Franklin to Clifford and Teysset, June 8, 1781, Franklin MSS., Misc. IV, L. of C.

not passing through Franklin's hands. Franklin's nephew, Jonathan Williams at Nantes, and the firm of Gourlade and Moylan at L'Orient were agents for Chaumont. The privateering business was still in Chaumont's charge and John Paul Jones was still complaining of the disgraceful contract which Chaumont had forced upon him and of the difficulty which he had in getting from him the prize money for himself and his crews. Chaumont was now practically in bankruptcy and it became necessary for Franklin to assist him. The Doctor wrote to Robert Livingston as though the contract of which Jones complained had been entered into voluntarily by the captains of Jones's ships, but Jones, though taking care to save his face with his employers, told a different story.[7]

One incident in this connection is quite revealing. A distinguished chemist of Vienna, Doctor Ingen-Housz, turned over eight thousand livres to Wharton, just before the American left for Philadelphia, to be invested in the commercial enterprises of the American mission. He was told that a profit of from twenty-five to eighty-fold might be expected. But after Wharton quitted France the Viennese doctor could hear nothing further from him, and he constantly plied Franklin with letters on the subject. For about three years he kept up his correspondence, and Franklin twice told him that he never heard from Wharton, although he was in correspondence with this defaulting merchant all the while.[8]

The firm of Richard Neave and Son of London had been before the War the financial backers of the old firm of Baynton, Wharton and Morgan, and Neave now complained that Wharton had left Paris without settling their accounts, thus ruining his house. Franklin apparently was unable to do anything for Neave, but through his agency Ingen-

[7] Arthur Lee, *Observations on Certain Commercial Transactions in France* (Philadelphia, 1780), pamphlet in L. of C.; R. H. to A. Lee, April 24, 1780, Lee MSS., Harvard U. library; John Bondfield to A. Lee, Jan. 22, 1780, *ibid.;* S. Wharton to John Brown, March 23, 1781, *ibid.; Journals of the Continental Congress,* XIX, 318; ——(?) to Holker, Oct. 5, 1781, Holker MSS., Mason collection; acct. of Franklin with Chaumont, 1780, Franklin MSS., VII, 4, H.S.P.; Jonathan Williams to Franklin, Aug. 23, 1782, Franklin MSS., Misc., III, H.S.P.; same to same, Oct. 10, 1782, *ibid.;* same to same, Oct. 18, 1782, *ibid.;* Williams, Moore and Co. to (Franklin), Nov. 6, 1782, *ibid.;* Wharton, *Diplomatic Correspondence,* VI, 113; Burnett, V, 425–426; Ford, *Letters of William Lee,* III, 812; J. P. Jones to Gourlade and Moylan, July 23, 1780, Cont. Cong. MSS., 193, f. 5; D. Coffyn to Franklin, March 10, 1781, Franklin MSS., XXI, 100, A.P.S.

[8] S. Wharton to Ingen-Housz, Feb. 29, 1780, Franklin MSS., LV, 90, A.P.S.; Ingen-Housz to Franklin, April 7, 1781, *ibid.,* XXI, 136; Wharton to Franklin, June 13, 1781, *ibid.,* XXII, 44; same to same, Oct. 22, 1785, *ibid.,* XXXIII, 224; Ingen-Housz to Franklin, Aug. 29, 1781, *ibid.,* XXII, 126; same to Wharton, June 12, 1782, *ibid.,* XXV, 94; same to Franklin, Feb. 26, 1783, *ibid.,* XXVII, 145; same to same, Nov. 19, 1783, *ibid.,* XXX, 95; same to same, June 11, 1785, *ibid.,* XXXIII, 133; Wharton, *Diplomatic Correspondence,* IV, 110–111; Isaac All to Franklin, (?) 15, 1780, Franklin MSS., Misc., II, H.S.P.; Franklin to Coffyn, Aug. 12, 1781, Franklin MSS., Misc., IV, L. of C.; Franklin to Ingen-Housz, Oct. 2, 1781, *ibid.;* same to same, Apr. 26, 1784, *ibid.,* VI; same to same, Sept. 2, 1786(?), *ibid.,* VII.

Housz was finally paid eight thousand pounds, a fair profit on his investment.[9]

Silas Deane was also a source of embarrassment to Franklin during these years. The lack of vouchers having prevented his getting his accounts settled by Congress, he returned to Europe during the spring of 1780. At the time of his departure he advised Robert Morris to invest in lands north of the Ohio, and though the connection of these two men with the united Illinois-Wabash Company did not become a matter of record until the next year, the relation was probably established at about this time. Deane was also to sell some lands for Joseph Wharton in Europe, and he was in correspondence with James Wilson of Pennsylvania about commercial matters.[10]

Early in 1781 Deane was again in Paris, and Franklin's old friend Thomas Walpole also was there. Walpole was trying unsuccessfully to insinuate himself into the peace negotiations as special agent in connection with the spoliation claims of the French merchants of St. Eustatia who had been plundered after Admiral Rodney's victory. Deane took this occasion to renew his speculations in London, but he was soon involved in more serious business.[11]

In July, 1781, he wrote a series of letters expressing a desire for reconciliation with England, thereby revealing himself as a traitor to the American cause. These he turned over to Lord North so that they might be published in America as intercepted correspondence. For this service he received remuneration from the British government. Both Lord North and the King thought that the letters were too obvious, but they were published as planned, North saying that Deane had acted fairly in putting himself in his power.[12]

In America the publication was suspected as a put-up job, but Deane's friends were placed in a quandary. Morris at once disowned him, as did Jay and most of his other friends. On March 4, 1782, Franklin wrote to

[9] Neave and Son to Franklin, March 5, 1780, Franklin MSS., XVII, 111, A.P.S.; same to same, March 25, 1781, ibid., XXI, 124; same to same; Oct. 31, 1781, ibid., XXIII, 36.

[10] Deane to Morris, April 8, 15, 1780, Morris MSS., N.Y.P.L.; same to same, April 17, 1780, Isham, Deane Papers, IV, 124–127; Deane to Joseph Wharton, May 10, 1780, ibid., IV, 146–148; Thos. Barclay to Robt. Morris, June 8, 1784, ibid., V, 300; Byars, Gratz, p. 66; Deane to James Wilson, Dec. 1, 1780, Wilson MSS., III, 15, H.S.P.; Deane to Franklin, Jan. 27, 1781, Franklin MSS., XXI, 34, A.P.S.

[11] Fortescue, Correspondence of King George the Third, V, 122–123; Donne, Correspondence of King George the Third, II, 332–333; Isham, Deane Papers, IV, 303–304, 547–548; Bancroft to Franklin (1782?), Franklin MSS., XLI, 94, A.P.S.; Deane certificate, Jan. 13, 1781, ibid., XXI, 21; de Castries to Walpole, April 19, 1781, P.R.O., F.O., 95, pkt. 2; Walpole to Germain, May 31, 1781, ibid.; Germain to Walpole, June 19, 1781, ibid.; same to same, Jan. 29, 1782, ibid.

[12] Fortescue, Correspondence of King George the Third, V, 200, 255–256, 260; Wharton, Diplomatic Correspondence, I, 565.

Congress that Deane was disaffected, but this was no news to Congress and it was no news to Franklin. Deane had begun denouncing his native land as soon as he returned to Europe, and Elkanah Watson, an American traveler and business man, visited him and heard him talk. Seeing Franklin shortly thereafter, Watson reported to him that Deane was disloyal; Franklin replied that he had heard such reports but had been unwilling to credit them. Deane continued to correspond with Franklin after the publication of his "intercepted" letters. When Franklin finally wrote to Congress about the matter, he urged that the traitor's accounts should be settled. On August 31, 1783, Franklin wrote Deane expressing "best wishes that you may hereafter so prudently conduct yourself as to recover the esteem and respect you once possessed among your countrymen." Franklin, in fact, never really denounced Deane, and to have done so would have been dangerous, for Deane knew too much.[13]

On January 22, 1780, John Jay arrived at Cadiz with the object of making a treaty with Spain, and on February 5 following John Adams reached Paris in the capacity of peace negotiator for Congress. They were both instructed to insist on the Mississippi River boundary and the free navigation of that river.

On March 18 Congress passed an act calling for the issuance of a new currency and devaluing the old issues at the rate of forty to one. Vergennes, Chaumont, and the French merchants objected strenuously to this arrangement, for the merchants expected to collect in specie value at the high rates which the old currency had necessitated, and much profit would be lost if they were not able to do this. Vergennes protested to Adams about the matter, and Adams informed him that France was under as much obligation to America as America was to her. Vergennes then announced that he would hold no further intercourse with Adams, and Franklin wrote to Congress saying that Adams was discredited at the French Court. He wrote to Vergennes also disapproving the conduct of his colleague.[14]

However undiplomatic Adams may have been, it is clear that Franklin,

[13] Isham, *Deane Papers,* IV, 400–402, 543–544, V, 15, 192; Sumner, *Morris,* I, 233; Reed, *Reed,* II, 373–374; Elkanah Watson, *Men and Times of the Revolution* (New York, 1856) pp. 130–131; Deane to Morris, Sept. 10, 1781, Morris MSS., N.Y.P.L., Morris to Ridley, July 8, 1782, *ibid.;* Paine to Morris, Feb. 20, 1782, *Collections of New York Historical Society, 1878,* I, 475; Simeon (?) Deane to Franklin, Jan. 18, 1782, Franklin MSS., XXIV, 30, A.P.S.; William Wilkinson to W. T. Franklin, Feb. 27, 1782, *ibid.,* CIV, 17; Silas Deane to Franklin, March 30, 1782, *ibid.,* XXIV, 159; Franklin to Livingston, March 4, 1782, A. Lee MSS., Harvard U. library; Byars, *Gratz,* pp. 218–219.

[14] Wood, *Congressional Control of Foreign Relations,* p. 85; *Journals of the Continental Congress,* XVI, 262–267, Sumner, *Morris,* I, 87; Bigelow, *Works of Franklin,* VIII, 281–282; Hale, *Franklin in France,* pp. 380–381; James Duane to Washington, Dec. 9, 1780, Sparks, *Letters to Washington,* III, 169–175.

having rid himself of Lee, wished to keep American affairs entirely in his own hands, for there was still much profit for his and Vergennes' friends in the situation. This fact is illustrated by further incidents. South Carolina sent Captain Alexander Gillon, and Pennsylvania dispatched James Searle to France to negotiate loans for those States. The States were under the same necessity of borrowing as was Congress. They certainly had a right to do so, but Franklin set himself to defeat the efforts of both agents, who reported that Franklin and his mercantile friends wished to keep all the profits in their hands. Searle wrote to Joseph Reed in regard to the matter, stating:

. . . unless some speedy and effectual measures are taken on our side the water to counteract the baneful influence that the conversation of the disappointed, mortified, and scheming G [Deane] has upon the minds of many people here, I fear very bad consequences may attend it.

This man has the countenance and protection of C [Franklin] to a very great degree, by which means he is attended to, and he is doing the greatest injury to 16 [Arthur Lee] in every company he can get admittance to.

There are others also, who make no scruple to treat the counsels of 16 [Lee] with every possible insult and misrepresentation, I mean a certain Doctor Bancroft, who does it openly at the public table of C [Franklin]. Mr. Cha-m-t, the great patron of O [C?], has also become outrageous and open-mouthed against the measures of A Z [Congress], which he represents and calls wicked and villanous, and has even threatened to expose, as he terms it, their base conduct to the world. All this is done in the most open manner at the place of residence of C [Franklin]. I find Mr. C. the declared enemy of private state loans, and have therefore not been able to get any assistance, or the offer of any, through that channel, and the two persons above mentioned, I mean G [Deane] and Bancroft, are using every means in their power to counteract the public as well as private loans, which loans, if effected through any other than a particular channel, would interfere with their connection in the public supply of our army, etc. Alas, Sir, there are, I fear, Arnolds in France, natives of America.[15]

Meanwhile at the instance of Spain the French government and its minister in Philadelphia, Luzerne, had set themselves against the Western ambitions of Congress. On January 31, 1780, Luzerne let it be known that it was desirable for the Western boundary of the States to be fixed at the proclamation line of 1763, and, of course, the navigation of the Mississippi was to be surrendered. Nevertheless, on October 4, 1780, Congress decided to adhere to its original instructions to Jay and Adams as to boundaries and the navigation of the Mississippi. Two days

[15] Reed, *Reed,* II, 455–457; Gillon to Stripps and Mey, June (?), 1780, Lee MSS., Harvard U. library; "J. B." to Arthur Lee, Feb. 24, 1781, *ibid.;* J. Adams to A. Lee, Oct. 10, 1782, *ibid.*

previously Franklin had written to Jay and expressed himself strongly as favoring this policy.[16]

But British forces were in occupation of Georgia and South Carolina, and France now began to suggest the possibility of a peace on the basis of *uti possidetis*. The assistance of Spain was sorely needed, and Jay's dispatches made it clear that no treaty could be had without surrendering the navigation of the Mississippi, which policy, however, Jay personally opposed.

On November 18 the Georgia delegation in Congress proposed that the demand for navigation below the thirty-first parallel be given up, and South Carolina, likewise alarmed over the prospect of being left in British hands, made a similar proposal. On November 22 Theodorick Bland of Virginia wrote to Governor Jefferson advocating this policy, but he was opposed by Madison. However, the situation was tense, Madison finally gave way, and on January 2, 1781, the Virginia House of Delegates voted to give in on the question of navigation. This was the same day on which that body offered to cede the Northwestern territory to Congress.[17]

On February 15, 1781, Jay was instructed by Congress to recede from the claim to navigation of the Mississippi below the thirty-first degree if that should be necessary in order to negotiate a treaty of alliance with Spain. Jay made the proposition in a guarded manner, and Spain still refused to negotiate. On August 10 at the instance of Morris a resolution was introduced to empower Jay to make "such further cession of the right of these United States to the navigation of the Mississippi as he may think proper." But the reaction to such concessions had been unfavorable and the resolution was unanimously defeated. On March 21, 1782, Congress congratulated Jay on his cautious conduct, and on August 7 he was instructed to make no further overtures.[18]

Meanwhile the complexion of Congress was changing. Luzerne, aided by his able secretary Barbé-Marbois—for whom Jefferson wrote his "Notes on Virginia"—and also by the use of bribery, was building up his strength in Congress. That this was not an extremely difficult matter is indicated by a memorial of November 16, 1783, from John Vardill to

[16] *Journals of the Continental Congress,* XVI, 114, XVIII, 900–902; Butler, *Kentucky,* pp. 139–141; Wharton, *Diplomatic Correspondence,* III, 488–490; Burnett, V, 28–29; Timothy Pitkin, *A Political and Civil History of the United States of America* (New Haven, 1828) II, 91–93.

[17] *Journals of the Continental Congress,* XVIII, 1070–1072, 1131–1132; Rives, *Madison,* I, 236–251; Bodley, *Kentucky,* I, 251ff.; Burnett, V, p. xxxiii, 455–456; Ford, *Letters of Joseph Jones,* pp. 51–52, 60–62.

[18] S. F. Bemis, *The Diplomacy of the American Revolution* (New York, 1935) p. 107; Wharton, *Diplomatic Correspondence,* IV, 257–258; *Journals of the Continental Congress,* XIX, 151–154, XXI, 853, XXII, 142, 449–451, 455–456.

Parliament in which the author said that he had secured much valuable information by a correspondence with Jay, Livingston, Gouverneur Morris, and James Duane and that he had secured the favor of two members of Congress by an offer of judgeships to be awarded at the end of the War. In 1780 Luzerne had written that members of Congress generally used their information for private speculations.[19]

Robert Morris was in close cooperation with Luzerne, and on February 20, 1781, Congress elected Morris Superintendent of Finance. Washington had hoped that the post would go to his aide, Alexander Hamilton. While holding this office Morris continued his speculating ventures with Deane, Holker, and others, and even speculated in the army contracts which he awarded. On March 14, 1783, Joseph Reed wrote to General Greene, "Mr. Morris has been for a long time the *Dominus Factotum* whose dictates none dare to oppose and from whose decisions lay no appeal. He has in fact exercised the power really of the three great departments, and Congress have only had to give their fiat to his mandates."

With the aid of this powerful financier and that of Luzerne, Robert R. Livingston of New York was, on August 10, 1781, elected Secretary for Foreign Affairs over Arthur Lee. The same group succeeded in having General Schuyler put in charge of the War Department.[20] Thus the organization of Congress fell entirely into the hands of the party of the Middle States, with Georgia and South Carolina—animated by their fear of being left out of the Union—usually acting in cooperation with them. The Adamses and their friends still held out against them in New England, but they could usually control only Massachusetts and Connecticut, Roger Sherman, Francis Dana, Artemus Ward, James Lovell, and General Joseph Warren being their principal supporters. Madison, Jones, Bland, and Randolph, who usually represented Virginia during this period, were no partisans of the Lees, but, having surrendered the Northwest, they stood for the Mississippi River boundary. They were supported in this by a majority of the North Carolina delegation. Thus two Southern and

[19] Lewis D. Einstein, *Divided Loyalties, Americans in England During the War of Independence* (New York, 1933) appendix C, quoting P.R.O., A.O., 12, 20, ff. 22–29; Sumner, *Morris*, I, 227; Wood, *Congressional Control of Foreign Relations*, pp. 87–88; Capt. William Armstrong to Sir Guy Carleton, April 1, 1783, Historical Manuscripts Commission, *Report on the American Manuscripts in the Royal Institution of Great Britain*, IV, 1–7.

[20] *Papeles de Cuba, legajo* 1354, 23, L. of C.; *ibid.*, 1281, 4, 13, 61, 64, 134, 170; Sumner, *Morris*, II, 81, 211–212, 298–299; Pringle and Holker vs. Duer and Parker, June, 1807, Holker MSS., Mason collection; note drawn by Benjamin Harrison & Co. on Holker, favor of Marbois, May 1, 1780, *ibid.*; Sparks, *Letters to Washington*, III, 252–254; Reed, *Reed*, II, 372–376; 392–394; Wood, *Foreign Relations*, pp. 97–98; Ford, *Letters of Joseph Jones*, pp. 68–70; J. B. Sanders, *Evolution of Executive Departments of the Continental Congress*, pp. 92, 99, 105–106, 128.

two New England States still stood together in the demand for the New-foundland fisheries and the Mississippi River boundary, but they could make little headway against the Morris-Luzerne group which was prepared to accept a restricted Western limit.[21]

On June 15, 1781, a new peace policy, signalizing the victory of Morris and Luzerne, was adopted by Congress. Vergennes had been trying all along to have Adams subordinated to Franklin in any negotiations which he might undertake. Not succeeding in this, another plan was now adopted. Luzerne notified Congress that Russia and Austria had proposed mediation, and that France was so hard pressed that she might have to accede to terms establishing the *uti possidetis* basis for the settlement of American affairs—in other words, threatening Congress with the loss of South Carolina and Georgia if that body was not more compliant with the wishes of France. On June 6 a motion was made in Congress to appoint Franklin, Jay, Laurens, and Jefferson as additional envoys to cooperate with Adams in the peace parleys, and they were to "make the most candid and confidential communications, upon all subjects, to the ministers of our generous ally the king of France; to undertake nothing in the negotiation for peace without their knowledge and concurrence." Massachusetts, Connecticut, and Virginia voted against this proposal, with North Carolina tied, and the motion failed for lack of a sufficient majority. The next day another vote was taken with the same result. On June 15, however, the instructions were spread on the journal, and on the 18th the committee appointed to confer with the French minister made a lengthy report. Luzerne protested against the currency legislation of Congress, mentioned that his government had made grants and loans amounting to fourteen million livres since the beginning of 1780, and again threatened *uti possidetis* settlement. The next day Congress addressed a letter to Franklin telling of the appointment of the new commissioners. No vote was taken in these final stages of the discussion, but it is clear that Luzerne had used all his resources and had finally broken the resistance of Congress. Under the new instructions everything was left to the discretion of the negotiators except the granting of independence. Luzerne wrote to Vergennes that he had found it easier to get Congress to subordinate the commissioners to him than to Franklin. Under this arrangement no Western boundary except the proclamation line of 1763 could have been expected. Robert Livingston and Gouverneur Morris, in fact, expressed themselves as favoring such a settlement. As late as August, 1782, the Massachusetts-Virginia group

[21] Paul C. Phillips, *The West in the Diplomacy of the American Revolution,* pp. 164, 182; Lee, *Arthur Lee,* II, 274–275, 281.

was still trying to secure more positive instructions to the commissioners on the question of the fisheries and the Western boundary, but the disputed land question prevented any positive action. Adams and Jay protested vigorously against the Congressional instructions which bound them to France.[22]

A detailed discussion of the peace negotiations is not necessary in this place, but certain of the steps which led up to the treaty have a special significance in connection with the situation existing in Congress. On March 5, 1782, Parliament voted for peace with the colonies. France had indicated a desire for peace, and Franklin made overtures to Shelburne. At first Shelburne thought that Franklin intended a separate peace, but it presently became clear that a separate negotiation and a final peace signed in conjunction with France was his idea. He apparently had hoped that his old friend Thomas Pownall would be commissioned by the British government to negotiate with him, and Thomas Walpole also had his aspirations, but Shelburne chose Richard Oswald as his agent to deal with the American commissioners. On April 12 Oswald met Franklin in Paris, but Jay did not arrive until June 23. For some time after his arrival Jay was ill with influenza, and Franklin carried on the discussions with Oswald. Vergennes became alarmed over indications that the British were trying to negotiate a separate peace, and wrote to Luzerne urging that Congress leave everything to the commissioners. On July 9 Franklin presented the British agent with his ideas as to peace terms. These required the recognition of complete independence, the confinement of the boundary of Canada to what it had been before the Quebec Act of 1774, freedom of fishing on the Banks of Newfoundland, and a settlement of the boundaries of the colonies. The surrender of Canada to the United States was mentioned as a desirable, but not an essential, article.[23]

It is amazing that nothing was said of the Mississippi River boundary

[22] Luzerne to Montmorin, May 1, 1780, Add. MSS., 24321, Br. Mus.; Sumner, *Morris*, I, 260; *Journals of the Continental Congress*, XX, 605–607, 608–610, 651–655, 669–676, XXIII, 471; Bemis, *Diplomacy of the American Revolution*, map. 5, p. 238; Gilbert Chinard, *Honest John Adams* (Boston, 1933) p. 168; Luzerne to Vergennes, Feb. 27, 1781(?), P.R.O., C.O., series 5, 40, pt. 3; Charles Thomson MSS., *Collections of the New York Historical Society, 1878*, I, 114–116; E. S. Corwin, *French Policy and the American Alliance of 1778* (Princeton, 1916), pp. 304–305n.; James C. Welling, *The States'-Rights Conflict over the Public Lands*, pp. 411–412.

[23] Bemis, *Diplomacy of the American Revolution*, p. 207; Thomas Pownall to Franklin, May 13, 1782, Franklin MSS., XXV, 70, A.P.S.; Fortescue, *Correspondence of King George the Third*, VI, 40–44; 61, V, 376–377; Shelburne to Oswald, May 21, 1782, P.R.O., F.O., 27, 2; Walpole to Fox, May 27, 1782, *ibid.*; Oswald to Shelburne, June 2, 1782, *ibid.*; Walpole to Grantham, Nov. 25, 1782, P.R.O., F.O., 27, 3; *Journals of the Continental Congress*, XXIII, 596–603; Bigelow, *Works of Franklin*, IX, 348.

or of the navigation of that river; the only inference that can be drawn is that Franklin was prepared to adopt the policy of Vergennes and of the Morris group in Congress on that head. It is true that he had previously written to Jay, on October 2, 1780, in a different tone, and on January 27, 1781, he reiterated his views. Furthermore, on August 12, 1782, about a month after he had given Oswald his views on peace terms he wrote to Livingston that Jay had learned from Count Aranda, the Spanish ambassador to France, that Spain was trying to "coop us up within the Allegheny Mountains," and he hoped Congress would insist on the Mississippi boundary and the free navigation of that river. But Franklin knew that it was now too late for Congress to change its instructions on that head, that the instructions, if followed, would lead to a result similar to that which he now professed to dread, and he had taken no steps to forestall those instructions or to prevent their substantial fulfillment.[24]

After the negotiations and after charges had been brought against Franklin on this head, both Jay and Adams wrote to him and acknowledged that he had not stood against them in their policy. They were right, for Franklin knew when to give in. To have put himself on record as having advocated an unfavorable peace would have been contrary to Franklin's nature, but there can be no doubt that if he had followed his intention to carry out the spirit of the instructions of Congress and consult Vergennes on the essentials of the negotiation, we should not have secured the Mississippi boundary. This is not usually denied, but Franklin's attitude is explained as an instance of complacency and loyalty to a generous ally. Yet the ally was not very generous in regard to boundaries, and Franklin certainly knew what Luzerne had been about in Philadelphia. He was simply but covertly taking the line which had been taken by his friends in Congress.[25]

On August 8 Oswald for the first time received a copy of his yet unsigned commission to treat with the American commissioners on terms of peace. The document was carefully worded so as not to recognize the sovereignty of the United States, but referred to them as "colonies." Jay insisted that the commission be changed so as to accredit Oswald to deal with the plenipotentiaries of the "United States," and the British Ministry agreed. Oswald received his new instructions on September 4,

[24] Sparks, *Works of Franklin*, IX, 382–387. For a different interpretation, see Kellogg, *British Régime*, pp. 186–190.
[25] Wharton, *Diplomatic Correspondence*, IV, 75, 241–242; Franklin to Jay, Jan. 27, 1781, Franklin MSS., Misc., III, L. of C.; Phillips, *West in the Diplomacy of the Revolution*, p. 216ff.; Bigelow, *Works of Franklin*, X, 179–180, 184–185.

and it looked as though the way was cleared for a peace settlement on the basis of Franklin's original proposals.

On September 6 Jay had a conference with Vergennes' secretary, Gérard de Rayneval, brother to Conrad Alexandre Gérard, the former French minister to the United States. In this conference de Rayneval outlined a compromise Western boundary settlement which presumably represented the ideas of Vergennes and his Spanish ally. The country north of the Ohio was to be left to Great Britain, and Spain was to have the territory bounded on the north by the Ohio and Cumberland Rivers, and on the east by a line running irregularly southward from the site of Nashville.[26]

That Franklin and his friends in Congress would have been glad to see the Northwest territory remain in British hands is not unlikely. Deane's and Morris's interest in those lands has already been discussed, and Virginia's cession, if accepted by Congress, precluded the validation of purchases from the Indians, on which ground alone the claim of the united Illinois-Wabash Company rested. British ministers had once proved amenable to the ideas of Thomas Walpole and his friends on American speculations, and they might do so again. But Jay was of another mind. He had been a member of the Morris group in Congress, but he seems to have been suspicious of French policy even before leaving America for Spain. He made his journey to Cadiz on board the same ship with Gérard, who was returning from his Philadelphia mission, and the Frenchman did much to heighten the suspicions of the American diplomat. Certain it is that from the time he set foot upon European soil Jay was the avowed opponent of French and Spanish ideas on the question of peace terms.[27]

These suspicions were still further heightened when, on September 9, de Rayneval, at the instance of Vergennes, left Paris for London to confer with Shelburne. Jay had reason to believe that the French were preparing to sell out their American allies, especially on the matter of the Western boundary, and he was not altogether wrong in his suspicion. The next day one of the British agents put into his hands an intercepted

---

[26] Bemis, *Diplomacy of the American Revolution*, pp. 215–222; Bemis, *Pinckney's Treaty*, pp. 38, 43n.; F. A. Ogg, *The Opening of the Mississippi* (New York, 1904) pp. 394–395; John Fiske, *The Critical Period in American History* (Boston, 1888) pp. 19–20.

[27] Phillips, *The West in the Diplomacy of the Revolution*, pp. 138–140; Sumner, *Morris*, I, 254–255; Daniel Walther, *Gouverneur Morris* (New York, 1934) p. 265; Corwin, *French Policy and the American Alliance of 1778*, 302n.; Elkanah Watson, *Men and Times of the Revolution*, p. 287; Willis F. Johnson, *America's Foreign Relations* (New York, 1916) I, 126.

letter which Luzerne's secretary, Barbé-Marbois, had written to Vergennes. This was quite revealing as to the policy of the French minister in Philadelphia. Jay at once dispatched Benjamin Vaughan, an English friend of Franklin who was preparing to migrate to America, to London in order to counteract the artifices of de Rayneval. Thus was Shelburne notified of the differences between the American and French diplomats, and he prepared to make the most of them. Without consulting Franklin, he defeated Vergennes' attempts to prevent a separate negotiation. New instructions were sent to Oswald, and on October 5 he and Jay agreed on a preliminary draft of the articles of peace. The Mississippi River boundary and the free navigation of the river for both America and Britain were stipulated. Canada was to remain in British hands. Thus it was Jay, with the support of Adams, who won the West for his country. Franklin, left to himself, was apparently prepared to sacrifice it. Secretary Livingston wrote to him protesting against the policy of Jay and Adams. On July 23, 1783, Arthur Lee wrote to Shelburne stating, "I had the pleasure of defending him [Jay] against those men, with whom he [had] cooperated in effecting my removal." [28]

Samuel Wharton had written to Temple Franklin asking that his friend send him a copy of the articles of peace at the first opportunity, but we do not know whether or not his request was granted. Jonathan Williams asked his uncle to use one of his ships in notifying Congress of the settlement. "This," the astute young business man stated, "will be making the public pay what I should otherways lose & what no Man can think unreasonable, . . . It is proper to inform you my Brig has a Cargo on board her. . . . I suppose there can be no objection to her having on board enough to ballast her ; & whether this be Brandy or stones is of no Consequence." This he realized was contrary to regulations as to flags of truce, but he thought the difficulty might be avoided. On April 11, 1783, D. Coffyn of Dunkerque, wrote to Franklin that three vessels had been dispatched for Philadelphia. "I hope," he wrote "my recommendation to the owners of these vessels in favor of Messrs. Bach and Shee (which your Excellency recommended to me in 1779) will make these gentlemen reap the first fruits of peace." Richard Bache was Franklin's

[28] Fortescue, op. cit., VI, 143–144, 161–162, 185–186; C. W. Alvord, Lord Shelburne and the Founding of British–American Goodwill (London, 1926) pp. 10–26; Lee, Arthur Lee, I, 174–176; Bemis, Diplomacy of the American Revolution, pp. 223–242; Sanders, Evolution of Executive Departments, p. 111; Lord Edmond Fitzmaurice, Life of William, Earl of Shelburne (London, 1875–1876) III, 243–244; Wood, Congressional Control of Foreign Relations, p. 97; Benjamin Vaughan to Franklin, March 5, 1782, Franklin MSS., XXIV, 123, A.P.S.; Jay's notes, Dec. 12, 1782, Lee MSS., Harvard U. library; Oswald to Townshend, Sept. 11, 1782, P.R.O., F.O., 27, 2; same to same, Oct. 5, 1782, ibid.; proposed articles of peace, Oct. 8, 1782, ibid.; Oswald to Townshend(?), Oct. 2, 1782, ibid.

son-in-law. Thus the end of the War was unwelcome news to these friends and kinsmen of Franklin, to Thomas Walpole, and doubtless to many others who had profited at the expense of their respective countries.[29]

[29] Fortescue, V, 464; (S. Wharton) to W. T. Franklin, June 21, 1782, Franklin MSS., CIV, 62, A.P.S.; Coffyn to Franklin, April 11, 1783, *ibid.*, XXVIII, 24; Jonathan Williams to Franklin, Dec. 6, 1782, Franklin papers, Misc., III, 70, H.S.P.

CHAPTER XXII

THE MOVEMENT FOR NEW WESTERN STATES, 1784–1785

DURING 1783 William Blount and his North Carolina company had obtained the consent of the Cherokee Indians to settle the Muscle Shoals country, but the transaction was not to be complete until the stipulated quantity of goods should be delivered to the natives. The fact that the Spanish were planning a settlement at the Shoals had a bearing upon the question. Blount now appealed to the Georgia assembly for a grant; on February 20, 1784, this object was accomplished to his satisfaction although an outright grant was not made. By a resolution of this date, a board of seven men was created to inspect and report on the Muscle Shoals lands. These seven were furthermore given the status of justices of the peace for the "District and County of Tennessee." They were authorized to appoint military officers and to grant lands at the rate of an eighth of a dollar per acre, but no person was to have more than a thousand acres. The next day Lachlan McIntosh, Junior, William Downes, Stephen Heard, John Morell, John Donelson, Joseph Martin, and John Sevier were named to constitute the commission. The four Georgians were members of the assembly; the three Carolina members were Blount's appointees. Patrick Henry was not apparently a member of Blount's company, but he took a lively interest in it.[1]

On May 31 Blount wrote to the Georgia commissioners saying that he supposed their object in going into the enterprise was the same as his own, namely, private emolument. He offered to make to each of them a donation of an equal share in the stock of the company. The resolution creating the commission had apparently provided that its members should be compensated for their services, but Blount interpreted the ambiguous wording to mean that they had a right to make a compensation to the company in the form of a land grant, and he urged that this should be as large as possible. He thought, in fact, that

---

[1] Allen D. Chester ed., *The Revolutionary Records of the State of Georgia* (Atlanta, 1908) II, 738–739, III, 492, 525–526; Henry to Joseph Martin, Feb. 4, 1785, Draper MSS., 15ZZ25–28; Alexander Martin to Joseph Martin, Feb. 11, 1784, *ibid.*, 1XX69; copy of Blount's petition, Feb. 28, 1784, J. G. Blount MSS., N.C.H.C.

it might include the whole of the area in the "Bend of the Tennessee," which he estimated to contain three hundred thousand acres "more or less." But if the entire area were not to be had in one survey he was prepared to take up as much as possible in thousand-acre tracts, and wrote to Martin, Donelson, and Sevier that fictitious names could be supplied for this purpose. He urged also that reports, "whether true or false," should be circulated as to the large numbers of people who were planning to settle in the country, alleging that he was going to establish himself there and take out at least fifty families with him. In conclusion, he wished the commissioners "an agreeable Journey and greate choice and great plenty of Chickamogga Squaws." [2]

Plans were made for sending the goods for the Indians to Martin at the Long Island of Holston, and the commissioners were to assemble there during the summer for the expedition to the Shoals. However, only one of the Georgia commissioners, Stephen Heard, arrived, and the goods did not come until he was ready to leave for home. No journey to the Shoals was made at this time, but Heard and Martin, possibly with the aid of Donelson and Sevier, proceeded to organize the county and to appoint officials. Sevier was made colonel-commandant, Donelson lieutenant-colonel, and Valentine Sevier, Junior, major. Donelson became the surveyor of the new jurisdiction. It was planned to open a land office at the Shoals in the following March. [3]

In September Martin was preparing to deliver the goods to the Indians and to get their deed to the "Bent," as the Bend of the Tennessee was commonly termed in the correspondence of the time. In December the commissioners apparently visited the Shoals but we know little of their activities at this stage. In fact, a serious interruption of the Shoals speculation occurred at about the same time. [4]

In August the western part of North Carolina began the process of setting up a government of its own, and the group of speculators who were interested in the "Bent" became entangled in the resulting imbroglio. Though Surveyor Donelson exercised his authority to issue warrants for thousand-acre tracts, no large grant seems to have been made to the company. Only one of the Georgia commissioners took any

[2] A. P. Whitaker, "The Muscle Shoals Speculation," M.V.H.R., XIII, 365–386; Blount to Donelson, March 9, 1784, Draper MSS., 1XX72; Blount to Donelson, Martin, and Sevier, May 31, 1784, J. G. Blount MSS., N.C.H.C.; Blount to Georgia commissioners, May 31, 1784, ibid.

[3] MS. journal, Georgia House of Assembly, Feb. 22, 1785, Georgia Department of Archives, Atlanta; Joseph Martin to William Blount, Aug. 28, 1784, J. G. Blount MSS., N.C.H.C.

[4] Martin to (Christian?), Sept. 6, 1784, William M. Bullitt MSS., Louisville; land warrant to John Sevier, signed by John Donelson, Dec. 22, 1785, Draper MSS., 11DD78a.

active part in the work, and McIntosh made complaints about the proceedings to the governor and council of Georgia. This body, which had not been consulted as to the affair, advised that it should be delayed if any good reason could be found for doing so. This advice was apparently followed for the time being, for no appreciable progress was made by the company during 1784. We shall see, however, that the project was revived, under somewhat altered circumstances, during 1785.[5]

On April 23, 1784, Congress adopted Jefferson's resolutions providing for the creation of new Western States. Among other things, they stipulated that conventions for the organization of territorial governments might be provided for on the initiative of Congress, or the people might take the initiative and petition Congress for that purpose. In either case, it is clear that Congress was to provide for the organization of the convention, and to control the public lands afterward.[6]

In July of the same year North Carolina ceded her Western territory to Congress, allowing one year within which that body might accept or reject the cession. Almost immediately the people of the Holston settlements elected a convention which met on August 23 following for the purpose of organizing a new government within the ceded area. Seeing that they were not yet under the protection of Congress and believing that North Carolina was not likely to pay them much attention while their fate hung in the balance, they thought they were entitled to care for their own interests.[7]

There was much justification for this feeling. During 1783 North Carolina had opened a land office and offered nearly the whole of the Western country for sale, though the Indian claim to a large part of it had never been extinguished. The natives were incensed, and the State made plans for negotiating a treaty with the Cherokee to quiet them, but as soon as the cession to Congress was made plans for the treaty were abandoned. The disparaging remarks about the West which had been made in the assembly while the question of cession was under debate further antagonized the frontiersmen.

The new-State movement in the Holston settlements evidently met with general approval. Both Sevier and Martin cooperated in it, but Arthur Campbell, commandant of Washington County, Virginia, was apparently the driving force behind it. Several leaders in the community vouched for the statement that "Colonel Campbell did, in a convention

---

[5] Alexander Martin to J. G. Blount, Feb. 26, 1785, J. G. Blount MSS., N.C.H.C.; *Revolutionary Records of Georgia*, II, 654–655.

[6] *Journals of the Continental Congress*, XXVI, 274–279; resolution of April 23, 1784, Cont. Cong. MSS., 30.

[7] Williams, *The Lost State of Franklin*, pp. 29–34.

of the North Carolina people, publicly propose to separate himself with the citizens of Washington and Montgomery in Virginia, and joining them declare themselves immediately independent of the States of Virginia and North Carolina, and moreover, stand in the front of the battle between these people and Virginia when necessary." [8] Campbell's brother David and his friend William Cocke were both leaders in the new-State movement. Cocke was he whom, according to his own statement, Lord Dunmore had singled out in 1775 to take command of all the Western country and to whom he offered thousands of British gold as a bribe to enter into the service of the King. The Virginian said he disdained the offer with contempt and "went hand in hand with your oldest & most beloved General in Suppressing enlistments for the British Service and cloathed their officers with Tar & Feathers, . . ." [9] The Holston convention now provided for the inclusion of the contiguous parts of Virginia in the new government, and Campbell was cooperating toward that end.

On November 18, 1784, Campbell wrote a letter to the president of Congress and enclosed with it a petition from the people of Washington County, Virginia. In these documents he based his appeal on the Congressional resolutions of April 23 as authorizing the creation of new Western States, though of course they were intended to apply immediately only to territory already ceded to Congress. However, the boundaries suggested in these resolutions for new States might have been applied to the unceded as well as to the ceded territory. Beginning with the forty-fifth parallel, each State was to have two degrees of latitude and to be marked by longitudinal lines running, one through the mouth of the Kanawha River, and the other through the lower end of the rapids of the Ohio. Campbell suggested that the boundary of the State in which he was interested be modified so as to be marked on the east by the Appalachian Mountains and the New River, on the north by a line running from the confluence of the New with the Greenbrier River in a southwestward direction to the thirty-seventh parallel, and along that parallel to the meridian line running through the Falls of the Ohio. On the south the boundary was to be the Tennessee River and the thirty-fourth parallel. Thus a strip of Virginia and a strip of Georgia were to be added to all of what is now eastern Tennessee, and a part of the Muscle Shoals tract would have been included. [10]

On December 14, 1784, the Holston convention met, as provided for

[8] Summers, *Southwest Virginia,* pp. 402–403.
[9] Memorial of William Cocke, undated, Draper MSS., 2U147.
[10] Henry, *Henry,* III, 268–270; Cont. Cong. MSS., 48.

by the assembly of the previous August. The Congressional resolutions of April had stipulated that the new governments should, in the first instance, adopt the constitution and laws of one of the existing States, subject to later change by ordinary legislative act. The "State of Frank-

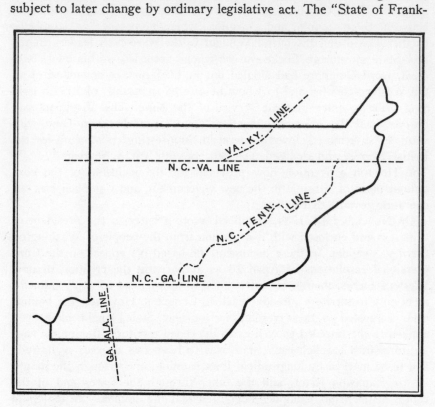

MAP 7. ARTHUR CAMPBELL'S PROPOSED STATE OF FRANKLIN

lin" conformed to this provision by adopting the constitution and laws of North Carolina, subject to change by a second convention which was to meet the following November. John Sevier was elected governor and William Cocke was chosen delegate to Congress. Cocke was to present to that body a petition, dated March 12, 1785, asking for the admission of the new State to the Confederation, with the boundaries stipulated in the cession act of North Carolina. But he carried a second petition from Arthur Campbell in which his ideas as to boundaries were set forth.[11] On January 13 Campbell's first petition was presented to Congress, and on May 16 his second address, which Cocke carried, was

[11] Williams, *The Lost State of Franklin,* pp. 39–44, 82–89.

presented also along with the one from the State of Franklin. No action was taken upon them.[12]

During the spring of 1785 Campbell continued to agitate for the separation of Washington County from Virginia with view to joining the State of Franklin. At his instance no delegates were returned from Washington to the House of Delegates in the March elections, and various meetings were held at which the State militia and tax laws were condemned as unduly oppressive upon the Western community.[13] Campbell addressed petitions to the House of Delegates as well as to Congress. They were entrusted to Archibald Stuart for presentation, and Stuart wrote Campbell that they arrived too late to be presented. Otherwise, he said, he should have submitted them even though he disapproved of their object. William Christian also, one of Campbell's supporters in his first secession movement of 1782, now opposed his plan, as did nearly all the Virginia leaders, but Christian approved of the separation of western North Carolina. A majority of the people and officials of Washington County supported Campbell.[14]

For a time Governor Patrick Henry, who had succeeded Harrison in November, 1784, took no notice of these disturbances, but the anti-Campbell faction in southwest Virginia was strong, and it pressed its case upon the governor. Finally, during the summer of 1785 Campbell accused the governor of favoring a "cabal," and he and the other secessionist members of the Washington County court were removed from office. Henry appointed William Russell to take over the military command with rank of brigadier-general. A personal quarrel had arisen between Campbell and Russell and this added fury to the fray. In July Russell appeared before the court over which Campbell was presiding and demanded that he be sworn into office, but Campbell refused to permit it, and the matter ended without a decision. When the Virginia assembly met on October 3 it proceeded at once to reinstate Campbell and the other deposed officials of Washington County, and the victory was theirs temporarily.[15]

[12] No mention is made in the journals of Congress of the presentation of the Franklin petition, but Williams cites *N.C.S.R.*, XVII, 464 to this effect. Franklin petition, March 12, 1785, Cont. Cong. MSS., 48, ff. 273–289; *Journals of the Continental Congress*, XXVIII, 4n.

[13] Deposition of William Russell, Feb., 1785, Campbell–Preston MSS., L. of C.; *Va. Mag. of Hist. and Biog.*, XVIII, 165–166.

[14] Archibald Stuart to Arthur Campbell, Jan. 5, 1785, Draper MSS., 9DD42; Christian to Campbell, March 27, 1785, *ibid.*, 9DD43; Christian to Thomas Madison, April 13, 1785, Durrett MSS., U. of C.

[15] Henry to Joseph Martin, April 16, 1785, Draper MSS., 15ZZ29–32; *C.V.S.P.*, IV, 31, 32, 37, 44–46, 100–101; Henry, *Henry*, III, 307–311; William Wirt, *Patrick Henry*, pp. 301–303.

In November the third Franklin convention assembled and took up the question of a definitive constitution. The resolution calling for the election of this body had defined the boundaries as stated in the Congressional resolution of April, 1784. According to this a part of southwestern Virginia would have been included in the new State, for thirty-seven and thirty-five degrees were the northern and southern limits proposed. The eastern boundary would have run north and south near the present site of Bristol. In cooperation with the Reverend William Graham, president of Liberty Hall Academy, Campbell had drawn up a liberal instrument of government about which he wrote enthusiastically to James Madison. It was strongly advocated before the convention by the Reverend Samuel Houston, cousin to the hero of San Jacinto. Governor Sevier and his supporters favored the retention of the North Carolina plan of government, and they won in the contest.[16]

North Carolina had repealed the cession of her Western territory before the first move for the creation of a new government in the Holston country, but this was unknown to the Western leaders at the time of their August assembly of 1784. The government of the State soon appointed Sevier and David Campbell to important Western offices, apparently hoping to wean them from the secessionist movement, but they persisted in their course. Joseph Martin, however,—probably under the influence of Patrick Henry—soon changed sides and began to oppose the Franklin movement. Blount and Governor Caswell, who were concerned with Sevier in the Muscle Shoals speculation, were anxious to proceed with this project, and the new-State agitation interfered with their plans. Both governors, Sevier and Caswell, would have been glad to reach an amicable settlement, but they had to save their faces with the public and they both had watchful enemies. The result was that the State of Franklin proceeded on its stormy way, but the victory of the Sevier party on the constitutional question safeguarded all North Carolina land claims in the Western country.[17]

If Campbell had been able to get his constitution adopted and the southwest Virginia counties annexed—for which latter proposition Sevier manifested no enthusiasm—he and his supporters might have been able to control the situation in regard to the public lands. As it was, the North Carolina speculators who had made such a coup under the public lands act of 1783 were protected in their claims. Campbell's interest in the State of Franklin soon began to wane.

[16] Abernethy, *From Frontier to Plantation in Tennessee,* pp. 76–80; resolution of the General Assembly of the State of Franklin, Aug., 1785, Madison MSS., L. of C.; Campbell to Madison, Oct. 28, 1785, *ibid.*
[17] *C.V.S.P.,* IV, 18–19, 53–54; Henry, *Henry,* III, 282–284, 322–323.

With the advent of peace, Virginia faced a new and complicated situation in regard to the West. The British had refused to surrender the Northwestern posts in accord with the terms of the treaty, and on June 26, 1784, Spain proclaimed the closure of the Mississippi to American commerce. The policy was actually put into force at New Orleans before July 22. During 1784 Washington made his famous Western tour to examine his lands on the Ohio and to consider the feasibility of a new effort to open the old Ohio Company trade route from the Potomac to the Monongahela. Immediately upon his return he wrote, on October 10, to Governor Harrison urging that this and the James River-Kanawha route to the West be developed by improvements. On May 17, 1785, the Virginia assembly created companies for the attainment of these objects. Washington was made president of the Potomac Company, and a block of its shares was offered to him for his services. Refusing to take them on his own account, he turned them over to Liberty Hall Academy in Lexington, which forthwith changed its name to Washington College and later became Washington and Lee University.[18]

Washington was not greatly disturbed about the closure of the navigation of the Mississippi. He believed that the West would be weaned from the East unless the two sections could be bound together by economic interest, and only by diverting the trade of the West to the eastward did he think this could be accomplished. He knew that New York and Pennsylvania were keen to develop routes of their own, but he considered the Potomac route superior to any other, as it certainly was so far as the length of land-carriage was concerned. He wished to see Virginia profit by the opportunity. Maryland cooperated with Virginia in the project, but the upper end of the route lay within Pennsylvania, and that State was not likely to promote the Virginia connection. Yet Washington favored an application to the Pennsylvania assembly for assistance, for he believed that the State would be afraid to thwart a work which would be so much to the interest of the settlers in the Pittsburgh area. At this time Richard Henry Lee, Jefferson, and doubtless a majority of eastern Virginians, agreed with Washington in his indifference to the navigation of the Mississippi.[19]

[18] Sparks, *Letters to Washington,* IV, 57, 89–90, 93–96; Sparks, *Writings of Washington,* IX, 58, XII, 264–267; Roy Bird Cook, *Washington's Western Lands* (Strasburg, Va., 1930) pp. 117, 127ff., 175–186; Elkanah Watson, *Men and Times of the Revolution,* p. 245; William Nelson to William Short, Jan. 11, 1784, Short MSS., L. of C.; John Girault to William Clark, July 22, 1784, Draper MSS., 1M98; *Journal of the House of Delegates,* Dec. 28, 1784, Jan. 1, 1785, pp. 91, 101, 105.

[19] Cook, *Washington's Western Lands,* pp. 100, 190, 195–196; Sparks, *Letters to Washington,* IV, 62–66; George Bancroft, *History of the Formation of the Constitution of the United States of America* (New York, 1903) I, 448; C. H. Ambler, *A History of Transportation in the Ohio Valley* (Glendale, Cal., 1932) pp. 67–68.

The attitude in Kentucky was, of course, quite different. Population there was increasing rapidly, Virginia and Pennsylvania furnishing the largest number of immigrants. Many of those coming down the Ohio landed at the mouth of the Limestone Creek where the town of Maysville was established in 1784 on land owned by the Virginian, John May. Land speculation was the principal occupation of the region, but trade also was increasing, and activities of this kind centered about Lexington and the Falls of the Ohio. The town of Louisville had been incorporated at the Falls in 1780 and commissioners appointed for laying it off on lands confiscated from the Tory, Dr. John Connolly. John Campbell owned an adjoining tract which had not been divided from that of Connolly, and he also held a mortgage on the Connolly tract, as did Joseph Simon. Campbell's land had orginally been confiscated along with that of Connolly but on satisfying the Virginia assembly that he was a loyal Whig it was restored to him, and the Louisville commissioners were directed to sell lots and pay off the Campbell and Simon mortgage on the Connolly tract. The two tracts were divided and the town grew apace. Campbell was appointed quartermaster at Fort Nelson and was engaged in surveying for the Gratz brothers, John Harvie of the Virginia land office, and others.[20]

The first merchant to establish himself at this place was Daniel Brodhead, Junior, son of the former commandant at Pittsburgh. He arrived during 1783 and soon established commercial relations with William Clark, cousin to the victor of Vincennes. The two Clarks were occupied at the time in founding the town of Clarksville, just across the river from Louisville. The Virginia assembly had made a grant of one hundred forty-nine thousand acres here to the veterans of the Illinois regiment, and a board to survey the tract and establish the town was created in October, 1783. George Rogers and William Clark, Alexander and Robert Breckinridge, William Croghan, and John Campbell were members of the board. Brodhead, Holker, Tardiveau, General Richard Butler and other traders had bought many of the soldiers' claims in this district. This was before Congress had accepted Virginia's cession, which provided for the grant to Clark's regiment, and before any treaty had been made to quiet the Indian claim; but William Clark lost no time in proceeding with his plans for development, and arrangements

---

[20] *Journal of the House of Delegates*, Nov. 24, Dec. 1, Dec. 9, 1783, pp. 31, 41, 55, Dec. 9, 1785, p. 81; Hening, *Statutes*, XI, 276–277, 321–322, 475–476; *Register of the Kentucky State Historical Society*, XV, 52; S. M. Wilson, *The First Land Court of Kentucky* (Lexington, 1923) p. 151; *Maryland Gazette*, Jan. 9, 1784, Durrett Misc. MSS., U. of C.; receipt of John Campbell, Jan. 15, 1784, Ohio Company MSS., H.S.P.; inventory of Nov. 24, 1784, Clark MSS., Virginia Archives.

for local self-government were made. Brodhead was soon engaged with John Craig, an associate of the Gratz brothers, in trying to invalidate some of Dunmore's old grants, and William Preston wrote to John Breckinridge in great perturbation about it. He thought that Patrick Henry and John Taylor of Caroline might be able to aid the original claimants.[21] On July 12, 1785, Judge Caleb Wallace wrote to Madison, "I wish I could say as much to vindicate the character of our Land Jobbers. This Business has been attended with much villainy in other parts, Here it is reduced to a system, and to take advantage of the Ignorance or of the Poverty of a neighbor is almost grown into reputation; which must multiply litigation and produce aversions that will not quickly subside."[22]

William Clark was interested also in trade down the Mississippi to New Orleans. In 1782 Captain John Girault, who had served in Clark's regiment, had gone on leave to Natchez and there established himself in trade as an agent for the up-river merchants. Many letters passed between him and William Clark in this connection, and Daniel Brodhead, Junior, as well as William Croghan, did business with him. He was also busy surveying for Clement Biddle, of Philadelphia, George Rogers Clark, Benjamin Harrison, Peter Tardiveau, and others.[23]

Tardiveau was one of two French merchants who had appeared in this region even before Brodhead arrived. The other was Bartholomew Lacassagne, and both he and Tardiveau had come from their native land during the War, the latter under the patronage of Benjamin Franklin. During 1778 he taught French in Philadelphia. The French consul-general, John Holker, took both Lacassagne and Tardiveau under his wing and on February 12, 1782, wrote a letter to Oliver Pollock in New Orleans, saying that they wished to engage in the Mississippi trade and recommending them to his care. Robert Morris also commended them to Pollock, thus showing his continued interest in the trade which

[21] Richard Butler to William Clark, Nov. 29, 1785, Draper MSS., IM130; Brodhead to Clark, Sept. 27, 1783, ibid., 1M48–51; minutes of Clarksville convention, Jan. 27, 1785, ibid., 1M103–105; Butler, Kentucky, pp. 142–143; Hening, Statutes, XI, 335–337; Preston to John Breckinridge, May 31, 1784, Breckinridge MSS., L. of C.; Thomas Madison to same, June 11, 1784, ibid.; P. Muhlenberg to President of Congress, July 5, 1784, Cont. Cong. MSS., 56, f. 113; Journals of the Continental Congress, XXVII, 625–626; Journal of the House of Delegates, Jan. 5, 1785, p. 108; Byars, Gratz, p. 230.

[22] Wallace to Madison, July 12, 1785, Madison MSS., L. of C.

[23] Girault to William Clark, March 13, 1783, Draper MSS., IM29; same to same, Aug. 5, 1782, ibid., 1M22; Brodhead to William Clark, June 11, 1784, ibid., LM83; Girault to W. Clark, July 9, 1784, ibid., 1M86; Brodhead to W. Clark, May 23, 1785, ibid., 1M111; diary of William Croghan, 1784, Draper MSS., 1N1; William Croghan to G. R. Clark, Nov. 3, 1785, ibid., 53J21; Virginia Land Office records, Grants, VI, 586–589; account book of William Croghan, Durrett MSS., U. of C.; Military Entry Book, no. VI, surveys of William Croghan, clerk's office, Jefferson County, Kentucky.

George Morgan and the American merchants of Kaskaskia had formerly carried on in association with him. Tardiveau established relations with John Dodge, and he and Lacassagne—who was for a time postmaster at the Falls of the Ohio—were active in the Kentucky country during 1785, but do not appear to have confined their efforts to any one community. Tardiveau bought some land claims from George Rogers Clark, which he later transferred to Holker. Lacassagne had some business relations with General William Irvine, and bought land claims from John Donne.[24]

The second merchant to establish himself at Louisville was General James Wilkinson. He set out for Kentucky during the latter part of 1783 and arrived at Louisville by January, 1784. One of his objects was trade. Dr. Hugh Shiell of Philadelphia, who spent much time during 1784 in Kentucky, was his principal associate. Shiell had a commercial partnership with Thomas Barclay, American vice-consul in France during the War. In France, the vice-consul had established the firm of Barclay, Moylan and Company at L'Orient in 1782. Stephen, John, and Jasper Moylan, sons to the Franco-Irish member of this firm, James Moylan, were residing in Philadelphia and had connections with the principal merchants of the city, and with David Duncan of Pittsburgh. John Holker was closely associated with the firm of Wilkinson and Shiell. Furthermore, Wilkinson was son-in-law to John Biddle, brother of Clement and Owen Biddle who were prominent in the commercial affairs of Philadelphia.[25]

But trade was not Wilkinson's only concern upon his arrival in Kentucky. He was a young man of chequered experience. Having figured in the Conway cabal and in the scandals of the clothier-general's department during the War, he still held the rank of brigadier and the office of adjutant-general in the Pennsylvania militia. On making up his mind to reside in Kentucky, he resigned these offices on November 9, 1784.

[24] Montaudouin to Franklin, May 7, 1777, Franklin MSS., VI, 11, A.P.S.; Jonathan Williams to Franklin, May 7, 1777, ibid., XXXVII, 87; Pennsylvania Packet, Dec. 8, 1778; Collins, Kentucky, p. 358; Alvord, Kaskaskia Records, p. 349; Holker to Pollock, Feb. 12, 1782, Pollock MSS., L. of C.; Holker vs. G. R. Clark, 1783, Durrett Misc. MSS., U. of C.; Lacassagne to Irvine, April 22, 1784, Irvine MSS., VII, 98, H.S.P.; C.V.S.P., III, 430–432; powers of attorney, April 26, 1785, etc., Filson Club, History Quarterly, VII, 43ff.; receipt of Lacassagne for land conveyance from John Donne, June 5, 1786, Durrett Misc. MSS., U. of C.

[25] Wilkinson to Shiell, n.d., Register of the Kentucky State Historical Society, XXIV, 260–262, 266; same to same, Sept. 2, 1784, ibid., XXIV, 264–265; Barclay to Shiell, Jan. 21, 1782, Ky. Historical Society MSS.; Brodhead to Wilkinson, Jan. 15, 1784, Filson Club, History Quarterly, VII, 36–37; James Hutchinson to Wilkinson, Feb. 7, 1784, Wilkinson MSS., Chicago Historical Society MSS.; Charles Biddle, Autobiography, p. 353; Marshall, Kentucky, I, 164–165; Thomas R. Hay, "Letters of Mrs. Anne Biddle Wilkinson from Kentucky, 1788–1789," reprint from Pa. Mag. of Hist. and Biog., LVI, 33–55.

Becoming thus a private citizen, he retained a keen interest in politics, and soon acquired a taste for land speculation.[26]

During the early period of his residence in Kentucky he was associated with Captain Isaac B. Dunn, of Philadelphia, late of the Third Pennsylvania Regiment and aide-de-camp to General St. Clair, and with James Armstrong, also Captain of the Third Pennsylvania, for the purpose of dealing in Western lands. Forming a connection with certain woodsmen who had explored the country north of the Ohio—probably Dorsey Pentecost and his party—Wilkinson acquired some kind of option on nearly two million acres which they claimed to have located and wrote to his brother-in-law, Dr. James Hutchinson, urging that he look for investors in such property. Of course this country was not open to settlement. The object of the speculators was merely to mark out choice tracts with view to having the first claim when they should be offered for sale by Congress. Wilkinson hoped Congress would give free rein to speculation when it put these lands upon the market and that it would employ him as one of its agents for transacting the business. Investments were made in Kentucky lands also, and William Clark and Tardiveau were witnesses to some of these transactions. Colonel William Grayson and Thomas Marshall also had some relations with Wilkinson. Various companies were organized for speculating in Kentucky lands and attempts were made to interest members of Congress in the enterprise.[27]

Wilkinson's mind, however, did not limit itself to mere ventures in trade and land speculation. On June 20, 1785, he wrote a letter to Dr. James Hutchinson giving his views on political matters. It shows that his eye took in the whole political and commercial situation of the West. Indian relations and the trade of the Mississippi River were the keys to the problem, and Wilkinson had ideas on both subjects. As to the trade, he said that Spain could easily be driven from Louisiana by the Western people, but the navigation of the Mississippi would be in jeopardy as long as England was able to block it with a single frigate. For this reason he thought it important to cultivate the friendship of the British.

[26] Wilkinson to President Dickinson, Nov. 9, 1784, Letters of Generals of the American Revolution, Dreer MSS., H.S.P.

[27] Wilkinson to Hutchinson, June 20, 1785, Pa. Mag. of Hist. and Biog., XII, 56–61; Wilkinson to Shiell, n.d., Ky. Historical Society MSS.; Grayson to Shiell, March 30, 1784, Emmett MSS., no. 9273, N.Y.P.L.; certificate of July 29, 1784, Gratz MSS., H.S.P.; Brodhead to Wilkinson, Jan. 15, 1784, Filson Club, History Quarterly, VII, 36–37; bond of James Patton and others, Feb. 11, 1784, ibid., p. 37; Wilkinson to Shiell, July 4, 16, 20, 1784, Register of the Kentucky State Historical Society, XXIV, 259–260, 262ff.; indenture dated Dec. 30, 1784, Innes MSS., XXIII, pt. 1, L. of C.; Thomas Gist to Samuel Chase, Feb. 4, 1785, Draper MSS., 1MM133–134.

This was a fundamental conception, and we shall see that it had an important bearing upon the later policy of the youthful General.[28]

As to the Indians, George Rogers Clark had carried the burden of dealing with them upon his shoulders for a long time and was still the dominant factor in the situation so far as Kentucky was concerned. It was important for Wilkinson to change this situation, for trade and land speculation, and even greater objects, could be promoted by a proper handling of the natives. Political reputation could also be enhanced by the acquisition of a reputation in Indian affairs, and Wilkinson avowed that this was one of his objects.

His letters of January 17, 1784, to the president of Congress, and of January 19 to Thomas Mifflin revealed these aims in a curious manner. Virginia made a treaty with the Chickasaws during the autumn of 1783, but these Indians were apparently not satisfied with their political situation. They desired further negotiations and to that end wrote letters to Governor Harrison of Virginia and to the president of Congress. One John Donne, an old associate of John Campbell in the Pittsburgh region, had migrated to Kentucky in 1779, and as late as 1786 he was living near Louisville and selling lands to John Holker and Lacassagne. He had formerly been a clerk in the commissary department under Colonel George Morgan, and in 1779 was employed by George Rogers Clark as "deputy conductor of stores." He had been sent by Clark to deal with the Chickasaws, among whom he resided for some time. These letters, one from Chief James Colbert to Harrison, and another from several other chiefs to Congress, were entrusted to Donne for delivery. On his way East he stopped at Louisville and there met Wilkinson, recently arrived at the place. Donne permitted the General to read the letters and Wilkinson then wrote to Mifflin and the president of Congress as though Donne were his agent rather than the agent of George Rogers Clark. He urged that a treaty be made and suggested that Donne would be a good man to handle the business. During the same period he was corresponding with the Shawnee and giving them the impression that he had the right to treat with them on behalf of Congress. It is clear that he hoped his services might be called into requisition in this connection.[29]

[28] Wilkinson to Hutchinson, June 20, 1785, Pa. Mag. of Hist. and Biog., XII, 56–61.
[29] Acct., Oct. 1–Dec. 31, 1777, Morgan MSS., Ill. Hist. Survey, Urbana; C.V.S.P., III, 513–517; Va. Mag. of Hist. and Biog., VII, 420; Wilkinson to Mifflin, Jan. 19, 1784, Cont. Cong. MSS., 78, XXIV, 431; Journals of the Continental Congress, XXVII, 461–462; Bodley, Clark, 265–266; Crumrine, Records of Deeds for the District of West Augusta, Annals of the Carnegie Museum, III, 289; Donne's commission, signed by Clark, Oct. 20, 1779, Durrett Misc. MSS., U. of C.; agreement

Though these early schemes of Wilkinson led to no immediate results, they reveal the bent of his mind and throw considerable light upon his later activities.

While the traders and speculators were establishing themselves at Louisville, a number of substantial Virginians, all of whom were interested in Western lands, were settling in the neighborhood. The most important of these was Colonel William Christian, who migrated from the lower Valley in 1785 and established himself on Beargrass Creek, near Louisville. The next year he was killed by the Indians. The same fate had, the previous year, overtaken his old friend John Floyd. Christian's son-in-law, Alexander Scott Bullitt, settled near him. This young man was the son of Judge Cuthbert Bullitt of Virginia and nephew to Thomas Bullitt who had surveyed the site of Louisville in 1773. On Beargrass the young Bullitt established his home at "Oxmoor," an estate which is now owned and occupied by a descendant of the original proprietor.[30]

Living temporarily with Bullitt was Alexander Breckinridge, who was attending to the land claims of his family, amounting to two hundred thousand acres, and whose brother John was a member of the Virginia House of Delegates and closely associated with the Preston interests of southwest Virginia. Walker Daniel, the attorney-general for the District of Kentucky, operated, in connection with Wilkinson, a salt works at Bullitt's Lick not far distant, but he was killed by Indians in August, 1784, and his place was taken by Harry Innes, who resigned the chief judgeship of the district court in order to accept the new appointment. Cyrus Griffin was then appointed to the chief judgeship, but on his declining, Colonel George Muter, who had been relieved from the post of commissioner of the Virginia War Office in 1781 on account of inefficiency, was selected to fill the vacancy. Samuel McDowell and Caleb Wallace were still serving as associate judges, and the former was engaging in trade at Limestone.[31]

There are significant implications in the fact that not one of the great

between John Donne and John Holker concerning land, June 5, 1786, *ibid.;* Lacassagne's receipt to Donne, same date, *ibid.*

[30] William Christian to Thomas Madison, Aug. 6, 1784, Draper MSS., 5ZZ78; same to Gilbert Christian, Aug. 13, 1785, *ibid.,* 5QQ124; *Register of the Kentucky State Historical Society,* XVII, 49ff.

[31] *Journal of the House of Delegates,* March 20–21, 1781, pp. 40–45; *ibid.,* Nov. 12, 23, 1785, pp. 34, 52; *C.V.S.P.,* IV, 67; *Register of the Kentucky State Historical Society,* XXIV, 263–264; contract dated July 27, 1784, Campbell-Preston MSS., L. of C.; William Johnson to Governor Harrison, Aug. 14, 1784, Clark papers, Va. Arch.; Alexander to John Breckinridge, Aug. 14, 1784, Breckinridge MSS., L. of C.; Preston to John Breckinridge, Oct. 28, 1784, *ibid.;* Alexander to John Breckinridge, Nov. 8, 1784, *ibid.;* same to same, Nov. 18, 1784, *ibid.;* same to John McDowell, Nov. 27, 1784, McDowell MSS., Presbyterian Historical Society, Philadelphia.

land speculators of the Philadelphia and Eastern coterie of comparable standing to that of Shelby, Christian, Henderson, Russell, Preston, and their ilk settled in the West. They wanted the land merely for speculation and had no intention of undergoing personally the hardships of the frontier. On the other hand, the Southerners coveted immense landed estates—the prerequisite of gentlemen, the basis of their semifeudal slave-holding society. Between 1779 and 1785 numerous well-born and influential men from Virginia, the Carolinas, Maryland, set their feet on the Wilderness Road; like Nathaniel Hart, of the Transylvania Company, who wrote to his wife from Kentucky that he was going down to Carolina "to make A Final End of all my Affairs below And then Push Out never to Return Again," these men planned to establish their homes on the hazardous frontier. Many, like Christian and Floyd, paid with their lives for their intrepidity.

One of the last official acts of Walker Daniel was to prosecute two agents, Pomeroy and Galloway by name, who had come into Kentucky for the purpose of agitating for the secession of the District from Virginia. They seem to have hailed from Pennsylvania, and all accounts indicate that they had the backing of certain members of Congress. Reviving an old statute against the spreading of false news, Daniel brought them into court and was able to force them to leave the District—not, however, before they had secured a considerable following in Jefferson County. Daniel's efforts were greatly assisted by General Wilkinson, who doubtless understood the men with whom he was dealing.[32]

This was the end of the first phase of the movement for the separation of Kentucky from Virginia. In the period from 1781 to 1784 it had been backed mainly by the non-Virginian element, who looked to Congress for assistance and hoped that that body would assume jurisdiction in the matter. In this case land claims based upon Virginia legislation would have been endangered, and consequently most of the settlers from the Old Dominion opposed the move. There were, however, a few influential Viriginians who had become associated with non-Virginian speculators on a large scale, and such men came out early in favor of separation.

It will be recalled that John Donelson, with the backing of Arthur Campbell, a non-resident, had agitated for Kentucky secession in 1782. Campbell's interest in Kentucky is accounted for by the fact that he owned lands there, to which he later removed his family. He also had some relations with Samuel Purviance, a Baltimore merchant who

[32] Marshall, *Kentucky*, I, 162; Bodley, *Clark*, pp. 263–264; *C.V.S.P.*, III, 555–556; James Speed to Governor Harrison, July 22, 1784, Smith, *Kentucky*, p. 234.

speculated heavily in Western lands in collaboration with Dorsey Pentecost. Campbell's first Washington County petition to Congress was entrusted to Purviance for delivery, and along with this Campbell sent some papers relating to the military situation in Kentucky.[33]

It is significant that it was the military situation which furnished the cause for the beginning of the second phase of the secession movement in Kentucky. Congress had failed to negotiate with the natives, and the people, still living in forts, were becoming restive. Arthur Campbell corresponded with a certain Ebenezer Brooks, tutor to the children of Thomas Marshall, about the situation, and Brooks gave himself credit for actually initiating the movement. There is no good reason for denying his claim.[34]

At the May session of the Virginia assembly an act was passed which levied a tax of five shillings the hundred acres on all Kentucky land grants of over fourteen hundred acres. This act was strongly objected to by Kentucky speculators, and the prominence given to it in the discussions during the second phase of the secession movement seems to warrant the statement that it was an acute cause of the agitation. Of course there were other grievances, such as the inconvenience of having to journey to Richmond in order to transact some kinds of legal business, the inadequate provision made for the district court of Kentucky, and the burdensome nature of some of the taxes. Particularly important, however, was the fact that no militia officer in Kentucky had the right to order punitive expeditions against the Indians, and the District was forced to stand on the defensive in its struggle with the natives.[35]

Under the assumption that the Cherokee were in need of punishment Colonel Benjamin Logan was induced to call a meeting of the leading citizens and militia officers who happened to be assembled at Danville on November 7, 1784, this being a court day. It was apparent from a letter received the next day from Colonel Joseph Martin that no danger threatened from the Cherokee, and, of course, Logan knew that he had no authority to send an expedition into North Carolina to punish them even if they had been on the war-path.[36]

[33] Margaret C. Pilcher, *Historical Sketches of the Campbell, Pilcher, and Kindred Families* (Nashville, 1910) pp. 52–56; Samuel Purviance to John Montgomery, April 17, 1784, Autograph Letters, LXX, 99, Chicago Historical Society MSS.; *Journals of the Continental Congress*, XXVIII, 4n.; Cont. Cong. MSS., 48, ff. 273–289.

[34] *C.V.S.P.*, III, 584–585, 588–589.

[35] Hening, *Statutes*, XI, 445; Christopher Greenup to Charles Simms, July 19, 1785, Charles Simms MSS., I, 34582, L. of C.; William Nelson to Short, Oct. 16, 1785, William Short MSS., L. of C.

[36] Brooks to Arthur Campbell, Nov. 9, 1784, Draper MSS., 11J37–38, printed in Bodley, *Kentucky*, I, 354–356; Bradford, "Notes on Kentucky," *Kentucky Gazette*, Dec. 1, 1826.

The meeting thus called by Logan lasted for two days. During the first, William Fleming, who happened to be in Kentucky at this time, acted as chairman; on the second, Isaac Shelby was put in the chair. A warm debate on the subject of the Cherokee expedition took place, with Fleming, Muter, and Wallace opposing it. The point was contested by Shelby, Greenup, and Brooks. The last-named had been invited by Logan to attend the meeting, though he could hardly have been called a prominent citizen. Martin's letter put a quietus to the agitation for the expedition, but, seeing that the District had no authority to organize such a campaign under any circumstances, Brooks, according to his own testimony, raised the question of a separate government for Kentucky.[37]

We have the testimony of a witness to the transactions that this was the real object of the meeting in the first place. It is even possible that the original idea came from Brooks, since he and Arthur Campbell had been corresponding about the desirability of a separate Kentucky government and making plans to coordinate the movements in that District and in southwest Virginia. One also wonders whether Thomas Marshall, Brooks' employer, may not have had a hand in it, for the surveyor of Fayette County and father of the great Chief Justice soon emerged as one of the leaders in the cause. Be this as it may, the discussions of November 7 and 8 ended in an agreement that elections should be held in the different militia districts of Kentucky and delegates should be chosen to meet at Danville on December 27 to discuss the question as to whether the District should be organized as a separate State.[38]

The situation had changed radically since the beginning of the year and the levying of the five shillings tax. No longer were non-Virginians the principal supporters of the secession movement. From this time forward the cause was upheld by most of the important Virginians who made their homes in Kentucky. Since the condition of affairs had not altered materially except for the enactment of the five shillings tax, it seems entirely reasonable to assume that this was the principal cause for the change. This practically amounts to saying that land speculation was the backbone of the movement in this second phase, as the tax affected few who were not speculators. There is also good evidence to the effect that the majority of the actual settlers of Virginia origin were either indifferent or opposed to the idea of a separate State. Such an establishment would lead to heavier taxation, and the claims of early settlers were protected under Virginia law. They had little to gain by the change.

[37] Grants to Pentecost and Purviance, Oct. 15, 1784, Virginia Land Office records, Grants, book M, p. 447.
[38] "Friend of the People," *Kentucky Gazette*, April 25, 1788; Temple Bodley, ed., *Littell's Political Transactions*, p. vi.

On December 27, 1784, the first Kentucky convention met as planned. Colonel William Fleming was elected president, and Isaac Shelby chosen chairman of the committee of the whole. The convention then proceeded to frame a series of resolutions setting forth the grievances under which the District of Kentucky was supposed to labor. Most of these complained of the special taxes levied upon the District and of the inconvenience caused by the remoteness of the capital of the State. The only vote recorded was that on the resolution protesting against the five shillings tax, and it is interesting to note that Richard Clough Anderson, the brother-in-law of George Rogers Clark, who had formerly been aide to Lafayette and was now surveyor of the area reserved in Kentucky for payment of military land bounties; John Campbell and Isaac Cox, both former residents of the Pittsburgh area; Christopher Greenup, clerk of the supreme court of the District, and future governor of Kentucky; James Harrod and Isaac Hite, both Kentucky pioneers; and Ebenezer Brooks voted, among others, for the resolution. Against it, among others, were John and Benjamin Logan, Judges Caleb Wallace and Samuel McDowell, Isaac Shelby, and William Kennedy. The last-named was presumably he who had visited the Cherokee country for Patrick Henry and his associates in 1774.[39]

In contrast to this was a resolution to the effect "That to grant any Person a larger quantity of Land than he designs Bona Fide to seat himself or his Family on, is a greevance, Because it is subversive of the fundamental Principles of a free republican Government to allow any individual, or Company or Body of Men to possess such large tracts of Country in their own right as may at a future day give them undue influence, and because it opens the door to speculation by which innumerable evils may ensue to the less opolent part of the Inhabitants and therefore ought not to be done in the future disposal of Lands in this District." [40]

It may be safely said that the views of the great majority of the frontier settlers were expressed by this resolution, but coming upon the heels of another one which condemned the levying of a special tax upon large estates, it causes some reflection. By this time Virginia had already granted nearly two million acres of Western lands to the Loyal and Greenbrier Companies, nearly five millions as bounties to Revolutionary soldiers, and thirty-eight millions on treasury warrants. Most of these claims were still pending, and practically all the good land in Kentucky

[39] T. P. Abernethy, ed., Journal of the First Kentucky Convention, *Journal of Southern History*, I, 75.
[40] *Ibid.*, pp. 75–76.

would be taken up by them. Speculators who had invested heavily in such claims—and it is a fair assumption that most of the treasury warrants and many of the soldiers' claims were in the hands of speculators —would lose rather than profit by the increase in the number of claimants. Thus the declaration against large grants, not having reference to previous ones, offered no threat to the speculator while it seemed to favor the interest of the actual settler. This was keen politics, of a type which has become quite familiar though not always recognized in its true colors.[41]

The only resolution which was proposed and rejected was one condemning the transfer of "the good People of the United States or any part of their Lands to any other State or to the United States." This apparently was intended to apply to the recent North Carolina cession, and it was rejected on the ground that it did not refer to any present grievance of Kentucky. Was it Arthur Campbell who suggested this to Ebenezer Brooks? [42]

Finally, the convention provided for the assembling of another similar body on May 23, 1785, to consider the question of separation from Virginia. Apparently no memorials were addressed either to the people, to the Virginia assembly, or to Congress, but the commanding officer in each district was to be furnished with a copy of the proceedings in order that he might inform the people thereupon.[43]

The second convention met at the appointed time. There were to have been eight delegates each from Jefferson and Fayette Counties and twelve from Lincoln. No representation had been allotted to the new county of Nelson, and on the appointed day none of the Jefferson delegates appeared. This was because John Campbell, who had charge of the State storehouse at Louisville, had interfered in the election. He had given it out that Fayette and Lincoln were planning a conspiracy against Jefferson, and, ostensibly in order to circumvent this plot, he secured the hasty election of twelve instead of the allotted eight delegates from the county. Nelson also chose twelve delegates in a similarly irregular manner. Fourteen of these, under the leadership of Campbell, appeared at Danville four days after the convention had assembled. At first they proposed to join the body if it would rescind all previous action and start work from the beginning again. This proposal was rejected, but consultations were held "out of doors," and when it was found that the two groups agreed in their desire for a separation of the District, the

[41] *Journal of the House of Delegates*, Nov. 24, 1784, p. 34; Journal of General Richard Butler, Oct. 10, 1785, Craig, *The Olden Time*, II, 443-446.
[42] Journal of the First Kentucky Convention, *loc. cit.*, I, 75.
[43] *Ibid.*, pp. 77-78.

delegates from Jefferson and Nelson, with the exception of Campbell himself, joined the others under an understanding that their credentials were not to be scrutinized.[44]

This was a peculiar proceeding, and its significance is obscure. The known facts indicate only that Campbell was trying to make himself a political power in Kentucky. If he had any special program of action, we do not know what it was. The non-Virginian element was apparently strongest in Jefferson County at this time, and it is probable that Campbell wished to organize that element and seize control from the Virginia leaders.

Despite the confusion caused by the action of Campbell, the convention proceeded with its business. Judge Samuel McDowell, who had once discussed the independence question with Arthur Campbell, was chosen president, and Thomas Todd acted as clerk. Addresses favoring separation from Virginia and adherence to the Confederation were directed to the House of Delegates and to the people of the District. The statute law of Virginia and the common law of England were to remain in force. Wilkinson was not a member of the convention, but it is usually stated that he was present at Danville and drafted the address to the people in florid terms and provocative style. Yet according to the General's own statement, he was ill at the time and did not visit Danville.[45]

It would seem that the irregularity of its composition accounts for the fact that this convention took no decisive action. It could hardly claim to speak for the people of the District, and it might have been dangerous to push matters to a conclusion under the circumstances. Therefore, it provided for the assembling of another convention in August, and the question of separation was left just where it had been before.[46]

The third convention met on August 8, 1785, and elected the same officials who had served on the previous occasion. A resolution condemning the five shillings tax was again adopted, and addresses, directed to the Virginia assembly and to the people of the District, were again framed. Wilkinson, taking his first active part in Kentucky politics, was a member of this convention, and it is usually said that he drafted these two addresses also. If so, the fact is not particularly significant, for there is nothing to indicate that he took any conspicuous part in the proceedings, and his correspondence of the time shows that he contemplated nothing

[44] Harry Innes to William Fleming, May 1, 1785, Fleming MSS., W. and L. U. library; same to same, June 20, 1785, *ibid.*

[45] The two addresses are printed in *Littell's Political Transactions,* pp. 62–66; Bradford, "Notes on Kentucky," *Kentucky Gazette,* Dec. 8, 1826; report of committee, May 27, 1785, Fleming MSS., W. and L. U. library; deposition of Samuel McDowell, Innes MSS., book 22, pt. 1, L. of C.

[46] Both addresses published in *Littell's Political Transactions,* pp. 66–72.

more than separation from Virginia. Humphrey Marshall, in his *History of Kentucky,* says that Kentucky now demanded a "free, sovereign, and independent republic" and implies that this meant independence from Congress as well as from Virginia. He considered Wilkinson responsible for this change of policy. Yet the resolutions were unanimously adopted by the convention and definitely express the intention of recognizing Congressional authority. It is obvious that no revolutionary intentions were entertained by this assembly. However, provision was made for launching an expedition against the Northern Indians and the people were addressed upon the subject in lurid terms. This move was to lead to important results during the following year.[47]

The most noteworthy act of the third convention was to delegate Innes and Muter, two of the Kentucky members of the House of Delegates, to present its petition for separation to that body. This was accomplished on October 8, and on January 10, 1786, an act was passed providing for the creation of the State of Kentucky.[48]

Little difference of opinion had appeared on the surface in Kentucky; practically all the Virginia leaders, with the exception of James Monroe, favored the creation of a separate State. The reasons given for this stand were various. Washington, Jefferson, Madison, and Richard Henry Lee thought it wise to follow the line of least resistance and make the best terms possible. But John Banister said he only regretted that the Kentuckians had not been a separate people from the beginning. Naturally the Revolutionary officers who had rights to land bounties in Kentucky opposed separation.[49]

The terms of separation stipulated by the assembly provided that Kentucky must become a member of the Confederation at the same time that she became a separate State and that all land claims set up under Vir-

[47] Smith, *Kentucky,* pp. 246–253; Butler, *Kentucky,* pp. 144–146; Marshall, *Kentucky,* I, 190–195; Cotterill, *History of Pioneer Kentucky,* 210–211; Thomas Marshall Green, *The Spanish Conspiracy* (Cincinnati, 1891) p. 56; Wilkinson to Hutchinson, June 20, 1785, *Pa. Mag. of Hist. and Biog.,* XII, 56–61; Bradford, "Notes on Kentucky," *Kentucky Gazette,* Dec. 8, 15, 22, 1826.

[48] Littell, *Political Transactions,* pp. 72–76; *Petitions of Early Inhabitants of Kentucky,* pp. 79–82; Hening, *Statutes,* XII, 37–40; *Journal of the House of Delegates,* Oct. 28, Nov. 14, Dec. 12, 1785, pp. 10, 36, 87–88; *Journal of the Senate of Virginia,* Jan. 10, 1786, pp. 82–83; Sparks, *Writings of Washington,* IX, 510.

[49] Jefferson to Madison, Feb. 20, 1784, *Writings of Thomas Jefferson,* (P. L. Ford, ed.), IV, 244; Jefferson to David Hartley, Sept. 5, 1785, *Writings of Thomas Jefferson* (Mem. ed.) V, 123–124; Madison to Monroe, May 29, 1785, Madison MSS., L. of C.; Madison to R. H. Lee, July 7, 1785, *ibid.;* William Grayson to Madison, Aug. 21, 1785, *ibid.;* Bancroft, *History of the Constitution,* I, 438, 451–452; Sparks, *Letters to Washington,* IV, 107–109; Ballagh, *Letters of Richard Henry Lee,* II, 382, 403; Filson Club, *History Quarterly,* VI, 230–233; Samuel McDowell to William Fleming, Nov. 11, 1785, Draper MSS., 2U137; John Banister to Jefferson, Dec. 2, 1785, Jefferson MSS., L. of C.; *Journal of the House of Delegates,* Nov. 29, 1785, pp. 63–64.

ginia law must remain equally valid under the jurisdiction of the new State. This latter was really the salient feature of the transaction.

It is noteworthy that the Kentucky conventions made no appeal to Congress, but addressed themselves to the government of Virginia only. It is clear that the Kentuckians intended that their State should become a member of the Confederation, but the terms upon which the new government was to be erected were to be settled as between the District and the State. This indicates that the Virginians who led the separation movement did not intend to have their land titles subject to Congressional authority. They may have preferred that the parent State should have left them more discretion in dealing with the matter, but there is ample evidence to the effect that the majority did not, at this time, intend to have Virginia grants called into question.[50]

By the end of 1785 it looked as though Kentucky would speedily become the fourteenth member of the Confederation, but during 1786 new factors entered into the situation, and seven years were to elapse before the business was finally settled.

While the new-State movement in Kentucky was making such progress, confusion reigned in the country north of the Ohio. The Virginia County of Illinois ceased to exist on January 5, 1782, and a year later Richard Winston, whom John Todd made commandant at Kaskaskia, departed the country. Jacques Timothe Boucher, Sieur de Montbrun [either he or a namesake of his helped to settle Nashville], a leader among the French inhabitants, succeeded him, but it cannot be said that he acted under the authority either of Congress or of Virginia. John Dodge, formerly an Indian agent under the Virginia régime, but who now had no legal authority of any kind, assumed military command at Kaskaskia and lorded it over the villagers in anything but pleasant fashion. There was friction between Dodge and the villagers and between him and de Montbrun, and, though jurisdiction passed definitely to Congress in 1784, that body took no action in regard to the situation.[51]

It is strange that this should have been the case, for Congress was not unaware of the Western problem. Indian commissioners were appointed for both the Northern and Southern Departments and treaties were made with the principal Western tribes. A cession of land in what is now eastern Ohio was acquired and Thomas Hutchins, having aided in the survey of the Virginia-Pennsylvania boundary, was commissioned to survey the new purchase. Jefferson's plan for the erection of new Western States

[50] *Petitions of Early Inhabitants of Kentucky,* pp. 78–79.

[51] John Todd's record book, *Chicago Historical Society Collections,* IV, 229; Alvord, *Cahokia Records,* pp. cxii, cxviii–cxix, cxxvii-cxxviii; Alvord, *Kaskaskia Records,* pp. 360–362; *C.V.S.P.,* III, 430–432.

was adopted, yet the Illinois country remained without a government.[52]

During the spring of 1784 Dorsey Pentecost explored the country while on his way to survey Kentucky lands for the company of which he was a member, and when he returned East, he took with him a petition, sponsored by Dodge, asking for the creation of a State government in the Illinois. But there were few signatures, and some of these were of doubtful authenticity.[53]

In the Pittsburgh area the new-State movement was not entirely dead. Washington pointed out its survival in his letter to Harrison on the question of the Potomac-Monongahela route, and a petition, without date but apparently of this period, asking for a separate State was presented to Congress. Virginia and Pennsylvania parties kept up their feud, and the town of Pittsburgh was surveyed for the Penns during 1784, but no political developments of signal import occurred during the years under discussion.[54]

[52] Edward Bancroft to William Frazer, Aug. 19, 1784, P.R.O., F.O. 4, III, 115–120; report of commissioners, Jan. 28, 1785, Cont. Cong. MSS., 30, ff. 203–205; James Dickinson to Hutchins, April 4, 1785, Hutchins MSS., H.S.P.; report of boundary commission, March 23, 1784, *ibid.;* Hutchins to John Montgomery, May 19, 1784, Autograph Letters, LXX, 97, Chicago Historical Society; Albach, *Annals,* p. 431; Mohr, *Federal Indian Relations,* pp. 108–109.

[53] Alvord, *Cahokia Records,* p. cxviii; Alvord, *Kaskaskia Records,* pp. 362–368; Pentecost to —— (?), Jan. 15, 1784, Etting collection, Misc. MSS., II, 23, H.S.P.; Pentecost to Levi Hollingsworth, Feb. 10, 1784, Ohio Company MSS., H.S.P.; Francis Preston to John Breckinridge, Dec. 22, 1784, Breckinridge MSS., L. of C.; Pentecost to President of Congress, Jan. 26, 1785, Cont. Cong. MSS., 30; Pentecost to M. Lecroiz, Nov. 6, 1785, Cont. Cong. MSS., 48.

[54] Ephraim Douglass to Gen. William Irvine, —— (?), 1784, *Pa. Mag. of Hist. and Biog.,* I, 52; Cook, *Washington's Western Lands,* pp. 90–91; C. M. Burton, *Ephraim Douglass and his Times,* p. 21; Tench Francis to George Woods, Sept. 30, 1784, Ross-Woods MSS., Historical Society of Western Pennsylvania; Pentecost to President Dickinson, Feb. 19, 1785, *Pa. Arch.,* series 1, X, 413–414; Henry Hamilton to Lord Sydney, July 8, 1785, P.R.O., C.O., 42, 48.

CHAPTER XXIII

THE WEST IN DISTRESS, 1786

DURING the years immediately following the Revolution Alexander McGillivray was perhaps the most important personage who figures in the history of the Spanish-American border. Much has been said, yet little is known, of this half-breed chieftain of the Creeks. His father, Lachlan McGillivray, was a Scottish merchant who took the Tory side during the War and quitted Georgia to live among the natives. When ten years of age the son was sent to New York to be educated, and on the outbreak of the War he was commissioned a captain in the British service, leading parties of Indians during the struggle. In 1783 he was made "King and Head Warrior" of the Creek Nation. During this year he continued to correspond with British officials at St. Augustine, hoping to secure their aid against the government of Georgia which was trying to get a cession of lands from the Creeks. The British cautiously advised him against precipitating hostilities, but sugges that he apply to the Spanish officials of Louisiana for supplies of munitions. The result of this was that in June, 1784, McGillivray became an agent of the Pensacola firm of Panton, Leslie and Company and an ally of the Spanish power on the Gulf, with the rank and pay of colonel.[1]

On November 1, 1783, Georgia made a treaty with the Creeks at Augusta whereby the Indian boundary was extended westward from the Ogeechee to the Oconee River. But McGillivray set himself against the surrender of any lands to the whites, and the treaty was not carried out. From May until November, 1785, the Creeks were at war with the Georgians, the conflict coming to a temporary end with the treaty of Galphinton on November 12, by which the boundary as set at the treaty of Augusta was reestablished. McGillivray would have nothing to do with this pacification, and the question of the boundary remained open for further dispute.[2]

[1] McGillivray to Lt. Col. Thomas Brown, April 10, 1783, P.R.O., C.O., series 5, 82; same to same, Aug. 30, 1783, *ibid.*; Thomas Brown to Lord North, Oct. 24, 1783, *ibid.*; William B. Stevens, *A History of Georgia* (Philadelphia, 1859) II, 431; Mohr, *Federal Indian Relations*, pp. 144–145; Littell, *Political Transactions,* p. xiii.

[2] Articles of the treaty of Augusta, Nov. 31, 1783, MS. vol., Bonds, Bills of Sale, etc., 1783–1792, G.D.A.; Articles of the treaty of Galphinton, Nov. 12, 1785, *ibid.*, (also in *A.S.P., Indian Affairs*, I, 16, dated Nov. 17); Thomas Brown to Lord North, July 30, 1783, P.R.O., C.O., series 5, 82; Bemis, *Pinckney's Treaty*, p. 57; Stevens, *Georgia*, II, 415–429; Mohr, *Federal Indian Relations*, pp. 146–147.

While involved in these difficulties Georgia was creating new ones for herself. Thomas Green was a Virginian who had moved during the War to Natchez on the Mississippi and established his family on a plantation at that place. When the enterprising young lawyer, Andrew Jackson, eloped from Nashville with the daughter of John Donelson, it was in the home of Green at Natchez that they found haven. After Spain wrested this country from the British, Green had trouble with the new rulers and on November 5, 1784, he presented a petition to the legislature of Georgia asking that the State establish a county to include the Natchez district. Of course Spain did not admit the American claim to the region under the treaty of 1783, and Natchez was still held by a Spanish garrison. But Georgia was not deterred by these considerations, and on February 7, 1785, created the county of Bourbon to include all the country which had been ceded by the Indians between the Yazoo River and the thirty-first parallel. Provision was made for surveying the Spanish boundary, and justices of the peace were appointed for the new jurisdiction. Tacitus Gilliard, Thomas Green, Sutton Banks, Nicholas Long, William Davenport, Nathaniel Christmas, William McIntosh, Junior, Benjamin Farrar, Cato West, Thomas Marston Green, William Anderson, Adam Bingamin, and John Ellis were named to the commission of the peace. They were instructed to claim the country for Georgia and to establish her authority, but not to bring on hostilities with Spain—a very large order for any thirteen men.[3]

Four of the new justices were in Georgia when the act creating Bourbon County was passed. To them the oath of office was administered, and they were to swear in their associates on reaching Natchez, for which destination they all presently set out. Davenport and Thomas Green decided to make their way to Kentucky and from thence float down the rivers to Natchez, while Long and Christmas journeyed overland.[4]

Green was the first to reach his destination. He arrived about June 1st and transmitted his instructions to Colonel Trevino, commandant at Natchez, who referred the matter to Governor Miró at New Orleans. Miró questioned the authority of Green's papers and on June 19 directed him to repair to New Orleans and appear before him. Instead of complying, Green undertook, in the capacity of colonel, to organize the militia of the new county for which purpose he was supplied with commissions.

[3] MS. Journal of the Georgia House of Assembly, Jan. 21, 1785, G.D.A.; *American State Papers, Public Lands,* I, 100; *American Historical Review,* XV, 70–73; Robert and George Watkins, *Digest of the Laws of Georgia* (Philadelphia, 1800) pp. 304–305; J. F. H. Claiborne, *Mississippi as a Province, Territory, and State* (Jamison, Miss., 1880) I, 95; A. P. Whitaker, *The Spanish-American Frontier,* pp. 55–58; R. G. Thwaites, *Early Western Travels* (Cleveland, 1904) IV, 325n.
[4] Madison to Monroe, June 21, 1785, Madison MSS., L. of C.

But to assemble the inhabitants without previous authority from the Spanish commandant was illegal, and Green soon found it expedient to quit the country. On June 24 Davenport arrived and found the district in confusion. A large part of the British inhabitants were American Tories who had taken refuge at Natchez under the British régime. Prominent among them were Alexander Ross, the erstwhile Pittsburgh trader; Anthony Hutchins, brother to Thomas of the chequered career; Richard Pearis, an inveterate land speculator and a kinsman of John Baynton, of the firm of Baynton, Wharton and Morgan; and William Dunbar, a Scottish merchant whose business partner was John Ross of Philadelphia. Such men had no great love for the Spanish, but neither were they inclined to submit to Georgia. Three of the local men who had been named as justices, Banks, Ellis and Gilliard—the last a wealthy Tory from South Carolina—now assembled the inhabitants in order to draw up a petition asking Congress to create a new State in the region. For this act they were jailed by the Spanish authorities.[5]

On July 25, Davenport, more cautious than the others, presented his credentials to Francis Bouligny, the Spanish commandant; four days later he received a reply advising him to repair to New Orleans, "where you will enjoy greater satisfaction and this district more quietness." But Davenport declined to make the journey and on August 25 he was joined by Long and Christmas. They reported their proceedings to Governor Elbert of Georgia, and presently Don Diego de Gardoqui, the Spanish *chargé d'affaires* at Philadelphia, was also apprised of their activities. He reported to John Jay, Secretary for Foreign Affairs, and Jay reported to Congress. The Georgia delegates, apparently having little information on the subject, disavowed the action of their State, and on October 10 Governor Esteban Miró of Louisiana ordered the Bourbon County officials to leave Natchez. In 1788 Georgia repealed the act creating the county.[6]

Georgia's other western county, established in 1784 in the "Bend of the Tennessee," maintained a precarious existence for some time longer. On November 28, 1785, commissioners appointed by Congress, of whom

<hr/>

[5] Thomas Green to Trevino, June (?), 1785, *A.H.R.*, XV, 76–77; *ibid.*, pp. 77, 96–97; Thomas Patterson to Oliver Pollock, June 28, 1785, Clark MSS., Va. Arch.; Davenport to Governor Elbert, July 20, 1785, G.D.A.; Governor Chester to Lord George Germain, Nov. 27, 1778, P.R.O., C.O., series 5, 595, f. 461.

[6] *A.H.R.*, XV, 297–299, 326, 328n; Monroe to Madison, July 12, 1785, Madison MSS., L. of C.; Davenport to Gov. Elbert, July 17, 1785, G.D.A.; Davenport to Bouligny, July 25, 1785, *ibid.*; Bouligny to (Davenport), July 29, 1785, *ibid.*; Davenport to Bouligny, July 20, 1785, *ibid.*; same to same, July 31, 1785, *ibid.*; Long and Christmas to Bouligny, Aug. 29, 1785, *ibid.*; Long, Davenport, and Christmas to Bouligny, Sept. 1, 1785, *ibid.*; same to Gov. Elbert, Sept. 13, 1785, *ibid.*; *Journals of the Continental Congress*, XXIX, 829–830; Martin to Henry, Sept. 19, 1785, *C.V.S.P.*, IV, 54–55.

Joseph Martin was one, signed the treaty of Hopewell with the Cherokee Indians. According to its terms the boundary line was fixed substantially as it had been in 1777, thus leaving to the Indians much land which was claimed by the whites, including the Bend of the Tennessee. Georgia and North Carolina were highly provoked by this turn of affairs, and William Blount, who attended the negotiations in the interest of his State, used all the influence which he and Governor Caswell possessed to change the result. But Martin, their partner in the Muscle Shoals venture, did nothing to help them and their efforts came to naught.[7]

Despite this situation and the untoward events which had occurred in the State of Franklin, the commissioners appointed by Georgia for the Bend country proceeded with their work. During December, 1786, they visited the Shoals, made some surveys, and on the 22nd of that month submitted a report to the Georgia assembly. During the early weeks of 1786 Blount visited Charleston in the interest of the company, and here he had the valiant support of General Wade Hampton. Through his influence the government of South Carolina, which State also had a claim upon the Bend country, made grants of land in that area to Blount's company. Some years before Wade Hampton, William Henry Drayton, and other South Carolina speculators with an interest in Western lands had endeavored to promote a union between Georgia and South Carolina, pleading that such a union would contribute to the wealth and dignity of each and would vastly increase the value of Georgia lands. They even offered to assume a part of Georgia's debt, but the scheme was defeated largely through the efforts of Button Gwinnet.[8]

In the summer of 1786 the Creeks took the war-path and all the Southern frontier became much alarmed. On June 25 Joseph Martin wrote to Patrick Henry that the Cumberland settlements were being attacked and that he feared the Powell Valley station would have to be abandoned unless relief could be sent. During July James Robertson, an associate of Judge Henderson in the establishment of Nashville, and Anthony Bledsoe, the old Long Hunter, entered into correspondence with McGillivray in the hope of securing peace for the Nashville area. They appar-

[7] R. G. Spaight to J. G. Blount, Mar. 27, 1785, J. G. Blount MSS., N.C.H.C.; William to J. G. Blount, Dec. 29, 1785, *ibid.;* Blount to Caswell, March 2, 1786, *ibid.:* Caswell to Blount, June 7, 1786, *ibid.;* William Blount to Joseph Martin, Dec. 23, 1785, Draper MSS., 2XX8; Martin to Henry, Feb. 6, 1786, *ibid.,* 1XX70; James White to Caswell, June 8, 1786, N.C. MSS., I, H.S.P.; Mohr, *Federal Indian Relations,* pp. 148–149; *Bureau of American Ethnology, Fifth Annual Report* (Washington, 1887) pp. 133–158; Whitaker, "The Muscle Shoals Speculation," *M.V.H.R.,* XIII, 372–373; Draper MSS., 14U1–108.

[8] Blount to Martin, Feb. 5, 1786, Draper MSS., 2XX9; Wade Hampton to John Sevier, Feb. 15, 1786, *ibid.,* 11DD79a; Wm. Henry Drayton to Humphrey Wells, June 8, 1777, White, *Georgia,* pp. 203–210.

ently had no intention of entering into a separate negotiation, but hoped to secure the aid of North Carolina in their efforts. The Georgia assembly decided that strenuous measures were necessary, and on August 3 and 4 created a commission and invested it with authority to make peace with the Creeks. Failing in this, war was to be declared, and provision was made for waging it with a force of fifteen hundred men. A few days later the commission was appointed and agents were delegated to concert measures with the Franklin settlers and to urge the Chickasaw and Cherokee Indians to cooperate. A land bounty was promised to all troops, whether from Georgia or elsewhere, and the governor of Virginia was asked for the loan of five hundred muskets.[9]

There is surely some significance in the fact that while this matter was being discussed the question of the Bend speculation was again taken up by the Georgia assembly. The legislation by which the "District and County of Tennessee" was established had been passed in a very peculiar manner. On February 20, 1784, a resolution was adopted providing for the creation of the District, and a bill was ordered to be brought in accordingly. The next day commissioners were appointed as provided in the resolution, but the journals showed no record of the passage of a bill. Now, on August 1, 1786, a motion was made to bring in a bill creating the county in regular form, but on the 12th it was defeated. After the adverse vote a resolution was adopted stating that all matters and interests relating to the county should stand just as they were before the futile attempt to pass the bill. Two days later the Tennessee commissioners were granted five thousand acres each for their services, but no additional surveys were to be made in the Bend until further orders should be issued.[10]

It was expected that further orders would be forthcoming, for Georgia now offered grants of land at the Shoals to the volunteers from the State of Franklin who were expected to serve in the war against the Creeks. Since Governor Sevier was a member of the Muscle Shoals Company, it was doubtless expected that he would take an interest in recruiting. The

[9] Martin to Henry, June 25, 1786, Cont. Cong. MSS., 71 II, f. 452; Henry to Va. delegates in Congress, *ibid.*, f. 441; McGillivray to Bledsoe and Robertson, July 22, 1786, Misc. MSS., series 1, I, N.C.H.C.; Bledsoe and Robertson to John McDonald and to McGillivray, Aug. 20, 1786, *ibid.*; Governor Telfair to Comrs. Robert Dixon and Stephen Scott, Aug. 27, 1786, Ga. Council Correspondence, L. of C.; Telfair to Sevier, Aug. 27, 1786, *ibid.*; same to Joseph Martin, Aug. 27, 1786, *ibid.*; same to William Davenport, Aug. 27, 1786, *ibid.*; same to Henry, Oct. 20, 1786, Executive Letter Book, 1786–1789; G.D.A.; MS. Journal of the Georgia House of Assembly, Aug. 3, 4, 8, 1786, pp. 470–485, 499–501, G.D.A.; James R. Gilmore, *John Sevier as a Commonwealth Builder* (New York, 1887) p. 99.

[10] MS. Journal of the Georgia House of Assembly, Aug. 1, 12, 14, 1786, pp. 456–458, 523–524, 540, G.D.A.

promoters of the company continued their activities and in August made a treaty with the Cherokee who again ceded the lands north of the Tennessee and held out prospect of selling a tract south of that stream, which would have given the Bend country an outlet to the Gulf. But the war with the Creeks did not materialize. The commissioners appointed to negotiate with the natives made peace with them, and on November 3 the treaty of Shoulder Bone was signed. By this instrument the Creek boundary was fixed at the Oconee River, as it had been done twice before —by the treaties of Augusta in 1783 and Galphinton in 1785. McGillivray, however, was still recalcitrant and the peace was no more than a truce.[11]

While the Congressional commissioners for the Southern Department were dealing so ineffectually with the Indian problem at Hopewell, those for the Northern Department were performing their functions with equal lack of success. On October 22, 1784, they made a treaty with the Six Nations at Fort Stanwix; on January 21, 1785, they signed the treaty of Fort McIntosh with the Wyandottes, Delawares, Chippewas and Ottawas; and on January 31, 1786, they concluded with the Shawnee the treaty of Fort Finney at the mouth of the Great Miami. By these instruments lands in what is now eastern Ohio and southern Indiana were ceded to Congress. On May 20, 1785, that body provided for the survey of a tract in the former area, and Thomas Hutchins was appointed to carry out the work. Colonel Josiah Harmar was put in command of a small Continental force to protect the area, but the Northwest country remained without a government.[12]

Meanwhile the British were making every effort to prejudice and incite the Indians against the United States, and their traders were trying to monopolize the commerce of the French villages. At Kaskaskia John Dodge maintained his military dictatorship in league with British agents, and with the support of Colonel Harmar, John Montgomery, and Peter Tardiveau. In desperation the French villagers appealed to Congress to

[11] Governor Telfair to Ga. Delegates in Congress, Nov. 15, 1786, Executive Letter Book, G.D.A.; same to Joseph Martin, Nov. 28, 1786, *ibid.;* same to Robert Dixon and Stephen Scott, Nov. 28, 1786, *ibid.;* same to John Sevier, Nov. 28, 1786, *ibid.;* same to William Davenport, Dec. 8, 1786, *ibid.;* same to John Habersham, Sept. 4, 1786, Ga. Council Correspondence, L. of C.; same to John Twiggs, Oct. 11, 1786, *ibid.;* same to Governor Henry, Oct. 30, 1786, *ibid.;* Martin to Henry, Nov. 21, 1786, *C.V.S.P.,* IV, 183; Alexander Outlaw to Governor Caswell, Oct. 8, 1786, *S.R.N.C.,* XVIII, 756–759; *Maryland Journal* copied in Draper MSS., 11J152; Stevens, *Georgia,* II, 380.

[12] General Richard Butler's Journal, Oct. 31, 1785, Craig, *The Olden Time,* II, 458; Journal of Thomas Hutchins, Nov., 1785, Hutchins MSS., H.S.P.; Josiah Harmar to Capt. Hamtramck, Oct. 26, 1786, *ibid.;* Walter Finney to G. R. Clark, March 24, 1786, Draper MSS., 53J25; Harmar to Hutchins, Nov. 6, 1786, George Morgan papers, L. of C.; *Register of the Kentucky State Historical Society,* VII, 29–33; Perkins, *Annals,* p. 273ff.

establish a government. At Vincennes the British had the upper hand, and the American element there had to fortify itself against hostile Indians, apparently encouraged by the British. Even in Kentucky the Shawnee and the Wabash tribes were making trouble despite the treaty of Fort Finney. When, in April, 1786, two conspicuous leaders of the frontier, John Donelson and William Christian, were killed, the Kentuckians decided that something must be done to stop the depredations.[13]

The Kentucky convention which met in the fall of 1785 had provided for an Indian expedition, and now Clark and the lieutenants of the Kentucky counties began an active agitation for one. Clark appealed to Governor Henry and Henry appealed to Congress. That body responded by ordering two companies of militia to the Falls of the Ohio. On June 25 Clark, urged thereto by the leaders of the Kentucky militia, decided to organize an expedition. Five days later Congress sanctioned an expedition under its own authority, and on July 12 Henry authorized the Kentucky officers to impress men and supplies. John May was made commissary of the expedition, and Christopher Greenup quartermaster.[14]

Thus the movement in Kentucky took shape under Clark's leadership before Henry's sanction was given, but his instructions reached their destination before the actual organization took place, and it was carried out under his authority. The action of Congress did not lead to any overt results, for no Continental expedition was organized and Clark acted on authority from Virginia only.

Clark was as much interested in the situation at Vincennes as he was in the plight of Kentucky. The American party there, being attacked by Indians and very doubtful of the attitude of the French, appealed to Congress for recognition of their land claims and to Clark for aid against their enemies. In July the latter sent Captains Hardin and Patton with a party of one hundred thirty men to their relief. The Indians were already in retreat when this force reached the vicinity, but it fell upon a detached party and Captain Hardin and several Indians were killed.[15]

On August 2 a meeting of Kentucky officers made plans for the main

[13] Anne to William Christian, March 22, 1786, Draper MSS., 2U140; Samuel McDowell to Governor Henry, April 18, 1786, Clark MSS., Va. Arch.; John May to Henry, April 19, 1786, ibid.; Benjamin Logan to Henry, April 19, 1786, ibid.; C.V.S.P., IV, 118–120; Alvord, Cahokia Records, p. cxxx; Alvord, Kaskaskia Records, pp. 381–383; Peter de la Valiniere to Congress, Aug. 24, 1786, Cont. Cong. MSS., 48.

[14] Bradford, "Notes on Kentucky," Kentucky Gazette, Dec. 22, 1826; Marshall, Kentucky, I, 247; Albach, Annals, pp. 442–444; Draper MSS., 46J98, 46J99, 53J42, 53J44, 53J48; Clark to Henry, May (?), 1786, Misc. MSS., Mason collection; Henry to President of Congress, May 16, 1786, Cont. Cong. MSS., 71, II, f. 427; Journals of the Continental Congress, June 30, 1786, XXX, 379–380; C.V.S.P., IV, 155, 156–157, 160–161; Henry, Henry, III, 362, 369–370.

[15] Draper MSS., 53J31; Filson's Journal, ibid., 10CC1–34; C.V.S.P., IV, 156–157.

campaign and bestowed the command upon Clark. On September 13, twelve hundred men assembled at Clarksville, but this was only half the number expected and the next day Colonel Benjamin Logan was sent back to raise an additional force. With the men thus assembled, Logan proceeded in October to destroy several Shawnee villages on the Great Miami. Clark marched his force to Vincennes and, after some delay, set out for the Wabash villages, but the natives had been warned of his approach. When within striking distance of the enemy a part of his troops mutinied and he returned to Vincennes. Here he established a garrison of over a hundred men enlisted for one year's service, and for their supply he impressed the stores of three Spanish merchants. The Wabash Indians, not realizing Clark's predicament, sued for peace, and Clark arranged to negotiate with them at Vincennes in April.[16]

These events gave rise to a storm in Kentucky which amounted to a major political crisis. While plans for the campaign were being discussed little objection was made, but when impressments began there was trouble. Henry exceeded his authority in sanctioning the impressment of men who were to be marched beyond the borders of the State, and the Kentucky officers knew that they were not on solid ground. They consulted the judges of the district court who gave an opinion favoring the measure, but many men opposed it, including some of the officers of Lincoln County. Logan, the commandant, was not of the number who worked against Clark, but it was the contingent from his county which was primarily responsible for the mutiny. Shortage of rations was the reason given for the insubordination of the troops, but trouble had broken out almost at the beginning of the march from Clarksville, and it was fomented by the Lincoln County officers. Opposition to Clark's policy was obviously at the bottom of it.[17]

Though impressments were often resented by the individuals affected and though they were doubtless illegal in this case, frontier leaders did not generally quibble over nice points when confronted by hostile savages on the war-path. It is a reasonable conjecture that there was a politi-

[16] James, Clark, pp. 352–359; Bodley, Clark, pp. 276, 289–291, 293–294, 297; Register of the Kentucky State Historical Society, XX, 210; resolutions of field officers, camp near Clarksville, Sept. 13, 1786, Clark MSS., Va. Arch.; Alexander to John Breckinridge, Sept. 22, 1786, Breckinridge MSS., L. of C.; Caleb Wallace to William Fleming, Oct. 23, 1786, Draper MSS., 9J244; Levi Todd to Patrick Henry, Aug. 29, 1786, ibid., 33J69–70; ibid., 53J51; William Morris to Hutchins, Oct. 27, 1786, Hutchins MSS., L. of C.; Clark to Henry, n.d., Cont. Cong. MSS., 71, II, f. 473; Logan to Governor Randolph, Dec. 17, 1786, ibid., f. 471; Clark to Henry, Dec. 30, 1786, C.V.S.P., IV, 213.

[17] Levi Todd to Robert Patterson, (1786), Draper MSS., 1MM166; same to same, Aug. 23, 1786, ibid., 1MM151; same to same, Sept. 13, 1786, ibid., 46J100; Logan to Randolph, Dec. 13, 1786, C.V.S.P., IV, 202; Pittsburgh Gazette, Dec. 16, 1786; Bodley, Clark, pp. 374–375; Butler, Kentucky, p. 154.

cal motive behind the imbroglio, and later developments give weight to such a conclusion.[18]

The movement for Kentucky independence marked time during the whole of 1786. The Virginia act of January 10 of this year provided that elections should be held in August and that a convention should meet in September to decide the question. The elections were held, but when September came a quorum failed to assemble at Danville on account of the absence of so many of the members who were with Clark on his Wabash campaign. On September 28 a group of those who did assemble, seeing their inability to act, petitioned the House of Delegates for an extension of the time within which Congress was to receive the new State into the Confederation. Another group sent in a contrary petition, but the Virginia assembly granted the extension of time and provided for the election of a new convention to pass on the question of separation. Thus nothing could be accomplished until the following year.[19]

Meanwhile Kentucky sentiment on the question of separation had undergone some change. The speculating gentry was not particularly pleased with the provisions of the Virginia act which left the disposal of most of the public lands in the hands of the parent State. Wilkinson came out strongly for independence and secured election to the convention by trickery. Others who at first had favored separation were now influenced to change their minds on account of the question of the navigation of the Mississippi. They felt that the aid of Virginia would be necessary in order to deal effectually with the Spanish problem. As early as January 25, 1786, Jefferson heard that there were those in Kentucky who desired separation from Congress as well as from Virginia, and Wilkinson is supposed to have been one of them but his letters which have survived do not prove the point.[20]

In New York, Jay and Gardoqui were endeavoring to negotiate a treaty which most Americans hoped would result in opening the great Western river to the commerce of their country. After extended conversations Jay realized that there was no chance of Spain's opening the river to our trade, and on August 3, 1786, proposed to Congress that a commercial treaty be concluded to run for a period of twenty-five or thirty

[18] Marshall, *Kentucky*, I, 249.
[19] Hening, *Statutes*, XII, 240–243; *Journal of the House of Delegates*, Jan. 10, 1786, p. 136; *ibid.*, Nov. 15, 1786, p. 41.
[20] Jefferson to A. Stuart, Jan. 25, 1786, *Writings of Jefferson* (Mem. ed.), V, 159; Innes to Fleming, Feb. 11, 1786, Fleming MSS., W. and L. U. library; James Speed to Fleming, Sept. 27, 1786, *ibid.;* John Brown to John Breckinridge, May 20, 1786, Breckinridge MSS., L. of C.; Caleb Wallace to Madison, Sept. 30, 1786, Madison MSS., L. of C.; "Friend of the People," *Kentucky Gazette*, April 25, 1788; R. O. Shreve, *The Finished Scoundrel* (Indianapolis, 1933) pp. 69–70; Marshall, *Kentucky*, I, 222–225, 242; Henry, *Henry*, III, 359–360.

years and that the navigation of the Mississippi be given up during the continuance of the agreement.[21]

Various votes were taken on the question, and in all of them the States north of Maryland favored Jay's proposal, while Maryland and all States southward opposed it. Except on the question of the acceptance of Virginia's cession of the old Northwest, this was the first clear-cut sectional division recorded in Congress on a major issue. The land companies, having been thwarted in all their purposes, no longer played a leading rôle, and the old Adams-Lee combination was not functioning. In a letter of October 10, 1786, Franklin expressed his views with characteristic shrewdness to Charles Pettit. He opposed surrendering the navigation, for the growth of the West depended upon it, but the Spaniards should be amused by dilatory tactics while the American settlements increased in strength until finally it would be cheaper to buy them out than to drive them out.[22]

The States which claimed Mississippi River boundaries were solidly opposed by those which had important commercial interests, but the stand of Maryland is hard to explain. The result was seven votes to five for Jay's proposal. Though nine votes were necessary for the ratification of a treaty, Jay was instructed, on August 29, to proceed with the negotiation along the lines which he had proposed. In Virginia, Washington and the Lees stood against the majority and favored this action, while Henry, who up to this time had often supported measures tending to increase the powers of Congress, now became an avowed leader of the State-rights group. It was feared by Madison that this situation would defeat all measures looking toward a more perfect union. The Kentucky members of the House of Delegates presented a protest against the reported action of Congress, and on November 29 the House instructed its Congressional delegation to oppose any attempt to surrender the navigation of the Mississippi.[23]

The West was, naturally, greatly aroused. Its future looked dark unless the Mississippi could carry its produce to New Orleans, and immi-

---

[21] Bemis, *Pinckney's Treaty,* pp. 95–97; *Journals of the Continental Congress,* XXIX, 658; XXXI, 480.

[22] Edmund Randolph to Benjamin Franklin, Dec. 6, 1786, Franklin MSS., XXXIV, 176, A.P.S.; Franklin to Pettit, Oct. 10, 1786, Franklin MSS., Misc., L. of C.

[23] Henry to Martin, Oct. 4, 1786, Draper MSS., 15ZZ33–40; *ibid.,* 11J82–106; Theodorick Bland to A. Lee, Nov. 20, 1786, Lee, *Arthur Lee,* II, 334–335; Madison to Washington, Nov. 1, 1786, Madison MSS., L. of C.; same to same, Nov. 8, 11, 1786, *ibid.; Journal of the House of Delegates,* Nov. 17, 29, 1786, pp. 46, 66; *ibid.,* Dec. 7, 1786, pp. 96–97; *C.V.S.P.,* IV, 209–210; Welling, *Land Politics of the United States,* pp. 16–20; S. M. Wilson, "George Washington's Contacts with Kentucky," Filson Club, *History Quarterly,* VI, 231ff.; Thomas Marshall Green, *The Spanish Conspiracy,* p. 106; Henry, *Henry,* III, 397–800; *Journals of the Continental Congress,* XXXI, 595–596, 600–601, 612–613, 697.

gration had fallen off sharply. The section, with an estimated population of about fifty thousand, was importing approximately two hundred thousand dollars' worth of goods annually from Baltimore and Philadelphia, paying about a fourth of the price in cash and furs and the remainder in land warrants. The trade with Natchez and New Orleans was closed to Americans, but the British and French merchants of the Illinois country were allowed to carry on the usual commerce, and Lacassagne and Tardiveau, with Holker and their associates, were able to continue operations. Furthermore, much flour reached New Orleans from Philadelphia by way of Port au Prince, and Daniel Clark acted as agent in the Louisiana capital for various American shippers.[24]

Even before Jay's proposal was made to Congress, several Western leaders feared that the pending negotiations would result in our acquiescence in the closure of the river and began to agitate against such an outcome. On May 4, James Wilkinson wrote to Dr. James Hutchinson expressing grave concern about the matter and condemning in strong terms the attitude of Congress. Shortly afterward a small group of Kentucky leaders, including Judges Muter and Sebastian of the district court; Harry Innes, the attorney-general; and John Brown, a nephew of William Preston who, after studying law under Jefferson had hung out his shingle in Danville, addressed a letter to the leaders of the Nashville district seeking cooperation against Congress in any attempt to close the river.[25]

This group along with Wilkinson was soon to emerge as leaders of the anti-Clark forces in Kentucky, but as yet they had evolved no distinctive policy. Muter was not enthusiastic about separation, and on August 18, Wilkinson wrote to Hutchinson:

I look forward to Independence & the highest Reputation in this Western World. . . . Our Convention will send an Agent to Congress in November, to solicit our admission into the Confederacy, . . . I could be this Man . . . if I would take it, but I have other Business to attend. The Gentleman, will I expect be Col. T. Marshall, Mr. Sebastian, Mr. Brower [Brown?], or Col. Bullett. I expect Sebastian will be the man. . . .

I carried my Election 240 ahead & I find . . . I spoke 3½ Hours, instead

[24] Unsigned paper, Dec. 28, 1784, P.R.O., C.O. 42, 16; geographical information by Thomas Hutchins, Hutchins MSS., H.S.P.; *Cahokia Records,* p. cxxvii; receipt of R. Brashear to William Clark, May 23, 1785, Draper MSS., 1M111; John Girault to W. Clark, July 13, 1786, *ibid.,* 1M136; John Holker to (John) Edgar, Jan. 26, 1786, Holker MSS., L. of C.; Lacassagne to Holker, April 19, 1786, *ibid.;* Daniel Clark to Holker, May 11, 1786, *ibid.;* Lacassagne to Holker, Sept. 18, 1786, *ibid.;* Terrasson *Frères et Cie.* to P. Tardiveau, Dec. 9, 1786, Tardiveau MSS., Ill. Hist. Library; William Christian to Thomas Madison, March 30, 1786, Draper MSS., 5ZZ82; James, *Clark,* p. 383; Bodley, *Clark,* p. 310.
[25] Wilkinson to Hutchinson, May 4, 1786, *Pa. Mag. of Hist and Biog.,* XII, 62; Draper MSS., 5XX18; *ibid.,* 6XX105.

of 1½. . . . I pleased myself, & . . . . every Body else. . . . I find myself now, much more easy, prompt, & eloquent in public debate, than I ever was in private conversation, . . .

Thus it seems clear that the schemes which this group was to promote were not hatched before the fall of 1786.[26]

It was Clark's expedition to the Wabash that gave his rivals their opportunity, and Kentucky politics a new turn. The mutiny which occurred in his ranks cannot be traced directly to Wilkinson, but it is clear that it was a "political" mutiny and that discrediting Clark was its object. Many stories were being circulated about his inebriety, and Wilkinson's hand is obvious here. Certainly the overthrow of the hero of Vincennes as the great man of Kentucky and the assumption of that rôle for himself was Wilkinson's prime objective, and the mutiny was the means toward that end.[27]

In November, 1786, a letter was written "from a Gentleman in North Carolina to a gentleman in Congress," saying "A gentleman just returned from Nashville informs me that Gen'l Clark and Col. Logan are now on their march with some militia from Kentucky to punish the Indians for their predatory excursions against our citizens. Clark is much exasperated against some Spaniards and others, settlers at Opost. He charges them with furnishing the Indians with military stores, and declares his intention of using them with a heavy hand as well as retaliating on the Spaniards for some of the Seizures and Confiscations of the property of our Citizens at Natchez. They add that Clark is constantly drunk." [28]

News, indeed, traveled fast, and it is probably significant that Wilkinson was carrying on an extensive trade in salt to Nashville at this time, and correspondence from that point to Kentucky sometimes passed through his hands. On November 29, 1786, "a gentleman in Danville" wrote to a "gentleman in Richmond" condemning Clark, and on December 12, "a gentleman in Kentucky" wrote to "his Friend in Philadelphia" saying "Clark is playing Hell. He is raising a Regiment of his own. . . . Seized a Spanish Boat with 20,000 Dollars. . . . I lead a plan to get the whole seized and secured for the owners, and [Alexander Scott] Bullett and [Richard C.] Anderson will execute it. Clark is eternally drunk, and yet full of design . . . a stroke is meditated against St. Louis and the Natchez." This letter is attributed, on good grounds, to Wilkinson,

[26] Wilkinson to Hutchinson, Aug. 18, 1786, *Pa. Mag. of Hist. and Biog.*, XII, 63–64; Muter to Madison, Sept. 23, 1786, Madison MSS., L. of C.
[27] Bodley, *Clark*, pp. 314–323, 329.
[28] *C.V.S.P.*, IV, 189.

and it is known that he did notify Spanish authorities of Clark's seizures, this being his first contact with the official agents of that nation.[29]

Granting that Wilkinson wrote this letter, he apparently had not yet seen one written eleven days earlier at the Falls of the Ohio by Thomas Green of Bourbon County fame. After leaving Natchez, Green had gone first to the Chickasaw country and then to Nashville, from which place he wrote on July 10, 1786, to Governor Telfair of Georgia saying that the Natchez country should be taken from the Spanish either under the authority of Georgia or under that of Congress. From there he had made his way to Kentucky, and it is clear that he consulted with Clark. His letter of December 3 from the Falls was directed to the governor, council, and legislature of Georgia. It condemned the closing of the Mississippi, told of Clark's seizure of the Spanish goods at Vincennes, which he said was done by way of retaliation, and affirmed that he and Clark were preparing to descend the Mississippi with a military force to seize Natchez as soon as Georgia should authorize the act. They also planned to take a large supply of goods for the Indian trade. Clark contributed to the expenses of the messenger who was to deliver this letter to Governor Telfair.[30] The next day a letter was written by "a Gentleman at the Falls of the Ohio," presumably Green, "to his friend in New England," which stated, "We have taken all the goods belonging to the Spanish merchants at Post Vincennes and the Illinois, and are determined they shall not trade up the river provided they will not let us trade down it." This letter was apparently intended as propaganda and was widely circulated in the Tennessee country. As early as May, 1785, McGillivray had heard rumors, presumably from the Georgia commissioners for Bourbon County, that Clark was preparing to descend upon the Spanish settlements. In July, John Girault had written from New Orleans that an American attack was expected, and the Spanish authorities were preparing for that event.[31]

Green's messenger was sufficiently indiscreet to show his papers to the group which was assembled at Danville awaiting the meeting of the con-

[29] Lardner Clark to William Croghan, May 2, 1786, Draper MSS., 1N3; *ibid.*, 29CC141–142, 33J34; Wilkinson to Nathaniel Massey, Dec. 19, 1786, Filson Club, *History Quarterly*, I, 172–173; Whitaker, *Spanish-American Frontier*, p. 97; Green, *Spanish Conspiracy*, p. 72; *C.V.S.P.*, IV, 202.

[30] Thomas Green to Governor, etc., of Georgia, Dec. 23 (should be Dec. 3), 1786, Ill. State Library; Thomas Green, Dec. 3, Draper MSS., 53J58; Thomas Green to Anthony Bledsoe, Sept. 10, 1785, *A.H.R.*, XV, 334; Green to Governor Telfair, July 10, 1786, *ibid.*, p. 352.

[31] The letter of Dec. 4th, 1786, from the Falls of the Ohio is often attributed to Wilkinson, Draper MSS., 19CC38; McGillivray to Miró, May 16, 1785, *A.H.R.*, XV, 73–74; Girault to William Clark, July 2, 1785, Draper MSS., 1N113; Harry and Anne Innes to John Coburn, Jan. 31, 1795, Draper MSS., 31CC23; *C.V.S.P.*, IV, 242; Green, *Spanish Conspiracy*, p. 387.

vention. At once it took action in the matter. On December 19, with Thomas Marshall in the chair, a committee was appointed to consult Clark and report on his activities. James Wilkinson, Harry Innes—who had married the widow of Wilkinson's former partner, Dr. Hugh Shiell —John Brown, James Garrard, Christopher Greenup, George Muter, and Edmund Lyne made up the committee. They began at once to take evidence, and the next day reported, by General Wilkinson, that a committee should be appointed to state the case to the governor of Virginia. They prepared to condemn Clark's acts, but to urge that his plans for the garrisoning of Vincennes and making treaties with the Indians should be carried out.[32]

Two days later this committee addressed its memorial to the governor. It accused Clark of corruption in connection with the impressment of supplies and referred to Green's hopes of raising troops in the Cumberland and Franklin settlements as well as in Kentucky. James Wilkinson, Benjamin Pope, John Brown, Caleb Wallace, John Craig, Christopher Greenup, Thomas Marshall, George Muter, Harry Innes, Edmund Lyne, Richard C. Anderson, Richard Taylor, James Garrard, Charles Ewing, John Logan, and John Edwards signed the document. This group shortly recommended to the governor that Congress be urged to appoint Wilkinson, Anderson, and Shelby to succeed Clark, Butler, and Parsons as commissioners to treat with the Indians.[33]

When they consulted Clark as to his activities he denied that he had planned to accompany Green to Natchez, but admitted that he had encouraged the enterprise in the hope of getting a grant of land. He said that he had no intention of molesting the Spanish, but he had advised the Kaskaskians to retaliate upon them for any seizures which they might make of American goods.[34]

In the controversy Clark was supported by the county lieutenants, Levi Todd, Benjamin Logan, and Robert Patterson. His opponents were mostly politicians and land speculators.[35]

[32] *Secret Journals of the Continental Congress,* IV, 301–329; deposition of Daniel Nieves, Dec. 20, 1786, Clark MSS., Va. Arch.; Minutes of Committee, Draper MSS., 53J59–61; Bodley, *Clark,* pp. 385–404.

[33] Address of the Danville committee to Governor Randolph, Dec. 22, 1786, Clark MSS., Va. Arch.; Perkins, *Annals,* p. 300.

[34] Report of the Danville committee, Dec. (?), 1786, Clark MSS., Va. Arch.

[35] Caleb Wallace to Madison, Nov. 20, 1786, Madison MSS., L. of C.; Levi Todd to Henry, Nov. 20, 1786, *C.V.S.P.,* IV, 182; same to same, Dec. 7, 1786, *ibid.,* p. 194; B. Patterson to Henry, Dec. 7, 1786, *ibid.,* p. 193; Robert Johnson to Henry, Dec. 5, 1786, Clark MSS., Va. Arch.; Benjamin Logan to Governor Randolph, Dec. 13, 1786, Draper MSS., 33J73; *ibid.,* 1MM171; Henry, *Henry,* III, 381.

CHAPTER XXIV

A YEAR OF CONFUSION, 1787

WHEN news of Clark's and Logan's expeditions first reached Richmond there was no expression of disapproval. The House of Delegates asked Governor Randolph for information on the subject, and the governor asked Congress to meet the expense of the expeditions. But when the Danville memorial arrived the matter took on another hue. On February 28, 1787, the governor consulted his council, which denied that it had authorized Clark to pursue the course followed by him. It forthwith adopted resolutions of censure, and notified the Virginia delegates in Congress of its action. During April Congress also condemned Clark's activities in the Wabash country. Spain was placated and Clark's reputation suffered. He, Butler, and Parsons were now replaced by Wilkinson, Anderson, and Innes as Indian commissioners. Not being themselves qualified for the work, they tried to induce Logan to act for them, with Innes as his secretary. Logan resented their conduct, and, though it seems that he did conduct some informal discussions, no treaty was even attempted by the new commissioners.

Since the capture of Kaskaskia and Vincennes, Clark had been the first citizen of Kentucky. It could hardly be denied that Wilkinson now supplanted him in that rôle. The merchant-adventurer from Philadelphia had done his work well, but only the first of his objects had been accomplished.[1]

After Clark's troops returned from the Wabash there was no reason why the fourth Kentucky convention might not have proceeded with its work and provided for the creation of the new State. But, as already related, the Virginia assembly had received a petition asking for delay and had accordingly provided for the election of a new convention. This

---

[1] Gov. Randolph to Speaker of the House of Delegates, Dec. 19, 1786, Clark MSS., Va. Arch.; proclamation by Gov. Randolph, Feb. 28, 1787, *ibid.;* Gov. Randolph to the General Assembly, Oct. 15, 1787, *ibid.;* same to G. R. Clark, Jan. 9, 1786, Draper MSS., 53J62; Clark to Gov. Randolph, May 11, 1787, *ibid.,* 11J174; A. S. Bullitt to Gov. Randolph, May 16, 1787, *ibid.,* 33J106; Logan to Randolph, Apr. 17, 1787, *ibid.,* 33J104; Gov. Randolph to the President of Congress, Jan. 24, 1787, Cont. Cong. MSS., 71, II, 467; Va. Council minutes, Feb. 28, 1787, *ibid.,* f. 491; *Secret Journals of the Continental Congress,* IV, 301ff.; *C.V.S.P.,* IV, 203, 267; James, *Clark,* pp. 378–379; Bodley, *Clark,* p. 300.

action was not in accord with the wishes of the Wilkinson-Innes group, but was the work of Dr. Ebenezer Brooks. It was he who had fathered the independence movement when Logan called his first assembly, and in the first convention Brooks was the only member to favor immediate separation. Since then his views had changed. He said that the closure of the Mississippi convinced him that Kentucky needed the support of Virginia in the struggle that must ensue with Spain. Actually, he seems to have resented the fact that the leadership in the movement had fallen into other hands, for he admitted his hostility to the Danville group which had been acting under the direction of Wilkinson and Innes.[2]

A preponderance of the Kentucky settlers owned no land, while enormous tracts were claimed by non-resident speculators. Virginia law protected the non-resident claimant, but there were those who hoped that the abrogation of Virginia's jurisdiction might be followed by a land policy more favorable to the actual settler. However, if Virginia's jurisdiction should be ended by accepting her terms of separation, existing claims would be protected. It was charged that Brooks and the men who now opposed legal separation were hoping that a forcible separation might be accomplished in the interest of the squatter.[3]

It does not appear that Brooks, who was probably acting in the interest of Colonel Thomas Marshall, was able to attract any appreciable number of followers, but there are numerous indications that the rank and file of Kentucky settlers were not greatly interested in the question of separation. The whole movement was apparently organized and carried through by a small group of leaders, most of whom were land speculators. The old differences between Virginian and non-Virginian claimants had disappeared, and now they stood together for legal separation since the protection of their extensive claims was at stake.

Thus, when in February, 1787, the members of the fourth convention who were present in Danville heard of the action of the Virginia assembly providing for the election of a fifth convention, they grudgingly adjourned without taking action. In August the balloting for members took place, and on September 5 the new convention assembled. On the 22nd it voted unanimously for separation on the terms proposed by Virginia and provided for a constitutional convention to meet the next year. The Virginia assembly was notified of this action, and an address was sent to Congress asking for admission to the Confederation. The Cumberland settlements had sent delegates to petition that they be admitted as mem-

[2] Muter to Madison, Feb. 20, 1787, Madison MSS., L. of C.; *Kentucky Gazette,* Aug. 18, Sept. 15, 22, Oct. 13, 1787, April 25, 1788.
[3] Caleb Wallace to Madison, Nov. 12, 1787, Madison MSS., L. of C.; *Kentucky Gazette,* Sept. 1, 8, Oct. 20, 1787.

bers of the new State, but no official action was taken upon this proposal. Apparently the prolonged agitation for statehood was about to end in success.[4]

For the greater part of this year there is an amazing lack of evidence as to the activities of the redoubtable General James Wilkinson. It is clear, however, that at about the time of his attack upon Clark's expedition he conceived a plan for visiting New Orleans. His letter of December 20, 1786, to the commandant at St. Louis, condemning the seizure of Spanish goods at Vincennes, was apparently the opening wedge. At about the same time he applied to Gardoqui, through the Baron von Steuben, for a passport, but the Spanish *chargé* refused to comply with the request. Through John Marshall, he approached Governor Randolph of Virginia for the same purpose, and with like result.[5]

These events occurred at the turn of the year, but it was not until June, 1787, that Wilkinson finally set out for New Orleans. His activities in the meantime constitute a mystery of real importance. During February, 1787, John Campbell, who had had many contacts with Innes and the General in Kentucky, visited Pittsburgh—a place which must have brought many memories. About the middle of this month a convention of Washington County, meeting at Pittsburgh, addressed a memorial to the government of Pennsylvania roundly denouncing the proposed surrender of the navigation of the Mississippi.[6]

H. H. Breckinridge, a Pittsburgh attorney, had been agitating the question ever since Jay first brought the matter up in Congress, but his main object evidently was to get elected to the assembly. This new agitation had a wider scope. A committee of correspondence, after the manner of 1775, was organized at Pittsburgh; its object was to carry on an agitation throughout the Western settlements. It addressed a letter to the Danville group, seeking its cooperation, and the request was immediately complied with. The Danville group consisted of the four men who constituted Wilkinson's council of State: Judges Muter and Sebastian, Harry Innes, the attorney-general, and John Brown. On March 29, they addressed a circular letter on the subject to the magistrates of Sumner County in the Cumberland region and received a favorable reply. Revo-

[4] Butler, *Kentucky*, pp. 144–146; Marshall, *Kentucky*, I, 251–252, 274–275; Madison to Muter, Jan. 7, 1787, *Tyler's Quarterly*, I, 29–30; *Kentucky Gazette*, March 9, 1827; Samuel McDowell to Arthur Campbell, Sept. 23, 1787, Draper MSS., 9DD46; same to Virginia delegates in Congress, Sept. 25, 1787, Cont. Cong. MSS., 71 II, 583.

[5] John Marshall to Wilkinson, Jan. 1, 1787, Durrett Misc. MSS., U. of C., published in *A.H.R.*, XII, 347–348; Manuel Serrano y Sanz, *El Brigadier Jaime Wilkinson*, p. 20; Wilkinson to Gardoqui, Jan. 1, 1789, in Charles Gayarré, *History of Louisiana*, (New Orleans, 1885) III, 247.

[6] Byars, *Gratz*, pp. 233–234; will of John Campbell, July 25, 1786, Durrett Misc. MSS., U. of C.

lution was certainly threatened if Congress did not change its policy, and an effort to consolidate the West behind the movement was already under way. The fact that it was not launched until long after Congress had acted upon Jay's proposal—and sufficient time had elapsed for the import of this action to sink in—indicates that it was not a spontaneous affair. John Campbell was one of the promoters, if not the main promoter, of the scheme, and the fact that the Pittsburgh "convention" sent its address to the men in Kentucky who happened to be closest to Wilkinson is not without significance.[7]

The Danville group proceeded to hold a meeting and to provide for the assembling of a Kentucky convention in May to discuss the whole question of the navigation of the Mississippi. The convention met as planned, but adjourned without taking action. Evidently the people of Kentucky were not as much concerned about such questions as were Wilkinson's friends. Yet on November 12 the Virginia House of Delegates adopted resolutions condemning surrender of the coveted navigation as repugnant to all confidence in the Federal government. But where was Wilkinson? He was probably in Kentucky until he left for New Orleans in June. Yet his name does not appear in connection with any of the events just described. The only obvious surmise is that he preferred to let his friends set the stage upon which he was soon to emerge as the principal actor.[8]

When the mercantile and mercenary General finally set out for New Orleans with his cargo of goods, he had no passport, and, according to his own statement, no connections in the city of his destination. But Daniel Clark was acting as agent for Tardiveau and the Holker connection, and Wilkinson had done much business with that group. When he got to New Orleans on July 2 he was cordially received by the governor, who had heard that it was he who had thwarted George Rogers Clark's proposed expedition against the Natchez. Wilkinson now arrranged with Daniel Clark to serve him in commercial matters.[9]

---

[7] Butler, *Kentucky*, pp. 158–160; Marshall, *Kentucky*, I, 258–269; Green, *Spanish Conspiracy*, pp. 109–111; *Pittsburgh Gazette*, Sept. 9, 16, Dec. 2, 1786, March 17, 1787; John Campbell to James Madison, Feb. 21, 1787, Madison MSS., L. of C.; Muter, Innes, Brown, and Sebastian to Magistrates of Sumner County, N. C., March 29, 1787, Draper MSS., 8CC5; Lacassagne to William Irvine, April 1, 1787, Irvine MSS., IX, 66, H.S.P.

[8] Bradford, "Notes on Kentucky," *Kentucky Gazette*, Feb. 9, 1827; Thomas Speed, *The Political Club of Danville, Kentucky* (Louisville, 1894) pp. 104–110; *Journal of the House of Delegates*, Nov. 12, 1787, p. 41.

[9] Temple Bodley says that Wilkinson communicated with Clark before going to New Orleans. Bodley, *Kentucky*, I, 401. Green, *Spanish Conspiracy*, pp. 124–125, 324; Byars, *Gratz*, p. 32; W. R. Shepherd, "Wilkinson and the Beginning of the Spanish Conspiracy," *A.H.R.*, IX, 490–506; Marshall, *Kentucky*, I, 313; Holker to John Edgar, *et al.*, Jan. 26, 1786, Holker MSS., L. of C.

After remaining in New Orleans for two months Wilkinson, on September 5, presented Governor Miró and the Intendant Navarro with a memorial. Upon this document, as far as Wilkinson is concerned, the "Spanish Conspiracy" was based. Much has been written of it, yet there are points which deserve special notice. It was proposed that Spain encourage the revolt of the West from the Confederation in order that it might form a connection with His Catholic Majesty. The navigation of the Mississippi was the bait which was to be used for this purpose. First, exclusive trading privileges should be granted to Wilkinson and his friends in order that they might build up a Spanish party in Kentucky, with Wilkinson acting as Spanish agent.

In his memorial the plotting General proceeded to outline his plan of operations, and this is the most significant part of the document. He alleged that a British agent had approached him in 1783 in regard to a Western revolt and intimated that officials in Detroit were still interested in promoting such a cause unofficially. British records do not disclose any evidence in support of these statements, but on July 28, 1786, Lord Dorchester, who came out as governor of Canada in this year, had recommended a plan for securing secret intelligence in regard to the American West, and he kept himself well informed as to events in that region. James Madison and Edward Carrington strongly suspected British activity along the line suggested by Wilkinson, and that individual stated that a British merchant [probably he referred to John Edgar] had offered to supply the expedition which Clark and Green were supposed to have planned against Natchez. On February 21, 1787, John Campbell said that the British agents at Detroit had been taking advantage of the West's indignation over the attitude of Congress on the navigation of the Mississippi to tamper with the people.[10]

Little is heard of George Rogers Clark during this year, but there were many men in the West who would have been glad to take matters in their own hands and drive the Spanish from the banks of the Mississippi. British support for such a movement was generally anticipated. On March 1, 1787, Captain John Sullivan wrote a letter to Gardoqui from the Georgia frontier, threatening such a movement. The more responsible leaders were less rash, yet there are evidences that an expedition against New Orleans would have found much support among the fron-

[10] Minutes of July 28, 1786, P.R.O., C.O., 42, 49; Dorchester to Sydney, Dec. 11, 1786, *ibid.*, 42, 50; John Edgar to Clark, Oct. 23, 1786, *Kaskaskia Records*, pp. 395–396; Edward Carrington to Gov. Randolph, Dec. 8, 1786, *C.V.S.P.*, IV, 197–199; John Campbell to Madison, Feb. 21, 1787, Madison MSS., L. of C.; Madison to Washington, March 18, 1787, Sparks, *Letters to Washington*, IV, 165–168; Green, *Spanish Conspiracy*, pp. 162, 294–298.

tiersmen. Orders from Congress and Virginia prohibiting punitive expeditions against the marauding Indians added to the general dissatisfaction in the West.[11]

Naturally, the Spanish were not unimpressed by Wilkinson's allegations. Miró was willing to listen further, and Wilkinson's propositions were plausible in the extreme. Kentucky, he said, had already petitioned Virginia for a separate government. Under the terms of separation it would be necessary to appeal to Congress for admission, but the East was jealous of the West and admission would probably be denied. Furthermore, seven States had already voted in favor of the closure of the Mississippi in connection with Jay's proposals for a Spanish treaty, and it was not likely that they would change their attitude. This would justify the West in setting up for itself, and many in the East would welcome that event. Certainly the East would be powerless to defeat such a move, and Congress could not object if Spain took advantage of the situation.[12]

Wilkinson urged that Spain should by no means surrender the navigation of the Mississippi, for in that case Western resentment against Congress would be appeased and revolt would die. It has been argued that he was trying merely to deceive Miró in order to promote his trading venture, but he wrote to his friend, Arthur St. Clair, now president of Congress, urging that a treaty with Spain be made according to Jay's proposal. Thus he used his influence to encourage Congress to do the very thing best calculated to promote revolt. When he reached Richmond on his return journey he denounced to Governor Randolph in strong terms the proposed treaty and the proposed constitution, and in Kentucky he took the same stand.[13]

The trade concession which he asked of Miró was merely a temporary expedient. It might prove lucrative for a few years, but Wilkinson knew that he could not deceive Spain indefinitely, and he proposed to leave his profits deposited in New Orleans until his plans could be carried through. These plans included a colonization venture on Spanish territory as well as a Western revolution. Gardoqui had been working on such a colonization scheme, and Wilkinson knew of his conversations with von Steuben

[11] John Sullivan to Gardoqui, March 1, 1787, *American Museum,* III, 436–437, also in *Kentucky Gazette,* Nov. 10, 1787, and Draper MSS., 18CC11–13; same to Governor Thomas Pinckney, Dec. 27, 1787, *American Museum,* III, 437–438; "Politics of the Ohio" (1787), paper in hand of Thomas Hutchins, Hutchins MSS., H.S.P.; J. Preston to John Breckinridge, March 24, 1787, Breckinridge MSS., L. of C.; *Secret Journals of the Continental Congress,* IV, 324–328; Gilmore, *Sevier,* pp. 113–115; Bodley, *Littell,* pp. 22–25.

[12] Miró and Navarro to Valdés, Sept. 25, 1787, inclosing Wilkinson's memorial of Sept. 5, 1787, "Pontalba" transcripts from the Louisiana Historical Society, Filson Club, Louisville, Kentucky.

[13] Bodley, *Kentucky,* I, 404; Bodley, *Littell,* pp. xliii–iv.

in that connection. He planned a similar venture and apparently intended to fall back upon that in case his revolution did not come off. But he was in earnest about revolution. If Congress did not change its policy there was every reason to believe that the West would be prepared to make its own terms with Spain, and Wilkinson meant to be the leader in that movement. When he stated that he planned to be the Washington of the West he meant just what he said. Events were marching fast. Only a little time should be needed for the maturation of his plans. On December 15 Harry Innes advertised in the newly established *Kentucky Gazette* for goods to be shipped to New Orleans on Wilkinson's account.[14]

That Wilkinson's Kentucky friends knew what he was about seems sufficiently clear. On December 27, 1786, there was organized a "Political Club" at Danville, Wilkinson's intimate friends being prominent members, and it began to hold debates on questions of public interest. In their first discussion they decided that the navigation of the Mississippi was not necessary to the welfare of the West. They decided also that Kentucky should be separated from Virginia and proceeded to frame what they considered would be a proper constitution for the new Republic. Perhaps their most significant debate was on the question of the right of an American citizen to expatriate himself. They came to the conclusion that he had the right to exercise that privilege of his own accord.[15]

It is not in the least likely that frontiersmen had any theoretical interest in such a question. Of what interest could it have been to Kentuckians unless they knew that Wilkinson planned to adopt Spanish citizenship when he visited New Orleans or planned to colonize Kentuckians on Spanish soil? On July 21, 1787, Innes wrote to Governor Randolph and predicted that within a few years the West would declare its independence. The governor, in connection with John May, John Craig, and Wilkinson, was investing heavily in Kentucky lands, and he gave no evidence of being perturbed. Wilkinson had told Miró that the notables of Kentucky sent him to Louisiana and that he would have brought credentials to that effect had he considered it safe. It cannot be doubted that Innes, Muter, Benjamin Sebastian—an ex-clergyman thought to have been from Virginia—and Brown knew much of his plans.[16]

The situation of Georgia and North Carolina in regard to the Western

[14] General James Wilkinson, *Memoirs of My Own Times* (Philadelphia, 1816) II, 108–111; Alceé Fortier, *A History of Louisiana* (New York, 1904) II, 128; *Kentucky Gazette*, Dec. 15, 1787; receipt, Dec. 19, 1787, Innes MSS., L. of C.
[15] Speed, *Political Club of Danville*, pp. x, 38, 100ff.
[16] Virginia Land Office, Grants, book VI, p. 543; John May to Robert Patterson, c. 1786, Draper MSS., 1MM168; John Crittenden to G. R. Clark, April 27, 1787, *ibid.*, 53J70; Innes to Gov. Randolph, July 21, 1787, Clark MSS., Va. Arch.; Robert Breckinridge to Innes, Nov. 24, Dec. 9, 1787, Innes MSS., L. of C.

problem was very similar to that of Virginia, the main difference being that Georgia had no settlements on the Western waters, and North Carolina had only the two quite isolated districts of Watauga and Cumberland. The former of these, as the State of Franklin, was in revolt. The latter was very weak. However, William Blount and his friend Governor Richard Caswell gave a certain unity to North Carolina policy, for they were practically the political "bosses" of the State. James Robertson and Anthony Bledsoe, the principal leaders of the Cumberland settlers, were much under their influence, and John Sevier, "Governor of the State of Franklin," was still concerned with them in the Muscle Shoals venture and willing to cooperate politically when possible.[17]

Dr. James White was a Philadelphian who had recently moved to North Carolina and been elected to the assembly. In December, 1785, that body sent him to Congress as a delegate of the State. For a new recruit to rise so suddenly in politics might seem a bit strange were it not for the fact that White was a business associate of the Blounts and a friend of Caswell. It is impossible to look upon him in any other light than as a tool of these magnates. On May 2, 1786, he took his seat in Congress; on August 26, he had a conference with Gardoqui and suggested that the West might accept the protection of Spain in case Congress did not succeed in opening the navigation of the Mississippi to its trade; and on October 6 he was elected Superintendent of Indian Affairs for the Southern Department.[18]

Arthur Campbell had aspirations to this office, and Joseph Martin, now dismissed by Governor Randolph as Indian agent for Virginia, was an active candidate with the backing of Patrick Henry. White was a Catholic, had studied law and medicine and spoke French, having been educated at the Jesuit school of St. Omer. He was well qualified to deal with the Spanish in New Orleans, but, though he bought lands in the Cumberland district, he had apparently never visited the West, and his qualifications for the Indian agency were not obvious, to say the least. But William Blount was his colleague in Congress, and he must have known his man.[19]

[17] Lardner Clark, the first merchant to settle at Nashville, was a partner in business with William Wickoff of Philadelphia, and they were associates in land speculations with the Blounts. Wickoff to J. G. Blount, Sept. 16, 1787, Blount MSS., N.C.H.C.; Nathaniel Rogers to J. G. Blount, Dec. 24, 1787, *ibid.*
[18] A. Ramsey to Caswell, March 13, 1786, Governors' correspondence, N.C.H.C.; Caswell to Blount, June 7, 1786, Blount MSS., N.C.H.C.; James White to J. G. Blount, Aug. 4, 1787, *ibid.;* White to Caswell, June 8, 1786, N.C. MSS., H.S.P.; *Journals of the Continental Congress,* Oct. 6, 1786, XI, 174.
[19] Ballagh, *Lee,* II, 486–488; Henry, *Henry,* III, 390; A. Campbell to Madison, Jan. 2, 1787, Madison MSS., L. of C.; same to Gov. Randolph, Nov. 20, 1787, *ibid.;* Randolph to Joseph Martin, Jan. 31, 1787, Draper MSS., 2XX12; *C.V.S.P.,* IV, 366–367, 375.

On February 16, 1787, White set out from Georgia for his negotiations with the Creeks. Georgia had made the treaty of Galphinton with them the previous year, but nothing had been done toward carrying out its terms. The State was evidently not over-enthusiastic about Congressional interposition, but if Congress could secure peace with her Indian neighbors, she was not inclined to complain. Accordingly, two State commissioners were appointed to assist White in his work. During April the commissioners held conferences with the Indians, but White's letters to Governor Matthews throw very little light upon what happened. At first he seemed to think that peace would be established but soon war threatened, and finally the Creeks granted a truce until August. White said that this concession was granted in order to give time for the creation of a new State which McGillivray was planning—a plan which he had had in mind since June 1, 1784, when he had suggested it to the Spanish governor at Pensacola.[20]

During this time the Congressional commissioner was in friendly correspondence with McGillivray, and Governor Caswell was also communicating with him. Gardoqui, the Spanish *chargé*, now in New York, was instructed by Floridablanca not to complete any treaty with the United States until he should be informed of the outcome of White's mission. He was also told that the commerce of New Orleans was to be opened to those frontiersmen who would attach themselves to Spain. This proves that White's proposal of 1786 had been taken up with the Spanish Ministry and that during 1787 the diplomatic Doctor was engaged in carrying it out. His close connection with Caswell and Blount indicates that he was only acting for men higher up, and we shall presently find further evidence to the same effect. It is clear that the North Carolina leaders did not wish to see the Western country cut off from the State, but if Spain should keep the Mississippi closed, and if the Creeks, with Spanish aid, should make life upon the frontier too hazardous for the development of Western lands, then it might be necessary to make the best terms possible with the enemy. A secession movement was the obvious way in which this might be accomplished.[21]

[20] Green, *Spanish Conspiracy*, pp. 123–124; Gov. Matthews to James White, Feb. 14, 1787, Ga. Council correspondence, L. of C.; same to Joseph Habersham, Feb. 15, 1787, *ibid.;* same to James White, April 14, 1787, *ibid.;* same to Gen'l. James Jackson, April 18, 1787, *ibid.; American State Papers, Indian Affairs,* I, 22–25; Gov. Matthews to Gen'l. Elijah Clarke, April 17, 1787, Executive Letter Book, G.D.A.; same to Few and Pierce, April 24, 1787, *ibid.;* same to Gen'l. Jackson, April 26, 1787, *ibid.;* same to Joseph Martin, April 28, 1787, *ibid.;* same to Timothy Barnard, April 28, 1787, *ibid.;* same to Gen'ls. Twiggs, Clarke, and Jackson, June 28, 1787, *ibid.*

[21] Bemis, *Pinckney's Treaty,* pp. 104–123, 143–145; Gov. Matthews to Timothy Barnard, Aug. 17, 1787, Ga. Council correspondence, L. of C.; Caswell to Bledsoe and Robertson, Feb. 27, 1787, *N.C.S.R.,* XX, 622; James White to McGillivray, April 4,

Governor Matthews was greatly disappointed over the result of White's negotiations, and White said that Georgia might have saved herself much trouble had she accepted his advice. He suggested also that the Georgians were too stupid to know their own interest and seemed to sympathize more with the Creeks than with his countrymen. When he reported to Congress on his mission that body responded by stating that it could not handle the Indian question adequately unless the States would cease to interfere and leave business entirely to the central authority. It also made another appeal to Georgia and North Carolina to cede their Western lands. Such a cession might have been the best way out of the difficulty, but certainly Congress had as yet done nothing to inspire confidence in its ability to handle the Indian question. In fact, the West—especially the Southwest—had much reason to believe that Congress had very little interest in any of its problems. [22]

The warlike intentions of the Creeks soon became unmistakable. In June they held a great council in the Alabama country with the Cherokee, Shawnee, and other nations. In August they sent a band of warriors to the Chickasaw Bluffs and killed several whites, William Davenport among the number. War was declared upon the Cumberland settlements, and James Robertson sent to Kentucky for aid. Georgia began to prepare for hostilities. [23]

Provision was made for raising three thousand men, and arrangements were concerted with the State of Franklin for enlisting another fifteen hundred there. Captain Augustus Christian George Elholm was a native of Denmark who came to America early in the Revolution and had been commissioned in Pulaski's corps. Governor Telfair had made him adjutant-general of the State of Georgia. The Dane, who was associated with Dr. White in his dubious plans, was later cashiered by Governor Matthews, but now he was aiding Sevier in enlisting and training the troops needed for the Creek campaign. Six hundred forty acres or one square mile of land was to be granted to each Georgian who served and fifty per cent more than that to each "Frank." The "Bend of the Tennessee" was again

1787, *A.S.P., I.A.,* I, 21–22; White to J. G. Blount, Sept. 14, 1787, Blount MSS., N.C.H.C.

[22] *Journals of the Continental Congress,* Aug. 3, 1787, XII, 120–128; James White to J. G. Blount, Aug. 4, 1787, Blount MSS., N.C.H.C.; Committee report, Oct. 20, 1787, Cont. Cong. MSS., 30.

[23] John Cobb to Gen'ls. Twiggs, Clarke, and Jackson, June 19, 1787, Executive Letter Book, G.D.A.; Gov. Matthews to John Sevier, Aug. 9, 1787, *ibid.;* same to Few and Pierce, Aug. 9, 1787, *ibid.;* same to William Pierce, Oct. 16, 1787, *ibid.;* same to Speaker of Assembly, Oct. 18, 1787, *ibid.;* Joseph Martin to Gov. Randolph, June 28, 1787, Clark MSS., Va. Arch.; Arthur Campbell to Gov. Randolph, Oct. 26, 1787, *ibid.;* Samuel McDowell to Arthur Campbell, Draper MSS., 9DD46; *C.V.S.P.,* IV, 333–334; *Kentucky Gazette,* Aug. 18, 1787; *Pittsburgh Gazette,* Sept. 29, 1787.

set aside for paying this bounty to the latter, thus keeping the Muscle Shoals venture alive. Governor Sevier readily accepted the terms, for next to land there was nothing he liked so much as an Indian war. So great was his reputation along this line that the Creeks and Chickamaugas left the Watauga settlements entirely alone while making life miserable for the Cumberland people.[24]

But Sevier was having his troubles at home. He had made treaties with the Cherokee and taken up land as far south as the French Broad River. This was done without the consent of North Carolina but with the advice of General Elijah Clarke of Georgia who said "seven states have agreed to give up the navigation. I know you must have the navigation of the Mississippi." The old North State, however, was not without resourcefulness, and she encouraged the election of loyal officials in the counties making up the State of Franklin. Sevier and Caswell were working for a compromise whereby a peaceful settlement of the differences between the two jurisdictions could be reached, but Caswell's enemies in the assembly, and John Tipton and William Cocke in Franklin prevented an agreement. Thus the dispute continued, with Sevier losing much of his support in the counties along the Virginia border. By this time Arthur Campbell had lost all interest in the State of Franklin and no longer had any ambition to separate southwestern Virginia from the State. He was still acting as lieutenant of Washington County, and its court now asked that he be restored to his old position as justice of the peace. The year ended with the rebel governor still in the midst of his difficulties with North Carolina and still awaiting the call for troops from Governor Matthews of Georgia for the expected war with the Creeks.[25]

North of the Ohio River the usual confusion continued. The Cahokians were disturbed about a grant of some common lands which Father Gibault

[24] Martin to Henry, Jan. 20, 1787, Henry, *Henry,* III, 382–385; MS. Journal of the Georgia House of Assembly, Jan. 23, 1787, pp. 77–78, G.D.A.; Gov. Matthews to John Sevier, Aug. 9, 1787, Ga. Council correspondence, L. of C.; same to same, Oct. 10, 1787, *ibid.;* William Cocke to Gov. Matthews, June 25, 1787, *American Museum,* II, 581; Sevier to Matthews, Aug. 30, 1787, *ibid.,* II, 580; George Elholm to Gen'l. Moultrie, Nov. 11, 1787, *ibid.,* II, 583; Matthews to Timothy Barnard, Aug. 7, 1787, Executive Letter Book, G.D.A.; same to Cocke, Nov. 8, 1787, *ibid.;* same to Col. Handley, Nov. 9, 1787, *ibid.;* same to Sevier, Nov. 12, 1787, *ibid.;* same to Pres. of Cong., Nov. 15, 1787, *ibid.*

[25] Abernethy, *Tennessee,* pp. 81–85; Arthur Campbell to Joseph Martin, June 10, 1786, Cont. Cong. MSS., 71, II, 453; Martin to (Randolph), March 25, 1787, *ibid.,* 71, II, 567; *ibid.,* 71, II, 531, 535; Gilmore, *Sevier,* p. 111; Arthur Campbell to Gov. Randolph, April 15, 1787, *C.V.S.P.,* IV, 268; *ibid.,* pp. 113–115, 236, 274–275; Thomas Hutchins to Gen'l. Shelby, April 22, 1787, Misc. MSS., series 1, I, N.C.H.C.; Arthur Campbell to Madison, May 12, 1787, Madison MSS., L. of C.; Caswell to Shelby, May 31, 1787, Durrett collection, Misc. MSS., U. of C.; *Kentucky Gazette,* Oct. 6, 1787; Sevier to Benjamin Franklin, Sept. 12, 1787, Franklin MSS., XXXV, 119, A.P.S.; John Tipton to Caswell, Nov. 27, 1787, Governors' correspondence, N.C.H.C.

had made to George Rogers Clark and which Clark had sold to Dorsey Pentecost. They petitioned Congress denying that Gibault had a right to dispose of the tract in question and asked that some kind of government be established among them. Tardiveau also was interesting himself in Illinois lands. He got up a petition to Congress asking that five hundred acres be granted to each male inhabitant in addition to what he might already hold and presented himself to that body as agent for the petitioners, both French and American. Of course he was to receive a part of the land for his services. On August 17, 1787, Harmar arrived in the Illinois country and took Tardiveau and Dodge under his wing. In connection with his campaign of the previous year, Clark had expelled Dodge from Kaskaskia, but he now returned and became the chief confidant of Harmar. Several prominent French residents protested to Congress against their rule, and M. Legras, "Colonel Commandant and Chief Magistrate of Vincennes," petitioned the "General Assembly of Kentucky," forwarding the appeal through General Wilkinson, but nothing was accomplished toward ameliorating the situation.[26]

The land between the Scioto and the Little Miami had been reserved by Virginia for bounties to her Continental line. This was to be used only after lands in the military reservation south of the Ohio and Green Rivers should be exhausted. By September, 1788, military warrants had been issued to State and Continental lines amounting to more than three and a half million acres. Of this, somewhat more than a million and a half acres had been located in Kentucky south of the Green River by August 1, 1787.

On January 25, 1787, Governor Randolph issued a proclamation opening the lands north of the Ohio to entry by the Continental line. The surveyor's office was opened for this purpose on August 1, 1787, and by September 6, 1788, nearly a million and a half acres had been located. This left more than a million acres in Continental warrants still outstanding. Colonel Richard C. Anderson was principal surveyor for all Virginia military bounty lands. George Muter and Thomas and Humphrey Marshall were superintendents for the State line, and William Croghan for the Continental line.[27]

Meanwhile Congress made a beginning toward the assertion of its authority in the eastern part of the Northwest Territory. On July 13, 1787, the famous Northwest Ordinance was passed, and on October 5 General

[26] Alvord, *Illinois Country*, pp. 363–371; *Kaskaskia Records*, pp. xlii, 424–429, 436–439; de la Valiniere to Congress, Aug. 25, 1787, Cont. Cong. MSS., 48; Cahokia petition, July 15, 1786, *ibid.*; Legras to Wilkinson, Feb. 3, 1787, *ibid.*; Tardiveau to Congress, Sept. 15, Aug. 27, 1787, Feb. 9, March 2, May 19, 1788, *ibid.*; Langlois to Charles Thomson, Sept. 20, 1787, *ibid.*; William Grayson to Madison, Aug. 31, 1787, Madison MSS., L. of C.; *Cahokia Records*, pp. cxxxiii–vi, cxxxviii–cxli, 580–589.
[27] *C.V.S.P.*, IV, 231, 475–476, 477.

Arthur St. Clair was chosen governor under that instrument. After two attempts Hutchins had failed to carry out the surveys which he had been directed to make next to the Pennsylvania boundary. The threatening attitude of the Indians contributed to his failure, and the British were doing all they could to encourage them to prevent American settlement. Nevertheless, during the year Congress made a grant of one and a half million acres to the Ohio Company, which had been organized the previous year by General Rufus Putnam, General Samuel Holden Parsons, Manasseh Cutler, and others, mostly from New England. The next year another grant of a million acres was made to John Cleves Symmes of New Jersey and his associates.[28]

During the following year General St. Clair organized his government and the land companies began the colonization of their grants. This was the beginning of a story which has often been told, the development of which belongs rather to the history of the new Federal Union than to the annals of the fading Confederation.

[28] Gen'l. Hope to Evan Nepean, Sept. 8, 1786, P.R.O., C.O., 42, 18; Daniel Claus to Evan Nepean, May 5, 1787, P.R.O., C.O., series 5, 42, 19; Rufus Putnam to Thomas Hutchins, July 7, 1786, Hutchins MSS., H.S.P.; A. A. Hoops to Hutchins, May 7, 1787, *ibid.;* narrative of John S. Gano (?), n.d., n.s., Draper MSS., 2U142; Beverley W. Bond, ed., *The Correspondence of John Cleves Symmes* (New York, 1926) pp. 278–280; Payson J. Treat, *The National Land System* (New York, 1910) pp. 42–43, 47–54.

CHAPTER XXV

SPANISH AND BRITISH INTRIGUE IN THE WEST, 1788–1789

DURING 1788 the efforts of Congress to deal with the Indian problem were as futile as ever. Richard Butler was now acting as sole agent for the Northern Department, and Richard Winn, a person with no special qualifications for the post, served for the Southern. Joseph Martin was appointed deputy agent to the Cherokee and Chickasaws. War between Georgia and the Creeks was threatening, but Congress provided for a treaty, to be negotiated by Winn. He was to have the assistance of agents appointed for that purpose by Georgia, North and South Carolina. North Carolina failed to make an appointment, but Georgia and South Carolina selected their ex-governors Matthews and Pickens. When Governor Handley of Georgia was notified of the Congressional arrangements he wrote on February 19 to Sevier, saying that preparations for hostilities would be suspended. It looked as though the Franklinites had lost their last chance of securing lands in the Bend of the Tennessee.[1]

But Sevier was not to be left without occupation. The anti-Franklinite party in Washington and Sullivan Counties had been growing apace and many of the early leaders of the new-State movement had fallen away from the cause. Under the leadership of John Tipton, some of Sevier's property was attached for payment of North Carolina taxes and an order was issued for the seizure of some county records supposed to be in Sevier's possession. A fight between the followers of the rival leaders occurred on or about February 3rd, and three men were killed in the fray.[2]

Tipton now appealed to Arthur Campbell to bring a force from Virginia to aid him in suppressing the rebel. Governor Randolph anticipated

[1] A group of Virginians from Botetourt County had offered to assist Georgia in the War in consideration of land bounties. Governor George Handley to Preston, Smith, and Hawkins, Jan. or Feb., 1788, Executive Letter Book, G.D.A.; Handley to Sevier, Feb. 19, 1788, *ibid.;* same to Elijah Clarke, Nov. 20, 1788, *ibid.;* Andrew Pickens to Joseph Martin, Nov. 10, 1788, Draper MSS., 33J144; Williamson to Martin, June 23, 1788, *ibid.,* 2XX17; appointment of Martin, *ibid.,* 2XX23; Joseph Martin to William (?) Blount, July 25, 1788, J. G. Blount MSS., N.C.H.C.; *C.V.S.P.,* IV, 401–402, 460; *A.S.P., I.A.,* I, 26.

[2] Samuel Johnston to J. G. Blount, April 12, 1788, J. G. Blount MSS., N.C.H.C.; Abernethy, *Tennessee,* p. 86.

an embarrassing situation in case North Carolina should call on him for assistance, but no such call was forthcoming. Joseph Martin was acting, under the authority of North Carolina, as brigadier-general of Washington District. He was not in the District when the Sevier-Tipton fight occurred, but returning soon afterward he applied himself to the task of making peace. Sevier, who said that he had been dragged into the Franklin movement and who was anxious to find a way out of it, appealed to Martin to mediate and offered to suspend all hostilities until the forthcoming session of the North Carolina assembly should have an opportunity to deal with the situation. Martin wrote to Governor Randolph that he had seen Sevier and settled the dispute. Apparently he had, for no further conflicts occurred and the State of Franklin passed quietly out of existence. North Carolina authority was reestablished in the rebel counties, and presently Sevier was invested with the brigadier-generalship which he had declined in 1784.[3]

While Sevier was embroiled in the stormy career of Franklin, Alexander McGillivray, in collaboration with his commercial partner William Panton, was engaged in the establishment of a trading post at St. Mark's in Florida. British goods were imported to this place for the supply of the Creeks. During the previous year a party of these Indians had visited British officials at Nassau, and now a certain William Augustus Bowles, under the patronage of Lord Dunmore, who was at this time governor of the Bahamas, came from the islands to reside for some months among the natives. Bowles was a Maryland Tory who had served as an officer in the British forces during the War. We have little information as to the object of his visit, but England was expecting a renewal of war in Europe. That an attack upon the Spanish possessions in America was looked upon as a possibility is shown by the activities of Lord Dorchester in Canada. For the present, however, McGillivray's Spanish connection was the more important. His attitude toward Bowles was not friendly, and the British adventurer shortly returned whence he had come.[4]

During April James Robertson sent two messengers from Nashville

[3] John Tipton and George Maxwell to Arthur Campbell, March 12, 1788, Draper MSS., 9DD47; Martin to Governor Randolph, March 13, 1788, Cont. Cong. MSS., 71, II, 597; Sevier to Martin, March 27, 1788, C.V.S.P., IV, 416–417, 421, 472.
[4] Gen. Richard McArthur to Lord Sydney, April 23, 1787, P.R.O., C.O., 23, 27; deposition of William Augustus Bowles, April 9, 1788, P.R.O., C.O., 25, 27; Gov. Handley to Few and Baldwin, April 26, 1788, Executive Letter Book, G.D.A.; same to Despedes, Nov. 25, 1788, ibid.; Arthur Campbell to Gov. Randolph, Aug. 1, 1789, C.V.S.P., V, 10–11; Henry Knox to Washington, July 6, 1789, A.S.P., I.A., I, 15–16; Arthur Campbell to Washington, May 10, 1789, Cont. Cong. MSS., 78, VI, 369; White, Historical Collections of Georgia, pp. 163–164; R. Faulder, Memoirs of William Augustus Bowles (London, 1791, reprinted in The Magazine of History, XII, 103–127).

with a letter to McGillivray. On the fourteenth of that month McGillivray answered the letter and mentioned that he had also had messages from Richard Caswell and Benjamin Hawkins of North Carolina. He was likewise in correspondence with Andrew Pickens, ex-governor of South Carolina, and on April 15 he invited Joseph Martin to visit him.[5]

We have no copy of Robertson's letter and we know nothing of its contents save what McGillivray said of it. In his reply to Robertson, he indicated only that peace was the object of the negotiation. Robertson sent a copy of the reply to Caswell and to Joseph Martin, who sent it to Governor Randolph. However, on April 25 McGillivray wrote to Governor O'Neill at Pensacola saying that Robertson had proposed that the Cumberland settlements should join with Kentucky in setting up an independent government and forming a connection with Spain.[6]

Since James White's conference with Gardoqui in August, 1786, this was the first suggestion of a Spanish intrigue which had come out of North Carolina. But Gardoqui had indicated that White's suggestion was being followed up. Wilkinson had returned from New Orleans to Kentucky in February, and Robertson's suggestion of collaboration with Kentucky indicates that he knew of the plans being made in the neighboring settlements.[7]

About the first of May James White, after a conference with Gardoqui, left New York to visit the Western settlements and gather into his hands the threads of Spanish intrigue. We cannot follow his movements in detail, but on May 16 he was at Pittsburgh in company with General Josiah Harmar and Samuel Holden Parsons. He accompanied Harmar to Fort Harmar and there we lose sight of him until he reached the Franklin country and called on John Sevier during July. On July 18 and again on September 12, Sevier wrote to Gardoqui and indicated his willingness to enter into such a scheme as Robertson had outlined to McGillivray.[8]

In order to facilitate this program Sevier organized a new State of Franklin in the southern counties of his old domain. He at once in-

[5] McGillivray to James Robertson, April 14, 1788, Misc. MSS., Series 1, I, N.C.H.C.; George Walton to Gov. Charles Pinckney, April 28, 1789, Executive Letter Book, G.D.A.

[6] McGillivray to O'Neill, April 25, 1788, Pontalba transcripts, Filson Club, Louisville; Miró to Valdés, June 15, 1788, *ibid.*; Robertson to Martin, May 7, 1788, Cont. Cong. MSS., 71, II, 619; Martin to Randolph, June 11, 1788, *ibid.*, f. 623; McGillivray to Martin, April 15, 1788, *ibid.*, f. 625.

[7] Bemis, *Pinckney's Treaty*, p. 143.

[8] *Ibid.*, pp. 158–159; Henry, *Henry*, II, 314–316; Gayarré, III, 257; A. P. Whitaker, "Spanish Intrigue in the Old Southwest," *M.V.H.R.*, XII, 155–176; *Journal and Letters of Col. John May of Boston*, Historical and Philosophical Society of Ohio, new series, I (Cincinnati, 1873) pp. 61–62.

stituted a war against the Cherokee and wrote to the council of his new State of Franklin that on January 12, 1789, he had won a bloody battle in the passes of the mountains. A letter written on the same day from Greene County, North Carolina, declared:

My hopes turn on the hinges of the treaty in May next. Last week a council of safety sat at French Broad. They disclaimed any present design of forming a new Gov. Resolved to put their volunteer corps under the direction of General Sevier. That they would aim at peace & court the protection of the United States, appointing Mr. Nelson and Mr. Ouitleau (Outlaw) to wait on Congress with their request. That they will petition for a division of the State at the Appalachian Mts; and have appointed Joseph Harden, Sen. to visit Cumberland and request concurrence of the inhabitants. Another meeting is appointed at Greensville in February so as to be more convenient to the counties of Washington and Sullivan, whose attendance by their Representatives is requested. General Sevier's messengers are returned from the Creek and Cherokee country with assurance Indians disposed to exchange prisoners and treat for peace agreeable to his proposals—an incorporating union is aimed at which there is some hopes of affecting from the apparent coalition of views between Sevier and McGillivray.[9]

Thus it is clear that Sevier was planning, in cooperation with the Cumberland settlements, to get Congressional assent to the creation of a new State in western North Carolina. McGillivray was to be brought into the movement and the Muscle Shoals country was to be incorporated in the new government. The half-breed Chief would certainly not have been expected to act without the good-will of Spain, and White was working on that end of the business but this was not being noised abroad at the moment.

Sevier also took a few amenable Cherokee chiefs under his wing and with the assistance of one Bennett Ballew began negotiating for a concession of land from this nation. Congress ordered troops to march to the protection of the Cherokee, and Patrick Henry and his agent, Joseph Martin, used their influence to thwart the efforts of Ballew. At about the same time Henry began to manifest an interest in Georgia's Western-land claims which, before the end of the year, took shape as the first Yazoo Company.[10]

[9] Sevier to Council of the new State of Franklin, Jan. 12, 1789, *Kentucky Gazette*, May 9, 1789; extract of a letter dated Greene County, N. C., Jan. 10, May 16, 1789, *ibid.*; George Nicholas to Madison, Nov. 2, 1789, Madison papers, L. of C.; Richard Winn to Secretary Knox, Aug. 5, 1788, *A.S.P., I.A.*, I, 28; ——(?) to Arthur Campbell, Aug. 20, 1788, Draper MSS., 9DD50; act creating the first Yazoo Companies, Dec. 21, 1789, *ibid.*, 11DD85a; Bodley, *Littell*, pp. 95–96; Abernethy, *Tennessee*, p. 87.

[10] Bennett Ballew to Gov. Samuel Johnston, Oct. 30, 1789, Governors' correspondence, N.C.H.C.; R. H. Lee to Henry, May 28, 1789, Henry, *Henry*, III, 387–389; Grayson to Henry, Sept. 29, 1789, *ibid.*, pp. 405–407; Joseph Martin to Henry, July 2, 1789, Draper MSS., 2XX30; same to same, Jan. 18, 1790, Southern History As-

On October 11, 1788, Gardoqui issued a passport to Sevier authorizing him to visit New Orleans. No use was made of this permit, but White returned to New York and at once set out on another journey, this time going to New Orleans by way of Havana. On April 15, 1789, he reached his destination and found the scheme in which he was concerned progressing nicely. On January 11 James Robertson and Daniel Smith had written separate letters to Miró proposing a connection between the Cumberland settlements and the Spanish power and saying that they were planning to send delegates to North Carolina in the fall to ask for a separation from the State. They had just succeeded in having the assembly of North Carolina organize their government as the "District of Mero," and the Spanish governor was apprised of the honor which had been conferred upon him.[11]

On April 18 and 22, 1789, White addressed letters to Miró discussing plans for the separation of the Franklin and Cumberland settlements from the American union and the extension of Spanish authority over these peoples. Miró wrote letters to White and to Smith in which he announced that the Western inhabitants would be permitted to ship their goods to New Orleans at a duty of fifteen per cent, with an even lower rate to men of political influence. He expressed interest in their plans, but said that Spain could do nothing in regard to the proposed separation until it had already been accomplished. Miró wrote to Wilkinson explaining the negotiations with White, Smith, and Robertson.[12]

These facts give a very imperfect picture of the Spanish intrigue so far as it applied to the Western settlements of North Carolina, but it is impossible to interpret them as fortuitous occurrences. They outline a movement which ramified from New York to Kentucky and from the Cumberland settlements to those of the new State of Franklin. It is hard to believe that Robertson, who had never acted except as agent for some one higher up, should have proceeded on his individual initiative in this instance.[13]

The Muscle Shoals speculators had planned an extension of their territory sufficiently southward to give their domain an outlet to the Gulf at Mobile Bay. In 1788 Sevier approached Miró in regard to a

sociation, *Publications,* VI, 30–32; Wm. Fleming to Gov. Randolph, July 31, 1789, *C.V.S.P.,* V, 9–10; Henry to R. H. Lee, Aug. 28, 1789, Jan. 29, 1790, Feb. 8, 1791, S. V. Henkels, *Patrick Henry Letters* (catalogue, Philadelphia, 1910) p. 42.

[11] Gayarré, III, 257–260.

[12] Miró to White, April 20, 1789, Pontalba transcripts, Filson Club, Louisville, Ky.; White to Miró, April 22, 1789, *ibid.;* Miró to Wilkinson, April 27, 1789, *ibid.;* Miró to Daniel Smith, April 24, 1789, *ibid.;* Maj. John Hamtramck to Gen. Harmar, July 29, 1789, *Kaskaskia Records,* pp. 506–508.

[13] James Robertson to William Blount, Sept. 21, 1789, J. G. Blount MSS., N.C.H.C.

proposed settlement at Muscle Shoals; at about the same time Joseph Martin wrote to McGillivray to obtain his consent to a settlement on the Tombigbee. Some of this correspondence was intercepted and turned over to the government of Georgia, which condemned Martin and protested to Congress concerning his conduct. The mysterious correspondence that was carried on simultaneously between Caswell, Pickens, and Martin on one side and McGillivray on the other can hardly be accounted for except by assuming that they were parties to the intrigue, and Martin, Caswell, and Sevier were all members of the Muscle Shoals Company. Dr. James White had no standing in North Carolina except as a protégé of Blount and Caswell. This phase of the Spanish conspiracy, then, was apparently an attempt of the Muscle Shoals group to secure the cooperation of McGillivray and his Spanish friends in helping to open the Bend of the Tennessee to settlement and give it an outlet to the Gulf. That this speculation was by no means dead is revealed by the fact that on December 2, 1789, the Georgia assembly passed an act confirming the former grant of five thousand acres to each of the commissioners who had been appointed to act for the company and allowing three months for the completion of titles to lands already surveyed under its authority in the Muscle Shoals area.[14]

It is true that Blount and Caswell, as well as White, Sevier, and Robertson, were all Federalists and intent upon securing adoption of the new Federal Constitution by North Carolina. The conspiracy would undoubtedly be quashed as a result of the establishment of the new government, and the conspirators must have looked upon that contingency with equanimity. The Bend country lay within the confines of Georgia and South Carolina, but Blount and Caswell and their friends also held claims to enormous tracts in western North Carolina. These lands would rise in value in case they were ceded to the central government and a stronger union created to protect them. No secret was made of the negotiation with McGillivray and the conspirators probably hoped that a knowledge of their plot might stimulate North Carolina to seek the protection of a more powerful union. But if that could not be accomplished, then it might be necessary to continue to bargain with McGillivray and the Spaniards in order to secure an outlet for Western produce and a rising market for Western lands.

[14] Alexander Outlaw to Gov. Caswell, Oct. 8, 1786, *S.R.N.C.*, XVIII, 756–759; MS. Journal of the Georgia House of Assembly, Jan. 24, Dec. 2, 1789, G.D.A.; Gov. George Walton to Washington, March 11, 1789, Executive Letter Book, G.D.A.; same to Governor of N. C., March 11, 1789, *ibid.; C.V.S.P.*, IV, 428–429; A. P. Whitaker, "The Muscle Shoals Speculation," *M.V.H.R.*, XIII, 379–382; A. P. Whitaker, "Spanish Intrigue in the Old Southwest," *M.V.H.R.*, XII, 155–176; Williams, *Franklin*, pp. 238–239; Abernethy, *Tennessee*, p. 115.

Governor Handley of Georgia was thoroughly suspicious of the dealings of White, Pickens, and Martin with McGillivray, believing that their influence with the Chief of the Creeks was not likely to aid in bringing about peace between his State and the natives. The superintendent, Richard Winn, fixed September 15, 1788, for the negotiation of a treaty with them, but neither Congress nor Georgia appropriated sufficient funds for the purpose, and McGillivray gave it out that he did not intend that any land cession should be made to the whites. Thus the end of 1788 found the situation between Georgia and the Creeks practically the same as it had been at the beginning.[15] During the following year another attempt was made under Congressional authority to negotiate a treaty with the Creeks. McGillivray was led to believe that the lands which his family had lost during the War might be restored to him. There is evidence suggesting that both the Congressional commissioners and the State of Georgia made overtures along this line, and on November 17, 1789, the Georgia assembly made McGillivray a citizen of the State. But this plan, like all previous ones looking toward a treaty with the wily half-breed Chief, ended in failure.[16]

It is obvious from the foregoing discussion that the Spanish intrigue in North Carolina had a different origin and varied in many details from the Kentucky phase of the plot. Yet the two movements paralleled each other and were used by the Spanish agents for the same purpose.

On his return from New Orleans, Wilkinson reached Kentucky in February, 1788. He had stopped in Richmond and accredited himself there as agent for Daniel Clark. There, too, he had heard from a returned member of Congress that Gardoqui had received news of his cordial reception in New Orleans. Since that official had not responded to his original advances, he had not intended that he should be apprised of the New Orleans venture, but he now wrote to him and entrusted the letter to his brother-in-law, Rudolph Tillier, in Philadelphia. Tillier was left to his own discretion as to the delivery of the letter and decided to withhold it. But later in the year Wilkinson's partner, Major Isaac B. Dunn,

---

[15] On February 1, 1788, Georgia made a partial cession of her Western lands to Congress and repealed the act creating Bourbon County, but Congress declined to accept the gift because of the conditions attached to it. MS. Journal of the Georgia House of Assembly, Jan. 23, 1788, G.D.A.; Watkins, *Digest of the Laws of Georgia*, pp. 370–371; Gov. Handley to Few and Baldwin, April 26, 1788, Executive Letter Book, G.D.A.; same to commissioners, Aug. 15, 1788, *ibid.;* committee report, July 14, 1788, Cont. Cong. MSS., 30; *A.S.P., I.A.,* I, 28–31.

[16] White, *Historical Collections of Georgia*, p. 154; MS. Senate Journal, Nov. 17, 1789, G.D.A.; George Walton to McGillivray, Feb. 7, 1789, Executive Letter Book, G.D.A.; same to Timothy Bernard, April 11, 1789, *ibid.;* Robert Hays to Daniel Smith, June 18, 1789, Draper MSS., 4XX6; Arthur Campbell to Oliver Spencer, Nov. 30, 1789, *ibid.,* 9DD54.

visited the East and had a conference with the Spanish *chargé,* who in this and other ways kept in touch with both phases of the conspiracy.[17]

On his way home Wilkinson sent Washington a present of some Indian fabrics, and the late Commander-in-Chief wrote to the late Clothier-General, whom he had dismissed from office and who had blabbed about the Conway cabal, that he was sorry he had not found it possible to visit him.[18]

Wilkinson arrived in the Kentucky wilderness in a coach and four—doubtless the first that had been seen in those parts—and his purchases of tobacco soon caused the price of the staple to rise and the fame of the purchaser to mount. In fact, Wilkinson had advised the Kentuckians to plant tobacco even before he had found a market for it.[19]

Immediately on his return Wilkinson dispatched Joshua Barbee, who had been recommended to him for that purpose by Harry Innes, to New Orleans with a letter for the governor. He later sent down several boatloads of goods under the care of Dunn and asked that a return in merchandise might be made forthwith. This was contrary to the original agreement whereby the proceeds were to be left in New Orleans until Wilkinson had made good his political engagement. But Miró did not wish to offend the powerful Kentucky magnate and complied with the request.[20]

Wilkinson, however, did not have a monopoly of the trade to New Orleans. Girault was still in Natchez and continued to correspond with William Clark. The former obtained a permit to import goods on paying a duty of twenty-five per cent, but he thought he might avoid the duty by landing the goods above Natchez and smuggling them in. Daniel Clark also obtained a similar permit for William Croghan. Such permits were supposed to be granted only to Spanish citizens, which Girault claimed to be. He thought that the granting of such permits was being kept secret for the time being, but that there was a general regulation concerning their issuance to Spanish subjects and that they would soon be very common. Furthermore, immigrants were allowed to bring in

[17] F. Webb to John Pendleton, Dec. 6, 1787, Clark MSS., Va. Arch.; James Innes to same, Dec. 18, 1787, *ibid.;* Miró and Navarro to Valdés, April 11, 1788, Pontalba transcripts, Filson Club, published in Gayarré, III, 206–207.

[18] Washington to Wilkinson, Feb. 20, 1788, James Wilkinson MSS., Chicago Historical Society.

[19] Marshall, *Kentucky,* I, 283–284; Green, *Spanish Conspiracy,* pp. 134–135; Draper MSS., 18CC15.

[20] Statement of Joshua Barbee, depositions in case of Innes vs. Marshall, Durrett MSS., p. 43; *A.S.P.,* XX, 923; Gov. Greenup to Kentucky delegates in Congress, Feb. 19, 1808, Innes MSS., L. of C.; Miró to Fray and Valdés, June 15, 1788, Pontalba transcripts, Filson Club; same to Valdés, Aug. 28, 1788, *ibid.;* Clark to Wilkinson, June 6, 1788, Wilkinson, *Memoirs,* II, appendix xiii.

their possessions duty free. Wilkinson, however, had a big advantage over such importers, for his tobacco was taken by the Spanish governor, under the pretense that it was the product of Louisiana, at a price of four dollars the hundred-weight. This was higher than the general market, and Miró reaped a share of the profits. All told, a considerable trade was being carried on with New Orleans, both from the Kentucky country and from Philadelphia.[21]

Gardoqui was anxious that the trade from Philadelphia to New Orleans should be handled by Eastern merchants who were his agents, one of whom was John Holker. When some of the New Orleans merchants failed to comply with his wishes in this matter he managed to impose penalties upon them until they conformed their practice to his desires.[22]

While Wilkinson was combining his trade and intrigue, politics in the West was crystallizing around the issue of statehood for Kentucky. Virginia had sent John Brown to Congress as representative for the Kentucky District, and on February 29, 1788, he presented to that body Kentucky's petition for admission to the Confederation. About the beginning of May an election was held in accord with Virginia's act of separation to choose delegates to a convention to frame a constitution for the new State. Kentucky's delegates to the Virginia convention which was to pass on the adoption of the new Federal Constitution were chosen at the same time.[23]

There was no question about Kentucky's desire for statehood, but there was considerable doubt about her desire for the new Constitution. The court of Fayette County, including McDowell, Wallace, Innes, Muter, Sebastian, Logan, and Greenup, had protested against it and asked that the delegates be instructed accordingly. Wilkinson and his powerful group of friends exerted all their influence toward the same end, and when, on June 28, the Virginia convention cast its fateful vote, eleven out of fourteen of the Kentucky delegates were in the negative, Humphrey Marshall and the two delegates from Jefferson County constituting the minority.[24]

There were several reasons for the opposition of Kentucky to the Federal Constitution. The attitude of Congress on the question of the

[21] Girault to William Clark, June 26, Aug. 27, 1787, April 12, July 21, Sept. 1, Dec. 5, 1788, March 20, Sept. 1, 1789, Draper MSS., IM143, 146, 151, 163, 171, 179, 185, 191; John Williams to William Clark, Feb. 11, 1789, *ibid.*, LM182; Wm. F. Switzler, "Report on the Internal Commerce of the United States," H. of R., 50th Cong., 1st session (1887–1888) XX, no. 6, pt. 2, p. 181; Clark to William Croghan, June 14, 1788, Draper MSS., 1N7; Isaac Dunn to Wilkinson, June 15, 1788, James Wilkinson MSS., Chicago Historical Society; Bemis, *Pinckney's Treaty*, p. 147.

[22] Wilkinson, *Memoirs*, II, appendix 6.

[23] *Kentucky Gazette*, May 3, 1788.

[24] Draper MSS., 11J182.

navigation of the Mississippi was certainly the foremost of these, and it was a powerful weapon in the hands of Patrick Henry and those who supported him in opposition to adoption. The fact that Congress had done nothing to aid Kentucky in its struggle with the Indians was another potent factor in the case, and so was the fear that when Federal courts should assume jurisdiction in cases involving land titles the interests of local land investors might suffer. But this fear was stronger in those parts of Virginia where the old land companies lay claim to the soil. In addition to all this, there is good evidence to the effect that Wilkinson and his friends knew that the creation of a stronger union would interfere with their intrigue with the Spanish, and thus they differed from their fellow-conspirators of North Carolina.[25]

On July 28 the seventh Kentucky convention assembled. It was supposed to frame a constitution for the new State, but nothing could be done until Congress had provided for its reception into the Confederation, and no such action had been taken. Consideration of the petition presented by Brown had been long delayed, and finally, on July 3, the whole question of the admission of Kentucky was referred to the new government which was soon to be established under the Federal Constitution.[26]

Brown looked upon this as merely another victory of the East over the South and West and thought that Kentucky could expect as little from the new as from the old union so long as it was dominated by the seven States north of Maryland. He at once got in touch with Oliver Pollock, who had just returned to America after a sojourn in a debtor's prison in Havana, and the two consulted Gardoqui. Brown informed the Spanish *chargé* that he was returning to Kentucky to work for the separation of that country from the union and for its alliance with Spain. On his return to New Orleans, Pollock gave Miró information to this effect.[27]

On July 10 Brown wrote to Muter stating that Gardoqui had said he had authority to open the navigation of the Mississippi to Kentucky in

[25] John Brown, however, wrote to Eastern friends favoring adoption. Testimony of John Fowler, n.d., Innes MSS., XX, pt. 2, L. of C.; Innes to Brown, April 4, 1788, *ibid.;* deposition of John Wilson, n.d., *ibid.,* XXII, pt. 2; Madison to Washington, April 10, 1788, Sparks, *Letters to Washington,* IV, 213–214; George Nicholas to Madison, May 9, 1788, Madison MSS., L. of C.; Bradford, "Notes on Kentucky," *Kentucky Gazette,* March 2, 1827; Marshall, *Kentucky,* I, 285, 310–311; Ambler, *West Virginia,* pp. 182–183; Green, *Spanish Conspiracy,* 142–143.

[26] Collins, *Kentucky,* I, 21; Bodley, *Littell,* pp. 26–32, 88–93; *C.V.S.P.,* IV, 461; Draper MSS., 18CC145–153; *Kentucky Gazette,* Aug. 30, 1788; Bradford, "Notes on Kentucky," *ibid.,* March 30, 1827.

[27] Information by Alexander McKee, May 31, 1785, P.R.O., C.O., series 5, 42, 48; testimony of John Brown, Innes MSS., XXII, pt. 1, L. of C.; Miró to Valdés, Nov. 3, 1788, Gayarré, III, 221–223; Green, *Spanish Conspiracy,* p. 155; Smith, *Kentucky,* pp. 435–436, 451; Wilkinson, *Memoirs,* II, appendix 1.

case that region became independent, but that it could never be done so long as it was a part of the United States. He wrote also to Samuel McDowell, president of the convention, and gave him similar information, but wrote it on a detached slip of paper. Innes, upon being shown the letter by McDowell, said "It will do." [28]

On May 15 Wilkinson had dispatched Dunn to New Orleans with a letter for Miró. He told the Spanish governor that he thought Congress would admit Kentucky, but that he planned to put his scheme through regardless of Congressional action. As soon as the new State government should be established agents were to be sent to treat with Spain. [29]

Muter had been one of Wilkinson's early group of Danville confederates, but he had lately moved from Danville and become a neighbor of Thomas Marshall near Frankfort. He had thus come under the influence of the veteran under whom he had served as lieutenant-colonel during the Revolution. Marshall had aided Wilkinson in his attack on Clark after the Indian campaign of 1786, but he and Muter now took the lead, aided by Dr. Ebenezer Brooks, in opposing Wilkinson's plans. [30]

When news reached the Kentucky convention that immediate admission had been denied by Congress indignation was expressed by many of the members, but Wilkinson must have been jubilant, for this event made his problem much simpler. Wallace, Innes, and Sebastian now, for the first time, openly advocated prompt separation from the union, but the Spanish connection was kept in the background. Wilkinson said that Marshall and Muter were the only Kentucky leaders who opposed his plans, although he had explained them fully only to Innes and Alexander Scott Bullitt. Yet, knowing that the majority of the people were not inclined to back anything more radical than a legal separation from Virginia in cooperation with Congress, the leaders hesitated. Resolutions were passed calling for the election of another convention "with full power to take such measures for obtaining admission of the district as a separate and independent state of the Union, and the navigation of the Mississippi, as may appear proper, and to form a constitutional Government in the District, . . . or to do and accomplish whatever on a con-

[28] Deposition of McDowell, n.d., Innes MSS., XXII, pt. 1, L. of C.; deposition of Humphrey (?) Marshall, n.d., *ibid.;* deposition of Samuel McDowell, n.d., *ibid.,* XXII, pt. 2; Collins, *Kentucky,* I, 21–22; Smith, *Kentucky,* pp. 282–283; Marshall, *Kentucky,* I, 304–306; Butler, *Kentucky,* pp. 171–172; Green, *Spanish Conspiracy,* pp. 180–181; Bodley, *Littell,* pp. 97–98; Shreve, *The Finished Scoundrel,* pp. 74–77.
[29] Wilkinson to Miró and Navarro, May 15, 1788, Pontalba transcripts, Filson Club, given in Gayarré, III, 208–211; Fortier, *Louisiana,* II, 129–142; Green, *Spanish Conspiracy,* pp. 129–130.
[30] *Journal of the House of Delegates,* Nov. 15, 1777, p. 27; Thomas Marshall to Washington, June 26, 1789, Sparks, *Letters to Washington,* IV, 261; Bodley, *Littell,* p. xi; Green, *Spanish Conspiracy,* pp. 210–211.

sideration of the state of the district may in their opinion promote its interests." Plenary powers were thus bestowed upon a body which could have no legal existence unless the authority of Virginia was first obtained.[31]

During September and October Kentucky waged an acrimonious contest over the election of members to this convention. Opponents of the Wilkinson group urged that no election should be held because there was no authority for the convention and because the wide powers which were proposed for it would make it a dangerous conclave. On October 15 Muter published a handbill, which later appeared in the *Gazette,* condemning the movement. Three days afterward another article appeared stating that the militia officers of the district had met and effected a compromise agreement. Elections were to be held and the convention was to meet as planned, but the voters were to instruct the delegates as to their stand on the question of separation. Opponents of the new State stressed the fact that taxes were not being collected in Kentucky, while proponents pointed out that militiamen were not being paid for their services.[32]

The Wilkinson clique argued that they proposed nothing revolutionary. Since Virginia had twice passed acts providing for the separation of Kentucky it now seemed unnecessary, so they said, to make another appeal to the State for permission to proceed. They, therefore, proposed that the convention should act without appealing again to Virginia; afterward an appeal could be made to Congress for admission to the Union.[33]

This sounded well, but it was nevertheless true that no authority existed for the separation of Kentucky without a previous arrangement with Congress for admission of the new State into the Confederation. Separation without this provision would have been revolution, and Wilkinson had written to Miró that he intended to carry through his plan for a Spanish alliance as soon as separation from Virginia had been accomplished. The sequel indicates that he meant what he said.[34]

[31] Wilkinson to Robert Clark, Jr., July 10, 1788, Innes MSS., L. of C.; Wilkinson to Miró, Feb. 12, 1789, Gayarré, III, 223–240; Marshall, *Kentucky,* I, 288–292; Green, *Spanish Conspiracy,* pp. 204–206; *Kentucky Gazette,* Aug. 16, 1788.

[32] Caleb Wallace to William Fleming, Aug. 13, 1788, Fleming MSS., W. and L. U. library; Butler, *Kentucky,* p. 167; Green, *Spanish Conspiracy,* pp. 180–185; *Kentucky Gazette,* Sept. 6, 13, 27, Oct. 11, 18, Nov. 1, 29, 1788; Draper MSS., 18CC157–159, 171–173, 175–179, 181–185, 187, 193.

[33] Bradford, "Notes on Kentucky," *Kentucky Gazette,* March 30, 1827; statement of Caleb Wallace, depositions in case of Innes vs. Marshall, p. 26, Durrett MSS., U. of C. library; paper in hand of Harry Innes, n.d., Innes MSS., XXII, pt. 2, L. of C.

[34] Testimony of William Green, n.d., Innes MSS., XXII, pt. 2, L. of C.; Marshall, *Kentucky,* I, 315.

On November 3 the eighth Kentucky convention assembled. John Brown had returned from Congress and had a seat in the body, as had Wilkinson and most of his friends. The contest which had occurred in connection with the elections had probably opened their eyes to the fact that, though most of the Kentucky politicians were on their side, the people were not inclined to follow them.[35]

Nevertheless they made an attempt to carry through their plans. Samuel McDowell was again chosen president, and from the chair he called upon Wilkinson to tell of his negotiations of the previous year with the Spanish governor in New Orleans. Wilkinson responded by reading the memorial which he had presented to Miró on that occasion. Then Brown was called upon to state his experiences in Congress. Having sensed the local opposition to the Spanish intrigue, Brown spoke in a guarded manner. There could have been no other object of this agitation but to demonstrate to the convention the hostility of Congress to the idea of a new State and the benefits held out by Spain in case Kentucky should set up a government independent of the Confederation.[36]

But the people had, for the first time, instructed their delegates, and it soon became clear that a majority favored continued cooperation with Virginia. Wilkinson's friends realized their defeat and acquiesced. After some controversy, a resolution was adopted which called once more upon Virginia to extend the time allowed for admission of Kentucky into the union and to provide for still another convention to draft a constitution. John Brown drafted this resolution, and on November 23 he wrote to Madison saying that he had abandoned his plan for setting up a government independent of Congress. Yet there can be no doubt about his original intentions, though he apparently favored a deal with the Spanish only because advantageous terms could not be had from Congress. This was probably true of the others except Wilkinson and perhaps Innes. Wilkinson now sent Dunn to petition Gardoqui for a grant of land on the Yazoo to which he might retire in case of necessity. At this time a correspondent of the *Independent Gazette* of Philadelphia said that the Western country "cannot from the nature of things, remain long subject to the old states. . . . If the navigation of the Mississippi be ceded by the States to Spain, this event will be facilitated. . . . The moment they attempt to give up the trade of the Mississippi, the Western Country, with all their territorial claims and pretentions, will be lost. The Court

[35] Cotterill, *Pioneer Kentucky*, p. 220.
[36] *Kentucky Gazette*, Jan. 30, 1789; Bradford, "Notes on Kentucky," *ibid.*, April 6, 1827; Green, *Spanish Conspiracy*, pp. 222–228; Marshall, *Kentucky*, I, 322–323; Smith, *Kentucky*, pp. 287–290; Butler, *Kentucky*, pp. 175–179; Bodley, *Littell*, pp. 102ff.

of London, through Lord Dorchester, will aid the new settlements against Old Spain and the natives of South America will unite with the Americans of Kentucke." [37]

On December 29 the Virginia assembly passed a third act providing for the separation of Kentucky. Its terms were less liberal than those of the two previous ones in that Virginia veterans were now to be allowed unlimited time in which to perfect their titles to bounty lands lying within the confines of Kentucky and the new State was asked to pay her proportionate part of Virginia's public debt.[38]

Under this act July 20, 1789, was fixed as the time for the assembling of the eighth Kentucky convention, which, if it accepted the terms, was to provide for the establishment of the first new State under the Federal Union. But the new conditions imposed upon Kentucky were not approved by many of the people of the District, and a controversy arose as to what should be done in the circumstances. Wilkinson and his supporters had come to the conclusion that if Kentucky accepted the terms Congress would receive the new State, and they were anxious to avoid such a conclusion of the matter. They longed to have the terms of separation rejected by the convention so that the District might retain its existing status until Congress, under the new union, should have time to express itself on the question of the navigation of the Mississippi. They believed that its stand would be similar to that of the old Congress and that separation from Virginia could then be accomplished under circumstances more favorable to the Spanish intrigue.[39]

There were others who now opposed separation on the ground that Kentucky needed the support of Virginia in Congress when the question of the navigation of the Mississippi should come up again. If Kentucky were a separate State, Virginia would no longer have any interest in working for the opening of the River. In fact, it would apparently be to her economic advantage to oppose it.[40]

[37] Extract from Philadelphia *Independent Gazette,* Sept. 1, 1788, copied in *Kentucky Gazette,* Nov. 22, 1788; Bradford, "Notes on Kentucky," *ibid.,* April 13, 20, 1827; Harry Innes to Arthur Campbell, Sept. 19, 1788, Draper MSS., 9DD51; John Brown to Madison, Nov. 23, 1788, Madison MSS., L. of C.; testimony of Judge John Allen, n.d., Innes MSS., XXII, pt. 2, L. of C.; Isaac B. Dunn to Wilkinson, Nov. (?), 1788, Wilkinson MSS., Chicago Historical Society; John Brown to Jefferson, Aug. 10, 1788, Jefferson MSS., L. of C.; Brown to Madison, Aug. 26, 1788, Madison MSS., L. of C.; Wilkinson to Gardoqui, Jan. 1, 1789, Gayarré, III, 247; *ibid.,* III, 221; Bodley, *Littell,* pp. lxi–lxiii, 52; Shreve, *The Finished Scoundrel,* pp. 79–80, 121; Green, *Spanish Conspiracy,* pp. 236–237; Marshall, *Kentucky,* I, 328–337.
[38] *Kentucky Gazette,* Feb. 14, 1789; Butler, *Kentucky,* p. 180; Marshall, *Kentucky,* I, 342–343; Bodley, *Kentucky,* I, 448; Bodley, *Littell,* p. 108; Hening, *Statutes,* XII, 788–791.
[39] Humphrey Marshall to George Nicholas, April 26, 1789, Innes MSS., L. of C.; George Nicholas to Madison, May 8, 1789, Madison MSS., L. of C.
[40] *Kentucky Gazette,* Jan. 3, 24, April 18, May 2, 23, 24, Aug. 15, 1789.

The establishment of the new Federal government was a propitious event, and a majority of the rank and file, but not a majority of the leaders, wished to accept the new terms and establish the State. This would enable Kentucky, after a time, to pass land laws favoring actual settlers, to control her own courts, and to make better provision for military protection.[41]

The combination of the first two groups was able to control the convention. An address was forwarded to the Virginia assembly complaining of the new terms of separation and asking that they be modified. Complaint was made also against a recent order of Governor Randolph recalling all scouts and rangers from the Western frontier. On December 18, 1789, the assembly passed a fourth act of separation. The objectionable features of the former act were removed, and it was provided that a ninth convention should assemble on July 26, 1790. On the appointed day the convention met and now at last arrangements were made for the organization of the State of Kentucky. On February 4, 1791, Congress agreed to admit the new member of the union, and on June 1, 1792, Kentucky became the fifteenth of the United States of America.[42] Isaac Shelby, who had labored long and honorably for the welfare of the frontier and who had initiated the memorable campaign of King's Mountain, was chosen its first governor.

In 1788 the population of Kentucky amounted to sixty-six thousand souls. New settlers were pouring in almost daily. Most of them came down the Ohio in boats and landed at the mouth of Limestone Creek, where John May, Simon Kenton, and their associates had established the town of Maysville in 1787. From this point the main road led to Lexington and thence to Louisville. Plantations were now to be seen all along the route, though settlement was sparse on account of large or scattered land holdings concentrated in the hands of a few men. At Danville another stream of settlers, who came in by way of Cumberland Gap and the Wilderness Road, joined that from Maysville. The Indians still made it necessary for them to travel well-armed and in large parties. The Kentucky papers of this period are full of advertisements for those wishing to go to the Eastern settlements to meet at a specified date at the Crab Orchard or elsewhere so that by banding together they might pass safely over the perilous Wilderness Road. Though many of the newcomers were from Pennsylvania and other States, the majority of the

---

[41] Levi Todd to Gov. B. Randolph, May 27, 1789, *C.V.S.P.*, IV, 630.
[42] *Kentucky Gazette*, Aug. 29, Sept. 5, 1789, April 20, 27, 1827; *Journal of the House of Delegates*, Oct. 20, 29, Nov. 3, Dec. 2, 1789; *P.E.I.K.*, pp. 140–141; Butler, *Kentucky*, p. 186; Collins, *Kentucky*, I, 21; Green, *Spanish Conspiracy*, p. 318; Bodley, *Littell*, pp. 109–115.

population was still of Virginian origin, and a traveler at a slightly later date commented upon their proneness to gamble, to drink, to discuss horses, and to ply strangers with questions.[43]

After the convention of 1789 had postponed the question of separation, Wilkinson made a second journey to New Orleans. On September 17 he addressed a memorial to Miró in which he discussed the new developments in the political situation in the West. The opening of the navigation of the Mississippi at a duty of fifteen per cent he thought very prejudicial to his political plans. He no longer favored the incorporation of Kentucky as a part of the Spanish domain, but now suggested an alliance between an independent Kentucky and the Spanish power. Apparently as compensation for this modification of his plan, he proposed to lend his aid to the Spanish policy of encouraging migration from the Western settlements to Louisiana and admitted to Miró that he had petitioned Gardoqui for six hundred thousand acres of land on the lower Mississippi to which he and his followers might repair in case their program were defeated in Kentucky. Furthermore, he reinforced a request which he had made on February 12 that pensions be granted to him and his principal coadjutors in Kentucky, as well as to some others whose cooperation he wished to enlist. Muter, Innes, and Sebastian were among the former, and Thomas and Humphrey Marshall among the latter.[44]

On December 31, 1789, Miró wrote to Don Antonio Valdés, the Secretary for the Indies, concerning this new communication of Wilkinson, and he credited him with having thwarted the intrigues of both Clark and Connolly in Kentucky. His faith in his American agent remained unshaken. He approved the main features of Wilkinson's plan and recommended that he and his lieutenants be pensioned. Five thousand dollars had already been used by Wilkinson (as he claimed) for the purpose of subsidizing his Kentucky supporters, and this was now repaid by Miró. Presently regular stipends were granted to Wilkinson himself and to the principal supporters for whom he had requested them. By granting free land to immigrants and the use of the Mississippi to certain traders at a duty of fifteen per cent, Spain was trying to conciliate the transmontane region and wean it from the United States. And Miró relied on Wilkinson and his supporters to promote the Spanish cause

[43] Dorchester to Sydney, Aug. 27, 1789, P.R.O., C.O., 42, 65, ff. 177–200; *Kentucky Gazette*, Jan. 24, Sept. 9, Oct. 3, 1789; *Pittsburgh Gazette*, June 2, 1787; Kenton, *Kenton*, p. 176; Hale, *Trans-Allegheny Pioneers*, p. 271; Cumming's "Tour of the West," R. G. Thwaites, *Early Western Travels*, IV, 212; F. A. Michaux, "Travels to the Westward," in *ibid.*, III, 247–248.

[44] Wilkinson to Miró, Sept. 17, 1789, and enclosure no. 3, Pontalba transcripts, Filson Club; statement of Daniel Clark, *A.S.P.*, XX, 704–705; *P.E.I.K.*, p. 121.

in Kentucky. The creation of the new union was an obstacle, but it by no means discouraged him.[45]

While Gardoqui and Miró were cooperating in the promotion of the Spanish conspiracy they did not lose sight of the original plan to colonize Americans on Spanish soil. Each had his own agents and his own scheme for carrying out this part of the program, and their failure to cooperate contributed to the miscarriage of their efforts along this line.[46]

Wilkinson's own plan for establishing a colony on Spanish soil, which he had discussed with Miró during his visit to New Orleans in 1787, was for a time lost sight of in face of the more important conspiracy. It was revived when Wilkinson, on January 1, 1789, dispatched Major Dunn to New York with a petition, signed by Innes, Sebastian and Brown as well as Wilkinson and Dunn, asking for a grant of land on the Yazoo. On February 14 he informed Miró of this move and asked his support. He was especially interested in thwarting certain other moves in the same direction under the patronage of Gardoqui.[47]

In 1785 a French Chevalier of the Order of St. Louis, Pierre Wouves d'Argès, established his residence in Kentucky and, according to his own account, began to enlist Kentuckians who would become members of an American colony on Spanish soil. Peter Tardiveau was his patron, and he apparently had the backing of the French legation in New York. In 1787 he visited Paris and discussed his plan with the Count Aranda, Spanish minister to France. In addition to proposing that an American colony be established in the Natchez district, he suggested that Western resentment against Spain should be placated by granting them the navigation of the Mississippi at a duty of twenty-five per cent and that free importation should be granted to such as would settle on Spanish soil and become Spanish citizens.[48]

Aranda thought well of the scheme and recommended it to Florida-blanca, with whom d'Argès was sent to consult at San Ildefonso. Instructions authorizing the program were sent to Miró and Gardoqui, and d'Argès set out for New York early in the fall of 1787. On his arrival in that city he was coldly received by the Spanish chargé, who was already plotting with Dr. James White and who did not relish the interposition of an agent not of his own choice.

Instructions directed that d'Argès should be dispatched to Kentucky

---

[45] Miró to Valdés, April 11, 1789, Pontalba transcripts, Filson Club; same to same, Dec. 31, 1789, *ibid.;* Green, *Spanish Conspiracy,* pp. 15–16.

[46] Gayarré, III, 252–254.

[47] Wilkinson to Gardoqui, Jan. 1, 1789, Gayarré, III, 247; same to Miró, Feb. 14, 1789, *ibid.,* 246–247.

[48] Whitaker, *Spanish–American Frontier,* pp. 78–89.

to promote his scheme, but, in order to delay his progress Gardoqui sent him by way of Havana and New Orleans instead of Pittsburgh.

By January 8, 1788, Miró had received the instructions relating to d'Argès, and since he was already involved with Wilkinson he protested to the Ministry against this new plan. In April d'Argès arrived in New Orleans, and Miró detained him there until August in order to prevent his interfering with the operations of Wilkinson in Kentucky. He presently set off for Martinique in a huff, and we hear no more of his activities in connection with the American West.[49]

A more amazing though less protracted scheme of colonization was hatched by none other than George Rogers Clark. Apparently disgruntled by the really shabby treatment which he had received at the hands of the administration of Governor Randolph, on March 15, 1788, he sent, by Major John Rogers, a letter to Gardoqui proposing to become a Spanish subject if that power would make him a large grant of land on which to establish an American colony. On May 26, Clark's associate and future brother-in-law, James O'Fallon, sent a similar communication to the same person. But apparently Gardoqui was not impressed by these offers and nothing more was ever heard of the scheme.[50]

George Morgan still harbored colonial ambitions, and on behalf of his "New Jersey Land Society" he petitioned Congress, on May 1, 1788, for a grant of two million acres in the Northwest Territory. It was his desire, in collaboration with Thomas Hutchins and their associates, to emulate the achievements of Symmes and Cutler, but Congress refused to make the grant in the location or to the extent desired, and Morgan broke off negotiations with that moribund body. In September he addressed Gardoqui on the subject of a grant in Spanish territory, his object being, of course, to found a colony. The *chargé* was favorably impressed with the project and authorized Morgan to explore the country and select a site for a city while he consulted his government as to authority for making an actual grant of about fifteen million acres on the west bank of the Mississippi opposite the mouth of the Ohio. Gardoqui furnished funds for the expedition, provided Morgan with a passport and wrote to Governor Miró at New Orleans about the scheme. Thomas Hutchins, who had recently completed the survey of the seven ranges north of the

[49] Miró to Valdés, Jan. 8, 1788, Pontalba transcripts, Filson Club; same to Floridablanca, Aug. 7, 1788, *ibid.;* same to Valdés, Aug. 8, 1788, *ibid.;* d'Argès to Miró, Aug. 12, 1788, *ibid.;* Miró to d'Argès, Aug. 13, 1788, *ibid.;* d'Argès to Miró, Aug. 21, 1788, *ibid.;* Fortier, *Louisiana,* II, 129–142.

[50] F. J. Turner, "The Origin of Genêt's Projected Attack on Louisiana and the Floridas," *A.H.R.,* III, 652; John C. Parish, "The Intrigues of Doctor James O'Fallon," *M.V.H.R.,* XVII, 230–263; Clark to Gardoqui, March 15, 1788, Draper MSS., 33J134; G. R. Clark to Jonathan Clark, April 20, 1788, *ibid.,* 2L26.

Ohio under Congressional authority, took an active part in these arrangements. He was to be the surveyor-general for the new colony and proposed to become a Spanish citizen for that purpose. Morgan was encouraged to expect local self-government, complete religious freedom, and free trade to New Orleans for his colonists. He planned to sell lands to actual settlers at an eighth of a dollar an acre.[51]

In November Morgan went to Pittsburgh and selected about seventy men to accompany him on his journey of exploration. Wilkinson's partner, Major Dunn, met him there and was much perturbed over his scheme, writing to Wilkinson that it would wreck their plans unless counteracted. Morgan's departure was somewhat delayed, but on January 3, 1789, he and his party set off down the Ohio in four armed boats. His thoughts must have turned back to the day twenty years before when as a young man he had set off with George Croghan for the Illinois country in the place of his faithless partner. He was instructed to investigate the situation in Kentucky as he passed through that country. He sent back a report saying that the settlers in that region were largely indiffent both to Wilkinson's plan for a Spanish alliance and to the British intrigue which Dr. John Connolly was engaged in fomenting.[52]

On reaching his destination he selected the site for his city on the west bank of the Mississippi a short distance below the mouth of the Ohio and christened it New Madrid. He proceeded to make surveys and to grant provisional titles to the colonists who had accompanied him. Completion of these titles was dependent upon approval of his plan by the Spanish government. In naming his city and in making provisional grants of land he had gone beyond the authority granted him by Gardoqui.

In May Morgan went to New Orleans to discuss his operations with Governor Miró and was greatly disappointed at finding that official quite cold to his project. Miró approved of religious toleration for colonists, but did not favor the exercise of public worship by non-Catholics. He objected also to the exercise of local self-government and believed that

---

[51] Gardoqui to Morgan, Sept. 17, 1788, Morgan MSS., Urbana, Ill.; Gardoqui to Miró, Oct. 4 (?), 1788, *ibid.;* same to Hutchins, Feb. 25, 1789, *ibid.;* minutes of the French legation in the U. S., extracts from the journal of M. de Moustier, Feb., 1788, L. of C.; J. H. and H. B. Peellnitz to Morgan, Sept. 10, 1788, Franklin MSS., XLVIII, 53, A.P.S.; Gardoqui to Morgan, Oct. 10, 1788, Franklin MSS., XLVIII, 53, A.P.S.; Gardoqui to Morgan, Oct. 10, 1788, Pontalba transcripts, Filson Club; J. Dawson to Gov. Randolph, Jan. 29, 1789, Draper MSS., 33J112; Hutchins to ——(?), Jan. 10, 1788, Hutchins MSS., H.S.P.; James, *Clark,* pp. 394–395; *Cahokia Records,* p. cxli; *Kaskaskia Records,* pp. 494–495.

[52] Savelle, *Morgan,* pp. 200–228; *Kaskaskia Records,* p. 503; William to J. G. Blount, March 3, 1789, Blount MSS., N.C.H.C.; Madison to Washington, March 8, 1789, Sparks, *Letters to Washington,* IV, 251–252; Tench Coxe to Madison, April 21, 1789, Madison MSS., L. of C.; John Rogers to William Clark, April 23, 1789, Draper MSS., IM188.

small grants of land should be made to settlers free of charge rather than sold to them, as Morgan was planning to do. However, Miró did not wish to alienate Morgan. He proposed to invest him with a military commission, to enlist his aid in bringing American settlers into the Spanish domain, and to make him a grant of one thousand acres of land with an equal amount for each of his sons. But he sent a military officer to New Madrid with instructions to build a fort and take over command of the country. Morgan immediately lost interest in the venture and returned to Princeton, whence he removed a few years later to "Morganza" on Chartiers Creek. Here, in 1806, he was visited by Aaron Burr, whose project of a great Western empire so aroused him that he reported his suspicions to President Jefferson and later went to Richmond to testify against Burr. Wilkinson had used all his influence with Miró to defeat the plans of Morgan, who, in August 1789, lost his principal lieutenant in the death of Thomas Hutchins. On September 2, 1789, Miró issued a proclamation inviting American immigrants to settle on Spanish territory, promising them freedom of worship, free lands, and the right to bring in their effects free of duty.[53]

Since his exploits at Fort Pitt in the days of Lord Dunmore, Dr. John Connolly had played no part in the affairs of the American West. In 1784 he was serving as storekeeper and clerk under Sir John Johnson, son and heir of Sir William, in the Canadian Department of Indian Affairs. In 1788 he returned to the American frontier. Believing that war between England and Spain was imminent, Lord Dorchester, the governor-general of Canada, began to take a lively interest in Kentucky affairs. On January 15, 1788, he dispatched an agent, presumably Connolly, to Detroit with instructions to investigate and report on the situation in the American settlements. Later in the year he sent Connolly, or an agent acting under him, to Pittsburgh with the same object in view. This agent consulted with General Samuel Holden Parsons, John Neville, and other magnates of the region and reported favorably on the situation. Apparently some Easterners also were involved, for Thomas Willing of Philadelphia wrote of the flame which "a few only of this city have kindled in the western country." Dorchester was in correspondence with leading characters both in Kentucky and at Pittsburgh and considered visiting both places. The British project was now revealed as a plan to encourage the separation of the West from the Confederation

[53] Isaac B. Dunn to Wilkinson, Nov. (?), 1788, Wilkinson MSS., Chicago Historical Society; list of persons who subscribed with Col. Morgan for land at New Madrid, n.d., Pontalba transcripts, Filson Club; Miró to Morgan, May 23, 1789, *ibid.;* Morgan to Miró, May 24, 1789, *ibid.;* Hugh Williamson to J. G. Blount, Aug. 8, 1789, Blount MSS., N.C.H.C.; *Kentucky Gazette,* Dec. 26, 1789.

and to furnish the settlers with military aid in the conquest of New Orleans, thus opening to them the navigation of the Mississippi.[54]

On October 25 Connolly appeared in Louisville, acting in the capacity of agent for Lord Dorchester. His old friend, John Campbell, now took him under his wing and introduced him to Wilkinson and Thomas Marshall, whereupon certain interesting conversations ensued. Marshall denied that he gave any encouragement and later wrote to Washington saying that Campbell had previously informed them of the proposition Connolly was about to make. Wilkinson said that he had got rid of the Doctor by employing an Indian to feign an attack upon his life and that Connolly escaped from the country in great fright. But before thus hastening his departure, if indeed he did so hasten it, Wilkinson heard what Connolly had to say and used it in his intrigue with Miró in order to strengthen his hold upon the Spanish governor.

In a letter of April 11, 1789, Dorchester wrote to the British Ministry that a committee of correspondence had been formed in Kentucky to further the British scheme, and he enclosed a memorial, apparently written by Wilkinson, encouraging the prosecution of the plan. It seems clear that Wilkinson would have been ready to undertake a British intrigue in case of failure of that with Spain. And it is likely that Connolly's proposals would have proved more to the taste of the settlers of Kentucky than would those of Wilkinson in case they had been forced to make a choice between the two.[55]

As it was, the majority of the Kentuckians had already proved themselves loyal to Virginia and the Confederation, and neither Wilkinson's nor Connolly's schemes had any great appeal for them. Campbell realized the danger of dealing in such intrigues with former Tories, and on November 8 he wrote to Governor Randolph telling of Connolly's return and denouncing his activities. On December 13 Governor St. Clair of the Northwest Territory wrote to John Jay telling of Connolly's visit to Louisville and denouncing him. On December 18 Harry Innes wrote to

[54] Return of officers and other appointments in the Northern Department of Indian Affairs, Nov. 20, 1786, P.R.O., C.O., 42, 18; Dorchester to Sydney, May (or June) 4, 1788, *ibid.*, 59; same to same, June 9, 1788, *ibid.*; same to same, Oct. 14, 1788, *ibid.*, 61; Thomas Willing to William Bingham, Balch, *Willing Letters and Papers*, pp. 136–137; Dorchester to Grenville, Oct. 25, 1789, Parker, *Guide to Materials in Canadian Archives*, p. 157.

[55] F. J. Turner, "The Diplomatic Contest for the Mississippi Valley," *Atlantic Monthly*, XCIII, 676–691, 807–817; Shreve, *The Finished Scoundrel*, pp. 122–123; Perrin, *Kentucky*, p. 283; Bodley, *Littell*, pp. liv–lv, lxv; *Journal of the House of Delegates*, Nov. 16, 1786, pp. 42–43; Thomas Marshall to Washington, Feb. 12, 1789, Sparks, *Letters to Washington*, IV, 245–251; Dorchester to Sydney, April 11, 1789, P.R.O., C.O., 42, 64; W. H. Siebert, "Kentucky's Struggle with its Loyalist Proprietors," *M.V.H.R.*, VII, 123–126.

Washington to the same effect, and the next day George Morgan wrote similarly to Gardoqui.[56]

Yet the "British Conspiracy" did not die a sudden death. On June 7 and again on August 27, 1789, Dorchester wrote to Lord Sydney stating that an influential group of Eastern Americans had proposed that Great Britain aid the West in carrying through a separation from the Union. It is impossible to know definitely to whom he referred, but he mentioned that General John Neville of the Pittsburgh area, Colonel John Stephenson, also of Pennsylvania, General Lincoln and Judge John Cleves Symmes had expressed the opinion that the new settlements north of the Ohio had interests similar to those of Kentucky. He evidently looked upon them as sympathetic toward his plan. Dorchester was instructed by his government that it was desirable for Britain to interest herself in the separation of the West from the East.[57]

It is obvious that during 1788 and 1789 a large proportion of the leadership of the West was convinced that the policy of the New England and Middle States would prevent Congress from adopting a policy favorable to Western development and that the best interests of the section would be served by a severance from the Union. Both England and Spain were prepared to assist in this program, and by playing off the one against the other the West might have been able to make a good bargain for itself. If the Federal Constitution had not been adopted when it was, or if a President unfamiliar with Western problems had been placed at the head of the new government, it is likely that the United States would soon have been bounded by the Allegheny Mountains.

These schemes to withdraw from the Confederation had been initiated by land speculators. But now they were aided by many frontiersmen who showed the same spirit that the colonists had shown in breaking away from England. Certainly Congress, the representative body of a government so newly established by rebels, was in no strong position, ethically or materially, to rebuke the rebellious West which felt that it was being sacrificed to the East. In the teeth of such forceful remonstrance that assembly began to give ground as early as 1788. In September of that year it introduced a

[56] S. M. Wilson, "George Washington's Contacts with Kentucky," Filson Club, *The History Quarterly*, VI, 234–235; John Campbell to Gov. Randolph, Nov. 8, 1788, *C.V.S.P.*, IV, 511, also in Draper MSS., 33J,119; *ibid.*, 33J,120–121; Innes to Washington, Dec. 18, 1788, Sparks, *Writings of Washington*, IX, 474; Mohr, *Federal Indian Relations*, p. 135; Green, *Spanish Conspiracy*, pp. 238–239; Henry, *Henry*, III, 389–395.

[57] F. J. Turner, "The Diplomatic Contest for the Mississippi Valley," *loc. cit.*; Dorchester to Sydney, June 7, 1789, P.R.O., C.O., 42, 65; same to same, Aug. 27, 1789, *ibid.*

resolution "designed to remove the apprehension and uneasiness produced by a report that Congress are disposed to treat with Spain for the surrender of their claim to the navigation of the river Mississippi." The resolutions stated that since the rumor was not founded in fact the delegates were at liberty to contradict it, that free navigation of the Mississippi was an essential right of the United States, and that negotiations on this subject should "be referred to the new government." This was a neat though temporary way out of the quandary.

Since Virginia's cession of her Western domain the land companies had been quiescent, waiting to see which way the tide might set. Soon George Morgan in behalf of Indiana would renew his suit in Virginia, which was to be kept up intermittently until the eleventh amendment put an end to such actions. Wise and crafty Ben Franklin was now back in Philadelphia, where visitors saw "a fat trunched old man in a plain Quaker dress, bald pate and short white locks sitting without his hat under the trees." Always cheerful, always prefacing every plea with a witty anecdote, he joined Samuel Wharton and other associates in attempts to salvage what they could from their land ventures. Long after the philosopher had been gathered to his fathers Congress continued to receive petitions from Vandalia and the Illinois-Wabash Companies, but the halcyon days of exploitation of the public lands were over and the companies got no comfort or recompense.[58] Presently Robert Morris over-reached himself in his trade and land speculations, languished for several years in debtor's prison, and died owing the United States nearly one hundred thousand dollars. Patrick Henry continued to fight his battles from the hearth-rug and the rostrum and to entertain delusive hopes for a fortune in Yazoo lands. For Silas Deane there was to be no paradise in Vandalia—that bold project which came so near to being our fourteenth colony; there was to be only exile in England and communion with such kindred spirits as Benedict Arnold. Wilkinson was to persist in his dabbling in intrigue and was destined likewise to die in exile. Improvident Sam Adams—who, from the day his neighbors outfitted him with clothes so that he might appear presentable in Congress, furnishes a relief to the greedy profiteers associated with him—remained indifferent to gain to the end of his days. Richard Henry Lee, whose family once dreamed of a princely domain stretching back through the ancient forests to the Mississippi, presided over the last Congress of the Confederation which now turned over to the States the question of the adoption of the Federal Constitution—an instrument framed by men with so

[58] *Secret Journals of the Acts and Proceedings of Congress* (1821) IV, 453–454; Manasseh Cutler's Journal, *Pa. Mag. of Hist. and Biog.,* XII, 110–111.

many foibles, and, in some cases, of such shameless rapacity, that it is passing strange it should have come to be considered sacred and immutable.[59] Soon Washington, whose record is the page without blemish in the history of the Revolution, was to prove himself as great a statesman as soldier when selected to guide the bantling nation, which now called itself the United States of America. To this rising new union, then, was transferred the vexed question of Western lands along with all other problems of the dying Confederation.

[59] Madison, who had so large a part in framing the constitution of the new union, thought it full of imperfections and likely to overthrow anything like a democratic government. "If it was to last only 10 or 20 years," he said, "it would be productive of ye happiest effects, but if much longer, of ye worst—the end of it a certain form of tyranny." James to Thos. Madison, Oct. 1, 1787, Madison MSS., Draper Collection, 5ZZ84.

CHAPTER XXVI

RETROSPECT

THE primary object of this study has been to investigate the political consequences of conflicting claims to Western lands rather than to pass upon the merits of the claims themselves. Yet Virginia's claim, under the charter of 1609, has entered so largely into all these disputes that it seems well to notice it before taking leave of the subject.

The boundaries of the province are described in the charter as follows: "from the Point of Land, called Cape or *Point Comfort,* all along the Sea Coast, to the Northward two hundred Miles, and from the said Point or *Cape Comfort,* all along the Sea Coast, to the southward two hundred Miles, and all that Space and Circuit of Land, lying from the Sea Coast of the Precinct aforesaid, up into the Land, throughout from Sea to Sea, West, and Northwest. . . ." [1] There has been much discussion as to what this verbiage may have meant, some finding it difficult to decide whether the northern or the southern boundary line was the one which should run northwest. This, truly, would have made a vast difference, but it is clear that the expression "up into the Land, throughout from Sea to Sea, West, and Northwest," did not refer to lines merely, but to the tract of country. This was to run west and northwest, and it is hard to see that the phrase could have been interpreted in any other way.

The revocation of the charter in 1624 did not change the boundaries, but after that time the King was able to change them at pleasure. The grants to the Calverts, to Penn, and to the Carolina proprietors did change them, and the sea to sea charters of Massachusetts and Connecticut set up conflicting claims. Otherwise the boundaries of Virginia remained the same down to the outbreak of the Revolution, except that the peace of 1763 established the Mississippi River as the western limit. The proclamation of 1763 did not change them. There can be no question that Hillsborough, under the plan of 1768, intended to establish a permanent boundary between the Southern colonies and the Indians; Donelson's line of 1771 was looked upon by some, especially by Richard Henderson,

[1] William Macdonald, ed., *Select Charters and other Documents Illustrative of American History* (New York, 1910) pp. 12–13.

as having accomplished this object. Yet the Treaty of Fort Stanwix purported to extend Virginia's frontier farther to the westward than did Donelson's line. Furthermore, England had claimed the land as her own in spite of the occupancy of the Indians, whom she never officially considered as a sovereign people.[2] Therefore, a cession by the natives conveyed merely their claim as occupants and did not involve sovereign rights. For this reason Indian cessions were not commonly looked upon as affecting colonial boundaries. It is for this reason that New York's claim to the country of the Six Nations cannot be taken seriously.

The official correspondence of the colonial period commonly assumed that Virginia extended to the Mississippi. Several of the governors made grants of land upon "the western waters," and, though few of these were ever perfected, the right to make the grants was not questioned. Moreover, when the King in Council in 1748 ordered the grant to be made to the Ohio Company, permission was given to take up land north and south of the Ohio River. The principal maps of the pre-Revolutionary period—Mitchell's, Evans', and Huske's—all show Virginia extending to the Mississippi south of its confluence with the Ohio, but to the north of that point there is no agreement as to the extent of the colony. Huske gives the fortieth parallel as marking her northern boundary, and on the map on which Hillsborough signified to Sir William Johnson his intentions as to the drawing of the Fort Stanwix line, the same northern boundary is indicated for Virginia.[3] Since no attempts were made by the colonists to settle this country before the Revolution the question during that period was largely an academic one, and Virginia, in spite of Lord Dunmore, took very little interest in the matter.

Neither Indiana, Vandalia, nor the Illinois and Wabash Companies ever obtained a royal confirmation of their claims, and hence they had no legal standing. The Camden-Yorke opinion was thoroughly spurious as far as its having application to any land claims in America is concerned. Yet the Indiana Company, on account of circumstances connected with the Treaty of Fort Stanwix, did have an equitable claim as against Virginia.

A fear of losing territory by the establishment of the colony of Vandalia is usually supposed to have aided the cause of the Revolution in Virginia. Yet it has been shown that the powerful interest of the Loyal Company in Virginia apparently favored the Vandalia project and that no official protest was made against it. Dunmore and Washington and the interests

[2] Opinion of Attorney-General J. T. Kempe, of New York, to Sir William Johnson, Aug. 12, 1765, *Sir William Johnson Papers*, IV, 817–819.
[3] Hillsborough to Sir William Johnson, March 12, 1768, P.R.O., C.O., series 5, 69. See Map II.

which they represented saw the matter in a different light, but it was admitted that the Crown had the right to make the grant, and they knew that they did not have sufficient influence in London to thwart it. Their activities extended no further than to the surveying of lands within the bounds marked out for Vandalia.

It may be permissible to remark at this point that our historians are practically unanimous in ascribing purely economic motives to Virginia when they attempt to account for the revolutionary activities of this Anglican, aristocratic colony. Beside the threat of Vandalia, there was the matter of debts owed by Virginia planters to British merchants, which were largely wiped out by the revolt of '76. For more than a hundred years the House of Burgesses had insisted that it alone had the right to lay taxes in Virginia. When the Stamp Act was proposed the House protested, and finally the colony was prepared for defense, but Dunmore struck the first blow in Virginia. She then took up arms to defend what she considered her constitutional rights, but independence was not proposed by any of her responsible leaders until the spring of 1776. Since the Revolution in Virginia, then, was begun a year before independence was proposed, it cannot be that a cancellation of debts was one of its original objects. Furthermore, it was not the leaders of the planter class who finally prevented the payment of those debts. Madison, with the backing of Mason, the Lees, and nearly all the prominent leaders of the State, did his best to secure the validation of these debts, even though a revolutionary act of 1777 had provided for their payment to the State,[4] and many of them had been so paid in depreciated currency. He came very near to succeeding. It was Patrick Henry and his "yeoman" following who bitterly fought the proposal and finally defeated it by the narrowest of margins.[5]

The Virginians took their political rights quite as seriously as the New Englanders took their Puritanism, and if the latter planted themselves on "the stern and rockbound coast" for sweet conscience's sake, the Virginians fought the Revolution, not because of the threat to their Western lands nor for the opportunity it might afford them to evade debts, but for a constitutional principle. An astonishingly large number of them had studied law in the Temple and knew their rights as Englishmen.

[4] Hening, *Statutes*, IX, 379–380.

[5] Mary Travers Armentrout, "A Political History of Virginia Finance, 1781–1789," (MS. dissertation in U. of Va. library), pp. 142–165. Under the leadership of Henry, on Dec. 12, 1789, the Virginia assembly passed an act providing that British debts could be collected when England complied with the treaty by surrendering the Western posts and making compensation for confiscated slaves. Hening, *Statutes*, XII, 528.

The dominant planter class had much to lose, both economically and socially, and it lost much.

During the first three years of the War the rivalry for Western lands was kept largely in the background by the struggle for freedom, but various ambitious men, unshackled by any kind of punctilio, were taking advantage of the screen which confusion and excitement threw around their actions to fasten their claim on Western territory. Clark's capture of Kaskaskia and Vincennes was made possible by the cooperation between Virginia and Pennsylvania speculators, but when the Indiana Company attempted to sell Virginia lands without having secured a title to them the State was spurred on to the establishment of a land office through which her Western domain south of the Ohio was put on the market. There then followed, on the floor of Congress and in the Ohio country, a bitter struggle between Virginia and her rivals. The capture of Detroit was prevented by this rivalry, and the adoption of the Articles of Confederation was long delayed. Virginia and her supporters had triumphed over Franklin, Dickinson, and their friends in withholding from Congress, under the Articles, the control of the Western lands. Under that instrument Congress could not interfere in the matter of State boundaries except through an elaborate system of arbitration, and Maryland, with her governor and her most influential politicians members of the great land companies, refused to confederate until Virginia had offered to cede her claims to the territory north of the Ohio—an area which the speculators expected to make their own. Maryland then gave in, but New Jersey, thoroughly under control of the speculators, led the movement which for the space of three years prevented Congress from accepting the proffered cession. This action arose from the conditions attached to the cession which provided for a guarantee of Virginia's remaining claims and an invalidation of all purchases made from the Indians in the territory to be ceded. Every time the matter came up a Virginian sprang to his feet and demanded that each member state on his honor before voting whether or not he was personally concerned in the land companies. This resulted in a deadlock, for, like the old trader Croghan when he sat down that day to write Sir William Johnson and Governor Franklin that it was better that they should not appear to be concerned in Indiana, the members were not willing to show their hands. Finally, in 1784, a compromise was affected and the cession accepted, Virginia having won a tacit acquiescence in the two points under dispute.

Indiana, Vandalia, and the Illinois and Wabash Land Companies had thus been defeated in Congress despite the overt sympathy of that body, during the latter years, with their ambitions. This was due to the fact that Virginia actually occupied, so far as any of the belligerents occupied, most of the territory which she claimed, and Congress lacked the means to dislodge her. There was yet another pitfall for those who aspired to part of the territory Virginia claimed: if her charter boundaries were denied, the other States would have a hard time showing how their boundaries were established. The circumstance of conflicting claims was not decisive, for there were few States whose boundaries were not contested, and the fact that Virginia's claims were extensive was really not pertinent to the question.

If the authority of Congress could have been made sovereign and the unoccupied lands placed under its control, then the matter would have assumed an entirely different aspect. But when the Articles were adopted in such form as to acknowledge the sovereignty of the States and deny that Congress owned any lands by devolution from the British Crown, that body was denied the power to deal with the land question except in the capacity of arbiter. It could appeal to the States for cessions, but it could not give orders.

But, if Congress could not come directly to the aid of the land companies, it could work for them in indirect ways, and it cannot be doubted that speculators were partly responsible for the instructions to our peace commissioners subjecting them to the will of the French Ministry, which, if carried out, would have resulted in a Western boundary considerably east of the Mississippi. The East would have been glad to see the Southwest restricted, and the Northwest, in British hands, might have been subject to further exploitation in which Americans could participate, whereas if Virginia's cession were accepted, the Illinois-Wabash Company could hope for nothing.

Thus that calculating sectionalism which was willing to sacrifice one part of the country to another and which later was to drench the land with the blood of a million of its sons, was coeval with the union itself, and economic motives then, as later, were back of it. When Robert Morris, hoping to influence the Western boundary and save his land claims, said to Gérard that the strength of the union must always lie in the North, he meant that the North hoped to so manipulate affairs that it could retain political control and use it for economic ends. This virus of sectional rivalry would have been hazardous even in a stable, vigorous government; it was almost fatal to the new union.

Even before Yorktown, secession movements began to spawn in the West, and they continued to show their heads all along the frontier from western Pennsylvania, through Kentucky and southwestern Virginia to western North Carolina, until the end of the Confederation period. In every case they were organized by land speculators for the furtherance of their own ends, and they were greatly aided by the habitual indifference of Congress toward Western interests, and particularly by its willingness, in 1786, to surrender to Spain the navigation of the Mississippi—the vital economic artery of the West. In every case these movements failed because the average settler could not be aroused to take sufficient interest in them and because Eastern legislatures displayed quite as much consideration for the welfare of frontiersmen as did Western speculators. There is, therefore, no spark of reality in the traditional view that these schemes for new Western States typified the free and independent spirit of the West in its quest for freedom. There is, in fact, very little evidence in the Revolutionary period for the belief that the West, on account of its greater democracy, was normally at odds with the East. Glorification of democracy—especially Western democracy—has become something of a cult with many historians, but we have seen that leadership on the frontier was concentrated in a few hands just as it was in the older settlements and that the rank and file of the one section had much in common with that of the other.

Many of the colonists had long chafed under British restrictions which prevented their occupying the West. They had seen bold individuals, through daring defiance of proclamations, and powerful companies, through virtue of influence in the seats of the mighty, lay claim to millions of acres. When the colonists definitely renounced British rule, like lads just released from school, they felt free to fight it out with those shrewd, far-sighted claimants who had beat them to Western lands. Consequently, a tumultuous rush to the West began—not for political freedom, but for private gain. Those who went for any other motive were not of the calibre to make their voices heard; they acquired no influence and wielded no power on the frontier. The leadership fell naturally into the hands of men who had come West definitely for the purpose of rising in the world, of acquiring that most obvious essential of a "gentleman"—a large landed estate or a substantial competence.

There were, of course, points in which the interests of the frontier differed from those of the older settlements, but on almost no question, including that of the Federal Constitution, does one find a clear-cut sectional alignment between East and West. And to pretend that the West, in the Revolutionary period, began at the fall line of the rivers is a patent error, at least so far as Virginia was concerned. The Piedmont distinctly represented an extension of Tidewater civilization which had been established for more than a generation. The frontier lay well beyond the Blue Ridge.

As Lord Macaulay pointed out, it is unimportant where Hannibal crossed the Alps or whether Mary of Scotland blew up Darnley. The inquiry may amuse us but the decision leaves us no wiser. It is of no moment, then, just how many acres various individuals and companies acquired or tried to acquire during the era of exploitation of public lands. But it does matter that usually the most successful speculators and traders were those who betrayed public trust and used official position to bilk the people. It matters that the specters of Vandalia and Indiana and Ohio could never be banished from the halls of council.

This study of land speculation would seem to point to the conclusion that a country cannot well afford to place its destinies in the hands of men who are engaged in the amassing of personal fortunes. When large profits are at stake neither their own consciences nor their country's distress often give pause, even to those who are loudest in the affirmation of their own righteousness. We have seen that this was not exclusively an American failing; men of high place in England and in France were equally concerned with the rebel colonists in this peculiar form of pillage of war. The Revolution was no exception to the fact that in time of war great fortunes are built from the distress of the country, the excitement fostering laxness and making it difficult for the public to be aware of what goes on behind closed doors. The eighteenth century, with all of its faults, did develop the ideal of a gentleman as a man rendered independent by his circumstances, liberal by his views, and public-spirited by his traditions. There are never many of this type in any age, but a democracy in particular has great need of them to save it from exploitation and demagoguery. The Revolution produced exploiters such as Robert Morris and opportunists such as Patrick Henry, but it produced also a John Adams and a George Washington. There were others of their mold and they were the true fathers of the country.

If the British government had adhered to its policy, inaugurated in 1754, of giving a thousand acres to every actual settler on the frontier, the West would have filled up rapidly with men who needed no other inducement. Its history would not be so largely a story of opportunism. The wavering, changing colonial policy of England and the unwise legislation of the new States resulted in most of the Western lands falling into the hands of a few speculators. These exploited the lowly settlers who bore the brunt of frontier hardship and protected the land for the absentee proprietors. Such settlers, not the speculators, were the real empire builders. Nevertheless, history has tended to transmute the vices of the land speculators into virtues, for they, too, played a part, regardless of the fact that their motive was pecuniary gain, in helping to open the way for the Westward moving caravan. They with their spurious grants and dubious titles, the settlers with their "tomahawk" rights, their squatters' rights, their military and treasury warrants soon covered the West with layer after layer of competing claims, which overlapped the land like shingles on a roof. This was later to present an almost hopeless snarl for the courts to unravel. But nothing could now stay the restless, land-hungry pioneer. He was definitely on his way to the Pacific.

Brown, Mrs. Percy (Charlottesville, Va.)
Campbell-Brown MSS.

Bullitt, William Marshall (Louisville, Ky.)
William Preston MSS.
William Christian MSS.

Carnegie Library (Pittsburgh, Pa.)
Letter books of George Morgan, 1774–1779

Chicago Historical Society
James Wilkinson MSS.
Autograph letters, vol. LXX

Filson Club (Louisville, Ky.)
Documents translated from the "Pontalba" collection belonging to the
Louisiana Historical Society, New Orleans, La.

Georgia Department of Archives (Atlanta, Ga.)
Bonds, Bills of Sale, Deeds of Gift, Powers of Attorney, 1783–1792,
Book C.
Bourbon County MSS.
William Davenport MSS.
Executive letter book, 1786–1789
Journal of the General Assembly of the State of Georgia, 1784–1789

Harvard University Library
Arthur Lee MSS.

Henderson Public Library (Henderson, Ky.)
Photostats from the collection of Mrs. Julia Alves Clore, San Antonio,
Texas

Historical Society of Pennsylvania (Philadelphia)
Autograph collection of the Society
Byars, William Vincent, "The First American Movement West" (original
manuscript)
J. F. Dreer collection
French Refugees, Colonial, and Indian Affairs
Generals of the American Revolution
Members of the Old Congress
Soldiers of the American Revolution
Etting collection
American and British Army
Generals of the Revolution
Governors
Miscellaneous MSS.
Simon Gratz, autograph collection
Gratz-Croghan MSS.
Benjamin Franklin MSS.
William Irvine MSS.
Journals of the Board of Trade (transcripts from Public Record Office,
London)

Lamberton Scotch-Irish collection
Thomas McKean MSS.
North Carolina MSS.
Ohio Company MSS.
Thomas Wharton letter book, 1773–1784
Wharton MSS.
James Wilson MSS.
Jasper Yeates MSS.

Historical Society of Western Pennsylvania (Pittsburgh)
  Denny-O'Hara MSS.
  George Morgan MSS.
  Ross-Woods MSS.

Illinois Historical Survey, University of Illinois (Urbana)
  George Morgan MSS.

Illinois State Historical Library (Springfield)
  Miscellaneous MSS.
  Tardiveau MSS.

Johnston, Juliet Alves (Henderson, Ky.)
  Alves MSS.

Kentucky Historical Society (Frankfort)
  Harry Innes account books
  James Wilkinson MSS.

Library of Congress
  British transcripts
    Thatcher notes from British documents
    Bancroft transcripts
    Virginia official correspondence
    Force transcripts
    B. F. Stevens, Facsimiles of Manuscripts Relating to America.
  French transcripts
  Affaires Étrangères, Correspondance Politique, États-Unis
    Minutes of the French Legation in the United States (photostats from
    the Library of William S. Mason, Evanston, Ill.)
  Spanish transcripts
    Archivo General de Indias, Papeles procedentes de la Isla de Cuba, Bour-
    bon County MSS., *legajo* 198.
  Breckinridge MSS.
  Daniel Brodhead MSS.
  Campbell-Preston MSS.
  Papers of the Continental Congress
    Indian affairs, no. 56
    Intercepted letters, no. 51
    Letters and papers of Thomas Paine, no. 55
    Letters and papers of Oliver Pollock, no. 50
    Pennsylvania State papers, no. 69
    Petitions from Kentucky, no. 48

    Reports of Committees, no. 30
    Territorial Claims, no. 77
    Virginia State Papers, no. 71
  Extracts from the Correspondence and Journals of William Dunbar
  Benjamin Franklin MSS., miscellaneous
  Georgia records, Council correspondence, 1782–1789
  Patrick Henry MSS.
  John Holker MSS.
  Harry Innes MSS.
  Thomas Jefferson MSS.
  James Madison MSS.
  George Mason MSS.
  George Morgan MSS.
  Robert Pleasants' letter book, 1771–1780
  William Short MSS.
  Charles Simms MSS.
  Adam Stephen MSS.
  George Washington MSS.

Louisiana Historical Museum (New Orleans)
  Miscellaneous MSS.

Mason, William S., library of (Papers now in Yale University Library)
  Benjamin Franklin MSS.
  John Holker MSS.
  Miscellaneous MSS.

New York Public Library (New York City)
  Robert Morris MSS.
  James Wilkinson MSS.

North Carolina Historical Commission (Raleigh)
  John Gray Blount MSS.
  Miscellaneous MSS.

Pennsylvania State Archives (Harrisburg)
  John Baynton letter book, 1764ff.
  Baynton, Wharton and Morgan letter book
  Baynton, Wharton and Morgan, miscellaneous letters
  George Morgan letter book, 1769–1771

Presbyterian Historical Society (Philadelphia)
  Bryan MSS.
  Hart MSS.
  Letters to Robert Patterson
  Henry Payne MSS.
  Andrew Steele MSS.

Public Record Office (London)
  Colonial Office papers

Series 5, nos. 7, 8, 38, 40, 43, 66–82, 101, 117–118, 129, 134, 156, 165, 175, 232, 595–597, 331–1334, 1346–1356, 1368–1369, 1374–1376.
Series 23, nos. 27–29
Series 42, nos. 14–20, 45–50, 58–65
Foreign Office papers, France, nos. 2–3, 27
Treasury papers, Series 1, nos. 470, 476, 549
War Office papers, Series 1, nos. 10–12, 28

Ridgway Library (Philadelphia)
Gratz MSS.

University of Chicago Library
Durrett collection
John Bradford, "Notes on Kentucky" (copied from the *Kentucky Gazette*, Aug. 25, 1826 to Jan. 9, 1829)
William Croghan, account book
Depositions in case of Harry Innes vs. Humphrey Marshall (typescript)
Robert B. McAfee, "Harrodsburg" (original manuscript)
A. W. Bascom, "George Nicholas, papers, letters, speeches, and biographical sketch"
Diary of James Nourse, 1775–1780
Miscellaneous MSS.

University of Virginia Library (Charlottesville)
Executive Journals of the Council of Virginia, 1752–1774 (photostat from the Public Record Office, London)
Thomas Jefferson MSS.
Lee MSS.
Hilldrup, R. L., "The Virginia Convention of 1776" (MS. dissertation)
Armentrout, Mary Travers, "A Political Study of Virginia Finance, 1781–1789" (MS. dissertation)

Virginia Historical Society (Richmond)
Thomas and Richard Adams MSS.
Campbell MSS.
Executive Journal of the Council of Virginia, 1740–1752 (photostat from the Public Record Office, London)
Lee MSS.
Edmund Randolph, "History of Virginia" (original manuscript. In process of publication in *Virginia Magazine of History and Biography*)

Virginia Land Office (Richmond)
Patent and Grant books, 1771–1789

Virginia State Library, Archives (Richmond)
Aspinwall transcripts from Public Record Office, London
Auditor's accounts with the Illinois Department, 1778–1783
Executive papers, George Rogers Clark MSS.
Journal of the Board of Western Commissioners (consisting of William Fleming, Thomas Marshall, Caleb Wallace, Samuel McDowell)
Legislative petitions, 1775ff.

Virginia Convention papers, 1775–1776 (including journal of Convention of 1775 and letters to the Committee of Safety, 1776)

Washington and Lee University Library (Lexington)
William Fleming papers, including journal of the First Kentucky Convention, 1785

Wisconsin Historical Society (Madison)
Draper collection
Boone MSS.
Brodhead MSS.
George Rogers Clark MSS.
Jonathan Clark MSS.
William Clark MSS.
William Croghan MSS.
Frontier Wars
Harrod MSS.
Historical Miscellanies
Joseph Martin MSS.
Robert Patterson MSS.
Pittsburgh and Northwest Virginia MSS.
William Preston MSS.
Shane MSS.
Shepherd MSS.
Virginia MSS.

COLLECTED WRITINGS

The Works of John Adams. Charles Francis Adams, ed., III. Boston, 1851.
The Journal and Correspondence of William Lord Auckland, I. London, 1861.
Beaumarchais the Merchant: Letters of Théveneau deFrancy, 1778–1780. John Bigelow, ed. New York, 1870.
Correspondence of Aaron Burr and his daughter Theodosia. Mark Van Doren, ed. New York, 1929.
George Rogers Clark Papers, 1771–1781. Collections of the Illinois State Historical Library, VIII, Virginia series, III. James A. James, ed. Springfield, 1912.
"Clark-Leyba Papers" in *American Historical Review,* XLI, 92–112. Lawrence Kinnard, ed.
George Rogers Clark Papers, 1781–1784. Collections of the Illinois State Historical Library, XIX, Virginia series, IV. James A. James, ed. Springfield, 1926.
Correspondence of Silas Deane, Delegate to the First and Second Congress at Philadelphia, 1774–1776. Collections of the Connecticut Historical Society, II, 129–368. Hartford, 1879.
"Papers Relating to the Case of Silas Deane," in *Seventy-Six Society Publications,* pp. 1–201. Edward S. Ingraham, ed. Philadelphia, 1855.
The Deane Papers. Collections of the New York Historical Society, 1886–1890. 5 vols. Charles Isham, ed. New York, 1887–1891.

The Official Records of Robert Dinwiddie, Lieutenant-Governor of the Colony of Virginia, 1715–1758, 2 vols. *Collections of the Virginia Historical Society,* new series, I–II. R. A. Brock, ed. Richmond, 1883–1884.

Duane Letters. Publications of the Southern History Association, IX, 389–400.

"Correspondence of Governor Robert Eden of Maryland," in *Maryland Historical Magazine,* II.

The Works of Benjamin Franklin. 10 vols. Jared Sparks, ed. Boston, 1856.

The Writings of Benjamin Franklin. 10 vols. Albert Henry Smyth, ed. New York, 1907.

The Works of Benjamin Franklin. 12 vols. John Bigelow, ed. New York, 1904.

Franklin and Galloway—Some Unpublished Letters. William Mason Smith, ed. Worcester, 1925. Reprinted from *Proceedings of the American Antiquarian Society.*

Correspondance Inédite et Secrète du Docteur B. Franklin, Ministre Plènipotentiaire des États-Unis d'Amérique près la Cour de France, depuis l'Année 1753 jusqu'en, 1790. Janet Pere, Libraire-Editeur. 2 vols. Paris, 1797.

The Correspondence of General Thomas Gage with the Secretaries of State, 1763–1775, I–II. Clarence Edwin Carter, ed. New Haven, 1931–1933.

The Correspondence of King George the Third with Lord North, 1768–1783. W. Bodham Donne, ed., I–II. London, 1867.

The Correspondence of King George the Third from 1760 to 1783, arranged and edited by Sir John Fortescue. 6 vols. London, 1927–1928.

B. and M. Gratz, William Vincent Byars, ed. Jefferson City, Mo., 1916.

Abstract of Unpublished Letters of Gen. Nathanael Greene, by Geo. H. Richmond. New York, 1906. (Pamphlet in University of North Carolina Library.)

Haldimand Papers in *Michigan Pioneer and Historical Society Collections,* IX, X, XI, XIX, XX.

The Papers of Sir William Johnson. James Sullivan and Alexander C. Flick, eds. 8 vols. Albany, 1921–1933.

Life and Correspondence of John Paul Jones, including the Narrative of the Campaign of the Liman, from Original Letters in the Possession of Miss Janette Taylor. New York, 1830. (Author not given.)

Letters of Joseph Jones of Virginia, 1777–1787. Worthington C. Ford, ed. Washington, 1889.

Correspondence of Henry Laurens of South Carolina. Printed for the Zenger Club. New York, 1861.

The Letters of Richard Henry Lee. James C. Ballagh, ed. 2 vols. New York, 1911–1914.

Letters of William Lee, 1766–1783. Collected and edited by Worthington C. Ford. 3 vols. Brooklyn, 1891.

"Letters to Robert Morris; Papers of Charles Thomson" in *Collections of the New York Historical Society, 1878, Revolutionary Papers,* I.

The Confidential Correspondence of Robert Morris. Stan V. Henkels, pub. Philadelphia, 1917.

Unpublished Letters of Edmund Pendleton. Proceedings of the Massachusetts Historical Society, second series, XIX (1905), 107–167. Boston, 1906.

The Writings of Thomas Paine, Secretary for Foreign Affairs to the Congress of the United States of America in the late War. Albany, 1792.

The Writings of Thomas Paine. 3 vols. Moncure D. Conway, ed. New York, 1894.

The St. Clair Papers. 2 vols. William Henry Smith, ed. Cincinnati, 1882.

"Correspondence between William Strahan and David Hall, 1763–1777" in *Pennsylvania Magazine of History and Biography,* XII, 116–122, 240–251. Philadelphia, 1888.

The Correspondence of John Cleves Symmes. Beverley W. Bond, ed. New York, 1926.

John Todd Papers. Chicago Historical Society's Collection, IV, 285–359.

The Letters of Horace Walpole. Peter Cunningham, ed., VII. London, 1866.

Correspondence of the American Revolution, being Letters of Eminent Men to George Washington. 4 vols. Jared Sparks, ed. Boston, 1853.

The Writings of George Washington. 12 vols. Jared Sparks, ed. New York, 1847.

Letters to Washington. S. M. Hamilton, ed., IV–V. Boston, 1901.

The Washington-Crawford Letters. C. W. Butterfield, ed. Cincinnati, 1877.

The Writings of George Washington. John C. Fitzpatrick, ed., I–IX. Washington, 1931–1933.

Letters from George Washington to Tobias Lear. William K. Bixby, ed. Rochester, 1905.

The Washington-Duché Letters. Worthington C. Ford, ed. Brooklyn, 1890.

The Diaries of George Washington, 1748–1799. 4 vols. John C. Fitzpatrick, ed. Boston, 1925.

"Selections from the Letter-books of Thomas Wharton of Philadelphia, 1773–1783," in *The Pennsylvania Magazine of History and Biography,* XXXIII, 319–339, 432–453.

Letters of Mrs. Ann Biddle Wilkinson from Kentucky, 1788–1789. Thomas Robson Hay, ed. Reprinted from *Pennsylvania Magazine of History and Biography,* LXI, 33–55.

"Letters of General James Wilkinson," in *Register of Kentucky State Historical Society,* XXIV, 254–267.

Willing Letters and Papers. Thomas Willing Balch, ed. Philadelphia, 1922.

MISCELLANEOUS DOCUMENTS

Almon, John, printed for, *A Collection of Interesting Authentic Papers relative to the disputes between Great Britian and America; Shewing the Causes and Progress of that Misunderstanding from 1764 to 1775.* London, 1777.

Anonymous pamphlet, *To the Honourable John Jay, Esquire, Chief Justice, and his Associate Judges of the Supreme Court of the United States Sitting in Chancery.* 179–? in Ridgway Library, Philadelphia.

Alvord, C. W., ed. *Cahokia Records, 1778–1790. Collections of the Illinois State Historical Library,* II, Virginia series, I. Springfield, 1907.

Alvord, C. W., ed., *The Illinois-Ouabache Land Company Manuscript*. Privately printed by Cyrus H. McCormick, 1915.

——————, *Kaskaskia Records, 1778–1790. Collections of the Illinois State Historical Library*, V, Virginia series, II. Springfield, 1909.

Alvord, C. W. and Carter, Clarence E., eds. *The New Régime, 1765–1767. Collections of the Illinois State Historical Library*, XI, British series, II. Springfield, 1916.

——————, *Trade and Politics, 1767–1769. Collections of the Illinois State Historical Library*, XVI, British series, III.

American State Papers, XVI–XVIII. *Public Lands, Indian Affairs*. Washington, 1832–1834.

Aspinwall Papers, Part II, *Collections of Massachusetts Historical Society*, X, fourth series. Boston, 1871.

Balch, Thomas, ed. "Papers Relating Chiefly to the Maryland Line During the Revolution" in *Publications of the Seventy-Six Society*. Philadelphia, 1857.

Beckwith, H. W., ed. *Collections of the Illinois State Historical Library*, I. Contains letters from Canadian Archives, pp. 290–457. Springfield, 1903.

Boyd, Julian P., ed. *The Susquehannah Papers, 1750–1772*. 4 vols. Wilkes-Barre, 1930–1933.

Burnett, Edmund C., ed. *Letters of Members of the Continental Congress*. 5 vols. Washington, 1921–1931.

——————, "Papers Relating to Bourbon County, Georgia" in *American Historical Review*, XV, no. 1, 66–111, no. 2, 297–353.

Chalkley, Lyman, ed. *Chronicles of the Scotch-Irish Settlement in Virginia*. Extracts from the original Court Records of Augusta County, 1745–1800. 3 vols. Rosslyn, Va., 1912.

Chandler, Allen D., ed. *The Revolutionary Records of the State of Georgia*. 3 vols. Atlanta, 1908.

Connolly, John. "A Narrative of the Transactions, Imprisonment, and Sufferings of John Connolly, an American Loyalist and Lieutenant-Colonel in his Majesty's Service" in *Pennsylvania Magazine of History and Biography*, XII, 310–324, 407–420; XIII, 61–70, 153–167, 281–291.

Craig, Neville B., ed. *The Olden Time*. 2 vols. Cincinnati, 1876.

Crumrine, Boyd, ed. "Minute Book of the Virginia Court held at Fort Dunmore (Pittsburgh) for the District of West Augusta, 1775–1776" in *Annals of the Carnegie Museum*, I, 525–568.

——————, *The Records of Deeds for the District of West Augusta, Virginia, for the Court Held at Fort Dunmore, 1775–1776*. Reprinted from *Annals of the Carnegie Museum*, III, no. 2.

——————, "Minute Book of the Virginia Court held for Yohogania County, first at Augusta Town and afterward on the Andrew Heath farm near West Elizabeth, 1776–1780" in *Annals of the Carnegie Museum*, II, 71–140, 205–429.

——————, *The County Court for the District of West Augusta, Virginia, 1776–1777*. Washington County, Pa., 1905.

Darlington, Mary Carson, ed. *Fort Pitt and Letters from the Frontier*. Pittsburgh, 1892.

Duane, John, ed., *New Materials for the History of the American Revolution.* New York, 1889.

Force, Peter, ed. *American Archives,* series 4, I–VI, series 5, I–III. Washington, 1837–1853.

Hazard, Samuel, ed. *Colonial Records, Pennsylvania Archives,* first series, 16 vols. Philadelphia, 1852–1856.

Hening, William Waller, compiler. *The Statutes at Large, being a Collection of all the Laws of Virginia, 1619–1792,* VIII–XII. Richmond, 1821–1823.

Hutchins, Thomas, *A Topographical Description of Virginia, Pennsylvania, Maryland, and North Carolina.* Reprinted from the original edition of 1778 and edited by Frederick C. Hicks. Cleveland, 1904.

Hulbert, A. B., ed. "Washington's Tour to the Ohio" and "Articles of the Mississippi Company" in *Ohio Archæological and Historical Quarterly,* XVII, 431–488.

Illinois and Ouabache [*sic*] Land Companies, Memorial of. Presented to the Honourable Congress of the United States at the sessions of 1802.

Illinois and Wabash Land Companies, Memorial of, to the Senate and House of Representatives of the United States. Baltimore, 1810.

Jillson, Willard R. *The Kentucky Land Grants. Filson Club Publications,* no. 33. Louisville, 1925.

Kellogg, Louise Phelps. *Frontier Advance on the Upper Ohio, 1778–1779. Publications of the State Historical Society of Wisconsin.* Madison, 1916.

—————, *Frontier Retreat on the Upper Ohio, 1779–1781. Publications of State Historical Society of Wisconsin.* Madison, 1917.

Lee, Arthur. Extracts of a letter written to the President of Congress by the Honourable, ———. Philadelphia, 1780.

—————, *Observations on Certain Commercial Transactions in France.* Report submitted to Congress. Philadelphia, 1780. (Rare Book Collection, Library of Congress.)

McIlwaine, H. R., ed. *Official Letters of the Governors of the State of Virginia,* I–III. Richmond, 1926–1928.

Munro, James, ed. *Acts of the Privy Council of England,* Colonial series, IV. London, 1911.

O'Callaghan, E. B., ed. *Documents Relative to the Colonial History of the State of New York,* VIII. Albany, 1857.

Palmer, William P., McRae, Sherwin, and Flournoy, W. H., eds. *Calendar of Virginia State Papers, 1652–1869.* 11 vols. Richmond, 1875–1893.

Ricord, Frederick W. and Nelson, Wm., eds. *Archives of the State of New Jersey,* first series, *Documents Relating to the Colonial History of New Jersey,* IX–X. Newark, 1886.

Robertson, James R., ed. *Petitions of the Early Inhabitants of Kentucky to the General Assembly of Virginia, 1769 to 1792. Filson Club Publications,* no. 27. Louisville, 1914.

Saunders, W. L. and Clark, Walter, eds. *Colonial* and *State Records of North Carolina.* 26 vols. Raleigh, 1886–1906.

Summers, Lewis Preston, ed. *Annals of Southwest Virginia, 1769–1800.* Abingdon, Va., 1929.

Taylor, Philip F., compiler. *Kentucky Society of Colonial Wars,* containing calendar of warrants for land in Kentucky granted for service in French and Indian Wars. Frankfort, 1917.

Thwaites, Reuben Gold and Kellogg, Louise Phelps, eds.

——————, *Documentary History of Dunmore's War, 1774.* Madison, 1905.

——————, *The Revolution on the Upper Ohio, 1775–1777.* Madison, 1908.

——————, *Frontier Defense on the Upper Ohio, 1777–1778.*Madison, 1912.

Washington, Bushrod. *Reports of Cases Argued and Determined in the Court of Appeals of Virginia.* 2 vols. Richmond, 1798–1799.

Wharton, Francis, ed. *The Revolutionary Diplomatic Correspondence of the United States.* 6 vols. Washington, 1889.

Wharton, Samuel. *Facts and Observations,* . . . London, 1775.

——————, *View to the Title to Indiana.* Published anonymously by. Philadelphia, 1776. (Rare Book Collection, Library of Congress).

—————— *Plain Facts.* Published anonymously by. Philadelphia, 1781.

Wilkinson, James. *Burr's Conspiracy Exposed and General Wilkinson vindicated against the slanders of his enemies.* Washington, (?) 1811.

OFFICIAL JOURNALS

Journals of the Continental Congress, 1774–1789. Gaillard Hunt and Worthington C. Ford, eds. I–XXVII. Washington, 1904–1928.

Journal of the United States in Congress Assembled, 1786–1788, XI–XIII. Philadelphia, 1787, 1801.

Secret Journals of the Acts and Proceedings of Congress (of the Confederation). 4 vols. Boston, 1821.

Debates in the Several State Conventions on the adoption of the Federal Constitution. Jonathan Elliott, ed. Philadelphia, 1888.

Journals of the House of Burgesses of Virginia, 1766–1776. John Pendleton Kennedy, ed. Richmond, 1905–1906.

Proceedings of the Convention of Delegates for the Counties and Corporations in the Colony of Virginia held at Richmond Town in the County of Henrico, on the 20th of March, 1775. Richmond, 1816. The same for the Convention held July 17, 1775. Richmond, 1816.

The Proceedings of the Convention of Delegates held at the Town of Richmond in the Colony of Virginia on Friday, the 1st of December, 1775, and afterward by adjournment in the City of Williamsburg. Richmond, 1816.

The Proceedings of the Convention of Delegates held at the Capitol in the City of Williamsburg in the Colony of Virginia, on Monday, the 6th of May, 1776. Richmond, 1816.

Journal of the House of Delegates of Virginia, 1776. Richmond, 1828.

Journal of Virginia House of Delegates, 1777–1791.

PRIVATE JOURNALS

Journal of a Tour to North Carolina by William Attmore, 1787. Lida T. Rodman, ed. *James Sprunt Historical Studies,* 17, no. 2. Chapel Hill, 1922.

Autobiography of Charles Biddle. Philadelphia, 1883.

"Journal of William Calk." Lewis H. Kilpatrick, ed., in *Mississippi Valley Historical Review,* VII, 365–377.

"Diary of Colonel Landon Carter" in *William and Mary College Quarterly Historical Magazine*, XIII–XXI.

The Journal of Nicholas Cresswell, 1774–1777. With an Introduction by A. G. Bradley. New York, 1928.

Cuming's Tour to the Western Country. Reuben Gold Thwaites, ed., in vol. IV, *Early Western Travels, 1748–1846*. Cleveland, 1904.

Christopher Gist's Journals with Historical, Geographical and Ethnological Notes and Biographies of his Contemporaries. William M. Darlington, ed. Cleveland, 1893.

Alexander Graydon's Memoirs of His Own Time with Reminiscences of the Men and Events of the Revolution. John Stockton Littell, ed. Philadelphia, 1846.

Journal of Capt. Jonathan Hart, to which is added the Dickinson-Harmar Correspondence, 1784–1785. C. W. Butterfield, ed. Albany, 1885.

Journal and Letters of Col. John May of Boston, 1788–1789, Historical and Philosophical Society of Ohio, new series, I. Cincinnati, 1873.

Three Journals by the Rev. James Smith of Powhatan County, Va. Josiah Morrow, ed. *Ohio Archæological and Historical Publications*, XVI. Columbus, 1907.

A Tour in the United States of America. J. F. D. Smyth, 2 vols. London, 1784.

A Tour of Four Great Rivers, the Hudson, Mohawk, Susquehanna and Delaware, in 1769, being the Journal of Richard Smith of Burlington, N. J. Francis W. Halsey, ed. New York, 1906.

First Explorations of Kentucky. J. Stoddard Johnston, ed. Containing Journals of Doctor Thomas Walker and Colonel Christopher Gist. *Filson Club Publication*, no. 13. Louisville, 1898.

Colonial Men and Times. Lillie DuPuy VanCulin Harper, ed. Containing the Journal of Col. Daniel Trabue. Philadelphia, 1916.

The Last Journals of Horace Walpole, during the Reign of George the Third from 1771–1783, with notes by Dr. John Doran. 2 vols. London and New York, 1910.

Washington and the West, being George Washington's Diary of September, 1784. Archer B. Hulbert, ed. New York, 1905.

NEWSPAPERS AND PERIODICALS

The Kentucky Gazette, Aug. 18, 1787—Aug. 22, 1789; Aug. 29, 1789—July 23, 1793. Lexington, Ky.

The Pennsylvania Packet or General Advertiser, July 4—Dec. 31, 1778, 1779. Philadelphia.

The Pittsburgh Gazette, Aug. 26, 1786—June 7, 1788 (Carnegie Library, Pittsburgh).

The Virginia Gazette, March 7—Oct. 3, 1766; 1774; 1777; 1779. Williamsburg, Va. (Va. State Library).

The American Museum, I–III. Philadelphia.

Annual Papers of the Winchester Virginia Historical Society, I. Winchester, 1931.

The History Quarterly, published by the Filson Club, and the University of Louisville. Louisville, Ky., I–VII.

Journal of the Department of History of the Presbyterian Church of the United States of America, XIV–XV. Philadelphia.

Louisiana Courier, 1808–1809. (La Historical Museum.)

Maryland Historical Magazine, I–V. Baltimore.

The Pennsylvania Magazine of History and Biography, I–XXX. Philadelphia.

Register of the Kentucky State Historical Society, H. V. McChesney, ed., I–XXIX. Frankfort, Ky.

The Remembrancer; or Impartial Repository of Public Events for the years 1776–1780. Printed for John Almon. London.

Tyler's Quarterly Historical and Genealogical Magazine. Lyon G. Tyler, ed., I–XIII.

The Virginia Historical Register and Literary Advertiser. William Maxwell, ed. 4 vols. Richmond, 1848–1851.

The Virginia Magazine of History and Biography, published by the Virginia Historical Society, I–XL. Richmond.

William and Mary College Quarterly Historical Magazine. Lyon G. Tyler, ed., I–XIII.

SECONDARY SOURCES

Abernethy, T. P., *From Frontier to Plantation in Tennessee.* Chapel Hill, 1932.

———, "Commercial Activities of Silas Deane in France" in *American Historical Review,* XXXIX, 477–485.

Adams, Herbert B., *Maryland's Influence upon Land Cessions to the United States, Johns Hopkins University Studies in Historical and Political Science,* I, third series, 1–54. Baltimore, 1885.

Albach, James R., *Annals of the West.* Pittsburgh, 1858.

Alden, George H., *New Governments West of the Alleghenies Before 1780.* Madison, 1897.

Allen, William B., *A History of Kentucky.* Louisville, 1872.

Alvord, Clarence W., and Bidgood, Lee., *The First Explorations of the Trans-Allegheny Region by the Virginians, 1650–1674.* Cleveland, 1912.

Alvord, Clarence W., *The Illinois Country, 1673–1818.* Chicago, 1922.

———, "Virginia and the West, an Interpretation" in *Mississippi Valley Historical Review,* III, 19–38.

———, *The County of Illinois.* Reprint from *Illinois Historical Collections,* II. Chicago, 1907.

———, "The British Ministry and the Treaty of Fort Stanwix" in *Proceedings of the State Historical Society of Wisconsin,* 1908, pp. 165–183. Madison, 1909.

———, *The Mississippi Valley in British Politics.* 2 vols. Cleveland, 1917.

———, *Mississippi Valley Problems and the American Revolution. Minnesota Historical Bulletin,* IV, 229–241.

———, "Lord Shelburne and the Founding of British-American Goodwill" in *Proceedings of the British Academy,* London, 1926.

Ambler, C. H., *A History of West Virginia.* New York, 1933.

———, *The Life and Diary of John Floyd.* Richmond, 1918.

Ambler, C. H., *George Washington and the West*. Chapel Hill, 1936.

——————, *A History of Transportation in the Ohio Valley*. Glendale, Cal., 1932.

Bacon-Foster, Corra, *Early Chapters in the Development of the Potomac Route to the West*. Washington, 1912.

Baker-Crothers, Hayes, *Virginia and the French and Indian War*. Chicago, 1928.

Bancroft, George, *History of the Formation of the Constitution of the United States of America*. 2 vols. New York, 1903.

——————, *Joseph Reed, A Historical Essay*. New York, 1867.

Beckwith, H. W., "General George Rogers Clark's Conquest of the Illinois" in *Collections of the Illinois State Historical Library*, I, 171–289.

Bemis, Samuel F., *Pinckney's Treaty*. Baltimore, 1926.

——————, *The Diplomacy of the American Revolution*. New York, 1935.

Blunt, Joseph, *A Historical Sketch of the Formation of the Confederacy*. New York, 1825.

Bodley, Temple, *George Rogers Clark, His Life and Public Services*. Boston, 1926.

——————,Introduction to Littell's *Political Transactions*. *Filson Club Publications*, no. 31. Louisville, 1926.

——————, *History of Kentucky before the Louisiana Purchase in 1803*, I. Chicago, 1928.

Boggess, Arthur C., "The Settlement of Illinois" in *Chicago Historical Society's Collection*, V. Chicago, 1908.

Bradford, John, "Notes on Kentucky" in *The Kentucky Gazette*, Aug. 25, 1826—Dec. 29, 1826; March 30—June 1, 1827.

Brenaman, J. N., *A History of Virginia Conventions*. Richmond, 1902.

Brock, Robert A., *Virginia and Virginians. Richmond, 1888*.

Burton, Clarence M., *John Connolly, a Tory of the Revolution*. Worcester, 1909. Reprinted from *Proceedings of the American Antiquarian Society*, Oct., 1909.

——————, "Ephraim Douglass and His Times, A Fragment of History, with the Journal of George McCully, and Various Letters of the Period" in *The Magazine of History with Notes and Queries*, III, extra numbers 9–12. New York, 1910.

Butler, Mann, *A History of the Commonwealth of Kentucky*. Louisville, 1834.

Butterfield, Consul W., *History of George Rogers Clark's Conquest of the Illinois and Wabash Towns, 1778 and 1779*. Columbus, 1904.

——————, *History of the Girtys*. Cincinnati, 1890.

Campbell, Charles, *History of the Colony and Ancient Dominion of Virginia*. Philadelphia, 1860.

Carter, Clarence E., "British Policy towards the American Indians in the South, 1763–1768" in *The English Historical Review*, XXXIII, 37–57.

——————, *Great Britain and the Illinois Country, 1763–1774*. Washington, 1910.

Cartmell, T. K., *Shenandoah Valley Pioneers and their Descendants*. Winchester, 1909.

Casseday, Ben, *The History of Louisville*. Louisville, 1852.

Caughey, John Walton, *Bernardo de Gálvez in Louisiana, 1776–1783*. Berkeley, 1934.

————————, "Willing's Expedition down the Mississippi, 1778" in *The Louisiana Historical Quarterly*, XV, 5–36.

Cambiarie, Celestin-Pierre, *Le Rôle de la France dans l'expansion des États-Unis*. Paris, 1935.

Chapman, T. J., *Old Pittsburgh Days*. Pittsburgh, 1900.

Chinard, Gilbert, *Honest John Adams*. Boston, 1933.

Claiborne, J. F. H., *Mississippi as a Province, Territory and State*. Jackson, 1880.

Clark, Daniel, *Proofs of the Corruption of Gen. James Wilkinson*. Philadelphia, 1809.

Clark, George L., *Silas Deane, a Connecticut Leader in the American Revolution*. New York, 1913.

Clement, Maud Carter, *The History of Pittsylvania County, Virginia*. Lynchburg, 1929.

Collins, Lewis, *History of Kentucky*. 2 vols. Covington, Ky., 1878.

Conway, Moncure Daniel, *The Life of Thomas Paine*. 2 vols. New York, 1892.

————————, *Edmund Randolph*. New York, 1888.

Cook, Roy Bird, *Washington's Western Lands*. Strasburg, Va., 1930.

Coombs, J. J., *The Trial of Aaron Burr for High Treason*. Washington, 1864.

Corwin, Edward S., *French Policy and the American Alliance of 1778*. Princeton, 1916.

Cotterill, R. S., *History of Pioneer Kentucky*. Cincinnati, 1917.

Coulter, E. Merton, *A Short History of Georgia*. Chapel Hill, 1933.

Craig, Neville B., *The History of Pittsburgh*. Pittsburgh, 1917.

Cribbs, George A., *The Frontier Policy of Pennsylvania*. Pittsburgh, 1919.

Crumrine, Boyd, *History of Washington County, Pennsylvania, with Biographical Sketches of many of its Pioneers and Prominent Men*. Philadelphia, 1882.

————————, "The Boundary Controversy between Pennsylvania and Virginia, 1748–1785" in *Annals of the Carnegie Museum*, I, 505–524.

Darlington, Mary Carson, *History of Colonel Henry Bouquet*. N. P. 1920.

DeHass, Wills, *History of the Early Settlement and Indian Wars of Western Virginia*. Wheeling, 1851.

Delaplaine, Edward S., *The Life of Thomas Johnson*. New York, 1927.

Doddridge, Joseph, *Notes on the Settlement and Indian Wars of the western parts of Virginia and Pennsylvania, from 1763 to 1783*. Albany, 1876.

Doniol, Henri, *Historie de la Participation de la France à l'Établissement des États-Unis d'Amérique*. 5 vols. Paris, 1890.

Douglas, Albert, "Major-General Arthur St. Clair" in *Ohio Archæological and Historical Society Publications*, XVI, 455–476. Columbus, 1907.

Downes, Randolph C., "Trade in Frontier Ohio" in *Mississippi Valley Historical Review*, XVI, 467–494.

————————, "Dunmore's War: an Interpretation" in *Mississippi Valley Historical Review*, XXI, 311–330.

Drake, Samuel G., *Indian Captivities, or Life in the Wigwam*, part second. New York, 1872.

Duer, W. A., *The Life of William Alexander, Earl of Stirling, with Selections from his Correspondence.* New York, 1847.

Durrett, Reuben T., *The Centenary of Kentucky.* Louisville, 1892.

Eckenrode, H. J., *The Revolution in Virginia.* Boston, 1916.

Einstein, Lewis D., *Divided Loyalties: Americans in England During the War of Independence.* New York, 1933.

Faulder, R., Printed for. *Authentic Memoirs of William Augustus Bowles, Esq., Ambassador from the United Nations of Creeks and Cherokees to the Court of London.* London, 1791. Reprinted, Tarrytown, New York, 1916, being extra number of *The Magazine of History*, XII, no. 46, 103–127.

Fernow, Berthold, *The Ohio Valley in Colonial Days.* Albany, 1890.

Filson, John, *The Discovery, Settlement, and present state of Kentucke.* Wilmington, 1874. Facsimile edition, W. R. Jillson, ed. Louisville, 1930.

Fisher, Sydney George, *Pennsylvania: Colony and Commonwealth.* Philadelphia, 1907.

Fiske, John, *The Critical Period of American History, 1783–1789.* Boston, 1888.

Fitzmaurice, Lord Edmond, *Life of William, Earl of Shelburne.* 3 vols. London, 1875–1876.

Fitzpatrick, John C., *George Washington Himself.* Indianapolis, 1933.

Flippin, Percy Scott, *William Gooch, Successful Royal Governor of Virginia.* Reprint from *William and Mary College Quarterly.*

Foote, William Henry, *Sketches of Virginia,* second series. Philadelphia, 1856.

Ford, Amelia Clewley, *Colonial Precedents of our National Land System as it Existed in 1800.* University of Wisconsin, 1910.

Fortier, Alceé, *A History of Louisiana.* 4 vols. New York, 1904.

Frischauer, Paul, *Beaumarchais.* Translated by Margaret Goldsmith. New York, 1935.

Gayarré, Charles, *History of Louisiana,* III: *The Spanish Domination.* New Orleans, 1885.

Gilmore, James R., *John Sevier as a Commonwealth Builder.* New York, 1887.

Green, Thomas Marshall, *The Spanish Conspiracy.* Cincinnati, 1891.

Greene, Katherine Glass, *Winchester, Virginia, and its Beginnings.* Strasburg, Va., 1926.

Griswold, Rufus W., *The Republican Court.* New York, 1867.

Hale, Edward E., and Hale, Edward E., Jr., *Franklin in France.* Boston, 1887.

Hale, John P., *Trans-Allegheny Pioneers.* Cincinnati, 1886.

Hall, James, *Sketches of History, Life, and Manners in the West.* 2 vols. Philadelphia, 1835.

Halsey, Francis W., *The Old New York Frontier.* New York, 1901.

Hanna, Charles A., *The Wilderness Trail.* 2 vols. New York, 1911.

Harding, Samuel B., *Party Struggles over the First Pennsylvania Constitution.* American Historical Association, *Annual Report,* 1894, pp. 371–402.

Harley, Lewis R., *The Life of Charles Thomson.* Philadelphia, 1900.

Harris, Alex, *A Biographical History of Lancaster County* (Pa.). Lancaster, 1872.

Haskins, Charles H., "The Yazoo Land Companies" in *Papers of The American Historical Association,* V, 395–437.

Hassler, Edgar W., *Old Westmoreland, A History of Western Pennsylvania During the Revolution.* Pittsburgh, 1900.

Haywood, John, *The Civil and Political History of the State of Tennessee.* Nashville, 1915.

Hemphill, W. Edwin, "The Jeffersonian Background of the Louisiana Purchase" in *Mississippi Valley Historical Review,* XXII, 177–190.

Henderson, Archibald, *The Transylvania Company and the Founding of Kentucky.* (Pamphlet.)

——————, *Dr. Thomas Walker and the Loyal Company of Virginia.* Reprinted from *Proceedings of the American Antiquarian Society.* Worcester, 1931.

——————, "A Pre-Revolutionary Revolt in the Old Southwest" in *Mississippi Valley Historical Review,* XVII, 191–212.

Hendrick, Burton J., *The Lees of Virginia.* Boston, 1935.

Henry, Wm. Wirt, *Patrick Henry, Life, Correspondence and Speeches.* New York, 1891.

Higgins, Ruth L., *Expansion in New York.* Columbus, 1931.

Hildreth, S. P., *Pioneer History: Being an Account of the First Examinations of the Ohio Valley and the Early Settlement of the Northwest Territory.* Cincinnati, 1848.

Hinsdale, A. B., "The Western Land Policy of the British Government from 1763 to 1775" in *Ohio Archæological and Historical Quarterly,* I, 207–229.

Holcombe, James P., *Sketches of the Political Issues and Controversies of the Revolution,* a discourse delivered before the Virginia Historical Society, Jan. 17, 1856. (Pamphlet in University of Virginia Library.)

Horner, Frederick, *The History of the Blair, Banister, and Braxton Families before and after the Revolution with a brief sketch of their Descendants.* Philadelphia, 1898.

Howe, Henry, *Historical Collections of Virginia.* Charleston, 1845.

Hulbert, A. B., *Historic Highways of America,* III: *Washington's Road.* Cleveland, 1903.

——————, *Ohio in the Time of the Confederation. Marietta College Historical Collections,* III.

Hutchinson, John A., *Land Titles in Virginia and West Virginia.* Cincinnati, 1887.

Imlay, George (*sic*), *A Topographical Description of the Western Territory of North America, to which is added The Discovery, Settlement and Present State of Kentucky by John Filson, etc.* London, 1793.

Jacob, John J., *A Biographical Sketch of the Life of the Late Michael Cresap.* Cincinnati, 1866.

James, James A., "Oliver Pollock, Financier of the Revolution in the West" in *Mississippi Valley Historical Review,* XVI, 67–80.

——————, "Oliver Pollock and the Free Navigation of the Mississippi River" in *ibid.,* XIX, 331–347.

——————, *The Life of George Rogers Clark.* Chicago, 1928.

James, James A., *The Significance of the Attack on St. Louis, 1780*. Mississippi Valley Historical Association, *Proceedings*, II, 199–217.

Jensen, Merrill, "The Cession of the Old Northwest" in *Mississippi Valley Historical Review*, XXIII, 27–48.

Jillson, Willard Rouse, *Tales of the Dark and Bloody Ground*. Louisville, 1930.

——————, *The Kentucky Country*. Washington, 1931.

Johnson, Cecil, "Expansion in West Florida, 1770–1779" in *Mississippi Valley Historical Review*, XX, 481–496.

Johnson, Willis F., *American Foreign Relations*. 2 vols. New York, 1916.

Kellogg, Louise Phelps, *The British Régime in Wisconsin and the Northwest*. Madison, 1935.

Kenton, Edna, *Simon Kenton*. Garden City, New York, 1930.

Knox, William, *The Controversy Between Great Britain and her Colonies Reviewed*. London, 1773. Printed for John Almon.

Koontz, Louis K., *The Virginia Frontier, 1745–1763. Johns Hopkins Studies in Historical and Political Science,* series XLIII, no. 2.

Leyland, Herbert T., "The Ohio Company" in *Quarterly Publication of the Historical and Philosophical Society of Ohio,* XVI, no. 1, 5–20.

Lee, Richard Henry, *Life of Arthur Lee*. 2 vols. Boston, 1829.

Lester, William Stewart, *The Transylvania Colony*. Spencer, Ind., 1935.

Lewis, Virgil A., *The Original Indiana Territory,* 1895. (Pamphlet in Library of Congress).

——————, *History of West Virginia*. Philadelphia, 1889.

——————, *History of the Battle of Point Pleasant*. Charleston, 1909.

Lincoln, Charles H., *The Revolutionary Movement in Pennsylvania, 1760–1776. Publications of the University of Pennsylvania,* series in History, no. 1. Philadelphia, 1901.

Lingley, Charles R., *The Transition in Virginia from Colony to Commonwealth. Columbia University, Studies in History, Economics, and Public Law,* XXXVI, no. 2. New York, 1910.

Lowdermilk, Will H., *History of Cumberland, Maryland*. Washington, 1878.

Lyle, Maria Catharine Nourse, *James Nourse and his Descendants*. Lexington, 1897.

Mahon, Lord (Stanhope, Philip Henry), *History of England from the Peace of Utrecht to the Treaty of Versailles, 1713–1783,* VI–VII. Boston, 1853.

Marshall, Humphrey, *The History of Kentucky*. 2 vols. Frankfort, 1824.

Massie, David Meade, *Nathaniel Massie, a Pioneer of Ohio*. Cincinnati, 1896.

Mershon, Stephen L., *English Crown Grants*. New York, 1918.

Mohr, Walter H., *Federal Indian Relations, 1774–1788*. Philadelphia, 1933.

Monette, John W., *History of the Discovery and Settlement of the Valley of the Mississippi*. 2 vols. New York, 1846.

Morton, Frederick, *The Story of Winchester in Virginia*. Strasburg, Va., 1925.

McWhorter, Lucullus Virgil, *The Border Settlers of Northwestern Virginia, from 1768 to 1795*. Dayton, Va., 1915.

Nasatir, A. P., *The Anglo-Spanish Frontier in the Illinois Country During the American Revolution, 1779–1783. Journal of the Illinois State Historical Society,* XXI, 291–358.

Nevins, Allan, *The American States During and After the Revolution, 1775–1789*. New York, 1924.

Ogg, F. A., *The Opening of the Mississippi*. New York, 1904.

Page, R. C. M., *Genealogy of the Page Family in Virginia*. New York, 1893.

Paxson, Frederick L., *History of the American Frontier*. Boston, 1924.

Pease, Theodore Calvin, and Marguerite J., *George Rogers Clark and the Revolution in Illinois, 1763–1787*. Springfield, 1929.

Pendleton, William C., *History of Tazewell County and Southwest Virginia, 1748–1920*. Richmond, 1920.

Perkins, James H., *Annals of the West*. Cincinnati, 1847.

Perrin, William Henry, *The Pioneer Press of Kentucky*. Louisville, 1888.

Perrin, W. H., Battle, J. H., Kniffin, G. C., *Kentucky, a History of the State*. Louisville, 1888.

Peyton, John Lewis, *History of Augusta County, Virginia*. Staunton, 1892.

Phillips, Paul C., *The West in the Diplomacy of the American Revolution. University of Illinois Studies in Social Sciences,* II, nos. 2 and 3. Urbana, 1913.

——————, *American Opinion Regarding the West, 1778–1783*. Mississippi Valley Historical Association, *Proceedings,* VII, 286–305.

Pilcher, Margaret Campbell, *Historical Sketches of the Campbell, Pilcher and Kindred Families*. Nashville, 1910.

Pitkin, Timothy, *Political and Civil History of the United States of America*. 2 vols. New Haven, 1828.

Pownall, Thomas, *A Topographical Description of such parts of North America as are contained in the* (annexed) *Map of the Middle British Colonies, etc. in North America*. Printed for John Almon. London, 1776.

Pound, Arthur, and Day, Richard E., *Johnson of the Mohawks*. New York, 1930.

Preston, Thomas Lewis, *Historical Sketches and Reminiscences of an Octogenarian*. Richmond, 1900.

Quaife, Milo M., "Jonathan Carver and the Carver Grant" in *Mississippi Valley Historical Review,* VII, 3–25.

Quisenberry, A. C., *The Life and Times of Humphrey Marshall*. Winchester, Ky., 1892.

Ranck, George W., *Boonesborough. Filson Club Publications,* no. 16. Louisville, 1901.

Randall, E. O., *Washington in Ohio. Ohio Archæological and Historical Society Publications,* XVI, 477–501. Columbus, 1907.

Rawle, William, "Sketch of the Life of Thomas Mifflin" in *The Memoirs of the Historical Society of Pennsylvania,* II, part II. Philadelphia, 1830.

Reed, William B., *Life and Correspondence of Joseph Reed*. 2 vols. Philadelphia, 1847.

Rives, William Cabell, *History of the Life and Times of James Madison*. 3 vols. Boston, 1859–1868.

Robertson, James A., *Louisiana Under the Rule of Spain, France, and the United States*. 2 vols. Cleveland, 1911.

Roosevelt, Theodore, *The Winning of the West*. New York, 1895.

Roselli, Bruno, *Vigo*. Boston, 1933.

Rowland, Mrs. Dunbar, *Life, Letters and Papers of William Dunbar*. Jackson, 1930.

Rowland, Kate Mason, "The Ohio Company" in *William and Mary College Quarterly*, I, 197–203.

——————, *The Life of George Mason*. New York, 1892.

Rupp, I. D., *Early History of Western Pennsylvania and the West*. Pittsburgh, 1846.

Rush, Ralph L., *The Adventures of Gilbert Imlay*. Indiana University Studies, X, no. 57. Bloomington, 1923.

Sabin, Lorenzo, *Biographical Sketches of the Loyalists of the American Revolution, with an Historical Essay*, I–II. Boston, 1864.

Sanders, J. B., *Evolution of the Executive Departments of the Continental Congress, 1774–1789*. Chapel Hill, 1935.

Sanz, Manuel Serrano y., *El Brigadier Jaime Wilkinson*. Madrid, 1915.

Savelle, Max, *George Morgan, Colony Builder*. New York, 1932.

Shaw, Helen Louise, *British Administration of the Southern Indians, 1756–1783*. Lancaster, 1931.

Shreve, Royal Ornan, *The Finished Scoundrel*. Indianapolis, 1933.

Siebert, Wilbur H., "Kentucky's Struggle with its Loyalist Proprietors" in *Mississippi Valley Historical Review*, VII, 113–126.

——————, *The Loyalists of Pennsylvania*. Ohio State University Bulletin, XXIV, no. 23. Columbus, 1905.

——————, *The Tory Proprietors of Kentucky Lands*. Columbus, 1919. Reprinted from *Ohio Archæological and Historical Quarterly*, XXVIII, no. 1.

Simms, H. H., *Life of John Taylor*. Richmond, 1932.

Sioussat, St. George L., *The North Carolina Cession of 1784 in its Federal Aspects*. Mississippi Valley Historical Association, *Proceedings*, II, 35–62.

——————, "The Breakdown of the Royal Management of Lands in the Southern Provinces, 1773–1775" in *Agricultural History*, III, 67–98.

Sipe, C. Hale, *Fort Ligonier and its Times*. Harrisburg, 1932.

Slaughter, Philip, *Memoir of Col. Joshua Fry, some time Professor in William and Mary College, Virginia, and Washington's Senior in Command of Virginia Forces, 1754, etc., etc., with an Autobiography of his Son, Rev. Henry Fry, and a Census of their Descendants*. Richmond, 1880.

Smith, Joseph, *Old Redstone, or Historical Sketches of Western Pennsylvania*. Philadelphia, 1854.

Smith, Z. F., *History of Kentucky*. Louisville, 1886.

Speed, Thomas, *The Wilderness Road. Filson Club Publications*, no. 2. Louisville, 1886.

——————, *The Political Club, Danville, Ky., 1786–1790. Filson Club Publications*, no. 9. Louisville, 1894.

Steele, Willis, *Benjamin Franklin of Paris*. New York, 1928.

Stillé, Charles J., *The Life and Times of John Dickinson, 1732–1808*. Philadelphia, 1891.

Sullivan, Kathryn, *Maryland and France, 1774–1779*. Philadelphia, 1936.

Summers, Lewis Preston, *History of Southwest Virginia, 1746–1786, Washington County, 1777–1870*. Richmond, 1903.

Sumner, William Graham, *The Financier and the Finances of the American Revolution*. 2 vols. New York, 1891.

Tatter, Henry, "State and Federal Land Policy During the Confederation Period" in *Agricultural History*, IX, 176–186.

Treat, Payson J., *The National Land System, 1785–1820*. New York, 1910.

Turner, Frederick Jackson, "Western State-Making in the Revolutionary Era" in *American Historical Review*, I, 70–87, 251–269.

Tyler, Lyon G., ed., *Encyclopedia of Virginia Biography*, II. New York, 1915.

——————, *Letters and Times of the Tylers*. 2 vols. Richmond, 1884–1896.

——————, *History of Virginia*. Chicago, 1924.

Van der Weyde, William M., *The Life and Works of Thomas Paine*. 3 vols. New Rochelle, 1925. (Much of the section dealing with the affair of Silas Deane is taken almost verbatim from Moncure D. Conway's *Life of Paine*.)

Veech, James, *The Monongahela of Old*. Pittsburgh, 1910.

Volwiler, Albert T., *George Croghan and the Westward Movement, 1741–1782*. Cleveland, 1926.

Waddell, Joseph A., *The Annals of Augusta County, Virginia, 1726–1874*. Staunton, 1902.

Wallace, David Duncan, *The Life of Henry Laurens*. New York, 1915.

Walther, Daniel, *Gouverneur Morris, Witness of Two Revolutions*. Translated by Elinore Denniston. New York, 1934.

Watkins, Robert, and George, *Digest of the Laws of the State of Georgia*. Philadelphia, 1800.

Watson, Elkanah, *Men and Times of the Revolution*. New York, 1856.

Watson, John Fanning, *Annals of Philadelphia and Pennsylvania, in the Olden Time*, I–II. Philadelphia, 1850.

Welling, James C., *The States-Rights Conflict over the Public Lands*. Papers of the American Historical Association, III, 411–432.

——————, *The Land Politics of the United States*. New York, 1888.

Whitaker, Arthur P., "Spanish Intrigue in the Old Southwest: an Episode, 1788–89" in *Mississippi Valley Historical Review*, XII, 155–176.

——————, "The Muscle Shoals Speculation, 1783–1789" in *ibid.*, XIII, 365–386.

——————, *The Spanish-American Frontier, 1783–1795*. Boston, 1927.

White, George, *The Historical Collections of Georgia*. New York, 1855.

Whitsitt, William H., *Life and Times of Judge Caleb Wallace*. Louisville, 1888. *Filson Club Publications*, no. 4.

Wilkinson, General James, *Memoirs of My Own Times*. 3 vols. Philadelphia, 1816.

Wilson, Goodridge, *Smyth County History and Traditions*. Kingsport, Tenn., 1832.

Wilson, Samuel M., *West Fincastle—Now Kentucky*. Reprinted from Filson Club, *History Quarterly*, IX, 65–94.

——————, *The First Land Court of Kentucky, 1779–1780*. Lexington, 1923.

——————, *The Ohio Company of Virginia*. Lexington, 1926. Offprint from *Kentucky Law Journal*, XIV, nos. 3 and 4.

Winsor, Justin, *The Westward Movement*. Boston, 1897.

——————, "Virginia and the Quebec Bill" in *American Historical Review*, I, 436–443.

Withers, Alexander Scott, *Chronicles of Border Warfare*. Reuben Gold Thwaites, ed. Cincinnati, 1920.

Wood, George C., *Congressional Control of Foreign Relations During the American Revolution, 1774–1789*. Allentown, Pa. 1919.

Woods, Neander M., *The Woods-McAfee Memorial*. Louisville, 1905.

Wroth, Lawrence C., "The Story of Thomas Cresap, a Maryland Pioneer" in *Maryland Historical Magazine*, IX.

INDEX

Abingdon, 15, 79
Act of Separation, 346
Adair, John, 261
Adamses, the, 131, 157, 169, 170, 186, 205, 215, 281
Adams faction, the, 236
Adams, John, 145, 156, 157, 158, 186, 212, 231, 278, 279, 282, 283, 284, 286, 368
Adams-Lee group, 170, 172, 186, 199, 237, 320
Adams, Richard, 213
Adams, Samuel, 186, 187, 360
Adams, Thomas, 213, 219
Administration, colonial, 33, 50
Agents:
    American, 206
    Imperial, 21
    Indian, see Indian agents
Albany, 14, 15
Albemarle County, 5, 7, 83, 105, 121, 135, 164, 174, 225
Albemarle Valley, 8
Allegheny Mountains, the, 10, 37, 46, 47, 53, 67, 76, 162, 258, 269, 284, 359
Alliance, the, 274, 275
America, 16, 17, 21, 22, 44, 45, 47, 53, 56, 57, 82, 89, 100, 114, 117, 122, 124, 141, 142, 143, 162, 173, 180, 181, 183, 185, 196, 203, 205, 209, 210, 211, 213, 249, 250, 274, 277, 286, 334, 363
    British forces in, 11
    cause of, 195, 197, 207
    democracy in, 228
    Spanish possessions in, 339
American lands, see Lands
Americans, 33, 141, 185, 188, 197, 199, 210, 235, 267, 321, 354, 359, 366
American trade, see Trade
Amherst, General Jeffrey, 11, 23
Ammunition, 6, 108, 198
Amsterdam, 172
Anderson, Col. Richard Clough, 305, 322, 324, 325, 336
Anderson, William, 312
"Anti-Gallican party," 237
"Anti-Proprietary party," 169
Anti-Transylvania movement, 164, 165

Anglicans, 169
Annapolis, 88
Appalachian Mountains, 1, 2, 9, 21, 291, 341
Appeals, Court of, 224, 259
Aranda, Count, 284, 354
Arbitration, 365
Arkansas River, 195
Armstrong, James, 299
Army, the:
    American, 206
    British, 230
    rebel, 209
    Revolutionary, 145, 170, 185, 219
    Washington's, 209, 226
Army contracts, speculation in, 281
Arnold, Benedict, 196, 244, 255, 360
Arthur, Gabriel, 2
Articles of Confederation, 122, 148, 171, 173, 223, 239, 242, 243, 245, 246, 247, 260, 272, 365, 366
Artillery, 252, 254
Assembly:
    Connecticut, 18
    Georgia, 288, 314, 315, 343, 344
    Kentucky, 336
    Maryland, 245
    North Carolina, 339
    Pennsylvania, 10, 15, 18, 23, 295
    Virginia, 12, 150, 159, 219, 223, 224, 225, 226, 227, 228, 243, 244, 249, 251, 256, 264, 265, 266, 270, 271, 272, 293, 295, 296, 303, 306, 307, 319, 325, 326, 352
Attainder, bills of, 158
Attorneys, 164
Auditor-general, 11
Augusta County, 4, 83, 86, 89, 94, 95, 101, 104, 132, 133, 134, 136, 256, 311
Augusta Town, 178, 241
Augusta, treaty of, 311, 316
Augusta, West, see West Augusta
Austria, 282

Bache and Shee, Messrs., 286
Bache, Richard, 146, 286

Bahamas, the, 339
Baker's Bottom, 106
Baltimore, 227, 241, 321
Ballew, Bennett, 341
Bancroft, Dr. Edward, 121, 122, 142, 143, 185, 206, 207, 211, 212, 216, 230, 231, 275, 279
Banister, John, 215, 219, 308
Banks, Button, 312, 313
Banyan, Goldsbrow, 73
Barbados, the, 183
Barbee, Joshua, 345
Barbé-Marbois, 280, 286
Barclay and Sons, David, 23
Barclay, Moylan and Company, 298
Barclay, Thomas, 298
Batts, Thomas, 2
Baynton and Wharton, 26, 211
Baynton, John, 26, 27, 29, 31, 40, 41, 42, 53, 175, 313
Baynton, Wharton and Morgan, 23, 24, 25, 26, 28, 32, 35, 36, 40, 41, 43, 57, 80, 81, 93, 117, 118, 146, 194, 276, 313
Beargrass Creek, 250, 301
Beaumarchais, 180, 181, 183, 185, 209, 210, 212, 214
Bedford, county of, 92
Bedford, Duke of, 7
Bend country, see Tennessee, Bend of the
Bend of the Tennessee, see Tennessee, Bend of the
Bentley, Thomas, 193, 195, 198, 202, 248
Berkeley, George, 3
Berkeley, Sir William, 1
"Beverly Manor," 4
Beverly, Robert, 2
Beverly, William, 3, 4
Bibliography, 370-392
Biddle, Clement, 297, 298
Biddle, John, 298
Biddle, Owen, 298
Big Sandy River, 75
Bingham, William, 172, 173, 183
Bird, Captain, 247
Bishop, American, 161
"Black Boys," 81
Blair, President John, 34, 38, 63, 64, 68, 154
Bland, Edward, 1
Bland, Richard, 138, 152
Bland, Theodorick, 244, 271, 275, 280, 281
Bledsoe, Anthony, 82, 192, 261, 314, 332
Bledsoe, Isaac, 82
Blois, 182
Bloomery, the, 71

Blount, John Gray, 260
Blount, William, 260, 261, 262, 288, 294, 314, 332, 333, 343
Blue grass region, 125
Blue Licks, 265
Blue Ridge Mountains, 2, 4, 368
Board of Trade, British, 6, 12, 24, 30, 33, 34, 43, 45, 49, 50, 52, 54, 56, 61, 62, 68, 72, 76, 101, 114
   see also Trade
Board of War, 186, 203, 275
Boats, 26, 198, 199
Boiling Spring, 126, 130
Boone, Daniel, 28, 80, 81, 82, 98, 109, 110, 125, 126, 130, 192, 249
Boonesborough station, 126, 129, 130, 191, 192
Borden, Benjamin, 3
Borneo, 122
Boston, 92, 107, 182, 185
Boston Port Bill, 107, 154
Botetourt County, 77, 83, 89, 101, 134
Botetourt, Lord, 47, 49, 64, 66, 67, 70, 71, 72, 73, 77, 133
Boucher, Jacques Timothe, 309
Bouligny, Francis, 313
Boundaries:
   charter, 271, 366
   colonial, 363
   determination of, 148
   inter-colonial, 36
   Mississippi River, 320
   State, 226, 246, 365
   Western, 233, 235
Boundary:
   Canadian, 107
   Cherokee, 67
   controversy, 94, 96, 97, 109, 139, 140, 166, 187, 223, 226, 227, 228, 241, 246
   Indian, 22, 32, 33, 43, 59ff, 311
   Mississippi, 236
   new, 70
   North Carolina-Virginia, 53, 277
   Pennsylvania, 91ff, 97, 227, 270, 309, 337
   Spanish, 312
   Tennessee River, 67
   Virginia, 53, 60, 62, 64, 67, 87, 91ff, 97, 125, 227, 270, 309
   Western, 91, 204, 230f, 237, 238, 271, 282, 283, 285
Bounties, 223
   land, 171, 335, 336, 351
   military, 210, 245, 336
Bounty claims, 47

Bouquet, Col. Henry, 11, 23, 25, 86
Bourbon County, 312, 313, 323
Bowles, William Augustus, 339
Bowman, Col. John, 191-192
Braddock, Gen., 10, 15, 16, 69, 80
Braddock's Road, 19
Bradshaw, Thomas, 45
Brandon, 213
Brant, Joseph, 16
Brant, Molly, 16
Braxton, Carter, 147, 148, 153, 154, 156,
    157, 159, 160, 169, 170, 172, 189, 215,
    217, 232
Breckinridge, Alexander, 296, 301
Breckinridge, H. H., 327
Breckinridge, John, 297, 301
Breckinridge, Robert, 4, 296
Breckinridges, the, 80
Breckinridge, William, 250
Bribery, 280
Bristol, 294
Britain, 57, 203, 209, 217
    see also Great Britain, England
"British Conspiracy," 359
British government, the, 69, 100, 122, 143,
    155, 156, 206, 211, 239, 283, 368
British Ministry, see Ministry, British
British, the, 9, 10, 19, 20, 188, 196, 200,
    240, 267, 274, 283, 295, 299, 311, 312,
    313, 316, 317, 329, 337, 338, 339, 366
Brodhead, Col. Daniel, 234, 251, 252, 254,
    296, 297
Brooks, Dr. Ebenezer, 303, 304, 305, 306,
    326, 348
Brown, John, 4, 250, 321, 324, 327, 331,
    346, 347, 350, 354
Buchanan, James, 5
Buchanan, John, 4, 256
Buffalo, 82, 83
Bullitt, Alexander Scott, 301, 322, 348
Bullitt, Judge Cuthbert, 301
Bullitt, Captain Thomas, 84, 85, 86, 87,
    88, 89, 102, 103, 130, 134, 301
Bullitt's Lick, 301
Bullitts, the, 80, 165
Burgesses, House of, 7, 9, 12, 61, 62, 67,
    68, 70, 71, 98, 107, 113, 138, 149, 150,
    151, 152, 153, 154, 155, 364
Burgoyne, defeat of, 206
Burke, Thomas, 132
Burlington Company, 22, 33, 42
Burlington, New Jersey, 22
Burr, Aaron, 357
Burwell, Robert, 134, 153
Bush-whacking, 106

Business, private, 22
Butler, Richard, 86, 106, 142, 174, 175,
    296, 324, 325, 338
Byrd group, the, 123
Byrd, John, 89
Byrd, Col. William, 73, 79, 80, 84, 100,
    103, 123, 134, 135, 153, 154, 156, 228

Cabell, Joseph, 256
Cabell, Nicholas, 256
Cadiz, 278, 285
Cahokia, 247
Cahokians, the, 335
California, 2
Calk, William, 126
Callender, Robert, 25, 32, 40, 52, 118, 143
Calloway, 191, 192
Calverts, the, 362
Camden, Lord, 45, 114, 116, 117
Camden-Yorke opinion, 21, 117, 118, 119,
    122, 123, 124, 131, 143, 144, 162, 363
Cameron, Alexander, 74, 75
Camm, John, 134, 156
Camp Charlotte, 113, 138
Campbell, Col. Arthur, 4, 79, 88, 99, 102,
    103, 108, 109, 124, 125, 131, 132, 166,
    191, 222, 235, 255, 256, 257, 258, 259,
    261, 262, 264, 265, 290, 291, 292, 293,
    294, 302, 303, 304, 307, 332, 335, 338
Campbell, Charles, 5
Campbell, David, 191, 291, 294
Campbell, John, 4, 17, 35, 79, 87, 93, 94,
    118, 121, 127, 136, 140, 143, 174, 177,
    187, 188, 193, 195, 240, 296, 300, 305,
    327, 328, 329, 358
Campbell, Gen. William, 4, 80
Canada, 20, 180, 203, 240, 286, 329, 339,
    357
    boundary of, 107, 283
Cannon, John, 268
Capitalists, French, 239
Corbin, Richard, 134
Carlisle, 6, 145
Carmichael, William, 208
Carolina, see North Carolina, South Car-
    olina
Carolina Blue Ridge, 2
Carolinas, the, 236, 302
    see also North Carolina, South Car-
    olina
Caroline County, 165
Caron, Pierre-Augustin, 180
Carrington, Edward, 329

Carroll, Charles, 122, 171, 239
Carter, Landon, 107, 150, 156
Carter, Robert, 8, 134, 135
Cary, Archibald, 149, 153, 157, 160, 180, 217, 220
"Castlewoods," 80
Caswell, Gov. Richard, 260, 261, 294, 314, 332, 333, 335, 340, 343
Catfish Camp, 167, 178
Caveats, 8
Cessions, land, 243, 244, 309, 344
    Connecticut, 245
    Indians, 363
    New York, 246, 272
    North Carolina, 294, 306
    Virginia, 246, 270, 271, 272, 273, 285, 296, 360, 365
Charleston, 64, 66, 127, 203, 260, 314
Charlotta, Province of, 52
Charlotte, Queen, 54
"Charlottina," 52
Charters, colonial, 54, 226
Chartiers' Creek, 110, 145, 267, 357
Chase, Samuel, 171, 239
Chatham, Earl of, 182
Chaumont, Donatien le Rey de, 182, 183, 206, 208, 209, 211, 212, 213, 216, 230, 231, 234, 239, 275, 276, 278
Cherokee, the, 33, 34, 53, 54, 60, 63, 64, 66, 67, 71, 74, 75, 77, 84, 88, 98, 101, 106, 123, 124, 125, 134, 220, 242, 256, 261, 288, 290, 303, 304, 305, 314, 315, 316, 334, 338, 341
    boundary of, 67
    campaign against, 257
    land claims of, 49
    treaty with, 190, 335
Chew, Joseph, 111
Chickamauga Indians, 223, 335
Chickasaw Bluffs, 334
Chickasaw country, 323
Chickasaw Indians, 259, 300, 315, 338,
    treaty with, 260, 262
Chillicothe, 86
Chippewas, 316
Chiswell, Col. John, 79, 153, 154
Chiswell's Mine, 60, 61, 63, 64, 79, 100
Cholmondeley, Robert, 11
Christian, Gilbert, 109, 132, 163, 191, 222, 259, 302
Christian, Israel, 80
Christian, Col. William, 80, 83, 99, 103, 123, 129, 250, 258, 264, 293, 301, 317
Christianity, 267
Christmas, Nathaniel, 312

Church, the, 134, 158, 159
Cincinnati, 240
Civilization, 23, 79
Claims, 104, 149
    bounty, 47
    conflicting, 366
    forfeiture of, 12
    Indian land, 12, 34
    land, 20, 224, 241
    see also Land claims
Clark, Daniel, 18, 142, 193, 265, 321, 328, 344, 345
Clarke, Gen. Elijah, 335
Clark, George Rogers, 18, 92, 105, 127, 128, 132, 165, 166, 167, 175, 192, 193, 196, 197, 198, 199, 201, 202, 216, 223, 228, 233, 234, 240, 247, 248, 249, 251, 252, 253, 254, 255, 259, 262, 263, 264, 265, 266, 270, 296, 297, 298, 300, 305, 317, 318, 319, 322, 323, 324, 325, 328, 329, 336, 348, 355, 365
Clark, Lucy, 92
Clarksville, 296, 318
Clark, William, 296, 297, 299, 345
Clifford, 172
Clinch River, 80, 81, 98, 109, 125
Clinch Valley, 123
Clymer, George, 200
Cocke, William, 130, 191, 291, 292, 335
Coffyn, D., 286
Colbert, Chief James, 300
Coldstream Guards, 10
Colebrook, Sir George, 45
Colonial troops, 100, 101
Colonial union, plan of, 14
Colonies, the, 1, 14, 19, 44, 60, 137, 139, 140, 141, 143, 167, 169, 181, 182, 193, 214, 243, 271, 284, 356, 359, 367
    boundaries of, 15, 60, 283
    British, 180
    dispute with, 57
    foreign commerce of, 172
    governors of, 21
    independence of, 149, 157
    inland, 50
    insurgent, 193, 205
    merchants in, 172
    middle, 33, 157, 170, 172
    new, 15
    Northern, 15, 205
    peace for, 283
    promotion of, 28
    proprietors of, 21
    rebel, 181, 203, 206, 368
    Southern, 205, 362

Colonies, *continued*
  united, 159
  Western, 24, 30, 70
Colonization, 4, 7, 235, 330, 337, 354, 355
Commerce, 173, 196
  Committee on, 196, 197, 210, 215
  foreign, 172
  Kaskaskia, 193f
  Virginia, 159
Commissioners:
  American, 230, 231, 283, 284
  Georgia, 288, 289, 323
  Indian, 309, 325, 333
  Louisville, 296
  Tennessee, 315
Common Sense, 214
Conciliation, 155
Confederation, the, 243, 244, 245, 292, 307,
  308, 309, 319, 326, 329, 337, 346, 347,
  349, 350, 357, 358, 359, 360, 361, 367
Confederation, Articles of, *see* Articles
  of Confederation
Connecticut, 18, 19, 37, 55, 131, 171, 181,
  236, 245, 246, 281, 282, 362
Connolly, Dr. John, 18, 74, 87, 88, 92, 94,
  95, 96, 97, 102, 103, 106, 107, 108, 114,
  115, 121, 136, 137, 138, 139, 140, 240,
  254, 268, 296, 353, 356, 357, 358
Conservatives, the, 149ff, 155, 156, 157,
  158, 189, 200, 217, 218, 219, 220, 221,
  222, 224, 231
Conspiracy, Spanish, 343, 354
Constitution:
  democratic, 170
  Federal, 343, 346, 347, 359, 360, 367
  Virginia, 157, 158, 159
Continental Congress, 114, 121, 130, 131,
  138, 139, 140, 141, 142, 144, 145, 147,
  148, 155, 156, 157, 159, 166, 167, 169ff,
  173, 174, 175, 176, 178, 179, 180, 183,
  185, 186, 187, 188, 189, 190, 196, 197,
  198, 199, 200, 201, 202, 203, 204, 208,
  209, 210, 211, 212, 213, 214, 215, 216,
  219, 222, 223, 225, 226, 231, 232, 233,
  234, 235, 237, 238, 239, 242, 243, 244,
  245, 246, 247, 248, 249, 251, 252, 257,
  258, 259, 260, 264, 266, 267, 269, 270,
  271, 272, 273, 274, 275, 277, 278, 279,
  280, 281, 282, 283, 284, 285, 286, 290,
  291, 292, 293, 296, 299, 300, 302, 303,
  308, 309, 310, 313, 316, 317, 319, 320,
  321, 323, 324, 325, 326, 327, 328, 329,
  330, 331, 332, 333, 334, 336, 337, 338,
  341, 343, 344, 346, 347, 348, 350, 351,
  352, 355, 359, 360, 365, 366, 367

Continental Congress, *continued*
  cessions to, 242
  crisis in, 212
  delegates to, 160
  expansionists in, 236
  foreign policy of, 184
  jurisdiction of, 226, 243, 244, 245,
    247
  and land question, 169ff
  members of, 281
  partisan situation in, 236
  politics in, 205ff
  Revolutionary, 58
  Virginia in, 236
  and the West, 230ff
Continental Line, the, 194, 336
Continental warrants, 336
"Conway Cabal," 186, 205, 298, 345
Conway, Henry S., 30
Conway, Col. Thomas, 185, 186, 187, 247
Conyngham, Captain Augustus, 232
Cook, Captain, 209
Cooper, Grey, 45
Corbin, Richard, 156
Cornstalk, 112
Council, Virginia, 7, 9, 12, 48, 49, 52, 63,
  68, 70, 73, 76, 89, 90, 94, 96, 98, 103,
  107, 109, 134, 135, 149, 151, 153, 154,
  178, 198, 201, 256
Counties:
  establishment of, 94
  Kentucky, 266
  new, 165, 166
  Western, 107, 224, 225
Courts:
  county, 191, 262
  Fayette County, 346
  Federal, 347
  Fincastle County, 166
  French, 206, 278
  Kentucky, 266-267
  Monongalia, 240
  organization of, 136
  Transylvania, 130
  West Augusta, 137
  Yohogania, 240-241
Coxe, Daniel, 20
Cox, Isaac, 305
Craig, David, 191
Craig, John, 164, 297, 331, 324
Crawford, Valentine, 137
Crawford, William, 68, 69, 70, 74, 87, 93,
  94, 104, 105, 107, 128, 133, 134, 136,
  137, 145, 174, 268, 270
Creek country, 341

Creek Indians, 259, 311, 314, 315, 316, 333, 334, 335, 338, 339, 344
  peace with, 315
  treaty with, 344
Cresap, Michael, 105, 106
Cresap, Thomas, 5, 6, 35, 74, 77, 92, 105
Cresswell, Nicholas, 127, 137
Croghan, George, 6, 7, 8, 16, 17, 18, 19, 21, 22, 23, 24, 25, 26, 27, 28, 29, 31, 33, 35, 36, 37, 40, 41, 43, 44, 45, 56, 59, 68, 69, 81, 87, 89, 92, 93, 94, 95, 96, 99, 102, 108, 110, 111, 112, 116, 117, 118, 119, 120, 121, 136, 137, 139, 142, 143, 145, 146, 167, 174, 176, 177, 189, 193, 194, 199, 225, 226, 227, 239, 240, 241, 245, 246, 253, 254, 267, 269, 270, 356, 365
Croghan-Morgan group, 194
Croghan-Virginia group, 268
Croghan, William, 18, 92, 296, 297, 336, 345
Cumberland County, 324, 332, 335, 341
Cumberland Gap, 46, 81, 82, 83, 85, 98, 123, 125, 126, 190, 352
Cumberland Mountains, 53, 72, 75, 76, 81, 223
Cumberland River, 82, 102, 125, 228, 260, 285
Currency, 22, 125, 151, 218, 225, 228, 232, 233, 263, 278, 282
  Virginia, 151, 248, 249, 364
Cutler, Manasseh, 337, 355

Dagge, Henry, 144
Dana, Francis, 281
Dandridge, Alexander Spotswood, 102, 129, 130
Daniel, Walker, 264, 266, 301, 302
Danville, 267, 303, 304, 306, 307, 319, 321, 322, 323, 325, 326, 327, 328, 331, 348, 352
D'Argès, Pierre Wouves, 354, 355
Dartmouth College, 16
Dartmouth, Earl of, 52, 54, 55, 56, 76, 89, 100, 101, 109, 110, 111, 120, 125, 128, 140
Davenport, William, 312, 313, 334
Davis, Azariah, 130
Deane, Silas, 131, 172, 173, 181, 182, 183, 185, 186, 187, 206, 207, 208, 209, 210, 211, 212, 213, 214, 215, 216, 219, 230, 231, 232, 234, 237, 238, 239, 247, 275, 277, 278, 281, 285, 360
Deane, Simeon, 211, 213, 239
De Berdt, Dennys, 180

Debts, 219
  planter, 160, 161
  Virginia, 364
Decatur, Alabama, 261
Defense, Virginia, 155
Delaware River, 34
Delap, S. and J. H., 172
Delaware, 170, 236, 239, 242
Delaware River, 91
Delawares, the, 11, 18, 19, 31, 34, 99, 106, 108, 112, 138, 141, 175, 201, 233, 267, 316
Delegates, House of, 130, 166, 197, 198, 202, 220, 254, 255, 256, 259, 280, 293, 301, 307, 308, 319, 320, 328
De Francy, 212, 213, 219
De Leyba, 199, 233
Democracy, 13, 228, 367, 368
Denmark, 334
Denny, Gov. William, 18
Detroit, 141, 175, 176, 178, 179, 196, 197, 200, 201, 233, 234, 248, 249, 252, 266, 329, 357, 365
De Warville, Brissot, 173
Dickinson, John, 148, 169, 170, 172, 365
Dinwiddie, Gov. Robert, 8, 9, 10, 24, 48, 49, 70, 89, 224
Diplomats, 286
Disraeli, 119
Dixon, see Mason and Dixon
Doak, Robert, 83
Dobbs, Gov. Arthur, 8
Dodge, John, 233, 248, 251, 298, 309, 310, 316, 336
Domain:
  public, 228
  Western, 8, 129, 221
Donegal, 4
Donelson, Col. John, 54, 71, 74, 75, 76, 84, 88, 102, 103, 123, 124, 125, 258, 259, 260, 261, 262, 263, 264, 288, 289, 302, 312, 317, 362, 363
Donelson, Stockley, 261
Donne, John, 298, 300
Dorchester, Lord, 329, 339, 351, 357, 358, 359
Douglas, James, 84, 85, 102, 103, 110, 130, 162
Downes, William, 288
Draper's Meadows, 5, 79, 80
Drayton, William Henry, 231, 237, 239, 314
Duane, James, 243, 281
Dunbar, William, 313
Duncan, David, 176, 255, 298
Dunkerque, 286

Dunmore, Lord, 40, 55, 56, 73, 74, 75, 76, 83, 84, 87, 88, 89, 90, 92, 94, 95, 96, 97, 98, 99, 100, 101, 102, 104, 105, 106, 107, 108, 109, 110, 111, 112, 113, 114, 115, 119, 121, 122, 123, 124, 125, 128, 129, 131, 132, 134, 136, 137, 138, 139, 140, 145, 155, 162, 166, 167, 173-174, 177, 190, 194, 224, 240, 254, 268, 291, 297, 339, 357, 363, 364
Dunmore's War, 97, 113, 120, 268
Dunn, Isaac B., 299, 344, 345, 348, 350, 354, 356
Duquesne, 10

East, the, 163, 201, 204, 219, 238, 295, 330, 345, 347, 359, 366, 367
Easterners, 73
East India Company, 45
Easton, treaty of, 18, 19
Edgar, John, 329
Edinburgh, University of, 80
Education, 80
Edwards, John, 324
Egremont, Lord, 20
Elbert, Gov., 313
Elkhorn, 127, 128
Elliott, Matthew, 176, 200
Ellis, John, 312, 313
Emancipation Act, Pennsylvania, 254
Embargo, 232
England, 1, 9, 15, 16, 19, 20, 22, 29, 30, 31, 44, 45, 53, 55, 56, 57, 58, 74, 100, 103, 118, 122, 143, 158, 169, 177, 180, 181, 182, 185, 208, 214, 237, 250, 299, 307, 357, 359, 360, 363, 368
    see also Britain, Great Britain
Europe, 184, 210, 213, 216, 265, 277, 278, 339
Evans' map, 75, 363
Ewing, Charles, 324
Exemption, 182
Expansion, Western, 51, 200, 236, 237
Exploration, Western, 1ff
Explorers, 81, 82

Fairfax, George, 8
Fallam, Robert, 2
Falls of the Ohio, see Ohio, Falls of the
Farrar, Benjamin, 312
Farrar, John, 125
Fauquier, Gov. Francis, 10, 11, 12, 20, 34, 38, 47, 60, 61, 63, 151, 152, 154
Fayette County, 249, 251, 263, 264, 304, 306, 346

Federal Constitution, see Constitution, Federal
Federalists, 157, 343
Field, Robert, 25
Fincastle County, 83, 85, 86, 89, 94, 99, 100, 101, 102, 123, 124, 128, 132, 134, 164, 166
Finley, Rev. James, 85, 270
Finley, John, 27, 41, 81, 82
Fish Creek, 105
Fisheries, the, 237
Fitzhugh, William, 222, 236, 238
Fleming, Col. William, 61, 62, 80, 103, 112, 153, 163, 222, 236, 239, 250, 265, 304, 305
Florida, 20, 203, 339
Floridablanca, Count, 202, 333, 354
Flour, 142, 176, 193, 232, 321
Floyd, John, 83, 102, 103, 104, 105, 109, 110, 111, 129, 130, 132, 133, 162, 163, 166, 191, 249, 250, 264, 266, 301, 302
Forbes, Gen. John, 10, 19, 20, 69, 80
Foreign Affairs, Committee for, 212, 214, 230
Forks of the Ohio, 5, 9, 10, 19
Fort Blair, 129, 142, 167
Fort Charlotte, treaty of, 113, 115
Fort Chartres, 26, 40
Fort Dunmore, 96, 107-108, 139
Fort Duquesne, 10, 20
Fort Fincastle, 107, 142, 167
Fort Finney, treaty of, 316, 317
Fort Henry, 1, 2, 142, 167, 188
Fort Jefferson, 223, 247, 251, 255
Fort McIntosh, 316
Fort Nelson, 255, 296
Fort Pitt, 11, 20, 25, 26, 27, 33, 35, 36, 37, 40, 42, 70, 80, 91, 93, 94, 95, 96, 127, 139, 140, 141, 142, 175, 188, 254, 357
Forts:
    chain of, 108
    erection of, 251
    frontier, 264
    Western, 167
Fort Stanwix, 33, 35, 36, 37, 43, 48, 53, 59, 64, 66, 67, 68, 69, 70, 87, 91, 103, 176, 220, 316, 363
    treaty of, 34, 35, 36, 37, 38, 43, 45, 86, 143, 189, 221, 242, 363
Fowey, the, 140, 155
Foy, Capt. E., 89
France, 23, 172, 173, 180, 182, 183, 185, 197, 208, 210, 211, 213, 214, 231, 332, 235, 237, 239, 249, 269, 275, 276, 278, 280, 282, 283, 284, 298, 354, 368

France, *continued*
  colonies of, 181
  Court of, 185, 203, 211, 231, 278
  fleet of, 232
  government of, 172, 214, 231, 279
  King of, 209, 212, 235, 248
  loans from, 279
  mission to, 181
  treaty with, 202
Franklin, Benjamin, 14ff, 18, 19, 20, 22, 23, 24, 25, 29, 30, 31, 32, 33, 35, 37, 44, 50, 56, 57, 59, 62, 111, 117, 119, 122, 138, 141, 142, 143, 144, 145, 146, 148, 169, 170ff, 177, 180ff, 205ff, 211ff, 230, 231, 238, 245, 247, 250, 274, 275, 276, 277, 278, 279, 280, 282, 283, 284, 285, 286, 287, 297, 320, 360, 365
Franklin-Deane group, 183
Franklin-Morris group, 172, 175
Franklin, State of, 191, 292, 293, 294, 314, 315, 324, 332, 334, 335, 339, 340, 341, 342
Franklin, Temple, 213, 275, 286
Franklin, Gov. William, 22, 29ff, 36, 40, 42, 43, 52, 55, 58, 77, 111, 119, 143, 144, 146, 177, 181, 213, 365
Frankfort, 127, 348
Franks, David, 16, 17, 117
Franks and Company, David, 24, 41, 45, 117, 143, 144, 193
Franks-Gratz group, 40, 117, 118
Franks, Moses, 17, 48
Fredericksburg, 8, 154, 155
French-American alliancé, 235
French and Indian War, 10, 12, 14, 15, 17, 20, 40, 59, 60, 79, 81, 84, 88, 91, 99, 100, 112, 151
French Lick, 83, 228, 260, 262
French, the, 9, 10, 14, 15, 20, 27, 28, 194, 247, 248, 285, 317, 332
Frontiersmen, 217, 218, 330, 331, 333, 367
Frontier, the, 4, 13, 20, 23, 25, 40, 60, 71, 73, 80, 83, 84, 107, 115, 137, 163, 166, 187, 189, 190, 194, 224, 234, 270, 302, 317, 333, 366, 368
  American, 357
  defense of, 15, 19, 140, 167
  disturbance on, 99
  forts on, 264
  Georgia, 329
  leadership on, 81, 318, 367
  settlements on, 263
  Virginia, 5, 7, 67, 100, Ch. 5, 363
  Western, 9, 60, 352

Fry, Col. Joshua, 7, 8, 10
Fry's and Jefferson's map, 5
Furs, 1, 15, 28, 79, 80, 321

Gage, Gen. Thomas, 25, 26, 27, 35, 55, 86, 92, 120
Galphinton, 311
  treaty of, 316, 333
Galloway, James, 45, 146, 147, 170, 302
Galloway, Joseph, 18, 23, 29, 32, 36, 111, 119
Galloway-Wharton group, 169
Gálvez, Don Bernardo de, 195, 196, 199, 202, 203, 240
Gardoqui, Don Diego de, 313, 319, 327, 329, 330, 332, 333, 340, 342, 344, 346, 347, 350, 353, 354, 355, 356, 359
Garrard, James, 324
Gates, Gen. Horatio, 186, 198
George III, 7, 9, 40, 47, 51, 52, 56, 76, 87, 124, 137, 148, 185, 277, 362, 363, 364
Georgia, 60, 171, 237, 261, 280, 281, 282, 288, 290, 291, 311, 313, 314, 323, 331ff, 338, 343, 344
  assembly of, *see* Assembly, Georgia
  commission, 315
Gérard, Conrad Alexandre, 203, 204, 206, 211, 212, 214, 215, 230, 231, 232, 234, 235, 237, 238, 248, 285, 286, 366
Germans, 3, 40, 169
Gibson, Col. George, 136, 143, 194, 195, 197, 198, 240, 254
Gibson, Col. John, 94, 136, 174, 175, 177, 194, 201, 240, 253, 268
Gilliard, Tacitus, 312, 313
Gillon, Capt. Alexander, 279
Girault, Capt. John, 297, 323, 345
Girty, Simon, 28, 188, 200, 240, 268
Gist, Christopher, 6, 7, 8, 9, 81
Gnadenhutten massacre, 267-268
Government, 157, 161, 163, 356, 361
  British, 21, 22, 23, 122, 230, 239, 277, 283
  colonial, 9, 14, 15, 157
  French, 172, 215, 279
  Kentucky, 304
  Proprietary, 46, 56, 57
  Virginia, 189
Gower, Lord, 45, 50, 117
Grand, Ferdinand, 211, 234, 239
Grand Ohio Company, 45ff, 46, 47, 48, 53, 54, 72
Grants, land, 2, 13, 27, 29, 37, 54, 57, 84, 104, 134, 239, 306, 309, 369

Gratz, Bernard, 17, 93, 118, 225, 226, 235, 245

Gratz brothers, 28, 42, 93, 117, 194, 221, 235, 253, 263, 269, 296, 297

Gratz, Michael, 17, 40, 99, 189, 227, 232

Grayson, Col. William, 144, 238, 299

Great Britain, 120, 149, 156, 187, 235, 285, 286, 359

Great Kanawha River, 9, 33, 34, 43, 44, 49, 62, 63, 64, 66, 70, 71, 75, 85, 100, 107, 111, 124

Great Meadows, 10, 70

Great Miami River, 316, 318

Greenbrier Company, the, 8, 90, 190, 259, 305

Greenbrier River, 7, 46, 220, 291, 336

Greene, Gen. Nathanael, 274, 281

Greene County, 341

Green, Thomas Marston, 312, 313, 323, 324, 329

Greenup, Christopher, 304, 305, 317, 324, 346

Grenville, George, 45

Griffin, Cyrus, 219, 222, 236, 238, 301

Gulf of Mexico, 342, 343

Hagerstown, 80

Haldimand, Gen., 86, 266

Hamilton, Gov. Alexander, 14, 179, 281

Hamilton, Henry, 178

Hampton, Wade, 261, 314

Hancock, John, 145, 169, 186, 211, 215

Hand, Gen. Edward, 187, 188, 196, 198, 199, 200

Handley, Gov., 338, 344

Hanna's Town, 94, 97, 137, 138

Hanson, Thomas, 102, 110

Hardin, Capt. Joseph, 317, 341

Harmar, Col., 316, 336, 340

Harrison, Benjamin, 147ff, 153, 154, 159, 160, 169, 170, 172, 200, 213, 215, 217, 219, 255, 259, 260, 262, 263ff, 269, 295, 297, 300, 310

Harrod, James, 82, 85, 105, 109ff, 126, 129, 130, 162, 163, 193, 305

Harrodsburg, 105, 126, 130, 162ff, 191, 192, 196, 249

Hart, Nathaniel, 124, 125, 302

Harvie, John, 7, 136, 164, 174, 189, 215, 219, 220, 225, 226, 263, 296

Havana, 342, 347, 355

Heard, Stephen, 288, 289

Heckwelder, John, 267

Henderson Company, 124, 126

Henderson group, 126, 133

Henderson, Judge Richard, 123-124, 125, 126, 128, 129, 130, 131, 132, 133, 135, 162, 163, 164, 189, 190, 191, 219, 220, 228, 257, 302, 314, 362

Henry, Patrick, 61, 62, 73, 80, 83, 100, 103, 114, 115, 121, 122, 123, 125, 131ff, 138, 141, 144, 149ff, 170, 174, 178, 184, 186ff, 195ff, 213, 219, 222, 223, 225, 227, 238, 240, 258ff, 261, 264, 271, 288, 293, 294, 297, 305, 314, 317f, 320, 332, 347, 364, 368

Hessians, 184

Hertford, Lord, 45, 47

Hewes, Joseph, 131, 172, 237

Hillsborough, Lord, 23, 30, 33, 43ff, 49ff, 55, 63, 66f, 71ff, 124, 362, 363

Hinkston's Station, 127

Hite, Isaac, 3, 85, 102, 110, 130, 162, 163, 165, 305

Hogg, James, 124, 130, 131

Holker, John, 211, 212, 213, 219, 231, 232, 234, 281, 296, 297, 298, 300, 321, 328, 346

Holston country, 82, 129, 165, 166, 223, 260, 261, 294

Holston-Kanawha line, 73

Holston River, 5, 66, 71, 79, 80, 81, 98, 123, 190, 257, 259, 289, 291

Hooper, Robert Lettis, 93, 131, 146, 172

House of Burgesses, see Burgesses, House of

Hughes, John, 29, 31, 182

Hunters, 81, 83

Hunting, 83, 113

Huske's Map, 363

Hutchins, Thomas, 17, 27, 230, 274, 309, 313, 316, 337, 355, 357

Hutchinson, Dr. James, 56, 57, 299, 321

"Illinois adventurers," 27, 32

Illinois Company, the, 29-30, 32, 34, 116ff, 122, 127, 131, 142, 193, 202, 211, 226, 234, 235, 363, 365, 366

Illinois country, 25ff, 36, 40, 53, 55, 81, 85, 118, 120, 122, 142, 179, 193ff, 202, 204, 233ff, 240, 247ff, 251, 255, 309, 310, 321, 323, 336, 356
    conquest of, 193ff, 197, 201, 202

Illinois River, 29, 118

Illinois-Wabash Company, 238ff, 245ff, 273, 277, 285, 360

Immigrants, 4, 13, 264, 296

Impressment, 254, 318, 324

Independence, 132, 139, 143, 149, 156, 157, 159ff, 170, 182, 206, 282, 283, 307, 308, 319, 321, 322, 326, 331, 364
War for, *see* Revolution, the
Independent Gazette, 350
Indiana, 41, 71, 136ff, 143, 148, 189, 226, 227, 360, 365
Indian affairs, 22, 37, 63, 66, 332, 357
Indian agents, 18, 22, 54, 74, 87, 93, 95, 123, 142, 174, 175, 190, 197, 201, 234, 242, 257, 259, 309, 332, 338
Indiana Land Company, 37, 38, 40, 43, 48, 80, 143, 164, 175ff, 189, 190, 194, 216, 219, 220, 235, 238, 245, 269, 272, 273, 316, 363, 365, 368
claim of, 144, 145, 148, 221, 223, 225, 226, 227, 238, 246
grants to, 37, 38, 43, 44, 48, 143, 145, 146, 189
reorganization of, 144f
Indian boundary, the, 31, 60, 64, 68, 70, 73, 83, 84, 91, 190
survey of, 74
Virginia, 59ff, 123
Indian campaign, 140, 348
Indian country, 31, 36, 63, 64, 66, 93, 112, 123, 141, 176, 233, 234, 266
Indian grants, 32, 56, 57, 69, 93, 94, 116
Indian Queen Tavern, 22, 146
Indians, the, 1, 2, 6, 8, 10, 15, 16, 18, 20ff, 32ff, 44, 45, 52, 54, 59, 64, 66, 69, 71, 75, 81ff, 95, 96, 98, 101, 106, 110, 112ff, 123, 125, 126, 137, 139, 141, 145, 147f, 155, 159, 164, 167, 174ff, 184, 187, 194, 195, 201, 202, 220ff, 234, 240, 242, 247ff, 255, 259ff, 264, 266ff, 272, 285, 288, 290, 299ff, 303, 311, 312, 314ff, 324, 325, 330, 333, 334, 339, 341, 344, 347, 352, 362, 363, 365
attacks of, 22, 24, 31, 104, 105, 142, 267
cessions, 144, 363
goods for, 6, 22, 117, 120, 289
hostility of, 84, 102, 108, 125, 191, 201, 268
neutrality of, 141, 178, 234
peace with, 21, 28, 112, 113, 138
purchases from, 120, 121, 171, 193, 200, 244, 245
trade with, 5, 6, 9, 22, 25, 26, 27, 35, 93, 108, 114, 142, 323
treaty with, 5, 8, 18, 141, 179, 200, 259, 296, 324
wars with, 32, 33, 73, 99, 106, 107, 109, 131, 132, 266, 335

Ingen-Housz, Dr., 276, 277
Innes, Harry, 124, 256, 266, 301, 308, 321, 324, 325, 326, 327, 331, 345, 358
Innes, James, 124, 189, 254, 268, 269, 346, 348, 350, 353, 354
Intrigue:
British, 356
Spanish, 34, 344, 351
and trade, 346
Ireland, 18, 30, 51, 82
Iroquois, the, 34, 37, 175, 242
Irvine, Gen. William, 266, 268, 269, 298

Jackson, Andrew, 71, 312
Jamaica, 27, 28
James River, 55, 295
Jay, John, 172, 204, 214, 238, 277ff, 313, 319ff, 327, 328, 330, 358
Jefferson County, 249, 263, 264, 302, 307, 346
Jefferson, Thomas, 7, 59, 129, 131, 132, 148f, 158ff, 164, 166, 169, 189, 198, 200, 217, 218, 219, 222f, 225, 228, 240, 243, 255, 264, 271, 280, 282, 290, 295, 306, 308f, 319, 321, 357
Jenyns, Soames, 3
Jesuit School of St. Omer, 332
Johnson, Benjamin, 254, 268
Johnson, Guy, 86
Johnson Hall, 28, 108
Johnson, Sir John, 175, 357
Johnson, Gov. Thomas, 122, 171f, 239, 245
Johnson, Sir William, 15ff, 21ff, 28ff, 43ff, 48, 52, 54f, 59f, 62ff, 73, 81, 86, 108, 111, 120, 124, 175, 242, 270, 357, 363, 365
Johnston, Samuel, 124, 189
Jones, Allan, 132, 166, 281
Jones, Capt. John Gabriel, 164, 165, 222
Jones, Capt. John Paul, 208, 209, 274, 276
Jones, Joseph, 243, 244, 272
Jones, Willie, 132, 189, 243

Kanawha River, 46, 54, 60, 61, 76, 79, 102, 104, 125, 167, 291, 295
Kaskaskia, 27, 28, 176, 179, 193, 195, 196, 197, 199, 201, 202, 216, 234, 298, 309, 316, 324, 325, 336, 365
Kennedy, Daniel, 142, 176, 179, 193, 194
Kennedy, William, 123, 305
Kentuckians, 309, 345, 358
Kentucky, 3, 27, 28, 62, 66, 81, 82ff, 97, 99, 101ff, 109, 110, 125ff, 131ff, 162ff, 188,

Kentucky, *continued*
190, 191, 199, 220, 221, 233, 242, 247,
249, 250, 255, 258ff, 263ff, 296, 298ff,
312, 317ff, 323ff, 334, 340, 342, 345, 347,
348, 351ff
  assembly of, *see* Assembly, Kentucky
  admission of, 347, 348
  counties of, 81, 98, 99, 249, 298, 303,
    317, 346
  conventions of, 305, 307, 308, 309, 317,
    347ff
  district of, 301, 305, 346
  explorers in, 81-82
  independence of, 319, 353
  lands of, 110, 221, 310, 331
  politics of, 307, 322
  secession of, 251, 252, 262, 349
  settlement of, 84, 98ff, 106, 109, 113,
    115, 126, 359
Kentucky Gazette, 331
Kentucky River, 54, 63, 75, 76, 84, 86, 88,
  101ff, 105, 110, 123, 125, 126ff, 162, 251,
  264
King's Mountain, 4, 352
Knox, James, 82, 102, 110

Lacassagne, Bartholomew, 297, 298, 300,
  321
LaFayette, Marquis de, 182, 185, 305
Lancaster, 5, 15, 16, 17, 25, 93, 187
  treaty of, 8, 34, 147
Land Act of 1779, 228, 249, 256
Land bounties, 171, 305
Land claims, 20, 99, 110, 111, 176, 219,
  236, 258, 302, 317, 366
Land companies, 3ff, 9f, 12, 68, 118, 126,
  150, 164, 171, 172, 173, 177, 187, 190,
  191, 193, 194, 199, 200, 202, 204, 215,
  219, 225, 238, 245, 271, 272, 320, 337,
  347, 360, 365, 366
  claims of, 218, 220, 222, 244, 247, 270
Land grants, 2, 5, 7, 12, 13, 24, 27, 29, 31,
  37, 47, 49, 59, 63, 67f, 76, 89, 100, 110,
  130, 162, 183, 201, 218, 288, 303, 306,
  324
Landjobbing, 28, 41, 244
Land office, 146, 190, 218, 219, 221, 365
  colonial, 224
  Virginia, 164, 250, 263, 296
Land office act, 224, 225, 227, 228, 238,
  241, 250, 253
Land question, 169ff, 215, 217ff, 221, 366
Lands, 2, 3, 21, 40, 49, 58, 68, 70, 84, 118,
  123, 125, 129, 142, 147, 169ff, 181, 187,

Lands, *continued*
200, 218, 223ff, 228, 234, 239, 247, 254,
261, 314, 364
  cessions of, 21, 35, 201, 260
  Kentucky, 263, 299, 310
  purchase of, 15, 21, 28, 124, 147, 148,
    159, 164, 200, 260
  titles to, 11, 21, 62, 253, 256, 343, 347
  Western, *see* Western lands
Land speculation, 5, 15, 31, 41, 60, 79, 89,
  108, 124, 134, 147, 217, 235, 237, 249,
  259, 296, 299, 300, 304, 360, 368
Land speculators, 20, 50, 116, 119, 132,
  136, 145, 162, 173, 201, 260, 263, 302,
  313, 324, 326, 367, 369
Land warrants, 263, 321
Laurens, Henry, 186, 196, 199, 214, 215,
  235, 237, 239, 282
Law, 321, 332
  Virginia, 241, 263, 270, 309, 326
Lawyers, 169, 170, 217
Lead mine, 79, 85, 88
Lee-Adams group, 189, 200, 231, 236
Lee, Arthur, 47, 49, 180ff, 185f, 189, 197,
  200, 202, 206ff, 212, 214, 216, 230f, 270f,
  274f, 279, 281, 286
Lee, Gen. Charles, 194
Lee, Francis Lightfoot, 219, 236
Lee, Hancock, 126ff, 133, 135, 148, 175
Lee, Philip Ludwell, 134, 158
Lee, Richard Henry, 8, 47, 107, 131, 147,
  149, 150, 151, 152, 154, 156, 158, 184,
  186, 206, 212f, 215, 217, 219, 223, 236,
  243, 295, 308, 360
Lees, the, 20, 132, 149f, 154, 157f, 160,
  169f, 184, 187, 205, 213, 215, 232, 235,
  237, 239, 271, 281, 320, 364
Lee, Thomas Ludwell, 5, 8, 149, 151, 180
Lee, William, 107, 180, 183
Lee, Willis, 127, 133, 134, 163
Legge, William, 52, 54
Levy, Levy Andrew, 16, 99
Lewis, Col. Andrew, 4, 34, 63, 64, 66, 103,
  107, 111, 112, 113, 138, 184, 201
Lewis, Major Charles, 4, 112
Lewis, John, 4, 7
Lewis, Thomas, 4, 5, 103f, 128, 132, 201,
  224, 256
Lexington, 137, 295, 296, 352
Liberals, 189, 200, 217ff, 222f, 227
Liberty Hall Academy, 294, 295
Licking River, 104, 128, 251
Limestone Creek, 264, 296, 301, 352
Lincoln County, 249, 251, 264, 306, 318
Linns, the, 195, 196, 198

Little Kanawha River, 37, 59, 70, 105, 112, 144
Little Miami River, 245, 336
Livingston, Robert R., 276, 281f, 284, 286
Lobbying, 142
Lochaber line, 73ff
Lochaber, treaty of, 54, 71, 84
Lochry, Col. Archibald, 92, 253, 255
Lochry, William, 94
Locke, John, 129, 158
Logan, Benjamin, 106, 129, 166, 191, 249, 251, 262, 303ff, 318, 322, 324ff, 346
Logstown, 6
  treaty of, 34
London, 6, 12, 17, 20, 22f, 25f, 29, 37, 40ff, 47f, 50, 53, 56ff, 76, 118, 121, 122, 142, 144, 180, 182, 197, 206f, 211, 212, 216, 230, 231, 274, 276f, 285f, 351, 364
Long Island, 71, 259, 289
Long, Nicholas, 312, 313
Lords of Trade, 21, 50
  see also Trade
Louisa River, 74, 75
Louisiana, 195, 299, 311, 313, 331, 346, 353
Louisville, 87, 240, 251, 255, 296, 298, 300, 301, 306, 352, 358
Lovell, James, 186, 231, 237, 281
Loyal Company, 8, 11, 12, 38, 49, 60, 72, 73, 76, 77, 83, 89, 90, 100, 125, 132ff, 150, 189, 190, 217, 220, 222, 224, 258, 259, 305, 363
Loyalist party, 139
Luttrell, John, 124, 125
Luzerne, Cesar Anne de la, 248, 251, 279, 280, 281, 282, 283, 284, 286
Lyman, Gen. Phineas, 37, 48, 49

Macaulay, Lord, 368
Macleane, Lachlan, 41, 45
Madison, John, 137
Madisons, the, 165, 217, 243, 244, 271, 272, 280, 294, 297, 281, 308, 320, 329, 350, 364
Maps, 75, 76
  pre-Revolutionary, 363
Marshal, James, 253, 267, 327
Marshall, Humphrey, 308, 336, 346, 353
Marshall, Thomas, 165, 249, 263ff, 299, 303f, 324, 326, 336, 348, 353, 358
Martin, Joseph, 83, 125, 163, 190, 257, 259ff, 288ff, 294, 303f, 314, 332, 338, 340f, 343f
Martin's Station, 126f, 247

Martinique, 172, 355
Maryland, 35, 46, 53, 60, 80, 91, 122, 140, 144, 170f, 174, 224, 231, 236, 238f, 242ff, 272, 295, 302, 320, 339, 347, 365
  assembly of, see Assembly, Maryland
Mason and Dixon line, 91
Mason, George, 8, 127f, 133, 135, 156ff, 160, 166, 198, 217f, 224ff, 243, 271, 364
Massachusetts, 55, 122, 157, 169, 171, 180, 205, 236f, 281f, 362
Matthews, Gov., 333ff, 338
Matthews, Sampson, 200
Maurepas, Comte de, 182, 183, 206
May, George, 192, 249f, 263
May, John, 89, 103, 133, 266, 296, 317, 331, 352
Maysville, 296, 352
McAfee, James, 86, 126
McAfee, Robert, 86, 126
McClelland's Station, 127
McDowell, Samuel, 265, 266, 301, 305, 307, 346, 348, 350
McGillivray, Alexander, 311, 314, 316, 323, 339ff, 343f
McIntosh, Gen. Lachlan, 200f, 233, 234, 288, 290
McKee, Alexander, 18, 87, 93ff, 108, 174, 188, 200
Medicine, 122, 332
Mercantile group, 170
  see also Merchants
Mercer, George, 8, 12, 20, 47, 48, 54, 70, 72, 74, 154
Mercer, James, 154, 189, 222
Mercer, John, 8, 154
Merchants, 18, 20, 109, 119, 124, 154, 159, 169f, 172f, 193ff, 199, 205, 210, 213, 216, 217, 239, 248, 266, 296, 297, 298, 302, 311, 313, 346
  British, 17, 23, 28, 160, 172, 321, 329, 364
  French, 239, 277, 278, 297, 321
  Jewish, 16, 17
  New Orleans, 265, 346
  Philadelphia, 19, 148, 221
  Spanish, 318, 323
Mercury, the, 150
Mexico, Gulf of, 43, 342, 343
Middle Department, 138, 169, 174, 201, 281, 359
Mifflin, Thomas, 186, 300
Military warrants, 263, 336, 369
Militia, 16, 83, 95, 106, 107, 115, 178, 197, 198, 293, 303, 312, 317

Militia, *continued*
    Kentucky, 322, 349
    Pennsylvania, 140, 298
    Transylvania, 130
    Virginia, 188
Mingoes, the, 138, 187
Mining, 79
Ministry:
    British, 12, 21, 22, 32, 37, 44, 45, 47,
        49, 54, 57, 101, 207, 284, 358
    French, 183, 206, 207, 208, 209, 366
Miralles, Don Juan de, 198, 203
Miró, Gov. Esteban, 312f, 329ff, 342,
    345ff, 353, 354ff
Mississippi, 196, 199
Mississippi Company, 20f, 47, 216
Mississippi River, 20, 28f, 61f, 66, 113,
    118, 142, 171, 174, 195f, 203f, 211, 236,
    247, 297, 312, 331, 333, 350, 355f, 360,
    362, 363, 366
    boundary, 237f, 278, 281ff, 286
    closure of, 295, 321, 323, 326
    navigation of, 199, 230, 235ff, 244,
        278, 279, 284, 295, 299, 319, 320,
        327ff, 332, 335, 347f, 351, 353f, 358,
        367
    trade on, 223, 299
Mississippi Valley, 235
Mitchell's map, 75, 363
Mobile, 28, 196, 199
Money, *see* Currency
Monongahela country, 105, 126, 140, 167,
    240f, 253
Monongahela River, 6, 97, 104, 107, 127,
    295
Monongalia, 187, 188
Montagu, Edward, 46, 72
Montgomery County, 256, 291
Montgomery, John, 174, 265, 316
Moore, Sir Henry, 30, 34
Morande, Théveneau de, 180, 210
Morgan, George, 24ff, 31, 36, 40, 52ff,
    56ff, 81f, 85, 118, 141ff, 175ff, 187ff, 193,
    196f, 199ff, 203, 226, 233, 234f, 238, 248,
    251, 267, 272, 298, 300, 355, 356f, 359, 360
Morris, Gouverneur, 204, 232, 238, 281,
    282
Morris group, 186, 199, 200, 235, 237,
    238, 282, 284, 285
Morris, Lewis, 141, 175, 233
Morris, Robert, 142, 146, 148, 159, 160,
    169ff, 176, 183f, 186, 193, 196, 203ff,
    210ff, 213, 215f, 219, 221, 228, 231ff,
    263, 277, 280, 281f, 285, 360, 366, 368
Morris, Thomas, 172, 173, 183

Mottin de la Balme, Col., 185, 247, 248,
    249
Mount Vernon, 87, 104
Munitions, 193, 275, 311
Murray, Daniel, 193, 195
Murray, William, 40f, 117ff, 127, 193ff,
    198, 202, 235
Muscle Shoals, 262, 288, 289, 291, 294,
    314, 315, 332, 335, 341ff
Muter, Col. George, 301, 304, 308, 321,
    324, 327, 331, 336, 346ff, 353

Nashville, 71, 82f, 228, 260, 285, 312, 314,
    321ff, 339
Natchez, 195, 223, 235, 297, 312, 313, 321,
    322, 323, 324, 328, 329, 345
Natchez country, 174, 323
Natives, *see* Indians
Nantes, 183, 208, 276
Navigation, *see* Mississippi River, navigation of
Negroes, 27, 155, 158, 184
Nelsons, the, 68, 72, 77
Nelson, Thomas, 8, 12, 134, 158, 222, 236,
    255
Nelson, William, 12, 49, 50, 72
Neutrality, 175, 176, 179, 195, 234
    broken, 201
    Indian, 142, 187
Neville, John, 136, 140, 141, 174, 177, 188,
    195, 226, 357, 359
New England, 157, 169, 171, 172, 236,
    237ff, 281, 282, 337
Newfoundland, 203, 282, 283
New Jersey, 3, 15, 17, 22, 23, 36, 55, 77,
    170, 236, 272, 273, 275, 337, 365
New Orleans, 17, 28, 82, 110, 142, 176,
    177, 183, 193ff, 202, 223, 240, 295, 297,
    312f, 320f, 323, 327ff, 340, 342, 344ff,
    350, 353, 354ff
Newport *Mercury,* 150
Newspapers, 382-383
New River, 2, 60, 83, 291
New-State movement, 288ff, 291, 294, 309,
    310
New World, the, 3, 4, 127, 155
New York, 16f, 21, 24, 30f, 33ff, 37, 42f,
    73, 141, 155, 171, 233, 236, 239, 242, 271,
    272, 275, 295, 311, 319, 333, 340, 342,
    363
Nicholas, Robert Carter, 149, 151f, 156,
    176, 196
North, the, 204, 205, 366
North, Lord, 45, 50, 52, 277

North Carolina, 5, 8, 14, 80f, 123ff, 131f, 171f, 189, 190, 220, 228, 236, 238, 239, 257, 259ff, 275, 281f, 289ff, 303, 306, 314, 315, 331, 332ff, 338ff, 347, 367
   assembly of, *see* Assembly, North Carolina
   boundary, 60, 227
   politics, 260
Northern Department, 60, 242, 309, 316, 338
Northern Neck, 8, 154, 157, 191
Northern Provinces, 61
Northwest, the, 28, 141, 199, 203, 236, 238, 255, 281, 320, 362, 366
Northwest Ordinance, 336
Northwest Territory, 280, 285, 336, 355, 358
Nova Scotia, 20, 111, 203

Oconee River, 311, 316
Ogeechee River, 311
Ohio Company, the, 5ff, 16, 20, 24, 35, 38, 47, 59, 68, 72, 77, 90, 127f, 133ff, 150, 157, 180, 216f, 220, 224, 295, 337, 363, 365, 368
Ohio country, 111f, 142, 167, 187, 199, 253, 254, 309
Ohio, Falls at the, 94f, 109f, 130, 162f, 240, 249ff, 255, 264, 291, 296, 298, 317
Ohio River, 5f, 8ff, 15, 24, 31, 33f, 37f, 43, 46, 47, 49, 53, 59, 61ff, 66f, 70, 75, 81f, 84ff, 94, 98, 99, 102, 105ff, 111, 113, 115, 117ff, 127, 131, 141, 144, 161, 167, 173, 178, 189, 195, 198f, 202, 204, 211, 216, 220, 223, 225, 233ff, 242ff, 247, 251, 254, 267, 277, 285, 291, 295f, 299, 309, 335f, 352, 355f, 359, 363, 365
Old Dominion, the, 60, 77, 101, 125, 144, 149, 159, 167, 170, 204, 254, 260, 302
Orange County, 80, 82, 123
Oswald, Richard, 283, 284, 286

Paca, William, 171, 231, 239
Pacific, the, 249, 369
Packet, Pennsylvania, 214
Page, John, 123, 134, 222
Paine, Thomas, 214, 215, 230, 235, 246
Paris, 181ff, 205, 207, 210, 213, 214, 216, 230, 250, 276ff, 285, 354
   Treaty of, 20
Parliament, 14, 44, 45, 150, 161, 209, 216, 281, 283

Parsons, Gen. Samuel Holden, 324, 325, 337, 340, 357
Passy, 183, 206, 212, 230, 245, 274
Patents, land, 74, 84, 224
Patton, Col. James, 4f, 7f, 11, 49, 72, 79, 256, 317
Peace, 26, 280, 282, 284, 295, 312, 339f
   with England, 283
   with Indians, 25, 27, 112, 138, 316, 318
   negotiations for, 277, 278, 283
   terms of, 235, 237, 284, 285
Peltry, 22, 82, 93, 193
Pendleton, Edmund, 5, 7, 79, 80, 100, 140, 149, 152, 153, 155, 157, 160, 177, 189, 194, 200, 217, 220, 243, 256
Penn, Gov., 36, 42, 92, 95, 96, 97, 108, 362
Penns, the, 18, 19, 48, 93, 94, 96, 310
Pennsylvania, 3, 6, 11, 14, 16, 18, 19, 20, 35, 36, 37, 42, 46, 52f, 61, 81, 87, 91ff, 109, 127, 137ff, 166f, 169f, 174ff, 180, 186, 194f, 200, 202, 213, 223, 227, 232, 235f, 240, 242, 246, 249, 253, 267ff, 273, 277, 279, 295f, 302, 310, 327, 352, 359, 365, 367
   assembly of, *see* Assembly, Pennsylvania
   boundary of, 11, 35, 68, 89, 337
   council of, 35
   emancipation act of, 254
   jurisdiction of, 92, 241
Pennsylvanians, 10, 15, 102, 107, 109, 115, 139, 177
Pennsylvania-Virginia boundary, 91ff, 227, 253, 267
Pensacola, 28, 196, 199, 202, 311, 333, 340
Pentecost, Dorsey, 92, 93, 94, 95, 107, 136, 167, 174, 178, 195, 253, 254, 263, 268, 299, 303, 310, 336
Periodicals, 382-383
Peters, Richard, 18, 36, 42
Philadelphia, 15, 17ff, 22ff, 28, 41, 43, 52, 56, 59, 62, 67, 72, 88, 92f, 114, 117ff, 121, 130f, 142, 144, 146, 156, 159, 176, 183f, 193, 202f, 208, 216, 231f, 234, 235, 237, 248, 250, 264f, 269, 274, 276, 279, 284ff, 297ff, 302, 313, 321, 325, 344, 346, 350, 357, 360
Phoenix, the, 232
Pickens, Andrew, 338, 340, 343, 344
Piedmont, the, 2, 7, 367
Pioneers, Western, 86, 98, 207, 224, 305, 369
Pittsburgh, 20, 26, 35, 68, 86, 87, 91ff, 106, 108ff, 113, 117, 118, 120, 136ff, 144f,

Pittsburgh, *continued*
147, 162, 166ff, 173ff, 187ff, 193ff, 226, 233f, 236, 240ff, 245, 248, 252ff, 266f, 295f, 300, 305, 310, 327f, 340, 355ff
"Pittsylvania," 52, 53, 76
Pittsylvania County, 71, 124
Planters, 124, 154, 156, 160, 161, 217, 364f
Point Pleasant, 4, 111, 112, 129, 142
Politics, 170, 194
    Congressional, 205ff
    Kentucky, 307, 322
    North Carolina, 260
    Virginia, 8, 149ff, 154, 217
    Western, 346
Pollock, Oliver, 142, 176, 183, 193ff, 197f, 203, 233, 240, 265f, 297, 347
Population, 3, 5, 132, 159, 219, 228, 249, 296
Postmaster-general, 44, 45, 180
Potomac River, 5, 6, 14, 55, 117, 295
Powder, 155, 166, 193, 194, 195, 196, 197
Powell's Valley, 81, 83, 98, 123, 125, 163, 314
Pownall, John, 15, 24
Pownall, Thomas, 15, 23, 24, 44, 45, 283
Preemption, 89, 90, 105, 148, 164, 190, 191, 218f, 225, 256, 262f
Preston, John, 4, 80
Preston, Robert, 83, 85, 86
Preston, Col. William, 4, 8, 68, 80, 83f, 88, 99f, 109, 125, 128ff, 132ff, 163, 222, 224, 250, 256, 257, 264, 297, 301, 302, 321
Privateering, 183f, 208, 213, 231, 276
Privateers, 183, 208, 209, 232, 250
Privy Council, 1, 44, 45, 50, 54ff, 67, 101
Proclamation of 1754, 24, 89, 104, 133, 224
Proclamation of 1763, 11f, 20ff, 25, 60, 61, 70, 76f, 84, 87ff, 100f, 103ff, 110, 129, 190, 224, 271, 279, 282, 362
Proprietary party, 19, 169
Public lands, 131, 133, 170, 219, 222, 249, 258, 294, 319
Purviance, Samuel, 302, 303

Quakers, 10, 14, 15, 18, 19, 23, 169, 170, 207, 360
Quebec, 17, 175
Quebec Act, 107, 161, 283
Queen Charlotte, 54
Quit-rents, 9ff, 46, 60, 63, 87, 100, 124, 128, 146, 191, 225

Radicals, 149ff, 150, 155, 156, 157, 158, 167, 170, 189, 200, 232

Raleigh Tavern, 79, 155
Randolph, Edmund, 149, 150, 158, 220, 222, 236, 239, 269, 271, 281, 325, 327, 330, 331, 332, 336, 338, 339, 340, 352, 355, 358
Randolph, John, 140, 149, 152, 156
Randolph, Peyton, 140, 149, 150, 152, 153, 154, 155, 156
Rattletrap, the, 196
Redemptioners, 4, 13, 79, 104
Redstone, 10, 35, 77, 92, 95, 105, 167
Reed, Joseph, 52, 156, 180, 184, 253, 279, 281
Religion, freedom of, 356, 357
Representation, 155, 158, 159
Revolution, the, 57, 60, 90, 112, 122, 142, 149, 155, 160, 161, 165, 167, 170ff, 175, 178, 183, 193, 204ff, 211, 217, 226, 234, 239, 266, 267, 271ff, 276, 281, 287, 297f, 305, 311, 312, 334, 339, 344, 348, 361ff
Richmond, 140, 165, 166, 188, 189, 251, 252, 262, 265, 303, 322, 325, 330, 344, 357
Rights, Bill of, 157, 158, 159
Robertson, James, 314, 332, 334, 339, 340, 342f
Robinson, John, 7, 8, 45, 79, 100, 149, 151ff
Rochford, Lord, 45, 181
Rogers, Col. David, 175, 177, 187, 198, 199, 240
Rogers, Col. John, 193, 198, 355
Ross, Alexander, 93, 94, 117, 174
Ross, George, 171, 235
Ross, John, 172, 183, 231, 313
Rumsey, James, 27, 41, 117
Russell, Capt. William, 9, 79f, 83, 98, 102, 109, 123, 129, 142, 222, 257, 293, 302
Russia, 274, 282

Safety, Committee of, 137f, 155, 194
St. Asaph's Station, 129, 130
St. Clair, Arthur, 92, 94, 95, 96, 108, 138, 141, 174, 175, 177, 299, 330, 337, 358
St. Louis, 195, 199, 249, 322, 327
Salt Licks, 82, 83, 103
Salt River, 86, 105, 109, 126
Salt springs, 85, 88
Saratoga, 82, 186, 206
Sargent, John, 45, 177
Sartine, Comte de, 183, 206
Schuyler, Gen., 243, 281
Scioto River, 46, 53, 85, 98, 106, 112, 115, 245, 336

Scotch-Irish, the, 4, 80, 169
Scott, Thomas, 167, 253
Sebastian, Judge Benjamin, 321, 327, 331, 346, 348, 353, 354
Secession, 257, 270
 Kentucky, 252, 302
 movement for, 254, 258, 262, 264, 266, 269, 294, 303f, 333, 366
Secessionists, 251, 259, 265
Secret Correspondence, Committee of, 172, 173, 180, 213, 215
Settlements, 67, 79, 82ff, 86, 105, 110, 125, 127, 137, 141, 161, 191, 195, 228, 256, 258, 262f, 320, 323, 337, 340, 342, 352, 367
 Cumberland, 314, 326, 334, 340, 341, 342
 Kentucky, 142, 195
 Western, 9, 11, 327, 340, 342, 353
Settlers, 12, 37, 60ff, 68, 77, 79, 83, 87, 89, 90, 94, 105, 123, 125f, 130, 144f, 148, 162ff, 166, 191, 218, 221f, 224f, 228, 240, 252, 254, 256, 259, 262, 267, 269, 295, 304, 315, 352, 356, 358, 367, 368f
 early, 4ff, 264
 frontier, 190, 305
 Kentucky, 251, 326, 356
 Virginia, 77, 251, 263
Sevier, John, 261, 288, 289, 290, 292, 294, 315, 332, 334, 335, 338, 339, 340, 341, 342f
Shawnee, the, 31, 34, 86, 88, 98ff, 102, 106, 108ff, 122, 138f, 141, 167, 175, 242, 247, 268, 300, 316ff, 334
Shelburne, Lord, 20, 30, 33, 41, 55, 60, 61, 62, 63, 180, 208, 266, 283, 285, 286
Shelby, Evan, 80, 112, 223, 262
Shelby, Isaac, 112, 260, 262, 302, 304, 305, 324, 352
Shepherd, Col. David, 136, 254
Sherman, Roger, 243, 281
Shiell, Dr. Hugh, 298, 324
Simms, Charles, 177, 189, 226
Simon, Joseph, 16, 17, 93, 121, 140, 296
Six Nations Indians, 8, 14, 16, 18, 24, 31, 32, 34f, 37, 44, 59, 62ff, 81, 86f, 91, 98f, 103, 108, 119f, 141, 143, 147, 220, 226, 242, 316, 363
Slavery, 27, 158, 159
Smallman, Thomas, 18, 93, 94, 136, 174, 268
Smith, Major Daniel, 5, 83, 123, 227, 342
Smith, Meriwether, 219, 222, 236, 239
Soldiers, 24, 47, 84, 90, 128, 219, 221, 263
South, the, 169, 205, 237, 274, 347

South Carolina, 231, 236, 237, 239, 261, 271, 279ff, 313f, 338, 340, 343
Southern Department, 55, 60, 257, 309, 316, 332, 338
Southwest, the, 83, 204, 238, 334, 366
Spain, 195ff, 203f, 232, 235, 244, 278ff, 284f, 295, 299, 312, 319, 325f, 329ff, 340ff, 348, 350, 353f, 357, 359f, 367
Spanish, the, 223, 236, 249, 288, 311, 313, 323f, 329, 330, 332, 338, 347
Speculation, 7, 31, 105, 122, 124, 142, 147, 162, 183, 185, 206f, 210, 217, 230, 260, 262, 263, 281, 285, 289, 299, 302, 315, 343, 360
 see also Land speculation
Speculators, 13, 18, 37, 100, 103, 104, 107, 119, 121, 123, 145, 189, 202, 213, 216, 218, 240, 249, 261f, 269, 289, 299, 301f, 306, 314, 319, 326, 342, 365, 366, 368, 369
Spies, 196, 197, 198, 209
Squatters, 164, 218, 326, 369
Stamp Act, 149ff, 154, 169, 170, 364
States-rights, 157, 320
Staunton, 3, 4, 79, 80, 94, 95, 97, 136, 137, 189
Strahan, William, 44, 45, 57
Stuart, John, 22, 33, 54, 59ff, 71, 73ff, 112, 123
"Suffering Traders," 31, 33, 35, 40, 43, 45, 48, 59, 69, 70, 80, 92, 143, 146, 221
Suffolk, Lord, 50, 55
Suffrage, the, 158, 159
Sullivan County, 338, 341
Sullivan, Daniel, 233
Surveyors, 83f, 105, 106, 107, 110, 124, 126, 128f, 132ff, 146, 163, 191, 224, 249, 254, 256, 263, 297, 336
Surveys, land, 70, 74, 90, 102ff, 132ff, 145, 219f, 224, 239, 256, 264, 269, 270, 315, 337, 356, 364
Susquehannah Company, 18, 19, 34, 37
Sycamore Shoals, 124, 125, 128
Symmes, John Cleves, 337, 355, 359

Tardiveau, Peter, 296, 297, 299, 316, 321, 328, 336, 354
Tayloe, John, 8, 128, 134
Taylor, Hancock, 82, 85, 102, 103, 110
Taylor, John, 217, 297
Taxation, 9, 155, 304
Taxes, 161, 191, 263, 338
Telfair, Gov., 323, 334

Tennessee, 5, 63, 71, 82, 242, 291, 316
    Bend of the, 289, 313, 314, 334, 338, 343
    County, 288, 315, 323
Tennessee River, 31, 34, 44, 59, 62, 63, 66, 67, 81, 124, 125, 223, 261, 291
Thompson, William, 85, 92, 93, 104, 105, 118
Tidewater, the, 3, 60, 73, 107, 150, 156, 158, 161, 368
Tipton, John, 335, 338
Titles, land, 11, 144, 190, 191, 200, 218, 221, 225, 227, 256, 262, 270, 347, 356, 368
Tobacco, 79, 159, 180, 181, 213, 215, 239, 345, 346
Todd, Col. John, 129, 130, 163, 166, 191, 202, 240, 248, 249, 251, 265, 309
Tories, the, 137, 147, 188, 311, 313, 358, 287, 339
Trade, 25f, 50, 109, 176, 178, 181, 184, 187, 193f, 202, 204, 213, 215, 223, 224, 239, 295ff, 330, 332, 360
    Board of, see Board of Trade
Traders, 18, 20, 22f, 31, 36f, 48, 59, 93, 99, 106, 145, 179, 198, 240, 276, 296, 301, 316, 353, 368
    see also Suffering traders
Transylvania, 130, 131, 164, 166, 225, 269
Transylvania Company, 123ff, 125ff, 130, 132, 164, 302
Treason, 57, 208-209, 270
Treasury, Board of, 186
Treasury, Virginia, 151, 152, 153
Treasury warrants, 224, 250, 251, 263, 306, 369
Treaties, 142, 260, 309, 319
Treaty of Fort Stanwix, see Fort Stanwix, treaty of
Treaty of 1783, 274ff, 312
Treaty, Spanish, 330
Trent, William, 6ff, 16ff, 22, 31, 33, 36, 40, 43ff, 57, 116, 117, 118, 121f, 124, 142ff, 238, 245f, 269
Trigg, Stephen, 222, 249, 250, 265
Troops, 26, 194, 252, 270, 318
    Clark's, 325
    Continental, 171, 234, 249
    lands for, 198
    Virginia, 141, 174, 233
    see also Army, Soldiers

United States, 199, 201, 202, 206, 211, 213, 240, 274, 281, 283, 284, 306, 316, 333, 341, 348, 349, 353, 359, 360, 361, 366

Vandalia, 40-58, 72f, 77, 89, 92, 94f, 99, 104, 111, 114, 119, 161, 173, 174, 177, 187, 211, 216, 246, 364
Vandalia Land Company, 54, 56, 71, 74ff, 84, 101, 109, 116, 117ff, 122, 142ff, 148, 176, 177, 189, 214, 221, 225, 230, 235, 238, 245, 246, 269, 273, 360, 363, 368
Vaughan, Benjamin, 286
Vergennes, 181, 185, 203, 206, 208, 211f, 231, 235, 237, 275, 278, 279, 282, 283, 284, 285, 286
Vincennes, 122, 233, 248, 296, 317f, 322f, 325, 327, 336, 365
Virginia, 1ff, 7, 8, 11, 13ff, 17, 19, 22, 24, 31, 34ff, 46ff, 53ff, 59, 61, 64, 66ff, 78ff, 87f, 90, 95, 96, 98, 99, 101, 103, 107, 109ff, 114, 115, 119, 121ff, 131ff, 147, 151, 154, 156f, 159, 160, 161, 163, 165ff, 186f, 189, 190, 193, 195, 197, 198, 199, 201ff, 236ff, 254ff, 280ff, 291ff, 324ff, 347ff, 363ff
    arming of, 155
    assembly, see Assembly, Virginia
    boundaries of, 3, 53, 66, 67, 81, 148, 272, 362
    cession of, 243, 244, 270, 272, 360
    claims of, 243, 245, 248, 249, 362, 365, 366
    conservatives in, 149ff
    constitution of, 148, 151, 158, 159
    convention, 121, 129, 131, 132, 133, 136, 139, 140, 144, 147, 148, 157, 158, 160, 163, 164, 165, 166, 175, 218, 346
    county, 240, 248, 253, 309
    frontier, 67, 363
    government of, 7, 12, 60, 89, 98, 101, 191, 309
    jurisdiction of, 145, 147, 148, 194, 253, 270, 326
    land office act of, 238, 249, 250
    North Carolina boundary of, 53, 66, 227
    Pennsylvania boundary of, 91ff, 227, 267, 308
    politics in, 8, 80, 159, 217
    Radicals in, 149ff
    Southwest, 53, 72, 191, 264
    Transylvania Company and, 123ff
    treasury warrants of, 250
    troops of, 59, 69, 174
    and the West, 242ff, 258ff
    Western boundary of, 11, 59, 61, 73, 75, 77
    Western claims of, 171

Virginia, *continued*
  Western land problem of, 162ff

Wabash Land Company, 142, 193, 202, 211, 226, 233, 234, 235, 317, 318, 325, 363, 365, 366
Wabash River, 29, 319, 322
Walpole, Horace, 44, 47, 51, 186
Walpole Company, 49, 50, 53, 54, 69, 70, 72, 74, 76, 86, 122, 176
Walpole, Thomas, 44, 45, 46, 49, 50, 52, 68, 72, 143, 177, 183, 185, 206, 216, 230, 277, 283, 285, 287
Walker, John, 121, 136, 138, 243
Walker, Dr. Thomas, 5, 7, 34, 38, 59ff, 63, 66ff, 69, 70, 73ff, 81, 83, 88, 89, 100, 102f, 120f, 131, 136, 138, 141, 163, 174, 178, 189f, 220ff, 225ff, 232, 244, 256, 264, 271
Wallace, Caleb, 222, 250, 265f, 297, 301, 304f, 324, 346, 348
War, Board of, 186, 198, 199, 200
Ward, Edward, 87, 93, 94
Warrants:
  land, 263
  military, 250, 263, 336
  soldiers', 263
  treasury, 250, 251, 263
Washington County, 253, 255, 256, 267, 270, 290, 291, 293, 327, 335, 338, 341
Washington, George, 4, 8, 9, 10, 19, 20, 25, 49, 68ff, 77, 84ff, 93ff, 103f, 111, 127, 132ff, 138, 141, 145, 156, 160, 170, 175f, 184, 219, 233, 243, 252, 254, 266, 281, 295, 308, 310, 320, 331, 345, 358f, 361, 363
  army of, 185, 209, 226
Watauga County, 332
Watauga River, 81, 124
West, the, 1ff, 15, 18, 20, 40, 105, 107, 124, 132, 159, 163, 166, 200, 216, 217, 222, 223, 230ff, 240, 259, 266, 286, 290, 295, 299, 302, 311ff, 320, 328, 329ff, 347, 353, 355, 357, 359, 362, 367, 368, 369
West Augusta, 136, 138, 139, 140, 165, 167, 174, 177
  court of, 137, 147
Western boundary, *see* Boundary
Western lands, 7, 9, 11, 37, 41, 48, 49, 74, 77, 78, 88, 89, 111, 122, 131, 132, 148, 149, 160, 161, 172, 177, 180, 205, 210, 211, 214, 215, 218, 219, 226, 227, 239, 243, 247, 250, 261, 271, 299, 301, 303, 305, 314, 333, 334, 361, 364, 365, 367, 368

Western States, New, 288ff, 290, 291, 309, 367
Western trade, *see* Trade
West Fincastle, 165, 166
West Florida, 199, 200, 203
Westmoreland County, 93, 94, 95, 96, 97, 137, 138, 139, 140, 174, 253, 270, 272
Westsylvania, 177, 179
Wharton, Charles, 31
Wharton, Joseph, 207, 216, 277
Wharton, Samuel, 24, 25, 26, 27, 29, 31, 32, 33, 36, 40, 41, 43, 44, 45, 46, 47, 48, 50, 52, 53, 54ff, 70, 72, 92, 95, 111, 117ff, 121, 122, 142, 143, 144, 146, 148, 170, 175, 177, 189, 207, 212, 216, 221, 230, 231, 245, 246, 269, 274, 276, 286, 360
Wharton, Thomas, 25, 41, 43, 52, 56, 58, 59, 114, 117, 118, 119, 120, 121, 122, 143, 145, 146, 147
Whigs, 139, 147, 174, 184, 296
White, Dr. James, 332ff, 341ff, 354
Wilkinson, James, 127, 298ff, 302, 307f, 319, 321ff, 336, 340, 342, 344ff, 353ff, 360
William and Mary, College of, 7, 80, 84, 85, 88, 104, 128, 133, 134, 191, 224, 250, 256
Williamsburg, 77, 79, 94ff, 100, 103, 113f, 121, 133, 135, 137f, 140, 154f, 159, 164, 193f, 197, 201, 226f, 239
Williams, Jonathan, 183, 208, 231, 271, 286
Williamson, Col. David, 267, 268
Willings, the, 169, 170, 183, 196, 197, 199, 203, 263, 357
Wilson, George, 92, 96, 138, 144, 171, 175, 239, 263, 277
Winchester, 3, 113, 136, 140, 141, 248
Winston, Richard, 142, 176, 179, 193, 194, 202, 309
Wolf Hills, 5, 79, 83, 123
Wood, James, 138, 141, 189
Wyandotts, 31, 175, 268, 316
Wythe, George, 131, 147, 148, 152, 154, 159, 198, 217

Yazoo Company, 341, 350, 354, 360
Yazoo River, 312
Yeates, Jasper, 174, 177, 179, 188
Yohogania County, 167, 178, 187, 194, 195, 240, 241, 253, 254
Yorke, Charles, 114, 116
  see also Camden-Yorke opinion
Youghiogeny River, 92, 268